The Collected Works of

MARY SIDNEY HERBERT

COUNTESS OF PEMBROKE

Volume II

The Collected Works of

MARY SIDNEY HERBERT

COUNTESS OF PEMBROKE

Volume II
THE PSALMES OF DAVID

Edited with Introduction and Commentary by

Margaret P. Hannay, Noel J. Kinnamon
and Michael G. Brennan

CLARENDON PRESS · OXFORD

1998

Oxford University Press, Great Clarendon Street, Oxford OX2 6DP
Oxford New York
Athens Auckland Bangkok Bogota Bombay Buenos Aires
Calcutta Cape Town Dar es Salaam Delhi Florence Hong Kong
Istanbul Karachi Kuala Lumpur Madras Madrid Melbourne
Mexico City Nairobi Paris Singapore Taipei Tokyo Toronto Warsaw
and associated companies in
Berlin Ibadan

Oxford is a registered trade mark of Oxford University Press

Published in the United States by
Oxford University Press Inc., New York

A catalogue record for this book is available from the British Library

Library of Congress Cataloging-in-Publication Data

Pembroke, Mary Sidney Herbert, Countess of, 1561–1621.
[Works. 1998]
The collected works of Mary Sidney Herbert, Countess of Pembroke /
edited with introduction and commentary by Margaret P. Hannay, Noel
J. Kinnamon, and Michael G. Brennan.
Includes bibliographical references and indexes.
Contents: v. 1. Poems, translations, and correspondence—
v. 2. The psalmes of David.
I. Hannay, Margaret P., 1944– II. Kinnamon, Noel J.
III. Brennan, Michael G. IV. Title.
PR2329.P2A12 1998 821'.3—dc21 97–25502
ISBN 0–19–811280–7 (v. 1)
ISBN 0–19–818457–3 (v. 2)

Typeset by Pure Tech India Ltd, Pondicherry
Printed in Great Britain
on acid-free paper by
Biddles Ltd,
Guilford and King's Lynn

12222433

CONTENTS

Volume 1 Poems, Translations, and Correspondence

Volume II The Psalmes of David

REFERENCES AND ABBREVIATIONS

Aggas, *Defence*	Philippe de Mornay, *The Defence of Death. Contayning a Most Excellent Discourse Written in Frenche. And Doone into English by E. A[ggas]* (1576), STC 18136.
APC	*Acts of the Privy Council*
Arundel Harington MS	*The Arundel Harington Manuscript of Tudor Poetry*, ed. Ruth Hughey (Columbus, Ohio: Ohio State UP, 1960).
Attridge, *Syllables*	*Derek Attridge, Well-Weighed Syllables: Elizabethan Verse in Classical Metres* (London: Cambridge UP, 1974).
Aubrey, *Brief Lives*	*Aubrey's Brief Lives*, ed. Oliver Lawson Dick (London: Secker and Warburg, 1949).
Barnes, *P and P*, ed. Doyno	*Barnabe Barnes, Parthenophil and Parthenophe 1593*, ed. Victor A. Doyno (Carbondale: Southern Illinois UP, 1971).
Baxter, *Ouránia*	Nathaniel Baxter, *Sir Philip Sydneys Ouránia, that is, Endimions Song and Tragedie. Containing all Philosophie* (1606), STC 1598.
BC	*The Book Collector*
Beal	Peter George Beal, *Index of English Literary Manuscripts, I: 1450–1625*, 2 vols. (London: Mansell, 1980).
Beilin, *Redeeming Eve*	Elaine Beilin, *Redeeming Eve: Women Writers of the English Renaissance* (Princeton: Princeton UP, 1987).
Bèze,	Théodore de Bèze, *The Psalmes of David, truly opened and explaned by paraphrasis, according to the right sense of everie Psalme*. Trans. Anthony Gilby (1581), STC 2033.
Bishops' Bible	*The holie bible conteynyng the olde testament and the newe* (1568), STC 2099.
BL	British Library.
Bloch, *Spelling*	Chana Bloch, *Spelling the Word: George Herbert and the Bible* (Berkeley: U of California P, 1985).
Bodenham, *Bel-vedére*	John Bodenham, *Bel-vedére or the Garden of the Muses*, [ed.], A. M.[unday?] (1600), STC 3189.

Brennan (D.Phil. diss.) | Michael G. Brennan, 'The Literary Patronage of the Herbert Family, Earls of Pembroke, 1550–1640', University of Oxford, D.Phil. diss., 1982.

Brennan, *Literary Patronage* | Michael G. Brennan, *Literary Patronage in the English Renaissance: The Pembroke Family* (London: Routledge, 1988).

Breton, *Pilgrimage* | Nicholas Breton, *The Pilgrimage to Paradise, Joyned with the Countesse of Penbrookes Love* (Oxford, 1592), *STC* 3683.

Breton, *Poems* | *Nicholas Breton Poems not Hitherto Reprinted*, ed. Jean Robertson (Liverpool: Liverpool UP, 1967).

Breton, *Wits Trenchmour* | Nicholas Breton, *Wits Trenchmour* (1597), *STC* 3713.

Breton, *Works* | *The Works in Verse and Prose of Nicholas Breton*, ed. Alexander B. Grosart (1879; rpt. New York: AMS P, 1966).

Briquet | Charles Moïse Briquet, *Les Filigranes: Dictionnaire historique des marques du papier dès leur apparition vers 1282 jusqu'en 1600*, 4 vols. (2nd edn., Leipzig: Hiersemann, 1923).

Bullough, *Sources* | Geoffrey Bullough, *Narrative and Dramatic Sources of Shakespeare* (New York: Columbia UP, 1966).

Buxton, *Sidney* | E. M. John Buxton, *Sir Philip Sidney and the English Renaissance* (London: Macmillan, 1954; rpt. 1964).

Calvin | *The Psalms of David and others. With M. John Calvins Commentaries*, trans. Arthur Golding (1571), *STC* 4395.

Camden, *Historie* | William Camden, *The Historie of the Most Renowned and Victorious Princesse Elizabeth... Composed by way of Annals*, trans. R. N.[orton] (1630), *STC* 4500.

Cary, *Mariam* | Lady Elizabeth Cary (Carey, Carew), *The Tragedie of Mariam, the Faire Queene of Jewry* (1613), *STC* 4613.

Cary, *Mariam*, ed. Weller and Ferguson | Elizabeth Cary, *The Lady Falkland, The Tragedy of Mariam the Fair Queen of Jewry with The Lady Falkland Her Life by one of her daughters*, ed. Barry Weller and Margaret W. Ferguson (Berkeley: U of California P, 1994).

Chamberlain, *Letters*	*The Letters of John Chamberlain*, ed. Norman Egbert McClure, 2 vols. (Philadelphia: American Philosophical Society, 1939; rpt. Westport, Conn.: Greenwood P, 1979).
Churchyard, *Conceit*	Thomas Churchyard, *A Pleasant Conceit penned in verse. Collourably sette out, and humblie presented on New-yeeres day last, to the Queenes Majestie at Hampton Court* (1593), STC 5248.
Constable, *Poems*	*The Poems and Sonnets of Henry Constable*, ed. John Gray (London: Ballantyne P, 1897).
Creation of a Legend	*Sir Philip Sidney: 1586 and the Creation of a Legend*, ed. Jan Van Dorsten, Dominic Baker-Smith, and Arthur F. Kinney (Leiden: J. J. Brill and Leiden UP, 1986).
Crowley	Robert Crowley, *The Psalter of David Newely Translated into English metre* (1549), STC 2725.
CSP	*Calendar of State Papers.*
Daniel, *Delia*	Samuel Daniel, *Delia. Contayning Certayne Sonnets* (1592), STC 6253.
Daniel, *Delia & Cleopatra*	Samuel Daniel, *Delia and Rosamond Augmented. Cleopatra* (1594), STC 6254.
Daniel, *Philotas*	Samuel Daniel, *Certaine Small Poems lately printed: with the tragedie of Philotas* (1605), STC 6239.
Davies, *Muses Sacrifice*	John Davies, *The Muses Sacrifice, or Divine Meditations* (1612), STC 6338.
Davies, *Poems*	*The Poems of Sir John Davies*, ed. Robert Krueger (Oxford: Clarendon P, 1975).
Davies, *Works*	*The Complete Works of John Davies of Hereford*, ed. Alexander B. Grosart (Edinburgh: Edinburgh UP, 1878).
Davison, *Rapsody*	Francis Davison (ed.), *A Poetical Rapsody Containing Diuerse Sonnets, Odes, Elegies, Madrigalls, and other Poesies, both in Rime, and Measured Verse* (1602), STC 6373.
De L'Isle MS	De L'Isle and Dudley Papers, Penshurst Place, Kent and Kent County Records Office.
DNB	*Dictionary of National Biography.*
Donne, *Divine Poems*	*John Donne: The Divine Poems*, ed. Helen Gardner (Oxford: Clarendon P, 1952).
Drayton, *Works*	*The Works of Michael Drayton*, ed. J. William Hebel. Introductions, notes, and variant

readings, ed. Kathleen Tillotson and Bernard Newdigate, 5 vols. (Oxford: Basil Blackwell, 1931–41).

EHR   *English Historical Review.*

ELH   *English Literary History.*

ELR   *English Literary Renaissance.*

England   Martha Winburn England, 'Sir Philip Sidney and François Perrot de Méssières: The Verse Versions of the Psalms', *Bulletin of the New York Public Library* 75 (1971), 30–54, 101–10.

Esplin (Ph.D. diss.)   Ross Stolworthy Esplin, 'The Emerging Legend of Sir Philip Sidney 1586–1652', University of Utah, Ph.D. diss., 1970.

Fisken, 'Education'   Beth Wynne Fisken, 'Mary Sidney's *Psalmes*: Education and Wisdom', in *Silent but for the Word*, 166–183.

Fisken, 'Parody'   Beth Wynne Fisken, '"The Art of Sacred Parody" in Mary Sidney's *Psalmes*', *Tulsa Studies in Women's Literature* 8 (1989), 223–9.

Fisken, 'World of Words'   Beth Wynne Fisken, '"To the Angell spirit…": Mary Sidney's Entry into the "World of Words"', in *Renaissance Englishwoman*, 263–75.

Fraunce, *Emanuel*   Abraham Fraunce, *The Countesse of Pembrokes Emanuel* (1591), *STC* 11339.

Fraunce, *Ivychurch*   Abraham Fraunce, *The Countesse of Pembrokes Ivychurch. Containing the Affectionate life, and unfortunate death of Phillis and Amyntas: That in a Pastorall; This in a Funerall; both in English Hexameters* (1591), *STC* 11340.

Fraunce, *Ivychurch. Third Part*   Abraham Fraunce, *The Third Part of the Countesse of Pembrokes Ivychurch. Entitul'd Amintas Dale. Wherein are the most conceited tales of the Pagan Gods in English Hexameters together with their auncient descriptions and Philosophicall explications* (1592), *STC* 11341.

Freer, *Music*   Coburn Freer, *Music for a King: George Herbert's Style and the Metrical Psalms* (Baltimore: Johns Hopkins UP, 1972).

Geneva   *The Bible and Holy Scriptures* (Geneva, 1560). Facsimile. (Madison: U of Wisconsin P, 1969).

Great Bible	*The byble in Englysche, that is to saye the content of all the holy scrypture* [First Great Bible]. Revised by M. Coverdale (1539), *STC* 2068.
Greville, *Prose Works*	*The Prose Works of Fulke Greville, Lord Brooke*, ed. John Gouws (Oxford: Clarendon P, 1986).
Hannay, *Philip's Phoenix*	Margaret P. Hannay, *Philip's Phoenix: Mary Sidney, Countess of Pembroke* (New York and Oxford: Oxford UP, 1990).
Harington, *Letters*	John Harington, *The Letters and Epigrams of Sir John Harington*, ed. Norman Egbert McClure (Philadelphia: U of Penn. P, 1930).
Harvey, *Letter*	Gabriel Harvey, *A New Letter of Notable Contents. With a Straunge Sonet, intituled Gorgon, or the wonderful yeare* (1593), *STC* 12902.
Harvey, *Pierces Supererogation*	Gabriel Harvey, *Pierces Supererogation or A New Prayse of the Old Asse. A Preparative to certaine larger Discourses, intituled Nashes S. Fame* (1593), *STC* 12903.
Harvey, *Works*	*The Works of Gabriel Harvey, D.C.L.*, ed. Alexander B. Grosart (1888; rpt. New York: AMS P, 1966).
Heawood	Edward Heawood, *Watermarks, Mainly of the 17th and 18th Centuries*, Paper Publication Society (Hilversum, 1950).
Heywood, *Gynaikeion*	Thomas Heywood, *[Gynaikeion]: or, Nine Bookes of Various History. Concerning Women* (1624), *STC* 13326.
Hiller	Geoffrey G. Hiller, ' "Where thou doost live, there let all graces be": Images of the Renaissance Woman Patron in Her House and Rural Domain', *Cahiers Elizabèthains* 40 (1991), 37–52.
HLB	*Harvard Library Bulletin*.
HLQ	*Huntington Library Quarterly*.
HMC	Historical Manuscripts Commission.
Howell, *Devises*	Thomas Howell, *Howell his Devises for his owne Exercise, and his Friends Pleasure* (1581), *STC* 13875.
Howell, *Devises*, ed. Raleigh	*Howell's Devises. 1581*, ed. Walter Raleigh (Oxford: Clarendon P, 1906).

Hunnis	William Hunnis, *Psalmes chosen out of the Psalter of David, and drawen fourth into English meter by William Hunnis* (1550), STC 2727.
JEGP	*Journal of English and Germanic Philology.*
JES	*Journal of European Studies.*
JMRS	*Journal of Medieval and Renaissance Studies.*
Jonson, *Poems*	*Ben Jonson: The Complete Poems*, ed. George Parfitt (New Haven: Yale UP, 1982).
Kay, *Melodious Tears*	Dennis Kay, *Melodious Tears: The English Funeral Elegy from Spenser to Milton* (Oxford: Clarendon P, 1990).
King, *Iconography*	John N. King, *Tudor Royal Iconography* (Princeton: Princeton UP, 1989).
King, *Reformation*	John N. King, *English Reformation Literature: The Tudor Origins of the Protestant Tradition* (Princeton: Princeton UP, 1982).
Lamb, *Gender*	Mary Ellen Lamb, *Gender and Authorship in the Sidney Circle* (Madison: U of Wisconsin P, 1990).
Lamb, 'Myth'	Mary Ellen Lamb, 'The Myth of the Countess of Pembroke: The Dramatic Circle', *Yearbook of English Studies* 11 (1981), 194–202.
Lamb, 'Patronage'	Mary Ellen Lamb, 'The Countess of Pembroke's Patronage', *ELR* 12 (1982), 162–79.
Lamb (Ph.D. diss.)	Mary Ellen Lamb, 'The Countess of Pembroke's Patronage', Columbia U, Ph.D. diss., 1976.
Lanyer, *Poems*	*The Poems of Aemilia Lanyer: Salve Deus Rex Judaeorum*, ed. Susanne Woods (New York: Oxford UP, 1993).
Lanyer, *Salve Deus*	Aemilia Lanyer, *Salve Deus rex Judæorum. Containing, the passion of Christ* (1611), STC 15227.
Leaver, 'Ghoostly Psalmes'	Robin Leaver, *'Ghoostly Psalmes and Spirituall Songes': English and Dutch Metrical Psalms from Coverdale to Utenhove 1535–1566* (Oxford: Clarendon P, 1991).
Lewalski, *Protestant Poetics*	Barbara Kiefer Lewalski, *Protestant Poetics and the Seventeenth-Century Religious Lyric* (Princeton: Princeton UP, 1979).
Lewalski, *Writing Women*	Barbara Kiefer Lewalski, *Writing Women in Jacobean England* (Cambridge, Mass.: Harvard UP, 1993).

Lok

Anne Lok [Prowse], 'A Meditation of a Penitent Sinner: Written in Maner of a Paraphrase upon the 51. Psalme of David', in *Sermons of John Calvin, upon the Songe that Ezechias made after he had bene sicke and afflicted by the hand of God*, trans. Anne Lok (1560), *STC* 4450.

Lok, *Ecclesiastes*

Henry Lok, *Ecclesiastes, otherwise called the Preacher. Containing Salomons Sermons or Commentaries* (1597), *STC* 16696.

Love, *Scribal Publication*

Harold Love, *Scribal Publication in Seventeenth-Century England* (Oxford: Clarendon P, 1993).

Martz, *Meditation*

Louis Martz, *Poetry of Meditation* (New Haven: Yale UP, 1962).

May, *Courtier Poets*

Steven W. May, *The Elizabethan Courtier Poets: The Poems and Their Contexts* (Columbia: U of Missouri P, 1991).

Mind's Melodie

Alexander Montgomerie, *The Mindes Melodie, Contayning Certayne Psalmes of the Kinglie Prophet David applyed to a new pleasant tune* (Edinburgh, 1605), *STC* 18051.

MLN

Modern Language Notes.

Moffet, *Nobilis*

Thomas Moffet, *Nobilis or a View of the Life and Death of a Sidney and Lessus Lugubris*, ed. Virgil B. Heltzel and Hoyt H. Hudson (San Marino, Calif: Huntington Library, 1940).

Moffet, *Silkewormes*

Thomas Moffet, *The Silkewormes and their Flies: Lively described in verse, by T.M. a Countrie Farmar, and an apprentice in Physicke* (1599), *STC* 17994.

Montgomery, *Symmetry*

Robert L. Montgomery, Jr., *Symmetry and Sense: The Poetry of Sir Philip Sidney* (Austin: U of Texas P, 1961).

Morton (Ph.D. diss.)

Lynn Moorhead Morton, ' "Vertue cladde in constant love's attire": The Countess of Pembroke as a Model for Renaissance Women Writers', U of South Carolina, Ph.D. diss., 1993.

N&Q

Notes & Queries.

New Ways

New Ways of Looking at Old Texts: Papers of the Renaissance English Text Society, 1985–91,

	ed. W. Speed Hill, *Medieval and Renaissance Texts and Studies*, in conjunction with the Renaissance English Text Society (Binghamton, NY, 1993).
NLH	*New Literary History.*
North	Plutarch, *The lives of the noble Grecians and Romanes. Translated out of Greeke into French by J. Amyot, out of French by T. North* (1579), *STC* 20065.
Old Version	*The whole booke of psalmes collected into English meter by Thomas Sternhold, J. Hopkins and others* (Geneva, 1569), *STC* 2440.
Osborne, *Memoires*	Francis Osborne, *Historical Memoires on the Reigns of Queen Elizabeth and King James* (1683), Wing 0515.
Parker	Matthew Parker, *The Whole psalter translated into English Metre, which contayneth an hundreth and fifty Psalmes* (1575), *STC* 2729.
Parry, *Victoria Christiana*	Henry Parry, *Victoria Christiana* (1594), *STC* 19336.
PBSA	*Papers of the Bibliographical Society of America.*
PMLA	*Publications of the Modern Language Association of America.*
PQ	*Philological Quarterly.*
Prescott, *French Poets*	Anne Lake Prescott, *French Poets and the English Renaissance: Studies in Fame and Transformation* (New Haven: Yale UP, 1978).
PRO	Public Records Office.
Psaumes	Clément Marot and Théodore de Bèze, *Les Psaumes de David mis en rime Francoise* (Geneva, 1562).
Rathmell (Ph.D. diss.)	John C. A. Rathmell, 'A Critical Edition of the Psalms of Sir Philip Sidney and the Countess of Pembroke', University of Cambridge, Ph.D. diss., 1964.
Renaissance Englishwoman	*The Renaissance Englishwoman in Print: Counterbalancing the Canon*, ed. Anne M. Haselkorn and Betty S. Travitsky (Amherst: U of Massachusetts P, 1990).
RES	*Review of English Studies.*
Rosenberg, *Leicester*	Eleanor Rosenberg, *Leicester: Patron of Letters* (New York: Columbia UP, 1955).

RQ	*Renaissance Quarterly.*
Schanzer, *Problem Plays*	Ernest Schanzer, *The Problem Plays of Shakespeare: A Study of 'Julius Caesar', 'Measure for Measure', 'Antony and Cleopatra'* (London: Routledge & Kegan Paul, 1963).
SEL	*Studies in English Literature 1500–1900.*
Shakespeare, *Works*	*William Shakespeare: The Complete Works*, ed. Stanley Wells and Gary Taylor (Oxford: Clarendon P, 1986).
Sidney, *Arcadia*	*The Countesse of Pembrokes Arcadia. Written by Sir Philip Sidney Knight. Now since the first edition augmented and ended* (1593), STC 22540.
Sidney, *Astrophel*	*Sir P.S. His Astrophel and Stella. Wherein the excellence of sweete Poesie is concluded* (1591), STC 22536.
Sidney, *Miscellaneous Prose*	*Miscellaneous Prose of Sir Philip Sidney*, ed. Katherine Duncan-Jones and Jan van Dorsten (Oxford: Clarendon P, 1973).
Sidney, *New Arcadia*	*The Countess of Pembrokes Arcadia [The New Arcadia]*, ed. Victor Skretkowicz (Oxford: Clarendon P, 1987).
Sidney, *Old Arcadia*	*The Countess of Pembrokes Arcadia [The Old Arcadia]*, ed. Jean Robertson (Oxford: Clarendon P, 1973).
Sidney, *Poems*	*The Poems of Sir Philip Sidney.* ed. William A. Ringler, Jr. (Oxford: Clarendon P, 1962).
Sidney, *Psalms*	*The Psalms of Sir Philip Sidney and the Countess of Pembroke*, ed. J. C. A. Rathmell (New York: New York UP, 1963).
Sidney, Mary. *Antonie*, ed. Freer	*The Tragedy of Antony by Robert Garnier. Translated by Mary Herbert, Countess of Pembroke*, ed. Coburn Freer, in *Women Writers*, 481–521.
Sidney, Mary. *Antonie*, ed. Luce	*The Countess of Pembroke's Antonie. 1592*, ed. Alice Luce (Weimar: Verlag von Emil Felber, 1897).
Sidney, Mary. *Discourse*, ed. Bornstein	*The Countess of Pembroke's Translation of Philippe de Mornay's Discourse of Life and Death*, ed. Diane Bornstein (Detroit: Michigan Consortium for Medieval and Early Modern Studies, 1983).

Sidney, Mary. *Triumph*	*The Triumph of Death and Other Unpublished and Uncollected Poems by Mary Sidney, Countess of Pembroke (1561–1621)*, ed. Gary F. Waller (Salzburg: U of Salzburg, 1977).
Sidney, Robert. *Poems*	*The Poems of Robert Sidney*, ed. P. J. Croft (Oxford: Clarendon P, 1984).
Silent but for the Word	*Silent but for the Word: Tudor Women as Patrons, Translators, and Writers of Religious Works*, ed. Margaret P. Hannay (Kent, Ohio: Kent UP, 1985).
SP	State Papers.
SP	*Studies in Philology*.
Spenser, *Astrophel*	*Edmund Spenser, Astrophel. A Pastorall Elegie upon the death of the most Noble and valorous Knight, Sir Philip Sidney* (1595), *STC* 23077.
Spenser, *Colin Clouts*	Edmund Spenser, *Colin Clouts Come Home Againe* (1595), *STC* 23077.
Spenser, *Complaints*	Edmund Spenser, *Complaints. Containing sundrie small poemes of the worlds vanitie* (1591), *STC* 23078.
Spenser, *Faerie Queene*	Edmund Spenser, *The Faerie Queene* (1590), *STC* 23080.
Spenser, *Mother Hubberds Tale*	Edmund Spenser, *Prosopopoia. Or Mother Hubberds Tale* (1591), *STC* 23078.
Spenser: Poetical Works	*Spenser: Poetical Works*, ed. J. C. Smith and E. de Selincourt (Oxford: Oxford UP, 1912; rpt. 1983).
Spenser, *Shepheardes Calender*	Edmund Spenser, *The Shepheardes Calender* (1579), *STC* 23089.
Spevack	*A New Variorum Edition of Shakespeare: Antony and Cleopatra*, ed. Marvin Spevack (New York: MLA, 1990).
STC	*A Short-Title Catalogue of Books Printed in England, Scotland, & Ireland...1475–1640*, completed by A. W. Pollard and G. R. Redgrave, 2nd edn. revised & enlarged by W. A. Jackson, F. S. Ferguson, and K. F. Pantzer, *Vol. I, A–H* (London: The Bibliographcial Society, 1986), *Vol. II, I–Z* (1976).
Strigelius	Victorinus Strigelius, *A Third Proceeding in the Harmony of King Davids Harp* [Psalms 45–61]. Trans. Richard Robinson (1595), *STC* 23361.

Taffin, *Children of God*   Jean Taffin, *Of the Markes of the Children of God, and of their Comforts in Afflictions...* *Overseene againe and augmented by the Author, and translated out of French by Anne Prowse* (1590), *STC* 23652.

TLS   *Times Literary Supplement.*

Vatablus   *Liber Psalmorum Davidis. Annotationes in eosdem ex Hebraeorum commentariis* (Paris, 1546).

Wall, *Gender*   Wendy Wall, *The Imprint of Gender: Authorship and Publication in the English Renaissance* (Ithaca: Cornell UP, 1993).

Waller, *Mary Sidney*   Gary Waller, *Mary Sidney, Countess of Pembroke: A Critical Study of Her Writings and Literary Milieu* (Salzburg: U of Salzburg, 1979).

Watson, *Amintae Gaudia*   Thomas Watson, *Amintae Gaudia* (1592), *STC* 25117.

Wing   *Short-Title Catalogue of Books Printed in England, Scotland, Ireland, Wales, and British America and of English Books Printed in Other Countries 1641–1700*, compiled by D. Wing, 3 vols. (New York: Index Society, Columbia UP, 1945–51; revised edn. New York: Index Society, Modern Language Association of America, 1972–88).

Witherspoon, *Garnier*   Alexander Maclaren Witherspoon, *The Influence of Robert Garnier on Elizabethan Drama* (New Haven: Yale UP, 1924).

Women in the Middle Ages   *Women in the Middle Ages and Renaissance: Literary and Historical Perspectives*, ed. Mary Beth Rose (Syracuse: Syracuse UP, 1986).

Women Writers   *Women Writers of the Renaissance and Reformation*, ed. Katharina M. Wilson (Athens, Ga.: U of Georgia P, 1987).

Woods, *Natural Emphasis*   Susanne Woods, *Natural Emphasis: English Versification from Chaucer to Dryden* (San Marino, Calif.: Huntington Library, 1984).

Wroth, *Love's Victory*   *Lady Mary Wroth's Love's Victory. The Penshurst Manuscript*, ed. Michael G. Brennan (London: The Roxburghe Club, 1988).

Wroth, *Poems*   *The Poems of Lady Mary Wroth*, ed. Josephine A. Roberts (Baton Rouge: U of Louisiana P, 1983).

Wroth, *Urania*   Mary Wroth, *The Countesse of Mountgomeries URANIA. Written by the right honourable the Lady MARY WROATH. Daughter to the right Noble Robert Earle of Leicester. And Neece to the ever famous, and renowned Sr. Phillip Sidney Knight. And to the most exelent Lady Mary Countesse of Pembroke Late Deceased* (1621), *STC* 26051.

Wroth, *Urania*, ed. Roberts   *The First Part of The Countess of Montgomery's Urania by Lady Mary Wroth*, ed. Josephine A. Roberts (Binghamton, NY: RMTS, 1995).

Wyatt   Thomas Wyatt, *Certayne psalmes chosen out of the psalter of David, commonly called thee vii. penytentiall Psalmes* (1549), *STC* 2726.

Yates, *Astraea*   Frances A. Yates, *Astraea: The Imperial Theme in the Sixteenth Century* (London: Routledge & Kegan Paul, 1975; rpt. Peregrine Books, 1977).

Young, *Mary Sidney*   Frances Berkeley Young, *Mary Sidney, Countess of Pembroke* (London: David Nutt, 1912).

Zim, *Psalms*   Rivkah Zim, *English Metrical Psalms: Poetry as Praise and Prayer, 1535–1601* (Cambridge: Cambridge UP, 1987).

EDITORIAL PROCEDURE

Transcription

1. The original spelling and punctuation of the copy-texts have been retained except for 'long s', 'VV' and 'vv' used for 'W' and 'w', typographical ligatures (excluding digraphs, which are preserved), and the abbreviations noted below, which have been silently expanded.

2. The use of 'i', 'j', 'u', and 'v' has been regularized, except where specific forms of these letters have been used in acrostics (e.g. Psalm 117. 4). Incidental use of capitals within words has also been regularized.

3. Deletions are printed in the textual notes within angle brackets: <>.

4. Interpolations are printed in the textual notes within slashes: /.

5. In MS *A* of the *Psalmes* all four sides of the pages are ruled in red, with a second rule used to align the text on the left. However, the gold majuscules used in the MS often extend to the left of this second rule so that all subsequent lines (including rhyming lines) are slightly indented. These left-hand indentations have been regularized in the texts.

6. All other departures from the copy-texts are acknowledged in the textual notes and the commentary; cruces are explained in the commentary; because many of the letters are holographs, the interpolations and deletions in the correspondence have been retained in the text (and printed in superscript) rather than moved to the textual notes.

Abbreviations

Abbreviations have been silently expanded, except for special cases in the textual notes where the relationship of particular manuscripts would otherwise be obscured.

1. Standard abbreviations:
ampersand;
tilde used for 'n' and 'm';
tilde used for 'i' in '-cion';

the symbol resembling a figure eight used in the manuscripts for final 'es';

superscripted letters such as 'th' (in 'with'), 'ch' (in 'which'), 'r' (in 'Sir', 'our', 'your', '-our'), 't' (in 'Knight');

superscripted letters (such as 't' and 'e') used with 'y' for words like 'that' and 'the' (the latter is also substituted for 'ye' where Woodforde uses it for the definite article in his transcript of the *Psalmes*, MS *B*).

2. Additional scribal abbreviations:

'Psal:' and 'Ps.' for 'Psalm' in MSS *A* and *B*, respectively (and variously in other manuscripts);

forms used by Woodforde in MS *B*: 'exp.' for 'expunged', 'Q' for 'qure', 'v' with a bisecting virgule for 'verse';

the special character used for '-que' in Latin texts;

two abbreviations used more than once in the endorsements to the letters: 'ex.' for 'examination' and 'touch.' for 'touching'.

3. Additional abbreviations, especially in the holograph letters:

superscripted letters such as 'w' used with 'y' for 'yow' (in addition to superscripted 'r' in 'yowr', as in the scribal practice cited above; the forms with 'w' are the preferred holograph spellings);

the special characters used for 'pre-' and 'pro-' and similar combinations involving 'p' and 'r';

'ld', 'Ld', 'L:', 'Lo:' and superscripted 'rd' (with 'L') used for 'lord' and 'lordship', depending on context;

superscripted 'pe' with 'L' for 'Lordship';

superscripted 'tie', 'ty' for 'Majesty' and 'ties' for 'Majesty's';

'Ph:' for 'Philip' (as also in some title pages of the *Psalmes* manuscripts).

Textual Notes

1. Limitations of space normally allow only verbal variants in manuscripts or editions other than the copy-texts to be reported in the textual notes; most variations in spelling, punctuation, indentation, and paragraphing are thus ignored. This principle applies especially to the *Psalmes* (and in particular to MS *I*, with its highly eccentric spelling, which is discussed in 'Manuscripts of the *Psalmes*'); fully reporting the divergences in all seventeen of the extant copies would amount to a nearly complete transcription of each of the manuscripts (the choice of MS *A* as the copy-text for the *Psalmes* is justified in 'Relationship of the Texts of the *Psalmes*'):

all substantive variants involving single words, phrases, and lines
are noted, but obvious scribal errors (e.g. 'th' for 'the' in 73. 49
and 'strangr' for the rhyme word 'strange' in 68. 42 [variant ver-
sion], MS *I*, and 'rembraunce' for 'remembrance' in 45. 60, MS
H) and routine, isolated corrections (e.g. 'right' corrected to
'ritch' in 49. 34, MS *K*) are usually ignored;

the main principle used in selecting substantive variants to report
is whether a word is given a separate, full entry in the *OED* in its
regular form (e.g. 'sperit' is treated as simply another spelling of
'spirit', but 'sprite' or 'spright' is considered to be a distinct
form and is thus cited as a substantive variant in the textual
notes); however, we do not apply the principle mechanically and
uncritically, but are guided by the context and sources of each
work and thus generally ignore unambiguous spelling variants
such as 'be' and 'bee', 'we' and 'wee', since citing them would
unnecessarily swell the textual notes;

to ensure the reporting of the complex transmission history of the
Psalmes, including the late rhymed versions of Psalms 120 to 127,
we discuss the seventeen extant manuscripts in 'Relationship of
the Texts of the *Psalmes*' and provide a multi-level presentation
of the texts themselves: the paraphrases as preserved in MS *A*,
the copy-text, with all emendations reported in the textual notes
and noted in the commentary; significant variants in the other
manuscripts reported in the textual notes and, when it is useful
to do so, noted in the commentary; and the alternative Psalm paraphrases, whether authorial or not, preserved in manuscripts other
than *A*, printed in their entirety;

other differences are cited to help establish the text in the copy-
texts or to clarify the relationship of the various editions and
manuscripts (to the copy-texts and to one another);

cruces are fully described;

emendations are noted and justified in the commentary (previous
editors are cited for support in the commentary when necessary,
but disagreements are usually passed over in silence);

lack of punctuation is indicated by a caret, and repeated text
is normally replaced by a tilde, except for complex cases (especially involving other variants), such as Pss. 64. 26, 69. 103, and
78. 161;

press variants are discussed in the introductions to the individual
works.

2. Handling of the *Psalmes* manuscripts requires additional comment, for not all of them are substantive witnesses:

two manuscripts, *L* and *P*, are ignored because *P* is copied from *L*, which is a copy of *E*;

two others, *F* and *J*, are cited selectively because *J* and Psalms 27–150 in *F* were copied from *A*;

the Greek letter χ represents the members of the χ tradition (*I*, *K*, *O*, *D*, *H*, *Q*, *E*, *L*, *P*, *G*, *M*) when there is no disagreement among them; θ similarly represents *O* and *D*, and σ represents *H*, *Q*, *E*, *L*, and *P*;

we have normally not reported minor variations in spelling (e.g. final 'y' vs. 'ie');

we have not reported in detail the verse numbers which were added later to *K* from the Prayer Book Psalter (even when it is clear that the source of the paraphrase was Geneva or another text) or the rubrics for morning and evening prayer added later to both *K* and *I*; the special features of these and the other *Psalmes* manuscripts are noted in 'Manuscripts of the *Psalmes*';

variants in the alternative Psalms are reported more fully, especially in the case of *G* and *M* because of the doubtful authority of those manuscripts in relation to one another (although *M*, which seems generally to preserve the latest state of the text, has been chosen as the copy-text for the rhymed Psalms 120–7, *G* occasionally appears to be a more reliable witness and is thus reported so that readers may make their own judgements).

Emendation

The need for and method of emendation vary for each work:

'Astrea' and 'Dolefull Lay': Correction of obvious printing errors (including one probable omission) adopted from subsequent editions.

Triumph of Death: Correction of scribal errors based on examination of context and comparison with the Italian text.

'Even now that Care' and 'Angell Spirit': Correction of scribal (and 1623 printing) errors based on examination of context.

Discourse: Silent reversal of turned characters and noted deletion of one obviously mistaken repetition.

Antonius: Silent reversal of turned letters, spacing within words, and font substitution; noted correction of obvious printer's misspellings (including faulty abbreviation of speech prefixes and mistaken punctuation); noted correction of other errors based on examination of context and comparison with the French text.

Psalmes: Correction of scribal errors based on comparison with sources and other manuscripts.

Spelling in the Holograph Letters

The correspondence reveals some distinctive, though not unique, spellings. For instance, 'w' is frequently used for 'u', especially in forms of the second person personal pronoun, hence, our expansion to 'yow' and 'yowr' when those forms are abbreviated. Other examples include the following: retention of 'e' before 'ing' ('loveing', Letter II; 'haveing', V, VII, XII; etc.), spelling of [i] without 'i' ('perceve', I; 'conceved', V, VI; etc.) or 'a' ('leve', IX, XVI; 'Cretur', IX, XV; etc.), use of 'i' for the now standard 'e' ('knowlidg', VII, VIII, XV; 'chaling', VII; 'Inglands', IX), use of 'e' for 'i' ('testemony', V, VII, XV; 'happenes' VII, X, XVI; etc.), use of 'c' for 's' ('beceching', I; 'bace', XII, XV; etc.), use of 's' for 'c' ('presious', VI, IX; 'embrased', VII; 'partisepating', IX; etc.), use of 'w' for 'u' in other words besides 'yow' and 'yowr' ('dowt', II; 'dwe', VIII, X, XV; 'trwth', XIII; etc.), 'oo' for 'ou' in the modal auxiliaries, 'could', 'should', and 'would' ('coold', II, V; 'shoold, V; 'woold', II; etc.), 'bin' and 'bine' for 'been' (I, II, VIII). A number of notable, but again not necessarily unique, spellings occur only once: 'hard' for 'heard' (I), 'faute' for 'fault' (I), 'unusiall' for 'unusual' (II), 'god' for 'good' as in some *Psalmes* manuscripts (II), 'arrant' for 'errand' (V), 'aughter' for 'author' (VIII), 'phelows' (XIII), among others. The use of 'o' for 'u' occurs in 'retorne' for 'return' (V, VI, X) and in 'most' for 'must' (I), which helps solve a crux in line 18 of 'Even now that Care', where 'must' appears as 'most'. Two distinctive features of the Italian hand used in these holographs could have led to scribal confusion: a single-stroke 't' (with the cross stroke made from the left after a long downward swoop without lifting the pen) sometimes resembling a fully looped 'long s', and an angular, cursive 's' sometimes resembling both secretary 'c' and secretary 'r'.

PSALMES

Literary Context

The biblical Psalms, a traditional part of Judaeo-Christian private and public worship, took on new resonance in the Reformation through their translation into the vernacular and their use in congregational singing. Some Psalms in English had circulated in manuscript Books of Hours during the second half of the fourteenth century, demonstrating the influence of the Wyclif translation, but the 'Constitution of Clarendon' (1408) ordered that 'no one shall in the future translate on his own authority any text of the holy scripture into the English tongue'.[1] The injunction was effectively enforced until Tyndale's publication of the New Testament in English on the Continent, begun at Cologne in 1525 and completed at Worms in 1526.

Vernacular Psalms also reached England through the Continent. Martin Luther advocated the use of vernacular songs for worship in his *Formula missae et communionis pro Ecclesia Vuittembergensi* (Wittenberg, 1523) and later that year told his friend Georg Spalatin that 'I intend to make German [vernacular] Psalms for the people, i.e., spiritual songs so that the Word of God even by means of song may live among the people. Everywhere we are looking for poets.'[2] Luther himself wrote metrical Psalms in German, as did Johann Agricola; these early Psalms were printed on broadsides for congregational singing and were collected by a printer in Nuremberg in 1524 as the first Reformation hymnbook. Subsequent vernacular Psalms in German, French, Italian, and Dutch are intimately connected to the ninety English versions published in the sixteenth century, because of the movement of Protestant exiles between England and the Continent.[3]

---

[1] C. C. Butterworth, *The English Primers (1529–1545): Their Publication and Connection with the English Bible and the Reformation in England* (Philadelphia, 1953), 5.

[2] Martin Luther to Georg Spalatin, 1523, translated in *Luther's Works: American Edition*, ed. U. S. Leupold and H. T. Lehmann (St Louis, 1955–86), LIII. 221. On the Psalms in Wittenberg, Nuremberg, and Strasburg, see Leaver, *'Ghoostly Psalmes'*, 2–33.

[3] For a list of sixteenth-century English Psalms, see Zim, *Psalms*, 211–59. R. Gerald Hobbs, 'Hebraica Veritas *and* Traditio Apostolica: Saint Paul and the Interpretation of the Psalms in the Sixteenth Century', in *The Bible in the Sixteenth Century*, ed. David C. Steinmetz (Durham, NC: Duke UP, 1990), 222–5, includes Continental Psalms and commentaries. For a list of seventeenth-century Psalm translations, see Philipp von Rohr-Sauer, *English Metrical Psalms from 1600 to 1660: A Study of the Religious and Aesthetic Tendencies of That Period* (Freiburg: Poppen and Ortmann, 1938), 119–24.

Martin Bucer, the Strasburg Reformer, is a central figure. The first
English Psalter in print was George Joye's translation of Bucer's 1529
Latin text, published under the pseudonym Aretius Felinus in
Antwerp in 1530.[4] Bucer, a strong advocate for congregational
Psalm-singing, later served as Regius Professor of Divinity at Cam-
bridge during Edward's reign and influenced the 1552 Book of Com-
mon Prayer as well as the form of worship used in Strasburg and in
Geneva. The connections continue in that while Bucer was pastor of
St Thomas' Church in Strasburg, Miles Coverdale sought safety there
(1540); Coverdale's translation of the Psalms was later printed with
the Book of Common Prayer, and he is said to have helped with the
translation of the Geneva Bible of 1560. During this same period
Bucer invited John Calvin to live with him and to become the pastor
of the French exiles there (1538–41). When Calvin found his Strasburg congregation singing the German Psalms, he sought to give
them a Psalter in their own language—a project that eventually produced the French-Genevan metrical Psalter, *Les Psaumes de David mis
en rime Francoise* by Clément Marot and Théodore de Bèze (1562), the
primary literary model for the Sidneian *Psalmes*, as for other metrical
versions such as the *Psalmi di David* by Philip Sidney's friend and correspondent François Perrot, which was published with the music of
the *Psaumes* (1581; complete edition 1603).[5] The revised Anglo-
Genevan Psalter familiarly known as 'Sternhold and Hopkins' or the
Old Version was also produced by this community of exiles, who
believed that 'there are no songes more meete, than the psalmes of
the Prophete David, which the holy ghost hath framed to the same
use, and commended to the churche, as conteining the effect of the
whole scriptures'.[6]

When the Marian exiles returned to England under Elizabeth, they
brought with them the Continental custom of singing Psalms. On 21

---

[4] *The Psalter of David in Englishe purely and faithfully translated aftir the texte of ffeline*
('Argentine' [Antwerp], 1530), STC 2370.

[5] See Prescott, *French Poets*, 15–17; and England, 30–54, 101–10. For listing of verse
forms from the *Psaumes* used in the Sidney *Psalmes*, see England, Appendix B, and Rathmell
(Ph.D. diss.), 530.

[6] *The forme of prayers and ministration of the sacraments, &c. used in the Englishe congregation at Geneva: and approved, by John Calvyn* (Geneva, 1556), STC 16561, sig. B2. For an
account of the gradual collection of the Psalms by 'Thomas Sternholde and others' and
Whittingham's revisions to make the verse closer to the Hebrew, see Leaver, 'Ghoostly
Psalmes', 241–56 and particularly the genealogical chart on 253. The Old Version was so
called after the appearance of *A New Version of the Psalms of David, Fitted to the Tunes
Used in Churches, by N. Tate and N. Brady* (1696), Wing B2598.

September 1559 the first known singing of metrical Psalms 'after Geneva fashion' took place at the 5 a.m. prayer service at St Antholin's Church in London. By 1560 the custom was so well established that John Jewel wrote to Peter Martyr on 5 March that 'You may now sometimes see at Paul's Cross, after the service, six thousand persons, old and young, of both sexes, all singing together and praising God'.[7] Once churches throughout England had adopted the custom, these Psalms became part of the popular culture. Coverdale wanted carters and ploughmen to whistle 'psalms, hymns, and such godly songs as David is occupied withal' and women to sing them as they spin, instead of *'hey nony nony, hey troly loly*, and such like phantasies'.[8] Apparently they did, for by 1579 Anthony Gilby was concerned that Psalms were being sung more 'for fashion sake, then for good devotion and with understanding'.[9]

Catholics also sang the Marot/Bèze Psalms, but as French Catholic attempts to parody or to suppress the *Psaumes* demonstrate, such Psalm-singing became increasingly partisan.[10] As George Wither records, Catholics 'have of late years disapprooved the translation of these *Psalmes* into the vulgar tongues, and scoffed at the singing of them in the reformed Churches' and 'in scorne termed them *Geneva Jigs*, and *Beza's Ballets*'.[11] When Protestants were persecuted, 'the psalmists' words seem to have come almost automatically to their lips', serving both as 'battle hymns' in the Continental religious wars

---

[7] Leaver, *'Ghoostly Psalmes'*, 240–1, quoting from *The Zurich Letters, Comprising the Correspondence of Several English Bishops and Others, with some of the Helvetian Reformers, during . . . the Reign of Queen Elizabeth*, ed. Hastings Robinson (Cambridge: Parker Society, 1847), I. 71.

[8] Miles Coverdale, *Remains of Myles Coverdale*, ed. George Pearson (Cambridge: Parker Society, 1846), 537. Cf. the subtitle of *The Whole Booke of Psalmes . . . Very mete to be used of all sortes of people privately for their solace and comfort: laying apart all ungodly Songes and Ballades, which tende only to the norishing of vyce, and corrupting of youth* (1562), STC 2430.

[9] Anthony Gilby, 'The Epistle to the Reader', in Théodore de Bèze, *The Psalmes of David, truely opened and explaned by Paraphrasis, according to the right sense of every Psalme* (1580), STC 2033, sig. *6.

[10] See, for example, the parody by Artus Désiré, *Le Contreparison des Cinquante-Deux Chansons de Clément Marot* (1560). Facsimile: Geneva: Librairie Droz SA, 1977; on Puritans and Psalm singing, see Percy Scholes, *The Puritans and Music* (London: Oxford UP, 1934), 266–74.

[11] George Wither, *A Preparation to the Psalter* (1619), STC 25914, sigs. B4ᵛ–B5. Attributing power to poetry in Sidneian terms, Wither claims that they 'feare the operation of the divine word expressed in *Numbers*' through 'our versified *Psalmes*', because 'there lurks in *Poesy* an enchanting sweetnesse, that steals into the hearts of men before they be aware'. On Catholic repudiation of Marot's Psalms, see Prescott, *French Poets*, 29–34.

and as personal consolation in times of persecution.[12] For example, when Adam de Sequart, emissary of Cardinal de Bourbon, Archbishop of Rouen, was sent to Dieppe in 1559 to suppress the Protestants, some 2,000 of them stood by his door singing Marot's Psalms in protest. A similar crowd of Psalm singers who marched to St Giles' Church in Edinburgh so terrified Esme Stuart, Duke of Lennox, that he fled in terror. Marching into battle, the Huguenots sang Psalm 68, 'Let God arise, let his enemies be scattered.' The direct application of Psalms to their own situation can be seen in the use of the popular Psalm 124 ('If it had not been the Lord who was on our side, now may Israel say') to the arrival of the Prince de Condé in Orleans, when the Huguenots changed the refrain to 'now may Orleans say'.[13]

Even reciting vernacular Psalms could become a political statement. For example, the recitation of Psalm 51, a standard part of the execution ritual, took on dramatic importance when the prisoner spoke in English instead of Latin.[14] Foxe recounts that when Dr Rowland Taylor began to recite the Psalm in English the sheriff struck him. ' "Ye knave", said he, "speake Latine, I will make thee." '[15] Foxe's account of Lady Jane Grey's death also emphasizes her use of the vernacular.[16] Awaiting execution, she recited 'the Psalm of "*Miserere mei Deus*" in English, in most devout manner throughout to the end'. Emphasizing her belief in the priesthood of all believers, Lady Jane ignored the Catholic priest and asked the crowd, 'assist me with your prayers'.[17]

Psalms were also considered particularly appropriate for private meditation. As the oft-reprinted comments of Athanasius direct, readers should apply the Psalms to their own condition because 'It is easy . . . for every man to finde out in the Psalmes, the motion and state of his owne soule'.[18] As Matthew Parker said in his Prefatory 'Of the vertue of Psalmes':

---

[12] W. Stanford Reid, 'The Battle Hymns of the Lord: Calvinist Psalmody of the Sixteenth Century', *Sixteenth Century Essays and Studies* 2 (1971), 36.

[13] Ibid., 43–53.

[14] Lydia Whitehead, '*A poena et culpa*: Penitence, Confidence and the *Miserere* in Foxe's *Actes and Monuments*', *Renaissance Studies* 4 (1990), 294.

[15] John Foxe, *The Acts and Monuments of John Foxe*, ed. George Townsend (New York: AMS Press, 1965), VI. 700.

[16] See Sidney accounts for 1573, De L'Isle MS U1475 A4/5.

[17] Foxe, *Acts and Monuments*, VI. 700.

[18] *The Whole Booke of Psalmes*, sig *7ᵛ. See also St Athanasius, as translated by Matthew Parker, *The Whole psalter translated into English Metre, which contayneth an hundreth and fifty Psalmes* (1567), *STC* 2729, sig. C1.

> In other bookes: where man doth looke,
> but others wordes seeth he:
> As proper hath: this onely booke,
> most wordes his owne to be.[19]

John Calvin demonstrated just how personal that application could become in the lengthy address 'to the godly Readers' that prefaced his commentaries on the Psalms. Believing that his interpretation gained resonance because his situation paralleled the Psalmist's, he explains that 'it availed mee not a litle that I had abiden the same things that [David] bewaileth or much like, at the handes of the householde enemies of the Churche'.[20] Others felt drawn to the Psalms because of tribulation. Psalm meditation became almost *de rigueur* for sixteenth-century prisoners, particularly those who believed that they were persecuted for their religious beliefs. Sir Thomas More, Henry Howard, Earl of Surrey, Queen Mary Stuart, John Dudley, Earl of Warwick, and his brother Robert, later Earl of Leicester, are just a few of those who translated appropriate Psalms of penitence, or, in the case of the Dudleys, prayers for vengeance against their enemies.

Translations and meditations on the penitential Psalms were frequently published, such as those by George Gascoigne, Thomas Potter, William Hunnis, and most notably Thomas Wyatt's reworking of Aretino's *Sette Salmi della Penitentia di David*. Wyatt stresses 'inwardness' when he speaks of 'Inward Sion, the Sion of the ghost' and of the 'heart's Jerusalem'.[21] Pembroke was probably familiar with some of these versions. She did know the 26 sonnets on Psalm 51 composed by Anne Lok, because she quotes Lok's phrase 'O god, god of my

[19] Parker, *The Whole psalter*, sig Aiiii^v.

[20] John Calvin, *The Psalms of David and others. With M. John Calvins Commentaries*, trans. Arthur Golding (1571), *STC* 4395, sig. *7^v.

[21] Thomas Wyatt, *Certayne psalmes chosen out of the psalter of David, commonlye called thee .vii. penytentiall psalmes* (1549), *STC* 2726; Stephen Greenblatt, *Renaissance Self-Fashioning: From More to Shakespeare* (Chicago: U of Chicago P, 1980), 115. George Gascoigne, [Psalm 130] *The Posies of George Gascoigne Esquire* (1575), *STC* 11636; Thomas Potter, *An Exposition upon the Cxxx. Psalme, Setting forth the comfortable doctrine of our justification and peace in Christ. Written by M. Luther: and nowe newley translated for the comfort of afflicted consciences, by Thomas Potter* (1577), *STC* 16979.3 (formerly 20137); William Hunnis, *Seven Sobs of a Sorrowfull Soule for Sinne* (1583), *STC* 13975. Penitential Psalms continued to be published in the seventeenth century, as R. Verstegan [Richard Rowlands], *Odes. In Imitation of the Seaven Penitential Psalmes* (1601), *STC* 21359; John Davies of Hereford, 'The Dolefull Dove: or Davids 7. Penitentiall Psalmes', in the *Muses Sacrifice, or Davids Meditations* (1612), *STC* 6338; and Sir John Hayward, *Davids Teares* (1625), *STC* 12991. George Chapman translated Petrarch's meditations on the penitential Psalms in 1612.

health' (51. 40) and adapts her phrase 'filthie fault' (51. 9).[22] Pembroke would undoubtedly have been familiar with Psalm paraphrases by other women. Lady Elizabeth Fane's meditations on twenty-one Psalms, published by Robert Crowley in 1550 (no longer extant), were available to her, and there were additional models in the Psalms attributed to Anne Askew and to Queen Elizabeth by John Bale, and women's prayers based on Psalms in Thomas Bentley's *The Monument of Matrones*, including those by Lady Elizabeth Tyrwhit.[23] Undoubtedly many others, like Pembroke herself, wrote but did not print Psalm meditations.[24] As Sidney said, the Psalms are appropriate for all persons in all occasions. 'Used with the fruit of comfort by some, when, in sorrowful pangs of their death-bringing sins, they find the consolation of the never-leaving goodness', they also may 'be used by whosoever will follow St. James's counsel in singing Psalms when they are merry'.[25]

Psalm translation provided more scope for independent statement than other scriptural translation, because the ambiguous 'I' of the Psalms leaves a space for the reader to insert a personal voice. 'David's infolded voices express Christ and ourselves as well as his own circumstance', as Anne Prescott reminds us.[26] Equally important is the complexity of the nested speakers. Translators usually speak in two voices, their own and that of the original author, but the divinely inspired Psalms are a special case. Anthony Gilby, referring to his English translation of Bèze's commentaries on the Psalms, made the sequence clear. Bèze, he says, has written 'a briefe and a plaine declaration of the meaning of the holy Ghost, who did endite the

[22] See Margaret Hannay, ' "Unlock my lipps": The *Miserere mei Deus* of Anne Vaughan Lok and Mary Sidney Herbert, Countess of Pembroke', *Privileging Gender in Early Modern England, Sixteenth-Century Essays and Studies* 23 (1993), 19–36.

[23] Queen Elizabeth, trans: Margaret of Angoulême, *A godly medytacyon of the christen sowle* (1548), STC 17320, sig. A7ᵛ–8; *The first examinacyon of Anne Askewe, latelye martyred in Smythfelde, by the Romysh popes upholders, with the Elucydacyon of Johan Bale* (Wesel, 1546), STC 848, sig. 4F7ᵛ–8. Bale apparently translated at least Psalm 13 himself. See King, *Reformation*, 219; Zim, *Psalms*, 221. Thomas Bentley, *The Monument of Matrones: conteining seven severall Lamps of Virginitie* (1582), STC 1892–3. Psalm paraphrases in Bentley's compilation are listed in Zim, *Psalms*, 244–6.

[24] *Odes in imitation of the seven poenitentiall Psalmes in seven severall kinde of verse* by Elizabeth Grymeston, for example, were published after her death by her husband in her *Miscelanea* (1604), STC 12407.

[25] Sidney, *Miscellaneous Prose*, 80.

[26] Anne Lake Prescott, 'King David as a "Right Poet": Sidney and the Psalmist', *ELR* 19 (1989), 134; Lewalski, *Protestant Poetics*, 301–2; Roland Greene, 'Sir Philip Sidney's Psalms, the Sixteenth-Century Psalter, and the Nature of Lyric', *SEL* 30 (1990), 19–40.

Psalmes, and set them foorth by his secretaries, David and others'.[27]
That is, the Psalms he is presenting have four authors, in descending
order from God, through David, to Bèze, and then to Gilby himself.
A similar pattern is seen in John Donne's poem 'Upon the translation
of the Psalmes by Sir Philip Sydney, and the Countesse of Pembroke
his Sister'. Saying that they make 'one *John Baptists* holy voyce', he
calls the brother and sister 'this *Moses* and this *Miriam*' and portrays
them as divinely inspired in their *Psalmes*, if at two removes:

> The songs are these, which heavens high holy Muse
> Whisper'd to *David*, *David* to the Jewes:
> And *Davids* successors, in holy zeale,
> In formes of joy and art doe re-reveale
> To us...[28]

That is, God speaks to David, who records God's words for the Jews;
the Sidneys, who have become '*Davids* successors', then 're-reveale'
those words to us in English. Pembroke also speaks through another
authorizing voice in addition to those of God and David, as Elaine
Beilin and Gary Waller remind us—that of her brother Philip,[29]
who had not only begun to paraphrase the Psalms, but had praised
them as the highest form of poetry, 'they that did imitate the uncon-
ceivable excellencies of God'.[30]

The Sidneian *Psalmes*, based on sophisticated Continental literary
models, were a conscious attempt to 'better grace' those Psalms than
'what the vulgar form'd', Pembroke's harsh, if accurate, assessment of
the thumping metres of the Sternhold and Hopkins Psalter decreed
for public singing by King Edward.[31] In dedicating the Psalms to
Elizabeth, Pembroke says that David would not be displeased by the
Sidneian version, 'Oft having worse, without repining worne' ('Even
now that Care', 32). Her contemporaries agreed with her assessment.
Thomas Moffet, for example, says that her 'pen divine and consecrated

---

[27] Gilby, *The Psalmes of David*, sig. *2v.
[28] Donne, 'Upon the translation of the Psalmes by Sir Philip Sydney, and the Countesse
of Pembroke his Sister', in *The Divine Poems*, ed. Helen Gardner (Oxford: Clarendon P,
1952; rpt. 1978), 34–5.
[29] Beilin, *Redeeming Eve*, 148–9; Waller, 'The Countess of Pembroke and Gendered
Reading', in *Renaissance Englishwoman*, 339.
[30] Sidney, *Miscellaneous Prose*, 80.
[31] Early version of 'To the Angell Spirit of Sir Philip Sidney' as printed in *The Whole
Workes of Samuel Daniel* (1623), II. 11. See [Variant] text. The revised version in the Tixall
MS is far more tactful.

Psalmes, | From wronging verse did *Royall Singer* raise'.[32] Donne
agreed, asking with patriotic concern if 'our Church' should sing
'More hoarse, more harsh than any other'.[33] Prior to the Sidneys,
he says, Continental versions shamed those in English; the Psalms
were 'So well attyr'd abroad, so ill at home' (38). Donne quotes
from Psalm 97. 1 to show the patriotic contribution of the Sidneys:

> And who that Psalme, *Now let the Iles rejoyce*,
> Have both translated, and apply'd it too,
> Both told us what, and taught us how to doe.
> They shew us Ilanders our joy, our King,
> They tell us *why*, and teach us *how* to sing.   (18–22)

Parallel to the tradition of Psalm singing and meditation was scholarly prose translation and commentary in Latin and in the vernacular.
Such application of Greek and Hebrew scholarship to the scriptures
became increasingly Protestant, because the Catholic Church chose
the Latin Vulgate as the authoritative text. To promote Protestant
scholarship, Francis I founded the Collège de Paris as a trilingual college, emphasizing the study of the three scholarly languages of Latin,
Greek, and Hebrew; the noted Hebraist Vatablus taught there. Trilingual studies flourished in Wittenburg and Geneva, as well as in
France and England. These studies produced more accurate vernacular translations of the Bible. Unlike Coverdale, Tyndale based his
translation of the Pentateuch (1530) on the Hebrew text. In one of
his final letters, he asks that he might have his Hebrew Bible, gram-
mar, and dictionary to continue work even as he awaits execution.[34]

Translation as a literary form presents significant challenges, particularly when one is presenting a sacred text. As George Wither noted
in his *Schollers Purgatory*, 'the Translater [of the scriptures]
is . . . bound, not only to the sence (according to the liberty used in
other Translations), but to the very words, or words of the same
power with those used in our allowed Interpretations'.[35] Pembroke's
own attitude toward Psalm paraphrase is reflected in her rendering
of the Psalmist's prayer, 'That in Thy lawes I may Thy Scholar be'
(Variant Psalm 119H. 32). She consulted the best translations and

---

[32] Moffet, *Silkewormes*, sig. G1.

[33] Donne, 'Upon the translation', ll. 43–4.

[34] *Tyndale's Old Testament Being the Pentateuch of 1530, Joshua to 2 Chronicles of 1537, and Jonah*, ed. David Daniell (New Haven: Yale UP, 1992), p. xvii.

[35] Wither, *Schollers Purgatory* (1624), STC 25919, sig. C2^v.

commentaries available to her, but she maintained a critical attitude toward these sources, which frequently disagreed with each other.[36]

Her interpretation is based on standard Protestant texts: the Coverdale Psalter, already beloved in the Book of Common Prayer; the Geneva Bible with the notes of 1560; and the commentaries of Calvin and of Bèze (in Latin and in the English translation of Anthony Gilby). Because she so frequently gives composite readings of these texts, she must have worked with them open before her. Occasionally she will echo other biblical translations, such as that by Bucer, the Tyndale/Coverdale Bible published by John Rogers under the pseudonym of Thomas Matthew, the Bishops Bible, and the Taverner Bible. Wording or repeated rhymes indicate that she also used or recalled other metrical Psalms, particularly those of Matthew Parker, but also those of Robert Crowley, Sternhold and Hopkins, George Gascoigne, and Anne Lok. Metaphors, interpretation, and wording indicate that she also consulted such additional sources as the commentaries of Victorinus Strigelius, Franciscus Vatablus, George Buchanan, and Immanuel Tremellius.

Much of her phrasing is adapted directly from her biblical sources, of course, like the opening of Psalm 45, 'My harte endites an argument of worth', from the Psalter (v. 1): 'My hart is enditing of a good matter'. More typically, she will restate biblical phrases. For example, she adapts a sentence from the Geneva Bible, 'thou hast made us to drinke the wine of giddines' (60: 3), into a doublet, 'dull horror was our drinck, | we drincking giddy grew' (60. 11–12); and she restates the biblical phrase, the wicked 'shall laugh him to scorn' (Psalter 52: 7), as the descriptive 'laughing shoote at thee | with scornfull glaunces' (52. 23–4). Often she incorporates notes from the Geneva Bible into her text, as the inexpressibility topos in 104. 78 or the angels in 89. 19–20. Sometimes she echoes the wording of other biblical translations, such as Bucer | Joye, 'heardsman' (80. 1), 'shine' (80. 2), 'anguishes' (120. 1), 'closeth' (125. 7); and the Bishops' Bible, 'A Vine thou didst translate' (80. 17).

Pembroke relied primarily on scholarly translations and commentaries, but she occasionally does echo other metrical versions of the

<hr/>

[36] On the sources for the Sidneian *Psalmes*, see Sidney, *Poems*, 505–9; Sidney, *Psalms*, pp. xv–xix; Waller, *Mary Sidney*, 184–90; Zim, *Psalms*, 152–202; England, 30–54; 101–10; Richard Todd, ' "So Well Atyr'd Abroad": A Background to the Sidney–Pembroke Psalter and Its Implications for the Seventeenth-Century Religious Lyric', *Texas Studies in Literature and Language* 29 (Spring 1987), 74–93.

Psalms. Many of her verse forms and some of her wording are derived from the *Psaumes* of 1562 by Marot and Bèze, such as 'fearfull dove' (55. 14), 'desert' (55. 17), 'Aspick' (58. 13), 'one quarter of a night' (90. 20), and 'fortes' (122. 13). She also develops the crow image (79. 10) from *Psaumes*, '*Aux corbeaux pour les paistre*'. (The biblical sources (v. 2) have only 'beasts'; Parker has 'byrdes'.) In 124. 6 Pembroke adapts '*la fureur*' (*Psaumes* v. 3) into a parallel, alliterated phrase, 'soe fell, so furious'. A few words apparently come from Crowley, such as 'darknesse' (88. 78) and 'targett' (115. 22). Both the simplicity of language and the opening rhyme of Psalm 113 are reminiscent of the Old Version: 'Ye children which do serve the Lord, | Praise his name with one accord' (v. 1). She also follows it in showing God lifting the needy out of the dust and making them rulers (113. 15–16) and echoes its phrasing in 'with skilfull song' (47. 15), adapted from 'all skillful prayses syng'.[37]

Occasionally Pembroke uses rhymes that are found in other metrical Psalms, but most of them are common enough to be coincidence or vaguely remembered, such as Parker's 'spake'/'quake' in 116, the Old Version's 'observe'/'swerve' in Psalm 119A, Crowley's 'paine'/'vaine' rhyme in Var. Ps. 127, or Gascoigne's 'word'/'Lord' in Psalm 130; Gascoigne's 'redeem'/'esteem' and 'prayeng'/'waighing' may be more indicative of influence.[38] Psalm 51 echoes 'so'/'snowe' and 'wall'/'fall' in Lok and 'me'/'iniquitie' in Crowley, but Pembroke's immediate source for her 'gladness'/'sadness' rhyme comes, surprisingly, from Golding's translation of Calvin, 'verely bicause the sadnes which tormenteth them, openeth them the gate to true joy...true gladnesse'. The 'gladness'/'sadness' rhyme is also used in Sidney's Psalm 43. A few other rhymes are repeated from Sidney, as his 'prating'/'hating' in Psalm 8, used in Pembroke's Psalm 69, or 'farr'/'starr' of Psalm 10, used in Psalm 57. The very infrequency of such rhymes repeated from sources that she regularly consulted would indicate a conscious effort to forge completely new versions.

The early versions of her Psalms transcribed by Samuel Woodforde give us a glimpse of her working process. Not all Psalms follow this

[37] See also 'trade' (119E. 15), 'bane' (119M. 14), and 'strayning' (142. 1). The idea of the path leading the Israelites through the dry bed of the Red Sea to 'glad pastures' (77. 89–96) is developed from the Old Version, as are her personification of the moon in 72. 23–4 and her use of the chain and robes of office as symbols of the wicked in 73. 16–18.

[38] Roy T. Eriksen argues for the influence of Gascoigne in 'George Gascoigne's and Mary Sidney's Versions of Psalm 130', *Cahiers Elisabethains* 36 (1989), 5.

exact pattern, but she usually began with the Book of Common Prayer or with the Geneva Bible to write a preliminary version. Then she consulted the Marot/Bèze *Psaumes*, adopting some of its metres as well as direct translations from the French. She frequently replaced the wording of the Coverdale Psalter with more precise or imaginative terms, relied on the Geneva Bible where it differs from the Psalter, expanded metaphors, supplied tighter connections between images that seemed unrelated in her originals, incorporated metaphors and interpretations from scholarly commentaries, and added rhetorical flourishes, such as figures of repetition, alliteration, word play, and rhetorical questions. (See I.58.) She also improved the quality of the verse. Some of the Variant Psalms recorded by Woodforde are clearly drafts, with occasional faulty rhyme, rough metre, or tangled syntax that is dramatically improved in MS *A* (as in Variant Psalms LXXI. 29–35; CV. 20, 23; and the ragged acrostic poem CXVII).

In Psalm 44, for example, the draft recorded by Woodforde is a close paraphrase of the Psalter. In the revised version in the Penshurst manuscript, Pembroke follows Calvin in expanding the plant metaphor (v. 3) and in rendering the biblical phrase 'the light of Gods countenance' as 'thie favors treasure' (14).[39] She follows Bèze in portraying God as the captain leading his armies (v. 10). From a Geneva note she adds (v. 12) the word 'slaves' (44) and the idea of 'hedshakings' (v. 14; l. 55). Here, as in many other passages, Pembroke adds 'blush' (60) to the biblical idea of shame or reproach (v. 15), a figure that parallels Philip Sidney's usage in Psalm 34. 20 and appears frequently in Bèze's Latin *carmina*.

Other *Psalmes* give composite readings from a variety of sources: for example, Psalm 51 relies primarily on Geneva, Coverdale, Calvin, and Lok, but 121 echoes the French *Psaumes*, Geneva, and Bèze. Some Psalms do rely more heavily on a single source, such as Psalm 48 on the Geneva text and notes, Psalm 55 on the French *Psaumes*, and Psalm 61 on Bèze.

Because of her concern to render the scriptures faithfully, she consulted the most scholarly translations and commentaries available in Latin, French, and English, and where her sources differ, she tends to follow the source closest to the Hebrew. For example, instead of relying primarily on Coverdale's Psalter in the Book of Common

---

[39] Calvin's commentary (44: 4): 'the lyght of thy countenance' means 'the declaration of his favour'.

Prayer, which was based on the work of Luther, Tyndale, and other translators, she favoured the 1560 Geneva Bible, 'Translated according to the Ebrue and Greke', as the title proudly states.[40] Noting that previous translations, such as Coverdale's, were based on 'imperfect knollage of the tongues', the Genevan translators claim that they 'have in every point and worde... faithfully rendred the text, and in all hard places moste syncerely expounded the same. For God is our witnes that we have by all meanes indevored to set forthe the puritie of the worde and right sense of the holy Gost.'[41] They used italics for places where the Hebrew text had been expanded, added notes on difficult words, supplied charts of doctrines and maps of biblical places, transliterated Hebrew names, and included a table interpreting those names. Calvin, Strigelius, Vatablus, and other commentators that Pembroke consulted give more extensive commentary on the Hebrew. She was particularly reliant on Bèze's Latin commentary, which is more closely tied to the Hebrew in the full Latin version than in Anthony Gilby's condensed translation. (The Latin original includes for each Psalm the *interpretatio* of Mollerus, as well as Bèze's own *argumentum*, *paraphrasis*, and *carmen*. Gilby does not translate the *interpretatio* or the *carmen*, sources that Pembroke uses repeatedly.)

Such concern for accurate translation was not confined to prose translations of the Psalms. Luther sought poets 'to turn a Psalm into a hymn' in simple language for the people, so that the meaning was 'cleare and as close as possible to the [Hebrew] Psalm'.[42] Marot studied Hebrew, but his *Psaumes* also rely on the scholarship of Vatablus and the Royal College; Bèze, who completed the French *Psaumes*, was a Hebrew scholar; Perrot studied Hebrew in Geneva.[43] Robert Crowley, who did not know Hebrew himself, prefaced his 1549 Psalter with the assurance that where his translation varies from the familiar English text (probably that of Coverdale), readers should 'consult men of learning and judgement in the knowledge of tonges' before criticizing his version, which is based on the translation of Leo Judas, to whom God has revealed 'thynges that were unknowne to them that before

---

[40] See also the first Anglo-Genevan Psalter, *The Psalmes of David, translated accordyng to the veritie and truth of th'Ebrue, wyth annotacions moste [profitable]* (Geneva, 1557), STC 2383. 6.

[41] 'To our beloved in the Lord', Geneva Bible, sig. ***iiii.

[42] Martin Luther to Georg Spalatin, 1523, *Luther's Works*, LIII. 36; Leaver, 'Ghoostly Psalmes', 3.

[43] England, 32–4. See also O. Douen, *Clément Marot et le Psautier Huguenot*, 2 vols. (Paris, 1878; Nievwkoop: B. de Graaf, 1967).

hym translated the Psalter out of the Ebrue'.[44] Matthew Parker, who knew that his readers would be concerned about the accurate rendering of the original, believes it necessary to justify his poetic expansion of the text:

> Who more will search: how here it goes,
>   let him the Hebrew trye:
> Where wordes were skant: with texts or glose
>   that want I did supplye.[45]

In a similar attempt to increase the accuracy of the familiar Sternhold and Hopkins Psalter, Genevan scholars revised—and, from a poetic standpoint, even further weakened—those metrical Psalms because 'we thought it better to frame the ryme to the Hebrewe sense, then to bynde that sense to the Englishe meter'.[46] Years later George Wither, who believed that their work was nevertheless a failure both as translation and as poetry, also 'sought...to make my *verse* speake the true word of God'.[47]

The Countess of Pembroke shared that Protestant goal of naturalizing the scriptures in her native tongue, although, unlike the revisers of *The Whole Booke of Psalmes*, she was concerned with poetic quality as well as scholarship. As Rathmell observed, she '*meditated*' on the Psalms, re-creating them as Elizabethan poems.[48] (See 'Methods of Composition and Translation'.) Dedicating the Sidneian *Psalmes* to Queen Elizabeth, she presented 'the Psalmist King | Now English denizend [made a citizen], though Hebrue borne' ('Even now that Care', 30). The Psalms as written by David are admired by 'all of tongues', all scholars who have a knowledge of Hebrew. Her task, she says, is to render the Psalms not 'transform'd | in substance' but only in 'superficiall tire' ('Angell Spirit', 8–9, 13). That is, she

---

[44] Robert Crowley, *The Psalter of David Newely Translated into Englysh Metre* (1549), *STC* 2725, sig. **ii.

[45] Parker, *The Whole psalter*, sig. Biii.

[46] *The Forme of Prayers... approved by... John Calvyn* (1556), sig. B4.

[47] George Wither, *A Preparation to the Psalter* (1619), sig. C5. Defending his own translation, he says that he would not presume to offer a new translation out of the Hebrew, even if he had been 'the greatest Hebrician of our time', but merely turned the translation 'which we already have, into verse', sig. C4^v. Five years later he complains that the Old Version is 'full of absurdityes...improprietyes, non- sence, and impertinent circumlocutions' as well as inaccuracies in translation and wonders 'what divine calling HOPKINS and STERN-HOLD had more than I have' that so many treat their words as sacred: *The Schollers Purgatory* (1624), *STC* 25919, sig. C3^r–v.

[48] Sidney, *Psalms*, p. xx.

attempted to retain the sense of the original Hebrew text while she clothed it in English verse.

It is not impossible that Pembroke also worked with the Hebrew original, although John Harington concluded that she consulted the Hebraicist Gervase Babington, who had at one time been chaplain at Wilton: Pembroke 'used this her chapleaen's advise, I suppose, for the translation of the Psalms'.[49] Harington was obviously wrong, however, when he said 'it was more than a woman's skill to expresse the sence so right as she hath done in her vearse'. In 1551 Petrucchio Ubaldini undoubtedly exaggerated when he said that in England 'the rich cause their sons and daughters to learn Latin, Greek, and Hebrew, for since this storm of heresy has invaded the land they hold it useful to read the scriptures in the original tongues'.[50] Yet there is some truth to his assertion, for educational reformers such as Lawrence Humphrey, Humphrey Gilbert, Thomas Cromwell, Robert Holgate, and Richard Mulcaster advocated Hebrew as part of the school curriculum for boys; the language was taught at least at the Merchant Taylors' School, St Paul's School, and Westminster School in the sixteenth century. By 1572, knowledge of Hebrew was required for admission to St John's College, Oxford.[51] Some Renaissance English women also learned Hebrew to study the scriptures. Paschali's flattery of Elizabeth in presenting his Italian Psalter, claiming that she was proficient in Hebrew and Aramaic, is rather doubtful, but Katherine Cooke was fluent in Hebrew, Lady Jane Grey's letters describe her desire to continue her study, and Elizabeth Falkland's daughters record her early study in that language so that even in her last days she 'could in the Bible understand well'.[52] Bathsua Makin not only knew Hebrew, but taught it to her pupils, including Princess Elizabeth, Lucy Hastings, Countess of Huntingdon, and her daughter Elizabeth Hastings.[53]

In the absence of conclusive external evidence, it is impossible to ascertain whether or not Pembroke did study Hebrew. There are no references to a Hebrew tutor in the account books, for example, as

[49] Sir John Harington, *Nugae Antiquae*, ed. Thomas Park (London: Vernor and Hood, 1804), II. 172–3.

[50] Cited in G. Lloyd Jones, *The Discovery of Hebrew in Tudor England: A Third Language* (Manchester: Manchester UP, 1983), 222.

[51] Ibid., 222–34.

[52] Ibid., 240–2; Cary, *Mariam*, ed. Weller and Ferguson, 186–7.

[53] Frances Teague, 'The Identity of Bathsua Makin', *Biography* 16 (1993), 7, 11. See also Jean R. Brink, 'Bathsua Reginald Makin: "Most Learned Matron"', *HLQ* 54 (1991), 313–26.

there are to 'Mistress Maria, the Italian', nor are there Hebrew books listed for young Mary Sidney.[54] Certainly Philip Sidney was interested in recovering the Hebrew metrical tradition of the Psalms, declaring that 'all learned hebricians agree' that the Psalms are written in metre 'although the rules be not yet fully found'.[55] This reference demonstrates Sidney's concern for accuracy to the original, but it does not necessarily imply that he had any direct knowledge of Hebrew.[56] Internal evidence is ambiguous because we must proceed by process of elimination—and no part of the Hebrew scriptures was studied and translated more often than the Psalms. Yet there are several instances when Pembroke's version may reveal direct access to the Hebrew, rather than reliance on commentaries. For example, her interpretation of Psalm 150. 1 incorporates an alternative meaning of the Hebrew, reading it as God's holiness rather than God's sanctuary or holy place, as it is interpreted in her usual sources.[57] Similarly, her phrase 'sonnes of dust' in Psalm 58. 3 highlights the word play from Genesis, where 'Adam' is made from 'Adamah' or dust (v. 1). Yet it is usually difficult to tell whether she has consulted the Hebrew or another source. In Psalm 139: 19 the Hebrew word meaning 'evil' or 'wicked' is a singular form usually translated as a collective term. Pembroke retains the singular 'but one' wicked man (l. 71) and uses a plural for the 'cursed brood | inur'd to blood' (l. 73–4) as in the original, whereas the English biblical texts have the plural for both the 'wicked' and 'the bloodie men'. The singular may have been suggested by direct access to the original—but it may come from Crowley (v. 19), ' If thou kill the wicked man', or perhaps from Parker, 'If thou now wouldst ... confound that wicked man: | bloud thursty men ... would leave me'.[58]

---

[54] De L'Isle MS U1475, A4 /4.

[55] Sidney, *Miscellaneous Prose*, 77.

[56] On Philip Sidney's possible knowledge of Hebrew sources, see Seth Weiner, 'Sidney and the Rabbis: A Note on the Psalms of David and Renaissance Hebraica', in *Sir Philip Sidney's Achievements*, ed. M. J. B. Allen *et al.* (New York: AMS Press, 1990), 157–62. On sixteenth-century discussion of the Psalms as verse, see Israel Baroway, 'The Bible as Poetry in the English Renaissance: An Introduction', *JEGP* 32 (1933), 472–8.

[57] Theodore Steinberg, 'The Sidneys and the Psalms', *SP* 92 (1995), 1–17 and ' "More then a woman's skill"? The Countess of Pembroke and the Hebrew Psalms', read at International Congress on Medieval Studies, Kalamazoo, Michigan, 7 May 1993. Deborah Hannay Sunoo contributed additional examples.

[58] The Variant 121 (which is probably not authorial) uses Alexander Montgomerie, *The Mindes Melodie, Contayning Certayne Psalmes of the Kinglie Prophet David applyed to a new pleasant tune* (Edinburgh, 1605), *STC* 18051, to add a sheep metaphor to the biblical text: 'The Lord doth keepe | Israell his sheepe'.

Another instance of her attempt to be faithful to the original is her habitual use of 'Jehovah' where the Psalter typically refers to 'God' or 'Lord', because contemporary Christian scholars erroneously believed that name to be closer to the Hebrew. (The strange hybrid uses the vowels of 'Adonai' with the consonants of the Tetragrammaton YHWH. The Hebrew text was printed that way by the sixteenth century, but Christian scholars did not understand that the vowels 'Adonai' were meant to be read aloud instead of—not with—the unpronounceable sacred name of God.) Pembroke would not need direct access to the Hebrew text for this usage, however, since Bèze's Latin volume (but rarely Gilby's translation) uses 'Jehovah' to translate the Tetragrammaton. For example, Psalm 105 begins in the Psalter, 'O give thanks unto the Lord, and call upon his Name: tell the people what things he hath done', a verse Pembroke renders:

> Jehovas praise, Jehovas holy fame
> 　ô show, ô sound, his actes to all relate.　(105. 1–2)

In Bèze, the *paraphrasis* and *interpretatio* both begin 'Celebrate Jehova' (translated by Gilby, 'Prayse the Lorde'). Pembroke also attempted to convey the sense of eternal being present in the Tetragrammaton. For example, her description of God as 'nam'd of eternall essence' in Psalm 68. 7 is based on the Geneva note (v. 4) that the name Jehovah does 'signify his essence'. Similarly, Psalm 72. 81–2 , 'o god who art . . . eternall lord' seems to play on the meaning of the name 'Jehova' (the word used here in Bèze's *paraphrasis*) as Pembroke understood it: the symbol of God's eternity (68. 7).[59]

Pembroke often attempts to render Hebrew verse forms into English. Psalm 111, as Calvin's heading notes, has the form of an 'Apcee', or alphabetical acrostic, in the original. Unlike her sources, she precisely renders the alphabetical form. But the acrostic Psalms 9, 10, and 37 are not so rendered by Sidney, nor are 112 and 145 by Pembroke, even when the form is clearly noted by Vatablus.[60] Where Calvin does not note that structure, the Sidneys do not write them as acrostics. Now, Pembroke could have known the verse form from the Hebrew and avoided repeating it on aesthetic principles, but the

[59] See also Psalms 85. 35; 93. 2; 94. 43, 46; and 102. 85–90. Sidney, in Psalm 25. 24, similarly describes God's kindness and lovingness as having 'Eternall Essence'.

[60] The commentary of Franciscus Vatablus is printed in *Liber Psalmorum Davidis. Annotationes in eosdem ex Hebraeorum commentariis* (Robertus Stephanus [Estienne], 1546).

correspondence to Calvin is noticeable. In Psalm 49, however, she does repeat the refrain exactly in lines 21–4 and 39–42, as does the Hebrew original. None of her usual sources retains the parallel structure. Parallelism and antithesis, so prominent in the Hebrew originals, are pervasive in her paraphrases, as they are in many of her sources. (See, for example, 47. 13; 109. 73–4; 114. 7, 9; and 119W. 7–8.)

Some of her Hebrew forms may derive from Parker. In the Hebrew, Psalm 119 is comprised of 22 groups of eight verses, each octave beginning with a successive letter of the Hebrew alphabet, as noted in most translations. Pembroke adopts this feature in her paraphrase, beginning each octave with the appropriate English letter, so that A opens 'An undefiled', B opens 'By what', and so on. Of her usual sources, only Parker retains the alphabetic initial words throughout; he is even more ambitious, for each couplet, and usually each line, begins with that letter.

Because the sources that she quotes attempt to reconstruct the original, we may never be able to prove conclusively whether or not she knew Hebrew. We can, however, establish that any access that Pembroke had to Hebrew, either by her own knowledge or by consulting scholarship, was usually filtered through Christian eyes.[61] Although the Reformers inserted fewer Christological references than medieval commentators, because they were more concerned about accuracy of translation, they did maintain that interpretation on occasion. Pembroke follows Calvin and Bèze in translating the word for the 'anointed one' or the 'messiah' in Psalm 132. 69 as 'Christ', the Greek term for 'anointed one' that had, by this date, specifically Christian connotations. (See also 89. 126.)[62] Her use of Jehovah may also be Christological, for, as Bèze argues in Psalm 93, that 'one word' contains all 'that is necessary to confirm our faith'. Since the Psalm 'hath respect unto Messias', Christ's 'verie true goodheade is proved hereby manifestly, that the name of Jehovah is attributed unto him'.

---

[61] On Christian readings of the Hebrew Psalms, see R. Gerald Hobbs, '*Hebraica Veritas* and *Traditio Apostolica*: Saint Paul and the Interpretation of the Psalms in the Sixteenth Century', in *The Bible in the Sixteenth Century*, ed. David C. Steinmetz (Durham, NC: Duke UP, 1990), 83–99. The central problem was discrepancies between the Hebrew text and New Testament interpretations of it; in his commentary on Psalm 22. 17, for example, Calvin is driven to conclude that 'the place is corrupted for the nonce by the Jewes'.

[62] In contrast, Sidney retains the word 'Anoynt' in 18. 91 and 'Anoynted' in 20. 22, and 28. 32.

Unlike most of her sources, Pembroke does not adopt the Christian practice of referring to the Church as the 'True Jerusalem',[63] nor does she ever mention the word 'Church' in her *Psalmes*, as does Philip Sidney in Psalm 29. 24. She does, however, paraphrase Bèze in giving a potentially Christian definition of 'Israel': 'I meane to men of undefiled hartes' (73. 2).[64] She also adds the idea of the Logos in Psalm 50. 1–3, in saying that God 'the ever-living lord', has summoned the nations, 'by his pursevant, his worde', probably from Strigelius (v. 1), who makes direct reference to 'the sonne of God, which is the lord of all cretures, and Logos the word, by whom the father hath made himselfe knowen unto us'.[65]

In other Psalms she develops central doctrines of Christian faith, as set forth by the Reformers. Her description of God as the one 'whose providence doth all enfold' (107. 120) echoes Calvin's heading for Psalm 107, for example, and in many Psalms she makes an interpretative reference to God's grace. The doctrine of God's grace is particularly emphasized in Pembroke's paraphrase of Psalm 51, where she incorporates that doctrine into her opening phrase, 'O lord, whose grace no limitts comprehend', and emphasizes that God does not demand sacrifices—or, implicitly, good works—'to gaine thy grace' (46). Her phrase 'free grace' (103. 9) comes directly from Calvin's statement of God's grace in 'freely forgiving and wyping away our sinnes' (v. 3). (See also 56. 43, 59. 89, and 119D. 40.) She also emphasizes the doctrine of prevenient grace in such passages as 59. 43–4.[66] Indeed 'gracelesse', or being without the grace of God, is one of her favourite epithets for the enemies of the godly. (See, for example, 44. 48, 106. 33, 119T. 21, and 139. 75.) The ungodly also hate 'to live in right reformed sort' (50. 43). She also incorporates the doctrine of election in 114. 3, from Calvin's discourse on the choosing of Israel (v. 1). Likewise, her verb 'renew' in 78. 2 echoes Calvin's interpretation of the Psalm as 'a second election . . . at what time he choze David out of the Tribe of Juda to have the government of the realme'. In

---

[63] See, for example, Vatablus' description of the Church as 'vera Jerusalem' (51. 1), and the interchangeable use of 'Hebrews' or 'Israel' and the 'Church' in Parker's heading for Psalm 83 and Bèze's heading for Psalm 109.

[64] Cf. Bèze 73: 1, 'It must needs be true and inviolable, that God can not be but favourable towardes Israel, that is, to them that worship him purely and devoutly'.

[65] Victorinus Strigelius, *A Third Proceeding in the Harmony of King Davids Harp* [Psalms 45–61], trans. Richard Robinson (1595), *STC* 23361.

[66] Calvin cites St Augustine's use of 'thys text oftymes ageinst the Pelagians, too prove Gods grace goeth before all the merits of men' (59: 11). He may have had in mind, for instance, *A Treatise of Nature and Grace, against Pelagius* (ch. 35 [XXXI]).

103. 53–6 her extended paraphrase may contain allusions to Calvin's use of the verse (12) to refute the view 'that the free remission of sinnes is given but once onely, and that afterwarde righteousnesse is gotten, or the possession of it is helde still by desert of works'. Instead, Pembroke says, God's mercy repeatedly forgives our 'faultes and follies'.

Pembroke regularly consulted Calvin's commentary on the Psalms. His commentary is the source of many of her metaphors, such as God's school (51. 21, 94. 21, and throughout 119), plant imagery (44. 6–8), images from carpentry (119B. 1–3), childbirth (58. 23), water imagery (115. 32–3), and the courtier making 'hott and harty sute' to God (119H. 4). Yet she ignores other promising metaphors, such as his references to the stage in Psalms 138. 1 and 142. 8. Sometimes she will follow Calvin's interpretation, as giving 'right' a moral sense in 45. 13–14. Some of her wording comes directly from Golding's translation of Calvin, such as 'ridled speech' (49. 6) and 'wandred from thie way' (51. 37).[67] Sometimes she summarizes his commentary, as in her phrase 'puffed hartes' (101. 14), which combines Calvin's translation (v. 5), 'Whosoever is... wide of harte, him can not I abyde', with his commentary, 'They must needs be puft up and swolen which gape after great things. For nothing is innough with them, onlesse, they may swalowe up the whole world.' In Psalm 51. 16–17, she adapts his explanation that the word usually translated 'conceived' means 'heated' in Hebrew. When she amplifies the metaphor used in Calvin's explanation that 'we be cherisshed and kept warme in sin, as long as we lye hid in the bowels of our mothers', she softens the passage, showing that the mother cherished the child as well as sin and corruption.[68] Her wording from Calvin is often incorporated with other sources, as in Psalm 124, which uses 'gulphes' (7) and 'grynn' (13) from Calvin, and 'greedy teeth' (12) from Parker, while most of the Psalm echoes the Psalter and the Geneva Psalms.

Although she does frequently echo Calvin in wording or interpretation, she uses his commentary with caution. Sometimes she uses an interpretation that Calvin discusses but specifically rejects, such as in the opening of Psalm 91. And in rendering Psalm 100 Pembroke wisely ignores Calvin, who includes ill-tempered fulminations against

---

[67] Other examples include 'wink' (50. 51), 'instant' (59. 18), 'blisse' (67. 25), the 'Date-bearing tree' (92. 35), 'Parlors' (104. 9), and 'blott' (130. 17).

[68] Fisken, 'Education', 178.

the reprobate even in his comments on this Psalm of joy. Where Bèze and Calvin disagree, she usually follows Bèze; in a Psalm like 120, for example, she followed Calvin's interpretation and therefore knew of his attribution of the Psalm to David—but she followed Bèze's attribution of the Psalm to the Babylonian exile.[69] She certainly rejects Calvin's attribution of Psalm 137 ('By the waters of Babylon') to David; departing from the standard interpretation as well as common sense, Calvin is reduced to crediting David with prophecy of the Babylonian exile. On many other occasions Pembroke follows Bèze instead of Calvin. For example, in Psalm 101. 5 she goes beyond most of her sources in portraying the enforced retreat as a time of deliberate preparation for public service, perhaps remembering her brother Philip's rustication with her at Wilton. Whereas Calvin comments that 'althoughe David continue styll a private person ... yet ceaseth he not to folow uprightnesse, all the meane whyle' (v. 2), her interpretation is closer to Bèze, who presents the opening verses as David's recognition that he must learn to govern his home and family before he can govern the kingdom.

Aside from the biblical sources, she tends to rely most heavily on the commentaries of Bèze. The meaning of Pembroke's sometimes difficult syntax, if unclear from the scriptural sources, can often be unravelled by reference to Bèze, as in 97. 12, 99. 21, 105. 91–93, 106. 17–18, 107. 13, 113. 10, and so on. (See Commentary.) So frequent is her reliance on Bèze that one may use his commentary, like the biblical phrasing and the Geneva notes, as a possible indication of the authorial reading. For example, in 68. 25 because *F, J* have 'They', the alteration in *A* to 'Ther' may not be contemporary. However, the phrasing in Bèze (v. 4) suggests that 'ther' is the correct reading: there in the desert where God gave them victories. Or in 69. 23 it would be tempting to adopt the emendation 'mote' (as in MS *I*) instead of 'note'; the latter is probably not a scribal slip, however, but used in the Latin sense of *nota*, a mark of infamy. The relevance of the Latin sense is indicated by Bèze's *carmen* on Psalm 70 (v. 3): '*Fac ignominiæ notam reportent, | Qui me ignominia volunt notatum*'. In this case, the corresponding line in the variant paraphrase confirms the reading: 'Thy cause it is I this disgracefull blame | And noted blot susteine' (Variant Psalm 70. 23–4).

[69] Her terms 'forgers' and 'poisoned abuse' (120. 6–8) retain Calvin's distinction between the two ways deceitful tongues work (v. 2): 'eyther in compassing them by wyles and captiousnes, or by deffaming them falsly'. She also follows Bèze over Calvin in 122. 1–5.

Echoes of Bèze, who had been praised in Sidney's *Defence*, are ubi-quitous.[70] Wording adapted from the Gilby translation includes the 'like a Carcasse' (102. 50), 'Arke the token of thy strength' (132. 32), and so on.[71] Psalm 74. 121 is almost quoted from Bèze (v. 22): 'Arise O Lord and plead thine owne cause', although she alters the biblical 'cause' to 'case', thereby sharpening the legal metaphor. In Psalm 79. 62 her phrase 'after goers' is a typical conflation of a longer phrase, 'to the worldes that shall come after' (v. 13). Similarly, her phrase, 'Tirantes hard yoke' (125. 9) where her biblical sources have 'rod', is a metaphorical distillation of Bèze (v. 3): the 'yron scepter of cruell tyrants do ly upon the shoulders of the godly'. She occasionally follows Bèze's spelling over that of the biblical sources, as 'Cham' rather than 'Ham' in 78. 158 and 105. 48.

Some wording seems to derive from Bèze's Latin, such as 'Avert' (119E. 13), 'abjected' (119P. 23), and 'declined' (119V. 20). She lists evils reigning in the land, 'Rape, murther, violence' (74. 112) directly from Bèze's *carmen*: '*Regnant undique vis, rapina, caedes*'. The image of the hawk (74. 103) is added from Bèze's *carmen* (19): '*Ah, ne, quæso, tuam hancce turturillam | Discerpi [sic] accipitum unguibus iubeto*' ('Ah, | pray that you not let the hawk tear this turtle-dove with its talons'). The idea of giving the first-born son the finest lodging as a privilege of primogeniture (89. 71) also probably derives from the *carmen*. In Psalm 110. 9–16 the extensive paraphrase is derived from Bèze (v. 3), but Pembroke adds the classical reference to Aurora, probably because of the Latin word for dawn, '*aurora*', used in his *carmen* and Mollerus' *interpretatio*. Her use of the Latin is also demonstrated by the variant incipits from Mollerus' translation which she presumably takes from Bèze, as in Psalms 80, 85, and 91. In Psalm 119L. 8 her addition of 'wine' to the biblical metaphor of the smoked bottle in v. 83, connecting with the wine of the gospel that cannot be contained in old bottles (Matt. 9: 17), probably derives from the Latin '*uter*' used by Bèze and Vatablus, and in both passages in the Vulgate.

Many of her metaphors are developed from Bèze, such as the mason image (141. 21), or the daughters as described as caryatids, both bearing and garnishing the palace, thereby emphasizing the structural, as well as the decorative, function of daughters in the

---

[70] Sidney, *Miscellaneous Prose*, 110.

[71] Other examples include 'foote stepps' (49. 8), 'glorious buildings' (49. 20), 'chang' (77. 52), 'balls' (83. 37), 'porter' (84. 39), 'decree' (87. 5), 'Majesty' (96. 17), 'Usurers' (109. 25), and 'porches' (122. 3).

palace (144. 53–6). Like Bèze, she expands scriptural metaphors, such as the vineyard (76. 28), God's adoption of Gentile peoples (87. 7–20), withered grass (102. 7–11), the bereaved bird (102. 19–24), clothing (102. 82–4), and eye imagery (138. 16–18). Like Bèze, Pembroke expands the metaphor of God leading his sheep from the standpoint of the shepherd in 78. 161–4, developed from his *carmen* (v. 52).

She often follows Bèze's interpretation, as in 78. 193, where the 'fire' that 'consumed their young men' is explained as 'The flame of [God's] wrath' (v. 63). Frequently she will choose his interpretation over Geneva, as in 74. 73–8. The Geneva note says the destruction of their enemies refreshed Israel like food, but Pembroke instead follows Bèze's interpretation of the drowned 'carkases to be devoured by the beasts of that wildernesse' (v. 14) as a metaphor for the destruction of Pharaoh. Likewise, she follows Bèze in interpreting the speaker in Psalm 75 as David rather than God Himself, and the journey in 119G. 11 as exile rather than pilgrimage. One of the clearest examples of her revision to follow Bèze is Psalm 113. 3, where MS *A* reads 'Jehova', following Bèze (v. 2), 'The blessed name of Jehovah'. The expunged variant in *B*, 'His name', which matches the biblical text, suggests that, in this case at least, Bèze was consulted after the paraphrase was first drafted. Similarly, in 76. 1 the variant recorded by Wood-forde is based on the Psalter (v. 1): 'In Jewry God is known', but the revision in MS *A* is based on Bèze: 'That true God of Israel is onely knowne in Judea'. Psalm 63. 6–7 demonstrates a similar process of revision. Yet even in the early version in MS *B* of Psalm 119G she relied on Bèze for the sense of exile (22) and the term 'Doctrin' (28), both of which are retained in her revision.

She does not follow Bèze slavishly, any more than she does Geneva or Calvin. In Psalm 93, for example, her description of the waves conforms to Bèze and yet she does not follow his allegorical interpretation of the storm (vv. 1 and 5). Despite her heavy reliance on Bèze in Psalm 77, she expands the metaphors and much expands the questioning of God, as well as pondering the role of the writer. Most intriguing is her interweaving of phrases from Bèze and from *Astrophil and Stella* in Psalm 73. (See 'Methods of Composition and Translation'.) She will often choose Bèze over the Psalter or Geneva, but on occasion she reverses that process for poetic reasons. For example, where the Hebrew is ambiguous in 140. 19, Pembroke follows the Psalter's rendering 'head' instead of Geneva (v. 9), 'chief', or Bèze, 'captaine', in order to continue the head imagery from line 16.

Pembroke demonstrates considerable independence in interpretation. Despite her usual reliance on Bèze and Calvin as her primary
authorities, she is not afraid to disagree with their scriptural interpretations. For example, in Psalm 131. 3 Pembroke applies the phrase
'too hygh' in v. 1 to the Psalmist's position before God, whereas Bèze
interprets it as social position and Calvin as a protest that the Psalmist
has no ambition and never sought high office in the Church. She also
rejects their interpretation when it is untrue to her own experience.
In the description of God's gift of children, for example, her phrasing
in 127. 13–16 paraphrases Bèze: children come 'not by chaunce, not
onely by force of nature, not by labor or industry, but . . . they are
given to the fathers by the goodnesse of the Lord' (v. 3). But Pembroke, who had borne at least four children, omits his absurd statement about the effortless appearance of children: 'Noe not thy
children has thou | by choise, by chaunce, by nature; | they are . . .
Jehovas, | rewardes'. In her class perspective, she also deviates from
her sources. (See I.73.)

One area in which Pembroke may erroneously be supposed to
depart from her Geneva sources is in her use of classical allusion.
As Zim observes, the Protestant tradition of Orpheus as a figure for
David and Urania as a Christian muse would be sufficient to justify
such classical interpolations into the Hebrew text. Pembroke did occasionally add such allusions to her text, such as the 'blasts of Eurus' for
the 'East winde' of Psalm 48. 20, the Zephyrs in 67. 30, and the cor-
nucopia in 73. 29.[72] In Psalm 89. 13 she alludes to the chariot of the
sun and in 55. 71–2 she renders the Geneva phrase about the death of
the speaker's enemies with a prayer that God will cut the thread of
life, a clear reference to the Parcae, the classical fates that spin and
then cut the thread of life. The reference is obviously not in the original Hebrew, although the image is used by Buchanan here and by
Bèze in Psalm 102. 23. Her Geneva sources, however, employed far
more classical allusion than she does. Pembroke does not follow Calvin,
for example, in quoting Caesar's famous statement, 'I came, I saw, I
wan' (Ps. 48: 5), which Calvin applies to Caesar's conquest of Egypt.

Pembroke does avoid the explicitly contemporary applications in
her Geneva sources. In Psalm 51. 50–1, for example, she does not
update Calvin's implied parallel to the actions of the French king
(v. 20), nor does she, like Bèze, apply the condemnation of unjust

---

[72] Zim, *Psalms*, 199.

judges in Psalm 82 specifically to 'our times', or add a personal note as he does in his heading of Psalm 120.[73] Perhaps because she does not share their personal experience of religious persecution, she incorporates no anti-Catholic polemic into her translation, as both Bèze and Calvin do in their commentary on Psalm 130, for example, as Morley does in his exposition of Psalm 94, and as the Geneva notes so notoriously do at every opportunity.[74] The Sidneys seem to have been able to separate their political concerns, such as their ardent defence of Continental Protestantism in the 1580s and 1590s, from their personal relations. Despite their involvement in the activist Protestant party of Leicester and their friendships with such Huguenots as Hubert Languet and Philippe de Mornay, the Sidneys also retained ties with Catholic friends and relatives. Sir Henry's niece Jane Dormer, for example, continued to correspond with him after she married the Duke of Feria and moved to Spain; Philip Sidney visited the English priest Edmund Campion during his European journey; and Sir Tobie Matthew was apparently a regular visitor to Pembroke's house in Spa around 1614–16.[75] By the time Pembroke had established that informal salon in Spa, one of her friends was the Countess of Barlemont, whose daughter was 'a *devota* designed to a convent'.[76] As we have seen, contemporary gossip suggests that the ladies were occupied with more frivolous pursuits than discussion of Christian doctrine— taking tobacco, dancing, gambling, shooting pistols, and carrying on flirtations with younger men—although they could, of course, have discussed their faith as well.

Another difference between the Sidneian *Psalmes* and their Geneva sources is their sense of 'devotion as a joyful game', in Freer's apt phrase.[77] Many of Pembroke's *Psalmes* have a lilt of joy, as in the

[73] Calvin: 'Seeing then that at this day in the papacie, Religion is defyled' (120: 5). Bèze: 'now also there is great use of this Psalme, seeing that the Godly are compelled oftentimes to flee into farre countries by the crueltie of the wicked' (Argument, Ps. 120). See also Bèze's Argument for Psalm 74.

[74] Henry Parker, Lord Morley, *The Exposition and declaration of the Psalme, Deus ultionum Dominus* [Psalm 94] (originally prepared 1534, pub. 1539), *STC* 19211, particularly sig. A5–7. Maurice S. Betteridge, 'The Bitter Notes: The Geneva Bible and its Annotations', *Sixteenth Century Journal* 14 (1983), 41–62.

[75] Katherine Duncan-Jones suggests that 'Given Campion's exceptional skill in arguing, Sidney may indeed have been all but persuaded' to become a Catholic: *Sir Philip Sidney: Courtier Poet* (London: Hamish Hamilton, 1991), 126.

[76] Sir Dudley Carleton to John Chamberlain, 2 Aug. 1616, *Dudley Carleton to John Chamberlain 1603–1624: Jacobean Letters*, ed. Maurice Lee (New Brunswick: Rutgers UP, 1972), 209.

[77] Freer, *Music*, 25.

'mery shout' of God's people in Psalm 100. 2 or the exuberance of Psalm 81, '*Exultate Deo*':

> All gladdnes, gladdest hartes can hold,
>> in meriest notes that mirth can yeld,
> lett joyfull songues to god unfold,
>> to Jacobs god our sword and shield.
>> Muster hither musicks joyes,
>> lute, and lyre, and tabretts noise:
> lett noe instrument be wanting,
>> chasing grief, and pleasure planting.   (1–8)

Waller is surely correct in explaining such passages as the interplay between Calvinism and courtliness, since she does incorporate ideas from both Calvin's commentaries and the conventions of courtly verse into her *Psalmes*.[78] The theological implications are somewhat more complex than that, however, for the Marian exiles in Frankfurt and Geneva had split over matters of doctrine and worship. Pembroke consulted the scholarship of both groups, those led by Calvin and Bèze, and those led by her father's friend and correspondent Matthew Parker, Archbishop of Canterbury.[79]

In her use of dance and music as appropriate forms of worship, she aligns herself with the more liberal group around Parker.[80] In Psalm 96. 36, for example, Pembroke adds dance to her usual sources, which have 'rejoyce' in v. 12. In Bèze the fields do 'leape for joy', but Pembroke's version calls on all of nature to 'daunce ô daunce, at such a good'. In Psalm 149 her three main Geneva sources—Geneva, Calvin, and Bèze—silently suppress the biblical reference to dancing, present in the Psalter and in the Bishops' Bible (v. 3): 'Let them praise his name in the dance.' Her version amplifies the sense of music and dance as part of a public celebration:

> Play on harp, on tabret play:
>> daunce Jehova publique daunces.   (9–10).[81]

[78] Gary Waller, 'A "Matching of Contraries": Ideological Ambiguity in the Sidney Psalms', *Wascana Review* 9 (1974), 124–33; ' "This Matching of Contraries": Bruno, Calvin and the Sidney Circle', *Neophilologus* 56 (1972), 331–43; ' "This Matching of Contraries": Calvinism and Courtly Philosophy in the Sidney Psalms', *English Studies* 55 (1974), 22–31.

[79] Sir Henry Sidney to Archbishop Matthew Parker, 1 Dec. 1574, De L'Isle MS 1475 C7/15.

[80] The Geneva disapprobation of dance is evident in the heading for Mark 6, 'The inconvenience of dancing', as the moral of the story of Salome, who danced before King Herod and claimed the head of John the Baptist as her reward.

[81] See also Sidney, Psalms 30. 34, 42. 16; Pembroke 53. 24, 68. 6–8, 75. 12, and 149. 10. Note that MS *I* twice removes references to 'daunce', at 51. 28 and 75. 12.

More surprising is her incorporation of sacred dance of joy into the penitential Psalm 51. The Psalmist prays for cleansing, and then that God will

> to eare and hart send soundes and thoughts of gladdnes,
> that brused bones maie daunce awaie their saddnes.   (27–8)

Pembroke's joyous phrase is not present in Bèze, Calvin, or Lok, and certainly not in Geneva, which takes out references to dancing even when present in the original Hebrew, as in Psalms 149. 3 and 150. 4.[82]

Calvin not only omits the dancing, but also warns against taking the references to musical instruments as warrant for their use in modern worship, for they 'belong to the tyme of their [the Israelites'] first traynment...[and] were peculiar to the people of old tyme' (149. 3). The use of music in worship was a point of serious doctrinal contention. Pembroke does not share Bèze's fear of the 'horrible abuses' (Argument, Psalm 149) of music put to the service of God. Bèze's Argument for Psalm 150 demonstrates his concern that music, even 'that grave and plaine singing of Psalms, which as I think hathe always bene in the Church, hath bene turned into a vicious curiosity'. Perhaps Pembroke was encouraged by Mollerus' *interpretatio*, printed by Bèze, that advocated choral dance: '*Laudent nomen eius choris.*'

The Geneva translators were nervous about descriptions of praise in Israel; for example, they translated Psalm 92. 3 to include praise on 'an instrument of ten strings, and upon the viole with the song upon the harp', remaining faithful to the original, but they added an apologetic note, 'These instruments were then permitted, but at Christs coming abolished.' Where the Geneva scholars suppress or attempt to discount references to dance and instrumental music as part of worship, Pembroke follows Parker, who cites biblical and patristic authorities to justify musical settings of the Psalms, as Ephesians 5: 19, which he renders, 'Syng Psalmes and hymnes'. Much of his prefatory poem, 'To the Reader', explains how his metrical Psalms should be sung, concluding,

> [The] princepall thing: your lute to tune,
> that hart may sing in corde:

---

[82] The Geneva translators are also wary of feasts. Cf. 81: 1 (note): 'It seemeth that this psalm was appointed for solemne feasts and assemblies of the people, to whome for a time these ceremonies were ordeined, but now under the Gospell are abolished.' Bèze, however, in his Argument for Psalm 81 identifies 8, 81, and 84 as Psalms for the 'feast of the vintage', without such explanations.

Your voyce and string: so fine to prune,
to love and serve the Lord.[83]

Like Parker, the Sidneys believed that the Psalms should be sung with
instruments, particularly the lute. Lute references abound in the
Psalms of Pembroke, who was celebrated for her lute-playing and
may have encouraged or even commissioned the settings of her own
Psalms 51 and 130, preserved in BL MS Additional 15117.[84] In her
paraphrases she adds the lute where her usual sources have 'harp',
as in Psalm 98. 15. (See also such passages as 81. 6, 87. 22, 92. 9,
98. 15, 144. 36, and 150. 6.) Most striking is her paraphrase of
Psalm 57. 8, which mentions only the psaltery and the harp in most
of her sources. Her phrase 'wake my tongue, my lute awake' (57.
34) is justified by reference to Parker, 'awake my tonge...awake
both harpe and lute' (v. 8), but both echo Sir Thomas Wyatt's popular
song, 'Awake my lute'. Finding her models in courtly verse and
scholarly commentary, Pembroke prays with the original Psalmist,
'prepared is my hart | to spread thy praise | with tuned laies'
(57. 31–3).

In addition to her joyous tone, some of her phrasing also echoes
Parker, such as 'waterlesse' (63. 5) and 'greedy teeth' (124. 12).[85]
Her phrase 'hilly bullwarkes' (125. 5) condenses Parker (v. 2): 'with
hils is set, | Envyroned: with bulwarkes great'. The 'Pilgrim' in
Psalm 119C. 7 and the metaphor of the tongue treading, or walking,
in Psalm 119D. 28 also seem to come from Parker. She quotes Parker
at the opening of Psalm 119R, 'Right wonderful...thy testimonies
be' and she improves Parker's cry in Psalm 120. 6, 'Ah long to
long', by addressing God directly, 'Ah God! too long' (120. 17).[86]
Probably because of Parker's example, Pembroke is emboldened to
form an acrostic of Psalm 117 so that the final phrase of v. 2 is rendered in the initial letters: PRAIS THE LORD. The form is without
precedent in her other sources; the closest analogue is Parker's 'A Pref-
ace to the Psalme. 119' where the initial letters form an acrostic for

---

[83] Parker, *The Whole psalter*, sig. Aii^v.

[84] On this intriguing miscellany, see Mary Joiner, 'British Museum Add MS. 15117: A
Commentary, Index and Bibliography', *Royal Musical Association Research Chronicle* 7
(1967), 51–109.

[85] Other examples include 'Adams' (66. 16), 'winck' (74. 50), 'plaine' as verb (77. 36),
'lovely' (84. 1), 'checks' (94. 17), 'sweete' manna (105. 84), 'Grave' [engrave] (119G. 1), 'roially' (126. 8), and 'painted' (142. 5).

[86] See also 102. 85 for a condensation of Parker. The revised Psalms 120–7, which may
not be authorial, rely on Parker as well as on the Psalter.

the Latin form of his name, Mattheus Parkerus, the only indication of the author of this metrical Psalter in the original edition. Although such rhetorical questions are characteristic of her style, she probably adapts his series of questions in Psalm 92. 13–15, and the parallel 'as' clauses in Psalm 109. 47–8. Her phrasing in Psalm 119T. 9–10 is as convoluted as Parker's and is probably modelled on his. Yet Pembroke does not always follow Parker. In her description of God's fatherly 'neerly touching touch' (103. 58), she rejects Parker's sense of punishment, 'For lyke hys chylde: the father useth, | To nurture hym: by chastisement'. Instead, she follows Bèze's gentler sense of 'embrace' (v. 13).

Although she did not follow Vatablus in the alphabetic Psalms 112 and 145 (see above), some wording does apparently echo his commentary, such as 'anguish' (50. 37), the reference to God listening as well as speaking (50. 5), the phrase 'high in Priesthood' (99. 18), and the idea of the balance in 58. 7. She may also have found in Vatablus (as well as Bèze) additional authority for making Psalm 68. 25–96 the words of the women, instead of the words of the Psalmist, as Calvin says. Her attacks on the false, slandering courtiers parallel Vatablus' commentary on Psalm 58, as does her use of the question/answer pattern in 58. 1. Her original phrase 'will either hand | clasp the rules of thy command' in Psalm 119F. 30–1 may also echo his phrase, '*admovebo manus meas praeceptis*' (v. 48), as Anne Prescott suggests (personal correspondence).

While there is little, if any, verbal correspondence between Pembroke's *Psalmes* and George Buchanan's Latin paraphrase or the text of the Tremellius–Junius Bible, her knowledge of both of them can hardly be doubted. Buchanan's Psalms were widely read both in Britain and on the Continent, and he himself was a friend to the young Sidney, who praised him for his 'piercing wit' and his Latin tragedies in the *Defence*.[87] Tremellius and Junius also have an important place in the *Defence* as authorities for including the Hebrew Psalms in 'the poetical part of the Scripture'.[88] Two of Pembroke's additions to the

---

[87] Sidney, *Miscellaneous Prose*, 110, 116. George Buchanan's Latin paraphrases of 18 psalms, *In Davidis psalmi aliquot latino carmine expressi a quatuor poetis* (Paris: Henri Estienne, 1556), were expanded, revised, and republished frequently, occasionally with music, including settings for Psalms 1–41 (Lyons, 1579, and settings by N. Chytraeus (Frankfurt, 1585). See I. D. McFarlane, *Buchanan* (London, 1981), 261, 271.

[88] Sidney, *Miscellaneous Prose*, 80. Israel Baroway, 'Tremellius, Sidney, and Biblical Verse', *MLN* 49 (1934), 145–9; Jan A. van Dorsten, 'Sidney and Franciscus Junius the

biblical text may perhaps be traced to Buchanan, the classical image of the thread of life in Psalm 55. 71 and the fertile Nile in 78. 153. Certainly Buchanan's version was well known as an aesthetic precedent for metrical paraphrase of biblical texts, including the use of quantitative verse.[89]

Pembroke may echo the wording of the Tremellius–Junius Bible occasionally, as in the added personal pronoun in 104. 71 and the appeal to the speaker's experience as a model in 131. 3. Although the text may not be any more of a major source for Pembroke than Buchanan, the annotations are relevant because of their emphasis on rhetorical analysis of the form and style of the biblical Psalms. Each note begins with a description of the type and structure of the Psalm, as in the case of Psalm 50, which is labeled '*didascalius*' and described as '*constans ex duobus partibus; narratione prophetica*' up to verse 7 and '*propositione doctrinae*' to the end. Such summary statements are then followed for each Psalm by glosses and references to any specific stylistic devices they may contain, such as metaphor, hyperbole, synecdoche, and Sidney's own example of prosopopoeia.[90] Thus, while Pembroke may rarely be indebted to any particular statement in Tremellius–Junius, the recognition of the Psalms as 'poetry' subject to the same kind of analysis that was applied to other literary texts could have given her warrant for the stylistic amplification that distinguishes her paraphrases. This is, of course, what Sidney acknowledges as part of the value of the Tremellius–Junius Bible.

Much of Pembroke's phrasing and interpretation comes from the Psalter and the Geneva Bible, of course, but the most striking aspect of her work is its composite use of Psalms and commentaries occasionally interwoven with phrases from Sidney's poems or those of her other contemporaries, as we have seen above. Indeed, her scholarship is so careful that it would be difficult to state categorically that she did *not* use any specific source available to her. The delight she took in her attempts to render the best biblical scholarship into English poems

---

Elder', *HLQ* 42 (1978), 1–13; Carol Kaske, 'Another Echo of the Tremellius–Junius *Libri Poetici* in Sidney's Biblical Poetics', *American Notes & Queries* 5 (1992), 83–6.

[89] Seth Weiner, 'The Quantitative Poems and the Psalm Translations: The Place of Sidney's Experimental Verse in the Legend', in *Creation of a Legend*, 193–220; and Richard Todd, 'Humanist Prosodic Theory, Dutch Synods, and the Poetics of the Sidney–Pembroke Psalter', *HLQ* 52 (1989), 278–87.

[90] Sidney, *Miscellaneous Prose*, 77.

can be glimpsed in her original addition to Psalm 75. 9 ('But I will declare for ever, and sing prayses unto the God of Jaakób'):

> And I secure shall spend my happie tymes
> in my, though lowly, never-dying rymes,
>   singing with praise the god that Jacob loveth.   (25–7)

Reporting variants in the seventeen manuscripts of the *Psalmes* presents special problems. To keep the apparatus within the limited space available to us, we have tried to include only substantive variants and have thus cited variations in spelling, for instance, only when doing so will help establish the copy-text or clarify the relationship of the various manuscripts (to the copy-text and to one another). For instance, we usually do not cite 'heart' in contrast to the invariable 'hart(e)' in MS *A* (Philip Sidney's Psalm 42. 1 would be another matter, of course); nor do we cite 'dear(e)', 'deer(e)', and 'dere', which are, on the whole, similarly insignificant variants in the context of the Psalm paraphrases. We do report variant spellings such as 'here', 'heer(e)', and 'hear(e)' and 'were' and 'wear(e)' because the context occasionally allows for variation in meaning. On the other hand, we normally ignore doubled letters, interchangeable letters such as 'i'/ y'y' and 'ie'/'y', and incidental 'e' (as in the examples cited above). When there are insignificant differences in the spelling of a variant shared by more than one manuscript, the spelling used is normally that of the first manuscript cited. Variations in the spelling of names and places, however, are usually noted more fully because they do not regularly appear in the *OED*, they sometimes help establish manuscript groupings, and they may occasionally point to Pembroke's sources. As explained in 'Editorial Procedure', neither MS *L* nor MS *P* is cited because they are relatively late copies of extant manuscripts and thus lack textual authority.

It will be convenient to note here some distinctive features of other manuscripts. The late seventeenth-century MS *B*, for instance, is the only one to use the spelling 'than'; all the others have 'then' without exception even in comparative constructins. Because of this consistency, the variation in *B* is not included in the apparatus (except for the correction in *B* at 118. 26, which suggests that Woodforde made a practice of changing the spelling of at least this one word in making his transcript). MS *B* also usually prefers 'heart' to 'hart(e)', as do *G*, *M*, and, often, *N*. (Pembroke writes only 'hart(e)' in the manuscript letters.) We fully report Woodforde's notes on the revisions in the original of *B*, but we print his underlined text in italics and we do not retain the marks he uses to key a passage in the main text to the corresponding passage in the margin because such marks have significance only in the context of the manuscript. The relatively late date of *G* and *M* (and sometimes *C*) is indicated partly by their use of the apostrphe, not just to indicate an elided 'e', but to signal the possessive form of nouns, as in the clear examples of 'The simple's surest guard' (Ps. 116. 13, MSS *M*, *C*) and 'His Sacred Name's eternall praise' (Ps. 145. 62, MSS *M*, *G*). The manuscripts of the σ group (*H*, *Q*, *E*) frequently double consonants and regularly have, for instance, 'holly(e)' or 'hollie' for 'holy'; the forms with double consonants are not normally reported. MS *D* invariably has 'wer' for 'were' and 'neclegt' for 'neglect'; the former variation is not noted in the apparatus, and the latter is cited only at Ps. 82. 6, where MS *O* is corrected in such a way as to suggest that θ may have had 'neclegt'. The eccentric spellings of MS *I* and routine scribal corrections in other manuscripts are reported selectively, as stated in 'Editorial Procedure'. In the case of the alternative Psalms, however, variations in the witnesses have been more fully reported because there is less certainty about the reliability of the copy-texts for those paraphrases than for the ones in MS *A*.

Deus auribus
Psalm 44.

Lorde, our fathers true relation
    often made, hath made us knowe,
howe thy pow'r in each occasion
    thou of old for them did'st showe.
    how thy hand the Pagan foe   5
        rooting hence, thie folke implanting,
    leavelesse made that braunch to grow,
        this to spring, noe verdure wanting.

Never could their sword procure them
    Conquest of the promist land: 10
never could their force assure them
    when theie did in danger stand.
    Noe, it was thie arme, thie hand,
        Noe, it was thie favors treasure
    spent uppon thy loved band,   15
        loved, whie? for thie wise pleasure.

Unto thee stand I subjected,
    I that did of Jacob spring:
bidd then that I bee protected,
    thou that art my god, my king.   20
    by that succour thou didst bring,
        wee their pride that us assailed,
    downe did tread, and back did fling,
        in thie name confus'd and quailed.

For my trust was not reposed   25
    in my owne, though strongest, bowe:
nor my scabberb held enclosed
    that, whence should my saftie flowe.

Psalm 44. Incipit and Psal: 44. *written in gold in the small space at the top of f. 39. Lacking in I.*
Variant in B.
Incipit: om. G, Q
4 showe.] ~∧ *K*, χ; ~: *C, M*   6 hence] out *E*   folke] folkes *Q*   7 braunch]
plant *J*   11 never] n *added in different hand and ink in A*   18 I] *added in darker*
ink in A; om. F   26 my] myne *K*, χ   though∧] thought, *H, E*   27 nor] n
added in different hand and ink in A; or F, J   enclosed] unclosed *C, G, M*

by reviling sclaundring foe
    inly wounded thus I languish:
wreakfull spight with outward blow
    anguish adds to inward anguish.

All, this all on us hath lighted,   65
    yet to thee our love doth last:
as wee weare, wee are delighted
    still to hold thie cov'nant fast.
    unto none our hartes have past:
        unto none our feete have slidden: 70
    though us downe to dragons cast
        thou in deadlie shade hast hidden.

If our god wee had forsaken,
    or forgott what hee assign'd:
if our selves wee had betaken   75
    Godds to serve of other kind.
    should not hee our doubling find
        though conceal'd, and closlie lurking?
since his eye of deepest minde
        deeper sincks then deepest working.   80

Surelie lord, this daily murther
    for thie sake wee thus sustaine:
for thy sake esteem'd no further
    then as sheepe, that must be slaine.
    upp O lord, up once againe: 85
        sleepe not ever, slack not ever:
    whie dost thou forgett our paine?
        whie to hid thie face persever?

Heavie griefe our soule abaseth,
    prostrate it on dust doth lie: 90
earth our bodie fast embraceth,
    nothing can the Claspe untie.

---

62 inly] I lie *σ*   63 wreakfull] wrackful *σ*   blow] shewe *Q*   66 doth] doe *O*
67 weare] *A, H, Q*; were *F, J, K, χ*   68 cov'nant] Covenants *N*   76 Godds] G
added in different hand and ink in A; \G/oddes *F (different ink and hand)*   80 then]
their *H, Q*   88 hid] hide *F, J, K, χ*

rise, and us with helpe supplie:
　　　lord, in mercie soe esteeme us,
95　that wee maie thie mercie trie,
　　　　Mercie maie from thrall redeeme us.

Eructavit cor meum.
Psalm 45.

My harte endites an argument of worth,
　　　the praise of him that doth the Scepter swaie:
My tongue the pen to paynt his praises forth,
　　　shall write as swift, as swiftest writer maie.
5　　then to the king these are the wordes I saie:
　　　　fairer art thou then sonnes of mortall race:
　　because high god hath blessed thee for ay,
　　　　thie lipps, as springs, doe flowe with speaking grace.

Thie honors sword gird to thie mightie side,
10　　O thou that dost all things in might excell:
with glorie prosper, on with triumph ride:
　　　since justice, truth, and meeknes with thee dwell.
　　soe that right hande of thine shall teaching tell
　　　　such things to thee, as well maie terror bring,
15　　and terror such, as never erst befell
　　　　to mortall mindes at sight of mortall king.

Sharpe are thie shaftes to clive their hartes in twaine
　　　whose heads doe cast thie Conquestes to withstand:
good cause to make the meaner people faine
20　　with willing hartes to undergoe thie hand.

---

93 us with] *written on a slip of paper pasted over* helpe *(eye-skip) in A*　　　94 soe] do *J*

Psalm 45. *Incipit and* Psal: 45 *written in darker ink than the text (here and through c. Ps. 138).
Lacking in I. B has verse numbers 1–17 by lines 1, 6, 9, 11, 17, 21, 25, 29, 33, 37, 41, 45, 49, 53, 57, 59, 63.*
Incipit: om. Q
2 that] who *B*　　　3 paynt] aynt *over erasure in A*　　　4 shall] s *added in different ink in A*　　　8 doe flowe with speaking grace] doe flowe with　speakeing grace *K*; doe speake with flowing grace *G*　　　10 O] *B, K, χ; om. F, J; A has* + *in left margin probably to note originally missing* O *which is added in ink not gold*　　things] mights *B, K, χ*
13 teaching] teachings *Q*　　　15 ∧and] (~ *N, C;* ∧An *Q*　　befell∧] ~) *N, C*　　　17 clive] cleave *B, K, χ*　　　18 heads] hedd *K, χ*　　Conquestes] conquest *θ, N*　　　19 faine] feign *B*　　　20 hartes] parts *N*　　hand] bande [?] *Q*

thie throne ô god doth never-falling stand:
    thie Scepter ensigne of thie kinglie might,
to righteousnes is linckt with such a band,
    that righteous hand still holds thie Scepter right.

Justice in love, in hate thou holdest wrong,   25
    this makes that god; who soe doth hate and love:
Glad-making oile, that oile on thee hath flong,
    which thee exaltes thine equalls farre above.
    the fragrant riches of Sabean grove
        Mirrh, Aloes, Casia, all thie robes doe smell: 30
when thou from Ivorie pallace dost remove
        thie breathing odors all thie traine excell.

Daughters of kings among thie courtlie band,
    by honoring thee of thee doe honor hold:
On thie right side thie dearest queene doth stand   35
    richlie araid in cloth of Ophir gold
    O daughter heare what nowe to thee is told:
        marke what thou hear'st, and what thou mark'st obey
forgett to keepe in memorie enrold
        the house, and folk, where first thou sawst the daie.   40

Soe in the king, thie king, a deere delight
    thie beautie shall both breed, and bredd maintaine:
for onlie hee on thee hath lordlie right,
    him onlie thou with awe must entertaine.
    then unto thee both Tirus shall bee faine   45
        presents present, and richest nations moe,
with humble sute thie Roiall grace to gaine,
        to thee shall doe such homage as they owe.

This Queene that can a king hir father call,
    doth only shee in upper garment shine?   50
Naie under clothes, and what shee weareth all,
    golde is the stuffe the fasshion arte divine,

21 ô] *om. N*   24 thie] the *B, E*   28 thine] Thy *B, K, χ*; her *O*   29 of]
which *C*   31 dost] doth *M*   32 *quadruply indented in A*   33 among]
amongst *θ*   35 side] hand *G, M*   37 O] *added in darker ink in A; om. F*   heare]
heere *C*   38 *not fully indented in A*   mark'st] hearst *M*   40 *quadruply indented
in A*   sawst] sav'st *B*   42 ∧bredd∧] *first d written over* e *in slightly darker ink in A*; (∼)
G, M; ∧breed∧ *F*   46 richest] riches *O*   49 This] The *σ, G, M*   a] the *B*
50 doth only shee] shee onely doth *G*   upper] utter *E*   garment] garments *D, C, σ,
G, M*   shine?] ∼∧ *K, χ*; ∼: *M*

brought to the king in robe imbrodred fine,
 hir maides of honor shall on hir attend:
55 with such, to whome more favoure shall assigne
 in neerer place their happie daies to spend.

Brought shall theie bee with mirth and mariage joy,
 and enter soe the pallace of the king:
Then lett noe grief thie minde O Queene anoy,
60 nor parents left thie sad remembraunce sting.
 in steed of parents, children thou shalt bring,
  of partad'gd earth the kings and lords to bee:
 my self thie name in lasting verse will sing,
  the world shall make no ende of thanks to thee.

Deus noster refugium.
Psalm 46.

God gives us strength, and keepes us sounde,
 a present helpe when dangers call;
then feare not wee lett quake the grounde,
 and into Seas let Mountaines fall,
5 yea soe lett Seas withall,
  in watry hills arise,
 as maie the earthlie hills appall,
  with dread and dashing cries.

For lo, a River streaming joy
10   with purling murmur saflie slides,
that cittie washing from annoy,
  in holly shrine where god resides.
  god in hir Center bides:
   what can this cittie shake?
15   god earlie aides and ever guides;
   who can this cittie take.

---

53 *om. D*   56 neerer] never *O*; meaner *M*   60–4 *60, 61, 63 triply indented, 62, 64*
quadruply indented in A

Psalm 46. *Lacking in I. Variant in B.*
Incipit: Deus noster *θ, N, C, H, E*; Deus nostrum *K*; Deus nostrum refugium *B*; *om. Q*
7 earthlie] earthy *K, χ*   8 and] of *C, G, M*   13 hir] his *altered to* her *D*; his *σ*

When nations goe against her bent,
    and kings with siege hir walls enround:
the voide of aire his voice doth rent,
    earth failes their feete with melting ground.   20
    to strength and keepe us sound,
      the god of armies armes:
    our rock on Jacobs god wee found:
      above the reach of harmes.

O come with me, o come and view   25
    the trophes of Jehovas hand:
what wracks from him our foes pursue,
    how cleerly he hath purg'd our land.
    By him warrs silent stand:
      he brake the Archers bow: 30
    made Charretts wheele a firy brand,
      and speare to shivers goe.

Bee still saith he; know, god am I:
    know I will be with conquest croun'd,
above all Nations raised high,   35
    high rais'd above this earthy round.
    To strength and keepe us sound
      the god of Armies armes:
    our Rock on Jacobs god we found,
      above the reach of harmes.   40

17 goe] come *M*   19 the] Thoe *H, Q;* Though *E; M alters the whole line:* Gods thundring voice, the *Earth* doth rent   21 strength] strengh *H*   23 on] in *F*   god] *added above caret in A*   25–40 *added in darker ink (like that used for incipits) in right margin opposite 9–24 in A; indentation irregular*   26 Jehovas] Jehovahs *D*; Jehovaes *Q, E*; Jehova's *J, N, C, G, M*   27 what] ffrom *E*   31 Charretts] *A, K, N*; Chariotts χ   wheele] wheeles *Q*   32 speare] speares *K*; spheere *O*   36 earthy] *A, D, Q*; earthly *K*, χ   37 strength] strenght *H*; strength' *N*

Omnes gentes plaudite.
Psalm 47.

All people to Jehovah bring
  a glad applause of clapping hands:
to god a song of triumph sing,
  who high, and highlie feared stands,
5 of all the earth sole-ruling king.

From whose allmightie grace it growes
  that nations by our power opprest,
our foote on humbled cuntries goes:
  who Jacobs honor loved best,
10 an heritage for us hath chose.

There past hee by: hark how did ring,
  harmonious aire with trumpetts sound:
Praise, praise our god; praise, praise our king,
  king of the world you judgments sound,
15 with skilfull song his praises sing.

On sacred throne, not knowing end,
  for god the king of kingdomes raignes
the folk of Abrahams god to frend
  hee, greatest prince, greate princes gaines;
20 Princes, the shields that earth defend.

Psalm 47. *Indentation unclear in A. Lacking in I. B has verse numbers 1–9 by lines 1, 4, 6, 9, 11, 13, 14, 16, 18.*

Incipit: Omnes gentes *B, K, θ, N, C, H, E; om. Q*

1 Jehovah] *A, D, N;* Jehova *F, B, K, χ* bring] singe *G* 3 triumph] Triumphs *B*
4 and] of *B* 5 king.] ~∧ *B, θ, G, M* 8 foote] feet *E* 9 loved] loveth
θ; M alters the whole line: For he (who *Jacob* loved best 11 past] pass'd *N*
12 aire] ayres *K* 13 Praise] P *added in ink (not gold) in A, and in different hand and
ink in F* god; praise] God, ô *G* 14 king] kinge *E;* Kings *K, χ* you] your *K,
χ* judgments sound] judgement sound *N, Q;* judgments round *G* 15 with . . . song]
In . . . tunes *K, χ;* in . . . noates *G, M* 16 On] O *written in ink (not gold) over erasure of* I
in A; an illegible letter corrected to O *in J;* In *F* 19 hee] the *K* 20 Princes]
P *added in ink (not gold) in A* shields] sheild *θ* that] *A, B;* the *K, χ* defend]
defends *D*

Magnus Dominus.
Psalm 48

Hee that hath eternall beeing
    glorious is, and glorious showes
    in the cittie hee hath chose,
        where stands his holie hill.
Hill Sion, hill of fairest seeing,   5
    cittie of the king most greate,
    seated in a northlie seate,
        all climes with joy doth fill
in each pallace shee containeth.
God a well-knowne rock remaineth.   10

One daie kings, a daie appointed
    there with joyned force to bee,
    see theie it? the things they see,
        amaze their mated mindes.
flyeng, trembling, disapointed,   15
    soe theie feare, and soe they fare,
    as the wife, whose wofull care
        the panges of child-bed findes.
Right as Shipps from Tarshis going,
crusht with blasts of Eurus blowing.   20

Now our sight hath matcht our heering
    in what state gods cittie stands
    how supported by his hands
        god ever holds the same.

Psalm 48. *Incipit and* Psal: 48 *written in small space at top of folio in A. Lacking in I. B has verse numbers 1–14 by lines 1, 5, 9, 11, 13, 15, 19, 21, 25, 27, 29, 31, 33, 39.*
Incipit: Magnus Deus *O; om.* K, Q
5 Hill∧ Sion, hill∧] ~, ~∧ ~∧ *B;* ~, ~, ~ *K;* ~, ~, ~, *O, N;* ~, ~∧ ~, *C;* ~∧ ~, ~, *H;* ~∧ ~∧ ~,
Q, E; Yea *Sion* hill *G;* Sweete hill *Sion M*   7 a northlie] a worthie *N, σ (a and* w *written over erasure in H)*   8 doth fill∧] ~./ *E;* doe fill∧ *H, Q, G;* doe fill; *M*   9–10 *these lines are in A, F, J, B (text); another version in K, χ is also in the margin of B, which notes:* The two last verses are putt in the margin instead of these expunged
                    Ev'ry pallace it enfoldeth
                    God for surest refuge holdeth.
9 containeth.] ~∧ *B*   12 force] powers *K, χ;* Peeres *C, M*   13 it?] yt: *Q, E*
17 care] case *J*   18 child-bed] childhood *N*   19 Tarshis] Tarshish *J, B, K, χ;*
Tharsis *Q, E*   20 crusht] Rusht *K* blasts] blast *K*   23 by] with *J*
24 ever] \for/ *[above caret; illegible characters stricken] K* holds] guard's *[written over erasure] K;* guards *χ*

25   In thie temples mid'st appeering
                wee thie favoure lorde attend:
                righteous lord both free from end,
                        thie fame doth match thie name.
          thie just hand brings Sion gladnes
30   turnes to mirth all Judaes sadnes

          Compasse Sion in hir standing
                tell hir towres, mark hir fortes:
                note with care the statelie portes
                        hir roiall houses beare.
35   for that ages understanding,
                which shall come, when wee shall goe,
                gladd in former time to know,
                        how manie what theie weare.
          For god, is our god for ever
40   us till death forsaking never.

                        Audite hæc omnes.
                        Psalm 49.

          World-dwellers all give heede to what I saie,
                to all I speake, to rich, poore, high, and low;
                knowledg the subject is my hart conceaves,
                wisdome the wordes shall from my mouth proceed;
5   which I will measure by melodious eare
                and ridled speech to tuned harp accord.

---

25 thie temples] the temples *F*; thy *Temple G*   mid'st] middest *K, H*   26 favoure]
succour *M*   27 righteous lord] Gratious god *K, χ*   30 Judaes] Judas *B, K, O,
H, M*; Juda's *C, G*; Judah's *J*   35 that] the *C*   38 weare] were *B, J, K, θ, N,
C, M*   40 us till death] us of his grace *G*; Us his folke *M*

Psalm 49. *Incipit and* Psal: 49 *written in small space at top of folio in A. Lacking in I. B has verse
numbers 1–20 by lines 1, 2, 3, 5, 7, 8, 11, 13, 15, 17, 19, 21, 25, 27, 31, 34, 36, 37, 39, 41. B
notes:* The very manner of this Psalms being crossd and alterd almost in every line and in
many words twice makes me beleive this was an originall book that is[,] that the book before
me was so for none but an author could or would so amend any Copy[.] The Italians call this
A Sestine: *Woodforde's parenthetical letters used to key marginal notes to affected portions of the
text are ignored.*
Incipit: Audite hec omnes *D, G, M; om. K, Q*
1 heede] *B notes: eare.* expungd.   6 ridled speech] *B notes: grave discourse* expunged:

The times of evill whie should theie mee dismaie,
    when mischief shall mie foote stepps overflow?
    and first from him whom fickle wealth deceaves,
    which his though greate vaine confidence doth breed   10
    since no man can his brothers life out-beare
    nor yeeld for him his ransome to the lord.

For deere the price that for a sowle must paie:
    and death his prisoner never will forgoe
    Naie tell mee whome but longer time hee leaves   15
    respited from the tombe for treasures meed?
    sure at his summons, wise and fooles appeare,
    and others spend the riches theie did hoord.

7–8 *B notes:*
       Why should I fearfull be in the evill day
       When mischeif treading on my heeles shal go expungd,
but it is further alterd and the first verse is sometime made to run thus[:] *Why should the time
of ev'ill my face affray* and then—*work my dismay* but both expungd.
8 shall mie foote stepps overflow] treading on my heele shall goe *K*; treading on my heeles
shall goe χ   9 and first from him] And first from men *K*, χ; *B notes: mischeif from
them* expunged: fickle] kl *written in slightly darker ink over* le *in A*; ficle *F*   wealth]
trust *B*   10 which his though greate] Of wealth which his *B*; while flowing store *K*,
χ; *B notes: their.* expunged: 11 since] *B notes: for* expunged: 12 yeeld] *B
notes: pay* expunged: for] to *N*
13–18 *B notes:* This third staffe is so blotted and often mended, that it is hardly perceptible
what should and what should not stand[.] At first it stood thus.
       For deer price they for their soulës must pay
       That from their treasures can for ever flow
       Tho so they live as life them never leaves
       With liveles limbs the greedy grave to feed
       For wise and foole deaths badg alike doth weare
       And strangers spend the riches they did hoord.
       Expunged.
The second verse is also thus mended[:] *Deaths service to an end doth never grow*[.] Expunged.
The fiffth also has *The wise and foole* expunged The sixth has And *others*, which is expungd,
then *And who then spends* expunged: Then the word<s> *others* instead of *strangers* is left to
stand as the last correction.
14 his] in *B*; A *K*; a χ   prisoner never will forgoe] bargaining is endlesse slow *B*
15 mee whome but longer time hee] me whom a longer time he *B*; whom hee but unim-
pris'ned *K*, χ; whome he\that/but ymprisoned *H*; whome hee, but he ymprisoned *Q*;
whome he but ymprisoned *E*   16 respited] Rejected *B*   tombe] grave *K*, χ
17 At his sure summons Wise and fooles appeare *B*; All, All wise, fooles, his badge alike
doe weare *K*, χ; all all wise, fooles his badge alike doe beare *D*; All all wise fooles his
badge alike doth weare *H, Q, G*; And all wise fooles: his badge alike doth weare *E*
18 hoord] *second* o *added in space left from erasure of ascending tail of* r *in A*; leave *B*

A second thinkes his house shall not decaie,
20   nor time his glorious buildings overthrow,
            nam'd proudlie of his name: where folly reaves
            exalted men of sence, and theie indeed
            a brutish life and death, as beasts they weare,
            doe live and die of whom is noe record.

25   Yea these, whose race approves their peevish waie,
            death in the pitt his Carrion foode doth stow
            and loe, the first succeeding light perceaves
            the Just installed in the greate mans steed;
            Nay farr his prince: when once that lovely cheere
30   lovely in house, in tombe becomes abhord.

            But god, my god, to intercept the praie
            of my life from the grave will not foreslowe
            for hee it is hee only mee receaves
            then though one rich doe grow, though glories seede
35   spring with encrease: yet stand thou free from feare,
            of all his pomp death shall him nought affoord.

---

19 A second thinkes] *B notes: yet who but* [*thinks*] expunged: *Another* [*thinks*]. expunged *yet who thinks not.* expunged: not decaie] *B notes: Last for aye* expunged   20 nor time his glorious buildings] Nor tyme his sumptuous labours *K, χ; B notes: That nor time shall his* [*buildings*] expunged   21 nam'd proudlie of his name] *B notes: Nor lands nam'd of his name* expunged: where] for *O*   22 exalted men] Such honourd fooles *B*   theie] such *O*   23 weare] *A, O, H;* were *J, K, χ*
25–30 *B notes:* This fifth staff stood thus.
            Yet their fond race admire their foolish way
            While death devours whole flocks of them below
            Where the just man when first his ey perceives
            The morning light shall in their state succeed
            Lording on them when their once lovely cheare
            A lothly tomb for house shall make abhorrd. expunged:
as also *Lord* in the fifth verse after the correction putt for, *prince*[.]
25 Yea these] These though *B;* And these *K, χ;* And those *M*   whose race] their race *B*   approves] approve *B;* applaud *K, χ*   peevish] wordes and *K, χ*   26 pitt] grave *K, χ; K notes in a different hand in the right margin:* hel.   foode doth stow] *descender of* e *and* doth sto *written on slip of paper pasted on f. 42ʳ in A;* foote doth stowe *D*   27 loe] lowe *σ*   light] lightes *O;* life *B*   28 steed] stead *B, F, M*   29 Nay] Yea *B*   when once] for soon *B*   30 tombe] *A, B, D;* earth *K, χ*   abhord] r *added above* od *in A*   31 intercept] interrupt *Q, E*   32 will] shall *B, K, χ*   34 doe grow] become *K, χ;* becomes *σ*   though glories] and honours *B;* though honnors *K, χ* though honour *N, H, E*   35 spring with encrease] *B notes: Full harvest bring him* expunged.   36 nought] naught *K*

Please theie them selves, and think at happiest staie
   who please them selves: yet to their fathers goe
  must theie to endles dark: for folly reaves
   exalted men of sence, and theie indeede   40
  a brutish life and death, as beastes theie weare,
   doe live, and die, of whome is noe record.

Deus Deorum.
Psalm 50.

The mightie god, the ever-living lord,
   all nations from earthes uttermost confines
sommoneth by his pursevant, his worde,
   and out of beauties beautie, Sion shines.
God comes, hee comes, with eare and tongue restor'd: 5
     his garde huge stormes, hott flames his usshers goe:
and called their apparrance to record,
     heav'n hasteth from above, earth from below.

He sits his peoples Judg, and thus commandes:
     gather mee hither that beloved line   10
whome solemn sacrifices holy bandes
    did in eternall league with me combine.
then when the heav'ns subsigned with their handes,
     that god in Justice eminentlie raignes:

37–9 B notes: instead of the three first Verses of this staffe there stood at first five thus for
which (\possibly/ because therby the staff was too long) the whole Psalm was crossd and
mended[:]

     The living thought his life at happyest stay
     So flatterers in his eares did whispering blow
     But they shall ly where erst their Fathers lay
     In shade of death where life shall never show
     And justly sure, for surely folly reaves etc. expunged.

37 and] which *B*   38 who] To *B*   39 must] shall *B, K, χ*   to endles dark] and
they are dead *K, χ*   40 theie] such *K, χ*   41 as] and *σ*   weare] were *B, J, K, O,
N, C, M*

Psalm 50. *Incipit* and Psal: 50 *(just beneath and to the right of the incipit) written in small space
at top of folio in A. Lacking in I. Variant in B.*
Incipit: om. K, Q
3 his worde] his *stricken before* his *in A;* the word *N*   4 beauties‸ beautie,] Beautie's‸
beawtie‸ *C;* bewties, bewtie‸ *O;* bewties, bewtie, *H, Q*   5 tongue] *a letter* (s ?) *stricken
after* e *in A*   7 apparrance] appearance *E*

15 Controlling soe, as nothing countermandes
   what once decreed his highest doome containes.

 You then my folke to me your god attend:
   hark Israell and heare thie peoples blame:
 not want of sacrifice doth mee offend,
20   nor doe I misse thy alters daily flame.
 To mee thie stall noe fatted bull shall send:
   should I exact one Hee-goate from thie fold?
 I, that as farr as hills, woodes, fieldes extende
   all birdes and beastes in known possession hold.

25 Suppose mee hungrie; yet to beg thie meate,
   I would not tell thee that I hungrie were:
 my self maie take, what needs mee then entreate?
   since earth is mine, and all that earth doth beare.
 But doe I long the brawnie flesh to eate
30   of that dull beast that serves the plowmans neede?
 or doe I thirst, to quench my thirsty heate,
   in what the throates of bearded cattell bleed?

 O no: bring god of praise a sacrifice;
   thie vowed debts unto the highest paie:
35 Invoke my name, to mee erect thie cries,
   thie praying plaints, when sorow stopps thie waie
 I will undoe the knott that anguish tyes,
   and thou at peace shalt glorifie my name:
 mildlie the good, god schooleth in this wise,
40   but this sharpe check doth to the godlesse frame:

 How fitts it thee my statutes to report?
   and of my covenant in thie talk to prate
 hating to live in right reformed sort,
   and leaving in neglect what I relate.
45 see'st thou a thief? thou grow'st of his consorte:
   dost with adultrers to adultrie goe:

---

15 countermandes] counterstandes *K, χ* 16 highest] sacred *K, χ* 17 then] *O*
M me your god] what I teach *K, χ* 21 bull] Bulles *K, χ* 22 one] on *D*
23 I] *added in darker ink in A; om. F* fieldes] feild *N* 24 all] as *O* and] all *K, χ*
26 not] no *Q* hungrie] hunger *H, Q* were] weare *H, Q* 28 since] *A, E*; Sith *K, χ*
32 bleed] bleedes *E*; breed *D* 33 god] *om. J* 34 debts] heastes *K, χ*
36 thie waie] the way *D, E, G, M* 37 I] *added in darker ink in A; om. F* that]
which *O* 41 How] *gold* H *over erased* gold N *in A*

thie mouth is slaunders ever-open porte,
  and from thie tongue doth nought, but treason, flow.

Naie ev'n thie brother thie rebukes disgrace,
  and thou in spight diffam'st thie mothers sonne: 50
And for I wink a while, thie thoughts imbrace:
  god is like mee, and doth as I have done.
But loe thou see'st I march another pace,
  and come with truth thie falshood to disclose:
thie sinne reviv'd, upbraides thie blushing face,   55
  which thou long dead in silence did'st suppose.

O laie up this in marking memorie
  you that are wont gods judgments to forgett:
in vaine to others for release you flie,
  if once on you I griping fingers sett.   60
And know the rest: my deerest worship I
  in sweete perfume of offred praise doe place:
and who directs his goings orderlie,
  by my conduct shall see gods saving grace.

Miserere mei Deus.
Psalm 51.

O lord, whose grace no limitts comprehend;
sweet lord, whose mercies stand from measure free;
to mee that grace, to mee that mercie send,
and wipe o lord my sinnes from sinnfull mee
O clense, o wash, my fowle iniquitie: 5

---

47 slaunders ever-open] ever slaunders open *D* 48 nought] naught *C* 52 doth]
does *K, N, C, σ, G, M* 54 with] in *Q* 56 dead] since *M* did'st] did *H*
59 release] releif *N, C, σ, G, M* 60 griping] grippinge *σ* 62 perfume] perfumes
χ 63 goings] goeing *O, E*

Psalm 51. *B has verse numbers 1–19 by lines 1, 6, 8, 11, 15, 19, 22, 27, 29, 31, 33, 34, 36, 40,
43, 45, 48, 50, 54.*
Incipit: Miserere mei Deus secundum *B*; Miserere mei deus secund magnam etc. *I*; Miserere mei *D, N, C, H, E*; meserere mei *O*; Miserere *K*; *om. Q*
2 mercies stand] mercy stands *D, G, M* 4 and wipe o lord my sinnes] and wipe [*H*:
whipe] O lord my sin *B, K, χ*; and wash awaye my sinn [wash awaye my *written in a different
hand over stricken* wype (o Lord) that] *I* 5 O clense] *F, B, K, χ*; clense *A (small space
left before* clense), *J*

clense still my spotts, still wash awaie my staynings,
till staines and spotts in mee leave noe remaynings.

For I alas, acknowledging doe know
my filthie fault, my faultie filthines
10   to my sowles eye unceasantlie doth show
which done to thee, to thee I doe confesse,
Just, judge, true wittnes; that for righteousnes
        thie doome maie passe against my guilt awarded,
        thie evidence for truth maie be regarded.

15   My mother, loe! when I began to be,
conceaving me, with me did sinne conceave:
and as with living heate shee cherisht me
corruption did like cherishing receave.
but loe, thie love to purest good doth cleave,
20   and inward truth: which hardlie els discerned,
        my trewand soule in thie hid schoole hath learned.

Then as thie self to leapers hast assign'd,
with Hisop, lord thie Hisop, purge me soe:
and that shall clense the leaprie of my mind.
25   make over me thie mercies streames to flow,
Soe shall my whitnes scorne the whitest snow.
        to eare and hart send soundes and thoughts of gladdnes,
        that brused bones maie daunce awaie their saddnes.

Thie ill-pleas'd eye from my misdeedes avert:
30   Cancell the registers my sinns containe:
create in me a pure, cleane, spottles hart:
inspire a sprite where love of right maie raigne.
ah! cast me not from thee: take not againe
        thie breathing grace: againe thie comfort send me,
35   and let the guard of thy free sprite attend me.

---

7 in mee leave] leave in me *B*   14 thie] thyne *Q*   15 when] where *B*
19 loe] lord *G, M*   love] good *θ*   22 leapers] Leapors *K, σ, C*; lepers *J*; lepors *O*;
leepers *G, M*   24 leaprie] leepry *N*   25 mercies] mercie *Q*   28 daunce]
leave *I*   30 cancell the registers [s *added?*], my sinns contayne *H*; Cancell the Register
my Sinnes Containe *C, E, G, M*; o cancell those records my sinn containe *I*   31 pure,
cleane] cleane pure *I, G*   32 sprite] sp'rite *C*; spright *I, σ*; spirit *B, D, N, G*
33 ah] and *I*   from thee] awaye *G, M*

Soe I to them a guiding hand wilbe,
whose faultie feete have wandred from thie way:
and turn'd from sinne will make retorne to thee,
whom turn'd from thee sinne erst had ledd astraie.
O god, god of my health, O doe away   40
       my bloodie crime: soe shall my tongue be raised
       to praise thy truth, enough can not bee praised.

Unlock my lipps, shut up with sinnfull shame:
then shall my mouth ô lord thy honor sing.
for bleeding fuell for thy alters flame,   45
to gaine thy grace what bootes it me to bring?
burnt-offrings are to thee no pleasaunt thing.
       the sacrifice that god will hold respected,
       is the hart-broken soule, the sprite dejected.

Lastly, O lord how soe I stand or fall,   50
leave not thy loved Sion to embrace:
but with thie favor build up Salems wall,
and still in peace, maintaine that peacefull place.
then shalt thou turne a well-accepting face
       to sacred fires with offred guiftes perfumed: 55
       till ev'n whole calves on alters be consumed.

Quid gloriaris?
Psalm 52.

    Tyrant whie swel'st thou thus,
       of mischief vanting?
    since helpe from god to us,
       is never wanting?

---

39 ledd] turnd *I*   40 god of my health] my god, of health *I*   41 soe] then *G*,
M   raise'd_∧_] se *written over erasure in A*; raised. *K*; raised: *C*; raised, *G, M*   44 thy]
thine *N*   45 for thy] of Thy *B*   49 *om. I*   sprite] sp'rite *C; N, G*; spirritt
Q, E   50 Lastly] And last *I*   soe] ere *I*   51 leave not thy loved Sion] leave
not thy holie Sion *O*; thie loved Syon leave not *I*   54 well-accepting] well accepted
F, G, M

Psalm 52. *Indentation irregular in A because of initial capitals; B groups stanzas into units of 8
lines (with a final stanza of 4 lines) and indents even numbered stanzas. Lacking in I. B has verse
numbers 1–9 by lines 1, 5, 9, 13, 17, 21, 25, 29, 37.*
Incipit: Quid gloriaris. *C; om. Q*

5   Lewd lies thy tongue contrives,
         lowd lies it soundeth:
    sharper then sharpest knives
         with lies it woundeth.

    Falshood thy witt approves,
10   all truth rejected:
    thy will all vices loves,
         vertue neglected.

    Not wordes from cursed thee,
         but gulphes are powred.
15 Gulphes wherin daily bee
         good men devoured.

    Think'st thou to beare it soe?
         God shall displace thee
    God shall thee overthrow,
20   crush thee, deface thee.

    The Just shall fearing see
         theis fearefull chaunces:
    and laughing shoote at thee
         with scornfull glaunces.

25 Loe, loe, the wretched wight,
         who god disdaining,
    his mischief made his might,
         his guard his gaining.

    I as an Olive tree,
30   still greene shall flourish:
    Gods howse the soile shall bee
         my rootes to nourish.

    My trust on his true love
         truly attending,
35 shall never thence remove,
         never see ending.

---

5 ∴ *in margin in A*   Lewd] Lowd *J*   6 lowd] Lewd *N*   13 Not] Noe *E*
17 Think'st] Thinks *N, σ*   19 God] G *added in darker ink (not gold) in A*   22 theis]
thus *F*; those *G*   24 scornfull] fearfull *B*   28 guard] God *G, M*   31 Gods]
G *added in darker ink (not gold) in A*   32 rootes] root *E* to] shalbe *O*   nourish] o
added above caret in darker ink in A   33 on] in *M*

Thee will I honor still
    lord for this justice:
There fix my hopes I will,
    where thy sainets trust is.   40

Thy sainets trust in thy name,
    therin they joy them:
protected by the same
    nought can anoy them.

Dixit insipiens.
Psalm 53.

There is noe god, the foole doth saie
    if not in word, in thought and will:
this fancie rotten deedes bewraie,
    and studies fixt on lothsome ill.
    not one doth good from heav'nlie hill   5
    Jehovas eye one wiser minde
could not discerne, that held the waie,
    to understand and god to finde.

They all have strai'd are cancred all:
    not one I saie, not one doth good.   10
But senslesnes, what should I call
    such careage of this cursed brood?
    My people are their bread, their food,
    upon my name they scorne to cry:
whome vaine affright doth yet appall,   15
    where no just ground of feare doth ly.

But on their bones shall wreaked be
    all thy Invaders force and guile,

---

38 this] his *O*; thy *N, σ, G, M*   39 There] T *added in ink in A*; There *B, K, χ*; heere *F*;
here *J*   44 nought] naught *B, K*

Psalm 53. *Lacking in I. Variant in B.*
Incipit: om. Q
3 this] his *χ*   6 Jehovas] Jehovahs *D*; Jehova's *J, N, C, G*   one] on *C, σ, G, M*; noe
O; no *D*   7 not] \not/ *[a different hand?] G*   held] heald *G*   9 have] are *Q*
12 this] that *J*   cursed] sinnefull *G*   15 appall] appale *σ*   16 of] I *N*
17 wreaked] wracked *σ*   18 thy] the *C, G, M*

in vile confusion cast by thee,
20   for god him self shall make them vile.
ah! why delaies that happy while
          when Sion shall our saver bring?
The lord his folk will one daie free:
          then Jacobs house shall daunce and sing.

Deus in nomine.
Psalm 54.

Lord let thy name my saving succor bee:
          defend my wronged cause by thy just might.
Lord let my crieng voice be heard of thee,
          lett not my heavie words be counted light.
5   For strangers I against me risen see,
          who hunt me hard, and sore my soule affright:
possest with feare of god in no degree.
          but god, thou art my helper in my right,
thou succour send'st to such as succour me.
10   then pay them home, who thus against me fight,
and let thy truth cut downe their trechery.
          soe I with Offrings shall thy Alters dight,
praising thy name which thus hast sett me free:
          giving me scope to soare with happie flight
15   above my evills: and on my enemy
          making me see, what I to see delight.

---

19 vile] vild *H, E*; vilde *Q*

Psalm 54. *Psalm number written to the right of the incipit at the top of the folio in A. Lacking in I. B has verse numbers 1–7 by lines 1, 3, 5, 8, 10, 12, 14.*
Incipit: Deus in nomine tuo *B*; *om. K, Q*
8 god] Lord *C, M*   10 home] whome *σ*   12 Alters] *Altars* [s *added?*] *G*; Altar *O, C, M*   13 hast] hath *E*   15 my enemy] myne enemye *F, J, D, G, M*   16 to] doe *M*

Exaudi Deus.
Psalm 55.

My god most glad to look, most prone to heere,
    an open eare o lett my praier find,
        and from my plaint turne not thie face away.
        behold my jestures, harken what I say
    while uttering mones with most tormented mind,   5
My body I no lesse torment and teare.
for loe their fearfull threatnings wound mine eare,
    who griefs on griefs on me still heaping laie,
        a mark to wrath and hate and wrong assign'd,
        therfore my hart hath all his force resign'd   10
to trembling pants, death terrors on me pray,
I feare, nay shake, nay quiv'ring quake with feare.

Then say I ô might I but cutt the wind,
    born on the wing the fearfull dove doth beare:
        stay would I not, till I in rest might stay.   15
        farr hence, ô farr, then would I take my way
unto the desert, and repose me there,
these stormes of woe, these tempests left behind,
but swallow them ô lord in darknes blind,
    confound their councells, leade their tongus astray,   20
        that what they meane by wordes may not appeare.
        for Mother Wrong within their towne each where,
and daughter Strife their ensignes soe display,
as if theie only thither were confin'd.

Psalm 55. *Lacking in I. B has verse numbers 1–23 by lines 1, 4, 7, 10, 12, 13, 16, 18, 19, 25, 26,
31, 37, 40, 43, 46, 48, 49, 53, 55, 58, 61, 67.*
Incipit: om. Q
1 heere] heare *F, B, K, χ*   3 thie face away] awaie thy face *O*; awaie a thy face awaie
[*first* awaie *underlined; second* awaie *added at the end of the line in a different hand but similar
ink*] *D*   4 jestures] gesture *σ*   5 mones] moane *C*   7 their] thie *E*   mine]
my *σ*   9 *B notes: As if no other tomb were mee assignd* Expunged, *and the verse in the
staffe enterlin'd in another hand.*   11 pants] plaints *F*; pathes *D*   death] Deaths *B*
pray] prey *B*; lay *N*   12 I] *added in ink (not gold) in A; om. F, J*   shake] quake *N*
with] for *θ*   14 wing] winges *D*   18 woe] woes *E*   19 swallow] *B notes: scat-
ter but expunged:*   20 councells] Counsels *B, K, O, N*; Counsailes *C*   22 towne]
tongue *J*; tounge *E*   23 daughter] daughters *N, E*   24 were] weare *F, H, Q*

25   These walk their cittie walles both night and day,
                oppressions, tumults, guiles of ev'ry kind
                        are burgesses and dwell the midle neere,
                                about their streetes his masking robes doth weare
                Mischeif cloth'd in deceit, with treason lin'd,
30   where only hee, hee only beares the sway.
        but not my foe with mee this pranck did play,
                for then I would have borne with patient cheere
                        an unkind part from whom I know unkind.
                        nor hee whose forehed Envies mark had sign'd,
35   his trophes on my ruins sought to reare,
        from whom to fly I might have made assay.

        But this to thee, to thee impute I may,
                my fellow my companion, held most deere,
                        my soule, my other self, my inward frend:
40   whom unto me, me unto whom did bind
                exchanged secrets, who togeather were
        gods temple wont to visit, there to pray.
        ô lett a soddaine death work their decay,
                who speaking faire such canckred malice mind,
45   let them be buried breathing in theyr beare
                        but purple morne black ev'n and midday cleare,
                shall see my praying voice to god enclin'd,
        rowzing him up and nought shall me dismay.

        Hee ransom'd me, hee for my saftie fin'd
50   in fight where many sought my soule to slay,
                        he, still him self to noe succeeding heire
                        leaving his Empire shall no more forbeare
                but at my motion, all these Athists pay,
        by whom, still one such mischiefs are design'd.

25 These] Those *O, N, σ, G, M*   walles] walks *F; om. O*   26 oppressions] *a dash before this word indicates mistaken indentation in A*   ev'ry] *apostrophe above stricken* e *in A;* every *F*   28 *aligned with mistakenly indented 26 in A*   their] the *E*   robes] roabe *M* 31 with mee this pranck] this prancke with mee *C, M*   33 an] d *erased after* n *in A;* and *F, K, N*   know unkind] knew unkind *B, σ, G*   34 had] hath *F*   35 ruins] ruine *K, C, M*   reare] weare *N*   38 held] heald *G*   41 exchanged] exchaingeinge *Q* were] weare *F, O, H*   42 there] then *σ*   45 in] on *E*; from *B*   beare] beere *B, D, E, C*   48 nought] naught *B*   51 noe] *written over erasure in A*   53 these] the *F*   Athists] *A, D*; Athests *E*; Atheists *K, χ*   54 one_∧] ~, *B*; ~_∧ *K, H, Q, E*; on, *N, C;* on_∧ *G, M*

who but such Caitives would have undermin'd   55
    nay overthrowne, from whome but kindnes meare
        they never found? who would such trust betray?
        what buttred wordes! yet warr their harts bewray.
    their speach more sharp then sharpest sword or speare
yet softer flowes then balme from wounded Rind.   60

But my oreloaden soule thy selfe upcheare
    cast on Gods shoulders what thee downe doth waigh
        long borne by thee with bearing pain'd and pin'd
        to care for thee hee shall be ever kinde
    by him the just in safty held allway   65
chaunglesse shall enter, live and leave the yeare:
but lord how long shall these men tarry heere
    fling them in pitt of death where never shin'd
        the light of life and while I make my stay
        on thee, let who their thirst with bloud allay   70
    have their life-holding threed so weakly twin'd
that it half-spunne, death may in sunder sheare.

Miserere mei Deus.
Psalm 56.

Fountaine of pitty now with pitty flow:
these monsters on me daily gaping goe.

58 harts] thoughtes *G, M*   bewray] *rounded* r *added above* a *in A*   60 wounded]
wounden σ   Rind] Ryne *F*   61–72 *written in a hand resembling the* J *hand on a slip*
of paper pasted in at bottom of f. 45^v *(letters not gilded; clubs of ascenders and descenders filled*
with ink, not open); A notes in a different hand: quere [*large arrow and three dots to the left of*
quere *pointing upward*]; *om. F*   61 oreloaden] ore=loaden *K*; ore loaden *O*; oreloden *J*,
D; oreladen σ, *G, M*; o're=laden *N*   upcheare] upreare *O*   62 cast] *B notes: Lay*
expunged: 65 held] heald *G*; *B notes: kept* expunged.   66 chaunglesse] *B*
notes: fearelesse expunged.   67 heere] here *B, J, E, N, G*; heare *H, Q*
69–72 *B notes:* The last 4 Verses stood thus before the Correction
           ———. *there let them ly for aye*
           Let such as would their thirst etc.
           Have, their l. h. t no longer twin'd
           But e're half spun let Death, the same off sheare.
The first of these foure further again thus corrected—*and while on Thee I stay.* but all
expungd as appeares [*in the text*] and corrected by the Authors own hand.
69 life] light *N*   70 with] on *K*

Psalm 56. *Psalm number written to the right of the incipit in A. Lacking in I. B has verse numbers*
1–13 by lines 1, 3, 6, 7, 11, 16, 18, 21, 26, 31, 33, 36, 41.
Incipit: Miserere mei *B, K, D, N, C, H, E;* meserere. mei. *O; om. Q*

dailie me devoure these spies
swarmes of foes against me rise,
5   ô god that art more high then I am low.

Still when I feare yet will I trust in thee:
thy word ô god my boast shall ever bee
god shalbe my hopefull stay
feare shall not that hope dismay
10   for what can feeble flesh doe unto me?

I as I can think, speake, and doe the best:
they to the worst my thoughts, wordes, doings wrest.
all their hartes with one consent
are to worke my ruine bent,
15   from plotting which they give their heads no rest.

To that entent they secret meetings make,
they presse me neere my soule in snare to take,
thinking slight shall keepe them safe.
but thou lord in wrathfull chafe
20   their league soe surely linckt in sunder shake.

Thou did'st ô lord with carefull counting looke
on ev'ry jorney I poore exile tooke:
ev'ry teare from my sad eyes
saved in thy bottle lyes,
25   these matters are all entred in thy book.

Then when soever my distressed sprite
crying to thee brings these unto thy sight,
what remayneth for my foes?
blames, and shames, and overthrowes,
30   for god him self I know for me will fight.

Gods never-falsed word my boast shalbe,
my boast shalbe his word to sett me free.

6 will I] I will *M*   in] on *M*   12 wrest] *rounded* r *added above* e *in A.*   17 neere]
sore *G, M*   my soule in snare] in snare my soule *D*   18 slight] flight *F*   19 lord]
god *O*   20 league] leagues *Q*   23 from] in *E*   25 are all] *written as a correc-*
tion of all *on a small piece of paper pasted onto f. 46 in A (original illegible);* all are *B*
26 when soever] whersoever *B*   sprite] spright *B,* σ; spirit *N*   27 crying] Coming
G   these] those *M*   31 never-falsed] never failed *G, M*

god shall be my hopfull stay,
feare shall not that hope dismay,
for what can mortall man doe unto me?   35

For this to thee how deeply stand I bound
lord that my soule dost save, my foes confound?
ah I can no paiment make,
but if thou for payment take,
the vowes I pay, thy praises I resound.   40

Thy praises who from death hast sett me free,
whether my feete did hedlong cary me.
making me of thy free grace
ther agayne to take my place,
where light of life with lyving men I see.   45

Miserere mei Deus.
Psalm 57.

Thie mercie lord, lord now thy mercy show,
on thee I ly
to thee I fly
hide me, hive me, as thyne owne,
till these blasts be overblown,   5
which now doe fiercely blow.

To highest god I will erect my cry,
who quickly shall
dispatch this all.

35–6 *the phrases,* for what can *and* For this to thee, *are written as a correction on a small piece of paper pasted onto f. 46 in A (original:* for what mortall *and* or to thee, *with space left for gold* F*)*
35 can] *om.* F   man] *A, B, K, G, M;* men χ   me] thee *N*   36 deeply] dearely *G*
stand] am *C*   38 ah] lord *G*   40 B *notes:* The last verse of this staffe before the
correction stood thus. *That still my song thy praryses do resound*[,] which not pleasing twas
thus changd[:] *That still I vow and still thy prayse resound*[,] but both expungd   thy] the
G, M   I resound] to resound *F*   42 whether] Whither *C, G, M*   45 lyving]
loving *N, C, σ, G, M*

Psalm 57. *Lacking in I. B has verse numbers 1–11 by lines 1, 7, 10, 13, 19, 25, 31, 34, 36, 43, 49.*
Incipit: Miserere mei *B, K, D, N, H, E;* meserere. mei. *O; om. Q*
1 lord, lord] lord, doth *F*   4 hive] hide *K*   thyne] thy *O*   6 doe fiercely]
fiercely *written over erasure in A;* so feirce doe *E*

10   hee shall downe from heaven send
          from disgrace me to defend
      his love and verity.

      My soule incaged lyes with lions brood,
                villains whose hands
15   are firy brands,
          teeth more sharp then shaft or speare,
          tongues farr better edg do beare
      then swords to shed my bloud.

      As high as highest heav'n can geve thee place
20   ô lord ascend,
              and thence extend
          with most bright, most glorious show
          over all the earth below
      the sunn-beames of thy face.

25   Me to entangle ev'ry waie I goe
              their trapp and nett
              is reddie sett.
          hoales they digg but their own hoales
          pitfalls make for their own sowles:
30   soe lord, o serve them soe.

      My hart prepar'd prepared is my hart
              to spread thy praise
              with tuned laies:
          wake my tongue, my lute awake,
35   thou my harp the consort make,
      my self will beare a part.

      My self when first the morning shall appeare,
              with voice and string
              soe will thee sing:

10 downe] *om. θ*   13 incaged] e *added,* ' *erased before* d *in A*; enraged *B*   16 shaft]
Sword G, M   17 farr] *B notes:* forte *that*   do] doth *G, Q*   18 shed] steed *H, Q*
19 heav'n] heaven *F, θ, σ, M*; Heav'ns *C*; heavens *G*   thee] *added as an abbreviation above
the line in A*   25 I] they *χ*   28 digg] have *D*   31 prepar'd] e *erased before* d
in A; *om. J*   35 harp] *B, K, χ*; hart *A*; har [*space left after* r] *O*   38 with] My *B*
39 soe will thee] To thee will *N, σ, G, M*

that this earthly globe, and all   40
    treading on this earthly ball,
my praising notes shall heare.

For god, my only god, thy gracious love
    is mounted farr
    above each starr,   45
    thy unchanged Verity
    heav'nly wings doe lift as hie
as cloudes have roome to move.

As high as highest heav'n can give thee place
    ô lord ascend   50
    and thence extend
    with most bright most glorious show
    over all the earth below,
the sunn-beames of thy face.

Si vere utique.
Psalm 58.

And call yee this to utter what is just,
    you that of justice hold the sov'raign throne?
and call yee this to yeld, O sonnes of dust,
    to wronged brethren ev'ry man his own?
    O no: it is your long malicious will   5
now to the world to make by practize known
    with whose oppression you the ballance fill,
Just to your selves, indiffr'ent els to none.

But what could they, who ev'n in birth declin'd
    from truth and right to lies and injuries?   10
to shew the venim of their canc'red mynd
    the Adders image scarcly can suffice.

---

40 earthly] earthy *D, M*   41 earthly] earthy *D, M*   47 doe] doth *D, Q*
49 heav'n] heaven *N, σ*; heavens *θ, G*; heav'ns *C*

Psalm 58. *Variant in B.*
Incipit: Si Vere *K, I, N, C, H, E; om. Q*
1 yee] you *I, Q, E, G, M*   3 yee] you *K, I, σ, G, M*   4 man] one *D*   5 O] O
K, I, χ; om. A   long] owne *G*   malicious] ambitiows *I*   6 by] thy *N*   7 whose]
what *θ*   9 declin'd] decline *I*   11 of] of of *N*   12 scarcly] hardly *G, M*

nay scarce the Aspick may with them contend,
on whom the charmer all in vaine applies
15   his skillfuls't spells: ay missing of his end,
while shee self-deaff, and unaffected lies.

Lord crack their teeth, lord crush these lions jawes,
soe lett them sinck as water in the sand:
when deadly bow their aiming fury drawes,
20   shiver the shaft er past the shooters hand.
so make them melt as the dishowsed snaile
or as the Embrio, whose vitall band
breakes er it holdes, and formlesse eyes doe faile
to see the sunn, though brought to lightfull land.

25   O lett their brood, a brood of springing thornes,
be by untymely rooting overthrowne
er bushes waxt, they push with pricking hornes,
as fruites yet greene are of by tempest blowne
the good with gladnes this reveng shall see,
30   and bath his feete in bloud of wicked one.
while all shall say: the just rewarded be
there is a god that carves to each his own.

Eripe me de inimicis.
Psalm 59.

Save mee from such as me assaile:
let not my foes,
ô god against my life prevaile:
save me from those,

---

15 skillfuls't] *a fourth* l *altered to long* s, 't *added in* A; skilfull F, *J*   16 self-deaff] a *added above* e *in* A; her selfe deafe *I*; herselfe deaf *N*   17 lord crush these] and crush theis *F*; Lord crush their *N*   18 sand] same *I*   19 fury] furies *I*   20 er] or *I* shooters] suters *E*   21 make] let *G, M*   23 doe] de *C*   27 er] as *altered to* er *or vice versa in* H; As *Q, E*   push] puff *I*   28 of] off *J*; off [*second* f *added*] H; offe *Q*; ofte *E*   by] with *G*; the *I*   tempest] *tempests G, M*   30 bath] *A, J, O, G, M*; bathe *F, I, K, χ*; both *N*   his] theire *C*   feete] foote *G, M*   32 carves] shares *D* to] for *M*

Psalm 59. *Lacking in* I. B *has verse numbers* 3–17 *by lines* 7, 13, 19, 25, 31, 37, 39, 43, 49, 55, 61, 67, 73, 79, 85.
Incipit: Eripe me B, K, χ; *om.* Q
4 *om.* B

who make a trade of cursed wrong   5
and bredd in bloud for bloud doe long.

Of these one sort doe seeke by slight
    my overthrow:
the stronger part with open might
    against me goe   10
and yet (thou god my wittnes be)
from all offence my soule is free.

But what if I from fault am free?
    yet theie are bent,
to band and stand against poore me,   15
    poore Innocent.
    rise god and see how these things goe:
and rescue mee from instant woe.

Rise god of armies, mighty god
    of Israell: 20
looke on them all who spredd abrode
    on earth doe dwell.
    and let thy hand no longer spare
such as of malice wicked are.

When golden sunn in West doth sett   25
    retorn'd againe,
as houndes that howle their food to gett
    they runn amaine
    the cittie through from street to street
with hungry maw some praie to meet   30

Night elder growne, their fittest day,
    they babling prate
how my lost life extinguish may
    their deadly hate.

5–6 *B notes:* The two last verses (before this Correction in the Authors hand) stood thus
    Who doing wrong by wrong do thrive
    And murdring souls by murder live.

but they are expungd
5 cursed] wicked *K*, χ; doeing *E*   6 doe] doth *E*   7 doe] doth *N*   11 thou
god] my God, thou *G*   14 *indented in A*   18 and] an *Q*   woe] foe *F*
19 Rise] R *written over erasure of* Ar *in A*; Arise *F*   22 doe] doth *N, G*   24 of]
om. C   25 doth] doe *G, M*   30 maw] mawes *B, O*   31 elder] older *B*
fittest] chiefest *D*   32 they] They *B, K,* χ; their *A*

35   they prate and bable voide of feare,
        for tush saie they who now can heare?

        Even thou canst heere, and heering scorne,
                all that they say
        for them (if not by thee upborne)
40   what propps doe stay?
            then will I as they wait for me
            ô god my fortresse wait on thee

        Thou ever mee with thy free grace
                prevented hast:
45   with thee my praier shall take place
                er from me past.
            and I shall see who me doe hate
            beyond my wish in wofull state.

        For feare my people it forgett
50   slay not outright
        but scatter them and soe them sett
                in open sight
            that by thy might they may be knowne
            disgrac'd, debas'd and overthrowne.

55   No witnes of their wickednesse
                I neede produce
        but their owne lipps, fitt to expresse
                each vile abuse:
            in cursing proud, proud when they ly
60   o lett them deere such pride aby.

        At length in rage consume them soe
                that nought remayne:
        lett them all beeing quite forgoe,
                and make it playne,

---

35 bable] prattle *E*   36 now can] can us *C, G, M*   37 Even] Lord *G*   heere]
heare *B, J, K, χ*   ᴧheeringᴧ scorne,] (hearing) ~ᴧ *G*; (hearingᴧ ~): *M*   40 doe]
can *B*   46 er] *A, O, σ, M*; ere *F, K, χ*; E're *B*   47 me doe] doe me *σ*   49 my]
thy *G, M*; the *σ*   it] yet *E*   50 slay] stay *J*   53–4 *written at top of f. 48ᵛ and
stricken in A*   53–90 *written with deeper indentation in right margin of A (f. 48ʳ) in a
hand resembling the J hand; that written lightly at bottom of folio*   54 debas'd] *B notes:
before the Correction it was* amaz'd *but expunged:*   55–90 *om. F*   58 vile] vilde *E*
60 such pride, O let them dearelie buye *G, M*   aby] a-buy *J*   61 length] lenghe
H, Q

that God who Jacobs rule upholds 65
rules all, all=bearing earth enfolds.

Now thus they fare: when Sunn doth sett
retorn'd againe,
as hounds that howle their food to gett
they runn amayne 70
the city through from street to street
with hungry mawes some pray to meet.

Abroad they range and hunt apace
now that now this,
as famine trailes a hungry trace, 75
and though they miss
yett will they not to kennell hye
but all the night at bay will lye

But I will of thy goodness sing
and of thy might 80
when early sunn againe shall bring
his cheerefull light
for thou my refuge and my fort
in all distress do'st mee support.

My strength doth of thy strength depend 85
to thee I sing
thou art my fort, mee to defend,
my God, my King
to thee I owe and thy free grace
that free I rest in fearless place. 90

Deus repulisti nos.
Psalm 60.

Thy anger erst in field
　　our scatt'red squadrons brake:
ô god bee reconcil'd,
　　our leading now retake.
5　this land at thee did quake,
　　　it chink't and gaping lay:
　O sound her ruptures make,
　　　hir quaking bring to stay.

Worse happes no hart could think,
10　　then did thy wrath ensue:
dull horror was our drinck,
　　we drincking giddy grew.
　but now an ensigne new
　　　re-chearing all dismaies
15　to guide thy fearers view
　　　thy truth our Chiefe, doth raise.

Then sett thy loved free,
　　preserve mee when I pray:
hark, hark, soe shall it be
20　　god from his howse doth say.
　then make a mery stay:
　　　and share we Sichems fields:
　the land in percells lay,
　　　that Sucoths valey yelds.

25　Mine Gilead lo by this,
　　Manasse lo mine own:
my soldier Ephraim is,
　　my law by Juda shown.

Psalm 60. *Lacking in I. Variant in B.*
Incipit: Deus repulisti B, K, I, θ, N, C, H, E; *om. Q*
1–3 *written in A as a correction on a slip of paper pasted onto f. 48ᵛ (Davies originally began to repeat Ps. 57 through line 2)*　　4 retake] betake N　　5 did] doth G　　6 and] as N, C, σ, G, M　　lay] clay N, C, σ, G, M　　9 happes] happ C　　22 Sichems] Sichem θ, C, M　　23 land] landes K　　25 Gilead] Gillead E; Gilliad H, Q; Giliad C　　26 Manasse] Manasseth J; Manasses D, E　　27 Ephraim] Ephraem G; Ephram σ　　28 Juda] A, E, C, G, M; Judah K, χ

my washpott Moab grown
  my shoe at Edom flong!   30
Philistia overthrown
  sing now thy triumph song.

But whom shall I attend,
  till I these conquests make?
on whose conduct depend   35
  till Edoms fortes I take?
  ô thine to whom we spake,
    but spake before in vayn:
  thine god that didst forsake
    our troupes for warr to trayn.   40

Against distressing foes
  lett us thy succour finde:
who trust in man repose,
  doe trust repose in winde.
In god lett hand and mind   45
    their force and vallor show
  hee, hee, in abject kind
    shall lay our haters low.

Exaudi Deus.
Psalm 61.

To thee I cry,
  my cryeng heare.
to thee my praying voice doth fly:
  lord lend my voice a listning eare.
  from country banished,   5
  all comfort vanished,
to thee I runn when stormes are nigh.

---

31 Philistia] Phelistia *H, Q*   39 didst] do'st *G*   41 distressing] dispersing *C*
43 man] mans *E*   44 winde] vaine *θ* (th'wind *written in a different hand and ink in the margin of D*) 45 hand] hart *C, M* 47 hee, hee] for he *J*

Psalm 61. *Lacking in I. B has verse numbers 1–6 by lines 1, 5, 8, 15, 22, 25; 7, 8 by original 29, 36.*
Incipit: om. Q
4 lend] send *θ* listning] lifteinge *H, Q*

Up to thy hill
　　　lord make me clyme;
which els to scale exceeds my skill:
　　　for in my most distressed tyme
　　　　　thy eye attended me,
　　　　　thy hand defended me,
against my foe my fortresse still.

Then where a tent
　　　for thee is made,
to harbor still is my entent:
　　　and to thy wings protecting shade
　　　　　my self I carry will,
　　　　　and there I tarry will,
safe from all shott against me bent.

What first I crave
　　　first graunting me,
that I the roiall rule may have
　　　of such as feare and honor thee:
　　　　　let yeares as manifold,
　　　　　as can be any told,
thy king, O god, keepe from the grave.

Before thy face
　　　graunt ever hee
maie sitt, and lett thy truth and grace
　　　his endles gard appointed bee.

10
15
20
25
30

9 make] let *G*　　　12 thy] Thine *E*　　eye] hand *G*　　　13 hand] power *G*
15 Then] There *G, M*　　　20 I] to *M*　　will] still *M*　　　21 safe] free *M*
22 What] W *written over erased gold* T *in A*; That *F, J*　　　23 graunting] graunt to *G, M*
29–35 *B notes*: This last staffe before the Correction (by the Author as I guess and under his own hand) stood thus in two staves.

　　　　　　　　7.　　　　*He ever shall*
　　　　　　　　　　　　　Sitt in Gods sight
　　　　　　　　　　While by set [?] turn of heavnly ball
　　　　　　　　Age unto age shall yeild his right
　　　　　　　　　　With favour gracing him
　　　　　　　　　　With truth embracing him
　　　　　　　Support him so he never fall
　　　　　　　　　8　　　*Then throned high*
　　　　　　　　　　　Who now sit low
　　　　　　　　With prayse I will Thee magnify
　　　　　　　And dayly pay the vowes I ow.
but expungd because as I think the last staff beginning at the 8th Verse was shorter than the rest.

then singing pleasantly,
praising uncesantly,
I dayly vowes will pay to thee.   35

Nonne Deo.
Psalm 62.

Yet shall my soule in silence still
    on god, my help, attentive stay:
yet he my fort, my health, my hill,
    remove I may not, move I may.
How long then shall your fruitlesse will   5
    an enimy soe farr from fall
with weake endevor strive to kill,
    you rotten hedg, you broken wall?

Forsooth that hee no more may rise
    advaunced eft to throne and crown: 10
to headlong him their thoughtes devise,
    and past reliefe to tread him down.
Their love is only love of lies:
    their wordes, and deedes, dissenting soe,
when from their lippes most blessing flyes,   15
    then deepest curse in hart doth grow.

Yet shall my soule in silence still
    on god my hope attentive stay:
yet hee my fort, my health, my hill,
    remove? O no: not move I may.   20
My god doth me with glory fill,
    not only shield me safe from harme:
to shunn distresse, to conquer ill
    to him I clime, in him I arme.

Psalm 62. *Lacking in I. Variant in B.*
Incipit: Tamen ad Deum *K, θ, N, H, E; om. Q*
3 health] help *F*   4 move] mone *K, N, C*; moane *θ*   6 fall] *altered in A*; thrall *D*
8 you...you] your...your *O, N, C, σ, G, M*   9 no] *om. O*   12 tread] pulle *D*
15 blessing] blessinges *E*   19 fort] hope *M*   health] help *F*

25 O then on god our certaine stay,
         all people in all times rely:
    your hartes before him naked lay,
         to Adams sonnes is vain to fly
    Soe vain, soe false, soe fraile are they,
30   ev'n he that seemeth most of might
    with Lightnesse self if him you waigh,
         then Lightnesse self will waigh more light.

    In fraud, and force noe trust repose:
         such idle hopes from thoughtes expell
35 and take good heed, when riches growes
         let not your hart on riches dwell.
    All powre is gods, his own word showes,
         once said by him twice heard by me:
    yet from thee lord all mercy flowes,
40   and each manns work is paid by thee.

                    Deus Deus meus.
                    Psalm 63.

    O god, the god where all my forces ly,
         how doe I hunt for thee with erly haste!
    how is for thee my spirit thirsty dry!
         how gaspes my flesh for thy refreshing taste!
5   wittnesse this waterlesse this weary waste:
              whence, ô that I againe transfer'd might be,
              thy glorious might in sacred place to see.

    Then on thy praise would I my lipps employ,
         with whose kind mercies nothing may contend;
10 No, not this life it self, whose care and joy
         in prayeng voice, and lifted hands should end.
         this to my soule should such a banquet send,

---

28 is vain to] s *in darker ink, possibly over erasure in* A; tis vaine to D, C, G, M; 'tis vaine N; in
vayne <to>\you/ E   34 thoughtes] thought<s> K; thought χ   36 hart] hearts
M   38 heard] hard O, K   39 yet] yᵗ E   thee] *second* e *added in* A; *the* C, G, M
Psalm 63. *Lacking in* I. *Variant in* B.
Incipit: Deus Deus K; *om.* Q
2 for] to D   erly] ly *written over erasure of* nest *in* A   4 flesh] soule D   5 waste]
place σ   6 transfer'd] transferd againe M   10 care] *written over erasure of* race *in*
A; race F

that sweetly fedd my mouth should sing thy name
    in gladdest notes contented mirth could frame.

And lo, ev'n heer I mind thee in my bedd,   15
    and interupt my sleepes with nightly thought,
how thou hast bene the target of my hedd,
    how thy wings shadow hath my safty wrought.
    and though my body from thy view be brought;
        yet fixt on thee my loving soule remaines,   20
        whose right right hand from falling me retaines.

But such as seeke my life to ruinate,
    them shall the earth in deepest gulph receave.
first murdring blade shall end their living date,
    and then their flesh to teeth of foxes leave,   25
    as for the king, the king shall then conceave
        high joy in god, and all that god adore,
        when lying mouthes, shall, stopped, ly no more.

Exaudi Deus.
Psalm 64.

With gracious hearing entertain
    this voice the agent of my woe:
and let my life, ô god, remain
    safe in thy guard from feared foe.
    hide me where none may know,   5
        that hatefull plotts contrive;
    and right to overthrow
        with tumult wrongly strive.

For tongues they beare, not tongues, but swordes,
    so piercing sharp they have them ground: 10
and words deliver, shaftes, not words,
    with bitter dint soe deepe they wound.

15 ev'n heer] even heare *H, Q*; ev'n now *C*; even now *G*   16 sleepes] sleepe *G, M*
19 thy] thie [ie *indistinct*] *H*; the *E*   22 such as] those that *M*   seeke] s *erased after*
final e *in A*; seekes *F*   23 deepest] *altered in A in darker ink*   27 in] to *G*

Psalm 64. *Lacking in I. Variant in B.*
Incipit: om. Q
3 god] Lord *N*   8 tumult] tumultes *G, M*   9 beare] have *M*   11 deliver]
delivered [*final* d *partly stricken*] *H*;   deliverde *Q, E*

        whose shott against the sound
          and harmlesse they direct:
15   in safe and fearelesse ground
          embusht with out suspect.

     Nay obstinate to ill they are,
        and meeting, all their talk apply
who can most closely couch his snare,
20   and who say they shall us discry?
        no guile so low doth ly,
          nor in so hidden part,
        but these will sound and try,
          even out of deepest hart.

25   But thou ô god from sodain bow
        death striking them a shaft shalt send:
and their own tongues to their own wo
        shall all their wounding sharpnes bend.
        thus wounded shall they end,
30   thus ending shall they make
        each mortall eye attend,
          each eie attending quake.

     Not one I say but shall behold
        this worke of God which he agayn
35   shall as he can in wordes unfold,
        if yet his feare he entertain.
        in who doth tymelesse raign
          the just shall joy and hope:
        the hartes uprightly playn
40   shall have their vaunting scope.

---

16 suspect] respect *Q*   18 meeting, all∧] ~∧ ~: *M*   19 closely] safely *M*
20 us] wee *N*   21 low] loe *Q*; soone *E*   22 nor] Not *N*   23 these] those
C, M   24 hart] parte *θ*   26 ∧death striking them∧] ∧death=strikeinge them∧ *K*,
C; (death strikeinge them) *σ, M*; (death-striking them) *G*   34 this] the *altered to* this *A*
36 if yet] yet if *F*   37 who] which *N*

Te decet hymnus.
Psalm 65.

Sion it is where thou art praised,
    Sion, ô god, where vowes they pay thee:
there all mens praiers to thee raised
    retorne possest of what they pray thee.
there thou my sinns prevailing to my shame   5
dost turne to smoake of sacrificing flame.

O he of blisse is not deceaved,
    whom chosen thou unto thee takest:
and whom into thy court receaved
    thou of thy checkrole number makest.   10
the dainty Viands of thy sacred store
shall feede hym so, he shall not hunger more.

From thence it is thy threatning thunder,
    lest we by wrong should be disgraced,
doth strike our foes with feare and wonder: 15
    ô thou on whom their hopes are placed,
whom either earth doe stedfastly sustayn,
or cradle rockes of restlesse wavy playn.

Thy vertue staies the mighty mountaynes,
    girded with pow'r, with strength abounding: 20
the roaring damm of watry fountaines
    thy beck doth make surcease hir sounding
When stormy uproares tosse the peoples brayn
that civill sea to calme thou bringst agayn.

Where earth doth end with endles ending,   25
    all such as dwell, thy signes affright them:
and in thie praise their voices spending
    both howses of the sonn delight them;

Psalm 65. *Lacking in I. B has verse numbers 1–12 by lines 1, 3, 5, 7, 13, 19, 22, 25, 31, 37, 41, 43.*
Incipit: om. Q
1 *not indented in A*   4 retorne] retornd *E*   5 sinns] sin *B, K,* χ   6 dost]
did'st θ   12 hym] them *F, D*   14 lest] *A, K, N*; least *F,* χ   17 whom]
Who θ   doe] doth *J, B, K,* χ   21 damm] Dame *B,* θ, *N, H, Q*; Damme *[with
tilde] K, C, G, M*   23–4 The raging *Sea,* to calme thou bringst againe | And
tumults which disturb the peoples braine *G, M*   24 that] The *B,* θ, *N, C,* σ   civill]
evill *J*   25 Where] When σ   28 sonn] sunne *J, K,* χ

both whence he comes, when early he awakes,
30   and where he goes, when ev'ning rest he takes.

Thy eie from heav'n this land beholdeth,
     such fruitfull dewes down on it rayning,
that storehowse-like hir lap enfoldeth,
     assured hope of plowmans gayning.
35   thy flowing streames hir drought doth temper so,
that buried seed through yelding grave doth grow.

Drunck is each ridg of thy cupp drincking;
     each clodd relenteth at thy dressing:
thy cloud-born waters inly sincking
40   faire spring sproutes foorth blest with thy blessing.
the fertile yeare is with thy bounty crown'd:
and where thou go'st, thy goings fatt the ground.

Plenty bedewes the desert places:
     a hedg of mirth the hills encloseth:
45   the fieldes with flockes have hid their faces:
     a robe of corn the valleies clotheth.
Desertes, and hills, and feilds, and valleys all,
rejoyce, showt, sing, and on thy name doe call.

Jubilate Deo.
Psalm 66.

All lands, the lymms of earthy round,
     with triumph tunes gods honor sound:·
          sing of his name the praisefull glory,
          and glorious make his praises story.
5   tell god: ô god, what frightfull wonder
               thy workes doe wittnes, whose great might,

29 both] This *K*, χ   30 and] that *K*, χ   31 Thy] Thie *[Greek* e *resembles* s] *H;*
This *E*   32 rayning] raigning *F, C, E, M*   35 doth] do *B, K,* θ, *N, C*
40 spring] springs *M*   sproutes] sproute *O*   41 fertile] frutefull *D*   46 clotheth]
closeth χ

Psalm 66. *Lacking in I. B has verse numbers 1–8 by lines 1, 5, 9, 13, 17, 21, 25, 29; 15–19 by*
49, 53, 55, 57, 61.
Incipit: Jubelate Deo *H, E;* om. *Q*
1 lymms] limbs *B*   earthy] earthly *Q, E, M*   3 praisefull] peacefull *B*

thy enimies so bringeth under,
    though frown in hart, they fawn in sight!

All earth and ev'ry land therefore
sing to this god, this god adore!   10
    all earth I say, and all earth dwellers,
    be of his worth the singing tellers.
O come, behold, ô note beholding,
    what dreadfull wonders from him flow:
more height, more weight, more force enfolding,   15
    then Adams earthy brood can show.

The Sea up-dried by his hand,
became a field of dusty sand:
    through Jordans streames we dry-shod waded,
    the joy whereof not yet is faded.   20
his thron of strength unmoved standeth:
    his eie on ev'ry coast is cast:
the rebell who against him bandeth,
    of Ruins cup shall quickly tast.

You folk his flock, come then, employ   25
in lawding him your songes of joy
    on god, our god, your voices spending,
    still praying, praising, never ending.
for he our life hath us re-given,
    nor would he let our goings slide: 30
though for our triall neerly driven,
    yea silver like in furnace try'de.

For god thou did'st our feete innett,
and pinching sadles, on us sett
    Nay (which is worse to be abidden),   35
    ev'n on our heads a man hath ridden.

---

8 though] They *N*   11 earth dwellers] earths dwellers *O*   16 earthy] earthly *K*,
O, N, C, σ, G   18 became] Becomes *N*   20 not yet is faded] is not yet faded *C*; is
not yet vaded *G, M*; not yeet is vaded *σ*   25 ∧his flock, come] (his flock) O *M*; ∧there-
fore, O *G*   26 your] *written in darker ink over erasure of* with *in A*   28 praying,
praising] praising, praying *F*   30 nor would he] *B* notes: *And would not* but
expunged: goings] goeing *E*   34 sadles] sadle *K*   36 *five slightly different versions are found in* χ: even our headds a man hath ridden *σ*; Even over our heades men have
ridden *N*; ev'n over our heades men hath ridden *C*; Over our heades ev'n man hath ridden
G; Over our heades, even men hath ridden *M*

hee road us through where fiers flashed;
    where swelling streames did rudely roare:
yet scorched thus, yet we thus washed,
40   were sett by thee, on plenties shoare.

I therefore to thy house will go,
to pay and offer what I owe:
    to pay my vowes, my lippes then vowed,
    when under grief my body bowed.
45 to offer whole burnt sacrifices,
    the fatt of Ramms with sweete perfume:
Nay goates, nay bulls, of greater sises,
    and greater prices to consume.

O come, all yee that god doe feare,
50 ô come, and lend attentive eare;
    while by my tongue shalbe expressed,
    how blessed he my soule hath blessed.
I cri'd to him, my cry procured
    my free dischardge from all my bandes:
55 his eare had not my voice endured,
    but that my hart unstained standes.

Now as my hart was inocent,
god heard the harty sighes I spent:
    what I to praiers recommended:
60   was gratiously by him attended.
praise, praise him then, for what is left me,
    but praise to him: who what I praid,
rejected not, nor hath bereft me
    my hopefull helpe his mercies aid.

---

37 hee] They *N, C, G, M*   39 scorched] *B notes: scalded* expunged: 40 were]
weare *F, H*   44 bowed] growed *K*   45 sacrifices] Sacrifizes *C, G, M*   46 Ramms]
lambes *θ*   47 nay bulls] and *Bulls M*   sises] sizes *F, J, B, H, E, N, C, G, M*
48 prices] prises *D, Q, E*; prizes *F, B, H, G, M*   49 come] then *M*   51 my]
added above caret in different ink in A; om. F   52 ∧blessed∧ he∧] ∧~∧ ~, *C, G*; ∧~, ~∧
E; ∧~∧ ~; *Q*; (~) ~∧ *M*   53 cri'd] e *erased after* i *in A*   54 from] *B, K, χ; in A*
58 spent] sent *G*   61 praise, praise] O praise *G, M*   63 hath] has *B*   64 my
hopefull] Of my true *G, M*

Deus misereatur.
Psalm 67.

God on us thy mercy show,
make on us thy blessings flow:
    thy faces beames
from heav'n uppon us show'r
    in shining streames: 5
    that all may see
    the way of thee,
and know thy saving pow'r.

God, the nations praise thee shall,
thee, shall praise the nations all: 10
    to mirth and joy
all such as earth possesse
    shall them employ:
    for thou their guide
    go'st never wide   15
from truth and righteousnes.

God the nations praise thee shall,
thee shall praise the nations all:
    then ev'ry field,
as farr as earth hath end,   20
    rich fruites shall yeld:
    and god our god
    with blisse shall load
who of his blisse depend.

God, I say with plenteous blisse   25
to enrich us shall not misse:
    and from the place
the father of the yeere
    begins his race,
    to Zephyrs nest,   30
    his races rest,
all lands his force shall feare.

Psalm 67. *Lacking in I. B has verse numbers 1–7 by lines 1, 4, 9, 12, 17, 19, 25.*
Incipit: Deus miseriatur *G, M; om. Q*
2 blessings] blessing *N*   3 thy] The *G*   4–5 *transposed in F*   5 in] Thy *N*
7 of] to *E*   20 hath] doth *θ*   24 of] on *G*   25 I say] it is *F*   30 nest] west *D*

Exurgat Deus.
Psalm 68.

Lett god but rise, his very face shall cast
    on all his haters flight and disarray:
as smoke in wind, as wax at fire doth wast,
    at gods aspect th'unjust shall flitt away.
5   the just meane while shall in Jehovahs presence
play, sing, and daunce. Then unto him, I say,
    unto our god, nam'd of eternall essence,
present your selves with song, and daunce, and play.

Prepare his path, who throned on delightes,
10   doth sitt a father to the Orphan sonn:
and in hir cause the wronged widow rights,
    God in his holy house late here begun.
    with families he empty howses filleth,
    the prisoners chaines are by his hands undone:
15   but barain sand their fruitlesse labour tilleth,
who crossing him rebelliously doe runn.

O god when thou in desert did'st appeare,
    what time thy folk that uncouth jorney tooke:
heav'n at the sight did sweat with melting feare,
20   earth bow'd hir trembling knee, mount Sinay shook.
    the land bedew'd; all wants by thee restored,
    that well thy people might the contry brook,
    as to a fold with sheep in plenty stored,
so to their state thy shepherds care did look.

25   Ther taught by thee in this tryumphant song
    a virgin army did their voices try:

Psalm 68. *Variant in B, I. K notes in right margin in a different hand:* This is otherwise translated
Incipit: om. Q
4 flitt] fleete *C*   5 Jehovahs] Jehovas *F, O*; Jehova's *K, N, C, G, M*; Jehovaes σ
7 our] your *J*   9 path] pathes θ   delightes] delight *O, C, G, M*   11 cause]
case *E*   widow] widowes *H*   14 hands] hand *K*, χ   15 sand] sandes *F*
16 doe] doth *F*   18 that] the *Q*   19 sweat with melting] melt with sweating *E*
20 hir] his *J*   Sinay] Sinai *N*; Syna σ; Sina *G*   21 wants] want σ, *G, M*
25 Ther] y *altered to* r *in darker ink in A*; There *K*, χ; They *F, J*   taught] brought *M*

fledd are these kings, fled are these armyes strong:
we share the spoiles that weake in howse did ly.
though late the Chymney made your beauties loathed,
now shine you shall, and shine more gracefully,   30
then lovely dove in cleare gold-silver cloathed,
that glides with feathered Oare through wavy sky.

For when god had (that this may not seeme strang)
expeld the kings with utter overthrow:
the very ground hir mourning Cloudes did change   35
to weather cleare, as cleare as Salmon snow.
Basan, huge Basan, that soe proudly standest,
scorning the highest hills as basely low,
and with thy top soe many topps commandest,
both thou, and they, what makes yee brave it so?   40

This Mountainett, not you, doth god desire:
here he entends his lodgings plott to lay:
hither Jehovah will him self retyre
to endlesse rest, and unremoved stay.
Heere twise ten thousands, doubled twise hee holdeth,   45
of hooked Charretts, clad in warrs array:
and hence more might more majesty unfoldeth,
then erst he did from Sinay mount display.

Ascended high, immortall God thou art,
and Captyves store thou hast led up with thee   50
whose gathered spoiles to men thou wilt impart:
nay, late thy rebells, now thy tenants bee.
Blest be the lord, by whom our bliss encreaseth
the god of might by whom we safty see:
God, our strong god, who us each way releaseth,   55
and ev'n through gates of death conducts us free.

---

27 these armyes] those armies *N*   29 Chymney] Chymneis *N*   beauties] beauty *σ*,
G, M   32 wavy] wavyd *K, H, Q*; waved *N, C, G, M*   33 may not] should *G*
35 ground] *aire M*   Cloudes] Cl *written over erasure in A*; clods *D*   36 Salmon] Sal-
man *C, G*; *Zalman M*; *Salmons F*   37 standest] standeth *N*   39 commandest]
comaundeth *N*   40 yee] you *M*   42 here] heare *H*   his lodgings] his lodging
D, σ; he lodging *O*   43 Jehovah] Jehova *K, O, σ, N, C, G, M*   45 Heere] Here
K, H, N, G, M; Heare *Q*   thousands] thousand *D*   46 Charretts] charriotts *θ, C, Q,
E, G, M*   warrs] warr *χ*   47 hence] thence *G*   unfoldeth] enfouldeth *O, σ, G, M*
50 Captyves] yves *written in darker ink over erasure of* aines (?) *in A*   up] s *corrected to* p *by
Davies*   52 *singly indented in A*   tenants] servants *K, χ*   54 safty] safely *F*

God of his enimies the head shall wound
        and those proud lookes that stiff in mischief go.
from Basan safe, and from the deepe undround,
60   I brought thee once, and oft I will do so.
                this said by hym, thy foote in bloud was stained,
        thy doggs tongues dide in bloud of slaughtred fo:
        and god, my king, men saw thee entertained
        in sacred house with this tryumphant show.

65 In vantgard marcht who did with voices sing:
        the rereward lowd on instruments did play:
    the battaile maides, and did with Tymbrells ring:
        and all in sweete consort did jointly say:
                praise god, the lord, of Jacob you descended,
70   praise him upon each solemn meeting day:
                Benjamyn, little, but with rule attended,
        Juda's brave lordes, and troupes in faire array.

    Stout Nepthaly with noble Zabulon:
        and sith our might thy bidding word did make,
75 confirme, ô god, what thou in us hast done,
        from out thy house, and that for Salems sake.
                So kings bring guiftes, so in thie check their ending
        these furious, wanton, Bulls, and calves shall take,
                these arrow-armed bands, which us offending,
80   are now soe ready warr to undertake.

    They shall bring silver stooping humbly low,
        Egipts greate peeres with homage shall attend:
    and Æthiop with them shall not forslow
        to god with speed like service to commend.

57 head] heads *D*   58 lookes] *second* o *added (?) in* A; lokes *D*; locks *K*   stiff] still
altered to stiff *in* A; still *E*   59 deepe] deepes σ, *G*, *M*   60 oft] eft *J*, *D* (*long*
s *?*)   do so] so doe *J*   62 tongues] tongue *G*, *M*   dide] died *D*, σ, *N*, *M*; di'de
C; di'd *G*   in] with *D*   65 marcht] martch *O*   66 on] with *G*, *M*   67 and
[*ampersand]*] that *E*   ring] sing *J*   68 in] with *D*   69 Jacob⌄] ~, *N*; ~: *H*
72 Juda's] Juda='s *F*; Judahs [s *altered to* h *(?)] J*; Judas *D*; Judaes σ   73 Nepthaly]
Nephthali *M*   with noble] next noble *K*, χ; next proude θ   74 did] doth *M*
75 what] that *J*   77 bring] bringes *C*, *M*   thie] thee *altered to* thie *in* A; thee *F*
79 these] The *N*   82 Egipts] Ægipts σ, *N*   83 Æthiop] Æthiope *C*, *G*, *M*;
Ethiope *K*, χ

Then kingdoms all to god present your praises,   85
   and on the lord your singing gladnes spend:
     above the heav'n of heav'ns his throne he raises,
     and thence his voice, a voice of strength doth send.

Then of all strength acknowledg god the well,
   with brave magnificence and glory bright   90
shining no less on loved Israell,
   then showing in the cloudes his thundring might.
     thou from the shryne where Jacob thee adoreth,
   all folk, ô god, with terror dost affright:
     he (prais'd be he) with strength his people storeth,   95
his force it is, in which their forces fight.

Salvum me fac.
Psalm 69.

Troublous seas my soule surround:
   save, ô god, my sincking soule,
sincking, where it feeles noe ground,
   in this gulph, this whirling hoale.
     waiting aid, with ernest eying: 5
     calling god with bootlesse crying:
dymm and dry in me are found
ey to see, and throat to sound.

Wrongly sett to worke my woe
   haters have I, more then heares: 10
force in my afflicting foe
   bettring still, in me impaires.
     thus to pay, and leese constrained
     what I never ought or gained,

85 your] *written as a correction over albumen (?) in darker ink in A*   88 strength] strengh
H   89 strength] strenghe *H*   91 loved] lovely *σ, G, M*   93 shryne] throane
σ, G, M   94 dost] doth *F*   95 be he] be thee *N*   strength] strenghe *H*   his]
all *G, M*   96 which] whom *N*   their] his *altered to* their *in A*

Psalm 69. *Variant in B.*
Incipit: Salvum me fac *A, G, M*; Salvum me *B*; Salvum me fac deus quoniam aqua etc: *I*;
Serva me *K, χ; om. Q*
1 my soule] doe mee *I*   2 god] lord *I*   3 feeles] s *added in A*   5 aid] and *N*
8 ey] eies *I*   9 my] mee *I*   10 heares] haires *J, K, χ*   11 force] For *N, C, σ,
G, M*   12 in me] *om. O*   13 leese] loose *I*   14 ought] ow'd *J*   or] nor *M*

15   yet say I: thou god dost know
            how my faultes and follies goe.

            Mighty lord, lett not my case
                blank the rest that hope on thee:
            lett not Jacobs god deface
20   all his frends in blush of me.
                    thyne it is, thyne only quarrell
                    dightes me thus in shames apparrell:
            Note, nor spott, nor least disgrace,
            but for thee, could taint my face.

25   To my kynn a stranger quite,
                quite an alian am I grown:
            in my very bretherens sight
                most uncar'd for, most unknow'n.
                    with thy temples zeale out-eaten,
30   with thy slanders scourges beaten,
            while the shott of piercing spight
            bent at thee, on me doth light.

            If I weepe, and weeping fast,
                if in sackcloth sadd I mourn,
35   in my teeth the first they cast,
                all to Jeast the last they turn.
                    now in streetes with publique prating
                    powring out their inward hating:
            private now at banquetts plac't,
40   singing songs of wyny tast.

            As for me to thee I pray,
                lord, in tyme of grace assign'd:
            gratious god, my kindest stay,
                in my aid be truly kind.
45   keepe me safe from such and myred
                    safe from flowing foes retyred:

---

15 say] said *I*   dost] do *M*   16 goe] grow *I*   18 on] in *θ, σ, G, M*   19 lett not]
nor let *I*   21 thyne only] 'tis thine owne *I*   23 Note] mote *I*   least] lesse *I*;
light *N*   25 kynn] frends *I*   28 uncar'd for] uncared *I*   31 while] whilst *I*
35 the] that *I*   37 in] the *I*   38 out] forth *I*   39 banquetts] banquet *K, χ*
42 of] for *K, I, χ*   43 kindest] kindnes *O*   45 safe] fast *I*   from such and
myred] from such and myred *F*; from su[n]ck & mynd [such *altered to* su[n]ck *with macron*

calme these waves, these waters bay,
leave me not this whirlpooles pray.

In the goodnes of thy grace,
   lord make answere to my mone: 50
ey my ill, and rue my case
   in those mercies told by none.
      lett not by thy absence languish
      thy true server dround in anguish.
Haste, and heare, come, come apace,   55
free my soule from foemens chase.

Unto thee what needes be told
   my reproch, my blott, my blame?
sith both these thou didst behold,
   and canst all my haters name.   60
      whiles afflicted, whiles hart-broken,
      waiting yet some frendshipps token,
some I lookt would me uphold,
lookt: but found all comfort cold.

Comfort? nay, (not seene before)   65
   needing food they sett me gall:
Vineager they fil'd me store,
   when for drinck my thirst did call.
      ô then snare them in their pleasures,
      make them, trapt ev'n in their treasures, 70
gladly sadd, and richly poore,
sightlesse most, yet mightlesse more.

placed over u *and* k *written over* h; & *written over albumen (?) covering illegible letter or word;* n *of* mynd *altered to* re] *A*; from sunk and myred *J*; <from>^un-sunck and mired [un-*added above stricken* from *in different ink*] *K*; unsunck and mired *θ, N, H*; unsunck unmired *I, C, Q, E, G, M*   47 bay] lay *I*   48 me not] not mee *I*   pray] play *I*   49 the] that *I*   54 server] servant *I*   55 Haste] hark *I*   come, come] Lord come *M* 57 needes] neede *C*   58 reproch] rebuke *I*   blame] shame *N, C, σ, G, M* 59 both these] both this *I*; all this *M* didst] doest *E*   61 whiles...whiles] whilst...whilst *I*; whilest . .. whilst *C*; while...whiles *O* 62 waiting] waiteing *altered to* wanteing [*stricken dot over* i *before* t] *in H*; wanting *Q, E* yet] still *I* frendshipps] d *added above* ns *and a caret in A*; freindship *N* 63 still I lookt that some man would *I* 64 lookt] looke *I* found] sawe *Q* 66 food] meate *I* sett] gave *I* 69 pleasures] pleasure *I* 70 treasures] treasure *I* 71 gladly] gladdest *I* and] *ampersand added in gold above a gold caret in A* richly] richest *I*

Downe upon them fury raine
    lighten indignation downe:
75   turne to wast, and desert plaine,
        house, and pallace, field and towne.
            lett not one be left abiding
            where such rancor had residing
whome thou painest, more they paine:
80 hurt by thee, by them is slaine.

Causing sinne on synne to grow,
    add still Cyphers to their summ.
righter lett them never goe,
    never to thy justice come.
85   but from out the booke be crossed,
        where the good men live engrossed:
while my God, me poore and low
high shall mount from need and woe.

Then by me his name with praise,
90   gladsome praise, shall be upborne.
that, shall more Jehova please,
    then the beast with hoofe and horne.
        with what joy, yee godly grived
        shall your harts be then relived?
95 When Jehova takes such waies
bound to loose, and falne to raise.

Laud him then ô heav'nly skies
    Earth with thine, and Seas with yours:
for by him shall Sion rise,
100   he shall build up Juda's towres.

---

73 raine] rayne *J, E*; raigne *D, H, Q*   74 lighten] light thie *I*   78–82 *the right half of these lines is obscured by an inkblot (?) in G; 78–80 are added in the left margin in a different hand and ink*   78 had] hath σ, *G (text and margin)*   81 sinne on] hym on σ synne to] singe to *O*   82 still] such *I*   summ] somm *I*   83 never let them righter goe *I*   85 the] thie *I*   86 where the] wherein *I*   men] doe *K, χ* live] been *I*   87 while] whilst *I*   low] loe *Q*   88 need] care *I*   89 his] thy *K, χ*   90 praise, shall be upborne] praiers shall adorne *I*   91 that, shall] for that *I*   Jehova] Jehovah *F, J, D*   please] wayes *I*   93 yee godly] ye gladlie *C*; how gladly *I*   94 your harts] our hearts σ, *G*; my soule *I*   be then] by them *E* 95 Jehova] Jehovah *D*   98 Earth] E *added in darker ink, not gold, in A*   100 Juda's] Judahs *J*; Judas *O*; Judaes *D, σ; Salems I*

there his servantes, and their races,
shall in fee possesse their places:
there his name who love and prize,
stable stay shall eternize.

Deus in adjutorium.
Psalm 70.

Lord hy thee me to save
lord now to help me hast:
shame lett them surely have
and of confusion tast,
    that hold my soule in chase.   5
    lett them be forced back,
    and no disgraces lack,
    that joy in my disgrace.

Back forced lett them be
and for a faire reward   10
their owne foule ruine see
who laugh and laugh out hard.
    when I most inly mone
    but mirth and joy renew
    in them thy pathes ensue   15
    and love thy help alone.

101 races] race *I*   102 their] the *K*, χ   places] place *I*   103 ∧who love∧ and
prize,] ∧who love∧ and prize∧ *K*, χ; ∧who love, and prize∧ *N*; (who love and prize) *M*;
∧who love∧ and prise∧ *D*; ∧who laud∧ and prize∧ *I*   104 ∧stable stay∧] (~) *G*; (Stable
staid) *M*

Psalm 70. *B notes:* Crost in the MS. *The apparently earlier version in B is shorter by two syllables in the second and third lines of each stanza. B has verse numbers 1–5 by lines 1, 3, 9, 13, 17.
Incipit:* Deus Adjutorium *N, C; om. Q*
1 *Written as a correction over* God to me take heede [take heede *stricken;* hy thee *written over*
to me] *in H*   Lord] God *K*, χ   2 lord now to help me hast] now to help me hast
added later by Davies in darker ink (gilded); Lord to my reskew haste *K*, χ; To help me
haste *B*   3 Shame lett their faces have *K*, χ; Shame let them have *B*; grant that
they shame may have *I*   4 and of] themselves *K*, χ   5 hold] have *K*, χ
6 forced] turned *B*   8 my] thy *G*   9 Back forced] Back-turned *B*   10 a faire]
a fowle *M; om. B*   11 foule ruine] fall *B*   12 and laugh] *om. B; B notes:* (This
Verse lacks a foot.)   13 when I most inly] Ah ha when most I *B*; when I in sorrow
K, χ   15 pathes ensue] trace ensue *B, K*, χ; trace pursue *C, M*   16 *indented
in A*   help] self θ

      Make them with gladdnes sing:
         to god be ever praise.
     and faile not me to bring,
20   my down-cast state to raise.
           thy speedy aid and stay.
            in thee my succour growes:
            from thee my freedom flowes:
          lord, make no long delay.

In te Domine speravi.
Psalm 71.

      Lord on thee my trust is grounded:
      leave me not with shame confounded;
         but in Justice bring me aide.
      lett thine eare to me be bended:
5   lett my life from death defended
         be by thee in safty staid.

      Be my rock, my refuge tower,
      show thy unresisted power,
         working now thy wonted will:
10   thou I say that never fainest
      in thy biddings but remainest
         still my rock, my refuge still.

      O my god, my sole help-giver,
      from this wicked me delyver,
15   from this wrongfull spightfull man:

---

17 with gladdnes] for ever *B*; in gladnes *K*, χ
18–19 *original version in B:*

              To God be Prayse
              And to me bring

22 From Thee my comfort growes *B*; On thee my succour lies *M*   23 flowes] flies *M*
Psalm 71. *Variant in B.*
Incipit: In te Domine *B, K, θ, N, C*; O In te domine *I; om. Q*
4 me be] <be> me be *O*; mee *D*   10 that] who *K*, χ   11 biddings] 'bidings *N*;
bydeinge σ; promise *M*   remainest] remainedst *N*   13 sole] soules *H (final* s *added),*
E   14 this] the *Q*

in thee trusting, on thee standing,
with my childish understanding,
     nay with life my hopes began.

Since imprison'd in my mother
thou me freed'st, whom have I other   20
     held my stay, or made my song?
yea when all me so misdeemed,
I to most a monster seemed,
     yet in thee my hope was strong.

Yet of thee the thankfull story,   25
fild my mouth thy gratious glory,
     was my ditty long the day,
Do not then now age assaileth,
couradge, verdure, vertue faileth,
     do not leave me cast away.   30

They by whom my life is hated,
with my Spies have now debated,
     of their talk and lo the summ:
God say they hath hym forsaken
now pursue, he must be taken,   35
     none will to his rescue come.

O my god bee not absented:
ô my god, now, now, presented
     let in haste thy succours be,
make them full disgraced, shamed,   40
all dissmighted, all diffamed,
     who this ill entend to me.

As for me, resolv'd to tary
in my trust, and not to vary:
     I will heape thy praise with praise   45

---

18 nay with life] \whence/my <with> life [whence *also added in left margin*] *I*   20 freed'st]
feed'st *K, I*   24 in thee my hope] in thee my trust *K, χ*; my trust in thee *E*
25 thee] *om. M*   thankfull] praisefull *K, χ*   28 Do] Doe *K, χ*; No *A*   29 vertue]
vetue *I (correction mark in right margin)*   31 They] Then *I*   by] of *G, M*   life]
Soule K, χ   32 my] their *K, χ*   33 summ] somm *I*   34–6 *last half of
these lines written in darker ink over a smudged erasure in A*   37 O] Then *K, χ*
38 ô] Nay *K, χ*   my] lord *G, M*   39 in] with *K, χ*   succours] succour *N, C, G, M*
40 make] Let *N*   full] fall *K, χ*   shamed] ashamed *N*   41 dissmighted] dismayed
O, N, C, E, G, M; dismay-ed *H, Q*   44 my trust] this hope *K, χ*

still with mouth thy truthes recounting,
still thy aides, though much surmounting
    greatest summ that number laies.

Nay my god by thee secured
50   where will I not march assured?
    (but thy truth) what will I hold?
who by thee from infant Cradle
taught still more, as still more able,
    have till now thy wonders told.

55   Now that age hath me attainted,
ages snow my hed hath painted,
    leave me not my god forlorn.
lett me make thy mights relation,
to this coming generation,
60   to this age as yet unborn.

God thy Justice highest raised,
thy greate workes as highly praised:
    who thy peere ô god, doth raign?
thou into these woes dost drive me:
65   thou againe shalt hence revive me:
    lift me from this deepe againe.

Thou shalt make my greatnes greater,
make my good with comfort better
    thee my lute, my harpe shall ring:
70   thee my god that never slidest
from thy word but constant bidest,
    Jacobs holy heav'nly king.

---

46 thy truthes] and truthes *F*; thy t<h>ruthes *I*; thy right *K*, χ; thy might *D*   47 aides, though much] helpe though both *K*, χ   48 summ] somme *I*; some *Q, E*; somes *G*; sumes *M*   49 my] lord *K*, χ   50 march assured?,] *J, K, N, C, G*; march? assured, *A* 51 in my talke who just but thou *K*, χ   54 have thy wonders spred till now *K*, χ 59 this] the *K*, χ   60 this] the *K*, χ   61 highest] high is *K*, χ   62 workes] Acts *K*, χ   64 into these woes] to deadly depth *K*, χ   65 againe shalt hence] wilt thence againe *K*, χ   66 this deepe] those gulfes *K*, χ; theise gulfes *C, G, M*   67 shalt] wilt *K*, χ   my greatnes] thy greatnes *O*; mee [x *in right margin*] *I*   69 my lute, my harpe] my harp, my lute *I*   ring] singe *K*, χ   70 that] who *G, M*   slidest] fainest *K*, χ   71 *rephrased in K*, χ: in thy biddings [*N*, σ: bidings] but remainest

Soe my lipps all Joy declaring,
soe my soule no honor sparing,
     shall thee sing by thee secure.   75
soe my tongue all tymes all places,
tell thy wreakes and their disgraces,
     who this ill to me procure.

Deus Judicium.
Psalm 72.

Teach the kings sonne, who king hym self shalbe,
    thy judgmentes lord, thy justice make hym learn:
to rule thy Realme as justice shall decree,
    and poore mens right in judgment to discern.
        then fearelesse peace   5
        with rich encrease
            the mountaynes proud shall fill:
        and justice shall
        make plenty fall
            on ev'ry humble hill.   10

Make him the weake support, th'opprest relyve,
    supply the poore, the quarrell-pickers quaile:
soe agelesse ages shall thee reverence give,
    till eies of heav'n, the sunn and moone, shall faile.
        and thou againe   15
        shalt blessings rayne,
            which down shall mildly flow,

---

73 all Joy declaring] noe honor sparing *K*, χ   74 no honor sparing] all joye declaring
K, χ; all joyes declaring *M*   77 thy] thy *altered to* theyr *H*; their *E*   wreakes] wr\e/
akes *H*; wracks *E*; wonks *I*; workes *N*   78 this ill to me] to me this ill *F*

Psalm 72. *Lacking in I. B has verse numbers 1–19 by lines 1, 3, 5, 11, 13, 15, 21, 23, 31, 34, 37,*
41, 43, 46, 51, 61, 71, 81, 83.
Incipit: Deus Juditium *E; om. Q*
2 judgmentes] judgement θ, *N, C, E*; justice *K, G, M*   justice] judgment *K, G, M*
make hym] may he *B*   4 judgment] justice *B*   9 fall] all *J*   11 Make
him] Hee shall *K*, χ   support] suborte *Q*   relyve] relieve *J, B, K*, χ   13 ages
shall thee] age<s> shall thee \due/ *K*   15 thou] then *D*   16 shalt blessings]
shall blessings *D*; Shalt blessing *N*   rayne] raigne σ

as showres thrown
on meades new mown
20   wherby they freshly grow.

During his rule the just shall ay be greene,
        and peacefull plenty joine with plenteous peace:
while of sad night the many-formed queene
        decreas'd shall grow, and grown again decrease.
25   from sea to sea
                he shall survey
                    all kingdoms as his own:
                and from the trace
                of Physons race,
30   as farr as land is known.

The desert-dwellers at his beck shall bend:
        his foes them suppliant at his feete shall fling:
the kinges of Tharsis homage guifts shall send;
        so Seba, Saba, ev'ry Iland king.
35   nay all ev'n all
                shall prostrate fall,
                    that crownes and Scepters weare:
                and all that stand
                at their command,
40   that crownes and Scepters beare.

For he shall here the poore when they complaine;
        and lend them help, who helplesse are opprest:
his mercy shall the needy sort sustaine;
        his force shall free their lyves that lyve distrest.
45   from hidden sleight
                from open might
                    hee shall their soules redeeme:

---

18 as showres] As showërs *B*; as showers *F, K, C, H, G, M*; His showers *N*; As shewers *θ*
19 on] o *written over erasure of* i *in A*   mown] sown *B*   22 joine] joine *altered to* Rome
[?] *K*; rome *D*; come *N, C, σ, G, M*   plenteous] plessant *σ*   23 while of sad] All
while of *K, χ*   night] might *D*   29 Physons] Perahs *K, D, M*; Perah's *G*; Perha's
C; Perhas *O, H, Q*; Perhaes *E*; Pyrrha's *N*   31–40 *om. K, χ*   41 here] heare *H*
43 the] thee *N*

           his tender eyes
         shall highly prise,
           and deare their bloud esteeme.   50

So shall he long, soe shall hee happy live;
    health shall abound, and wealth shall never want:
they gold to hym, Arabia gold, shall give,
    which scantnes dere, and derenes maketh scant.
           they still shall pray   55
         that still he may
           so live, and flourish so:
         with out his praise
         no nights, no daies,
           shall pasport have to go.   60

Looke how the woods, where enterlaced trees
    spread frendly armes each other to embrace,
joyne at the head, though distant at the knees,
    waving with wind, and lording on the place:
           so woods of corne   65
         by mountaynes borne
           shall on their showlders wave:
         and men shall passe
         the numbrous grasse,
           such store each town shall have.   70

Looke how the Sunne, soe shall his name remayne;
    as that in light, so this in glory one:
all glories that, at this all lights shall stayne:
    nor that shall faile, nor this be overthrowne.
           the dwellers all   75
         of earthly ball
           in hym shall hold them blest:

---

48 *a mistaken* shall *(anticipating 49) has been covered with albumen (?) at the end of the line
in A*   49 highly] dearly σ   prise] *A, D*; prize *B, K, χ*; price *J*   50 deare]
highe σ   53 Arabia] Arabian *K*   59 nights] night *B*   no] nor *Q*   61 where]
with θ, *E*   62 frendly] *A, B (text)*; out their *K, χ; B notes: out their*, but expunged:
embrace] ymprace *H*   63 head] heads *B, N, C, G, M*   64 on] in *altered to* on
in *H*; in *N, E*   67 *not fully indented in A*   72 in glory] in *added above caret in
different ink in A*; glorie *F*   73 at] as *K, D, σ, C, M*   76 of] on θ   earthly] earthie
F, J, B, K, D, C, σ, M

as one that is
of perfect blisse
80   a patterne to the rest.

O god who art, from whom all beeings be;
        eternall lord, whom Jacobs stock adore,
all wondrous works are done by only thee,
        blessed be thou, most blessed evermore.
85   and lett thy name,
                thy glorious fame,
                        no end of blessing know:
                lett all this Round
                thy honor sound,
90   so lord, ô be it so.

Quam bonus Israel.
Psalm 73.

It is most true that god to Israell,
        I meane to men of undefiled hartes,
        is only good, and nought but good impartes.
Most true, I see, albe, allmost I fell
5   from right conceit into a crooked mynd;
        and from this truth with straying stepps declin'd
for loe my boiling brest did chafe and swell
        when first I saw the wicked proudly stand,
        prevailing still in all they tooke in hand.
10   and sure no sicknes dwelleth where they dwell:
        nay so they guarded are with health and might,
        it seemes of them death dares not claime his right.

80 to] for *O*   81 bee;] ~: *C*; ~ₐ *F, K, χ*   82 lord] god *D*   83 all] *B, K, χ*;
and *A*   87 blessing] blessings *B, χ*

Psalm 73. *B has verse numbers 1–28 by lines 1, 4, 7, 10, 13, 16, 19, 22, 25, 28, 31, 34, 37, 40,
43, 46, 49, 52, 55, 58, 61, 64, 67, 70, 73, 76, 79, 82.*
Incipit: Quam bonus *B, I, K, θ, H, E*; Quam bonus Deus *N, C*; *om. Q*
4 albe] albeet *K, H*; allbe 't *I*; albe't *C*; Albeit *M*   allmost I fell] I almost fell *F, G*
8 stand] *over erasure in A*   12 dares] dare *B*

They seeme as priviledg'd from others paine:
    the scourging plagues, which on their neighbours fall,
    torment not them, nay touch them not at all.   15
therefore with pride, as with a gorgious chaine,
    their swelling necks encompassed they beare:
    all cloth'd in wrong, as if a Robe it were:
so fatt become, that fattnes doth constraine
    their eies to swell: and if they thinck on ought,   20
    their thought they have, yea have beyond their thought.
they wanton grow, and in malicious vaine
    talking of wrong, pronounce as from the skies!
    soe high a pitch their proud presumption flyes.

Nay heav'n it self, high heav'n, escapes not free   25
    from their base mouthes; and in their common talk
    their tongus noe less then all the earth do walk.
wherefore ev'n godly men, when so they see
    their horne of plenty freshly flowing still,
    leaning to them, bend from their better will: 30
And thus, they reasons frame: how can it bee
    that god doth understand? that he doth know,
    who sitts in heav'n, how earthly matters goe?
see here the godlesse Crue, while godly wee
    unhappy pine, all happines possesse: 35
    their riches more our wealth still growing lesse.

Nay ev'n within my self, my self did say:
    In vain my hart I purge, my hands in vain
    in cleanes washt I keepe from filthy stayn,
since thus afflictions scurge me ev'ry day: 40
    since never a day from early East is sent,
    but brings my payne, my check, my chastisment.

---

13 from] by *I*   14 plagues] plauges *O*, σ   15 them not] not them *I, K*, θ, *N*, σ
17 necks] neck σ   encompassed] encompasseing θ   18 if] in *I*   were] weare *H, Q*
20 and] as *Q*   ought] aught *B*   21 thought] thoughtes *G*   yea] yee *I*; yet *N*
beyond their] beyond y^r: *N*   22 vaine] veine *B*   23 wrong] wrongs *N, C*
pronounce] they speake *B, I, K*, χ; they spake *Q*   27 do] *A, K, Q*; doth *I*, χ
28 so] as *M*   31 reasons] reason *M*   33 earthly] earthy *D*   34 here] heare
H, Q   39 cleanes] cleames *I*; clearnes *N*   keepe] kept *E*   40 afflictions] affliction *H, Q, G*

and shall I then these thoughtes in wordes bewray?
  ô lett me lord give never such offence
45   to children thine that rest in thy defence.
so then I turn'd my thoughtes another way:
  sounding, if I, this secrets depth might find;
  but combrous cloudes my inward sight did blynd.

Untill at length nigh weary of the chase,
50   unto thy house I did my stepps direct:
  there loe, I learn'd what end did these expect,
and what? but that in high, but slippery place,
  thou didst them sett: whence, when they least of all
  to fall did feare, they fell with headlong fall.
55 for how are they in lesse then momments space
  with ruine overthrowne? with frightfull feare
  consum'd soe cleane, as if they never weare?
right as a dreame, which waking doth deface:
  so, lord, most vaine thou dost their fancies make,
60   when thou dost them from carelesse sleepe awake.

Then for what purpose was it? to what end?
  for me to fume with malecontented hart,
  tormenting so in me each inward part?
I was a foole (I can it not defend)
65   so quite depriv'd of understanding might,
  that as a beast I bare me in thy sight.
but as I was yet did I still attend,
  still follow thee, by whose upholding-hand,
  when most I slide, yet still upright I stand.
70 then guide me still, then still upon me spend
  the treasures of thy sure advise, untill
  thou take me hence into thy glories hill.

---

47 secrets] secret *K, C, E, M* 48 did] *om. I* 49 length] lenght *I*; lengh *H*
50 thy] my *N* 51 these] those *B* 52 but slippery] and slipprie *G*; and slipperie
E, M 53 least] left *B, N, C*; lift *O* 57 soe] of *I* weare] *A, Q*; were *B, J, I, K, χ*
58 as] like *M*; as as *E* 61 for] t *altered to* f, *rounded* r *written above* o *in A*; to *F, θ*
63 so] sore *K* 65 understanding] understandings *C, G, M* 66 bare] beare *I, Q*
67 did I still] still I did *χ* 68 follow] follow'd *θ* 69 yet still upright I] yet still
I upright *B*; yet most upright I *I*; I still upright yet *D* 71 advise] advice *C, G, M*
72 glories] glorious *C, E, G*

O what is he will teach me clyme the skyes?
    with thee, thee good, thee goodnes to remaine?
    no good on earth doth my desires detaine.   75
often my mind, and oft my body tries
    their weake defectes: but thou, my god, thou art,
    my endlesse lott, and fortresse of my hart.
the faithlesse fugitives who thee despise,
    shall perrish all, they all shalbe undone,   80
    who leaving thee to whoorish Idolls runn.
but as for me, nought better in my eyes
    then cleave to god, my hopes in hym to place,
    to sing his workes while breath shall give me space.

Ut quid Deus.
Psalm 74.

O god, why hast thou thus
    repulst, and scattred us?
shall now thy wrath no lymmitts hold?
    but ever smoke and burne?
    Till it to Asshes turne   5
the chosen flock of thy deare fold?

Ah! think with milder thought
    on them, whom thou hast bought,
and purchased from endlesse daies:
    thinck of thy birthright lott.   10
    of Sion, on whose plott,
thy sacred house supported staies.

Come lord, ô come with speed,
    this sacrilegious seed
    roote quickly out, and hedlong cast: 15

74 thee good] thee good *[second* o *added]* H; Thee God B, Q, E; (thee God) G; (O God) M;
my God C   thee goodnes] the goodnes G   75 good] god E   77 defectes]
desersts I   but thou] but then B   78 my hart] mine hart I   82 my] mine I
84 shall] doth K

Psalm 74. B *has verse numbers 1–23 by lines 1, 7, 13, 19, 25, 28, 31, 37, 43, 49, 55, 61, 67, 73,
79, 85, 91, 97, 103, 109, 115, 121, 124.*
Incipit: Ut quid θ; *om.* Q
6 folk] flock B, I, K, χ   7 think] thing I   9 daies] *om.* I   10 of] on M
11 of] On M   14 seed] deed E

all that thy holy place
did late adorne and grace,
their hatefull hands have quite defast.

Their beastly trumpetts rore,
20   where heav'nly notes before
in praises of thy might did flow:
within thy temple they
their ensignes eft display,
their ensignes, which their conquest show.

25   As men with axe on arme
to some thick forrest swarme,
to lopp the trees which stately stand:
they to thy temple flock,
and spoiling, cutt and knock
30   the curious workes of carving hand.

Thy most most holy seate
the greedy flames do eate,
and have such ruthlesse ruyns wrought,
that all thy house is raste,
35   so raste, and so defast,
that of that all remayneth nought.

Nay they resolved are,
we all alike shall fare,
all of one cruell Cupp shall taste.
40   for not one house doth stand
of god in all the land,
but they by fire have laide it waste

We see the signes no more,
we wont to see before,
45   nor any now with sp'ryt divine

---

16 that] those *F*   21 praises] praise *θ*   23 eft] oft *B, I, K, χ*   24 which]
with *K*   their conquest] their conquests *I, E*; they conquest *N*   26 to] so *F*
28 thy] the *θ, N, σ*   30 workes] worke *C, M*   31 seate] Place *B*   32 flames]
slaves *I*   33 have] hath *G*   ruthlesse] ruth kess *I*; ruthfull *M*   34 raste] raz't
C; rac't *J*; rac'd *N*   35 raste] raz't *C*; rac'd *N*   so defast] quite defas't *G, M*
40 doth] shall *σ*   41 god] gods *χ*; God's *C, M*   45 now] more *D*   sp'ryt]
Spi'rit *B*; sp'rite *K*; sprite *θ, H, Q, G*; spirit *F, I, E, N, C, M*

amongst us more is found,
who can to us expound,
what tearme these dollors shall define.

How long, ô god, how long
wilt thou winck at the wrong
of thy reviling railing foe?
shall he that hates thy name,
and hated paintes with shame,
so do, and doe for ever soe?

Woe us! what is the cause
thy hand his help withdrawes?
that thy right hand farr from us keepes?
ah lett it once arise,
to plague thine enimies,
which now embosom'd idely sleepes.

Thou art my god, I know,
my king, who long ago
did'st undertake the chardg of me:
and in my hard distresse
did'st work me such release,
that all the earth did wondring see.

Thou by thy might didst make
that Seas in sunder brake,
and dreadfull dragons which before
in deepe or swamme or cral'd,
such mortall strokes appal'd,
they floted dead to ev'ry shore.

Thou crusht that monsters head,
whom other monsters dread,
and soe his fishy flesh did'st frame.

50

55

60

65

70

75

46 amongst] amongs *N*; Among *B, I, K, θ, C*   more] now *G*   51 railing] slaundring
G   52 hates] hartes *I*   53 *om. N (space left)*   and] With σ   hated] *B, K, θ*;
hates *[final* d *altered to* s *(?)] I*; hating *C, G, M*; painless σ; hatred *A*   paintes with] points
wth *O*; painte with *C, G, M*; painled *I*; hated σ   59 plague] plauge *Q, E*   thine] theis
F; their *K*   64 my] <thie> my *E*; thy *H, Q*   66 wondring] working *θ*   68 that]
The *E*   71 strokes] stokes *Q*   73 crusht] crush'st *B*   that] the *E*   monsters]
Monsters *written over erasure of* Serpents *in G*; monstrous *N*   75 soe] *added above
caret in A*   his] this *I*; theire *G*

to serve as pleasing foode
to all the ravening brood,
who had the desert for their dame.

Thou wondrously didst cause
80   repealing natures lawes
from thirsty flynt a fountayne flow
and of the rivers cleare,
the sandy bedds appeare,
soe dry thou mad'st theyr chanells grow.

85   The day arraid in light,
the shadow-clothed night,
were made, and are maintain'd by thee
the sunn and sunn-like raise,
the boundes of nightes and daies,
90   thy workmanshipp no lesse they be.

To thee the earth doth owe,
that earth in sea doth grow,
and sea doth earth from drowning spare:
the summers corny crowne,
95   the winters frosty gowne,
nought but thy badge, thy lyvery are.

Thou then still one, the same,
thinck how thy glorious name
these brain-sick mens dispight have borne,
100   how abject enimies
the lord of highest skies,
with cursed taunting tongues have torne.

Ah! give noe hauke the pow're
thy Turtle to devowre,
105   which sighes to thee with moorning mones:

---

82 rivers] River *N*   84 theyr] them *altered to* theyr *in A*; they *Q*   87 were] weare *H*
88 raise] raies *F, J, θ, C*; rayes *B, I, K, N, σ, G, M*   95 gowne] growne *D*; grownd *I*
96 lyvery] lyveries *K*   97 Thou then] Thou thou *D*; Thoe then *E*   one] on *I, θ*
99 mens] men *F*   dispight] despite *C*; despights *B, I, K, χ*   have] hath *B, I, K, O, σ*
102 cursed] cursinge *σ, G, M*   tongues] tongue *D*   torne] borne *M*   105 which]
with *D*   sighes] sightes *H*   moorning] mourning *F, J, I, K, χ*; mornings *O, N*

nor utterly out-rase
from tables of thy grace
the flock of thy afflicted ones.

But call thy league to mynd,
for horror all doth blind,   110
no light doth in the land remayne:
Rape, murther, violence,
each outrage, each offence,
each where doth range, and rage and raigne.

Enough, enough we mourne: 115
let us no more returne
repulst with blame and shame from thee:
but succour us opprest,
and give the troubled rest,
that of thy praise their songues may be.   120

Rise god, pleade thyne owne case,
forgett not what disgrace
these fooles on thee each day bestow:
forgett not with what cries
thy foes against thee rise,   125
which more and more to heav'n doe grow.

Confitebimur tibi.
Psalm 75.

Thee god, ô thee, wee sing, we celebrate:
thy actes with wonder who but doth relate?
so kindly nigh thy name our need attendeth.

---

106 out-rase] - out race *F*; outrace *J, C*; out race *Q, E*   115 we] no *I*   mourne] more *I*
120 thy] their *I*   their] our *M*   123 these] Those *B*   on thee each day] each daye
on thee *Q*   125 thee] mee *N*   126 heav'n doe grow] heaven growe *B, I, K, D, σ, G,*
M; heav'n growe *O, N, C*

Psalm 75. *B and K contain the variant only; I and N contain both versions. K notes in a different*
hand: This is otherwise translated.
Incipit: Confitebimur *B, I, θ, N, C*; confitebor tibi *G*; *om. Q*
1 Thee god, ô thee] Thee God (O thee) *C, G*; Thee ô god thee *E*; Thee (O God) *M*
2 wonder] wonders *I, Q*   doth] doe *Q, E*

sure I, when once the chardg I undergo
5   of this assembly, will not faile to show
          my judgments such, as justest rule commendeth.

The people loose, the land I shaken find:
this will I firmly propp, that straitly bind;
          and then denounce my uncontrolled pleasure:
10   bragg not you braggardes, you your saucy horne
lift not lewd mates: no more with heav'ns scorne,
          daunce on in wordes your old repyning measure.

Where sunn first showes; or last enshades his light;
divides the day; or pricks the midst of night;
15   seeke not the fountayne whence preferment springeth.
gods only fixed course that all doth sway,
lymitts dishonors night, and honors day,
          the king his crowne, the slave his fetters bringeth.

A troubled Cupp is in Jehovas hand,
20   where wine and wyny lees compounded stand,
          which franckly fild, as freely hee bestoweth;
yet for their draught ungodly men doth give,
gives all (not one except) that lewdly lyve,
          only what from the dreggs by wringing floweth.

25   And I secure shall spend my happie tymes
in my, though lowly, never-dying rymes,
          singing with praise the god that Jacob loveth.
my princly care shall cropp ill-doers low,
in glory plant, and make with glory grow
30   who right approves, and doth what right approveth.

---

4 once the] once [once *written over* I] this *I*   5 faile] feare *G, M*; shame *N*   6 my]
A, I, C, N; thy *K, χ*; my *altered to* thy *H*   judgments] judgment *C*   commendeth]
comaundeth *θ, N, σ*   8 that] that will I *θ*   straitly] straightly *I, χ*   10–17 *written between stricken lines 43–50 of Ps. 71 (including the spelling,* thruthes*) as at the top of f. 36ᵛ
in* I   10 braggardes] braggers *I, K, χ*   12 daunce] glaunce *I*   13 Where]
When *K, σ, G, M*   sunn] sonne *I*   enshades] enchardgde *I*   14 the midst of]
the mids of *I, N, H*   15 fountayne] fountanes *I*   springeth] springseth [eth
added?] *D*; springs *O*   18 bringeth] brings *I*   19 Jehovas] Jehova's *N, C, G, M*;
Jehovaes *I, σ*; Jehovahs *D*; Jehova'hs *J*   20 where] weare *I*   21 freely] frankly *I,
N, Q*   23 except] exempt *G, M*   25 And] So *I, K, χ*   26 though] thought *σ*
28 care] cares *I*   cropp] drop *I*   29 and] to *I*   30 and doth] *A, O*; and does *K,
χ*; or doth *I*

Notus in Judea.
Psalm 76.

Only to Juda god his will doth signify;
　　only in Jacob is his name notorious;
his restfull tent doth only Salem dignify;
　　on Syon only stands his dwelling glorious;
　　　　Their bow, and shaft, and shield, and sword he shivered,　　5
　　　　drave warr from us, and us from warr delivered.

Above proud princes, proudest in their theevery,
　　thou art exalted high, and highly glorified:
their weake attempt, thy valiant delivery,
　　theire spoile, thie conquest meete to be historified.　　　　10
　　　　the mighty handlesse grew as men that slumbered
　　　　for hands grew mightlesse, sence and life encombered.

Nay god, ô god, true Jacobs sole devotion,
　　thy check the very Carrs and horses mortifide,
cast in dull sleepe, and quite depriv'd of motion.　　　　15
　　　　most fearefull god, ô how must he be fortifide!

Psalm 76. *B has verse numbers 4–12 by 7, 9, 13, 16, 19, 20, 22, 25, 28.*
Incipit: Notus in Judæa Deus *B*; In Judeæ *I*; In Judæa *N*; In Judea *C*; In Juda *D*; In Judas *O*;
om. Q, M
1, 3 *B notes:* Before the Correction (by the Author under his own hand) the first and third
verse stood thus though upon the Correction expungd
　1) *That only land knowes God that jury named is.*
　3) *His restfull tent in only Salem framed is*
2 Jacob] Israel *B*　　　　4 on] In *N, M*　　Syon] him *O*　　5 Their] Theire *O*; there *B,*
K, χ; them *I*; the *D*　　bow] bowes *E*　　shaft] shafts *E*　　6 drave warr from us] Drave
us from warre *K, N, C, σ, G, M*　　7 theevery] lyvery *I*　　9 attempt] attempts
B, C　　valiant] valiand *B*　　10 thie] their *altered to* thie [r *erased*] *A*
11–12 *B notes:* The two last verses before correction stood thus, tho by the Author expungd.
　　　　　　As men whose senses had to sleep resignd their right
　　　　　　Nor mighty they their hands nor lands could find their might
11 grew] were *B*　　　　12 grew] were *B*
13–18 *B notes:* [A] This staffe standeth thus expunged
　Nay God O God etc. [*true Jacobs sole Devotion*]
　At Thy rebuke the v. c. and h. were
　As cast in slumber quite. [sic] *d. of m.*
　M. f. G. what arms must he what forces beare
　W. f. f. before thy presence stayes it
　　self (or) [sic]
　When bloody ensign of thy wrath displays it self/.
13 ô] o^r *Q, E*　　true] *om. θ*　　　　14 very] wearie *N, C, σ, G, M*

　　　　whose fearelesse foote to bide thy Onsett tarieth,
　　　　when once thy wrath displaied ensigne carieth.

From out of heav'n thy Justice judgment thundred
20　　　　when good by thee were sav'd, and bad were punished,
while Earth at heav'n with feare and silence wondred.
　　　　yea, the most ragefull in their rage astonished
　　　　　　fell to praise thee: whom thou, how ever furious
　　　　shalt eft restraine, if fury prove injurious.

25 Then lett your vowes be paid, your Offrings offered
　　　　unto the lord, ô you of his protection:
unto the fearefull lett your guiftes be proffered,
　　　　who loppeth princes thoughts, prunes their affection.
　　　　　　and so him self most terrible doth verify,
30　　　　　　in terrifying kings, that earth doth terrify.

　　　　　　　　Voce mea ad Dominum
　　　　　　　　　　Psalm 77.

　　　　　　To thee my crying call,
　　　　　　　　to thee my calling cry!
　　　　　　　　I did ô god, adresse,
　　　　　　　　and thou didst me attend:
5　　　　　　　　　　to nightly anguish thrall.
　　　　　　　　from thee I sought redresse;
　　　　　　　　to thee unceassantly
　　　　　　　　did praying handes extend.

17 foote] feete *C*　　thy Onsett] the onsett *σ*, *G*; thy onsent *I*　　　20 thee were] thee
weare *H*, *Q*　　bad were] bad weare *Q*　　punished] <punnished> \stet./ <sundered>
[stet. *added above* punnished *in a different hand*] *I*　　　22 most] more *F*
23–4 *B notes:* (b)—*and what as it remayning is*
　　(c) *Of rage in them reserv'd of thy restraining is* (or)
　　(c) *Shalt force restrain if eft they prove injurious.*
　　　　　　　　　　expungd
23 thee] God *G*　　　24 shalt eft] shall eft *N*, *G*　　　25 paid] pd *[single tilde above both*
letters] *B*　　your Offrings] your offring *B;* with offrings *I*　　27 unto the] To him most
N, *C*　　　28 princes] *[altered]* \princes/ *[added in a different hand and ink]* *I*　　their]
there *I*　　affection] affeccons *[tilde over* n] *E*　　　29 terrible] terribly *B*　　　30 that]
who *B*; the *I*　　doth] do *B*, *K*

Psalm 77. *B has verse numbers 1–20 by lines 1, 5, 9, 17, 25, 29, 33, 41, 45, 49, 53, 57, 60, 65,*
69, 73, 77, 81, 89, 93.　　　　　　　*Incipit:* Voce mea ad *K*; Voce mea *B*, *I*, *θ*, *N*, *C*; *om. Q*
1 crying] cryeings *K*　　　2 calling cry] callings crie *[*calli *written over erasure;*r
altered] *K*　　5 nightly] mightly *I*; mightie *K*, *N*

All comfort fled my soule:
   yea god to mind I cal'd,
   yet calling god to mynde
   my thoughts could not appease:
      nought els but bitter dole
   could I in thincking finde:
   my sprite with paine appal'd,
   could entertaine no ease.

Whole troupes of busy cares,
   of cares that from thee came,
   tooke up their restlesse rest
   in sleepie sleeplesse eies:
      soe lay I all opprest,
   my hart in office lame,
   my tongue as lamely fares,
   no part his part supplies.

At length with turned thought
   a new I fell to thinck
   uppon the auncient tymes
   uppon the yeares of old:
      yea to my mynd was brought,
   and in my hart did sinck,
   what in my former Rimes
   my self of thee had told.

Loe then to search the truth
   I sent my thoughts abroade;
   meane while my silent hart
   distracted thus did plaine:
      will god no more take ruth?
   no further love impart?
   no longer be my god?
   unmoved still remayne?

9 soule] fowle *I*   10 yea] Yet *B*   15 sprite] Sp'rite *B, K*; spirit *N, G, M*   16 could]
cold *I*   17 Whole] Whose *N*   20 sleeplesse] restles *E*   21–3 *Q puts 23 be-*
fore 21–2   21 lay I all] all I lay *N*   22 in] of θ   lame] prest *E*   23 tongue]
lunge [?] *N*   as lamely fares] doeth faye but lame *E*   25 length] lenghe *H*
26 a new] Anew *I, Q*; A-new *N*   30–1 *transposed in Q*   31 Rimes] tymes *E*
32 my self] what I *Q*   33 Loe] So *B, I, K,* χ   35 hart] hard *I*   37 will
god] god will *F*

Are all the Conduites dry
of his erst flowing grace?
could rusty teeth of tyme
to nought his promise turne?
45   can mercy no more clyme
and come before his face?
must all compassion dy?
must nought but anger burne?

Then lo, my wrack I see,
50   say I, and do I know
that chang lies in his hand,
who changlesse sittes aloft?
          can I ought understand,
and yet unmindfull be,
55   what wonders from hym flow?
what workes his will hath wrought?

Nay still thy acts I minde;
still of thy deedes I muse;
still see thy glories light
60   within thy temple shine.
          what god can any find?
(for tearme them so they use)
whose majesty, whose might,
may strive ô god with thine?

65   Thou only wonders do'st;
the wonders by thee done,
all earth do wonder make,
as when thy hand of old
          from servitude unjust
70   both Jacobs sonnes did take;
and sonnes of Jacobs sonne,
whom Jacobs sonnes had sold.

The waves thee saw, saw thee,
and fearefull fledd the field:

53 ought] ofte *Q, E*   56 hath] has *B*   57 I] *om. I*   59 glories light] glorious
light *G*; glourious sight *E*   64 may] My *M*   ô] oʳ *E*   65 do'st] gost *O*   67 do]
doth *B, I, K, χ*   68 thy hand] they had *I*   70 did] didst *C*   73 thee saw]
saw thee *I*

the deepe with panting brest   75
engulphed quaking lay:
   the cloudes thy fingers prest,
did rushing Rivers yeld;
thy shaftes did flaming flee
through firy airy way.   80

Thy voices thundring crash
from one to other pole,
twixt roofe of starry Sphere
and earth then trembling flore,
   while light of lightnings flash   85
did pitchy cloudes encleare,
did round with terror role,
and rattling horror rore.

Meane while through dusty deepe
on seas discovered bed,   90
where none thy trace could view,
a path by thee was wrought:
   a path whereon thy crue
as Shepherds use their sheepe,
with Aron Moises ledd,   95
and to glad pastures brought.

Attendite popule.
Psalm 78.

A grave discourse to utter I entend;
the age of tyme I purpose to renew,

75 the deepe] Thee deep *N*; the deede *I*   79 flee] flie *N*; glide *I*   80 airy] aery *I*;
aërie *N*   81 thundring] thunder *D*   82 other] th'other *C, G, M*   pole] poole *F*
83 Sphere] speare *H, Q*   84 earth] earthes *I, K, χ*; Earth's *C, G*   85 while]
Whilst *B*   lightnings] lightning *I, G, M*   87 role] roll *B*; rolle *D, E, M*; rowle *C, G*
88 rattling] deadlie *θ*   89 dusty] dusky *χ*   93 whereon] wherin *I*   95 Moses [*K:*
Moises] and *Aaron* led *I, K, χ*; *B notes*: Moses with Aaron led *but expunged*:   96 glad]
good *E*

Psalm 78. *B has verse numbers 1–43 by lines 1, 2, 5, 9, 13, 17, 21, 25, 29, 33, 35, 37, 41, 45, 49,
51, 53, 55, 57, 61, 65, 71, 73, 75, 78, 81, 85, 89, 93, 97, 99, 103, 105, 108, 111, 113, 115, 117,
121, 125, 128, 129, 133; 45–72 by 137, 139, 141, 143, 145, 149, 153, 161, 167, 169, 175, 177,
180, 182, 185, 187, 189, 191, 193, 195, 197, 199, 201, 203, 205, 209, 211, 214.*
Incipit: Attendite Populi *J, I, θ, N, C*; Attendite popule meus *B*; *om. Q*

you ô my charge to what I teach attend;
heare what I speake, and what you heare ensue.
5   the thinges our fathers did to us commend,
the same are they I recommend to you:
which though but heard wee know most true to be:
we heard, but heard, of who them selves did see.

Which never lett us soe ungratefull grow,
10   as to conceale from such as shall succeed:
let us the praises of Jehova show,
each act of worth, each memorable deede
chiefly since he him self commanded so:
giving a law to Jacob and his seed,
15   that fathers should this use to sonnes maintayne,
and sonnes to sonnes, and they to theirs again.

That while the yong shal over-live the old,
and of their brood some yet shalbe unborn;
these memories in memory enrold
20   by freating tyme may never thence be worn
that still on god their anchor, hope may hold;
from him by no dispairefull tempest torn;
that with wise hartes and willing mindes they may
think what he did, and what he bidds obay.

25   And not ensue their fathers froward trace,
whose stepps from god rebelliously did stray:
a waiward, stubborn, stailesse, faithlesse race;
such as on god no hold by hope could lay
like Ephraims sonnes, who durst not show their face,
30   but from the battaill fearefull fledd away:
yet bare, as men of warrlike excellence,
offending bowes, and armor for defence.

4 what...what] <things> \what/...that *I*   8 we heard] Wee heare *B*   who]
whome *G, M*   9 us] *A, B (text)*; mee *I, K, χ; B notes: me* expunged.   10 suc-
ceed] succred *I*   11 us] *A, B (text)*; me *I, K, χ; B notes: me* expunged.   Jehova]
Jehovah *D*; Jehovah<s> [?] *K*; Jeho< >\vath/ *[a letter stricken] I*   12 each] *B*
notes: and expunged.   15 that] *dash before* that *indicates mistaken triple indentation*
in A   this use to sonnes] to sons this use *B*   16 and sonnes] *dash before* and *indicates*
mistaken triple indentation in A   19 in memory] in memories *D*   21 on] in *E*
22 dispairefull] disgracefull *O*   torn] born *I*   25 froward] forward *E*   28 could]
did *O*   29 Ephraims] Ephram's *K*; Ephrams *H, Q, G, M*   31 bare] bore *B*

And why? they did not hold inviolate
the league of god: nor in his pathes would go.
his famoues workes, and wonders they forgate,　　　　35
which often hearing well might cause them know.
the workes and wonders which, in hard estate
he did of old unto their fathers show:
　　　whereof all Egipt testimony yeelds,
　　　and of all Egipt, chiefly Zoan fields.　　　　40

There where the deepe did show his sandy flore,
and heaped waves an uncouth way enwall:
whereby they past from one to other shore,
walking on seas, and yet not wett at all.
he ledd them so, a cloud was them before　　　　45
while light did last: when night did darknes call,
　　　a flaming piller glitt'ring in the skies
　　　their loadstarr was, till sunne again did rise.

He rift the Rocks and from their perced sides,
to give them drinck, whole seas of water drew:　　　　50
the desert sand no longer thirst abides;
the trickling springs to such huge Rivers grew.
yet not content their furie further slides;
in those wild waies they anger god anew.
　　　as thirst before, now hunger stirrs their lust　　　　55
　　　to tempting thoughtes, bewraying want of trust.

And fond conceites begetting fonder wordes:
can god say they, prepare with plentious hand
deliciously to furnish out our boordes
here in this waste, this hunger-starved land?　　　　60

---

34 pathes] path *G, M*　　　36 well might] well may *Q*　　　cause] make *B*　　　39 Egipt]
Ægipt *E*　　　40 Egipt] Ægipt *Q, E*　　　41 his] its *B*　　　sandy] sand *F*　　　flore]
shore *J*; flowre *H*; flower *E*　　　42 an uncouth] did all the *I, K, χ*　　　43 other]
th'other *G, M*　　　44 on] twixt *M*　　　45 a cloud] aclowd *I*; acould *O*　　　46 light]
life *altered to* light *in A*　　　47 glitt'ring] glistring *I, O, C, E, Q, G, M*; glisteringe *K,
D, N, H*　　　48 loadstarr] lead=starr *J*　　　sunne] sonne *I*　　　49 *horizontal pencil
stroke in the margin just above this line in A*　　　rift] riv'd *J, B, K, χ*; riv\e/d *H*; rived *I,
Q, E*　　　perced] peirceinge *H, Q*　　　50 seas] streames *O*　　　water] water [s *stricken
after* r *(?)] K*; waters *J, I, D, N, C, E, M*　　　51 sand] sande<s> *K*; sandes *G*
52 grew] growe *E*　　　55 as] a *I*　　　now] so *B*　　　56 thoughtes] thought *K*
58 say they] they say *B*　　　60 here] hee *I*

we see indeed the streames, the Rock affordes:
we see in pooles the gathered waters stand:
    but whither bread and flesh so ready be
    for him to give as yet we do not see.

65 This heard, but heard with most displeased eare,
that Jacobs race he did so dearly love,
who in his favoure had no cause to feare,
should now so wav'ring, so distrustfull prove;
the raked sparkes in flame began appeare,
70 and staied Choller fresh again to move;
    that from his trust their confidence should swerve,
    whose deedes had show'n, he could and would preserve.

Yet he unclos'd the garners of the skies,
and bade the cloudes Ambrosian Manna rain:
75 as morning frost on hoary pasture lies,
so strawed lay each where this heav'nly grain.
the finest cheat that princes dearest prise,
the bread of heav'n could not in fines stain:
    which he them gave, and gave them in such store,
80   each had so much, he wish't to have no more.

But that he might them each way satisfie,
he slipt the raines to east and southerne wind;
these on the Cloudes their uttmost forces try,
and bring in raine of admirable kind.
85 the dainty Quailes that freely wont to fly,
in forced showrs to dropp were now assign'd:
    and fell as thick as dust on sunn-burnt field,
    or as the sand the thirsty shore doth yeld.

61 the streames] that streames θ   the Rock] s *stricken after* k *in* A; the Rocks F, C, E, G, M
62 in] the J   waters] water B, D, C, M   stand] stande<s> K   63 whither] h *added*
above w *in* A; whether F, J, B, I, θ, σ   bread] a *added above* re *in* A   and] or E   flesh]
fish J   65 heard, but heard∧] ~ (~∧ K; ~∧ ~, O; ~ (~) G, M most] much B
eare,] ~∧ B, I, K, χ; ~) K   66 so] *added above caret in* A   69 appeare] t'appeare θ
70 Choller] choler B; chollar O; colour I, K; Collour N, H, Q; collour E; Cullour C, G, M
73 garners] garner I   74 rain] raigne K, D, C   76 strawed] strewed B   77 cheat]
wheat [c *altered to* w *by scribe]* F; wheate O   princes dearest] deerest princes I, K, χ
prise] A, D; prize B, I, K, χ   78 could not in fines] in fineness could not D   82 raines]
reins B; raigns I   southerne] northerne θ   wind] windes F 84 in raine] in raigne
Q; forth raine D   kind] kindes F   87 on] in F   field] feilds I

Soe all the plain, whereon their army lay,
as farr abroad as any tent was pight,   90
with feathred rain was wat'red ev'ry way,
which showring down did on their lodgings light.
then fell they to their easy gotten pray,
and fedd till fullnes vanquisht had delight:·
        their lust still flam'd still god the fuell brought   95
        and fedd their lust, beyond their lustfull thought.

But fully fild, not fully yet content,
while now the meate their weary chapps did chew:
gods wrathfull rage uppon these gluttons sent,
of all their troupes the principallest slew.   100
among all them of Israells descent
his stronger plague the strongest overthrew.
        yet not all this could wind them to his will,
        still worse they grew, and more untoward still.

Therfore he made them waste their weary yeares   105
roaming in vain in that unpeopled place;
possest with doubtfull cares, and dreadfull feares:·
but if at any time death show'd his face,
then lo, to god they su'de and su'de with teares:
then they retornd, and earely sought his grace: 110
        then they profest, and all did mainly cry
        in god their strength, their hope, their help did ly.

But all was built uppon no firmer ground
then fawning mouthes, and tongues to lying train'd:
they made but showes, their hart was never sound: 115
disloiall once, disloiall still remain'd.
yet he (so much his mercy did abound)
purged the filth, wherwith their soules were staind:

---

89 Soe] See *F, J*   the] their *N*   whereon their] wheron the *B*   91 way] day *B*
93 gotten] gotte *I*   pray] prey *B, N*   98 while] whilst *C*   102 stronger] wrathfull *B, I, K, χ*; fearefull *G*   104 still worse] All worse *N*   106 roaming] roueinge
[first e *added above caret] H*; roveiinge *[first* e *added above caret] E*; roueinge *Q*; roaving *G*;
Roving *M*; wayninge *K*   107 and] with *E*   109 to god they su'de] they sude to
god *I*   110 retornd] return *I*   112 help] health *B*   114 train'd] bent *M*
115 hart was] hartes was *σ*; hartes were *C, G, M*   117 so much his mercy] so much
his goodnes *G;* his mercie did so much *N*   118 were] weare *H*   staind] staid *I*

destroid them not, but oft revok'd his Ire,
120   and mildly quencht his indignations fire.

For kind compassion called to his mynd,
that they but men, that men but mortall were,
that mortall life, a blast of breathing wind,
as wind doth passe, and past no more appeare,
125   and yet (good god) how ofte this crooked kind
incenst him in the desert every where?
        againe repin'd, and murmured againe,
        and would in boundes that boundles pow'r contain.

Forsooth their weake remembrance could not hold
130   his hand, whose force above all mortall hands
to Ægipts wonder did it self unfold,
loosing their fetters and their servile bands:
when Zoan plaines where christall Rivers rold,
with all the rest of those surrounded lands,
135   saw watry clearnes chang'd to bloudy gore,
        pining with thirst in middst of watry store.

Should I relate of flies the deadly swarmes?
of filthy froggs the odious anoy?
grashoppers waste, and Catterpillers harmes,
140   which did their fruites, their harvest hope enjoy?
how haile and lightning breaking of the armes
of Vines and figgs, the bodies did destroy?
        lightning and haile, whose flamy, stony blowes
        their beastes no less and cattell overthrowes?

145   These were but smokes of after-going fire:
now, now his fury breaketh into flame:
now dole and dread now pine and paine conspire
with angry Angells wreak and wrack to frame.
nought now is left to stopp his stailesse ire;
150   so plaine a way is opened to the same.

119 oft] eft *B*   122 mortall] mortalls *E*   were] weare *H, E*   123 life] lyfe's *K*
124 as] and *K*   126 him] <t>hem *H*; them *Q*   131 Ægipts] *A, E*; Ægypts *Q*;
Egipts *I, K,* χ   wonder] wonders *I, Q*   133 Rivers] waters *I*   134 with]
whith [?] *I*   those] these *O, N*   135 chang'd] turn'd *F, I, K,* χ   136 store] shore *E*
139 waste] wastes *G, M*   140 fruites] fruite χ   harvest] havest *Q*   hope] hopes *Q*
141 of] off *I*; oft *B*   143 lightning...haile] lightnings...hailes *D*   144 and]
then θ   148 wreak] wreck *Q*

abroad goes Death, the uttermost of ills,
in house, in field, and men and cattell kills.

All that rich land, where-over Nilus trailes
of his wett robe the slymy seedy train,
with millions of mourning cries bewailes   155
of ev'ry kind their first begotten slain.
against this plague no wealth, no worth prevailes:
of all that in the tentes of Cham remayn,
    who of their house the propps and pillers were,
    them selves do fall, much lesse can others beare.   160

Meane while, as while a black tempestuous blast
drowning the earth, in sunder rentes the skies,
a Shepheard wise to howse his flock doth haste,
taking nere waies, and where best passage lies:
god from this Ruine, through the barrain wast   165
conductes his troupes in such or safer wise:·
    and from the seas his sheepe he fearelesse saves,
    leaving their wolves intombed in the waves.

But them leaves not untill they were possest
of this his hill, of this his holy place,   170
whereof full Conquest did him lord invest,
when all the dwellers fledd his peoples face,
by him subdu'd, and by his hand opprest.
whose heritage he shared to the Race,
    the twelv-fold race of godly Israell,   175
    to lord their landes, and in their dwellings dwell.

But what availes? not yet they make an end
to tempt high god, and stirre his angry gall:
from his prescript another way they wend,
and to their fathers crooked by-pathes fall.   180

152 in field] and field *J, B, N, σ, G, M*   153 that] the *Q*   154 slymy] slying *N*
156 their] the *D*   158 remayn] remaines *N, E*   159 were] weare *H, Q*
161 Meane while, as while∧] Meane while, as when∧ *F;* Meane while∧ as while∧ *I, K, Q;*
Meanewhile (as while∧ *N;* Meane while, (as while∧ *C;* Meane while, as while, *H;* Meane
while, (as while∧ *G, M*   blast∧] ~, *N, C;* ~) *G*   162 rentes] rent *Q;* rends *G, M*
skies,] ~∧ *I, K, χ;* ~: *N, C;* ~) *G;* ~:) *M*   163 a] As *Q*   164 passage] pasture *O*
lies:] ~∧ *I, K, χ;* ~. *O, M;* ~:) *N;* ~) *C*   165 this] t *added in different ink in D;* his *χ*
167 seas] sea *O*   168 their] i *added,* r *added above* i *in A;* the θ   waves] graves *F*
169 But] But \them/ *O*   174 shared] showed *I*   176 landes] land *B*   dwel-
lings] dwelling *I*

so with vaine toile distorted bowes we bend:
though level'd right, they shoote not right at all.
　　　the idoll honor of their damned groves,
　　　　when god it heard, his jealous anger moves.

185　For god did heare, detesting in his hart,
　　　the Isralites a people soe perverse:
　　　and from his seate in Silo did depart
　　　the place where god did erst with men converse,
　　　right well content that foes on every part
190　his force captyve his glory should reverse:
　　　　　right well content (so ill content he grew)
　　　　　his peoples bloud should tyrantes blade imbrue.

　　　Soe the yong men the flame of life bereaves:
　　　the virgins live despair'd of mariage choise:
195　the sacred priests fall on the bloudy glaives;
　　　no widow left to use hir wailing voice.
　　　but as a knight, whom wyne or slumber leaves,
　　　hearing alarm, is roused at the noise:
　　　　　soe god awakes: his haters fly for feare,
200　　　　and of their shame eternall marks do beare.

　　　But god chose not, as he before had chose,
　　　in Josephes tents, or Ephraim to dwell:
　　　but Juda takes, and to mount Syon goes,
　　　to Syon mount, the mount he loved well.
205　there he his house did Castle-like enclose;
　　　of whose decay no after times shall tell:
　　　　　while hir own weight shall weighty earth sustain,
　　　　　his sacred seate shall here unmov'd remain.

　　　And where his servant David did attend
210　　a shepherds charge, with care of fold and field:

181 we] they *O, G*　　bend] sind *I*　　　185 heare] here *Q*　　detesting] detest even *Q*
188 converse₍] ~₍ *K, χ*; ~: *F*; ~, *N*; ~; *M*; ~. *A, J*　　189 on] in *θ*　　　192 his]
That *M*　　tyrantes] tircints *N*　　blade] bloud *N, C, σ, G, M*　　　194 despair'd] dis-
paire *N*　　195–7 *B brackets these lines, has three dots each in the left margin by 195 and
197, and notes:* thus pricked *[then in different ink]* so markt possibly for correction as also
above　　197 knight...slumber] *written as a correction over stricken last six words of
line 198 in I*　　or] and *θ, Q*　　198 alarm] a Larrum *E*　　200 do] they *I, K, χ*
beare] bearth *I*　　201 had chose] did chose *I, K;* did choose *χ*　　202 tents] tent *E*
or] and *O*　　Ephraim] Ephraims *J, I, K, χ*　　203 Juda] Judah *B*　　206 decay]
decayes *F*　　after] other *J*　　208 his] as *J*　　seate] seates *O*

he takes him thence and to a nobler end
converts his cares, appointing him to shield
his people which of Jacob did descend,
and feede the flock his heritage did yeld:
      and he the paines did gladly undergoe,   215
      which hart sincere, and hand discreet did show.

Deus venerunt.
Psalm 79.

The land of long by thee possessed,
the heathe'n, lord, have now oppressed:
thy temple holily maintained
till now, is now, prophanely stained.
      Jerusalem quite spoil'd and burned,   5
          hath suffred sack
          and utter wrack,
to stony heapes hir buildings turned.

The livelesse carcases of those,
that liv'd thy servants, serve the Crowes: 10
the flock, soe derely lov'd of thee
to ravening beastes dere foode they be
      their bloud doth streame in every streete
          as water spilled:
          their bodies killed   15
      with sepulture can no where meete.

    To them that hold the neighbour places
    we are but objects of disgraces:

---

211 nobler] noble *B*   212 converts] conducts *C, M*   216 which] With *B*; with *E*
hand] hands *N*   discreet] discrete *B*

Psalm 79. *Lacking in I. B has verse numbers 1–14 by lines 1, 9, 12, 17, 21, 25, 29, 33, 37, 40,*
45, 49, 53, 57.
Incipit: om. Q
1 long] late *E*; livinge *N*   2 have] hath *M*   3 *rephrased in K, χ, σ, G*: Thy temple
holily <by thee> maintayned *K*; thy temple holilie by thee maintained *θ, N, C, M*; Thy
temple holly by thee maintained *σ*; Thy holie *Temple*, so maintained *G*   6 sack]
sacks *B*   7 wrack] wracks *B*   8 buildings] houses *B, K, χ*   10 serve] *second*
e *over erasure of* 'd *(?) in A*; serves *F*   11 of] by *θ*   13 doth] doe *O*   14 water]
waters *D*   16 can no where] no where can *G, M*

on ev'ry coast who dwell about us,
20   in ev'ry kind deride and flout us.
    ah lord! when shall thy wrath be ended?
    shall still thine yre,
    as quenchles fire,
    in deadly ardor be extended?

25   O kindle there thy furies flame,
    where lives no notice of thy name:
    there lett thy heavie anger fall,
    where no devotions on thee call.
    for thence, they be who Jacob eate,
30   who thus have rased,
    have thus, defaced,
    thus desert laid his ancient seate.

Lord ridd us from our sinnfull cumbers,
count not of them the passed numbers:
35   but lett thy pitty soone prevent us,
    for hard extreames have nerely spent us.
    free us, ô god, our freedome giver;
    our misery
    with help supply:
40   and for thy glory us deliver.

Deliver us, and for thy name
with mercy cloth our sinnfull shame:·
ah? why should this their byword be,
where is your god? where now is he?
45   make them, and us on them behold,
    that not despised,
    but deerly prised,
    thy wreakfull hand our bloud doth hold.

Where grace, and glory thee enthroneth,
50   admitt the grones the prisoner groneth:

19 on] one *H*   21 ah] *dash before* ah *indicates mistaken triple indentation in A*   22 shall still] still shall *K, O, N, σ*   24 ardor] order *θ*   25 furies] *A, B, M*; furious *K, χ* 29 for] ffrom *K, χ*   30 rased] razed *θ, G, M*; raced *J*   32 thus] This *σ*   laid] Land *σ*   33 our] or *D*   35 lett] with *M*   36 for hard] foe=hard *altered to* for hard *K*; foe-hard *C*   have nerely] hath meerely *N*   38 misery] *a letter stricken after* misery *(?) in A*   45 and us on] on us and *θ*   47 deerly] highly *M*   prised] *A, θ*; prized *J, K, χ*

the poore condem'd for death reserved
let be by thee in life preserved.
    and for our neighbours, lord, remember
    th'opprobrious shame
    they lent thy name   55
with seav'n-fold gaine to them thou render.

Soe we thy servantes, we thy sheep,
whom thy lookes guide, thy pastures keepe:
till death define our lyving daies,
will never cease to sound thy praise.   60
    Nay when we leave to see the sunn,
        the after goers
        we will make knowers
from age to age what thou hast done.

Qui regis Israel.
Psalm 80.

Heare thou greate heardsman that dost Jacob feed:
    thou Josephs shepheard shine from Cherubs throne:
in Ephraim, Benjamyn, Manasses need,
    awake thy power, and make thy puisance knowne.
    free us distressed, raise us overthrowne,   5
        Reduce us straid, ô god, restore us banish'd:
display thy faces skies on us thine owne,
    soe we shall safly dwell, all darknesse vanish'd.

Lord god of hosts, what end, what meane appeares
    of thy wrathes fume against thy peoples cry?   10

---

55 lent] bent *θ*   58 pastures keepe] pasture keepes *θ*   59 lyving] livinge *[first* i
written over o] *K*; loninge *H*; loaninge *Q*; lovinge *E*   62 the] *om. N*   63 we]
om. K, θ

Psalm 80. *Variant in B.*
Incipit: Qui ducis Israel *K*; Qui ducis *I*; *om. Q*
1 heardsman] d *added above* rs *and caret in A*; heardman *I, K, χ*   that dost] *A, θ*; that doth
K, N, C, σ, G, M; the dost *I*   2 Josephs] *A, I, K, N*; Joseph *χ*   3 Ephraim]
Eph\r/aym *H*; Ephram *Q*   4 and] *om. E*   6 banish'd] d *written over* t *in A*
7 thy faces skies on us] thy faces skie on us *θ*; on us (thy faces skies) *G*   thine] thy *M*
8 darknesse] h *altered to* k *in A*   10 fume] fame *N*

whom thou with teares for bread, for drink with teares
    so diettest, that we abandon'd ly,
to foes of laughter, and to dwellers by,
    a field of brall. but god restore us banish'd
15   display on us thy faces cleered sky,
        so we shall safly dwell all darknes vanish'd.

A Vine thou didst translate from Zoan playnes,
    and weeding them that held the place of old,
nor planting care didst slack, nor pruning paines,
20   to fix hir rootes, whom fieldes could not enfold.
    the hills were cloked with hir pleasing cold:
      with Cedars state hir branches height contended:
    scarse here the sea, the River there controld
      hir armes, hir handes, soe wide she both extended.

25   Why hast thou now thy self dishedg'd this vine,
      carlesly left to passengers in pray?
unseemly rooted by the woodbred swine,
    wasted by other beasts that wildly stray?
    ô god, retorne, and from thy starry stay
30   Review this Vyne, reflect thy looking hither;
this Vineyard see, whose plott thy hande dyd lay,
    this plant of choise, ordained not to wither.

Consum'd with flames, with killing axes hewne
    all at thy frown they fall, and quaile, and dy:
35   but heape thou might, on thy ellected one,
    that stablisht man in whom we may affy.
    then we preserv'd thy name shall magnify
      without revolt, lord god restore us banish'd:
display on us thy faces cleered sky,
40   soe we shall safly dwell all darknes vanish'd.

12 we] they *G, M*   abandon'd] abandond *[altered] I*; abandd ∫an *written over* ou, n *stricken*; ~ *added above* e*] K*; abounded [u *(or* n*) added above caret between* o *and* n *(or* u] *H*; abounded *Q, E, G, M*   13 laughter] slaughter *F, M* to dwellers] of dwellers *N* 14 brall] Brale [?] *Q*; brawle θ, *C, G, M*   15 cleered] cleerest *I,* θ, *E*   16 we shall] shall wee *C* all] as *I*   21 were] weare *H, Q* pleasing] plesent *I* 22 height] high *E, G, M*   23 River] rivers *K*   24 she] they *G*   25 dishedg'd] discharg'd *I*   29 *not indented in A* thy] the *J* starry] starly *I*   31 lay] say *I* 35 on] one *O*   36 stablisht] stablest *K, C, G, M*; stablist θ, *H*; sablest *N* in] on *I* 39 cleered] cleerest θ, *E, G, M*   40 we shall] shall wee θ

Exultate Deo.
Psalm 81.

All gladdnes, gladdest hartes can hold,
     in meriest notes that mirth can yeld,
lett joyfull songues to god unfold,
     to Jacobs god our sword and shield.
     Muster hither musicks joyes,   5
      lute, and lyre, and tabretts noise:
     lett noe instrument be wanting,
     chasing grief, and pleasure planting.

When ev'ry month begining takes,
     when fixed tymes bring sacred daies;   10
when any feast his people makes;
     lett trumpetts tunes report his praise.
     this to us a law doth stand,
     pointed thus by gods owne hand;
of his league a signe ordained,   15
     when his plagues had Ægipt pained.

There heard I, erst unheard by me,
     the voice of god, who thus did say:
Thy shoulder I from burthen free,
     free sett thy hand from baked clay.   20
     vexed, thou my aide did'st crave;
     thunder-hid I answer gave:·
till the streames where strife did move thee,
     still I did with triall prove thee.

I bade thee then attentive be,   25
     and told thee thus: O Israell,
this is my covenant that with thee
     no false, nor forrein god shall dwell.

Psalm 81. *Lacking in I. B has verse numbers 1–16 by lines 1, 4, 9, 12, 15, 19, 21, 25, 28, 30, 33, 35, 37, 39, 41, 45.*
Incipit: om. Q
1 gladdnes] n *added above caret in A*   hold] ho *written over erasure in A* (y *visible under* h)
2 mirth] earth *θ*   5 musicks] Musick *E*   9 month] moneth *C, σ, G, M*   10 *not
indented in A*   tymes bring] tyme bring *K, C, H, Q, G, M*; time brings *θ, N*   16 pla-
gues] plauges *Q*   had] held *N*   Ægipt] *A, Q*; Egipt *F, K, χ*; Egypt *B*   pained] stained *E*
17 There] Then *altered to* Ther [n *partly erased?*] *D*; Then *O*   23 where] when
O; of *G*   strife] striffs [?] *Q*   28 nor] no *K, χ*   shall] should *B*

I am god, thy god, that wrought
30   that thou wert from Ægipt brought:
open me thy mouth; to feede thee
I will care, nought els shall neede thee.

But ah, my people scorn'd my voice,
and Israell rebelled still:
35   so then I left them to the choise
of froward way and wayward will.
why alas? why had not they
heard my voice, and held my way?
Quickly I their foes had humbled,
40   all their haters hedlong tumbled.

Subdu'd by me who them anoi'd,
had serv'd them now in base estate:
and of my graunt they had enjoy'd
a lease of blisse with endlesse date.
45   flower of the finest wheate
had byn now their plenteous meate:
honny them from Rocks distilled
filled had, yea over filled.

Deus stetit.
Psalm 82.

Where poore men plead at Princes barre,
who gods (as gods vicegerents) ar:
the god of gods hath his tribunall pight,
adjudging right
5   both to the judg, and judged wight.

30 Ægipt] *A, Q*; Egipt *F, K, χ*; Egypt *B*
34, 36 *B notes:*
    (a) before the Correction but expunged:
    Nor Israël would me obey
    (b) *Of wayward will and froward way*
37 had] did *F*   38 heard] hard *C*   40 all] And *B*   42 base estate] servile
state *B, K, χ*   46 byn] bin *D*; bine *H, Q, E*; been *F, K, χ*   47 them from]
from the *B*

Psalm 82. *Lacking in I. B has verse numbers 1–8 by lines 1, 6, 8, 11, 16, 21, 23, 26.*
Incipit: Deus stetit in Sinaque [que *abbreviated*] *H*; Deus stetit in Si: *E*; *om. θ, Q*
1 plead] pleades *θ (s stricken?)*   2 who] what *B*   as gods] as God's *G*

How long will ye just doome neglect?
　　how long saith he, bad men respect?
you should his owne unto the helplesse give,
　　the poore releeve,
　　ease him with right, whom wrong doth greeve.　　　10

　　You should the fatherlesse defend:
　　　you should unto the weake extend
your hand, to loose and quiet his estate
　　through lewd mens hate
　　entangled now in deepe debate.　　　15

　　This should you doe: but what doe ye?
　　　you nothing know, you nothing see:·
no light, no law; fy, fy, the very ground
　　becoms unsound,
　　soe right, wrong, all, your faultes confound.　　　20

　　Indeed to you the stile I gave
　　　of gods, and sonnes of god, to have:
but err not princes you as men must dy:
　　you that sitt high,
　　must fall, and low, as others ly.　　　25

　　Since men are such, ô god arise:
　　　thy self most strong, most just, most wise,
of all the earth king, judg, disposer be;
　　since to decree
　　of all the earth belongs to thee.　　　30

6 neglect] ne<c>glect *O*; neclegt *D*　　7 respect] protect *B*　　10 him] them *G*
15 entangled] just angledd *H*; Juste angled *Q*; Just angled *E*　　now] nowe, now *E*
in deepe] *B notes*: interlined *in quarel and* but expungd because a foot too long
16 you] yee *θ*　　21 Indeed] I *written in darker ink over erasure of* Ii *in A*　　22 god]
gods *K, N, C*　　24 sitt] sett *N*　　25 *B notes*: *As others fall with others low must ly.* |
So it was at first corrected and the other expungd but this being after expung'd, *stet* is putt to
the other.　　low] lie *θ*　　as] with *K, χ*; where *θ*

Deus quis similis.
Psalm 83.

Be not, ô be not silent still
   rest not, ô god, with endlesse rest:·
     for lo thine enemies
     with noise and tumult rise;
5 hate doth their hartes with fiercnes fill,
   and lift their heades who thee detest.

Against thy folk their witts they file
   to sharpest point of secret sleight:
     a world of trapps and traines
10   they forge in busy braines,
that they thy hid ones may beguile,
   whom thy wings shroud from serching sight.

Come lett us of them nothing make:
   lett none them more a people see:
15   stopp we their verie name
     within the mouth of fame.
such are the counsells these men take;
   such leagues they linck, and these they be.

First Edoms sonnes, then Ismaell,
20   with Moab, Agar, Geballs traine:
     with these the Amonites
     the fierce Amalekites,
and who in Palestina dwell,
   and who in tentes of Tyre remaine.

Psalm 83. *B has verse numbers 1–18 by lines 1, 3, 7, 13, 17, 19, 21, 25, 27, 29, 31, 33, 37, 40, 43, 45, 49, 52.*
Incipit: Deus quis *I, N, C; om. θ, Q*
5 doth] doe *M*   hartes] heart *J*   6 heades] *altered in A*   7 witts] witt θ; waies *E*
8 sleight] slights *E*   11 they thy hid ones] they thy hidd-ones [i *written over* e, *or* e *over* i] *N*; they thy headd ones *H, E*; they thy *head=ones* [hid=ones *in margin*] *Q*; they they hidd ones *M*   12 wings] winge *Q*   from] for *I, N, H*   13 of them nothing] *A, B, G*; nothing of them *I (written over erasure), K, χ*   15 stopp] stoop *I*   their] the *C, G*
17 counsells] Councells *F, I, K, D, σ, G, M*; Counsell *B*   18 and these they be] and such they bee *K, χ; om. I*   20 Agar] Hagar *χ*   21 Amonites] Amorites *K*
22 fierce] feire *N*   23 Palestina] palesna *I*

Ashur, though further of he ly,   25
    assisteth Lotts incestious brood.
        but lord as Jabin thou
        and Sisera didst bow:
as Midian did fall and dy
    at Endor walls, and Kyson flood: 30

As Oreb, Zeb, and Zeba strong,
    as Salmuna who ledd thy foes:
        (who meant, nay said no lesse
        then that they would possesse
gods heritage) became as donge: 35
    soe lord, ô soe, of these dispose.

Torment them, lord, as tossed balls;
    as stuble scatt'red in the aire:
        or as the branchy brood
        of some thick mountain wood,   40
to naught, or nought but asshes falls,
    when flames doe sindg their leavy haire:

Soe with thy tempest them pursue,
    so with thy whirlewind them affright:
        so paint their daunted face,   45
        with pencell of disgrace,
that they at length to thee may sue,
    and give thy glorious name his right.

Add feare and shame, to shame and feare:
    confound them quite, and quite deface;   50
        and make them know that none,
        but thou, and thou alone,
dost that high name Jehovah beare,
    high plac't above all earthly place.

---

25 Ashur] shur *written over erasure in* A; Assur N, C, G   of] off B, O   he] thie I
26 assisteth] assisted O   27 thou] show N   29 dy] *altered to* ly *in* F; die χ
31 Zeba] Saba K   32 Salmuna] Salmana B, I, K, χ   who] that θ   33 (who
meant,] (~∧ B, C; ∧~∧ I, K, θ, G; ∧~, Q, E, M   ∧nay] (~ G, M   lesse∧] ~, N; ~) G, M
35 ∧gods heritage)] ∧~, K; ∧~, θ; ∧~∧ Q; (~) E   38 *not indented in* A   40 mountain]
Mountains B   41 naught] nought F, O, M   or nought] or naught I, K, D, N, C, σ, G
but] to χ   42 leavy] l *(loop not gilded) over erasure of* h *in* A   haire] *om.* I   49 feare
and shame] shame and feare F   52 and thou] (O lord) M   53 high] *om.* O   Jeho-
vah] A, D; Jehova B, J, I, K, χ   54 earthly] earthy D; earth by I

Quam dilecta.
Psalm 84.

How lovely is thy dwelling,
greate god, to whom all greatnes is belonging!
   to view thy Courtes farre, farre from any telling,
my soule doth long, and pine with longing.
5   unto the god that liveth
        the god that all life giveth
    my hart and body both aspire,
    above delight, beyond desire.

    Alas? the Sparow knoweth
10   the house, where free, and fearelesse she resideth:
   directly to the neast the Swallow goeth,
where with hir sonnes she safe abideth.
        ô Alters thine, most mighty
        in warre, yea most allmighty:
15   thy Alters lord: ah? why should I
    from Alters thine excluded ly?

    O happy who remaineth
thy houshold-man, and still thy praise unfoldeth;
   ô happy who him self on thee sustaineth,
20   who to thy house his jorney holdeth?
        me seemes I see them going
        where mulberies are growing:
    how wells they digg in thirsty plaine,
    and Cesternes make, for falling Rayne.

25   Me seemes I see augmented
still troop with troop, till all at length discover
   Sion, wherto their sight is represented
the lord of hostes, the Sion lover.

Psalm 84. *B has verse numbers 1–12 by lines 1, 4, 9, 17, 19, 21, 25, 29, 33, 37, 41, 47.*
Incipit: Quam dilecta Tabernacula *H; om. θ, Q*
3 Courtes] courtis *I;* coutes *H*   telling] dwellinge *K*   4 long] *om. N*   7 both]
doth *J, I, K, χ; B notes: doth* expunged   10 she] hee *I*   12 sonnes] younge *χ*
13 Alters] Altar *K*   20 whose hart thie waies [*G:* lawe] ingraved holdeth *I, K, χ; B
notes on this variant line:* expunged.   24 for] *B notes: from* expunged.   26 all at]
all all at *E;* at the *N*   27 wherto] where, to *J*

ô lord, ô god, most mighty
    in warre, yea most allmighty: 30
heare what I begg, harken I say,
    ô Jacobs god, to what I pray.

Thou art the shild us shieldeth:
then lord, behold the face of thine anointed.
    one day spent in thy courtes more comfort yeldeth,   35
then thousands otherwise appointed.
    I count it cleerer pleasure
    to spend my ages treasure
waiting a porter at thy gates:
    then dwell a lord with wicke'd mates.   40

Thou art the sunn that shineth,
thou art the buckler, lord, that us defendeth:
    glory and grace Jehovas hand assigneth:
and good without refusall sendeth
    to him who truly treadeth   45
    the path to purenes leadeth.
ô lord of might, thrice blessed he,
whose confidence is built on thee.

Benedixisti Domine.
Psalm 85.

Mighty lord from this thy land,
    never was thy love estrang'd:
Jacobs servitud thy hand
    hath we know to freedome chang'd.

---

31 harken] marck what *G, M*   32 what] whome χ   33 us] that *I*   35 com-
fort] profitt *O*   yeldeth] *om. I*   36 otherwise] otherwaies *E*   40 a lord] o Lord
K, χ; olord *I*; *om. θ*   41 Thou] That *θ*   sunn] same *θ*   42 thou art] Thou art
B, I, K, χ; that art *A*   that us] us *I*   43 Jehovas] Jehova's *J, N, C, G*; Jehovahs *K, θ*;
Jehovaes *σ*   hand] hands *O*   44 good] *second* o *added by scribe in F*; godd *I*   45 to]
Lo *N*   47 thrice] most *B*

Psalm 85. *B has verse numbers 1–13 by 1, 4, 9, 12, 15, 18, 20, 23, 26, 30, 34, 38, 42. B notes:*
This Psalm is Crossd through the body of it. *Contrary to his usual practice, Woodforde did not
transfer the marginal revisions of Psalm 85 to the body of the text, but recorded them in the margins of his transcription.*
Incipit: Benedixisti *N, C, G, M*; Bendixisti *B*; Benevolus fuisti *I, K*; *om. θ, Q*

5
    all thy peoples wicked parts
      have byn banisht from thy sight
      thou on them hast cured quite
    all the woundes of synnfull dartes.
        still thy Choller quenching soe,
10
        heate to flame did never grow.

Now then god as heretofore,
    god, the god that dost us save,
change our state, in us no more
    lett thine anger object have.
15
      wilt thou thus for ever grive?
      wilt thou of thy wrathfull rage
      draw the threed from age to age?
      never us againe relive?
      lord yet once our hartes to joy
20
      show thy grace, thy help employ.

What speake I? ô lett me heare
    what he speakes: for speake hee will
peace to whome he love doth beare,
    lest they fall to folly still.
25
      ever nigh to such as stand
      in his feare, his favour is:·

---

6 *Original line preserved in B (which has the A version in the margin):* Have by Thee been hidd from sight   byn] bin *D*; bine *H, Q, E*; been *F, I, K, χ*; bene *G*   8 dartes] Dearth *I*
9–10 *original in B (text):*

    All Thy wrath Thou hast asswag'd
    Weakning so thy angers might
    That it never grew enrag'd.

B notes: Ex Correctione Auctoris su sub manu duobq [*vertical stroke through ascender of* b, *for us ?*] versiculis pro tribq [*vertical stroke through ascender of* b, *for us ?*] positis [*quotes 9–10*] et sic per totum psalmum
9 still] *All B (margin)*   Choller] collour *E*   10 to] in *I*   11 god] o god σ, *G, M*
12 god, the god] Thou the God *G, M*   15 wilt thou thus] *B notes: Why wilt Thou* expunged   18 relive] *B notes: revive!* Expunged
19–20 *original in B:*

    Make us once Thy prayses sing
    Make us once Thy mercys staye
    (Once again Thy succours bring.

B notes: ex correctione [*quotes 19–20*]
19 Lord our hartes yet once to joye θ; *Lord on us Thy folk to joy B (margin).*   21 What] Why *B*   23 whome he love doth beare] whom he love dos beare *B*; them hee love doth beare *N*; *B notes: them, that do him feare* expunged   24 lest] Least *B, I, K, χ*   25 nigh] might σ

how can then his glory misse
    shortly to enlight our land?
        Mercy now and truth shall meete:
        Peace with kisse shall Justice greete.   30

Truth shall spring in ev'ry place,
    as the hearb, the earthes attire:
Justices long absent face
    heav'n shall show, and Earth admire.
        then Jehova on us will   35
        good on good in plenty throw:
        then shall we in gladdnes mow,
    wheras now in grief we till.
        then before him in his way
        all goe right, not one shall stray.   40

Inclina Domine.
Psalm 86.

Æternall lord, thine eare incline:
    heare me most helplesse, most oppressed:
this Client save, this servant thine,
    whose hope is whole to thee addressed.
        on me Jehova, pitty take: 5
        for daily cry to thee I make.

---

28 land] lawe *O*   30 *B notes: ex* Correctione: *Peace with kisse shall Justice greet*[.] *Original in B (text):*
        Right peace with loving kisse
        Friendly shall each other greet
greete] mete *I*   33 *B notes: While of Right the lovely face* expunged   34 heav'n]
heev'ns *I, K, C*; heavens χ   35 Jehova] Jehovah θ; the Almighty *B*   38 wheras]
when as *I, K, N, σ, G, M*
39–40 *B notes: Ex* Correctione [*quotes* 39– 40] *Original in B (text):*
        Then before his presence shall
        Right direction rightly go
        Guiding right the stepps of All
40 stray] stay *I*

Psalm 86. *Variant in B.*
Incipit: om. θ, *Q*
1 Æternall] Eternall *I, K,* χ   lord] God σ, *M*   thine] thy *I, K, N, C*   2 helplesse]
helps *I*   3 this Client . . . servant] Thy Servant . . . Client *M*   5 Jehova] Jehovah θ

thy servantes soule from depth of saddnes
that climes to thee, advance to gladdnes.

O lord, I know thee good and kind,
10   on all that aske much mercy spending:
then heare ô lord with heedfull mynd
        these carefull suites of my commending.
        I only call when much I neede:
        needes of thy help I then must speed:
15   a god like whom, (if gods be many)
        who is, or doth, there is not any.

And therefore, lord, before thy face
        all Nations which thy hand hath framed,
shall come with low adoring grace,
20   and praise the name upon thee named.
        for thou art greate, and thou alone
        dost wonders, god, done els by none:·
        ô in thy truth my path discover,
        and hold me fast thy fearing lover.

25   Lord all my hart shall synge of thee:
        by me thy name shall still be praised,
whose goodnesse richly powr'd on me
        from lowest pitt my soule hath raised.
        and now againe mine enimies
30   doe many, mighty, prowd arise:
        by whom with hate my life is chased,
        while in their sight thou least art placed.

But thou, Jehova, swift to grace,
        on light entreaty pardon showest:
35   to wrath dost goe a heavy pace,
        and full with truth and mercy flowest.
        then turne and take of me remorse:
        with strength my weaknesse reenforce:
who in thy service have attended,
40   and of thy handmaid am descended.

9 kind] king *I*   12 these] those *C*   22 by] by by *E*   23 path] pathes *C*
26–7 *transposed in I; 27 repeated after 26, top of f. 41ᵛ*   28 lowest pitt] *underlined in*
K, glossed in a different hand in left margin: hell.   32 their] their *altered to* thy *in D*;
thy *O*   art] are *N*   33 Jehova] Jehovah *θ*   36 with] of *I, K, χ*   and] in *I*
38 strength] strenght *I*   40 am] have *I*

O lett some token of thy love
    be eminently on me placed;
some Cognisance, to teach and prove,
    that thine I am, that by thee graced.
        to dye their cheekes in shamefull hue   45
        that now with spite my soule pursue.
    eye taught how me thou doo'st deliver
    my endlesse aid and comfort giver.

Fundamenta ejus
Psalm 87.

Founded upon the hills of holinesse
    gods city stands: who more love beareth
to gates of Sion high in lowlinesse,
    then all the townes that Juda reareth.
        City of god, in gods decree   5
        what noble things are said of thee!

I will, saith he, hence foorth be numbered
    Egipt and Babell with my knowers:
that Palestine and Tyre, which combered
    the fathers, with the after-goers   10
        shall joyne: soe Æthiope from whence
        the borne shall be, as borne from hence.

Yea this, men shall of Sion signify:
    to him, and him it gave first breathing;
which highest god shall highly dignify,   15
    eternall stay to it bequeathing.

---

42 on] o *I*   44 thine I am, that] I am thine, and σ, *G, M*   45 dye] die θ, *C, G, M*
in] with σ, *G, M*   47 eye taught] Yea taught *N; om. (space left) I*   doo'st] *second* o
written over erasure of didst *in A*

Psalm 87. *Lacking in I. B has verse numbers 1–7 by lines 1, 2, 5, 7, 13, 16, 19.*
Incipit: Fundamenta *N, C, G, M; om.* θ, *Q*
3 high] hige *E*   4 that] wch *B;* of *E*   7 saith he, hence foorth] said he, hence forth
B; hencefoorth saith hee *K,* χ   numbered] *first* e *added in A*   8 Egipt] Ægypt *Q;*
Ægipt *J, E*   9 Tyre, which combered] Tyre∧ which combred *K, H, E;* Tyre∧ which
cumbred θ; Tire (which combred *N; Tire* (which cumbred *C;* Tire, (which cumbred *M*
10 after-goers∧] after-goers,) *N;* aftergoers) *C;* after goers) *G;* after-goers) *M*   11 Æthiope]
Ethiope *B, K,* χ   13 this] theis *O*   men shall] shall men *G, M*   14 gave first]
first gave *M*   15 highly] high *O*

Jehova this account shall make,
when he of his shall muster take.

That he and he, who ever named be
20   shall be as borne in Sion named:
in Sion shall my musique framed be,
of lute and voice most sweetly framed:
I will, saith he, to Sion bring
of my fresh fountaines ev'ry spring.

Domine Deus.
Psalm 88.

My god, my lord, my help, my health;
to thee my cry
doth restles fly.
both when of sunn the day
5   the treasures doth display,
and night locks up his golden wealth.

Admitt to presence what I crave:
ô bow thine eare
my cry to heare,
10   whose soule with ills and woes
so flowes, soe overflowes,
that now my life drawes nigh the grave.

With them that fall into the pitt
I stand esteem'd:
15   quite forcelesse deem'd,

---

17 Jehova] Jehovah θ this] thus *K*   24 fountaines] fountayne *J*
After Psalm 87, *B has*, Ps. LXXXVIII, *then notes (with a pointing hand in left margin):* But
here all the leaves are torn off, to the 23 verse of the CII. Psalms, to be supplyd if possible
from some other Copy, of which there is a fayre one in Trinity Colledg library in Cambridg,
and of which many yeares since I had the sight when I first began my Paraphrase[.] Sam:
Woodforde.
Psalm 88. *Lacking in B.*
Incipit: om. θ, *Q*
6 locks] lock *I*   9 cry] plaint *C*   11 overflowes] ever flowes *N, H*   12 nigh
the] neer the *I, K*; neere my χ grave] *K underlines* grave *and notes in different ink in a
different hand in the right margin:* hell.

          as one who free from strife,
          and sturr of mortall life,
among the dead at rest doth sitt.

Right like unto the murdred sort,
          who in the grave   20
          their biding have:
                  whom now thou dost no more
                  remember as before,
quite, quite cut of from thy support.

Throwne downe into the grave of graves   25
          in darknes deepe
          thou do'st me keepe:
                  where lightning of thy wrath
                  upon me lighted hath,
all overwhelm'd with all thy waves.   30

Who did know me, whome I did know,
          remov'd by thee
          are gone from me
                  are gone? that is the best:
                  they all me so detest,   35
that now abrode I blush to goe.

My wasted ey doth melt away
          fleeting amaine
          in streames of paine
                  while I my praiers send,   40
                  while I my hands extend,
to thee my god and faile noe day.

Alas, my lord, wilt then be tyme,
          when men are dead,
          thy truth to spread?   45
                  shall they, whome death hath slaine,
                  to praise thee live againe,
and from their lowly lodgings clime?

---

18 dead] deed *I*   21 biding] bodies *θ*   22 now] *om.* χ   no] never *Q*   24 of]
off *J*   28 lightning] lightninges *Q*   30 overwhelm'd with all] overwhelmed with
G, M   33 *the whole line is repeated at the top of f. 72ᵛ and stricken in gold in A*   35 me
so] wee see *θ*   43 my lord] (my God) *M*   wilt] wil't *J*; will *I, K,* χ   be tyme]
betime *O, H*   48 lodgings] *A, C, G, M*; lodging *I, K,* χ

Shall buried mouthes thy mercies tell?
50   dust and decay
              thy truth display?
                    and shall thy workes of mark
                    shine in the dreadfull dark?
thy Justice where oblivions dwell?

55   Good reason then I cry to thee,
              and ere the light
              salute thy sight,
                    my plaint to thee direct.
                    lord why dost thou reject
60   my soule, and hide thy face from me?

Ay me, alas, I faint, I dy,
              so still, so still,
              thou dost me fill,
                    and hast from yongest yeares,
65   with terrifying feares,
that I in traunce amaz'd doe ly.

All over me thy furies past:
              thy feares my mind
              doe fretting bind
70   flowing about mee soe,
                    as flocking waters flow:
no day can overrun their haste.

Who erst to me were neare and deare
              farr now, ô farr
75   disjoyned ar:
                    and when I would them see,
                    who my accquaintance be,
as darknesse they to me appeare.

---

49 mercies] mercie *I, K, χ*   54 oblivions] oblivion *F, I, θ*; oblivious *σ*; *the letter before*
s *in K is unclear,* n *or* u   56 ere] er *I, σ, C, M*   the] thy *θ*   57 thy] my *N, C, G, M*
61 Ay] Ah *N*   alas] alay *I*   65 feares] teares *M*   66 doe] doth *G*   69 fret-
ting] fettring *I, χ*; fetteringe *K, M*   bind] finde *E*   70 flowing] flocking *Q, E, G, M*;
floweinge *altered to* flockinge *in H*   mee] *added in a hand resembling the J hand above caret in*
A; om. F, J   71 flocking] floweing *E, Q, G, M* flockinge *altered to* floweinge *in H*
72 their haste] theiy hast *I*   73 were] weare *H, Q*   74 farr now] fall now *I*
ô farr] o fall *I*   76 would] should *θ*   78 they] thy *H*

Misericordias Domini.
Psalm 89.

The constant promises, the loving graces,
    that cause our debt, eternall lord to thee,
till ages shall fill up their still void spaces,
    my thankfull songues unalt'red theme shalbe.
    for of thy bounty thus my thoughtes decree: 5
It shalbe fully built, as fairely founded:
    and of thy truth attesting heav'ns shall see
the boundlesse periods, though theirs be bounded.

Loe I have leagu'd, thou saist with my ellected,
    and thus have to my servant David sworne: 10
thy Ofspring kings, thy throne in state erected
    by my support all threates of tyme shall scorne.
    and lord, as running skies with wheeles unworne
cease not to lend this wonder their commending:
    soe with one minded praise no lesse adorne   15
this truth the holy troopes thy Court attending.

For who among the cloudes with thee compareth?
    what angell there thy paragon doth raigne?
whose majesty, whose peerelesse force declareth
    the trembling awe of thine immortall traine.   20
    lord god whom Hostes redoubt, who can maintaine
with thee in powrfullnes a Rivalls quarrell?
    strongest art thou, and must to end remaine,
whome compleate faith doth armor-like apparrell.

Psalm 89. *Lacking in B. K notes in a different hand:* This is otherwise translated[.] *Variant, as well as regular version, in I.*
Incipit: Misericordias Domine *K*; Miserecordias Domine *H, E*; Miserecordias Dei *N*; Miserecordias *I, C; om. θ, Q*
3 ages] ages ages *J*   still void] still void <void> *A*; still void *J*; void void *F*; endles *I, K, χ*
4 theme] theme *written (in different ink and in a hand resembling the* J *hand) over erasure of* thine *in A*; thine *altered to* theme *in J*; thine *F*; theames *N*   8 periods] period *θ, σ*
theirs] their<s> *E*   9 my] mine *M*; thine *G*   11 Ofspring] offspring *J, N, C, M*
12 my] *added in gold above gold caret in A*   14 lend] laud \lend/ [*added in a different hand*] *K*   their] ther *K*; there *H*   15 minde$_\wedge$ praise] mind \with/ praise [with *added above caret in different ink*] *K*; minde$_\wedge$ praises *θ, σ, Q*; mine$_\wedge$ and praise *I*; mind$_\wedge$ our praise *N, C*; minde, praises *E, M*; mynd, (praises *G*   adorne$_\wedge$] ~, *N*   16 truth$_\wedge$] ~, *I, K, D, σ, M*; ~,) *G*   the] thy *M*   17 among the cloudes with thee] with thee among the clowds *I, K, χ*   20 thine] thy *K, χ*   traine] fame *I*   21 whom] of *O* who] who<m> *O*

25   Thy lordlie check the Seas proud courage quailed,
          and highly swelling lowly made reside:
      To crush stout Phaaro thy arme prevailed:
          what one thy foe did undisperst abide?
          the heav'n, the Earth, and all in bosome wide
30   this huge rounde Engin clipps, to thee pertaineth:
          which firmly based, not to shake, or slide,
      the unseene hinge of North and South sustaineth.

      For North and South were both by thee created,
          and those crosse pointes our bounding hills behould,
35   Thabor and Hermon, in whose joy related
          thy glorious grace from West to East is told.
          thy arme all pow'r, all puisance doth enfold:
      thy lifted hand a might of wonder showeth:
          Justice and Judgment doe thy throne uphold;
40   before thy presence Truth with Mercy goeth.

      Happy the people, who with hasty running
          poast to thy Court when trumpets tryumph blow:·
      on pathes enlighted by thy faces sunning
          their stepps, Jehova, unoffended goe.
45   thy name both makes them gladd and holds them soe:
      high thought into their hartes thy Justice powreth:
          the worshipp of their strength from thee doth flow,
      and in thy love their springing Empire flowreth.

      For by Jehovas shield stand we protected,
50   and thou gav'st Israel their sacred king,
      what time in vision thus thy word directed
          thy loved Prophet: ayd I will you bring

---

26 highly swelling lowly made] swelling high, did lowly make *M*   27 stout] proude *O*,
σ, G, M   Phaaro] Pharoh *O*; Pharo *D*; Pharaoh *J, σ, C*; Pharoah *N*; Pharoa *G, M*   arme]
hand *M*   prevailed] u, *i.e.* v, *added above caret in darker ink in A*   28 one] on *K, σ*
foe] face *N*   29 heav'n] *heavens G, M*   31 or] to *I, K, χ*; <nor [not?]> to
H   32 hinge] kinge *E*   34 bounding] bordering *G, M*   36 from West to
East] from East to west *J*; to East and West *I, K, χ* 37 arme] armes *E*; name *C*   all
pow'r] of powre *F*   enfold] unfould *θ*   38 hand] *Arme G*   39 doe] doth *σ*
42 Court] *Courtes M*   tryumph] triumphes *I, K, θ, N, C, σ*   43 enlighted]
enlightned *N, G, M*   by] with *θ*   44 Jehova] Jehovah *K, θ*   45 both] *om. I*
46 thought] thoughts *I, N, C, G, M*   47 worshipp] glory *G, M*   flow] growe
G   48 flowreth] flow\r/eth *K*; floweth *θ, N, C, Q*   49 For] So *N*   Jehovas] Jehova's
N, C, G, M; Jehovahs *I, K, O*; Jehovaes *σ*   52 ∧thy loved Prophet:] (~,) *G*; ∧~) *M*

against that violence your state doth wring
from one among my folk by choise appointed;
    David my servant: him to act the thing   55
have I with holy oile my self anointed.

My hand shall bide his never-failing piller,
    and from myne arme shall he derive his might:
not closly undermin'd by cursed willer,
    nor overthrown by foe in open fight.   60
    for I will quaile his vexers in his sight:
all that him hate by me shall be mischaunced
    my truth my clemency on him shall light
and in my name his hed shall be advaunced.

Advaunced so that twixt the watry borders   65
    of seas and flouds this noble land define,
all shall obay, subjected to the orders,
    which his imperious hand for laws shall signe.
    he unto me shall say: thou father mine,
thou art my god the fort of my salvation: 70
    and I my first-bornes roome will him assigne,
more highly thron'd then king of greatest nation.

While circling time, still ending and begining,
    shall runne the race where stopp nor start appeares:
my bounty towards him, not ever linning,   75
    I will conserve nor write my league in yeares.
    nay more, his sonnes, whome fathers love enderes,
shall find like blisse for legacie bequeathed;
    a stedfast throne I say, till heav'nly Spheares
shall faint in course, where yet they never breathed.   80

Now if his children doe my lawes abandon,
    and other pathes then my plaine Judgments chuse:

54 from] for *θ*   55 the] *F, J, I, K, χ;* the the *A*   58 myne] my *F, G, M*   60 foe]
foes *G, M*   61 *bracket and* I 168 *or* I 169 [8 *altered to* 9 *or vice versa*] *written in pencil in
margin of A*   his sight] h sight *I*   62 hate] harme *G, M*   64 hed] *horne G*
68 laws] s *added in darker ink in A;* law *F, θ*   signe] singue *I*   70 my god] the
God *M*   71 my first-bornes roome will him] my first borne roome [*K:* rowme] will
him *K, χ;* will him my first borne roome *C*   72 greatest] highest *G, M*   74 stopp_∧
nor start] stopp, no start *σ;* start_∧ nor stopp *G, M*   75 linning] endinge *θ*
79 Spheares] speers [?] *I*   82 pathes_∧ then_∧] ~, ~, *I, H, Q*   Judgments] judgment
θ, N, σ

breake my behestes prophanely walke at randon,
and what I bidd with froward hart refuse:
85   I meane indeede on their revolt to use
correcting rodd, their sinne with whipps to chasten:
not in their fault my loves defect excuse
nor loose the promise, once my faith did fasten.

My league shall hold, my word persist unchanged:
90   once sworne I have, and sworne in holinesse;
never shall I from David be estranged,
his seede shall ever bide, his seate no lesse.
the daies bright guide, the nightes pale governesse
shall claime no longer lease of their enduring:
95   whome I behold as heav'nly wittnesses
in tearmlesse turnes, my tearmlesse truth assuring.

And yet, ô now by thee abjected, scorned,
scorcht with thy wrath is thy anointed one:
hated his league, the crowne him late adorned,
100   puld from his head, by thee, augments his moane.
raz'd are his fortes: his walls to ruine gone:
not simplest passenger but on hym praieth:
his neighbours laugh: of all his haters none,
but boasts his wrack and at his sorrow plaieth.

105   Takes he his weapon? thou the edge rebatest:
comes to the field to fight? thou makest him fly:
would march with kingly pomp? thou him unstatest:
ascend his throne? it overthrowne doth ly:
his ages spring and prime of jollity
110   winter of wo before the day defineth
for praise, reproche, for honor, infamy,
he over-loden beares, and bearing pineth.

How long ô lord, what still in dark displeasure
wilt thou thee hide? and shall thine angry thought

83 prophanely] and plainly *I, K, χ*; and loosely *G, M*   84 hart] hearts *M*; hard *I*
87 their] *added in gold above gold caret in A*   fault] faultes *M*   88 loose] lose *D*; breake
G, M   the] my *O*   96 tearmlesse turnes] turnless turne *χ*; turneles turnes *C, G, M*
98 one] me *I*   101 raz'd] ras'd *θ*   fortes] forces *J, Q, E*   102 praieth] preyeth *N*
104 boasts] boast *K*   105 rebatest] abatest *D*   106 comes] *A, I, K, C*; Come *χ*
makest] *A, J, H, E*; makst' *F, I (* h *altered to* t*), K, χ*; makes *O*   107 with] in *O*   un-
statest] understand *I*   109 prime] time *I, K, χ*   112 over-loden] overladen *K, C,*
G, M   113 How] H [*hole in paper*] *I*   114 thine] *A, C*; thy *I, K, χ*

still flame? ô thinck how short our ages measure;   115
    thinck if we all created were for nought,
    for who is he whom birth to life hath brought,
but life to death, and death to grave subjecteth?
    from this necessity (let all be sought)
no priviledg exemptes, noe age protecteth.   120

Kind lord, where is the kindnesse once thou swarest,
    swarest in truth thy Davids stock should find?
Show lord, yet show thou for thy servant carest,
    holding those shames in unforgetting mind,
    which we embosom'd beare of many a kind: 125
But all at thee and at thy Christ directed:
    to endlesse whom be endlesse praise assign'd,
be this, againe I saie, be this effected.

Domine, refugium.
Psalm 90.

Thou our refuge, thou our dwelling,
    ô lord, hast byn from time to time:
long er Mountaines proudly swelling
    above the lowly dales did clime:
    long er the Earth, embowl'd by thee   5
      bare the forme it now doth beare:
    yea thou art god for ever, free
      from all touch of age and yeare.

O but man by thee created,
    as he at first of earth arose,   10

115 short] short's *N, G, M*; shall *I*   116 were] weare *F, H*   117 life] light *K*
119 necessity (let all be sought)] ~∧ ~∧ *K, θ*; ~, ~, *N, G, M*; ~∧ ~: *C*   120 exemptes]
exempteth *I*   age] *A, M*; aide *K, χ*   121 swarest] swareth *I*   122 should find]
om. I   123 Show] thow *I*   servant] servants *K, χ*   125 we] me *altered to* we in
D; me *O*   kind] king *I*   128 I saie, be this] be this I saie *D*

Psalm 90. *Lacking in B, I.*
Incipit: om. θ, Q
2 byn] bin *D*; bine *H, Q, E*; been *F, K, χ*   3 er] ere *F, K, θ, H, N, C, G*   4 lowly]
lov'lie *K*   5 er] ere *F, K, O, N, G*   the Earth] th'earth *K, N, C*   embowl'd]
emboweld *N*   6 bare] beare *σ*   7 for] from *O*   8 and] or *E*

when thy word his end hath dated,
 in equall state to earth he goes.
  thou saist, and saying makst it soe:
   be noe more, ô Adams heyre;
15   from whence you came, dispatch to goe,
    dust againe, as dust you were.

Graunt a thousand yeares be spared
 to mortall men of life and light:
what is that to thee compared?
20   one day, one quarter of a night.
    when death upon them storm-like falls,
    like unto a dreame they grow:
    which goes and comes as fancy calls,
    nought in substance all in show.

25 As the hearb that early groweth,
  which leaved greene and flowred faire
ev'ning chang with ruine moweth,
  and laies to rost in withering aire:
   soe in thy wrath we fade away,
30   with thy fury overthrowne:
    when thou in sight our faultes dost lay,
    looking on our synns unknown.

Therefore in thy angry fuming,
 our life of daies his measure spends:
35 all our yeares in death consuming,
   right like a sound that sounded ends.
    our daies of life make seaventy yeares,
    eighty, if one stronger be:
    whose cropp is laboures, dollors, feares,
40   then away in poast we flee.

Yet who notes thy angry power
 as he should feare soe fearing thee?
make us count each vitall hower
 make thou us wise, we wise shall be.

11 hath] had *F, E* 13 makst] makes *M* 15 you] *A, E;* yee *K,* χ 16 you]
A, E, G, M; yee *K,* χ were] weare *H, Q* 18 men] man *C, G, M* 19 thee] bee
K, χ 23 goes and comes] comes and goes *C* 24 nought] naught *K, H, N*
25 that] which σ 27 ev'ning] Evenings *M* 29 thy] *om. E* 34 our] his *C*
daies] joyes *M* 35 death] dearth *F* 39 laboures] labor *K,* θ, *C* 40 flee] flie θ

turne Lord: shall these things thus goe still?   45
    lett thy servantes peace obtaine:
us with thy joyfull bounty fill,
    endlesse joyes in us shall raigne.

Glad us now as erst we greeved:
    send yeares of good for yeares of ill: 50
when thy hand hath us releeved,
    show us and ours thy glory still.
      both them and us not one exempt,
      with thy beauty beautify:
      supply with aid what we attempt,   55
      our attempts with aid supply.

Qui habitat.
Psalm 91.

To him the highest keepes
    in closet of his care:
who in thallmighties shadow sleepes,
    for one affirme I dare:
      Jehova is my fort   5
    my place of safe repaire:
      my god in whom of my support
    all hopes reposed are.

From snare the fowler laies
    he shall thee sure unty: 10
the noisome blast that plaguing straies
    untoucht shall passe thee by.
      soft hiv'd with wing and plume
    thou in his shrowd shalt ly
      and on his truth noe lesse presume,   15
    then most in shield affy.

47 joyfull] wilfull *σ*   53 not one] and not *E*   56 still with help lord us supplie *G*
(a word erased before still*)*; Still with aide lord us supply *M*   attempts] attempt *K*

Psalm 91. *Lacking in B.*
Incipit: Habitans in *I; om. θ, Q*
3 thallmighties] th'allmightie *K*   5 Jehova] Jehovah *θ*   my] *om. M*   10 thee] be *I*
11 blast] blastes *C, M*   plaguing] plaugeinge *Q*; plauginge *H, E*   13 soft] sast *I*

Not mov'd with frightfull night
    nor arow shott by day:
though plague I say in darknesse fight,
20   and wast at noontide slay.
        nay all be thousands here,
    ten thousands there decay:
        that Ruine to approch thee nere,
    shall finde no force nor way.

25 But thou shalt live to see,
    and seeing to relate,
what recompences shared be
    to ev'ry godlesse mate.
        when once thou mak'st the lord
30   protector of thy state;
        and with the highest canst accord
    to dwell within his gate:

Then ill, nay cause of ill,
    shall farr excluded goe:
35 nought thee to hurt, much lesse to kill,
    shall nere thy lodging grow.
        for Angells shall attend
    by him commanded soe:
        and thee in all such waies defend,
40   as his directions show.

To beare thee with regard
    their hands shall both be spred:
thy foote shall never dash to hard,
    against the stone misled.
45   Soe thou on Lions goe
    soe on the Aspicks head:
        on Lionet shalt hurtlesse soe
    and on the Dragon tread.

---

17 night] might *altered to* night *in K, D*; might χ   19 plague] plauge *H, Q*   say] ay *written in darker ink over* ee *in A*   21 all be] allbee *J, I, K, N, C, H, G*; albeet *E*; albe't *M* here] heare *H, Q*   23 that Ruine] <th ten [?]> that *I*   24 no] nor *I, K,* χ 25 to] *om. O*   27 recompences] recompence shall *M*; recompence σ   31 canst] cause *I*   33 nay] way *N,* σ   34 excluded] x *written over* n *in A*; x *written over erasure in J*; encluded *F*   35 nought] naught *C*   42 be] hee *I*   44 against] againe *O*   47 Lionet] Lyonesse *F*; Lyones [s *written over* t *or vice versa*] *H, E*   shalt hurtlesse] shall hurtles *N, C, H, Q*; shalt hartless *E*; that hurtles *I*   soe] goe *Q*

Loe me saith god he loves,
I therfore will him free:
my name with knowledg he approves,
that shall his honor be.
he asks when paines are rife,
and streight recev'd doth see
help, glory, and his fill of life,
with endlesse health from me.

50

55

Bonum est confiteri.
Psalm 92.

O lovly thing,
to sing and praises frame,
to thee, ô lord, and thy high name
with early spring
thy bounty to display,
thy truth when night hathe vanquisht day
yea soe to sing,
that ten string'd instrument
with lute, and harp, and voice consent.

5

For, lord my mind
thy works with wonder fill;
thy doings are my comfort still.
what witt can find,
how bravely thou hast wrought?
or deeply sound thy shallowst thought?
the foole is blind,
and blindly doth not know,
how like the grasse the wicked grow.

10

15

The wicked grow
like fraile, though flowry grasse:

20

55 glory] gro'rie *I*   56 health] help *I*

Psalm 92. *Lacking in B, I.*
Incipit: Bonum est Confitere *H, E*; Bonum est *N, C, G, M*; *om. θ, Q*
1 O] *written over erasure of* A *in A*   6 night hathe] u *altered to* th *in* hathe *in A*; night
have *F*; night hat *C*; might hath *N*   vanquisht] *A (* qu *added in gold above gold caret), F, J,
N*; vanisht *K, χ*   20 though] through *F*

> and falne, to wrack past help doe passe.
> But thou not soe,
> but high thou still dost stay:
> and loe thy haters fall away.
25   thy haters loe,
> decay and perish all;
> all wicked hands to ruine fall.
>
> Fresh oiled I
> will lively lift my horne,
30   and match the matchlesse Unicorne:·
> Mine ey shall spy
> My spies in spightfull case:
> mine eare shall heare my foes disgrace.
> like Cedar high
35   and like Date-bearing tree,
> for greene, and growth the just shall be.
>
> Where god doth dwell
> shall be his spreading place:
> gods Courts shall his faire bowes embrace.
40   even then shall swell
> his blossoms fatt and faire,
> when aged rinde the stock shall beare.
> and I shall tell
> how god my Rock is just,
45   so just, with him is nought unjust.

Dominus regnavit.
Psalm 93.

> Cloth'd with state and girt with might,
> Monark-like Jehova raignes:

---

21 doe] doth *E*   22 But] Yet *G, M*   24 loe] loe [e *writen over* w] *E*; lo<we> *D*;
lowe *K, O, N, C, G, M*   26 all] shall *C*   33 mine] my *F*   35 and] Or *C*
39 Courts] s *added in different ink in A and J*; Court *F, K, χ*   bowes] bowghes *C*; boughes
θ, N, G, M   40 swell] dwell *θ*   41 blossoms] blessinge *Q*   42 rinde] ryne *E*
45 is] *om. F*

Psalm 93. *Lacking in B.*
Incipit: Dominus regna. *I*; Dominus Regnavitt *H*; *om. θ, Q.*
1 with state] in *State I, K, χ*   2 Jehova] Jehovah *I, K, O*

he who Earthes foundation pight,
     pight at first, and yet sustaines.
     he whose stable throne disdaines   5
Motions shock, and ages flight:
     he who endles one remaines,
one, the same, in changlesse plight.

Rivers, yea though Rivers rore,
     roring though sea-billowes rise;   10
vex the deepe, and breake the shore,
     stronger art thou lord of skies.
     firme and true thy promise lies
Now and still, as heretofore:
     holy worshipp never dies   15
in thy howse where we adore.

Deus ultionum.
Psalm 94.

God of revenge, revenging god, appeare:
     to recompence the proud, Earthes judge arise.
how long, ô lord, how long, unpunisht beare
     shall these vile men their joyes, their jolities?
     how long thus talk, and talking tiranize?   5
        cursedly doe and doing proudly bost?
        this people crush by thee affected most?
this land afflict, where thy possession lies?

For these the widow and the stranger slay:
     these work the Orphans deadly overthrow.   10
god shall not see then in their thoughts they say,
     the god of Jacob he shall never know.
     o fooles this folly when will you forgoe,
        and wisdome learne? who first the eare did plant,

---

3 foundation] foundations *N, M*   5 throne] state *M*   9 yea] you *θ*   though]
thought *I*   12 thou] then *O*   13 lies] *A, I, K, N*; ties *χ*
Psalm 94. *Lacking in B.*
Incipit: om. θ, Q.
6 cursedly] Cursed *E*   7 affected] afflicted *E*   11 see] so *I*   then] them *θ, G, M*
ᴧin . . . sayᴧ] (~ . . . ~) *G, M*   13 you] yee *θ, C, G, M*

15   shall he him self not heare? sight shall he want,
     from whose first workmanshipp the eye did grow?

     Who checks the world shall he not you reprove?
          shall knowledg lack, who all doth knowledg lend?
     nay ev'n the thoughts of men who raignes above,
20   he knowes, and knowes they more then vainly end.
          then blest who in thy schoole his age doth spend;
              whom thou ô lord dost in thy law enforme.
              thy harbour shall him shrowd from ruines storme,
     while pitts are dig'd where such men shall descend.

25   for sure the lord his folk will not forsake,
          but ever prove to his possession true;
     Judgment againe the course of Justice take,
          and all right hartes shall god their guide ensue.
          see, if you doubt: against the canckred crue,
30   those mischief-masters, who for me did stand?
              the lord, none els: but for whose aiding hand,
     scilence by now had held my soule in mew:

     But lord thy goodnes did me then uphold,
          ev'n when I said now, now I faint, I fall:
35   and quailed in mind-combats manifold
          thie consolations did my joyes recall.
          then what society hold'st thou at all,
              what frendshipp with the throne of missery?
              which law pretends, intends, but injury,
40   and Justice doth unjust vexation call?

     To counsell where conspired Caitives flock
          the just to slay, and faultlesse bloud to spill?
     O no: my god Jehova is my Rock,
          my rock of refuge, my defensive hill,

---

18 all doth] doth all *I*   19 thoughts] thought *θ, N, σ*   raignes] raigne *I*   20 knowes, and knowes∧] ~, (~) *G*; ~, (~ knowe) *M*   vainly] vainlier *I*   21 thy] the *N*   22 law] lay *I*   23 ruines] ruyns *or* rayns *H*; raynie *Q, E*   24 while pitts] wher pits *D*; where pigc [?] *O*   25 his folk will not] will not his folke *K*   29 see] so *σ*   30 those] Theis *G, M*   35 quailed in mind-combats] quail<e>d in minde \with/ combatts *K*; quailed in minde with combats *Q, E*; quald in mind in combats *I*   36 consolations] consolation *J*   joyes] woes *θ*   37 hold'st] shouldst *O*   39 intends] intend *I*   40 doth] dost *I*   41 counsell] councell *I, θ, σ, G, M*   Caitives] *om. M*   43 O no] on *I*   Jehova] Jehovah *θ*

he on their heades shall well repay their ill: 45
    Jehova, loe! the god in whome we joy,
    destroy them shall, shall them at once destroy:
and what the meane? their owne malicious will.

Venite exultemus.
Psalm 95.

Come, come lett us with joyfull voice
    record and raise
    Jehovas praise:
come lett us in our safties Rock rejoyce.
        into his presence lett us goe 5
        and there with Psalmes our gladdnes show
    for he is god, a god most greate,
    above all gods a king in kingly seate

What lowest lies in earthy masse,
    what highest stands, 10
    stands in his hands:
the Sea is his, and he the Sea-wright was.
        he made the Sea, he made the shore:
        come let us fall, lett us adore:
    come let us kneele with awfull grace, 15
    before the lord, the lord our makers face.

He is our god, he doth us keepe:
    we by him ledd,
    and by him fedd,
his people are, we are his pasture sheepe. 20
        to day if he some speach will use,
        doe not, ô doe not you refuse

45 their ill] them ill χ   46 Jehova] Jehovah θ   loe] lord N   in] on I   47 shall them] yea them M   48 the] they I, K, χ

Psalm 95. *Lacking in B, I.*
Incipit: om. θ, Q
1 Come, come lett us] Come now, let us G; Come, let us now M   3 Jehovas] Jehova's H, C, G, M; Jehovahs D; Jehovah's (?) N; Jehovaes H, Q; Jehovah O   6 Psalmes] P *written in gold over erased* S *in* A; phalmes O   7 he is] he's a C   8 gods] goodes E
11 stands] is G, M   15 kneele] fall σ, G, M   16 the lord, the lord] the lord θ
20 pasture] pastures θ

with hardned hartes his voice to heare,
as Masha now, or Meriba it were.

25   Where me your fathers, god doth say,
did angring move,
and tempting prove:
yet oft had seene my workes before that day.
twise twenty times my poast the sunn,
30   his yearly race to end had runn,
while this fond Nation bent to ill,
did tempt, and try, and vex and greeve me still.

Which when I saw, thus said I, loe,
these men are madd,
35   and too too badd
erre in their harts; my waies they will not know.
thus therefore unto them I sweare:
(I angry can noe more forbeare)
the rest for you I did ordaine,
40   I will soe work you never shall obtaine.

Cantate Domino.
Psalm 96.

Sing and let the song be new,
unto him that never endeth:
sing all Earth and all in you.
sing to god and blesse his name,
5   of the help, the health he sendeth,
daie by day new ditties frame.

Make each country know his worth;
of his actes the wondred story

25 me . . . doth] mee . . . did *G*; once . . . did *M*   26 angring] angry *θ, Q, M*   29 times]
yeeres *θ*   33 thus] this *K*   35 too too] two to *K*   36 erre] err *σ, C, G, M*; er
K, θ   38 angry] anger *N*   can noe] cannott *F*   40 obtaine] attaine *θ*

Psalm 96. *Lines 17, 20 not indented in A because of gold capitals,* M, O. *Lacking in B. Top half
of f. 68ᵛ blank in K.*
Incipit: om. θ, Q
3 and] om. *K*   4 *not fully indented in A*   5 help] health *Q*   health] help *I, Q*

paint unto each people forth.
    for Jehova greate alone   10
  all the gods, for awe and glory
    farre above doth hold his throne.

For but Idolls what are they,
    whom besides madd Earth adoreth?
he the skies in frame did lay: 15
    Grace and Honor are his guides
    Majesty his temple storeth:
    Might in guard about him bides.

Kindreds come Jehova give,
    give Jehova all together,   20
force and fame whereso you live.
    give his name the glory fitt:
    take your Offrings gett you thither,
    where he doth enshrined sitt.

Goe adore him in the place   25
    where his pompe is most displaied:
Earth ô goe with quaking pace.
    goe proclaime Jehova king:
    staylesse world shall now be staied;
    Righteous doome his rule shall bring.   30

Starry roofe, and earthy floore,
    sea and all thy widnesse yeldeth:
now rejoyce and leape and rore.
    leavy Infants of the wood,
    fieldes and all that on you fieldeth,   35
    daunce ô daunce, at such a good.

For Jehova commeth loe!
    loe to raigne Jehova commeth:

---

10 Jehova] Jehovah θ   12 his] *om. I*   13 For but] For *added at the beginning of the
line in different ink and a hand resembling the J hand; original* B *erased, replaced by* b; *original
for stricken after* but *in A*; For but *written over erasure of* But for *in same ink and hand in J*; But
for *F*; ffor but *I, K, χ*   14 whom] what *I*   ∧besides∧] *F, J, K, χ*; ∧bsides∧ *A*; (~) *M*
madd Earth adoreth] made earth adoreth *O*; *om. (space left) I*   16 Honor] glorie *G*
18 bides] guides *E*; rides *M*   19 Kindreds] Kinreds *K, O, N, C, G*   Jehova]
Jehovah θ   20 give] *I, K, χ*; O give *A*   Jehova] Jehovah θ   28 Jehova] Jehovah θ
31 floore] flooaer [oa *written over* w (?)] *H*; flower *E*   32 sea] see *I*   thy] your *M*
35 fieldes] ffeild *H, E*   fieldeth] feedeth *I, K, χ*   36 ô daunce] advance *I*
37 Jehova] Jehovah *J, θ*   38 loe] Now *M*   Jehova] Jehovah θ

under whome you all shall goe.
40   He the world shall rightly guide:
truly as a king becommeth,
for the peoples weale provide.

Dominus regnavit.
Psalm 97.

Jehova coms to raigne
rejoyce ô Earthy maine:
you Isles with waves enclosed,
be all to joy disposed.
5   Cloudes him round on all sides,
and pitchy darknesse hides.
Justice and judgment stand
as propps on either hand,
whereon his throne abides.

10   The fire before him goes,
to asshes turnes his foes:
his flashing lightnings maketh,
that Earth beholding quaketh.
The mountaines at his sight,
15   his sight that is by right
the lord of all this all,
doe fast on melting fall;
as wax by fiers might.

The heav'ns his justice tell,
20   noe lesse they all that dwell
and have on earth their beeing
are gladd his glory seeing.
shame then, shame may you see,
that Idoll-servers be:

39 you] *A, M*; yee *K, χ*; ye *I*   goe] rightly guide *I*

Psalm 97. *Lacking in B, I.*
Incipit: om. θ, Q
1 Jehova] Jehovah *θ*   2 Earthy] *A, θ*; earthly *K, N, C, σ, G, M*   4 joy] mirth *M*
8 propps] propp *H, E*   on] in *θ*   9 whereon] Wherein *σ, G*   12 lightnings]
light\n/ings *F*; lightlings *K*; lighnings [h *altered to* n *after* i (?)] *D*; lightning *N, C, G*
23 you] they *G, M*

and trust in Idolls place. 25
but let before his face
all Angells bow their knee.

When Sion this did heare,
how did hir joyes appeare!
    how weare to mirth invited 30
    all townes in Juda sited!
        for thou lord rulest right:
        thou thron'd in glory bright
            sitt'st high: they all by thee
            be rul'd who Rulers be, 35
        thy might above all might.

Who love god, love him still:
and haters be of ill.
    for he their lives preserveth,
    whome he as his reserveth 40
        Now light and joy is sowne
        to be by good men mowne.
            you just with joyfull voice
            then in the lord rejoyce:
        his holynesse make knowne. 45

Cantate Domino.
Psalm 98.

O sing Jehova, he hath wonders wrought,
    a song of praise that newnesse may commend:
his hand, his holy arme alone have brought
    conquest on all that durst with him contend.
    he that salvation his elect attend, 5
        long hid, at length hath sett in open view:

---

28 heare] a *added above* r *in A* 30 weare] *A, H;* were *K, χ* 31 sited] cited *O*
34 by] be *O* 37 Who love] Who loves *G, M* 39 lives] lawes *Q*
Psalm 98. *Lacking in B.*
Incipit: om. θ, Q
1 Jehova] Jehovah *θ* wonders] wondrous *I* 2 that] the *I* 3 have] hath *F, I,*
K, χ 4 all] *om. O* 6 hid] held *E*

and now the unbeleeving Nations taught
        his heavn'ly justice yelding each their due.

His bounty and his truth the motives were,
10   promis'd of yore to Jacob and his race
which ev'ry Margine of this earthy spheare
        now sees performed in his saving grace.
        then earth, and all possessing earthy place,
        ô sing, ô shout, ô triumph, ô rejoyce:
15   make Lute a part with vocall musique beare,
        and entertaine this king with trumpetts noise.

Rore Sea, and all that trace the bryny sands:
        thou totall globe and all that thee enjoy:
you streamy Rivers clapp your swymming hands:
20   you Mountaines echo each at others joy.
        see on the lord this service you imploy,
            who comes of earth the crowne and rule to take:
and shall with upright justice judg the lands,
        and equall lawes, among the dwellers make.

                Dominus regnavit.
                Psalm 99.

            What if nations rage and frett?
            what if earth doe ruine threate?
                Loe! our state Jehova guideth,
                he that on the Cherubs rideth.

5   Greate Jehova Sion holdes,
                high above what earth enfolds:

---

8 yelding] yeedinge *Q*   their] his *altered to* their [s *erased;* t, r *added*] *in A*   9 bounty]
Bounties *σ*   the] his *σ, G, M*   were] weare *H*   11 this earthy] his earth<l[?]>ye *Q*;
his earthlye *E*; this *Earthly M*; this heav'nly *C*; this *heavenly G*   13 earthy] Earthly *N, C*
14 shout] short *I*   ô rejoyce] and rejoyce *I, K, χ*   17 Sea] Seas *σ, G, M*   the] thy *M*
19 streamy] streaming *J*   clapp] claspe *K, N, C, σ, G, M*   20 at] to *O*   22 crowne
and rule] rule and Crowne *σ, G, M*   23 *indented in A*   lands] lande *I, σ*   24 among]
amongst *Q, E*

Psalm 99. *Lacking in B.*
Incipit: Dominus regn: *K*; Dqminus regnabit [b *altered to* v (?)] *I*; om. *θ, Q*
2 doe] doth *N, M*   3 Jehova] Jehovah *D*   5 Jehova] Jehovah *θ*

thence his sacred name with terror,
forceth truth from tongues of error.

Thron'd he sitts a king of might,
mighty soe, as bent to right: 10
    for how can but be maintained
    right by him who right ordained?

O then come Jehova sing:
sing our god, our lord our king:
    at the footstoole sett before him,   15
    (he is holy) come, adore him.

Moses erst and Aron soe,
(there did high in Priesthood goe)
    Samuell soe unto him crying,
    gott their sutes without denying.   20

But from cloudy Piller then
god did daine to talk with men:
    he enacting they observing,
    from his will there was no swerving.

Then our god Jehova thou,   25
unto them thy eare didst bowe:
    gratious still and kindly harted,
    though for sinne they somwhile smarted.

O then come Jehova sing:
sing our god, our lord our king.   30
    in his Sion mount before him
    (he is holy) come adore him.

---

10 bent] bend *I*   12 him] *written over* so *in I*   who right] whome right *O*; <as, bent>
\that right/ [*canceled eye skip to* 10] *I*   13 O then] O *written in gold over erased* T, t
added in A   Jehova] Jehovah θ 15 the] his θ, *G, M*   sett] *A, M*; sitt *I, K,* χ
18 there] theis *I, K,* χ 21 But] Out *I, K,* χ 24 there] their *I, N*   25 Jehova]
Jehovah θ 26 thy] thyne *J*   didst] did *N*   27 harted] hartly *F*   28 sinne]
some σ they somwhile] somewhile they *G*   29 Jehova] Jehovah θ

Jubilate Deo.
Psalm 100.

O all you landes the treasures of your joy
      in mery shout upon the lord bestow:
your service cheerfully on him imploy,
        with triumph song into his presence goe.
5   know first that he is god; and after know
this god did us, not we our selves create:
      we are his flock, for us his feedings grow:
we are his folk, and he upholds our state.
with thankfullnesse, ô enter then his gate:
10   make through each porch of his your praises ring.
all good, all grace, of his high name relate,
      he of all grace and goodnesse is the spring.
Tyme in noe termes his mercy comprehends,
from age to age his truth it self extends.

Misericordiam et judicium.
Psalm 101.

When, now appointed king, I king shall be,
      what mercy then, what justice use I will,
I here, ô lord, in song protest to thee.

Till that day come thou me the crowne shalt give,
5   deepe study I on vertue will bestow:
and pure in hart at home retired lyve.

My lowly eye shall levell at no ill:
      who fall from thee with me not one shall stand:
their waies I shall pursue with hatred still.

Psalm 100. *Lacking in B.*
Incipit: Jubilate deo omnes *θ*; *om. Q*
1 you] ye *G, M*   treasures] treasure *J*   2 mery shout] me<a>rie shoute *K*; merrye
showe *E*; pleasant songes *M*   4 song] songes *M*   5 and] then *O*   6 this]
that *C*   7 feedings] feeding *I, θ*   9 his] this *I*   12 and] all *I, K, χ*
13 Tyme] T *added in darker ink in A*   comprehends] comprehendeth *I*   14 truth it
self] blessed *truth M*   extends] extendeth *I*

Psalm 101. *Lacking in B, I.*
Incipit: Misericordiam *K*; Miserecordiam *χ*; *om. Q*
3 here] *A, M, Q*; heere *K, χ*; heare *E*   6 home] whome *H*; whom *θ*

Mischievous heads farre of from me shall goe: 10
   malicious hartes I never will admitt:
and whisp'ring biters all will overthrow.

Ill shall I brooke the proud ambitious band,
   whose eyes looke high, whose puffed hartes doe swell:
but for truth-tellers seeke and search the land.   15

Such men with me my Counsailors shall sitt:
   such evermore my Officers shall be,
men speaking right, and doing what is fitt.

Noe fraudulent within my house shall dwell:
   the cunning coyning tongue shall in my sight   20
be not endur'd, much lesse accepted well.

As soone as I in all the land shall see
   a wicked wretch, I shall him hate outright;
and of vile men Jehovas city free.

Domine exaudi
Psalm 102.

   O lord my praying heare:
     lord lett my cry come to thine eare.
   hide not thy face away,
     but haste, and aunswer me,
   in this my most most misserable day,   5
     wherein I pray, and cry to thee.

---

10 of] off *J, O*   16 Counsailors] Counsailers *E*; counsellers *O*; Councellors *D, G, M*
17 my] *A, G*; myne *K, χ*   18 right] *om. θ*   19 fraudulent] fradulent *H, E*
20 cunning coyning] cunninge=coyninge *K*; cunning-coyning *N*   23 hate outright]
roote owt=right *K, θ, N, C*; roote outquight [qui *written over* ri] *H*; roote out quite *Q, E,*
G, M   24 vile] vild [*or* vile] *O*; vilde *D*   Jehovas] Jehovahs *J, Q*; Jehovaes *σ*; Jehova's
N, C, G, M

Psalm 102. *Lines 1–72 lacking in B. Top third of f. 71ᵛ blank in K. B has verse numbers 23–7 by*
lines 73, 76, 79, 82, 85.
Incipit: Dominus exaudi *G, M; om. Q*
1 praying] praying *written above underlined* cryinge *in K*; crieing *χ*   2 lett] led *I*
4 and] *ampersand added in gold above gold caret in A*   5 my most most] my <hast
hast> most most *I*; most *χ*

My daies as smoke are past:
          my bones as flaming fuell waste:
     mowne downe in me (alas)
               with Sithe of sharpest paine,
     my hart is withered like the wounded grasse,
               my stomak doth all foode disdaine.

          Soe leane my woes me leave,
               that to my flesh my bones do cleave:
     and soe I bray and howle,
          as use to howle and bray
     the lonely Pellican and desert Owle,
          like whome I languish long the day.

          I languish soe the day,
               the night in watch I waste away;
     right as the Sparow sitts,
          bereft of spowse, or sonne:
     which irk'd alone with dolors deadly fitts
          to company will not be wonne.

               As day to day succeeds,
                    so shame on shame to me proceeds
     from them that doe me hate:
          who of my wrack soe boast,
     that wishing ill, they wish but my estate,
               yet think they wish of ills the most.

          Therefore my bread is clay,
               therefore my teares my wine alay:·
     for how els should it be,
          sith thou still angry art,
     and seem'st for nought to have advaunced me,
          but me advaunced to subvert?

10 Sithe] Sieth *M*; sigh *F, O*   11 withered] wounded *M*   the] *om. M*   wounded]
withred *M*   12 foode] good *I*   13 woes] boaes *I*   14 flesh] bones *C; Skynne
[written over erasure of* flesh] *M*   bones] flesh *C*   16 as use] and us *I*   17 lonely]
A, D; lovely *I, χ*; lov'ly *K*   18 whome] home *E*   long] all *E*   22 bereft] breav-d
[?] *Q*   23 irk'd] *om. (space left) N*   24 company] compaine *D*   28 soe] doe *K*
29 that] the *I*   30 think] thicke *K*   they wish] *om. I, K, χ*   33 how els] else,
how *M*   34 sith] since *C*   35 seem'st] seemes *Q*   for] of *O*   nought] naught *C*

The sunn of my life daies
   inclines to west with falling raies,
and I as hay am dride:
   while yet in stedfast seate   40
eternall thou eternally dost bide,
   thy memory noe yeares can freat.

   O then at length arise:
   on Sion cast thy mercies eyes.
now is the time that thou   45
   to mercy shouldst incline
concerning hir: ô lord, the tyme is now,
   thy self for mercy didst assigne.

   Thy servauntes waite the day
   when she, who like a Carcasse lay   50
stretch'd forth in Ruines beare
   shall soe arise and live,
that Nations all Jehovas name shall feare,
   all kings to thee shall glory give.

   Because thou hast a new   55
   made Sion stand, restor'd to view
thy glorious presence there?
   because thou hast I say
beheld our woes, and not refus'd to heare
   what wretched we did playning pray.   60

   This of record shall bide
   to this and ev'ry age beside:
and they commend thee shall
   whome thou a new shalt make,
that from the prospect of thy heav'nly hall   65
   thy eye of earth survey did take.

---

37 sunn] Sonne *H*   38 falling] failinge *O*   raies] raise *O*   39 am] *gold* I *stricken*
in ink before am *in A*; I am *F*   46 shouldst] shoulds *O*   47 tyme] tymes *H*
51 stretch'd] stretch *G*; shretcht *I*   in] i *written over* o, *or vice versa, in H*; on *Q, E, G, M*
beare] beere *I, K, χ*; bere [b *altered*] *N*   53 Jehovas] Jehova's *J, N, C, M*; Jehovahs
θ; Jehovaes *σ*   feare] beare *K*   54 glory] honnor *M*   55 a new] anew *F, J, I,*
K, N   59 refus'd] refuse *σ*   60 we] men *I*   playning] plainly *E*   63 com-
mend] comaund *σ*   64 a new] *A, F, C, H, E, G, M*; anew *J, I, K, χ*   65 hall] hill *I*
66 thy] The *N*   did] doth *N*

    Harkning to prisoners grones,
    and setting free condempned ones:
  that they, when Nations come,
70   and Realmes to serve the lord,
  in Sion, and in Salem might become
    fitt meanes his honor to record.

    But what is this? if I
    in the mid way should fall and dye?
75 My god to thee I pray,
    who canst my praier give;
  turne not to night the noonetide of my day,
    since endlesse thou dost aglesse live.

    The Earth the heaven stands
80   once founded, formed by thy hands:·
  they perish, thou shalt bide:
    they olde, as clothes shall weare,
  till changing still, full change shall them betide,
    uncloth'd of all the clothes they beare.

85   But thou art one, still one:
    tyme interest in thee hath none,
  then hope, who godly be,
    or come of godly Race:
  endlesse your blisse; as never ending he,
90   his presence your unchanged place.

     Benedic anima
     Psalm 103.

   My soule, my hart,
   and every inward part,

---

67 grones] cries *I*   73 *B* notes *(to the right of a pointing hand):* Here at this 23 verse My
Copy again begins   74 way] day *I*   76 praier] prayers *I, K*   77 to night]
added above caret in B   79 heaven] heavens *C, M*   83 full] all *I*   84 beare]
weare [a *written over another letter] K*; weare χ; wer *D*; were *Q*; wee are *I*   86 hath]
have *C*   87 hope] help *Q*   88 or] are *I*   89 endlesse your] Your endles *G*
90 Shall ever be, before his face *G*

Psalm 103. *Lacking in I. B has verse numbers 1, 2 by lines 1, 4; 4–22 by 12, 17, 20, 25, 28, 33, 36, 41, 49, 57, 65, 68, 71, 73, 76, 81, 84, 89, 92. Two leaves (stubs remaining) are torn out after Ps. 103 in K.*
Incipit: Benedic anima mea *B*; Benidic anima mea *H, E; om. Q*

praise high Jehova, praise his holy name:
  my hart, my soule,
  Jehovas name extoll: 5
    what gratious he
    doth, and hath done for thee,
be quick to mind, to utter be not lame.

  For his free grace
  doth all thy sinnes deface,   10
he cures thy sicknesse, healeth all thy harme.
    from greedy grave
    that gapes thy life to have,
    he setts thee free:
    and kindly makes on thee   15
all his Compassions, all his mercies swarme.

  He doth thee still
  with flowing plenty fill:
he Eagle-like doth oft thy age renew.
    the lord hys right   20
    unto the wronged wight
    doth ever yeld:
    and never cease to shield
with Justice them, whome guile and fraude pursue.

  His way and trade   25
  he knowne to Moses made,
his wonders to the sonnes of Israell
    the lord, I meane,
    Jehova; who doth leane
    with mildest will   30
    to Ruth and mercy still;
as slow to wrath, as swift to doing well.

  When he doth chide
  he doth not chiding bide:
his anger is not in his treasures laide.   35

---

3 Jehova] Jehovah *θ*; Jehova<s> *K*   5 Jehovas] Jehova's *J, N, C*; Jehovahs *O*; Jehovaes *σ*
6 gratious] graces *I, N*   7 thee] mee *O*   11 harme] harmes *H*; harme<s> *Q, E*
19 thy] thyne *J, E*   20 hys] *written over* 1 *and another letter in A*   29 Jehova]
Jehovah *θ*   31 Ruth] truth *σ*   35 treasures] a *added above* es *in A*; *Treasure G*

he doth not serve
our synnes, as sinnes deserve:
nor recompence
unto us each offence,
40   with due reveng in equall ballance waide.

For looke how farre
the Sphere of farthest starre
drownes that proportion earthly Center beares:
soe much, and more
45   his never empty store
of grace and love
beyond his synnes doth prove,
who ever hym with due devotion feares.

Nay looke how farre
50   from East removed ar
the westerne lodgings of the weary sunne:
soe farre, more farre,
from us removed are,
by that greate love
55   our faultes from him doe prove,
what ever faultes and follies we have done.

And looke how much
the neerly touching touch
the father feeles towards his sonne most deare,
60   affects his hart,
at evry froward part
plaid by his child:
soe mercifull, soe mild,
is he to them that beare him awfull feare.

65   Our Potter he
knowes how his vessells we

39 us] *om. N*   40 waide] waid [wai *written over erasure of* lai (?)] *J*; Way'd [W *written over* l (?)] *B*; layde *E*   43 that] the *Q*   earthly] earth<|>y *K*; earthy *B, θ, C, G, M* 47 doth] doe *M*   50 East] <each>\East/ [*different ink*] *K*   removed ar] remov'd we are *B*   51 westerne] wasterne *O*   lodgings] lodging *B*   weary] wearied *E*   sunne] sonne *O*   58 neerly] meerelie *N, σ*   touching] *om. N* 59 towards] towerdes *C, G, M*; toward *J, K*   sonne] sunn *K*   62 plaid] *B notes:* Done *expunged:*   64 is he] He is *O*   that] which *O*   65–96 *lacking in K (torn out)*

in earthy matter lodg'd this fickle forme:
    fickle as glasse
     as flowres, that fading passe,
      and vanish soe,   70
      no not their place we know,
blasted to death with breath of blustring storme.

    Such is our state;
     but farre in other rate,
gods endlesse Justice and his mercy stand,   75
     both on the good,
      and their religious brood;
       who uncontrol'd
       sure league with him doe hold,
and doe his lawes, not only understand.   80

    Jehova greate
     sitts thron'd in starry seate:
his kingdome doth all kingdoms comprehend.
     you Angells strong,
      that unto him belong,   85
       whose deedes accord
       with his commanding word,
praises and thanks upon Jehova spend.

    Spirits of might,
     you that his battaills fight,   90
you ministers that willing work his will:
     all things that he
     hath wrought, where soe they be,
      his praise extoll:
      thou with the rest my soule,   95
praises and thanks spend on Jehova still.

---

67 earthy] earthly *Q*   68 fickle] k *added in darker ink in* A   71–2 *B notes:* mark'd
thus [*correction symbol in parentheses*] in the margin, Quære whether for correction at
16.   74 but] bu [bee (?)] *Q*   75 gods] god *E*   Justice] bounties *N*; bountie *C*
mercy] bounty χ; justice *N, C*   79 doe] doth σ   81 *bracket and* K 193 *written
in pencil in margin of* A   Jehova] Jehovah θ   83 his] Whose *N*   kingdome doth]
Kingdom dos *B*; kingdomes doth *M*   88 Jehova] Jehovah θ   89 might] night *N*
91 that] who *N*   92 all things] And all *N*   93 they] it *N*   96 spend on]
upon *B*; yeild to *N*   Jehova] Jehovah θ   still] spend *B*

Benedic anima mea.
Psalm 104.

Make ô my soule the subject of thy songe
    th'eternall lord: ô lord, ô god of might,
to thee, to thee, all roiall pompes belonge,
    clothed art thou in state and glory bright:·
5   for what is els this Eye-delighting light;
but unto thee a garment wide and long?
    the vauted heaven but a Curtaine right,
a Canopy, thou over thee hast hunge?

The rafters that his Parlors roofe sustaine,
10   in Chev'ron he on christall waters bindes:
he on the windes, he on the cloudes doth raigne,
    riding on cloudes, and walking on the windes.
    whose winged blasts his word, as ready findes
to poast from him, as Angells of his traine:
15   as to effect the purposes he mindes
he makes no lesse the flamy fier faine.

By him the earth a stedfast base doth beare,
    and stedfast soe, as tyme nor force can shake:
which once round waters garment-like did weare,
20   and hills in seas did lowly lodging take.
    but seas from hills a swift descent did make,
when swelling high by thee they chidden were:

Psalm 104. *B has verse numbers 1–18 by lines 1, 4, 9, 13, 17, 19, 21, 25, 28, 31, 33, 37, 41, 45, 49, 52, 57, 62; 20–35 by lines 69, 72, 73, 75, 77, 81, 85, 88, 89, 92, 95, 97, 100, 103, 105, 108.*
    Incipit: Benedic anima mea domino: *I;* Benidic Anima mea *H;* Benidic: Anima mea: *E;* Benedic anima *K, C, G, M; om. θ, Q*
3 to thee, all] \to Thee/all *B*   4 clothed art thou] thow clothed art *I*   6 but unto thee] *caret placed over* o *after* t *of* but; unto *written in a different ink and hand above caret in A*   7 vauted] vaulted *J, B, I, O, N, C, G, M*   heaven] heav'en *F, I;* heavens *θ, C, G, M*   but a] is but *I;* but even a *θ*   9 roofe] roofes *I*   10 in Chev'ron] inchevron *K;* encheveron *C, G;* Enchevron'd *M*   he on] be whome *E*   11 windes ...cloudes] Cloudes... windes *G, M*   raigne] reign *B;* raine *K*   12 riding on] hee rides on *I*   walking] walketh *I*   13 as ready] allreadie *F*   14 from] for *B, I, K, χ;* <from> for *H*   15 as] and *I, θ*   16 flamy] flaming *I*   17 the] this *I* 18 force] age *O*   20 lodging] lodgings *E*   22 high] hills *I*   thee] *added above caret in A*   they chidden] theire children *I*   were] weare *F, H*

thy thunders rore did cause their Conduites quake,
hastning their haste with spurr of hasty feare.

Soe waters fledd, soe mountaines high did rise,   25
   so humble Valleis deepely did descend,
all to the place thou didst for them devise:
   where bounding Seas with unremoved end,
   thou badst they should them selves no more extend,
to hide the earth which now unhidden lies: 30
   yet from the mountaines rocky sides didst send
springs whispring murmurs, Rivers roring cries.

Of thes the beasts which on the plaines doe feede
   all drinck their fill: with these their thirst allay
the Asses wild and all that wildly breede: 35
   by these in their self-chosen mansions stay
   the free-borne fowles, which through the empty way
of yelding aire wafted with winged speed,
   to art-like notes of Nature-tuned lay
make earelesse busshes give attentive heed.   40

Thou, thou of heav'n the windowes dost unclose,
   dewing the mountaines with thy bounties raine:
Earth greate with yong hir longing doth not lose,
   the hopfull ploughman, hopeth not in vayne.
   the vulgar grasse, whereof the beast is faine,   45
the rarer hearbman for him self hath chose:
   all things in breef, that life in life maintaine,
from Earths old bowells fresh and yongly growes.

---

23 thunders] *B notes: thundry* expunged.   24 hastning] hastinge θ; \and/hast<ing>
[*ampersand added in left margin*] *I*   their haste] theyr speed *D*; with speede *O*; their
<haste>\speed/ *I*; their\speed/<hast> [*hast underlined*; speed *added in different ink*] *K*
29 them selves no more] no more themselves *I, K* (themselves *written over erasure*),
N, σ   30 the] this *I*   33 thes the beasts] the *added as an abbreviation in gold
above gold caret in A*   plaines] plaine θ 34 fill] fills *I*   36 these] thee *J*   man-
sions] stations *I, K*; stacon [*tilde over* n] *O*; stacion *D*; *B notes: stations* expunged
37 the free-borne] Thee free-borne *N*   fowles] fowle *G, M*   which through the
empty way] that in the region play *I*   38 wafted] wasted [?] *Q*   winged] wingy *B*
39 Nature-tuned] natures tuned *I*   41 heav'n] heav'ns *I*; Heavens *C, G, M*   dost]
didst θ unclose] unclose [v, *i.e.* u *written over* e] *K*; enclose θ, Q 42 dewing the]
\be/ Dewing <the> [be *added in margin*] *I*   raine] rayne *F, K, O, H, E, C*; raigne *Q*
43 yong] child θ lose] *A, F, I, K, D, Q, G*; loose *B, J, χ*   46 hath chose] doth
choose *N*   48 fresh and yongly] <younge>, freshe, and youngly *H*; younge
and freshlye *E*   growes] groes *K*; g\r/oes *N*

Thence Wyne, the counter-poison unto care:
50   thence Oile, whose juyce unplaites the folded brow:
thence bread, our best, I say not daintiest fare,
      propp yet of hartes, which els would weakly bow:
      thence, lord, thy leaved people bud and blow:
whose Princes thou, thy Cedars, dost not spare,
55   a fuller draught of thy cupp to allow,
that highly rais'd above the rest they are.

Yet highly rais'd they doe not proudly scorne
      to give small birdes an humble entertaine,
whose brickle neastes are on their branches borne,
60   while in the Firrs the Storks a lodging gaine.
      soe highest hills rock-loving Goates sustayne;
and have their heads with clyming traces worne:
      that safe in Rocks the Connyes may remaine,
to yeld them Caves, their rocky ribbs are torne.

65   Thou makst the Moone, the Empresse of the night,
      hold constant course with most unconstant face:
thou makst the sunne the Chariot-man of light,
      well knowe the start, and stop of dayly race.
      when he doth sett and night his beames deface,
70   to roame abroade wood-burgesses delight,
      Lions, I meane, who roreing all that space,
seeme then of thee to crave their food by right.

When he retornes they all from field retire,
      and lay them downe in Cave, their home, to rest:

49 Thence] Then *I*   50 thence] then *I*   juyce] juce *F, M*; joyce *H, Q*; juice *[?]*
altered to joye *in I*; *vertue G*   unplaites] unpleats *I, O*; smoothes *G*   folded] wrinkled *G*
51 thence] Then *I*   bread] bredd *Q*; bread [*a* written over d (?)] *H*   best, I] ~ (~ *C,*
G, M   daintiest ^fare,] ~ ^~^ *I, K* (; ~ ^~: *N*; ~) ~^ *G*; ~^ ~) *C, M*   53 thence]
then [ce *stricken after* n] *K*; Then *I, θ*   leaved] loved *I*   56 that] *B notes:* forte
Though.   rest] earth *σ*   59 brickle] bricklye *E*; brittle *J, I, θ*   on] in *I, θ*
60 while] whiles *I, θ*   Storks] Storke *F*   gaine] gaynes *F*   61 soe] The *θ*
62 traces] *B notes:* forte pro *tresses*   63 Rocks] Caves *G, M*   64 Caves] rest *G, M*
ribbs] sides *G*   65 the Empresse] our Empresse *I*   66 hold] <know>\hold/
D; knowe *O*   unconstant] inconstant *I, θ*   68 knowe] *B, I, χ*; knowe<s> *K*; knowes *A*
69 *underlined in B, which notes:* a Crosse at this line possibly for correction   doth] dos *B*
70 roame] rove *I*   72 crave] clayme *K, N, C, σ, G, M*   73 retornes] retires *B*
74 Cave] caves *K*   home] whom *D*; whome *Q*; <w>home *H*

they rest, man stirrs to wyn a workmans hire,   75
    and works till sunn have wrought his way to west.
    eternall lord who greatest art and best,
how I amaz'd thy mighty workes admire!
    wisdome in them hath every part possest,
wherto in me, no wisdome can aspire.   80

Behold the Earth: how there thy bounties flow!
    looke on the Sea extended hugely wide:
what watry troopes, swymme, creepe, and crawle, and goe,
    of greate, and small, on that, this, ev'ry side!
    there the saile-winged shipps on waves doe glide: 85
sea-Monsters there: their plaies and pastymes show:
    and all at once in seasonable tyde
their hungry eyes on thee their feeder throw.

Thou giv'st, they take; thy hand it self displaies,
    they filled feele the plenties of thy hand: 90
all darkned lye deprived of thy Raise,
    thou tak'st their breath, not one can longer stand.
    they dye, they turne to former dust and sand,
till thy life-giving sp'rit doe mustring raise
    new companies, to reenforce each band,   95
which still supplied, never whole decaies.

Soe may it, oh! soe may it ever goe,
    Jehovas workes his glorious gladdnesse be,
who touching Mountaynes, Mountaynes smoaking grow,
    who eyeing Earth, Earth quakes with quivering knee.   100
    As for my self, my seely self, in me
while life shall last, his worth in song to show

---

75 stirrs] works *I*   76 have] hath *I, θ, C, G, M*   77 lord] *added above caret in different ink in* K; god *σ*   greatest] glorious *θ*   78 mighty] heavnly *O*; heavenly *D* 79 them] thee *I*   part] worke *I*   80 wisdome] goodnes *θ*   82 Sea] seas *I, θ* 83 swymme, creepe, and crawle] there swim, creepe, craule *I*   84 of] both *θ*   and] of *K, N, C, σ G, M*   that, this] this, that *I, θ, C, G, M*   85 waves] wave *written in darker ink over erasure in* A   87 and] at *G*   88 hungry] hungries *F*   90 feele the] with the *F*; full, with *I*   91 lye] lies *C*   94 life-giving] *A, B, K, θ*; life-living *N, C, σ, G, M*   sp'rit] sprite *F, I, H*; spright *Q*; spiritt *K, χ*   doe] doth *I, θ*   96 whole] wholye *E*   98 Jehovas] Jehova's *I, N, C, G, M*; Jehovaes *σ*; Jehovahs *K, O*   glorious] glories *σ*   101 seely] silly *σ, C, G, M*   102 while] whilst *I*   shall] doth *θ*   his worth in song] in song his Worth *B, I, K, χ*; his worth in praise *C,*   *G, M*

I framed have a resolute decree,
and thankfull be, till being I forgoe.

105   O that my song might good acceptance finde:
       how should my hart in greate Jehova joy!
    ô that some plague this irreligious kinde,
       ingrate to god, would from the earth destroy!
       meane while my soule uncessantly employ.
110   to high Jehovas praise my mouth and mynd:
       nay all (since all his benefitts enjoy)
    praise him whom bandes of time nor age can binde.

Confitemini Domino.
Psalm 105.

Jehovas praise, Jehovas holy fame
    ô show, ô sound, his actes to all relate:
to him your songs, your psalmes unto him frame;
    make your discourse, his wonders celebrate.
5   Boast ye god-serchers in his sacred name,
    and your contracted hartes with joy dilate:
       to him, his arke, his face, lett be intended
       your due inquest, with service never ended.

Record I say in speciall memory
10   the miracles he wrought, the lawes he gave,
    his servantes you ô Abrahams progeny
       you Jacobs sonnes, whome he doth chosen save.

---

103 decree] degree *N*   104 and thankfull be] And thanked bee *O*; thankfull to bee *I*; <and> thankefull\to/bee *K*; *B notes* (*on* thankfull be): *thankfully* expunged 106 Jehova] Jehovah *I*, θ, *H*   107 plague] plauge σ   108 ingrate] ungrate θ   earth] world *I*   109 while] whilst *I*   uncessantly] incessantly *I*, θ   110 to] On *G*, *M* Jehovas] Jehova's *I*, *N*, *C*, *G*, *M*; Jehovaes σ; Jehovahs *K*, *O*   my] thie *I*;   both θ and] my *E*   111 since] sith *I*, *Q*   112 whom] whose *K*, χ   bandes] bounds *I* nor] *A*, *I*, *D*; no [*superscript* r *erased*] *K*; no χ

Psalm 105. *Variant in B.*
Incipit: Confetemini Domino *H*, *E*; Confitemini *I*; *om. Q*   1–8 *F puts this stanza after stanza 2*   1 Jehovas praise] Jehova's praise *J*, *G*; Jehovahs praise *I*, *O*; Jehovaes praise *H*, *Q*; *Jehovah* praise *K*; Jehova praise *N*, *C*   Jehovas] Jehova's *J*, *N*, *C*, *G*, *M*; Jehovahs *I*, *K*, *O*; Jehovaes *Q*, *E*   fame] name *E*   5 ye] yea *I*; you *K*, *C*, *M*   his] has *I* 6 your] yow *I*, *K*, χ   8 your] With *G*   inquest] request *F*, *N*   10 the lawes] and lawes *F*   11 Abrahams] Abrams *E*

we first and most on him our god relye:
    all be noe boundes his jurisdiction have:
    and he eternally that treaty mindeth,   15
    which him to us untearmed ages bindeth.

A treaty first with Abraham begun,
    after againe by oth to Isaack bound,
lastly to Isaacks god-beholding sonne
    confirm'd, and made inviolably sound.   20
I give in fee (for soe the graunt did runne)
    thee and thine heirs the Cananean ground:
        and that when few they were, few, unregarded,
        yea strangers too, where he their lott awarded.

They strangers were and roam'd from land to land,   25
    from Realme to Realme: though seatlesse, yet secure;
and soe remote from wrong of meaner hand
    that kings for them did sharp rebuke endure.
touch not I chardge you my anointed band,
    nor to my Prophetts least offence procure.   30
        then he for Famyn spake: scarse had he spoken,
        when Famyn came, the staff of bread was broken.

But he for them to Ægipt had foresent
    the slave-sold Joseph kindly to prepare:
whose feete if freating Irons did indent,   35
    his soule was clog'd with steely boultes of care.
till fame abroad of his divining went,
    and heav'nly sawes such wisdome did declare;
        that him a message from the king addressed
        of bondage ridd, of freedome repossessed.   40

14 all be] albee *K*, χ; albeyt *E*; Albei't *G*   noe . . . his] his . . . no *G*   jurisdiction] jurisdictions *J, H*   15 he] *added above caret in A in a hand resembling the J hand*; *om. F, J*
16 which] with *I*   18 Isaack] Isaak *K*; Isack *F*, θ *E*; Isak *H, N, C, G, M*   19 Isaacks]
Isaaks *K*; Isackes *O*; Isakes *N, C*; Izacks *D*; Isaac's *J*; *Jacobs F* \Jacob:/<sakes> *H*; Jacob *Q,
E, G, M*   god-beholding] gods behouldinge *Q*; God's beholding *G*; Gods-beholding
M   20 inviolably] inviolable *Q, G, M*   22 thine] thy σ, *M*   Cananean] Cannanaan *K*; Cananaans *I*   23 that] thoe [?] *Q*   were] weare *H, Q*   24 too,] ~∧ *I, K, O*;
to∧ *D*; to, (*, C, G, M*   25 strangers were] strangers weare *F, H, Q*; stangers where *I*
27 from . . . of] of . . . from *Q*   30 least] lest *I, E*   31 spake] sent *C*   33 Ægipt] *A,
K, Q, E*; Egipt *I*, χ   34 slave-sold Joseph] slave=sod Joseth *I*   35 if] two [*written
over erasure*] *I*   36 steely] sterly σ   37 till] <his>\Till/ [*lighter ink*] *K*   38 sawes]
shewes *Q, E*   39 him] he θ   a] *om. I*

Noe sooner freed, the Monark in his handes
    without controll both house and state doth lay;
he Rulers rules, Commanders he commandes;
    wills and all doe: prescribes and all obay.
45   while thus in tearmes of highest grace he stands,
    loe, Israell to Ægipt takes his way,
      and Jacobs lyne from Holy Sem descended,
    to sojourne comes where Cham his tentes extended.

Who now but they in strength and number flowe?
50   rais'd by their god their haters farre above?
for, chang'd by him, their entertainers grow
    with guile to hate, who erst with truth did love.
But he with sacred Moses wills to goe
    Aron his choise, those mischiefes to remove:
55   by whose greate workes their senders glory blazed
    made Chams whole land with frightfull signes amazed.

Darknes from day the wonted sunne doth chase,
    (for both he bidds and neither dares rebell)
late watry Nilus lookes with bloudy face:
60   how fisshes die, what should I stand to tell?
or how of noisome froggs the earth-bred race
    croak where their princes sleepe, not only dwell?
    how lice and vermyn heav'nly voice attending
    doe swarming fall, what quarter not offending?

65   Noe rayny cloude but breakes in stony haile:
    for cheerefull lightes dismayfull lightnings shine:
not shine alone, their firy strokes assaile
    each taller plant: worst fares the figg and Vyne
nor, cal'd, to come doe Catterpillers faile
70   with Locustes more then counting can define:

42 doth] did *F, G, M*   44 prescribes] prescribe *I*   45 while] whiles *C*   46 Israell]
I sarell *I*   Ægipt] *A, K, Q, E*; Egipt χ; Egiot *I*   takes] take *I*   47 lyne] lyme *I*
48 comes] come *H, Q, G, M*; came *E*   50 haters] harters *I*   53 hewith] heerwith
K, N, C, σ, G, M   54 Aron] Arron *H*; Aaron θ, *Q, E, N*   55 blazed] blayd *I*
56 Chams] Cham's *G*; Chaims *[?] I*   whole] whose *I*   signes amazed] *om. I*
57 doth] did *E*   58 dares] dare *K, N, C, σ, G, M*; doth *I*   60 what] how *N*
62 croak] Croakes *O, D (?)*   65 rayny] *first* y *added in gold above gold caret in A*
66 lightes] light *G*   lightnings] lightning *I, C, G*   67 shine] thine *I*   firy] furie
Q   68 figg] figges *K*

by these the grasse, the grace of fieldes is wasted,
the fruites consum'd by owners yet untasted.

Their eldest-borne, that Countries hopefull spring,
   prime of their youth, his plague doth lastly wound;
then rich with spoile, he out his folk doth bring;   75
   in all their tribes not one a weakling found.
Ægipt once wisht, now feares, their tarrying,
   and gladdly sees them on their journey bound:·
      whome god in heate a shading cloude provideth
      in dark with lamp of flamy piller guideth.   80

Brought from his store at sute of Israell
   Quailes in whole Beavies each remove pursue;
him self from skies, their hunger to repell,
   candies the grasse with sweete congealed dew.
He woundes the Rock, the rock doth, wounded, well: 85
   welling affoordes new streames to Chanells new.
      all for gods mindfull will can not be dryven,
      from sacred word once to his Abraham given.

Soe then in joyfull plight, his loved bands
   his chosen troopes with triumph on he traines: 90
till full possession of the neighboure lands,
   with painelesse harvest of their thancklesse paines,
he safly leaves in their victorious hands,
   where nought for them to doe hence forth remaines,
      but only to observe and see fullfilled,   95
      what he (to whome be praise) hath said and willed.

---

71 grace] grass *E*   fieldes] feilde *σ*   72 fruites] fruite *I, K, χ*   73 that] theire *O*;
the *C*   74 youth] youths *I*   plague] plauge *σ*   lastly] lastlie [*initial* h *stricken*, l
added in different ink] *K*; hastely *σ*;   hast'ly *N*; hastlie *C, G, M*; hasty [?] *I*   75 folk]
I, K, χ; flock *A, M,*   doth] did *N*   77 Ægipt] *A, Q, E*; Egipt *I, K, χ*   wisht]
wist *E*; wishe *I*   80 piller] pillars [s *written over another letter?*] *Q*   82 whole]
whole [s *altered to* l] *E*; whose *F*   Beavies] leavies *N, C, σ, G, M*   84 dew] due *Q*
85 Rock] rockes *K*   86 welling] willinge *σ*   87 for] from *O*   88 word] *om. O*
Abraham] Abram *J, E*   92 with] wih *Q*   94 to doe hence forth] henceforth to
doe *I, K, χ*

Confitemini Domino.
Psalm 106.

Where are the hymmes, where are the honors due
　　　to our good god, whose goodnes knowes no end?
who of his force can utter what is true?
　　　who all his praise, in praises comprehend?
5　　　　ô blessed they whose well advised sight
of all their life the levell straight doe bend,
　　　with endlesse ayming at the mark of right.

Lord for the love thou dost thy people beare,
　　　graunt thought of me may harbor in thy mind:
10　make me with them thy safeties liv'ry weare,
　　　that I may once take notice in what kinde
　　　thy kindnes is on thine ellected showne:
　　　that I may gladdnes in their gladdnes finde,
　　　boasting with them, who boast to be thine owne.

15　Indeede we have as our fore-fathers done
　　　done ill, done wronge, unjustly, wickedly:
for (that I may begin where they begun)
　　　thy workes in Egipt, nought they passed by.
　　　　quite out of thought thy many bounties fell,
20　　　and at the sea they did thy pacience try:
　　　　at the red sea, they did I say rebell.

Yet god (o goodnes) saved for his name
　　　these Mutiners that this his might might show,
for he the waters did rebuking blame,
25　　　the waters left at his rebuke to flow

Psalm 106. *Lacking in I. B has verse numbers 1–27 by lines 1, 3, 5, 8, 11, 15, 17, 22, 24, 27, 29, 31, 33, 36, 39, 41, 43, 47, 50, 52, 55, 57, 61, 64, 66, 68, 70; 29 by both 71 and 74; 30–48 by 76, 77, 78, 82, 85, 88, 90, 92, 94, 96, 99, 101, 103, 105, 106, 108, 110, 113, 116.*
Incipit: om. Q
2 to our good] *A, N*; To Our *B*; unto our *K, χ*　　3 force] power *N, C*　　what] all *N, C*
5 blessed] happie *N, C*　　6 straight] strait *B*　　doe] doth *θ, N, C, Q, E*　　7 of
right] aright *E*　　12 on thine] on theine *K*; on thy *N, C*; to thine *M*　　13 their]
thie *F*　　14 boast] hope *θ*　　thine] theine *K*　　17 begun] beganne *J*　　18 Egipt]
Ægipt *J, Q*　　nought] naught *B, N, C*　　19 quite] quit *K*　　21 they did I say] I
saie they did *N, C*　　23 Mutiners] mutinous *N, C*

on sandy deepe as on the desert sands,
   unwett in waves he made his people goe:
      setting them safe from all their haters hands.

For look how fast their foes did them pursue,
   soe fast, more fast the sea pursu'd their foes: 30
all drent, all dead, not one left of the Crue.
   then loe beliefe, then thankfullnesse arose
      in faithlesse, gracelesse hartes: but in a trice
   Oblyvion all remembraunce overgrowes
      of his greate workes, or care of his advise.   35

For gluttonous they flesh in desert crave,
   that they forsooth might try th'allmighties might:
as gluttons fitts, they flesh in desert have,
   for fully fedd, yet far'd in pining plight.
      what should I utter how from Moses they   40
   and holy Aron sacred in gods sight,
      through envy sought to take the rule away?

The very Earth such mischiefe griv'd to beare
   and opning made hir gaping throate the grave,
where Dathan and Abiran buried were,   45
   buried alive with Tentes and all they have.
      whose complices the flash of angry fire
   surprised soe, none could from burning save,
      in asshes rak'd they found their treasons hire.

A molten god they did in Horeb frame,   50
   and what? forsouth the suckling of a Cow;
their heav'nly glory chang'd to beastly shame,
   they more then beasts, before a beast did bow.

26 as] and σ   sands] sand *J*   28 setting] And sett *N*   haters] *B, K, χ; om. A*
hands] hande *Q*   29 foes] fees *N*   30 sea] Seas *C*   31 drent] drownd *M*
32 then∧ loe] Then∧ to *B*; Lo, then *N, C*   thankfullnesse] thanfullnesse *K*   33 but]
where *N*   35 his greate] Gods great *N, C*   workes] worke θ   or] and *N*   37 that
they forsooth might try] With scope t'experiment *N*; *B notes: With scope t'experiment* Expunged   38 desert] desarts *N*   39 for] But *N, C*; Though *M*   far'd] liv'd *N, C*
41 Aron] Aaron *E*; A'aron *B*   42 to take the rule] the rule to take *B, K, χ*   44 gaping]
verie *G*   45 Abiran] *Abiron F*; Abiram *J, B, N, C, σ, G, M*   buried] burned *C*
46 buried] burned *C*   47 flash] fashe *F*   fire] *B notes: flame*, but that expungd. *fire*
is putt.   49 found] had *M*   *B notes:* before the Correction it stood, *They raked lay in
ashes of their shame* which is expungd   treasons] on *written over erasure of* us (?) *in A*
50 they] y *written over* n *in different ink in A*; then *F*   51 suckling] sucking *N*
52 chang'd] turn'd *F*; turned θ

a Calfe, nay image of a Calfe they serv'd,
55   whose highest worshipp, hay they should alow,
God was forgott, who had them soe preserv'd;

Preserv'd them soe by miracles of might,
done in the plaines where fertile Nilus flowes:
and wondred workes; which fearefully did fright,
60   the Oker bancks their passage did inclose.
therefore their wrack he meant; which while he meant
Moses his chosen in the gapp arose,
and turn'd his wrath from wrackfull punishment.

What more? the land that well deserv'd desire
65   with fond disdaine mistrustfull they reject:
their tentes doe flame with hott rebellious fire,
Jehovas wordes receav'd with no respect.
for which he in the desert overthrew
them selves, their sonns, their fathers fault infect,
70   scatt'red, exil'd, no certaine Country knew.

For they to Pehor, filthy Idoll, went,
and what had bin to dead things sacrific'd,
forbidden foode, abhominably spent.
soe god with anger mightely surpris'd
75   his hurtfull hand against their health did raise:
but Phinees, justice done, their lives repris'd,
and for that justice purchas'd endlesse praise.

Could this suffice? Nay farther at the brooke,
the brooke of brall, they did the Lord incense:
80   which then his name of their contention tooke:
where Moses self did smart for their offence
for inly angred that he rashly spake,
forgetting due respect and reverence,
which for his rashnesse god did angry make.

55 hay] haye [y *written over* v (?)] *K*; *om. (space left) F*   60 their] which *B*; that *K, χ*   passage] ferry *is underlined (but not stricken) and* passage *is written above it in A (in a hand resembling the J hand)*; ferry *F*; passage *J, B, K, χ*   67 Jehovas] Jehova's *N, C, G, M*; Jehovaes *σ*   receav'd with] receav<e>\'/d with *K*; receaved *θ*   69 their fathers] with fathers *J, K, χ*; which fathers *B*   71 Pehor] Pëor *B*   72 bin] *A, D*; bine *H, Q, E*; been *F, K, χ*   73 abhominably] abhominable *M*   76 Phinees] Phinies *C, G, M*; Phinyes *Q, E*   78 farther] further *B, K, θ, E, M*   79 brall] Braul *B*; brawle *C*; Beall *σ*   did] <did> *H*; *om. Q, E*   80 his] its *B*   their] then *F*

After their sonnes came to that lovely land,   85
    noe better minded, albe better blest,
would not roote out, as stoode with his command
    the Pagan plants, who then the place possest.
        but grew togither up, and did as they,
        in Idoll service forward as the best: 90
        in Idoll service roote of their decay.

For they both sonnes and daughters offered
    unto their gods; gods? no, they devills were:
whose guiltlesse bloud, which wastfully they shed,
    imbru'd the Idolls Canaan did beare,   95
        the land defiled was with murthers done,
        whiles they in workes no filthines forbeare,
        and in conceiptes a whooring mainly runn.

Soe god incensed grew against his owne,
    and plainly did his heritage detest: 100
left them to be by strangers overthrowne,
    lorded by foes, by enimies opprest.
        often he freed them by his force divine:
        but when their witts would give his wrath no rest.
        left them at length in worthy plagues to pine.   105

He left them long yet left them not at last
    but saw their woes, and hear'd their waylfull cries
which made him call to thought his cov'nant past.
        soe chang'd, not only in him self did rise
        repentant pitty of their passed paines: 110
        but their Captivers now relenting eyes
        his ruth of them to tender yelding traines.

Goe on ô god, as them, soe us to save:
    Rally thy troopes that widly scattred be,
that their due thankes, thy holynesse may have;   115
    their glorious praise, thy heav'nly powr may see.

85 came] com'n *B*   86 albe] allbe *B*; albee *N*; all-be *K*; all be θ, *H Q*; albeyt *E*; albeit
G; albet *M*   87 his] is *H*   88 place] land *M*   90 forward] froward *B*
best] rest θ   93 gods?] Gods∧ θ, *Q, E*; Gods; *H*   were] weare *H, Q*   94 wast-
fully] wrongfully θ   95 imbru'd] Inbru'd *B*   98 conceiptes] conceipt *E*
103 force] fore\ce/ *D*; power *O*   105 plagues] plauges *Q, E*   106 yet] *B notes:*
but expunged: 107 waylfull] wailinge *O*; woefull *C*   109 chang'd] change θ, *E*
113 ô] *om.* θ   114 Rally] recall θ   that] which *M*   widly] wildlie θ, *E*

ô god of Izrael our god, our lord,
eternall thankes be to eternall thee:
lett all the Earth with praise approve my word.

Confitemini Domino.
Psalm 107.

O celebrate Jehovas praise,
    for gratious he and good is found;
and noe precinct, noe space of daies,
    can his greate grace and goodnes bound.
5   say you with me, with me resound
      Jehovas praise with thankfullnes:
    whose bands of perill he unbound,
      when tirants hate did you oppresse.

How many, and how many tymes,
10   from early East, from evening West,
from thirsty coastes, from frosty clymes,
    hath he dispersed brought to rest!
how many sav'd, who deepe distrest,
    and straying farre from path and towne,
15   with want and drouth soe sore were prest
    that drouth well neer their lives did drowne!

They cri'd to him in woefull plight;
    his succour sent did end their woe.
from error train'd he led them right,
20   and made to peopled places goe.

---

117 Izrael] Israell *F, K, χ*; Israel *M*; Israël *B*   119 my] thy *N*

Psalm 107. *Lacking in I. B has verse numbers 1–43 by lines 1, 5, 10, 13, 15, 17, 19, 21, 23, 25,
28, 31, 33, 35, 37, 39, 41, 45, 49, 51, 53, 55, 57, 59, 65, 69, 73, 81, 83, 84, 85, 87, 89, 91, 93,
97, 99, 101, 105, 108, 111, 113, 117.*
Incipit: om. K, Q   1 Jehovas] Jehova's *N, C, G*; Jehovahs *O*; Jehovaes *σ*   2 gra-
tious] glorious *θ*   3 precinct] præcinct *B*   noe space] or space *G*   5 say you]
Then saye *M*   6 Jehovas] Jehova's *N, C, G, M*; Jehovaes *σ*   9 How] H *written
over erased* N *in A*; Now *F*   10 from evening] to eveninge *θ, E*   11 coastes] Wasts *B*
from frosty] to frostie *D, σ*   13 who deepe] *B, K, χ*; how deepe *A*   15 sore]
neere *θ, C*   were] weare *H*   16 neer] nigh *M*   17 cri'd] Crye *E, G, M*
18 did] doth *G, M*

such then in song his mercies show,
   his wonders done to men display:
who in the hungry hunger soe,
   soe doth in thirsty thirst alay.

How many fast imprisoned lye   25
   in shade of death, and horror blind,
whose feete as Iron fetters tye,
   soe heavy anguish cloggs their mind!
whom though the lord did Rebells finde,
   despising all he did advise;   30
yet when their hart with grief declin'd
   now helplesse quight and hoplesse lies.

They cry to him in wofull plight;
   his succour sent doth end their wo.
from death to life, from darke to light   35
   with broken boltes he makes them goe.
such then in song his mercy show,
   his wonders done to men display;
the gates of brasse who breaketh so,
   so makes the Iron yeld them way.   40

How many wantonly missled,
   while fooles, they follow Follies traine,
for sinne confined to their bedd
   this gwerdon of their folly gaine.
their loathing soule doth foode refraine,   45
   and hardly, hardly failing breath
can now his ending gasp restraine
   from entring at the gate of death.

They cry to him in wofull plight:
   his succour sent doth end their woe.   50
his word putts all their paine to flight
   and free from sicknesse makes them goe.

---

21 song] songs *B*; <seeing>*song[?]/ *K, which has a stricken note in left margin:*
<*soeing[?]>   mercies] mercy *B, E*; praises *O*   24 alay] allway *altered to* alay *in K*
(*1 and* w *stricken), altered in H (*aye *written over* wa; ie *stricken)*   30 advise] devise *θ, E*
31 their hart with grief] theire hart<s> with greife *K*; their hearts with greif *N, C, σ, G,*
M; with greife theire harte *θ*   36 makes] make *K*   37–8 *indentation of these lines*
reversed in A   37 mercy] mercys *B, K, χ*   40 them] him *B*   45 loathing] a
added above o *in A*   soule] Soules *G, M*   50 doth] th *above caret in A*   51 word]
words *E*

such then in song his mercy show
his wonders done to men display
55 tell gladly of his workes they know
and sacrifice of praises pay.

How many mounting winged tree
for traffique leave retiring land
and on huge waters busied be,
60 which bancklesse flow on endlesse sand!
these, these indeed, well understand,
enform'd by their feare-open ey,
the wonders of Jehovas hand
while on the waves they rocking ly.

65 He bids and straight on moisty maine
the blustring tempest falling flies:
the starrs doe dropp bedasht with raine,
soe huge the waves in combat rise.
now shipp with men do touch the skies:
70 now downe more downe then Center falls;
their might doth melt, their courage dies,
such hideous fright each sence appalls.

For now the whirlwinde makes them wheele:
now stop'd in midst of broken round
75 as drunckards use, they staggring reele,
whose head-lame feete can feele noe ground.
what helpes to have a Pilot sound?
where wisdome wont to guide the sterne
now in dispairfull danger droun'd,
80 with wisdoms ey can nought discerne?

They cry to him in wofull plight;
his succour sent doth end their woe.

---

53 mercy] mercies *J*, *B*, *K*, χ   55 tell] till *[?]* *Q*   57 mounting] mounted θ, *N*
tree] trees *E*   63 Jehovas] Jehova's *N*, *G*, *M*; Jehovaes σ   64 waves] wawes *K*
65 straight] strait *B*   66 the] His *B*   67 dropp] droop *K*   68 huge] high
M   combat] combate [u *altered to* o] *B*; cumbate *K*, *H*; Cumbatt *Q*; cumbat *G*   69 do]
doth *K*, *C*, σ, *M*   70 falls] fallse *Q*   72 fright] sight *K*, θ, *N*, σ; sightes *C*, *G*, *M*
appalls] appales *B*, σ; appalles *O*   78 wont] want\s/ *D*   sterne] storm *altered to*
sterne *in B*   79 danger] daungers θ; tempest *M*   80 with] w<t>\c/h *D*   can
nought] can naught *B*; cannot θ, *E*

of Seas and winds he partes the fight:
  to wisshed port with joy they row.
  such then in song his mercies show;   85
    his wonders done to men display:
  Make peoples presse his honor know,
    at princes thrones his praise bewray.

How many whers doth he convert
  well watred grounds to thirsty sand?   90
and saltes the soile for wicked hart
    the dwellers beare that till the land!
  how oft againe his gratious hand,
    to watry pooles doth desertes change?
  and on the fields that frutlesse stand,   95
    makes trickling springs unhoped rang?

Suppose of men that live in want
  a Colony he there do make.
they dwell, and build, and sow, and plant,
  and of their paines greate profitt take.   100
  his blessing doth not them forsake,
    but multiplies their childrens store:
  Nay ev'n their Cattaill, for their sake,
    augmentes in number more and more.

They stand while he their state sustaines: 105
  then comes againe that harmefulle day
which brings the enterchange of paines,
    and their encrease turnes to decay.

84 row] goe *O*   85 song] songs *B*; songes *K*   mercies] mercy *B, K, θ, Q*
87–8 *B notes:* It stood before Correct.
  Both unto men that stand more low
  And such as sit on higher sway expungd
87 peoples presse] people prest [*a letter altered before* t (?)] *E*   his] with *K, χ*   honor]
honors *J*   88 bewray] *written on a slip of paper pasted over* display *in A*   89 whers]
where *K, χ*   doth] dos *B*   90 grounds] grounde *Q*   thirsty] baren *B*   91 soile]
B notes: earth. expunged.   hart] hartes *O*   92 land] <ground> land *D*; ground *O*
94 doth] dos *B*   95 fields] groundes *G, M*   that] which *G*   96 makes] Make
G, M   unhoped] *a lightly stricken after* o *in A*   98 do] did *K, χ*   99 and sow]
they sow *M*   101 blessing] Blessinges *H, E*   doth] dos *B*   102 childrens] children *Q* 103 ev'n] even *I, θ, N, Q, G, M*; ever *H*; ere *E*   105 while] whiles *C*
107 the enterchange of] an interchange of *B, K, χ; B notes: the*   *surprising* expunged:

nor strang; for he exiled stray
110   makes greatest kings, scorn'd where they goe:
the same from want the poore doth waigh,
     and makes like heards their howses grow.

See this, and joy this thus to see,
     all you whose judgmentes judg aright:
115 you whose conceites distorted be,
     stand mute amazed at the sight
how wise were he, whose wisdome might
     observe each course the lord doth hold,
to light in men his bounties light,
120   whose providence doth all enfold?

Paratum cor meum.
Psalm 108.

To sing and play my hart is bent,
     is bent gods name to solemnize
thy service ô my tong, present:
     arise my lute, my harp arise.
5   My self will up with dawning skies,
          and so in song report thy praise,
          no eare but shall conceave my laies
          as farre as Earth extended lies.

For, lord, the heav'ns how ever hy,
10   are lower farre then thy sweete grace:
thy truth on stedfast wings doth fly,
     aspiring up to cloudy space.
          ô then thy self in highest place
          above the heav'ns, Jehova, show:

109 nor] not *E*   110 makes] mak'th *θ*   111 the poore] the power *σ*   waigh]
waye *E*   112 howses] households *B*   114 aright] upright *B*   115 distorted]
B notes: disorderd expunged: 117 were] weare *Q*   wisdome] judgment *Q*
120 enfold] *B notes: unfold expunged*

Psalm 108. *Variant in B.*
Incipit: Parat cor *K, O*; Paratum Cor *D, C, M*; *om. I, Q, G*   6 thy] his *G, M*
11 stedfast] te *written over another letter in A*   wings] winge *σ*   doth] doe *M*
12 aspiring] Ascending *M*   space] place *Q, E*   13 then] thou *Q*   place] space *E*

and thence on all this Earth below 15
display the sunn-beames of thy face

To sett thy dearly loved free,
  to helpe and heare me when I pray.
hark, hark, so shall, so shall it be,
  him self doth from his temple say. 20
  then make we heere a mery stay,
    and let me part out Sichems fields:
    the land that Succothes valley yelds,
  by Pearch and pole divided lay.

Myne Gilead is Manashe mine: 25
  Ephraims armes shall guard the king:
my law shall Juda right define,
  while I my shoe at Edom fling.
  thee Moab I will humbled bring
    to wash my feete in servile place: 30
    thou Palestine my late disgrace,
  triumphed, shalt my triumph sing.

But who shall cause us Edom take,
  and enter Edoms strongest towne;
who; but thou god, us'd to forsake 35
  our troopes, and at our sutes to frowne?
  then help us ere distrest we drowne:
    who trusts in man doth vainly trust.
    in only god prevaile we must,
  he, he shall tread our haters downe. 40

---

15 this] the *θ, C, M*   16 face∧] *I, K, D, M*; face. *A, X*   21 we] mee *I, Q, E*
heere] heere [a *altered to* e *before* r *(?)*] *J*; here *Q, E*; heare *I, N, M*   mery] merry *F, I,*
σ, N, C, G, M; mearie *K*; mirry *θ*   22 Sichems] *Sichem C*   23 Succothes] Succoths
K, N; Sucothes *O, E*; Sucoths *I, D, H, Q*   24 pole] poole *O*   25 Gilead] Gillead *σ*
M; Giliad *C*   Manashe] Manasseh *J*; Manasse *I, K, χ*; Manasses *G, M*   26 Ephraims]
Ephrams *Q, M*   armes] arme *I, K, χ* stronge arme *G, M*   27 law shall] lawfull *F*
28 shoe] shoes *N*   29 I will] will I *θ*   32 triumphed] triumphinge *O*   34 enter]
Endor *I*   strongest] strongest *F, J, I, K, χ*; stronget *A*   35 thou] <thou> *K*
37 ere] er *θ, H, Q, C*; err *Q*   38 trusts] *final long* s *added in darker ink in A*; trust *O*
doth] shall *M*   39 only] oly *I*   prevaile] u *i.e.* v *added above caret in A*   40 he, he]
Even he *M*

Deus laudem.
Psalm 109.

Since thus the wicked, thus the fraudulent,
    since liers thus enforce my blame:
        ô god, god of my praise,
be not in silence pent:
5   for their malitious wordes against me raise
Engins of hate, and causelesse battry frame.

Causelesse? ay me! quite contrary to cause
    my love they doe with hate repay:
        with treasons lawlesse spight
10   they answer frendshipps lawes
        and good with ill, and help with harme requite:
    what resteth now, but that to thee I pray?

I pray then what? that lorded at command
    of some vile wretch I may him see:
15   that fittly still his foe
to thwart his good may stand:
        that judg'd from judgment, he condempn'd may goe,
    yea to his plague, his praier turned be.

That speedy death cutt of his wofull life,
20   another take his place and port:
        his children fatherlesse,
and husbandlesse his wife,
        may wandring begg, and begg in such distresse
    their beggred homes may be their best resort.

25 That Usurers may all he hath ensnare,
    and strangers reape what he hath sowne:
        that none him frend at all,
none with compassions care

Psalm 109. *B has verse numbers 1–3 by lines 1, 3, 5; numbers 4 and 5 by line 7; 6–31 by lines 13, 16, 19, 21, 23, 25, 27, 29, 31, 34, 37, 43, 45, 49, 51, 55, 58, 61, 65, 67, 70, 72, 73, 76, 79, 81. Incipit: Deus Laudum H; Deus Laudem meam θ; Deus laudem tuam C, M; om. I, Q, G* 6 Engins] E *added in darker ink in A*   14 vile] vild θ   15 fittly] filthie σ 17 condempn'd may] condemned B, I, K, χ   goe] *om.* I   18 plague] plauge H, Q; plagues B   19 of his] *a second* f *added, without gilding and in different ink, in a hand resembling the J hand in A*   20 port] part B   23 wandring] wardring I   24 homes] home G   26 sowne] sowen θ   28 compassions] compassion I

embrace his brood, but they to wrack may fall
and falne may lye in following age unknowne.   30

That not his owne alone but ev'ry cryme
      of fathers, and forefathers hand,
            may in gods sight abide:
yea to eternall tyme
            synne of his mother and his mothers side   35
      may in his mind, who is eternall, stand.

That he and they soe farre may be forgott,
      that neither print of being leave:
            what humane nature will
for he remembred not,   40
            but sought a wretch inhumanly to spill
      and would of life an humbled hart bereave.

He loved mischif; mischief with him goe:
      he did noe good; then doe him none,
            be wretchednes his cloake,   45
into him soaking soe
            as water dronken inwardly doth soake
      as oile through flesh doth search the hidden bone.

Be woe, I say his garment large and wide,
      fast girt with girdle of the same.   50
            so be it, be it aye,
such misery betide
            unto all such as thirsting my decay,
      against my soule such deadly falshood frame.

But thou ô lord, my lord soe deale with me   55
      as doth thy endlesse honor fitt:
            and for thy glories sake
let me deliverance see,
            for want and woe my life their object make
      and in my brest my hart doth wounded sitt.   60

29 may] might *θ*   32 fathers] Father *G, M*   36 stand] bide *O*   37 soe farre
may be forgott] may be so farr begott *B*   42 an] my *I*   humbled] humble *χ*; humane *E*
hart] soule *O*   bereave] berave *I*   44 noe] *written over erasure in A*   47 doth]
dos *B*   48 as] And *B*   49 Be] But *σ*   garment] garments *χ*   large] fresh *N*
53 thirsting] thirst in *O*   55 ô lord] O God *B*   56 doth] dos *B*   thy] thine *J*
honor] glorie *Q*

I fade and faile as shade with falling sunn:
  and as the Grasshopper is tost,
    place after place I leese.
  while fast hath nigh undone
65   the witherd knotts of my disjoynted knees,
    and dried flesh all juyce and moisture lost.

Worse yet alas! I am their scorne, their nod,
  when in their presence I me show
    but thou, thou me uphold,
70 my lord, my gratious god:
    ô save me in thy mercies manifold,
    thy hand, thy work, make all men on me know.

They curse me still, but blesse thou where they curse:
  they rise, but shame shall bring them downe.
75   and this my joy shall be,
  as bad disgrace or worse
    shall them attyre then ever clothed me,
    trailing in trayne a synnfull shamefull gowne.

Then, then will I Jehovas workes relate
80   where multitudes their meeting have:·
    because still nigh at hand
  to men in hard estate
    he in their most extreamities doth stand,
    and guiltlesse lives from false condempners save.

Dixit Dominus.
Psalm 110.

Thus to my lord, the lord did say:
  take up thy seate at my right hand,

61 fade] vade *Q*   and] I *N*   faile] *B notes: fall* expunged   sunn] sonne *Q, E*; sum *I*
64 nigh] nighe [e *written over* t (?)] *H*; night *I, E*   66 juyce] joyce *H, Q*; joye *E*
lost] left [?] *O*; lest *D*   67 their nod] and nodd *B*
B, I, K, χ; thou *A*; butt thou *J*; thou do'st *G, M*   69 thou, thou] Thou, Thou
shame shall] shall shall *O*   77 then] that *E*   73 where] when *B*   74
full] shameles *B*   gowne] growne *H, E*; grownde *Q*   78 trailing] Training *B*   shame-
C, G, M; Jehovahs *O*; Jehovaes σ   workes] praise θ   79 Jehovas] Jehova's *J, I, N,*
G, M have] make *O*   83 extreamities] extremitie θ, *E*   80 meeting] meetings *J,* θ,
    84 save] saves *K*

Psalm 110. *B has verse number 1 by line 1.*   *Incipit: om. Q*
1–11 *partly obscured by stain from a dried flower in J*   2 my] m *written over erasure in A*

till all thy foes that proudly stand,
I prostrate at thy footestoole lay.
      from me thy staffe of might   5
      sent out of Sion goes:
      as victor then prevaile in fight,
      and rule repining foes.

But as for them that willing yeld,
      in solempne robes they glad shall goe: 10
attending thee when thou shalt show
triumphantly thy troopes in field:
      in field as thickly sett
      with warlike youthfull trayne
      as pearled plaine with dropps is wett,   15
      of sweete Auroras raine.

The lord did sweare, and never he
      what once he sware will disavow:
      as was Melchisedech soe thou.
an everlasting priest shalt be.   20
      at hand still ready prest
      to guard thee from anoy,
      shall sitt the lord that loves thee best,
      and kings in wrath destroy.

5–8 *B notes:* It stood before Corr:
                      Thy staff of might
                      From Sion goes
                      Be victor then in fight
                      And rule repining foes. expunged.
5 from me] For lo! *B*; Behold *K*, χ; <beheeld[*?*]>\behold/ *I*   6 sent] From *B, I, K,* χ
8 and] all *O*   10 solempne] sacred *B*   12 triumphantly] triumphanly *K*   13 in
field as] So each side *B, which also notes on* each side: added upon Correction.   thickly sett]
thick beset *B*; thickest sett [*?*] *I*; quickly sett σ, *G*   14 warlike] *B notes (at line 13):*
added upon Correction.   15 plaine] trayne *K*; field *B*   with dropps] *B notes (at
line 13):* added upon Correction.   wett] sett θ   16 *B notes:* The last verse [16]
stood before[:] *With dropps of s. A. r.* expunged.   Auroras] Aurora's *N, C, M*; Auroraes
σ, *G*   raine] rayne *K*, σ, *M*; rayn *B*; raigne *D*   18 sware] sweare *Q*   19 Melchis-
edech] Melchisedec *B*; Melchesedech *O*; Melchisadech *I*; Melchisadeck *Q, E*; Melchisadeth
H   20 an] And *Q*   shalt] shall *B, N*
21–4 *B notes:* It stood before
                      At thy right hand
                      To guard thee well
                      The lord shall carefull stand
                      And kings shall in his [?] fury quell expunged.
B also records another version of 21: Shall prest at thy right hand expunged   23 shall] So
B, which notes: Shall/first writen on the Correction and then expungd.   thee] the *F, N*

25   Thy Realme shall many Realmes containe:
           thy slaughtred foes thick heaped ly:
           with crusshed head ev'n he shall dy,
      who head of many Realmes doth raigne.
            If passing on these waies
30   thou tast of troubled streames:
           shall that eclips thy shyning raies?
           nay light thy glories beames.

Confitebor tibi.
Psalm 111.

    At home, abroad most willingly I will
    Bestow on god my praises uttmost skill:
    Chaunting his workes, workes of unmatched might,
    Deem'd so by them, who in their search delight.
5   Endlesse the honor to his powre pertaines:
    From end as farre his justice eake remaines.
    Gratious and good and working wonders soe,
    His wonders never can forgotten goe.
    In hungry waste he fedd his faithful Crue,
10   Keeping his league, and still in promise true.
    Lastly his strength he caus'd them understand,
    Making them lords of all the heathens land.
    Now what could more each promise, doome, decree,
    Of him confirme sure, just, unmov'd to be!

26 thick heaped] thick heap'd *B, which notes: in heapes* expunged: 27 Ev'n he with
crushed head shall dy *B*   28 doth] doe *M*
29–32 *B notes:* before it was

              yet in the way
              With troubled streames
              Thou shalt thy thirst allay
              But that shall light etc. expunged.

This last correction seems to be written by the Author   29 these] those *M*   32 glories]
glorious *G, M*

Psalm 111. *B has verse numbers 1–10 by lines 1, 3, 5, 7, 9, 11, 13, 14, 15, 17.*
Incipit: Confitebor *B; om. I, Q*   1 home] whome *Q*   2 praises uttmost] utmost
praises *θ*   4 search] a *added above* er *in A*   6 eake] take *E*; still *G, M*   7 and
working] as working *I, K, N, C, σ, G, M*   11 caus'd] *A, B (text);* made *I, K, χ; B
notes: made* expunged   12 them] then *I*   heathens land] heathen land *B, θ, N, G,
M*; heathen landes *D*   13 promise] promisd *E*   doome] done *I*   14 confirme
sure] *A, B (text);* approve sure *K, θ* a prove sure *C, σ;* a prove-sure *N;* a proofe sure *G,
M; B notes: approve* expunged

Preserv'd his folk, his league eternall framd, 15
Quake then with feare when holy he is nam'd.
Reverence of him is perfect wisdoms well:
Stand in his lawe, so understand you well.
The praise of him (though wicked hartes repine)
Unbounded bides, noe time can it define: 20

Beatus vir.
Psalm 112.

O in how blessed state he standeth,
    who soe Jehova feareth,
that in the things the lord commandeth
    his most delight appeareth!

The branches from that body springing 5
    on the earth shall freshly flourish:
their pedigree from good men bringing
    the lord with blisse will nourish.

The happy howse wherein he dwelleth
    well stored shall presever: 10
the treasures justly gott he telleth,
    shall bide his owne for ever.

For he when woe them over-cloudeth
    the darkned hartes enlighteth:
his mildnes them and mercy shrowdeth 15
    his justice for them fighteth.

He is both good and goodnes loveth,
    most liberall and lending:
all businesses wherein he moveth
    with sound advice attending. 20

---

15 folk] flock *G, M*

Psalm 112. *B has verse numbers 1–10 by lines 1, 5, 9, 13, 17, 21, 23, 25, 29, 33.*
Incipit: om. Q
1 in how] how in *B*   blessed] happie *E*   3 things] thing *B, σ*   5 springing]
springeth *E*   6 the earth] th'earth *χ*; the-earth *H*; earth *Q*; *Earth G*   freshly]
freely *B*   10 stored] standing *M*   13 woe them] woes him *G*   14 the]
their *G, M*   enlighteth] inlightneth *B*; enlightneth *I, Q, E, G*   15 them] then *K*
19 businesses] busnesses *J*; busines *N, C, G, M*

He firmly propt for ever falling,
  his name exempt from dying:
can heare ill newes without appalling,
  his hart on god relying.

25 Hys hart (I say) which strongly staied,
  is free from feare preserved:
till on his foes he view displaied
  the plagues by them deserved.

He gives where needs, nay rather straweth,
30 his justice never ending:
soe honors hand him higher draweth
  with gladd applause ascending.

Of good I meane: for wicked wretches
  shall seeing fume, and fuming
35 consume to nought, their frutles fetches
  to nought with them consuming.

Laudate pueri.
Psalm 113.

O you that serve the lord,
to praise his name accord:
Jehova now and ever
commending, ending never,
5 whom all this earth resoundes,
from East to Westerne boundes.

He Monarch raignes on high;
his glory treades the sky.

---

24 god] good *O* 25 staied] *B, K, χ*; staid *A, N, C* 27 displaied] *B, K, χ*; dis-
plaid *A, N* 28 plagues] plauges *J, H, Q* 29 needs] need *N* 32 ascending]
ascendend *I* 33 good] God *J* 35 nought] naught *B, I, N* 36 nought]
naught *B, I, N* them] then *O*

Psalm 113. *Variant in I. B has verse numbers 1–9 by lines 1, 2, 3, 5, 7, 9, 13, 14, 17.*
Incipit: om. Q
1 serve] *B notes:* first *feare* then *praise* but both expunged. 2 accord] record *E*
3 Jehova] Jehovah *D*; *B notes: His name* expunged. 5 whom] *B notes: which*
expunged. 6 boundes] bound *B* 7 raignes] raynes *H, Q* 8 treades] fills *M*

like him who can be counted,
that dwells soe highly mounted?　　　　　　　　10
yet stooping low beholds
what heav'n and earth enfolds.

From dust the needy soule,
the wretch from miry hole
he lifts: yea kings he makes them,　　　　　　　15
yea kings his people takes them.
he gives the barren wife
a frutfull mothers life.

In exitu Israel.
Psalm 114.

At what tyme Jacobs race did leave of Ægipt take,
　　and Ægipts barbrous folk forsake:
then, then our god, our king elected Jacobs race
　　his temple there and throne to place.
The sea beheld and fledd; Jordan with swift returne　　5
　　to twinned spring his streames did turne.
The mountaines bounded soe, as fedd in frutfull ground
　　the fleezed Rammes doe frisking bound.
The hillocks capreold soe, as wanton by their dammes
　　we capreoll se the lusty lambes.　　　　　　　　10

9–10 *B notes:*
　　　　　　　　By whom can he be faced
　　　　　　　　He who most highly placed
but expungd by the Author and set as in the text only it was first *His like* etc but *His like* is
changd to *like him*　　12–13 *A has a dash and* L 217 *in the margin between these
lines*　　13 From] ffor *O;* ff<o>r\o/ *K (tilde over first* o)　　14 miry] merrie *altered
to* meiry *in K*　　15 yea] ye *K, D, N*　　16 yea] he *K, N, H*
17–18 *B notes:*
　　　　　　　　The barren Wife before
　　　　　　　　He stores with children store expunged
18 mothers] s *added in A;* mother *F*

Psalm 114. *Lacking in I. B has verse numbers* 1–8 *by lines* 1, 3, 5, 7, 11, 13, 17, 19.
Incipit: In exitu [*added in the left margin in a different hand*] *K; om. Q*　　1 Ægipt] *A, Q,
E, M;* Egipt *K,* χ; Egypt *B*　　2 Ægipts] *A, Q, E;* Egipts *K,* χ; Egypts *B*　　3 our
god] o^r god *H;* ô god *E; om. N*　　elected] c *added above caret in A*　　5 beheld] l *added in
same ink and hand, gilded in A*　　6 spring] *final* s *erased in A;* spring *F;* springs *J, B, K,*
χ; streames *E*　　8 fleezed] fleeced *J, B;* feeced *N;* fleesinge θ　　9 hillocks] hillock *B*
capreold] capred σ, *G, M*　　by] with *Q*　　dammes] damms *B, K, H, E;* dams θ, *Q, N;*
dames *G, M*　　10 capreoll] capre *H, Q;* Caper *E, G, M*

O sea, why didst thou fly? Jordan, with swift returne
    to twinned spring what made thee turne?
Mountaines why bounded ye, as fedd in frutfull ground
    the fleezed Rammes doe frisking bound?
15 Hillocks why capreold ye, as wanton by their dammes
    we capreoll see the lusty lambes?
Nay you, and earth with you, quake ever at the sight
    of God Jehova, Jacobs might.
Who in the hardest Rocks, makes standing waters grow
20   and purling springs from flints to flow.

Non nobis Domine.
Psalm 115.

Not us I say, not us,
    but thine owne name respect, eternall lord:
and make it glorious,
    to show thy mercy and confirme thy word.
5 why lord, why should these nations say,
where doth your god now make his stay?

You ask where our god is?
    In heav'n enthron'd, no marke of mortal ey.
nor hath, nor will he misse
10   what likes his will, to will effectually.
what are your Idolls? we demaund:
gold, silver, workes of workmens hand.

11 didst] dids *E*   Jordan, with swift] ~‸ why swifte *B*; *om. D*   12 spring] springes *O*, *C*, *σ*, *G*, *M*   thee] the *F*   13 bounded] bounde *σ*   ye] yea *O*   in] with *K*, *χ* 14 fleezed] fleeced *B*, *N*; fleesed *D*; fleesinge *O*   15 capreold] capre *H*, *Q*; caper *E*, *G*, *M*   ye] yea *C*   by their] with their *B*, *θ*, *σ*; with your *K*, *N*, *C*, *G*, *M*   dammes] *A*, *G*; damms *B*, *K*, *E*, *C*; dams *θ*, *Q*, *N*; dames *H*, *M*   16 capreoll] caper *H*, *E*, *G*, *M*; capre *Q*   17 Nay you] Naye yee *M*   ever] even *N*   18 of] O *B*   Jehova, Jacobs] ~‸ ~ (, *H*; Jehovah‸ ~ *K*, *N*; ~: ~ *Q*; Jehovas *B*   19 makes] makst *E*   20 flints] flinte *C*, *G*

Psalm 115. *Lacking in I. B has verse numbers 1–18 by lines 1, 5, 7, 9, 13, 15, 17, 19, 21, 23, 25, 27, 31, 33, 35, 37, 43, 47.*
Incipit: Non nobis *G*, *K* (*added in left margin in a different hand*); *om. Q*   1 us I say, not] s I say, not *written over erasure in A*   8 marke] worke *O*   9 nor hath] r *written over* t *in A*   he] his *E*   10 effectually] eternally *G*   12 workes] worke *D* hand] hands *B*, *G*; hand<es> *C*

They mouthes, but speachlesse, have:
       eyes sightlesse: eares, no newes of noies can tell:
who them their noses gave,   15
       gave not their noses any sence of smell.
nor handes can feele, nor feete can goe,
nor signe of sound their throates can show.

And wherin differ you,
       who having made them, make of them your trust?   20
but Israel pursue
       thy trust in god, the targett of the just.
O Arons howse, the like doe yee:
he is their aid, their targett he.

All that Jehovah feare,   25
       trust in Jehovah, he our aid and shield:
he us in mind doth beare,
       hee will to us aboundant blessings yeeld.
will evermore with grace and good
blesse Jacobs howse, blesse Arons brood.   30

Blesse all that beare him awe,
       both great and small the conduites of his store,
he never dry shall draw,
       but you and youres enrich still more and more.
blest, ô thrice blest, whom he hath chose,   35
who first with heav'ns did earth enclose.

Where height of highest skies
       removed most from floore of lowly ground
with vaughted roofe doth rise:
       him self tooke up his dwelling there to found.   40
to mortall men he gratious gave
the lowly ground to hold and have.

---

14 noies] noise *F, J, B, K (altered), N, C, H (altered), Q, E, G, M*   16 sence] sent *N*
17 feele] feeld *Q*   20 of them] of *O*   your] theire *θ, N*   23 Arons] Aarons *B, E*
yee] you *D*   25 Jehovah] Jehova *B, K, χ*   26 Jehovah] Jehova *B, K, χ*   and]
ampersand (different from Davies's usual ampersand) added in gold above gold caret in A;
our *O*   27 doth] doe *M*   28 blessings] blessing *E*   29 will] And *G*
30 Arons] Aarons *B, E*   36 earth] him *E*   39 vaughted] vawted *θ*; vaulted *J,*
B, K, N, C, σ, G, M   40 tooke up] *B notes: hath chose expunged.*

And why? his praise to show:
    which how can dead men, lord, in any wise?
45 who downe descending goe
    into the place where silence lodged lies.
But save us: we thy praise record
will now and still: ô praise the lord.

Dilexi quoniam.
Psalm 116.

The lord receaves my cry,
    and me good eare doth give:
then love hym still will I,
    and praise him while I live.
5   fast bound in bonds of death,
        with deadly anguish thralled:
      when greef nigh stopt my breath,
        upon his name I called.

I call'd, and thus I said;
10   ô lord my bands unbind.
I found him prone to aid,
    I found him just and kind.
      the simples surest guard
        by me of right esteemed:
15   whom he distressed hard,
        from hard distresse redeemed.

My soule turmoild with woes,
    now boldly turne to rest,
such changes on thee showes
20   who greatest is and best.
      My life from death is past,
        mine eies have dried their weeping:

---

46 place] pitt *G*   48 the] thee *M*

Psalm 116. *Lacking in I.*
Incipit: Dilexi quoniam [*added in left margin in a different hand*] *K*; *om. Q*
2 good eare doth] doth good eare *F*   3 hym] *added in gold above gold caret in A*
5 bonds] bandes *C, G, M*   11 prone] quick *M*   13 simples] simple's *C, M*;
sympless *Q*; simplest *J*   14 esteemed] *B, K, C, H, Q, G, M*; redeem'd *A*   15 hard]
heard *B, K, χ*   16 hard] heard *σ*   redeemed] *B, K, C, H, Q, G, M*; esteem'd *A*
18 rest] d *erased before* r *in A*   19 thee] her *σ*   22 mine] my *θ*

my slipping foote stands fast:
my self live in his keeping.

Beleeving as I spake,   25
    (such woe my witts did blind)
I said when I did quake,
    I all men liers finde.
        which finding false, to thee
            what thancks lord shall I render,   30
        who showring blisse on me
            dost me soe truly tender?

My cup with thancks shall flow
    for freedom from my thrall:
which I in flames will throw,   35
    and on thy name will call.
        to thee my vowes will pay,
            thy people all beholding:
        who deere their deaths dost weigh,
            that are to thee beholden.   40

This I thy servant taste,
    thy slave thy handmaids sonne:
whose bands thou broken hast,
    and fettring chaines undone.
        Who unto thee for this   45
            a sacrifice of praising
        to offer will not misse,
            thy name with honor raising.

Thou, whom no times enfold,
    shalt have what I did vow: 50
and they shall all behold,
    who to thy Scepter bow.
        the place, that holy place,
            before thy howse extended:
        the very midle space   55
            in Sion comprehended.

24 keeping] keeinge *K*   26 woe] woes *G, M*   did] do *N*   blind] binde *K*, χ   31 show-
ring] showring [r *written over another letter*] *K*; showing *B*   35 throw] trowe *O*
39 dost weigh] doe waigh *F*   40 are] art *H*   beholden] behouldeing *K*, χ   41 thy]
thie thy *H*   42 slave] flame σ   44 fettring] frettinge *K*, χ   50 did] doe *E*
53 holy place] hollye place *E*; hollie place *H*; hollie hill *Q*   56 comprehended] Comph/ *O*

Laudate Dominum.
Psalm 117.

P raise him that ay
R emaines the same:
A ll tongues display
I ehovas fame.
5   S ing all that share
T his earthly ball:
H is mercies are
E xpos'd to all.
L ike as the word
10   O nce he doth give,
R old in record,
D oth time outlyve.

Confitemini Domino.
Psalm 118.

The lord is good, you see and know;
    acknowledg then and praise him soe:
for soe his bounty it extendeth,
noe age can say, loe here it endeth.

5   Thou chosen Israel allway,
    with me be prest the same to say:
for soe his bounty it extendeth,
noe age can say, loe here it endeth.

Psalm 117. *Variant in B. Only A, F, J as well as the variant in B, clearly emphasize the acrostic by means of initial capitals and lack of indentation. I, θ do not indent, but do not capitalize all initial letters. K, N, M indent even lines. C has quatrains and indents even lines. G indents 2, 4, 10, 12; doubly 5, 7; triply 6, 8. H combines pairs of lines into a six-line stanza and indents 2–6; Q, E also have only six lines and indent even lines.*
Incipit: om. Q
2 R emaines] remaine *E*   3 display] explaie *O*   4 I ehovas] Iehova's *N, C, G,*
M; Iehovahs *I, K*; Iehovaes *σ*   6 earthly] earthie *K, χ*   7 H is] His *N, M*;
H his *A*; his *I, K, χ*   9 as] so *I, K, χ*

Psalm 118. *Lacking in I. B notes:* It has a crosse thus (X) in the margin + Upon correction added and interlin'd in the first verse of each staff. a word of two syllables
Incipit: Confitemini *K, C, G, M; om. Q*
1, 5, 9 *B notes (in darker ink):* added by interlining[:] see and [*1*], chosen [*5*], sacred [*9*].
1 good] god *D, σ*; God *O*

You that of sacred Aron came,
  be prest with me to say the same: 10
for soe his bounty it extendeth
noe age can say, loe here it endeth.

  And you his fearers all the rest,
  the same to say with me be prest:
for soe his bounty it extendeth,   15
noe age can say, loe here it endeth.

  I somtime straitned lay in thrall:
  so lying I on god did call,
god answere gave me, when I called,
and me unlarging me unthralled.   20

  Jehova doth my party take;
  should feare of man then cause me quake?
Nay with my frends sith god is placed,
how can my foes but be disgraced?

  More safe it is on god to stay,   25
  then confidence on man to lay:
more safe who god his refuge taketh,
then he who kings his succour maketh.

  Of enimies all sortes that be,
  on ev'ry part inviron'd me: 30
but I their sinewes cut and quailed,
Jehovas name soe much prevailed.

  They me inviron'd yet againe,
  againe they did me straitly strayne:

---

9 Aron] Aaron *B, E*   came] come *J*   10 be prest] Accord *C*; Joine you *G, M*
12 here] heere *F, K, D*; heare *Q*   13 And you] *B notes:* Added.   14 the same
to say] the same [f *altered to* s] to saie *K*; His praise to sound *G, M*   16 here]
heere *F, K, θ, H*; heare *Q*   17 somtime] *B notes:* Added; sometimes *G, M*
straitned] straightned *θ, N (second* t *added), C, Q, E, G, M*; straighned *H*;   strenghtened *K*
19 god] g *written in darker ink in A*   20 unlarging] *A, F, σ*; enlarging *J, B, K, χ*
21 *B notes:* it stood before Correction. *The lord my part doth take* expunged.
22 should] Shall *G* man] men *σ, G* cause] make *B, K, χ*   23–4 *B notes:* in the
margin [*correction mark in parentheses*]   25 it is] *B notes:* Added.   26 then] Then
altered to Than *(?) in B*   on] *A, B, N, C*; in *K, χ*   29 enimies] *B notes:* twas *Foes*
expunged for *Enemys* a word of 3 syllables to be putt   31 quailed] quailes *N*
32 Jehovas] Jehova's *N, C, G, M*; Jehovaes *σ*   33 They me] *B notes:* Added.
34 straitly] straightly *θ, σ, C, G, M*

35   but I their sinewes cut and quailed,
      Jehovas name soe much prevailed.

      They me inviron'd yet a new,
        and swarming fast like Bees they flew.
      as fire in thornes they quickly quailed,
40   soe to their wrack his name prevailed.

      In-deede thou sore at me dids't thrust:
        yet by his succour stand I must.
      in him my strength, of him my ditty,
      he did my soule in thralldom pitty.

45   You righteous troupe with me rejoyce:
        consort with mine your joyfull voice:
      say prais'd his hand, yea double praised,
      be his strong hand so highly raised.

      For be assur'd I shall not dy;
50   but live gods works to testify:
      who though he sore did scurging paine me
      he hath but scurg'd, he hath not slaine mee.

      Who opens to me Justice gate?
        I entring may Gods praise relate.
55   this gate unto Jehova showeth
      by this to him the righteous goeth.

      Here, here ô Lord, I will thee praise,
        who didst my life to safty raise:
      the stone the builders erst refused,
60   in corner now is laied and used.

---

36 Jehovas] Jehova's *N, C, G, M;* Jehovaes σ   37–40 *added in the left margin in* H
37 They me] *B notes:* Added.; They yet *M*   yet] me *M*   38 they] that *K,* χ
40 *E repeats* 36   his] thy θ   41 In-deede] *B notes:* Added; Andeede *O*   thou]
they *Q*   dids't] did *Q*   43 in] on *O*   44 thralldom] tharldome *O*   45 right-
eous] *B notes: just* expunged for 3 syllables to be putt in its stead   46 mine] mee *G*
47 prais'd] praise θ   hand] hands *G*   yea] ye *B*   48 be his strong] he his strong
F; by his stronge *E;* be stronge his *Q*   49 For be assur'd] ffor hee assur'd *F; B notes:*
Twas first *For lo* then *For lo behold.* expunged   51 scurging] scouring *O*   53 opens to
me] open to me *K,* χ; *B notes: ope's me* expunged   56 this] thuss σ   57 Here,
here ô Lord] Heere O Lord *N, C,* σ, *G;* Heare O lord θ, *M;* O Heere mee Lord [O *added;*
mee *added above caret written over* o] *K; B notes on* ô lord: Added.   58 to] from *O*
60 In head of Corner now is used *G, M*

This workmanshipp in deed divine
doth in our eyes with wonder shine.
god made this day, he did us send it,
in joy and mirth then lett us spend it.

O help us Lord, ô help we say,   65
ô prosper, prosper us we pray.
blest in thy name who comming rideth,
blest in thy house who dwelling bideth.

Thy house, Lord mighty God, whence we
both have our light and sight to see: 70
ty fast the lambe on Alter lying,
the cords to horned corners tying.

O god, my mighty god thou art,
and I to thee will praise impart:
ô god thou art my god, and ever   75
I will extoll thee, ceasing never.

The lord is good you see and know:
acknowledg then and praise him soe.
for soe his bounty it extendeth,
no age can say, loe here it endeth.   80

61 workmanshipp] k *added in gold above gold caret in A; B notes on the last two syllables:*
Added.   63 god] g *written in darker ink in A*   64 joy and mirth] mirth, and joye
M 65 O help us] *B notes: Before* Help. expunged.   66 prosper us] <us> prosper us
K; us, prosper us θ   69 *B notes: The Lord is God and hee* expunged   whence]
when *N* 70 both have our light] have both our sight *G; B notes: Both gives us light* expunged:
sight] light *G*   73 mighty] *B notes: Added.*   77–80 *Lacking in F (*The *appears as
a catchword at the bottom of f.* 133*); the lines are at the top of f.* 102^v *in A.*   77 good] god θ,
E   see and] *B marks the phrase as usual—*see and*—but omits the marginal note,* 'Added'.

Beati immaculati.
A Psalm 119.

An undefiled course who leadeth,
and in Jehovas doctrine treadeth,
  how blessed he?
  how blest they be
5   who still his testimonies keeping,
   doe seeke him self with harty seeking?

For whom in walke Gods way directeth,
sure them no sinnfull blott infecteth
  of deede or word:
10   for thou, ô lord,
   hast to be done thy lawes commanded,
   not only to be understanded.

O were my stepps soe staid from swerving,
that I me to thy heasts observing
15 might wholy give.
   then would I live
   with constant cheere all chaunces brooking,
   to all thy precepts ever looking.

Then would I worshipp thee sincerly,
20 when what thy Justice bidds severely.
  thou shouldst me teach:
  I would noe breach
  Make of thy law to me betaken:
  ô leave me not in whole forsaken.

Psalm 119. *Lacking in I.*
A.
Incipit: om. K, Q. The incipits of subsequent octaves (groups of eight verses) are omitted in A, F, J, B, K, and χ (except for N and all the σ group but Q). The octaves (with or without incipits) are preceded by capital letters in A, F, J, B, K, θ, N, C; by letters and numerals in H, G (except for octave A), M; by Parte *(or its abbreviation) and numerals in Q, E (and its descendants). Folio 94ᵛ (following Ps. 119) blank in K; next leaf torn out, stub remaining.*
1 course] life *G, M* 2 Jehovas] Jehova's *J, C, G, M*; Jehovaes *σ* 6 him self] him still *G, M* harty] hearty *B, G, M*; hardie *H, Q* 7 way] word *M* 10 thou] then *altered to* thou (en *partly erased*) *in A* 11 hast] haste *C, M* 13 were] a *lightly stricken before* r *in A*; weare *F, H* swerving] r *added above caret in darker ink in A* 15 wholy] holie *N* 20 when] Where *B* thy] the *C* 24 leave] lead *N* not in whole] wholy not *M*; not then quite *C*

B.

By what correcting line,
     may a yong man make streight his crooked way?
by levell of thy lore divine.
       sith then with soe good cause
     my hart thee seekes, ô lord, I seeking pray   5
       let me not wander from thy lawes.

Thy speeches have I hidd
     close locked up in Caskett of my hart:
fearing to do what they forbidd.
       but this can-nott suffice: 10
     thou wisest lord, who ever-blessed art,
       yet make me in thy statutes wise.

Then shall my lipps declare
     the sacred lawes that from thy mouth proceed:
and teach all nations what they are   15
       for what thou dost decree
     to my conceit farre more delight doth breed,
       then worlds of wealth, if worlds might be

Thy precepts therefore I
     will my continuall meditation make: 20
and to thy pathes will have good eye
       the orders by thee sett
     shall cause me in them greatest pleasure take,
       nor once will I thy wordes forgett.

C.

Conferre, ô Lord;
this benefitt on me,

B.
Incipit: In quo corriget *N*; In quo corigett *H, E*   2 streight] straight *θ, σ, N, G, M*;
streit *B*   of] at *θ*   4 sith] Seeth *H, Q*   6 lawes] *Written over erasure of* wayes *in*
A; waies *F*   8 Caskett] closett *θ, C, M*   14 the] Thy *altered to* The *in B*
that] which *B*   thy] the *altered to* thy *in B*   18 then] the\m/ *H*   worlds . . . worlds]
world . . . world *E (final letters in H unclear)*   20 meditation] meditacons *E*   22 orders]
order *F, θ*

C. *B notes:* In the margin this mark [*correction mark in brackets*]
Incipit: Retribue servo *N, E*; Retrube servo *H*

that I may live, and keepe thy word.
 open mine eyes,
5   they may the riches see,
 which in thy law enfolded lies.

  A Pilgrim right
  on earth I wandring live:
   o barre me not thy statutes light.
10 I wast and spill,
  while still I longing grieve,
 grive longing for thy judgments still

  Thou proud and high
  dost low and lowly make:
15   curst from thy rule who bend awry.
 what shame they lay
  on me then from me take:
 for I have kept thy will allway.

  Let Princes talk,
20 and talk their worst of me:
   in thy decrees my thoughts shall walk.
 all my delight
  thy wittnest will shalbe:
 my councell to advise me right.

D:

Dead as if I were,
  my soule to dust doth cleave:
   lord keepe thy word, and doe not leave
me here:
5   but quicken me a new.
  when I did confesse

---

3 and] to *H, E, G, M*; to- *Q* 4 mine] my *K* 5 the] The [*altered to* Thy] *B*; thy *N*
6 enfolded] enfoldeth *H, E* 10 *added by Woodforde in the right margin in B* wast]
waste *F, D, H, Q, C, M* 15 bend] leade *C* awry] aw\r/y *B* 17 then] Lord
M 23 wittnest] witness'd *B*; witnesse *K, σ* 24 councell] *A, Q*; counsell *B, K, O,*
σ, N; Counsaile *C* me] men *K*
D.
Incipit: Adhæsit pavimento *N, E*; Adhæsitt pavimento *H*
1 were] weare *H, Q, C* 3 lord] l *added in darker ink, loop not gilded, in A* 4 here]
heere *Q, N, C, M*; heare *K, θ, H* 5 a new] anew *F, K, θ, Q, E, N*

        my sinnfull waies to thee,
          as then thy eare thou did'st to me
adresse:
      soe teach me now, thy statutes true.   10

Make that I may know,
     and throughly understand
      what waie to walk thou dos't command
then show
       will I thy wonders all.   15
         very woe and greif
           my soule doe melt and fry;
             revive me lord, and send me thy
relief;
       and lett on me thy comfort fall.   20

From the lyers trace,
     from falshoods wreathed way,
      ô save me lord, and graunt I may
embrace
       the law thou dost commend.   25
         for the path ay right,
           where truth unfained goes,
             my tongue to tread hath gladly chose:
         my sight
       thy judgmentes doth, as guides, attend.   30

Since therefore, ô lord,
     still did I, still I doe
      so neerly, deerly cleave unto
thy word:
       all shame from me avert.   35
         then loe, loe then I

---

8 thy eare thou did'st] my eare thou didst' *F*; thou didst thy eare *O*; thine eare thou didst *E*
17 soule] hart *C*   doe] doth *B, K, χ*   and] *added above caret (different from Davies's usual caret) in A*   18 revive] receaue *F*   22 wreathed] writhed *B*; wretched *χ*; *om. K*
23 graunt] make *B, K, χ*   25 commend] comeund [e *written over* a] *C, G*; command *M*
26 the] thy *O*   path ay right] path aright *O*; pathwaie right *G, M*   27 unfained] unfeigned *B*   28 tread] speake *G, M*   gladly] dayly *B*   30 judgmentes] judg-ment *B*   35 all] And *N*; as *σ*   36 loe, ∧loe∧ then] loe, (lord) then *G*; loe∧ then *θ*

will tread, yea running tread
   the trace, which thy commandments lead:
when thy
40   free grace hath fully freed my hart.

E

Explaine, ô lord, the way to me,
   that thy divine edicts enfold:
      and I to end will runne it right.
O make my blinded eyes to see,
5   and I thy law will hold: yea hold
         thy law with all my hartes delight.

O be my guide, ô guide me soe,
   I thy commandments path may pace:
      wherein to walk my hart is faine.
10 O bend it then to things that show
   true wittnes of thy might and grace,
      and not to hungry thirst of gaine.

Avert mine eye, it may not view
   of vanity the falsed face:
15   and strength my treadings in thy trade.
lett doings prove thy sayings true
   to him that holds thy servants place,
      and thee his awe, his feare hath made.

Thou then my feare, remove the feare
20   of comming blame from carefull me:

---

39 when thy] *piece of paper over* free gra *after* thy *in A*
E.
B indents even stanzas
Incipit: Legem pone N, H, E
2 enfold] unfold *J, B*   6 thy law] most sure *G*   7 ô guide] and guide *M*   8 path]
pathes *G*   10 bend] binde *G, M*   13 mine] my *B*   eye, it] eyes, it *H*; eyes$_\wedge$ yt
Q, E; eyes$_\wedge$ they *G*; eyes, they *M*   15 treadings] treading *B, σ*   17 him] them *σ,*
G, M holds] hould *H, E*   18 his feare] and feare *G, M*   19 the] my *O*
20 comming] Cousning *B*; *B notes:* forte *comming.* winning expunged   carefull] fearfull *E*

for gratious are thy judgmentes still:
behold, to me thy precepts deare,
most deare, and most delightful be:
ô let thy justice aid my will.

F

Franckly poure ô Lord on me
saving grace, to sett me free:
that supported I may see
promise truly kept by thee.

That to them who me defame,   5
roundly I may answere frame:
who because thy word and name
are my trust, thus seeke my shame.

Thy true word ô do not make
utterly my mouth forsake: 10
since I thus still waiting wake,
when thou wilt just vengaunce take.

Then loe I thy doctrine pure,
sure I hold, will hold more sure:
nought from it shall me alure,   15
all the time my time shall dure.

Then as brought to widest way
from restraint of straitest stay,
all their thincking night and day:
on thy law my thoughtes shall lay.   20

Yea then unto any king
wittnesse will I any thing,
that from thee can wittnesse bring:
in my face no blush shall spring.

---

22 behold] b *added in darker ink, loop not gilded, in A*   23 most delightful] so delightfull *G*
24 my will] me still *B*
F.
Incipit: Et veniat super me *N, H, E*
1 poure] powre χ   5 who] whome *K, O*   6 roundly] ly *added above caret in A*
13 loe] lord *G, M*   14 sure I hold, will] I will hould, yea *C*; sure will hould, yea *G, M*
more] most *B, G*; it *N*   16 my time] my life *G, M; om. N*   18 straitest] straight-
est *K,* χ; streightest *B*   19 their] my *G, M*   20 law] lawes *F*

25   Then will I sett forth to sight
          with what pleasure, what delight,
          I embrace thy preceptes right,
          whereunto all love I plight.

          Then will I, will either hand
30   clasp the rules of thy command:
          there my study still shall stand,
          striving them to understand.

G

          Grave deeply in remembring mind
             my trust, thy promise true:
          this only joy in griefe I find,
             thy words my life renue.
5   though proudly scorn'd, yet from thy lore
          I no way have declin'd:
             I hold for comfort what of yore
          thy doomes, ô lord, defind.

          I quake to view how people vile,
10   doe from thy doctryne swerve:
          thy just edicts ev'n in exile
             did me for musick serve.
             I keepe thie learning, and in night
          record Jehovas stile:
15   observing still thy precepts right,
          loe this I have the while.

H

          High Jehova once I say,
             for my choise and lott I take,
          I will sure his wordes obay.
          hott and harty sute I make,

---

26 what delight] and delight *E*   29 will either] *A, B (text)*; with either *K,* χ; *B notes*
(*on* will): forte pro *with*

G. *This version is in A, F, J. Variant in B, K, χ.*

H. *This version is in A, F, J. Variant in B, K, χ.*
3 sure] obay *stricken in ink and gold after* sure *in A*

praying thus ev'n to thy face: 5
pitty me for thy words sake.
Ev'ry path, and evr'y pace
   taught by thee, observing well,
   to thy rule I frame my race.
lest upon delaies I dwell   10
   but to keepe contend with speed
   what to me thy precepts tell.
by lewd robbers brought to need
   from my losses of thy lawes
   never did neglect proceed.   15
midnights watch thy praises cause,
   while that me from bed and rest
   thought of thy just judgments drawes.
felowshipp and frendshipps hest,
   with thy fearers all I hold,   20
   such as hold thy biddings best.
Lord the earth can scarse enfold,
   what thou dost beningly give:
   let me then by thee be told
in thy learning how to live.   25

I.

In all kindnes thou ô lord,
hast to me perform'd thy word:
   this now resteth that I learne
     from thy skill a skillfull tast,
   good from evill to discerne,   5
     on thy lawes whose trust is plac't.

Yet unhumbled I did stray:
now I will thy words obay.
   thou that art soe highly good
     nothing can thy goodnes reach,   10

---

7 pace] place *F*   9 thy] \thy/ [*above caret by scribe*] *F*   10 lest] least *F, J*
16 thy] my *F*   20 thy] my *F*   23 beningly] benignly *J*
I.
Incipit: Bonitatem fecisti *N, H, E*
2 hast] Haste *M*   3 resteth] restest *E*

thou where floweth bounties flood,
willing me thy statutes teach.

What if proud men on me ly?
I will on thy lawes rely.
15   wallow they in their delights,
fatt in body, fatt in mind;
I the pleasures of my sprightes
will unto thy doctrine bind.

Now I find the good of woe,
20   how thy hests it makes me know:
of whose mouth the lectures true,
are alone all wealth to me
millions then, and Mines adue,
gold and silver drosse you be.

K.

Knitt and conformed by thy hand
hath been evr'y part of me:
then make me well to understand,
conceiving all thou dost command.
5   that when me thy fearers see,
they for me may justly joy:
seeing what I look't from thee
on thy word I now enjoy.

O Lord thy judgmentes just I know;
10   when thy scurges scurged me,
thou, in that doing, nought didst show
that might thy promise overthrow.
let me then thy comfort see
kindly sent as thou hast said:
15   bring thy mercies life from thee:
on thy lawes my joyes are laid.

17 pleasures] pleasure *K*, χ   22 alone] above θ   23 adue] adieu *B, J, θ, N, G, M;*
adieue *H, Q;* adiew *C, K;* adiewe *E*

K.
Incipit: Manus tuæ fecerunt me *N, H, E*
1 conformed] confirmed *M*   2 of] in σ   5 me] wee θ, *N,* σ   8 word] lawe *M*
11 nought] naught *B*   14 sent] send *K*   15 bring] send *G, M*   16 are] have *O*

Let blame and shame the proud betide
    falsly who subverted me:
whose meditations shall not slide,
but fast in thy command'ments bide.   20
    so shall I thy fearers see
        on my part who know thy will:
while I purely worshipp thee,
    blott nor blush my face shall fill.

L.

Looking and longing for deliverance
    upon thy promise, mightlesse is my mind,
sightlesse myne eyes, which often I advaunce
        unto thy word,
        thus praying: when, ô lord,   5
    when will it be I shall thy comfort find?

I like a smoked bottle am become:
    and yet the wine of thy command'ments hold.
ay me! when shall I see the totall summe
        of all my woes?   10
        when wilt thou on my foes
    make wronged me thy just reveng behold?

Their pride hath digged pitts me to ensnare,
    which with thy teachings how doth it agree?
true or more truly, Truth thy precepts are: 15
        by falshood they
        would make of me their pray:
    let truth ô lord from falshood rescue me.

Nigh quite consum'd by them on earth I ly:
    yet from thy statutes never did I swerve.   20

---

18 subverted] subvertetd [d *written over* h] *H*; subverteth *Q, E*   19 meditations] med-
itacion *E*   20 in] on *B, K, χ*
L.
Incipit: Defecit anima mea *N, E*; Defecitt annima *H*   2 promise] promises *E*   is] in
K, χ   7 smoked] smoakinge *O*   8 wine] waie *G, M*   13 hath] have *O*
14 teachings] *teaching G*; *precepts M*   doth it] *A, B, G, M*; it doth *K, χ*   15 thy
precepts] they allwaies *M*   17 pray] prey *B, J*   19 Nigh] Night *E*   quite] quitt *K*

Lord, of thy goodnes quicken me, and I
will still pursue:
thy testimonies true,
and all the biddings of thy lipps observe.

M.

Most plainly, lord, the frame of sky
doth show thy word decayeth never:
and constant stay of earth descry
thy word, that staid it, staieth ever.
5   for by thy lawes they hold their standings,
yea all things do thy service try:
but that I joy'd in thy commandings;
I had my self bene sure to dy.

Thy word that hath revived me
10   I will retaine, forgetting never:
lett me thine owne be sav'd by thee,
whose statutes are my studies ever.
        I mark thy will the while their standings
the wicked take my bane to be:
15   for I no close of thy commandings,
of best things els an end I see.

N.

Nought can enough declare
how I thy learning love:
whereon all day my meditation lies.
by whose edicts I prove

---

21 quicken] quickne *O*   24 the] thy *O*   biddings] bidding *M*
M.
Incipit: In æternum Domine *N*; In eternum Domine *H, E*
2 word] words *E*   3 earth] Earth *B, F, J, K,* χ; Eearth *A*   5 thy] theire
O lawes] lawe *G*   7 joy'd] 'd *added above caret in A*   8 B notes: *My self had
perisht utterly* expungd   9 hath] *om. Q* revived] relieved *K,* χ   16 ∧of best
things els] ∧~, *H, Q;* ∧~: *E;* (~) *N, G;* (~,) *C*
N.
Incipit: Quomodo dilexi? *N;* ~∧ *H, E*
3 whereon] Wherein *M*   all] on *O*

farre then my foes more wise,   5
  for they a wisdome never-failing are.

  My teachers all of old
    may now come learne of me,
whose studies tend but to thy wittnest will:
      nay who most aged be,   10
thought therefore most of skill,
    in skill I passe, for I thy precepts hold.

  I did refraine my feete
    from ev'ry wicked way,
that they might firmly in thy statutes stand.   15
      nor ever did I stray
from what thy lawes command:
    for I of thee have learned what is meete.

  How pleasing to my tast!
    how sweete thy speeches be!   20
noe touch of hony soe affects my tong.
      from whose edicts in me
hath such true wisdom sprong;
    that all false waies quite out of love I cast.

                    O.

O what a lanterne, what a lampe of light
    is thy pure word to me!
to cleere my pathes, and guide my goings right.
      I sware and sweare againe,
    I of the statutes will observer be,   5
      thou justly dost ordaine.

The heavy weightes of greif oppresse me sore:
    lord raise me by thy word,

9 tend] tendes *F*   wittnest] wittnesse *K, σ*   11 thought] Though *σ*   13 refraine]
reform *B*   15 they] I *M*   20 speeches] precepts *N*   23 true] sure *B*
sprong] sprung *B, K, χ*
O.
Incipit: Lucerna pedibus *N*; Lucerna pedibus meis *H, E*
1 lanterne] Lanthorne *C, Q, G*; lantorne *M*   3 goings] goeing *G*   4 sware] swear
B, σ   5 the] Thy *B, K, χ*   observer] observed *H*; observant *Q, E*   7 weightes]
waight *C*   greif] griefes *C*   8 lord] l *added in darker ink and different hand, loop not
gilded, in A*

as thou to me didst promise heretofore.
10   and this unforced praise:
I for an offring bring, accept ô lord,
        and show to me thy waies.

What if my life ly naked in my hand,
        to evr'y chaunce expos'd!
15   should I forgett what thou dost me command?
            no, no, I will not stray
from thy edicts though round aboute enclos'd
        with snares the wicked lay.

Thy testimonies as mine heritage,
20   I have retained still:
and unto them my hartes delight engage.
        my hart which still doth bend,
and only bend to doe what thou dost will,
        and doe it to the end.

P.

People that inconstant be,
      constant hatred have from me:
but thy doctrine changlesse ever
      holds my love that changeth never.
5   for thou the closett where I hide
      the shield whereby I safe abide:
my confidence expects thy promise just.
        hence, away you cursed crue,
        gett you gon, that ridd from you
10   I at better ease and leisure,
        maie performe my Gods good pleasure.
ô Lord as thou thy word didst give,
      sustaine me soe that I may live:
nor make me blush, as frustrate of my trust.

9 didst] did *G*   10 this] that *M*   13 What] h *written over* i *in A*   14 chaunce]
chaunge *θ*   19 as mine] as my *B, K, χ*; are my *E*   22 doth] dos *B*
P.
Incipit: Iniquos odio habui *N, E*; Inicos odio habui *H*
2 from] for *B*   5 thou] thou'rt *N*   hide] bide *C*   6 shield] seild *N*   9 gon]
hence *M*   12 didst] dost *N*   14 my] thy *θ*

Be my Piller, be my stay,
   safe then I shall swerve no way:
all my witt and understanding
   shall then work on thy commanding
for under foote thou treadst them all,
   who swerving from thy preceptes fall:
and vainly in their guile and treason trust.
     yea the wicked sort by thee
     all as drosse abjected be:
   therefore what thy proof approveth,
   that my love entirely loveth.
   and such regard of thee I make,
   for feare of thee my flesh doth quake:
and of thy lawes, thy lawes sevearly just.

15

20

25

Q.

Quitt and cleere from doing wrong,
   ô lett me not betraied be
unto them, who ever strong
   doe wrongly seeke to ruine me.
     nay my lord
     baile thy servant on thy word:
       and lett not these that soare to high,
       by my low stoope yet higher fly.

5

Eye doth faile while I not faile
   with eye thy safty to pursue:
looking when will once prevaile,
   and take effect thy promise true.
     all I crave,
     I at thy mercies hand would have:

10

16 I shall] shall I *θ*   18 thy] thee *K*   19 foote] feete *G*   22 yea] you *θ*
25 love] hart *F*; soule *E*   28 lawes, thy] lawe∧ thy *θ*
Q.
Incipit: Feci judicium *N*; Feci Juditium *H*; ffeci Juditium *E*
1 Quitt] Quite *C*, *M*   3 ever strong] over=strong *J*; overstronge *O*; over strong *D*,
N, *σ*   4 doe] *om. G*, *M*   5 my] ô *M*   7 these] those *B*, *C*, *G*, *M*   to]
too *F*, *J*, *C*; so *B*, *G*, *M*   9 Eye doth] Eyes doe *G*; Mine eyes *M*   while I] while
I'le *M*; *B notes: I do* expunged   14 thy] *om. B, which notes: thy* expunged

15   and from thy wisdome, which I pray
                           may cause me know thy law and way.

        Since thy servaunt still I stay,
            my understanding lord enlight:
        so enlight it that I may
20   thy ordinances know aright.
                    now, ô now,
                        the time requires, ô lord, that thou
                            thy lawes defence shouldst undertake:
                        for now thy law they sorely shake.

25   Hope whereof makes, that more deere
            I thy edicts and statutes hold,
        then if gold to me they were,
                yea then they were the purest gold.
                    makes that right
30   are all thy precepts in my sight:
                        makes that I hate each lying way,
                        that from their truth may cause me stray.

                            R.

        Right wonderfull thy testimonies be:
                my hart to keepe them I therefore bend.
                    their very threshold gives men light,
                    and gives men sight,
5   that light to see:
                    yea ev'n to babes doth understanding lend.

        Opening my mouth: I dranck a greedy draught,
                and did on them my whole pleasure place.
                    looke then ô lord, and pitty me
10   as erst I see

---

16 know] keepe *G*   17 stay] say *K*, χ   22 the] *om. B, which notes: The*
expunged: 24 they] doth *B, K*, χ   sorely] shurely *E*   27 were] weare *F, H*,
Q, C   28 purest] pure of *O*   29 right] aright *K*   30 all thy] all
<my>\thy/ *K*; all my *O*; thy *B, which notes: all* expunged.   my] <thy>\my/ *K*; <th>
my *O*   32 their] thei<re> *K*; thei<r> *H*; th<e>y<r [erased]> *D*; thy *O*; thie *E*
R.
Incipit: Mirabilia *N, H*; Mirabillia *E*
3 men] them *K*, θ; me *E*   6 doth] doe *E*

ordain'd and taught
    by thee for them whose hartes thy name embrace.

Of all my goings make thy word the guide,
    nor lett injustice upon me raigne:
        from them that false accusers be   15
        lord sett me free:
soe never slide
    shall I from what thy statutes do ordayne.

Shine on thy servant with thy faces beames,
    and throughly me thy command'ments teach.   20
        from fountaines of whose watry eyes
        doe welling rise
of teares huge streames,
    viewing each where thy doctrines daily breach.

S.

    Sure, lord, thy self art just,
        thy lawes as rightfull be:
    what rightly bid thou dost,
        is firmly bound by thee.
        I flame with zeale to see   5
        my foes thy word forgett:
        pure wordes, whereon by me:
        a servantes love is sett.

    Though bare, and though debast
        I yet thy rules retaine: 10
    whose doomes do endlesse last,
        and doctrine true remayne.
        In presure, and in paine
        my joyes thy preceptes give:
        no date thy judgmentes daine,   15
        ô make me wise to lyve.

12 for] from σ, *G*, *M*   13 thy] my *C*   the] *B notes: my* expunged   14 injustice]
injustice\(lord)/ *G*   20 throughly] h *added above caret in* *A*; thoroughly *G*
21 fountaines] fountaine *C*   22 welling] *A, B, θ*; swelling *K, N, C, G, M*; dwellinge *θ*
S.
This version is in A, F, J. Variant in B, K, χ.   9 bare] r *written over erasure of another*
letter (c?) in A   10 rules] words *J*   13 presure] *first* r *written over erasure of* l *in A*

T.

To thee my harty plaint I send:
lord turne thine eare
my plaint to here;
for to thy law my life I bend.
since I have envoked thee;
lett me lord thy succour see:
and what thy ordinaunces will
I will persist observing still.

My cry more early then the day
doth daily rise:
because mine eyes
upon thy promise waiting stay.
eyes, I say, which still prevent
watches best to watching bent:
esteeming it but pleasing paines
to muse on that thy word containes.

O in thi mercy here my voice,
and as thy lawes
afforde the cause
so make me lord, revyv'd rejoyce.
lord, thou seest the gracelesse crue
presse me neere, who me pursue.
as for the doctrine of thy law
they farre from it them selves with-draw.

That, lord, thou seest, and this I see:
thou evr'y where
to me art neere,
for true, nay truth thi precepts be.

T.
Incipit: Clamavi *N*; Clamavi toto Corde *H*; Clamavi in toto Corde *E*
1 plaint] plaints *I, θ*   3 here] heare *B, F, J, K, χ*   4 life I] life doth *N*; selfe doth *K*
5 *A has bracket and* M 241 *in left margin.*   6 me] my *E*   7 thy] thine *J*
12 thy] the *E*   15 pleasing] pleasant *N*   17 thi] *added (as abbreviation) above*
caret in A   here] heare *B, F, K, χ*   22 pursue] *F, J, K, χ*; pusue *A*   23 thy]
the *F*

now, though not now first, I know,
for I knew it long ago:
that firmly founded once by thee
thy ordinance no end can see.

V.

View how I am distressed,
and lett me be released:
for looke what me thy word hath bidden
out of my mind hath never slidden.

Then be my causes deemer:
be then my soules redeemer.
and as good hope thy word doth give me,
lett with good help thy worke relive me.

Where wickednesse is loved,
there health is farre removed.
for since thy sole edictes containe it,
who serch not them, how can they gaine it?

Thy mercies are so many,
their number is not any:
then as thou usest, lord, to use me,
revive me now, and not refuse me.

Exceeding is their number,
that me pursue and cumber:
yet what thy wittnesse hath defined,
from that my stepps have not declined.

I saw, and greeved seeing
their waies, who waiward being,

29 now, though] ~∧ ~ K; ~, (~ G, M   not now∧ first,] ~∧ ~∧ B, θ Q; ~, ~, H; ~, ~∧ E;
~∧ ~) N, C; ~) ~∧ G, M; \now/not<nowe>first, K   30 knew] know K, Q
31 founded] founded [final n *altered to* d] H; founden Q
V.
Incipit: Vide humilitatem N, H, E
4 my] *om.* B   6 then] thou J, C, G, M   8 good] god E   thy] the E   relive] redeem
B   10 there] theire O; theyr D; there [*dot above* r] N; their H, Q   11 sole]
blest M   16 revive] Receave G, M   21 greeved] grieved K

with guilefull stubburnes withstanded
what by thy speeches was commanded.

25   Since therefore plaine is proved,
      that I thy lawes have loved:
looke lord, and here thy bounty showing
restore my life now feeble growing.

    This in thy doctrine raigneth,
30   it nought but truth containeth:
this in thy Justice brightly shineth,
thy just edictes no date defineth.

W.

Wrong'd I was by men of might
    hottly chas'd and hard assailed:
little they my hart to fright,
    but ô much thy words prevailed:
5 wordes to me of more delight,
then rich booty wonne by fight.

Fraud doe I with hate detest,
    but with love embrace thy learnings
seav'n times daily er I rest,
10   sing thy doomes and right discernings.
whome who love with peace are blest
plentious peace without unrest.

Doing what thy precepts will
    I thy help have long expected:
15 my soule by thy doctrine still,
    loved most, is most directed.
thy edicts my deedes fullfill
who survaist my good and ill.

24 speeches] *Precepts M*   25 plaine] plaie *E*
    27 here] *A, Q*; heere *altered to* heare
in M; heare *B, K, χ*   30 it] Yet *E*

W. *This version is in A, F, J. Variant in B, K, χ.*
6 fight] ffight [l *altered to second* f] *F*

Y.

Yeeld me this favour, Lord.
my plaint may presse into thy sight:
and make me understand aright
    according to thy word.

Admitt to sight I say, 5
the praier that to thee I send,
and unto me thy help extend,
    who on thy promise stay.

Then from my lipps shall flow
a holy hymn of praise to thee: 10
when I thy scholer taught shalbe
    by thee thy lawes to know.

Then shall my tongue declare,
and teach againe what thou hast taught:
all whose decrees to triall brought 15
    most just, nay justice are.

O then reach out thy hand,
and yeeld me aid I justly crave,
since all things I forsaken have
    and chosen thy command. 20

I looke, I long, ô lord
to see at length thy saving grace:
and only doe my gladnes place,
    in thy glad-making word.

I know my soule shall live, 25
and living thee due honor yeeld:
I know thy law shalbe my shield
    and me all succour give.

Y.
Incipit: Appropinquet deprerecatio [*abbreviation duplicating* re] *N*; Appropinquet deprecatio
E; Appropinquett Deprecatio *H*
8 on] *A, B, C*; in *K, χ*   10 a] An *B*   18 justly] Justice *K*   22 length] lenght
K, H   23 only] gladdlie *C*

As sheep from shepherd gon
30   so wander I: ô seeke thy sheep,
who soe in mind thy precepts keep,
that I forgett not one.

Ad Dominum.
Psalm 120

As to th'Eternall often in anguishes
erst have I called, never unanswered,
againe I call, againe I calling
doubt not againe to receave an answer.

5   Lord ridd my soule from treasonous eloquence
of filthy forgers craftily fraudulent:
and from the tongue where lodg'd resideth
poisoned abuse, ruine of beleevers.

Thou that reposest vainly thy confidence
10   in wily wronging, say by thy forgery
what good to thee? what gaine redowndeth?
what benefitt from a tongue deceitfull.

Though like an arrow strongly delivered
it deeply pierce, though like to a Juniper

---

29 shepherd] sheephearde [*?*] *H*; sheepeards *K*, *θ*, *Q*, *E*   gon] grone *K*

Psalm 120. *Variant in G, M, which have rhymed versions of Psalms 120–7 instead of the quantitative versions in the other manuscripts. B notes:* This and the seven following Psalms without Rhymes seeme to be made in Imitacion of the Greek and Latin lyricks, by quantity of syllables and diversity of foot, a project about Sir Philips age, though our language is not suited so well for it[.] This present Psalm seemes to be made in Imitation of those of Horace *Vides ut altâ stet nive candidum* etc *Musis amicus* and severall others of the same measure which is this

$-/^{\smile}-/-/-^{\smile\smile}/-^{\smile\smile}/$
$-/^{\smile}-/-/-^{\smile\smile}/-^{\smile}/$
$-/^{\smile}-/-/^{\smile\smile}/-/$
$-^{\smile\smile}/-^{\smile\smile}/-^{\smile}/-/$ [*final* – *altered?*]

[in darker ink:]
    Ode Scilicet Tricolos
    Tetrastrophos.
Incipit: om. Q
1 th'Eternall] th\'/<e>Eternall *K*; the eternall *O*; the Æternall *E*   often] oft'n *D*;
ever *C*   2 never] *om. K*   4 an answer] an swer *I*   6 craftily] craftie *F*
8 poisoned] Poisned *B, K*; poisoned *F, I (?), N, C, σ*   abuse] abuses *Q*   9 that]
hast *N*   reposest] apposest *F*   11 to] doth *D*   14 deeply] deeplier *θ*   to] *om. N*

it coales doe cast which quickly fired,   15
flame very hott, very hardly quench'ing?

Ah God! too long heere wander I banished,
to long abiding barbarous injury:
 with Kedar and with Mesech harbour'd,
 how? in a tent, in a howslesse harbour.   20

Too long, alas, to long have I dwelled here
with frendly peaces furious enemies:
 who when to peace I seeke to call them,
 faster I find to the warre they arme them.

Levavi oculos.
Psalm 121.

What? and doe I behold the lovely mountaines,
whence comes all my reliefe, my aid, my comfort?
ô there, ô there abides the worlds Creator,
whence comes all my reliefe, my aid, my comfort.

March, march, lustily on, redoubt no falling: 5
god shall guid thy goings: the lord thy keeper
sleepes not, sleepes not a whit, no sleepe no slumber
once shall enter in Israells true keeper.

But whome named I Israells true keeper?
whome? but only Jehovah: whose true keeping   10
thy saving shadow is: not ever absent
when present perrill his reliefe requireth.

---

15 it] yeet *E* 16 quench'ing?] quenching. *B, N, Q*; quenching~ *I, O, C, H, E*;
quenched. *K*; quenching~ *altered to* quenched~ *in D* 17 too] to *θ* 19 Mesech]
Mesec *B* harbour'd] harbor'd *B, I, K*; harbour\e/d *F*; harboured *θ, C, σ* 20 how?]
how *K, H*; howe, *Q*; howe: *E* in a howslesse] a hopeless *σ* 24 warre] warrs *I*

Psalm 121. *Variant in G, M. B notes:* Carmen Phaleucium seu Hendecasyllabum. –/-˘˘/-
˘/-˘/-˘/
Incipit: Levavi occulos *H*; Levavi olulos *O*; *om. Q*
1 What?] ~~ *B, K*; ~: *H, E*; ~, *Q* 2 comfort?] ~~ *B, I, K, χ*; ~, *N*; ~: *C* 3 ô
there, ô there] other, o there *I*; o ther~ o<r> ther *D* abides] bides *θ* 4 all] *om. Q*
5 lustily on] on lustilie *O*; on lustely *D* no] not *N, C* 9 whome] who *θ* named]
nam'd *θ* 10 Jehovah] Jehova *J, B, K, χ* 11 is:] ~; *B*; ~, *O*; ~~ *I, D, C, H, E*
12 present] presen *H*

March then boldly by day: no sunne shall hurt thee
with beames to violently right reflected.

15   feare no jorny by night: the Moony vapors
shall not cast any mist to breed thy grevaunce.

Nay from evr'y mishapp, from ev'ry mischief
safe thou shalt by Jehovas hand be garded:
safe in all thy goings, in all thy commings,

20   now thou shalt by his hand, yea still be guarded.

Lætatus sum.
Psalm 122.

O fame most joyfull! ô joy most livly delightfull!
loe, I do heare godds temple, as erst, soe againe be frequented,
and we within thy porches againe glad-wonted abiding,
lovly Salem shall find: thou Citty rebuilt as a Citty,

5   late disperst, but now united in absolute order.
Now there shalbe the place for gods holy people appointed
first to behold his pledg, then sing allmighty Jehova.
Now there shalbe the seate, where not to be justiced only.
all shall freely resort whom strife, hate, injury vexeth:

10   but where Davids house and ofspring heav'nly beloved
shall both Judges sitt and raigne Kings throned in honor.
Pray then peace to Salem: to hir frends all happy proceeding
wish to hir walls all rest, to hir fortes all blessed aboundance.
This with cause I doe pray, since from these blisses a blessing

---

13 then] on *O*   14 reflected] respecked *I*   15 night: the∧] *B*, *K*; ~∧ ~: *A*
16 thy] thee *B*   grevaunce] greevancye σ   17 evr'y...ev'ry] every...every θ, *C*, σ
18 thou shalt] shalt Thou *B*   Jehovas] Jehova's *C*, *N*; Jehovaes σ   garded] guided *N*

Psalm 122. *This version is in A, F, J, I, K, θ, N, C. Another quantitative version is in B, I, σ. A
rhymed version is in G, M. K notes in a different hand:* This is otherwise translated[.] *I puts the
B version second and notes:* Idem. *In the margin in a later hand, I also notes (in pencil):* Printed
in Sidneiana.
Incipit: Letatus sum F, I, θ; om. Q*
1 ô joy] joy *N*   delightfull] dispightfull *F*   2 heare] a *added above caret in A*   3 we]
mee *N*   4 lovly] lovely *F, I, K, θ, N, C*   find:] ~, *K, θ, C*; ~∧ *I, N*   5 disperst]
dispersts *D*   in] an *stricken in gold after* in *in A*   6 people] temple *F*; Temple *J*
7 then] there *I*   8 only] oly *I*   10 but] b *added in darker ink, not gilded, in A*
ofspring] offspring *N*; of spring *I*   heav'nly] heavenlie θ, *N*   12 frends] frend
and *I*   13 fortes] ports *N, C*   14 I doe] doe I θ   pray] wishe *C*   these] those
θ, *N, C*

my brother and kinsman, my frend and contry deriveth   15
This I doe wish and more, if more good rest to be wished
since our god here builds him an howse, allmighty Jehova.

Ad te levavi oculos meos.
Psalm 123.

Unto thee, oppressed, thou greate commander of heaven
    heav'nly good attending, lift I my earthy seeing.
right as a waiters eye on a gracefull master is holden:
    as the look of waitresse fix'd on a lady lieth:
soe with erected face, untill by thy mercy relived,   5
    ô Lord expecting, begg we thy frendly favour.
scorne of proud scorners, reproch of mighty reprochers
    our sprights cleane ruined fills with an inly dolor.
then frend us, favour us, lord then with mercy relive us,
    whose scornfull misery greatly thy mercy needeth.   10

Nisi quia Dominus.
Psalm 124.

Say Israel, doe not conceale a verity
    had not the lord assisted us,
    had not the lord assisted us what tyme arose.
    against us our fierce enimies:

15 frend] friends *N, C*   16 This] T *added in different ink and hand in A*   I doe] doe I
θ, C   17 an] a *θ, N, C*   Jehova] Jehovah *O*

Psalm 123. *Variant in G, M. B notes:* Hexametrum and Elegiacum carmen.
Incipit: Ad te levavi oculos *N*; Ad te levavi occulos *H, E*; Ad te levavi *B, I, K, θ, C; om. Q*
1 thee, oppressed] Thee'Oppressed *B*; th'oppressed *I*; the oppressed *K*   heaven] heav'en
F, K   2 heav'nly] heavenlie *θ, N, C, σ*   good] God *B, O, N, C*; god *I, K, D, σ*
earthy] earthly *I*; earlye *E*   3 waiters] waighters *E*   on a] on *B*   master] mast *O*
is holden] *om. O*   4 look] lookes *O*; loks [?] *D*   of] *A, B, K, H*; of a *I, χ*   fix'd]
fixed *F*   a lady] her ladie *Q, E*   7 reprochers] reproches *I, K, θ*   8 sprights]
Sprits *B, H*; sprites *I, θ*; spirits *N, C, Q, E*   ruined] ruyn'd *F*   fills] fill *θ*   an] *om. I*
9 then with] thou with *σ*   mercy] thy mercie *χ*   10 misery] miseries *χ*

Psalm 124. *Variant in G, M. B notes:* Carmen Iambicum cum Dimetro.
Incipit: Nisi quia *B, I; om. Q*
2 assisted] afflicted *E*   3 assisted] afflicted *E*   4 us] *om. O*

5   us all at once long since they had devoured up:
          they were soe fell, soe furious.
       if not, the angry gulphes: the streames most horrible
          had drowned us: soe drowned us,
       that in the deepe bene tombed at the least on the deepe
10   had tumbled our dead Carcases.
    But lord, what honor shall thy people yeeld to thee,
          from greedy teeth delivered?
       escaped as the fowle, that oft breaking the grynn,
          beguiles the fowlers wilyines.
15   for sure this is thy work, thy name protecteth us,
          who heav'n, and earth hast fashioned.

                    Qui confidunt.
                    Psalm 125.

       As Sion standeth very firmly stedfast,
       never once shaking: soe on high Jehova
       who his hope buildeth, very firmly stedfast
                    ever abideth.

5   As Salem braveth with hir hilly bullwarkes
       roundly enforted: soe the greate Jehova
       closeth his servantes, as a hilly bullwark
                    ever abiding.

       Though Tirantes hard yoke with a heavy pressure
10   wring the just shoulders: but a while it holdeth,
       lest the best minded by too hard abusing
                    bend to abuses.

---

6 were] weare *F, H, Q*   7 if] Yeet *E*   gulphes] gulfe *Q, E*   9 at the] at *B, I, K, χ*
10 tumbled] tomb\l/ed *I*; tombled *K*; toombed *θ, C*; tombedd [u *altered to* o, l *altered to*
first d] *H*; tombed *N, Q, E*   Carcases] carcase *I*   11 to] *Added above caret in A*
13 fowle] foule *F, B, K, E*   breaking] breaketh *E*   grynn] grine *[?] H*; ginne *J, Q, E*;
gynnes *C*; *om. I*   14 beguiles] because *E*   16 heav'n] heaven *K, θ, N, σ*
and] who *B, I, K, χ*   hast] hath *B, I, K, χ*

Psalm 125. *Variant in G, M. B notes:* Carmen Sapphicum cum Adonico.
Incipit: om. Q
3 buildeth] buildet *I*   6 enforted] enforced *B*   7 bullwark] bullworke *O*; bull-
warks *I*   9 Tirantes] Tyran's [y *altered*] *N*   10 just] justs *E*   a] *om. θ*
11 abusing] abrusinge *K, H, Q*; a bruseing *E*   12 bend] bent *O*

As the well-workers, soe the right beleevers;
lord favour, further; but a vaine deceiver,
whose wryed footing not aright directed   15
                   wandreth in error.

Lord hym abjected set among the number
whose doings lawles; study bent to mischiefe
mischief expecteth: but upon thy chosen
                   peace be for ever.   20

In convertendo.
Psalm 126.

When long absent from lovly Sion
by the lords conduct home we retorned,
we our sences scarsly beleeving
thought meere visions moved our fancy.

Then in our merry mouthes laughter abounded,   5
tongues with gladdnes lowdly resounded
while thus wondring Nations whispered:
god with them most roially dealeth.

Most true: with us thou roially dealest,
woe is expired, sorow is vanished: 10
now lord, to finish throughly thy working
bring to Jerusalem all that are exiles.

---

13 the well-workers] well the workers *E*; *B notes on* workers: *doers expunged.*   15 not
aright] a- *added above caret in K*; not right χ; not rightlie *O*   18 study] sturdy *F*   to]
to doe *E*

Psalm 126. *Variant in G, M. B notes:*
  $-/-/-\smile\smile/-/$
  $-\smile\smile/-/-\smile\smile/-/$
  $-\smile\smile/-/-\smile\smile/-$
  $-/-\smile\smile/-\smile\smile/-/$

Incipit: om. Q
1 lovly] lovely *F, K,* χ; lovëly *B*   Sion] *Salem C*   2 home] whome *I, D,* σ   3 our]
our own *B*   4 fancy] fancies *I, E*   5 merry] merre *E*; mercie *I*   6 lowdly]
gladly *I* resounded] resoundeing *E*   7 while] Whie *E* wondring] whispring *C*
whispered] wispered *I, Q, E*; whispred *D, N, H* (h *written over* o [?]); w<oondred> [*partly
erased*] *C*   9 with us] yt is *E*   10 woe] who *H*; w<h>oe *E*   11 finish]
furnish *E*

Bring to Jerusalem all that are exiles,
soe by thy comfort newly refreshed:
15   as when southern sunn-burnt regions
be by cold fountaines freshly relived.

Oft to the plowman soe good happ hap'neth,
what with teares to the ground he bequeathed,
season of harvest timly retorning,
20   he, before woefull, joyfully reapeth.

Why to us may not as happly happen,
to sow our businesse wofully weeping:
yet when businesse growes to due ripnes,
to see our businesse joyfully reaped?

Nisi Dominus.
Psalm 127.

The house Jehova builds not,
we vainly strive to build it:
the towne Jehova guards not,
we vainly watch to guard it.

5   No use of early rising:
as uselesse is thy watching:
not ought at all it helpes thee
to eate thy bread with anguish.

As unto weary sences
10   a sleepie rest unasked:
soe bounty commeth uncaus'd
from him to his beloved.

Noe not thy children hast thou
by choise, by chaunce, by nature;

13–16 *B notes:* Written as I judg by the Author himself and added.   14 newly] lively
B, I, K, χ   16 freshly] freshed *O*   17 hap'neth] happeneth *θ*   18 bequeathed]
A, F, I, Q, E; bequeathed [d *altered to* t (?)] *H*; bequeatheth *J, B, K, χ*   21 happly]
happily *B, I, K, χ*   23 growes] grow *I*   due] deepe *J*

Psalm 127. *Variant in G, M. B notes:* ˘-/˘-/-˘/-
Incipit: Nisi quia *B*; om. *Q*
5 of] or *Q*   6 uselesse] *final* se *stricken in A*   thy] o^r *[?] B*   9 weary] wearied *Q*
11 uncaus'd] uncawsed *C, E*   14 choise...chaunce] chaunce...choice *K*

they are, they are Jehovas,   15
rewardes from him rewarding.

The multitude of infantes,
a good man holdes, resembleth
the multitude of arrowes,
a mighty Archer holdeth.   20

Hys happines triumpheth
who beares a quiver of them:
noe countenance of haters
shall unto him be dreadfull.

Beati omnes.
Psalm 128.

All happines shall thee betide,
  that dost Jehova feare:
and walking in the pathes abide,
    by him first troden were
      the labours of thy handes   5
    desired fruit shall beare.
      and where thy dwelling stands,
    all blisse, all plenty there.

Thy wife a vine, a fruitfull vine
  shall in thy parlor spring: 10
thy table compasse children thine
    as Olive plants in ring.
      on thee I say, on thee:
    that fearst the heav'nly king,
      such happinesse shall he   15
    he shall from Sion bring.

---

15 are, they] wholie *C*   18 a] the σ   21 Hys] *B notes: This* expunged   22 beares]
beare *B*

Psalm 128.
Incipit: om. Q
2 dost] doth *G*   4 first troden] Comanded *M*   were] weare θ, *H, Q, C*   5 labours]
labour *C, M*   thy] thine *I, K, χ*   11 thy] The *E*   15 he] be *B*   16 he
shall] To thee *M*

Yea while to thee thy breath shall hold,
   though running longest race,
Thou Salem ever shalt behold
20   in wealth and wished case:
       and childrens children view
     while Jacobs dwelling place
       noe plagues of warre pursue,
     but guiftes of peace shall grace.

Sæpe expugnaverunt.
Psalm 129.

Oft and ever from my youth,
   soe now Israel may say;
Israel may say for truth,
   ofte and ever my decay
5   from my youth their force hath sought:
     yet effect it never wrought.

Unto them my back did yeeld
   place and plaine (ô height of woe)
where as in a plowed field,
10   long and deepe did furrowes goe.
       but ô just Jehova, who
     hast their plow-ropes cutt in two!

Tell me you that Sion hate,
   what you thinck shalbe your end?
15 terror shall your mindes amate:
     blush and shame your faces shend.

---

17 thy] *om. θ*   18 running longest] longest running *B*   21 childrens] *final* s *added*
in darker ink in A children] childrens *H*   23 plagues] plauges *Q, E*   24 shall]
and *θ*

Psalm 129.
Incipit: Sepe expugnaverunt *F, θ, H, E, G, M;* Sæpe expug: *I; om. Q*
1 my] <my> *K*   2 now…may] maye…nowe *E*   3 Israel] Israël *B;* Isr'ell *N*
5 hath] have *Q*   6 wrought] brought *B*   7 Unto] But unto *θ* my] by *O*
8 and plaine] and pain *I, K, χ; B notes: of pain* expunged: 11 who] thou *χ*
13 you] yee *I, K, χ*   15 mindes] minde *O, D (?), Q, E*

mark the wheate on howses topp:
such your harvest, such your cropp.

Wither shall you where you stand;
    gather'd? noe: but wanting sapp: 20
filling neither reapers hand,
    nor the binders inbow'd lapp.
        nay who you shall reape or bind,
        common kindnesse shall not find.

Such as travail by the way,   25
    where as they their paines imploy;
shall not once saluting say,
    god speed frendes, god give you joy:
        he in whome all blessing raignes,
        blesse your selves, and blesse your paines.   30

De profundis.
Psalm 130.

From depth of grief
    where droun'd I ly,
lord for relief
    to thee I cry:
my ernest, vehment, cryeng, prayeng,   5
graunt quick, attentive, heering, waighing.

O lord, if thou
    offences mark,
who shall not bow
    to beare the cark?   10
but with thy justice mercy dwelleth,
and makes thy worshipp more, excelleth.

18 such your . . . such your] y *added in each case in A* ; such our . . . such our *F*   19 Wither]
Whither *F, C*   22 inbow'd] in=bowd *I*; in bow'd *C, G*; in boude *H, E (third letter of*
second word unclear); in bond *Q*; empty *M*   23 who you] yow who *N, C*   or] and *E*
24 common] commond *I*   25 travail] travell *θ, N, σ, M*   29 blessing] blessinges
θ, C   raignes] reigns *B*; raygnes *Q*; raynes *K, N, H, E*
Psalm 130. *Indentation unclear in A.*
Incipit: Deprofundis *A*; De prefundis *I*; De deprafundis clamavi *H*; De deprafundis *E*
2 where] When *N*   droun'd] drowd *B*   6 attentive] attending *B*   11 thy] thee *E*
12 and makes] *F, J, I, K, χ*; whereby *written in different ink over erasure in A*; Whereby *B*
(text); *B notes:* and makes *expunged*

Yea makes my soule
        on thee, ô lord
15   dependeth whole,
        and on thy word,
though sore with blott of sinne defaced,
yet surest hope hath firmly placed.

Who longest watch,
20   who soonest rise,
can nothing match
        the early eyes;
the greedy eies my soule errecteth,
while gods true promise it expecteth.

25   Then Israel
        on god attend:
attend him wel,
        who still thy frend,
in kindnes hath thee deere esteemed,
30   and often, often erst redeemed.

Now, as before;
        unchanged he
will thee restore
        thy state will free;
35   all wickednes from Jacob driving
forgetting follies, faultes forgiving.

13 Yea makes] *F, J, I, K, χ*; On thee *written above stricken* And nowe (e *of* nowe *separately stricken), which was originally written over erasure of* yea makes *in A; the later phrases are in different ink and seem not to be written in Davies's hand; original catchword,* yea makes my, *stricken, with stricken* And *under my and* On *(not stricken) to the right of* And; On thee *B (text); B notes:* yea makes *expunged*   17 sore] store *I*   20 soonest] *Second* o *added above caret in A*   22 the] thy *G*   early] earlier *N*   23 eies] eye *I* errecteth] directeth *O*   25–6, 27–8 *written as single lines in E (which marks the error in 25–6), G*   31 Now] Noe *θ*   35 Jacob] *Jacobs K, N, C, H, G, M*   36 follies] follie *O*

Domine non est.
Psalm 131.

A lofty hart, a lifted ey
    Lord thou dost know I never bare:
lesse have I borne in things to hygh
    a medling mind, or clyming care.
looke how the wained babe doth fare,   5
O did I not? yes soe did I:
    none more for quiett might compare
ev'n with the babe that wain'd doth ly.
    Heare then and learne ô Jacobs race
    such endlesse trust on god to place.   10

Memento Domine.
Psalm 132.

Lord call to mind, nay keepe in mynd
    thy David and thy Davids paines:
who once by othe and vow did bind
    him self to him who ay remaynes,
    that mighty one,   5
    the god in Jacob known.

My howse shall never harbor mee,
    nor bedd alow my body rest,

Psalm 131. *N contains two versions, one unique, then the common version, which is preceded by* the note: The same, another way. *B has Psalm number and incipit, but then notes:* But from this place to the end my Copy is defective the leaves being torn off/ Ita testor Sam: Woodforde who for sir Philip Sidnys Sake, and to preserve such a remaine of him undertook this tiresome task of transcribing. 169$\frac{4}{5}$
Incipit: Domine non *K*; Dominus non: *I*; *om. Q*
5 wained] weaned *I, E, G*   6 O] *I, K, χ; om. A*   7 more] none *I*   might] migh
H; maie *θ*   8 wain'd] wean'd *I, C, E, G, M*   9 Heare] H *added in different ink and hand (similar to those used for the added capitals in Ps. 132) in A;* heere *I*

Psalm 132. *A lacks gilding throughout and red ruling under incipit and number; initial capitals and capitals in* 2, 6, 18, 19, 20, 24, 32, 34, 37, 46, 49, 68, 69, 70, 76, *as well as* M *of* Memento *and* P *of* Psalm, *added in different ink and hand; text written in different ink and in a slightly different hand from those of Pss. 131 and 133. Lacking in B.*
Incipit: om. Q
1 nay] lord *C*   3 did] didst [*altered*] *D*

nor eyes of sleepe the lodging bee,
10   nor ey-lidds slendrest slumbers nest:
untill I finde
a plott to please my mind.

I find, I say, my mind to please
a plott wherin I may errect
15   a howse for him to dwell at ease,
who is ador'd with due respect:
that mighty one
the god in Jacob known.

The plott thy David then did name,
20   wee heard at Ephrata it lay:
wee heard, but bent to find the same,
were faine to seeke an other way:
ev'n to the fields,
that woody Jear yeelds.

25   And yet not there, but heere ô heere
wee find now settled what wee sought:
before the stoole thy feete doth beare
now entring in, wee, as wee ought,
adore thee will,
30   and duly worship still.

Then enter lord thy fixed rest,
with Arke the token of thy strength,
and let thy priests be purely drest
in robes of Justice laied at length:
35   let them bee glad
thy gracefull blisse have had.

For David once thy servants sake
doe not our kings, his seede reject:

---

9 the] tho' *N*; thoe *σ*; though *G, M*   10 slumbers] slumber *K*   14 wherin]
whereon *J, I, K, χ*   17 one] on *I*   20 heard] hard *O*   Ephrata] Euphrata *Q*
21 heard] h\e/ard *I*; hard *θ*   22 an other] another *J, I, K, χ*   24 Jear] J *added
as* I *in different ink in* A; Jear *J, I, K, θ, N, C, Q, G, M*; feare *H* (?), *E*; *om. (space left)* F
27 feete] foote *C, G, M*   28 as wee] wee *added above caret in* A   30 duly] daily *J,
E, G, M*   32 strength] strenght *H*; strengh *J*   33 purely] partly *E*   37 David]
Davids *θ*   servants] *final* s *added* (?) *in* A   38 kings] kinge *O, C, σ, G, M*

for thou to him this othe did'st make
    this endles othe: I will erect,   40
        and hold thy race
        enthron'd in Roiall place.

Nay if thy race my league observe,
    and keepe the cov'nants I sett down,
their race againe I will preserve   45
    eternally to weare thy Crown:
        no lesse thy throne
        shall ever bee their owne.

For Syon which I loved best,
    I chosen have noe seate of change: 50
heere heere shall bee my endles rest,
    heere will I dwell, nor hence will range:
        unto the place
        I beare such love and grace.

Such grace and love that evermore   55
    a blisse from gratious loving mee,
shall blesse hir vittaile, blesse hir store,
    that ev'n the poore who in hir bee
        with store of bread
        shall fully all bee fedd.   60

In hir my priests shall nought anoy:
    nay cladd they shall with safty bee.
Ô how in hir with cause shall joy
    who there as tenants hold of mee!
        whose tenure is   65
        by grace my fields of blisse.

Ô how in hir shall sprowt and spring,
    the scepter Davids hand did beare!
how I my Christ, my sacred king,
    as light in Lantern placed there   70

43 Nay] Say *F*   if] of *N*   51 heere heere] heere, here *Q, N*; here, here *C, G, M*; Heare heare *θ*; heere *F*   52 heere] heare *D*   hence] here *M*   56 a] as *I, K, χ* 57 blesse] blisse *N*   vittaile] victuall *J, χ*   58 who] that *F, I*   65 tenure] tresure *J*   66 my] the *C, M*   fields] field *H, Q, G, M*   68 Davids] David *I* 70 Lantern] lanthorn *I, Q*; Lanthorne *C, G, M*

with beames devine
will make abroad to shine!

But as for them who spite and hate
    conceave to him, they all shall down,
75   down cast by mee to shamefull state,
    while on him self his happy Crown
      shall up to skies
      with fame and glory rise.

Ecce quam bonum.
Psalm 133.

How good, and how beseeming well
      it is that wee,
      who brethren be,
as brethren, should in concord dwell.

5   Like that deere oile, that Aron beares,
      which fleeting down
      to foote from crown
embalmes his beard, and robe he weares.

Or like the teares the morne doth shedd
10   which ly on ground
      empearled round
on Sion or on Hermons hedd.

For join'd there with the Lord doth give
      such grace, such blisse:
15   that where it is,
men may for ever blessed live.

76 him self] him himself *C*   his] this *Q*, *E*
Psalm 133. *Lacking in B.*
Incipit: Ecce quam *θ, C, G*; Exe [?] quam *M*; *om. Q*
4 brethren] brothers *C*   5 Aron] Aaron *E*   9 the morne] that morne *σ*,
M   doth] doe *Q*   shedd] spread *σ, G, M*; cladd *I*   13 For] F *added without gilding*
in different ink and hand in A   there with] therewith *I, K, χ*   14 such blisse] and
blisse *G*   16 men] Man *σ*

Ecce nunc.
Psalm 134.

You that Jehovas servants are,
  whose carefull watch, whose watchfull care,
    within his house are spent;
    say thus with one assent:
      Jehovas name be praised. 5
      then let your hands be raised
        to holiest place,
        where holiest grace
          doth ay
            remaine: 10
          and say
            againe,
      Jehovas name be praised.
      say last unto the company,
        who tarryeng make 15
        their leave to take,
      all blessings you accompany,
from him in plenty showered,
whom Sion holds embowered,
      who heav'n and earth of nought hath raised. 20

Laudate nomen.
Psalm 135.

O praise the name whereby the Lord is known
  praise him I say you that his servants be:

Psalm 134. *Indentation unclear in A. Lacking in B.*
Incipit: Eece nunc *O*; Ecce nunce benidicite *H*; *om. Q*
1 Jehovas] Jehova's *N, G, M*; Jehovahs *K*; Jehovaes *Q, E*   2 whose watchfull] who
watchfull *Q*   4 assent] consent *Q, E, G*   5 Jehovas] Jehova's *N, G, M*; Jehovaes *σ*
13 Jehovas] Jehova's *K, N, G, M*; Jehovaes *σ*   17 blessings] blessing *I*   18 showered]
second e *added above caret in A*   19 Sion] Sions *I*   embowered] *second* e *added above*
caret in A   20 nought] naught *K, N*   hath] th *written over partial erasure of* st *in A*
Psalm 135. *Lacking in B.*
Incipit: om. Q

you whose attendance in his howse is shown,
   and in the courtes before his howse we see,
5   praise god, right tearmed god, for good is he:
      ô sweetly sing
      unto his name, the sweetest, sweetest thing.

For of his goodnes Jacob hath he chose,
   chose Israel his own Domain to be.
10   my tongue shall speake, for well my Conscience knowes,
    greate is our god, above all gods is he.
    each branch of whose inviolate decree
      both heav'ns doe keepe,
      and earth, and sea, and seas unsounded deepe.

15 From whose extreames drawne up by his command
   in flaky mists, the reaking vapors rise:
then high in cloudes incorporate they stand:
    last out of cloudes raine flowes, and lightning flies.
    no lesse a treasure in his storehouse lies
20   of breathing blasts,
      which oft drawn foorth in wind his pleasure wasts.

He from best man to most dispised beast
   Ægipts first borne in one night overthrew:
and yet not so his dreadfull showes he ceas'd,
25   but did them still in Egipts mid'st renew.
    not only meaner men had cause to rue,
      but ev'n the best
      of Pharos court, the king among the rest.

He many Nations, mighty Kings destroi'd:
30   Sehon for one, who rul'd the Amorites,
and huge-lim'd Og, who Basans crown enjoy'd,
    yea all the kingdoms of the Cananites
    whose heritage he gave the Izralites,
      his chosen train,
35   their heritage for ever to remain.

---

5 for good] for god θ, σ   8 hath he] he hath *M*   9 Domain] Demaine *K*, χ; Demeasne θ   12 inviolate] inviola\t/<ble> *K*; inviolable χ   14 unsounded] unfounded σ   15 by his] with some *E*   16 flaky] flakinge θ   23 Ægipts] *A, Q, E*; Egipts *F, K*, χ; Egypts *N*   25 Egipts] *A, F, K*, χ; Ægipts *J, Q, E*   28 Pharos] Pharohs *J*; Pharaoes σ; Pharaos *C*; Pharoes *G, M*; Phara's *N*   among] amongst *J*   31 huge-lim'd] huge θ

Therefore ô Lord, thy name is famous still,
   the memory thy ancient wonders gott,
Tyme well to world his message may fulfill
   and back retorne to thee, yet never blott
     out of our thoughts: for how should be forgott   40
       the lord that so
     forgives his servant, plagues his servants fo?

What difference, what unproportion'd odds
   to thee these Idolls gold and silver beare?
which men have made, yet men have made their godds.   45
   who though mouth, ey, and eare, and nose they weare
   yet neither speake, nor looke, nor smell, nor heire.
      ô Idolls right
     who Idolls make, or Idolls make your might.

But you that are of Israells descent,   50
   ô praise the lord: you that of Aron came
ô praise the lord, you Levies howse assent
   to praise the lord: you all his fearers, frame
   your highest praise, to praise Jehovas name.
      his praises still.   55
     Salem resound, resound ô Sion hill.

Confitemini.
Psalm 136.

O praise the Lord where goodnes dwells,
   for his kindnes lasteth ever:
ô praise the god all gods excells,
   for his bounty endeth never.

Praise him that is of lords the lord,   5
   for his kindnes lasteth ever:

40 should] can *K*, χ   42 plagues] plauges σ   servant] servants *K*, χ   45 yet
men have made] yet make of them *M*   46 who] And *G*   49 make, or] make︿
or: *E*; right︿ or *F*   50 Israells] Isralites *K, N, H, Q*   51 Aron] Aaron *E*
52 Levies] Levites *Q*   53 you all] all you *G*   54 to praise] to high *G*   Jehovas]
Jehova's *N, G, M*; Jehovaes σ
Psalm 136. *Lacking in B, I.*
Incipit: Confitemini Do *G, M*; Confitemine Domino *H, E*; *om. Q*
3 god] lord θ

who only wonders doth afford,
　　for his bounty endeth never.

Whose skillfull art did vault the skies,
　　for his kindnes lasteth ever:
made earth above the waters rise,
　　for his bounty endeth never.

Who did the Luminaries make,
　　for his kindnesse lasteth ever:
the Sunn of day the charge to take,
　　for his bounty endeth never.

The Moone and Starrs in night to raign,
　　for his kindnesse lasteth ever:
who Egipts eldest born hath slayn,
　　for his bounty endeth never.

And brought out Israel from thence,
　　for his kindnes lasteth ever:
with mighty hand and strong defence,
　　for his bounty endeth never.

Who cutt in two the russhy sea,
　　for his kindnes lasteth ever:
and made the middest Jacobs way,
　　for his bounty endeth never.

Who Pharo and his Army droun'd,
　　for his kindnes lasteth ever:
and ledd his folk through desert ground,
　　for his bounty endeth never.

Greate kings in battaile overthrew,
　　for his kindnes lasteth ever:
yea mighty kings most mighty slue,
　　for his bounty endeth never.

10

15

20

25

30

35

7 only] mighty *M*　　　10 lasteth ever] etc. *N*　　　11 waters] water *M*　　　12 endeth
never] etc. *N*　　　14 lasteth ever] etc. *N, E*　　　16 endeth never] etc. *N, E*　　　18 his
kindnesse lasteth ever] his kindnes etc. *N*; his etc. *E*　　　19 Egipts] Ægipts *J, Q, E*
20 his bounty endeth never] his bountie etc. *N*; his etc. *E*　　　22–52 *N, E substitute* etc.
for ends of second and fourth lines of each stanza, with these exceptions: N completes 52; E com-
pletes 38, 40, 50, 52　　　25 two] too *E*　　russhy] ruddie *N*; rushing *G, M*　　　29 Pharo]
Pharao *σ*; Pharaoh *N, C*; Pharoh *G, M*　　　30 kindnes] kindest *D*　　31 folk] flocke *θ*
33 Greate] Who *C*　　　35 most mighty] and Princes *M*

Both Sehon king of Amorites,
    for his kindnes lasteth ever:
and Ogg the king of Basanites,
    for his bounty endeth never.   40

For heritage their kingdoms gave,
    for his kindnes lasteth ever:
his Israell to hold and have,
    for his bounty endeth never.

Who minded us dejected low,   45
    for his kindnes lasteth ever:
and did us save from force of foe,
    for his bounty endeth never.

Who fills with foode each feeding thing,
    for his kindnes lasteth ever: 50
praise god who is of heav'ns the king,
    for his bounty endeth never.

Super flumina.
Psalm 137.

Nigh seated where the River flowes,
    that watreth Babells thanckfull plaine,
which then our teares in pearled rowes
    did help to water with their raine,
the thought of Sion bred such woes,   5
    that though our harpes we did retaine,
      yet uselesse, and untouched there
      on willowes only hang'd they were.

Now while our harpes were hanged soe,
    the men whose captives then we lay,   10

40 endeth never] lasteth ever *F*   49 foode] good *E* feeding] living *K, O, M*
51 who] he *M* heav'ns] heav'n *F*

Psalm 137. *Lacking in B.*
Incipit: om. I, Q
1 Nigh] Nighe [e *written over* t (?)] *E*   River] Rivers *I* flowes] floes *I*   3 rowes]
roes *I*; Roaes [R *written over another letter?*] *K*   4 their] the *Q, E* raine] rayne *F, E,*
C, M; raigne *H, Q*   8 were] weare *F*   9 while] whilst *I*; whiles *H, E, G, M*
were] weare *H*   10 then] there *O*

did on our greifs insulting goe,
   and more to greeve us, thus did say:
you that of musique make such show,
   come sing us now a Sion lay.
15   ô no, we have nor voice, nor hand
      for such a song, in such a land.

Though farre I ly, sweete Sion hill,
   in forraine soile exil'd from thee,
yet let my hand forgett his skill,
20   if ever thou forgotten be:
and lett my tongue fast glued still
   unto my roofe ly mute in me:
      if thy neglect with in me spring,
      or ought I do, but Salem sing.

25   But thou, ô lord, shalt not forgett
    to quitt the paines of Edoms race,
who causlessly, yet hottly sett
   thy holy citty to deface,
did thus the bloody victors whett
30   what time they entred first the place:
      downe downe with it at any hand
      make all platt pais, lett nothing stand.

And Babilon, that didst us wast,
   thy self shalt one daie wasted be:
35 and happy he who what thou hast
   unto us donne, shall do to thee,
like bitternes shall make thee tast,
   like wofull objects cause thee see:
      yea happy who thy little ones
40   shall take and dash against the stones.

11 greifs] greife θ   goe] groe *I*; growe θ, *N, C, G, M*   14 Sion] Sions *N, E*   17 ly]
bee *I*   19 his] her *I, O*   21 and] yea *I*, θ   23 with in me] in mee doe *I*, θ
24 ought] ofte *Q*   25 shalt] wilt *I*, θ   27 hottly] whotly *K*   30 they] the *Q*
32 platt pais] flat, plaine *I*; flatt plaine θ   33 that] which *I*   34 shalt] shall *N, C, E*
35 and] Yea *G*   36 unto us] to others *I*, θ   37 bitternes] miseries *I*   thee] the *H*
38 cause] make *I*, θ, *E*   39 happy] blessed *I*

Confitebor tibi.
Psalm 138.

Ev'n before kings by thee as gods commended,
and Angells all, by whom thou art attended,
   in harty tunes I will thy honor tell.

The pallace where thy holines doth dwell,
shall be the place, where falling downe before thee,   5
   with reverence meete I prostrate will adore thee.

There will I sing how thou thy mercy sendest,
and to thy promise due performance lendest,
   whereby thy name above all names doth fly.

There will I sing, how when my carefull cry   10
mounted to thee, my care was streight released,
   my courage by thee mightily encreased.

Sure lord, all Kings that understand the story
of thy contract with me, nought but thy glory
   and meanes shall sing whereby that glory grew.   15

Whose highly seated ey yet well doth view
with humbled look the soule that lowly lieth,
   and farr aloofe aspiring things espieth.

On ev'ry side though tribulation greive me,
yet shalt thou aid, yet shalt thou still relive me,   20
   from angry foe thy succor shall me save.

Thou lord shalt finish what in hand I have:
thou lord I say whose mercy lasteth ever,
   thy work begun shall leave unended never.

Psalm 138. *Lacking in B. Lines 10, 16, 22 not indented in A. Sestets, rather than tercets, in K, C, E.*
Incipit: Confitebor tibi Dom *H*; Confitebor tibi Do: *E; om. Q*
1 by thee as gods] as Gods by thee *G*   commended] commanded *F*   3 thy] thine *I, E*
7 mercy] mercies χ   8–12 *K transposes 8 and 11, 9 and 12*   9 doth] do\th/ *D*; doe
O, Q, E   12 by thee mightily] mightelie by thee *I, K,* χ   13 Kings] K *written in gold over another, illegible letter in A;* \k/<th>ings *D*; thinges σ   16 yet] ye σ   17 look] lookes *O*   that] the *I*   19 though] th<o>ough *(first o stricken in gold) A*   21 foe] foes σ, *G, M*   22 hand] u *altered to* n *in A*   24 shall] shalt *K,* χ

Domine probasti.
Psalm 139.

O lord in me there lieth nought,
 but to thy search revealed lies:
  for when I sitt
  thou markest it:
5 no lesse thou notest when I rise:
yea closest clossett of my thought
 hath open windowes to thine eyes.

Thou walkest with me when I walk,
 when to my bed for rest I go,
10 I find thee there,
  and ev'ry where:
 not yongest thought in me doth grow,
no not one word I cast to talk,
 but yet unutt'red thou dost know.

15 If foorth I march; thou goest before;
 if back I torne, thou com'st behind:
  soe foorth nor back
  thy guard I lack,
 nay on me too, thy hand I find.
20 well I thy wisdom may adore,
 but never reach with earthy mind.

To shunn thy notice, leave thine ey,
 ô whether might I take my way?
  to starry Spheare?
25 thy throne is there.
 to dead mens undelightsome stay?
there is thy walk. and there to ly
 unknown, in vain I should assay.

O sunn, whome light nor flight can match,
30 suppose thy lightfull flightfull wings

Psalm 139. *Lacking in B, I.*
Incipit: Domini probasti *F, M; om. Q*
12 not] no *F* 13 one] *added in gold above gold caret in A* 14 yet] it *F* 16 torne]
turne *K,* χ; tourne σ; come *F* 19 too] to *C,* σ, *G, M* 21 earthy] markinge θ
22 thine] thy *O* 23 whether] whither *D, N, C, G, M* 26 undelightsome]
undelight<full>\some/ *O;* undelightfull *M* 29 nor] and *O*

thou lend to me;
and I could flee
as farr as thee the ev'ning brings;
ev'n ledd to West he would me catch,
nor should I lurk with western things.   35

Doe thou thy best, ô secret night,
in sable vaile to cover me:
thy sable vaile
shall vainly faile:
with day unmask'd my night shall be.   40
for night is day, and darknes light,
ô father of all lights, to thee.

Each inmost peece in me is thine:
while yet I in my mother dwelt,
all that me cladd   45
from thee I hadd.
thou in my frame hast strangly delt;
needes in my praise thy workes must shine
so inly them my thoughts have felt.

Thou, how my back was beam-wise laid,   50
and raftring of my ribbs dost know:
know'st ev'ry point
of bone and joynt,
how to this whole these partes did grow,
in brave embrodry faire araid,   55
though wrought in shopp both dark and low.

Nay fashonles, ere forme I toke,
thy all and more beholding ey
my shaplesse shape
could not escape: 60
all these, with tymes appointed by,
ere one had beeing, in the booke
of thy foresight, enrol'd did ly.

34 West] <west>\Easte/ *D*   35 lurk] reste *Q*   36 night] might *Q*   43 peece]
parte *Q*   47 frame] forme *θ*   48 thy] thou *N*   51 dost] didst *D*   52 know'st]
knew'st *θ*   61 with tymes appointed by] with times appointed by *K*, *χ*; which tymes
appointed by [which, s, *and* appointed by *stricken;* fram'd successively *added above stricken*
appointed by *in different ink and in a hand similar to the J hand*] *A*; which tymes appointed by
F; tyme fram'd successively *J*   62 the] thy *Q*   63 did] <doth>did *D*; doth *O*

My god, how I these studies prize,
that doe thy hidden workings show!
whose summ is such,
noe summe soe much:
nay summ'd as sand they summlesse grow.
I ly to sleepe, from sleepe I rise,
yet still in thought with thee I goe.

My god if thou but one would'st kill,
then straight would leave my further chase
this cursed brood
inur'd to blood:
whose gracelesse tauntes at thy disgrace
have aimed oft: and hating still
would with proud lies, thy truth outface.

Hate not I them, who thee doe hate?
thyne, lord, I will the censure be.
detest I not,
the canckred knott,
whom I against thee banded see?
ô lord, thou knowst in highest rate
I hate them all as foes to me.

Search me, my god, and prove my hart,
examyne me, and try my thought:
and mark in me
if ought there be
that hath with cause their anger wrought.
if not (as not) my lives each part,
Lord, safly guide from danger brought.

64 prize] prise θ, E   65 thy] theis θ   workings] working G   66 summ] some σ, C
is such] soe much O   67 summe] some σ, C   68 summlesse] endlesse θ   69 from]
for I, K   71 one] once E   75 gracelesse] gacelesse Q   78 not] not not E
who] whome O   doe hate?] ~∧ θ, σ   79 the] thy θ   80 a slip of paper is pasted
over the canckred knott *(text of line 81) at the end of this line in A*   81 knott] not D
82 see?] ~∧ θ, σ, G   84 foes to] foe<s> <doe>\to/ K   85 my god] ô god E
89 their] thy θ   90 lives] lifes G

Eripe me Domine.
Psalm 140.

Protect me lord, preserve me sett me free
from men that be: soe vile, soe violent:
in whose entent both force and fraud doth lurk
my bane to work: whose tongues are sharper things
then Adders stings: whose rusty lipps enclose   5
a poisons hurd, such in the Aspick growes.

Save I say Lord, protect me, sett me free
from those that be so vile, so violent:
whose thoughts are spent in thincking how they may
my stepps betray: how nett of fowle misshape   10
may me entrapp: how hid in traitor grasse
their conning cord may catch me as I passe.

But this ô Lord, I hold: my god art thou:
thou eare wilt bowe, what tyme thy aid I pray
in thee my stay, Jehova: thou dost arme   15
against all harme, and guard my head in feild.
ô then to yeeld these wicked their desire,
do not accord: for still they will aspire.

But yeeld ô Lord, that ev'n the head of those
that me enclose, of this their hott pursute   20
may tast the frute: with deadly venome stong
of their own tongue, loe, loe, I see they shall,
yea coales shall fall, yea flames shall fling them low
ay unrestor'd to drown in deepest wo.

Psalm 140. *Lacking in B, I. N divides 2, 3, 4, 5 to emphasize internal rhyme and produces 10-line stanzas. Q emphasizes internal rhyme with colons and initial capitals (e.g.: Soe, line 2). E emphasizes internal rhyme with colons and raised periods (:·).*
Incipit: Eripe me *C*; *om. Q*
1 Protect] Preserve θ   2 vile] vilde *K, θ, σ, N*   soe violent] and violent *N*   3–8 *om.*
M   6 poisons] poisonous *K, χ*; poisoned *C, G*   hurd] hoord *J, K, χ*; hoorde *H, Q*
7 I say Lord] \lord/I saie <Lord> *K*   8 vile] vild *K, σ, N*   so violent] and violent *N*
10 fowle] foule *F, K, Q*   misshape] mishappe *O*; misshapp *C, M*; mishapp *F, J, K, σ*; mishap *D, N*   12 conning] cunning *F, J, K, χ*   cord] lord *O*   13 hold] know
M   art thou] thou art *F*   15 in] On *M*   thou dost] thou didst θ; I doe *G*   16 head]
bedd *K, χ*   17 these] this σ   18 they] th\e/y *O*; thy *D*   21 tast] taste [t *written over* c] *D*; cast *O, H*   stong] stronge *K, χ*   22 loe, loe] for loe θ; loe, so *M*

25 For liers, lord, shall never firmly stand
 and from the land who violently live
  Mischief shall drive: but well I know the poore
  thou wilt restore: restore th'afflicted wight.
  that in thy sight the just may howses frame,
30 and glad record the honor of thy name.

Domine clamavi.
Psalm 141.

To thee Jehova, thee, I lift my cryeng voice,
ô banish all delay, and lett my plaintfull noise,
 by thy quick-hearing-eare be carefully respected.
  as sweete perfume to skies lett what I pray assend:
5 lett these uplifted hands, which prayeng I extend,
  as ev'ning sacrifice be unto thee directed.

Ward well my words, ô Lord, (for that is it I pray)
a watchfull Sentinell at my mouthes passage lay:
 at wickett of my lipps stand ay a faithfull porter.
10 incline me not to ill, nor lett me loosly goe
  a mate in work with such, whence no good work doth grow
  and in their flattring baites, lett me be no consorter.

But lett the good-man wound, most well I shall it take,
yea price of his rebukes as deerest balme shall make,
15 yea more shall for him pray, the more his wordes shall grive me,
  and as for these, when once the leaders of their crue
  by thee be brought to stoope, my wordes most sweetly true
  shall in the rest soe work, that soone they shall belive me.

---

25 firmly] firmely [*?; altered*] E   30 thy] my E

Psalm 141. *Lacking in B, I. The lower half of f. 104ᵛ (after Psalm 141) is blank in K. Incipit: om. K, Q*
1 To thee Jehova, thee] O Lorde to thee to thee *Q*; To thee Jehova *θ*   3 quick-hearing-eare] quicke hearinge voice *θ*   4 perfume] perfumes *E* skies] skie *G*
5 triply *indented in A*   7 is it] *A, N*; it is *K, χ*   8 watchfull] watching *N*
my] \my/ *E; om. H, Q* lay] staye *N*   9 lipps] mouth *M*   11 grow] flowe *E*
12 me be no] bee no more *F*; me not be *Q*   14 yea] ye *H*   16 once] one *H, Q*; on *E*

Meane while my bones the grave, the grave expects my bones,
soe broken, hewn, disperst, as least respected stones,   20
   by careles Mason drawn from cave of worthles Quarry
   but thou ô Lord, my lord, since thus thi servants ey
   repleate with hopfull trust doth on thy help rely,
   faile not that trustfull hope, that for thy helpe doth tarry.

O soe direct my feete they may escape the hands   25
of their entangling snare, which for me pitched stands:
   and from the wicked netts for me with craft they cover.
   nay for these fowlers once, thy self a fowler be,
   and make them fowly fall where netts are laid by thee,
   but where for me they lay, let me leap freely over.   30

Voce mea ad Dominum.
Psalm 142.

My voice to thee it self extreamly strayning
   cries prayeng, lord; againe it cryeng praieth.
before thy face the cause of my complayning,
   before thy face my cases mapp it laieth.
      wherein my soule is painted   5
        in doubtfull way a stranger:
      but, Lord, thou art accquainted,
        and knowst each path, where stick the toiles of danger.
        for me, mine ey to ev'ry coast directed
           lights, not on one that will so much as know me: 10
        my life by all neglected,
           ev'n hope of help is now quight perish'd from me.

---

21 *added in an italian hand in left margin in K (insertion marks to the right of 20 and in the left
margin above 21)*   23 on thy] onely *K*   25 soe] *om. F*   27 they] thy *Q*
28 these] those *Q*

Psalm 142. *Lacking in B.*
Incipit: Voce meæ ad Do *H*; Voce mea *I, θ, C; om. Q*
1 to thee it self] it self to thee *G, M*   3 the] a *θ*   my] a *θ, σ*   5 painted] t
added above caret in A   6 way] waies *C, G, M*   8 stick] sticks *E, G, M*   the] thy *O*
toiles] *Netts M*   danger.] *F; final* r *(and conjectural punctuation) lost in A because of a closely
trimmed right margin*   10 on] on *I, K, χ;* on<e> *D; om. A*   12 help] life *σ*
from] froe *H, Q;* fro *E;* fr<o>' [*o blotted?*] *K*

Then with good cause to thee my spiritt flieth,
    flieth, and saith: ô lord my safe abiding
15 abides in thee: in thee all-only lieth
    lott of my life, and plott of my residing.
      alas then yeeld me heiring,
        for wearing woes have spent me:
      and save me from their tearing,
20   who hunt me hard, and daily worse torment me.
      ô change my state, unthrall my soule enthralled:
        of my escape then will I tell the story:
      and with a crown enwalled
        of godly men, will glory in thy glory.

Domine exaudi.
Psalm 143.

Heare my entreaty Lord, the suite, I send,
    with heed attend.
      and as my hope and trust is
        reposed whole in thee:
5   so in thy truth and justice
        yeeld audience to me.
        and make not least beginning
         to judge thy servants sinning:
        for lord what lyving wight
10   lives synnlesse in thy sight?

O rather look with ruth upon my woes,
    whom ruthlesse foes
      with long pursute have chased,
        and chas'd at length have cought,

---

15 thee all-only] whome all onely *M*   16 my residing] thy residinge *K*   18 wear-
ing] weareing *G, M*; wearyinge *I, K, χ*   have] hath *E*   20 worse] most *E*
21 enthralled] unthralled *I*   24 godly men] godlines *N*

Psalm 143. *Lacking in B.*
Incipit: Domini exaudi *M*; *om. Q*
7 make] ma\r/ke *H, E*   9 for] what *θ*   13 have] hath *altered to* have *(stem of final*
h *erased) in A*; hath *F, E*   14 at length have] now have *N*; nowe hath *C*; have *I, K, χ*

and cought in tombe have placed   15
with dead men out of thought.
  ay me! what now is left me?
  alas! all knowledg reft me,
    all courage faintly fledd,
    I have nor hart, nor hedd.   20

The best I can is this, nay this is all;
that I can call
  before my thoughts, survayeng
  tymes evidences old,
  all deedes with comfort waighing,   25
  that thy hand-writyng hold.
    soe hand and hart conspiring
    I lift, no lesse desiring
     thy grace I may obtayne,
     then drougth desireth raine.   30

Leave then delay, and let his cry prevaile;
whom force doth faile.
  nor lett thy face be hidden
  from one, who may compare
  with them whose death hath bidden   35
  adiew to life and care.
    my hope, lett mercies morrow
    soone chase my night of sorrow.
     my help, appoint my way,
     I may not wandring stray.   40

My cave, my clossett where I wont to hide,
in troublous tyde:
  now from these troubles save me,
  and since my god thou art,
  prescribe how thou wouldst have me   45
  performe my duties part.

---

18 knowledg] comfort *M*   reft] rest [?] *I*   28 lift] list *I*   31 his] <t>his *D*; this *O*
32 whom] Where *G*   34 one] me [*first half of* m *in darker ink over erasure*] *F*; him *M*
35 death] life *E*   37 my hope] *A, I, K, G*; my hopes *χ*; Ô lord *M*   38 chase]
chuse *K*   39 my help, appoint] And so direct *M*   40 may] will *θ*   41 my]
the *C*   43 these] those *χ*   troubles] trobless *Q*; troublous *E*

and lest awry I wander
in walking this Meander,
  be thy right sprite my guide,
  to guard I go not wide.

50

Thy honor, justice, mercy crave of thee
ô lord that me
  reviv'd thou shouldst deliver
  from pressure of my woes,

55

and in destructions river
  engulph and swallow those,
  whose hate thus makes in anguish:
  my soule afflicted languish:
  for meete it is so kind

60

  thy servant should thee find.

Benedictus Dominus
Psalm 144.

Prais'd bee the lord of might,
  my rock in all allarms,
by whom my handes doe fight,
  my fingers mannage armes.

5

My grace, my guard, my fort,
  on whom my safty staies:
To whom my hopes resort
  by whom my realme obaies.

Lord what is man that thou

10

  should'st tender soe his fare?

47–8 Transposed and rephrased in E:
              In walking this *Meander*
              least I awrie, doe wander

47 lest] least χ   49 sprite] spirit *N, C, Q, G*; hand *M*   53 shouldst] wouldst *O*
54 pressure] presence σ   60 servant] servants *I*

Psalm 144. Initial letters of first and fifth lines (except for line 13), as well as B *of incipit,* P *of* Psalm, *and* D *in 40, added in ink, not gold, in a hand resembling the* J *hand; text written in different ink from that of Pss. 143 and 145, but in a similar hand. Davies makes three errors involving stanza breaks by beginning new stanzas with lines 61 (top of f. 130ᵛ) and 69 and by neglecting to space between lines 64 and 65. Lacking in B, I.*
Incipit: Benidictus deus *H, E;* Benedictus *G, M; om. Q*

what hath his child to bow
    thy thoughts unto his care?
Whose neerest kinn is nought,
    no Image of whose daies
more livly can bee thought,   15
    then shade that never staies.

Lord bend thy arched skies
    with ease to let thee down;
and make the stormes arise
    from mountaines fuming crown.   20
Let follow flames from sky,
    to back their stoutest stand:
lett fast thy Arrowes fly,
    dispersing thickest band.

Thy heav'nly helpe extend   25
    and lift mee from this flood:
let mee thy hand defend
    from hand of forraine brood
whose mouth no mouth at all,
    but forge of false entent,   30
wherto their hand doth fall
    as aptest instrument.

Then in new song to thee
    will I exalt my voice:
then shall ô god with mee   35
    my tenn-string'd Lute rejoyce.
Rejoyce in him, I say,
    who roiall right preserves
and saves from swords decay
    his David that him serves.   40

O lord thy help extend,
    and lift mee from this flood:
lett mee thy hand defend
    from hand of forrain brood

13 nought] naught *N*   21 *aligned with 19 and 23 in A*   24 thickest] quickest *θ*
28–9 *a mistaken space between these lines is corrected with a large bracket in each margin
in A*   31 hand] handes *E*   37 Rejoyce] Revive *N*   38 right] rights *E*

45   whose mouth no mouth at all,
                but forge of false entent:
      whereto their hand doth fall
                as aptest instrument.

      Soe then our sonnes shall grow
50   as plants of timely spring:
      whom soone to fairest show
                their happy growth doth bring.
      As Pillers both doe beare
                and garnish kingly hall:
55   our daughters straight and faire,
                each howse embellish shall.

      Our store shall ay bee full,
                yea shall such fullnes finde,
      though all from thence wee pull
60   yet more shall rest behind.
      The millions of encrease
                shall breake the wonted fold:
      yea such the sheepy prease,
                the streetes shall scantly hold.

65   our heards shall brave the best:
                abroad no foes alarme:
      at home to breake our rest,
                no cry, the voice of harme.
      If blessed tearme I may
70   on whom such blessings fall:
      then blessed blessed they
                their god Jehovah call.

---

52 growth] groweth *σ*   doth] did *O*   53 Pillers] *Pallace M*   doe] doth *C, G, M*
55 our] o\r/<r> *K; Or θ*   straight] straigh *H*; straite *E*   58 fullnes∧ finde,] *K, N*;
~∧ ~: *C, G;* ~, ~∧ *A* (finde *added in a different hand*)   60 rest] stay *F*   61 *Davies*
mistakenly begins a new stanza with this line (top of f. 130ᵛ) in A   64–5 *no space between*
these lines in A   67 home] home [w *erased and stricken before* h] *Q*; whome *H, E*
68–9 *mistaken space between these lines in A*

Exaltabo te.
Psalm 145.

My god, my king to lift thi praise
   and thanck thy most thanck-worthy name
I will not end, but all my daies
   will spend in seeking how to frame:
   recordes of thy deserved fame   5
      whose praise past-praise, whose greatnes such,
      the greatest search can never touch.

Not in one age thy works shall dy,
   but elder eft to yonger tell
thy praisefull powre: among them I   10
   thy excellences all excell
   will muse and marke: my thoughts shall dwell
      upon the wonders wrought by thee,
      which wrought beyond all wonder be.

Both they and I will tell and sing   15
   how forcfull thou, and fearefull art:
yea both will willing wittnes bring
   and unto comming tymes impart
   thy greatnes, goodnes, just desert:
      that all who are, or are to be,   20
      this Hymne with joy shall sing to thee.

Jehova doth with mildnes flow,
   and full of mercy standeth he:
greate doubt if he to wrath more slow,
   or unto pardon prompter be.   25
   for nought is from his bounty free:
      his mercies do on all things fall
      that he hath made, and he made all.

Psalm 145. *Lacking in B, I.*
Incipit: Exultabo te Deus *N*; Exaltabo te Deus *N, H, E*; *om. K, Q*
9 tell] telling [ing *added in different ink*] *K*   11 excellences] Excellencies *J*; excellenc\i/
es *O*; excellencies *D*   excell] excelling [ing *added in different ink*] *K*   12 shall]
<shall>\ay/ [*added in different ink*] *K*   dwell] dwelling [ing *added in different ink*] *K*
14 wonder] wonders *O, σ, M*   17 bring] bee *J*   18 comming tymes] cunning
tunes *N*   20 or] and *θ*   21 with] of *G, M*   sing] *om. O*   22 doth] still *E*
flow] show *F*   24 more] were *N*   26 his] is *Q*   27–8 *added in different ink at
the bottom of f. 107ʳ in K* (*catchwords,* his mercies, *stricken*)   27 mercies] mercie *O, M*

Thus Lord, all creatures thou hast wrought,
30   though dombe, shall their creator sound:
but who can utt'raunce add to thought,
they most whom speciall bonds have bound.
(for best they can, who best have found)
shall blase thy strength, and glad relate
35   thy more then glorious kingdoms state.

That all may know the state, the strength,
thy more then glorious kingdom showes:
which longest tyme to tymlesse length
leaves undefin'd: nor ages close
40   as age to age succeeding growes
can with unsteedfast chang procure
but still it must, and steedfast dure.

Thou dost the faint from falling stay,
nay more, the falne againe dost raise:
45   on thee their lookes all creatures lay,
whose hunger in due tyme alaies
thy hand: which when thy will displaies,
then all that on the aire do feede,
receave besides what food they neede.

50   Each way, each working of thy hand
declare thou art both just and kind,
and nigh to all dost alway stand
who thee invoke, invoke with mynd,
not only mouth: ô they shall fynd,
55   he will his fearers wish fullfill,
attend their cry, and cure their ill.

He will his lovers all preserve:
he will the wicked all destroy:

29–33 *added in a different hand at the top of f. 107ᵛ in K*   30 their] t *written over another letter* (c [?]) *in A*   33 who] which *K*   37 kingdom] kingdome [*final* s *lightly erased*] *K*; kingdomes *F, Q*   42 must] most *N*   44 more, the falne₍] more, then falne₍ *K, N*; more₍ then falne₍ *O*; more₍ then fallne, *D*; more, then fallne, *C, E, M*; more, them fallne, *H*; more, (then fallne) *G*   dost] doth *O*; doe *G*   raise] rise *O*   46 tyme] times *G*   alaies] allayees *H*; allaies *Q*; all<w>aies *K*; allwaies *χ*   47 hand: which] ~, ~ *H, E*; ~₍ ~ *Q, G*; ~, (~ *N*; ~ (~ *M*   will₍ displaies,] ~₍ ~₍ (, *C*, (, *G*; ~₍ ~) *N*; ~) ~₍ *M*   48 do] doth *K, N, Q, E*   49 receave] *A, θ, C*; receaves *K, N, σ, G, M*   besides] beside *N*   neede] feede *D*   52 alway] allwaie [*final* s *lightly erased*] *K*; allwaies *χ*   58 destroy:] *C, M*; ~, *J*; ~₍ *A, F, K, χ*

to praise him then as these deserve,
　　ô thou my mouth thy might employ:　　　　　　　60
　　nay all that breath, recorde with joy
　　　his sacred names eternall praise,
　　　　while race you runne of breathing daies.

Lauda anima mea
Psalm 146.

Upp, up, my soule, advaunce Jehovas praise.
　　his only praise: for fixed is in me
to praise Jehova all my living daies
　　and sing my god, untyll I cease to be.
　　ô lett not this decree　　　　　　　　　　5
　　　a fond conceite deface,
　　　　that trust thou maist in earthy Princes place:
　　　　　that any sonne of man
　　　　　can thee preserve, for not him self he can.

His strength is none: if any, in his breath:　　　10
　　which vapor'd foorth to mother earth he goes:
nay more, in him, his thoughts all find their death.
　　but blessed he, who for his succour knowes
　　the god that Jacob chose:
　　　whose rightly level'd hope　　　　　　　　15
　　　his god Jehova makes his only scope,
　　　　so strong, he built the skies,
　　　　the feeldes, the waves, and all that in them lies.

60 thou] then *K*, χ　　　　63 you] who *O*　　runne] runn [*a letter erased at the end*] *K*

Psalm 146. *Lacking in B, I. In K, the lower half of f. 108ʳ (after* Psalm 146*) and all of f. 108ᵛ are blank.*

Incipit: Lauda anima *C; om. Q*

1 Jehovas] Jehova's *J, N, C, G, M;* Jehovaes σ　　　　7 earthy] Earthly *C, Q, E, M*
9 preserve] prefer *D*　　　10–16 Om. *K,* χ, *but restored in G, M; K notes in a different hand:* [stanza] 2 want[ing]; *Lines 17–18 of stanza 2, however, are attached to stanza 1 in all ten of these copies; the first stanza is, thus, eleven lines long.*　　　10 none: if any, in his breath:] none (if any∧ in his breath) *G, M* ‖ none (if any∧ in his breath) *A*　　　12 him, his] him∧ his *G, M;* his, his *A*　　15 rightly] h *added above caret in A*　　　17 strong] stronge [o *written over another letter*] *H;* strange θ, *N*　　18 waves] Seas *G, M*

He endles true doth yeeld the wronged right,
20   the hungry feedes, and setts the fett'red free:
the lame to lymms, the blind restores to sight
          loveth the just, protects who strangers be.
          the widowes piller he,
              he Orphans doth support:
25   but heavy lies upon the godlesse sort.
              he everlasting raignes,
                  Syon, thy god from age to age remaines.

Laudate Dominum
Psalm 147.

Sing to the Lord: for what can better be,
          then of our god that we the honor sing?
with seemly pleasure what can more agree,
          then praisfull voice, and touch of tuned string?
5   for lo the lord againe to forme doth bring
          Jerusalems long ruinated walls:
and Jacobs house, which all the earth did see
          dispersed erst, to union now recalls.
              and now by him their broken hartes made sound,
10   and now by him their bleeding wounds are bound.

For what could not, who can the number tell
          of starrs, the torches of his heav'nly hall?
and tell so readily, he knoweth well
          how ev'ry starre by proper name to call.
15   what greate to him, whose greatnes doth not fall,
              with in precincts? whose powre no lymitts stay?
          whose knowledges all number soe excell,
              not numbring number can their number lay?

19 wronged] wronge his *O*   21 lymms] lymbes *Q*; lymbs *N*   25 godlesse] godlie
N

Psalm 147. *Lacking in B. Psalm number altered in I.*
Incipit: om. *Q*
2 god] lord *I*   the] thee *N*   4 praisfull] praising *N*   7 earth] world *G, M*
8 now] he *E*   12 of his] of the σ   14 by] his *F*   17 knowledges] knowledg
doth *E*

easy to him to lift the lowly just:
easy to down proud wicked to the dust.   20

O then Jehovas causfull honor sing,
  his, whom our god we by his goodnes find:
ô make harmonious mix of voice and string
  to him, by whom the skies with cloudes are lin'd:
    by whom the rayne from cloudes to dropp assign'd   25
      supples the clodds of sommer-scorched fields,
fresheth the mountaines with such needfull spring,
  fuell of life to mountaine cattaile yeeldes.
      from whom yong Ravens careles old forsake,
      croaking to him of Almes their diett take.   30

The stately shape, the force of bravest steed
  is farre to weake to work in him delight:
no more in him can any pleasure breed
  in flying footman foote of nymblest flight.
    nay which is more, his fearers in his sight   35
      can well of nothing, but his bounty brave;
which never failing, never letts them neede,
  who fixt their hopes upon his mercies have.
      ô then Jerusalem Jehova praise,
      with honor due thy god ô Sion raise.   40

His strength it is thy gates doth surely barre:
  his grace in thee thy children multiplies:
by him thy borders ly secure from warre:
  and finest flowre thy hunger satisfies.
    nor meanes he needes: for fast his pleasure flies, 45
      borne by his word, when ought him list to bid.
snowes woolly locks by hym wide scatt'red are,
  and hoary plaines with frost, as asshes, hid.
      gross icy gobbetts from his hand he flings,
      and blowes a cold to strong for strongest things.   50

21 Jehovas] Jehova's *J, I, K, N, C, G, M*; Jehovaes *σ*   22 goodnes] godness *Q*
23 string] *om. I*   24 with] which *I*   25 rayne] raine *I, θ, N, G, M*; raigne *H, Q*
28 mountaine] maintaine *I, χ*   30 of] for *G, M*   diett] foode doe *χ*; foode to *θ*
31 stately] stateliest *E*   34 footman] footmen *H, Q*   37 letts] let *C*   38 fixt]
fixe *G*   hopes] thoughtes *G, M*   mercies] mercie *O, E, G, M*   41 it] t *written
over another letter (s [?]) in A*   43 warre] *final e written over partial erasure of s in A*;
warre *F, I, K, χ*; warrs *J*   44 flowre] flower *K, χ*   49 gross] *second s altered in A*
50 strong] cold *F*   strongest] sharpest *I*

He bidds again, and yce in water flowes,
  as water erst in yce congealed lay:
abroad the southern wind, his melter, goes,
  the streames relenting take their wonted way
55   ô much is this, but more I come to say,
    the wordes of life he hath to Jacob tolde:
taught Israell, who by his teaching knowes
   what lawes in life, what rules he wills to hold.
    no Nation els hath found him half soe kind,
60   for to his light what other is not blynd.

Laudate Dominum.
Psalm 148.

Inhabitants of heav'nly land
  as loving subjectes praise your king:
you that among them highest stand,
  in highest notes Jehova sing.
5   sing Angells all on carefull wing
    you that his heralds fly,
and you whom he doth soldiers bring
   in feild his force to try.

O praise him Sunne the sea of light,
10   o praise him Moone the light of sea:
you preaty starrs in robe of night
  as spangles twinckling do as they.
   thow spheare within whose bosom play,
    the rest that earth emball:
15   you waters banck'd with starry bay,
    ô praise ô praise hym all.

All these I say advaunce that name,
  that doth eternall beeing show:

---

52 congealed] congrated *θ* 55 ô] *erasure of* T *before* ô *in A* 58 wills] will *I*
59 soe] to *I*

Psalm 148. *Lacking in B. Lines 17–56 lacking in K (leaves torn away).*
Incipit: Laudate *I, K; om. Q*
1 Inhabitants] Inhabitans *I* 3 among] amongst *I, K, χ;* amongest *D, H, Q* 5 carefull]
care *N* 7 soldiers] soldierd [i *altered*] *I* 11 night] might *I* 14 that] of *E*
15 banck'd] banke *N, C, σ*

who bidding, into forme and frame,
   not beeing yet, they all did grow.   20
all formed, framed, founded so,
   tyll ages uttmost date,
they place retaine they order know,
   they keepe their first estate.

When heav'n hath prais'd, praise earth anew;   25
   you Dragons first, her deepest guests,
then soundlesse deepes, and what in you
   residing low or moves, or rests.
   you flames affrighting mortall brests:
     you stones that cloudes do cast: 30
     you feathery snowes from wynters nests,
     you vapors, sunnes appast.

You boistrous windes, whose breath fullfills
   what in his word his will setts down:
ambitious mountaines, curteous hills: 35
   you trees that hills and mountaines crown:
   both you that proud of native gown
     stand fresh or tall to see:
   and you that have your more renown,
     by what you beare, then be.   40

You beasts in woodes untam'd that range:
   you that with men famillier go:
you that your place by creeping change,
   or airy streames with feathers row.
   you statly kings, you subjects low   45
     you Lordes, and Judges all:
   you others whose distinctions show,
     how sex or age may fall.

All these I say, advaunce that name
   more hygh then skies, more low then ground.   50
and since advaunced by the same
   you Jacobs sonnes stand cheefly bound;

28 moves] lives *E*   or rests] as [os (?)] rests *I*   31 feathery] feathered *F*   34 his]
added above caret in A   37 native] Nature σ, *G, M*   gown] grownd *I*; ground θ, *N, C*;
growne [*added in right margin in different ink;* grounde *stricken*] *H*; growne *Q, E, G, M*
38 or] and θ   44 or] our *E*   row] rawe *I*   49 these] these [o *before* s *altered to*
e (?)] *I*; those σ, *M*   50 skies] skie *Q*

you Jacobs sonnes be cheefe to sound
your god Jehovas praise:
55   so fitts them well on whom is found,
such blisse on you he laies.

Cantate Domino.
Psalm 149.

In an erst unused song
to Jehova lift your voices:
make his favorites among
sound his praise with cheerefull noises.
5   Jacob, thou with joy relate
him that hath refram'd thy state:
sonnes whom Sion entertaineth,
boast in him who on you raigneth.

Play on harp, on tabret play:
10   daunce Jehova publique daunces.
he their state that on him stay,
most afflicted, most advaunces.
ô how glad his saincts I see!
ev'n in bed how glad they be!
15   heav'nly hymnes with throat unfolding,
swordes in hand twice-edged holding.

Plague and chastise that they may
Nations such as erst them pained:
yea, their kings in fetters lay,
20   lay their Nobles fast enchained.
that the doom no stay may lett
by his sentence on them sett.

---

54 Jehovas] Jehova's *N, C, G, M*; Jehovaes *σ*   55 well] *om. O*   56 *indented in A*
such] The *I, χ*   on you he] he on you *D*
Psalm 149. *Lacking in B, K.*
Incipit: om. I, Q
1 song] tounge *Q*   2 lift] list *I*   6 refram'd] reformd *θ*   8 in] on *θ, G, M*
raigneth] rayneth *H, E*   12 afflicted] afflictet *I*   15 throat] voice *N, C, G, M*
16 hand] hands *O, Q*   twice-edged] two edged *C, M*   17 Plague] plauge *σ*
18 them] they *C*   20 enchained] *second* e *added above caret in A*; enchaynet *I*
21 the] thee *θ*   22 by] Aye *χ*   his] this *θ*

lo what honor all expecteth
whom the Lord with love affecteth!

Laudate Dominum
Psalm 150.

O laud the Lord, the God of hoasts commend,
  exault his pow'r, advaunce his holynesse:
  with all your might lift his allmightinesse:
your greatest praise upon his greatnes spend.

Make Trumpetts noise in shrillest notes ascend: 5
  make Lute and Lyre his loved fame expresse:
  him lett the pipe, hym lett the tabrett blesse,
him Organs breath, that windes or waters lend.

Lett ringing Timbrells soe his honor sound,
  lett sounding Cymballs so his glory ring,   10
that in their tunes such mellody be found,

As fitts the pompe of most triumphant king.
conclud: by all that aire, or life enfold,
  lett high Jehova highly be extold.

Psalm 150. *Lacking in B, K (a few letters remain visible on the stubs of leaves torn from K).*
Incipit: om. I, Q
1 O] *written over erasure of* L *in A*   3 lift] list [?] *I*   7 the tabrett] the *added above*
caret in A   9 soe] to *N*   10 so] to *F*   12 pompe] pomps *I*   most trium-
phant] triumphant *written in gold on a slip of paper pasted over illegible original in A; God*
our Heavenly [the first word written over erasure of most *(?)]* G   13 life] earth θ

After Psalm 150 *in A:* Finis *[then on separate lines:]* John Davies of the Citty of Hereford
hand-writer hereof:·; *F, C, H, E, G, M also have* Finis; *N has* The End.; *G adds to the*
right of Finis, Sir Philip: Sydney: Knight; *H and E end with a list of the Penitential Psalms*
(followed in H by a Greek motto on f. 148ᵛ):

The. 7. Penitentiall
Psalmes of David./
vizt:
Psal:: 6: 32: 38: 51 ⎫
    :102: 130: 143 ⎭
Μονώ τό [sic] Θεώ [sic]
H
The 7°: penitentiall
psalmes of David./
Psals. ⎱ 6°: 32°: 38°: 51°: ⎱
       ⎰ 102: 130: 143:   ⎰

Variant *Psalmes*

[*Variant: MS B*]

Psalm XLIV
Deus auribus

1. Our Fathers lord by hearing
   Have made us understand
   Thy works before their eyes appearing
   In time gon long ago
5 2.   How rooting nations, them thy hand
       Did plant and planted nourish
   The stock prophane did leafeless grow
   The faithfull branch did flourish.

3. Their Sword did not procure them
10   Possession of the land
   Nor more did their own arms assure them
       In doubtfull time and place
   Thy arm it was it was thy hand
       Thy favor passing measure
15   Sent on them from thy lightsom face
       Why? only for thy pleasure

4. To thee I stand subjected
   O God my only King
   Let Jacob then by thee protected
20   As erst so now remain
5.   By Thee Our Foes we back did fling
   Thy name us so defended
   Our feet trodd down the rising traine
   That ill to us intended

Psalm XLIV [*Variant*]. *Copy-text: B. Lines 2, 4, 6, 8 indented, 5, 7 not indented in B, but Woodforde notes his error.* The First staffe ought to have been written as is the second and the rest[.] SW. *B notes:* The next Psalm has in the topp of it three little crosses thus [$^x_x{}^x$] and the whole Psalm is lightly crossed with the pen, Quaere whether further corrected or new made[.] *Verse number 25 om. in B. On the verso of each leaf, the verse numbers are in the right margin.*

6   My trust was not reposed   25
        In force of bended bow
     My scabard did not hold enclosed
            With sword my saving might.
7.   But thou hast kept us from the Foe
            Our haters all confounding   30
8   Thee will we prayse still day and night
            Thy name O God resounding

9.   Now Thou aloof dost hover
        And dost us quite disgrace
     And utterly hast given over   35
            Our Armys forth to lead
10.   Thou makst us shew our back for face
            To men with malice boyling
         Whose troops upon our goods do tread
            At their owne pleasure spoyling   40

11. As sheep to be devoured
        Thou hast us left alone
     Thou scattringly hast us out poured
            Among our heathnish foes
12.   Thou sellest us but coin hast none   45
            Thy folk thou so hast prized
         As things from whence no profit growes
            Base, worthless, vile, despised.

13. To them that are about us
        Thou makest us a scorn   50
     That borderers do laugh and flout us
            Who neare unto us dwell
14.   And wee a Proverb tost and worn
            By tongues of forreign places
         At whom to nod it suteth well   55
            And use all vile disgraces

15. My shame before me goeth
        As I do dayly go
     Confusion so upon me groweth
            That I my face do hide   60

48 despised] despis'd *B*

16.   Fearing to feel the bitter blow
      Rebuking slander giveth
      Wherwith me lord like, on each side
      Revengeful malice grieveth.

65 17   All this on us hath lighted
      Yet Thee to have in mind
      Wee for all this are still delighted
      And hold Thy Cov'nant fast
    18.   Our hearts have not from thee declin'd
70   Nor feet away have slidden
    19.   Though thou us down to dragons cast
      In deadly Shade hast hidden

    20   If we Our God had shifted
      Out of forgetfull thought
75   If we adoring hands had lifted
      To any God but Hee
    21.   Should not God seek it out, and sought
      Find out though closly lurking
      Since of the deepest hearts his ey
80   Descrys the deepest working

    22   For Thy Sake sure sustain we
      Thus dayly kild to be
      Nor better estimate obtain we
      Than sheep to slaughter prest
85 23.   Up lord, O Lord shake sleep from thee
      Be not farr off for ever
    24.   Why dost (forgetting us opprest)
      To hide thy face persever.

    25.   Our greived Soul down beaten
90   On lowest dust doth ly
      Our grovling belly almost eaten
      By earth to earth doth cleave
    26.   O rise, with Succours us supply
      Let mercy so esteem us
95   That we thy mercy may receive
      From thraldom to redeem us.

[*Variant: MS B*]

Psalm XLVI.
Deus noster Refugium.

1.   Our hope is God, God is our stay
      A sheild to keep us sound
      Still ready to be found
  When troubles would our minds dismay
2.   Then albeit the Earth quake all   5
      And highest hills do fall
      Into the deepest deep
  Yet still We will us fearless keep.

3.   Yea tho the deep up boyling make
      Such watry mountains rise   10
      As at their dashing cryes
  The Earthy mountains seeme to shake
4.   Yet shall a Rivers streaming joy
      With myrth wash from annoy
      The Citty God hath chose   15
  His Holy dwelling to enclose.

5.   God in this Cittys Center bides
      What can this Citty shake
      Who can this Citty take
  Wher God a present ayd resides?   20
6.   When Nations rage against it came
      And empires did the same
      Ayr did with thunder sound
  Earth faild their feet with melting ground

7.   The God of Armys for us armes   25
      When any tumult moves
      The God that Jacob loves
  Our fortresse is against all harms
8   O Come yourselves, O come and see
      How clean, how throughly hee   30

Psalm XLVI [*Variant*]. *Copy-text: B. B notes*: This Psalm is dasht with the pen as is the
XLIV. *Verse number 11 om. in B.*
Incipit: Deus nostrum Refugium *B*
14 wash] wash'd *B*

Hath purgd the earth of those
That unto him or his were foes.

9   By him each where all warrs are dread
As farr as land doth go
35   He shiverd hath the bow
Crusht pikes, and flames with chariots fedd
10.   Be still sayth he and know that I
Am God who will on high
My peerless power and prayse
40   Above all lands and people rayse

11.   The God of armys, for us arms
When any tumult moves
The God that Jacob loves
Our fortresse is against all harms

[*Variant: MS B*]

Psalm L
Deus Deorum

1.   The ever living God the mighty lord
Hath sent abroad his pursevant his Word
To all the Earth, to which in circling race
Rising or falling Sun doth shew his Face
5   2.   Beauty of Beautys Sion is the place
Which he will beautify by his appearing
3.   God comes, he comes and will not silent stay
Consuming Flames shall usher him the way
A guard of storms about him shall attend
10   4.   Then by his voice he for the Earth shall send
And make the vaulted heav'n to earthward bend
That he may judg his people in their hearing.

---

33 dread] dead *B*   41–4 *B notes*: I suppose this Psalm may bee crosst because of the conclusion or last staffes not answering the rest being shorter by foure verses. as in the former Psalms above, which are therfor corrected

Psalm L [*Variant*]. *Copy-text: B. B places verse number 19 by 52.*
1 *indented in B*

5   Before me here let their appearance make
    My Saints saith he who league did undertake
    With me to hold my pledg of sacrifice   15

6   (This justest doome the Audience of the skys
    Shall wondring shew, for no injustice lyes
        Where God himself as judg the judgment frameth.)

7. My people heare to you I speech will use
    Heare Israël, and I will Thee accuse   20
    For I am God Thy God, and thus do say

8. Because Thou dost not dayly offrings pay
    Nor Sacrifice to me present alway
        This is not that in Thee my censure blameth.

9. Nor bullock I Thy house enstalled holds   25
    Nor goate will take selected from Thy folds

10. For all the Cattle woody forests shield
    For all the flocks a thousand downs do yeeld

11. All birds all beasts wide wanderers of the field
        Are mine, all known to mee, and me all knowing   30

12. If I were hungry that I hungry were
    Since earth is mine, and all that earth doth beare
    I would not tell it Thee to begg thy meate

13. But do I long the flesh of bulls to eate
    Or do I thirst to quench my thirsty heat   35
        With blood from throats of bearded cattle flowing

14   A Sacrifice to God of Prayses frame
    Perform Thy vowes made in the Highest name

15   In troublous times to me for succour send
    The playning voice, and when I succor lend   40
    For lending succour to my glory bend
        All that Thou art; these offrings I demand Thee

16   This to the Good. Now to the Godles sort
    How fitts it Thee my statutes to report
    And of my Cov'enant in thy talk to prate   45

17. Wheras to live in right reformed state
    Thou dost refuse, nay in Thy heart dost hate
        Casting behind Thy back what I command Thee.

13 *indented in B*

18.   Seest Thou a thief? a theif with him Thou art
50   Adulterers findst? Thou tak'st Adulterers part
19.   Thy mouth a denn where Serpent slaunder lyes
      Thy tongue a stamp that coines but fraud and lyes
20.   Ev'n to disgrace of him; whom to thee tyes
      The sweet strait band of calling one your mother
55 21.   Thus while Thou didst, because I silent staid
      Thus in Thy thought thy wicked fancy said
      God is like me, and like his like doth love
      But my true deeds shall Thy false thoughts reprove
      And to thy face from point to point shall prove
60   Against thee all that thou hast sought to smother.

22   Mark this all you, whose crazed holely braine
      Cannot one thought of God in you contain
      Mark this I say, least if with griping hand
      I once lay hold of you, none may withstand
65   My matchless might, nor loose the pinching band
      So straitly straind, as to be loosed never
23.   In Summe who will that I take in good part
      His offring must on Altar of his heart
      Offer an earnest love of honouring me
70   And He whose stepps aright disposed be
      That man will I keep still from danger free
      And place with God in safty lasting ever.

[*Variant: MS B*]

Psalm LIII.
Dixit insipiens.

1.   The foole in foolish Fancy says
      There is no God that marks mens wayes
      So he and all the Witless train
      Such deeds both do, and don maintain
5   Whose hatefull touch the earth doth stain,
      Who good among them? None

Psalm LIII [*Variant*]. *Copy-text: B. B notes*: This Psalm is crossd in the body of it\and/with three Crosses at the beginning[.] *B places verse numbers 2, 6 by 6, 21.*

2. Even God that can most nearly pry
    Hath cast on them his searching eye
    Searching if any God would know

3. What finds he? All astraying go   10
    All so corrupt and cankred so
        Not one doth good, not one.

4. O Fury! Are Gods people bred
    For as they were so are ye fedd.
    On them, ye Wolvish Canibals   15
    And unto God, which of you calls?

5. But lo great feare upon you falls
        From what you feared least
    For God shall so his people wreake
    That He whole armys boanes shall breake   20
    Chased by them with shame and scorn

6. Ah! when shall time away be worne
    That Israel Syons Saviour born
        May joy and Jacob rest.

[*Variant: MS B*]

Psalm LVIII
Si vere utique

1.   You that in judgment sitt
    Is this to speake what is in judgment fitt
    Is this aright to sentence wronged case
            O you but earthly Adams race
            Though higher sett in honourd place?   5

2.   Nay is not this the wrong
    which in your hearts you have revolved long
    Now to the World in practice to display?
            To whom where justice you should weigh
            Oppression you in ballance lay   10

3.   But never did I look
    From you for better, since the shape you took

Psalm LVIII [*Variant*]. *Copy-text*: B. B *notes*: This Psalm is cross'd in the MS. for correction or change. Quære.

Of men; since first you fedd on breathing wind
With lying mouth, and wronging mind
15   From truth and right you still declin'd.

4.   Not only Serpents hisse
But Serpents poyson in them lodged is.
Poyson such as the Subtile Aspick beares
5.   Whose tayle ev'n then doth stop her eares
20   When shee the skilfull'st charmer heares

6.   Their teeth, Lord, where they stand
Crack in their mouths: crush with thy bruising hand
These lions jawes; as water in dry ground
7.   So make them sink: when they would wound
25   Breake thou their shafts, their shott confound

8.   O let them so decay
As the dishoused snail doth melt away
Or as the Embryo, which formless yet
Dyes e're it lives, and cannot get
30   Though born to see sun rise, or sett.

9.   O let their springing thorns
Ere bushes waxt they push with pricking horns
Be by untimely rooting overthrown
With whirlwinds topside turfway blown
35   As fruits which fall ere fully grown.

10.   Now when the just shall see
This justice justly done by justest Thee
On the unjust, and their no juster brood
They shall glad at so great a good
40   Bath righteous feet in wicked blood

11.   And thus in heart shall say
Sure a reward doth for the righteous stay
There is a God whose justice never swerves
But good or ill to each man carves
45   As each mans good or ill deserves.

[*Variant: MS B*]

Psalm LX
Deus repulisti

1.   O God, who angry leftst us in the field
       Repuls'd, disorderd, scattred, slain
       Again to us be reconcil'd
       O be our guide again

2.   The very Earth Thou madest with trembling quake   5
       With chinks and chaps it gaping lay
       O sound again her ruptures make
       Stay her in former stay

3.   What most displeasing any heart could think
       Displeasd Thou didst Thy people show   10
       Dull horror drank they as a drink
       That makes men giddy grow

4.   But now again Thou hast an ensign spredd
       To cheere Thy last dismayed band
       Which by Thy truths conduction ledd   15
       In stout array shall stand

5.   March on O God, set Thy beloved free
       Be deafe no more to what we pray

6   Hark, hark, I heare so shall it be
       God from his Temple say!   20
   March then no further make a merry stand
       Here will I part out Sichems feilds
       By perch and pole I'll meate the land
       That Succoths vally yeilds

7.   Mine Gilead Manasse also mine   25
       Ephram yeilds me men for warr
       Judah shall right by law define
       When strife breeds doubtfull Jarr

8.   Moab shall wash my feet in servile place
       At Edom I my shoe will fling   30
       Thou Palestine (O alterd case)
       Shall of my triumph sing

Psalm LX [*Variant*]. *Copy-text:* B. *B notes:* This whole Psalm in the MS has a Crosse
through the body of it

9.   But who shall bring us to the walled town
     But who shall cause us Edom take
35   10.   Who but the God, that threw us down
     And did our hosts forsake
     11   Long long we thus in servitude have layne
     Come heavnly God O come at length
     And ridd us out for vain most vain
40   Is help of human strength.
     12.   Then Victory shall us with glory crowne
     When not in men, in God we trust
     And then our foes by him cast down
     Shall lick the deadly dust.

[*Variant: MS B*]

Psalm LXII
Nonne Deo.

1.   Yet shall my Soul not grutch, but silently
     Waiting on God his gracious will attend
     His will wheron my health and help depend
2.   For He my rock my Saftys Treasury
5   He is my mount his strength even to the end
     Tho sore I shake from fall shall me defend.
3.   How long then will you vain attempts contend
     To pull him down whom God hath raysed high.
     You envy him and envy makes you dy
10   As aged walls, whose crooked backs do bend
     By their own weight, or hedges thoroughly
     Windshaken so, they standing seem to ly.
4.   But what makes them, these biusy paines apply?
     They see I do to Excellency ascend
15   And therfore thus my ruin still entend

Psalm LXII [*Variant*]. *Copy-text: B. B places verse number 10 by 38, omits verse numbers 4–7.*
1 *not indented in B*
14–15 *B notes:* These two verses first stood thus.
     Sure that I faln may not again ascend
     To tread me lower yet they do intend
which not pleasing were expungd The second then was thus alterd *And therfore thus my trea-*
cherous fall intend Treacherous, was then blotted out and *greater* putt in instead, which not yet
pleasing it was lastly put as in the text But indeed after all the whole Psalm stands crossd

They say they love; Indeed they love to ly
They speake so well, none can their speech amend
But think so ill, none worser thoughts can spend

5.　　　Yet O my Soul grutch not, but still attend
Gods gracious will persever silently　　　　　　20
To wait on God Thy help with patient eye
6.　Make him Thy rock Thy fort thee to defend
Make him Thy Mount Thy Safetys treasury
Wheron Thy hopes unshaken may rely.

7.　　　From him that is my Saving succours grow　　25
By him that is, my glory shines so bright
He is my rock, a rock so firmly pight
As naught can shake much lesse can overthrow
When dreadfull danger would my Soul affright
In him I trust, to him I take my flight　　　　　30
8　　　Your trustfull faith O all you people plight
To God; to God your hearts uncloathed show
And God your help your only refuge know
9　For who possesse This earth in Adams right
Are all so vain, that if to weights they go　　　35
Ev'n Vanity for weight will fall more low
10　　　Look in good ground your confidence you sow
Be skilfull husbands, chuse your seed aright
Think not to have good harvest of your slight
Nor of your ravin many sheaves to mowe　　　40
Nay tho with fruits your barns be throughly dight
Yet on such sand build not your best delight.
11　　　Rather in choyse set this before your sight
Twice said in heav'n, I heard in earth below
God is the ffountain whence all might doth flow.　45
12.　True lord most true, and yet not only might
But mercy with a purpose naught to owe
But as the Worke to pay the workman so.

44 Twice] *B notes: Which* expunged:

[*Variant: MS B*]

Psalm LXIII
Deus Deus meus.

1.   O God, thou art both God, and good to me
        Thee to find I therfore will
           Employ my skill
  When first my Sight the morning light shall see

5   Within my Soul a thirst of thee dos dwell
        Nay my body more doth crave
           Thy tast to have
  Than in this desert dry a springing Well

2.   This desert whence when I my thoughts do reare
10   I no lesse behold thy might
           And glory bright
  Than if I in Thy Sanctuary were

3.   For mercys thyne, so kind Thy mercys are
        All life joyes nay life surmount
15   Which to recount
  My thankfull lips no time, no paine shall spare

4.   As long as life Thy gift, Thy loving gift
        Leaves me not, my joyfull prayse
           Thy name shall rayse
20   Wherin to Thee I praying hands will lift

5.6.   My hungry Soul most dainty food doth tast
        When of Thee I dreame in night
           Or think in light
  Or have my tongue upon thy prayses plac't.

25   7.   Thy Safeguard me from perill hath preserv'd
        Hiv'd by Thee I dry have lain
           From showres of pain
  Thy hand to me this life hath still reserv'd.

8.   But who persue, and would me headlong throw
30   Headlong shall themselves be thrown

Psalm LXIII [*Variant*]. *Copy-text: B. B notes:* This Psalm is crossed in the MS.

9.   With tempest blown
          Into the place in lowest earth most low.

10   The murthring blade shall first their life devoure
                    Carkasses of life bereft
                        Shall there be left   35
          Where foxes teeth shall have them in their power.

11   As for the King, The King in God shall joy
                    So shall they who evermore
                        His name adore
          Who lying mouths will stop, lyars destroy.   40

                    [*Variant: MS B*]

                    Psalm LXIV.
                    Exaudi Deus.

1.   This voice wherin my grief I show
          With gracious eare lord entertaine
          And let my life in rest remain
          By Thee preserv'd from feared foe
2.   O hide me where they may not know.   5
                    Whose wicked witts in wiles are spent
                    And rage to working wrong is bent

3.   For their sharp tongues such edg do beare
          As fretted stones give whetted Swords
          They levell so with bitter words   10
          As if not words but shafts they were
4.   Which they embusht and free from feare
                    When none could think, where none could see
                    Discharg upon poore harmless me

5.   Nay obstinate to ill they go   15
          Discoursing how they Snares may lay
          They say who sees? And well they may
6.   For sure they search each corner so

Psalm LXIV [*Variant*]. *Copy-text: B. B notes:* This Psalm is crosst too. *B omits verse numbers*
3–10.
5 placed to the right of 4 in B (2 in parentheses)

No guile no fraud can ly so low
20   But these will find in any part
Ev'n in the depth of deepest heart

7.   But Thou O God a shaft shalt send
Death striking them with suddain blow
8.   And their own tongues to their own Woe
25   Shall all their wounding sharpness bend
Then all shall quake that see their end
9.   And all the earth their end shall see
And seing, prayse Gods just decree

10.   Mean while on his Almighty Name
30   The just man vext by man unjust
Shall cast the Anchor of his trust
And land his comfort on the same
And such whose Consciences not lame
Upright can stand, and march aright
35   Shall boast in God their Captains might.

[*Variant: MSS B, I*]

Psalm LXVIII
Exurgat Deus.

1.   Do Thou O God but rise, and in a moments space
Thy foes shall scatred be, and cast in disarray
Who hate to Thee conceale, or hate to thee bewray
Affrighted at Thy fearfull look shall fly before Thy face
5   2.   Yea so they all shall fly, as smoke away doth go
Which going go'eth to naught, or like the waxy ball
At least aspect of Fire doth into water flow
So naughty men at sight of God from naught to nought shall
fall.

3.   Meane while who justice love, who set their hearts aright
10   When they behold how God doth wicked men destroy

Psalm LXVIII [*Variant*]. *Copy-text: B. Line 1 not indented in B; verse number 25 placed by 78.*
I indents 2–3, 5, 7 (2–3, 6, 8 indented in stanza 1; 2, 4, 6–7 indented in stanza 2). B notes: This
Psalm is crost in the MS. *I notes in pencil in a later hand:* Printed in Sidneiana.
6 go'eth] grows *I*   or] and *I*   like] liken *I*   8 nought shall] nothing *I*

In mapp of outward prayse shall paint their inward joy
And in his gracious ey shall find but triumph and delight.
4. Delight then triumph then, then joy before him show
Then prayse his name *Who is*, who on the heaven rides
5. Who most right judging judg the Widdows cause doth know   15
Who father of the Fatherless in Sacred Temple bides.

6. Thou God with Childrens store the empty house dost fill
Thou of the fetterd foot dost loose the fretting band
But that Rebellious rout, who stiff against Thee stand
Exiled from the fields of blisse the cursed sand do till   20
7. When Thou O God didst march before thy faithfull train
When through the wastfull wayes Thou didst Thy journy take
8 The heavns at sight of Thee with sweating drops did raine
The earth did bow her trembling knee, yea Sinay mount did
     shake.

Mount Sinay shook O God Thou God of Israël   25
At sight of Thee, a sight exceding sight and thought
9. Who when to promisd soyle Thou hadst thy people brought
Upon Thy weary heritage refreshing showërs fell
10. There Thou Thy flock didst feed, ther for Thy sheep distrest
Thou hadst in store layd up each good and healthfull thing   30
11. A virgin army there, with chastness armed best
While armys fledd, by Thee was taught this triumph Song to
     sing.

12. These Kings, these Sons of Warr, lo, lo they fly they fly
Wee house=confined maids with distaffs share the spoyle
13. Whose hew though long at home the chimnys glosse did foyle   35
Since now as late enlarged doves wee freer skyes do try
As that gold-featherd fowle so shall our beautys shine
With beating wavy aire with oare of silverd winge
So dasleth gazing eyes that eyes cannot define
If those sweet lovely, glittring streames from Gold or Silver
     spring.   40

12 but] *B notes:* forte for *both*   14 who on] whom' [?] *I*   16 in Sacred] god in his
sacred *I*   17 Childrens] children *I*   18 of the] god of *I*   loose] looke *I*   fret-
ting] pinching *I*   20 fields] sea *I*   22 wastfull] desart *I*   23 heavns] heav'n *I*
27 Who] and *I*   soyle] land *I*   29 didst] doth *I*   ther for] there for *I*; therfore *B*; *B*
notes: forte pro *there for*   30 healthfull] fruitfull *I*   33 fly they] <they>\fly/thy *I*
34 distaffs] distares *I*   36 doves] dames *I*   38 With] which *I*   40 those] that *I*

14   For when th'Almighty had with utter overthrow
       The Kings extirpate hence (that this may not seem strange)
       The very ground her robes black mourning clouds did change
   And clad herself in weather cleere, as cleare as Salmon snow.

45 15   Mount Basan be Thou proud of thy fatt feeding lands
       Of thy empyreall site, mount Basan boast thy fill
       Whose proudly perking top so many tops commands
   Mount Basan tho thou boast and burst Gods hill is Sion hill.

16.   You other hills, whose topps so many topps command
50   What makes you then to leap, what makes you then to swell
       This humble mount is that where God desires to dwell
17.   Here here his house, Who Ever is, shall everlasting stand
       Here He twice thousands ten, yea doubled twice retaines
       Of chariots fit for warr, which carve with hooked wheele
55   In midst of whom the lord in sacred seat remains
   As glorious now, as when his weight mount Sinais back did feele.

18   Thou art gon up on high, with Thee Thy Captive bands
       Whose spoiles Thou hast receiv'd, and wilt to Thyne impart
       O God, Eternall God, so reverenc't Thou art
60 19.   That even thy Rebels dwell with Thee, as tenants to Thy lands
       The lord our healthfull help, our blessing prayse shall have
       Who on us day by day doth good on good amasse
20.   He only is our God, the God who doth us save
   The lord Eternall keepes the keyes wherby from death wee passe

65 21.   God of their hatinge heads the crounes with wounds shall
                crowne
       Who are against him bent, and who still onward go
       In way of wicked will, the bloody streames that flow
   Their growing Perrukes water shall in tresses hanging down
22   As I my self, said God did once from Basan bring
70   And then from drowning death in deepest Seas did keep
       I now will do again the same, the self same thing
   From Basan I will bring my folk, and keep them from the deep.

---

43 clouds] cloud *I*   46 empyreall] empertall [?] *I*   50 what] with *I*   51 humble]
mountains *I*   54 chariots] charrets *I*   which] with *I*   55 midst] widds [?] *I*
63 our] the *I*   who] that *I*   65 hatinge] horting *I*   67 that] the [?] *I*
69 self] flock *I*   70 then] them *I*   71 will do again] again will doe *I*   72 folk]
flock *I*

23   He said; and out of hand, thou didst Thy foot engrain
       In blood: In blood of foes thy doggs their tongues did dye
24. And all O God, my King, beheld with open ey   75
       Thy marching to Thy Holy place, they saw, they saw Thee plain.
25. The Vantguard was of them, that did with voyces sing
       They in the rereward plac'd, on instruments did play
       The middleward was maids, and did with timbrells ring
       The voices, tymbrells, instruments in sweet consort did say   80

26   Praise God O prayse our lord, when you your meetings make
       You blessed Jacobs root, you race of Israël
27. Of whom young Benjamin with sword his foes doth quell
       And bullets shott from Judas sling, make more than armours ake
       We noble Zabulon and Nepthali could name   85
       Two thunderbolts of warr, but God we turn to Thee
28. Thou gavest to us this force, O God confirm the same
       And what by Thee hath been begun, by Thee let ended be

29   God for Thy temple sake, for Salem when it stands
       Where Kings with offred gifts, Thy Altars heads shall croune   90
30. These furious bulls rebuke, these wanton calves knock down
       These furious wanton bulls and calves, these arrow-arm'd bands
       I meane defeat these troops that do in wars delight
       Make them with humble grace their silver tributes pay
31. Let Egypt send to Thee her men of greatest might   95
       Let Ethiope with lifted hands Thy speedy favor pray.

32   And you, you Kingdoms all, that Earthy Kings do share
       The King of Kings extoll, I meane the heavnly King
       A Song to God the lord a Songe of prayses sing
       Let your melodious Instruments his past-praise worth declare   100
33. For bravely mounted he on highest Heavens back
       The rolling spheres to rule doth coachmanlike persist

---

74 thy] the *I*   doggs] doge *I*   75 And] *I*; An *B*   78 on] in *I*   79 timbrells
ring] timble bring *I*   80 in sweet consort] with one accord *I*   81 our] the *I*
82 root] brood *I*   Israël] Isräel *B*; Israell *I*   83 with sword his foes] his foes with
force *I*   84 bullets shott from Judas sling, make] Juda with sling whirled stones
makes *I*   85 could] call'd' [?] *I*   86 warr] fight\warr/ *I*   87 to us] us *I*
88 be] *om. I*   89 God] Lord *I*   temple] temples *I*   when] where *I*   91 wanton calves] lesser\wanton/clues *I*   92 furious wanton] *I*; wanton² furious¹ *B*   arrow-
arm'd] arrow armed *I*   93 defeat] *added above caret in B*   wars] warr *I*   94 humble]
humbled *I*   97 that Earthy] which earthly *I*   102 rolling] running *I*

And from the hight of hights in thundring cloudy crack
Sends down his voice, a voyce of strength, a strength none can
  resist.

105 34.   Then give to God all strength, of strength the mine and spring
           Whose brave magnificence, whose sunlike glory showes
           No lesse on Israels line, the line himself hath chose
           Than in the thundring cloudy crack, his powerfull might doth
             ring.

    35.   Thou fearfull art O God, and fearfull things didst show
110   Down from Thy starry Seat, from out Thy Sacred hill
           From Him from Him it is his peoples might doth grow
           The mighty God of Israel, to him be prayses still.

[*Variant: MS B*]

Psalm LXIX
Salvum me

  1   Save me O God, O Save my drowning Soul
  2   For fast I stick in depth of muddy hole
           When I no footing find
       Now, now, into the watry gulfs I fall
5   And with the streame I go
  3.   Hoarse is my throat so long I cry and call
       So long look for my God, that dymm nay blind
           Mine eyes with looking grow.

  4.   Who hate to me and causeless hate do beare
10   Are more than that to every one one haire
           I from my head can give
       Who with no juster cause seek my decay
           More mighty are than I
  5.   So what I never took I must repay

---

103 from] for *I*   105 God] god<the> *I*   106 brave] bright *I*   glory] grory *I*
107 Israels] *B has a dotted line under* Israels *and* Isaacks *written above it*; Isaacs *I*
108 thundring cloudy crack] cloudie thundring cracks *I*   might] strength *I*   109 things
didst] signes dost *I*   110 Seat] throne *I*

Psalm LXIX [*Variant*]. *Copy-text: B. B notes*: This Psalme is crost in the MS *B places verse
numbers 5, 12, 25, 28 by 14, 35, 77, 83.*

But God my Follys in Thy knowledg live   15
    Thou dost my faults descry.

6   O mighty Lord, let not discount'nanct be
    By my occasion such as trust in Thee
       Let never blushing shame
    O God of Isrell flowing from my fall   20
       Thy Servants faces staine

7. For what I beare for Thee I beare it all
    Thy cause it is I this disgracefull blame
       And noted blot susteine.

8   My Brethren me did for a stranger hold   25
    My mothers children so did me behold
       As one they did not know

9. Zeale of Thy house my Soule did eate and burn
       What shame on Thee was layd
    Transferrd on me to my reproach did turn   30

10. I wept, I fasted, yet for doing so
       How did they me upbraid?

11. Changing my weeds in sackcloth sad I mournd
    My Sackcloth these to jeasts and jybings turnd
12.   And both in public place   35
    Of me did prate, and private in their wyne
       On me did ryme and sing.

13. But I, when Thou the season dost assigne
    To Thee will pray, lord let Thy saving grace
       Not faile me help to bring!   40

14. Lift me out of this mire; let me not sink
    In pudled poole, from such whose thoughts can think
       But hatred to my Soul
    And from this bottomless, and banckless deep
       O save, and set me free   45

15. Keep, that these streames o'erwhelm me not, O keep
    This gulf engulf me not, this gapeing hole
       Shut not her mouth on me

16 Answer me lord in that sweet grace of thyne
    And in Thy mercys numberless encline   50
       To me Thy abiding eye
17. Ne from Thy Servant hide Thy helpfull face

For ev'ils me streightly close

18   O haste, O heare, O come, and come apace
55   Unto my Soul, O free it presently
                 Redeeme it from my foes.

19   My shame, my ignominious disgrace
         To Thee is known, and still before Thy face
                 Are all that beare me spight
60 20. Which so did rack so rent my tender heart
                 That languishing I pin'd
         I lookt from Somebody for some kind part
         That some would stirr, but all were frozen quite
                 No comfort could I find.

65 21. Comfort? Nay more to aggravate my Woe
         They gave me gall, when I did hungry grow
                 And vinacre for drink
    22. Lord make their tables to themselves a snare
                 Their happyness a nett
70 23. Make that their eyes, in only darkness stare
         And when they go with weakness make them sink
                 Such weights upon them sit.

    24. Thy never ceasing indignations shower
         Show'r down on them, and in whole rivers poure
75   Let Fury of Thyne Ire
         On evry side of them lay griping hold:
    25.   Their house be desert ground
    26   Quite desolate their tents, for they are bold
         To plague, whom thou but strik'st, and still aspire
80   Thy wounded more to wound.

    27. Add still more cyphers to their sinfull summ
         But to Thy justice let them never come
    28.   And from the blessed book
         The book of life, that Godly men contains
85   Let them clean rased be
    29. But I poore destitute, whose heart sustains
         The heavy weight of wo to Thee will look
                 Thou God shalt Succour me

85 them clean] them [*erasure*] clean B   be] *written over erasure in* B

30 Then shall O God my Song extoll Thy name
    My thankfull prayses magnify Thy Fame   90
31.   Which Thou shalt dearer hold
    Than any Sacrifice, which horned head
                Or hoofed foot doth beare
32. The Godly grieved ones, who seeking tread
    The Paths of God, when they my change behold   95
                Their hearts to joy shall reare.

33. For God doth hearken to the poore mans cryes
    And never dos the Prisners plaint despise
34.   Praise him you circling Spheres
    Thou steadfast earth, Thou Sea, and what in thee   100
                Doth either swim or saile
35. For Sion shall his safe protection see
    And every towre his loved Juda beares
                To build he shall not faile

36 He shall not faile to build up evry place   105
    And builded bring in habitable case
                That such as do him serve
    Not only may therin themselves reside
                But their succeding seed
    Heires to their heritage may still abide   110
    And all, whose loves of his name well deserve
                No other seate may need.

                [*Variant: MS B*]

                Psalm LXXI
                In te Domine

    1.   On thee my trust is grounded.
                Lord let me never be
                With shame confounded
    2.   But set me free
                And in Thy justice rescue me   5

91 Which] Wher *B*

Psalm LXXI [*Variant*]. *Copy-text: B. B notes: Cross'd in the MS. B aligns 4 and 7 with 3 in
stanza 1, and 2 with 1 in stanza 2; verse numbers 5, 11, 15, 17, 24 placed by 16, 50, 67, 73, 110.*

Thy gracious eare to me ward bend
And me defend.

3.   Be Thou my rock my Tower
My ever safe resort
10   Whose saving power
Hath not been short
To work my safety, for my Fort
On Thee alone is built; in Thee
My strong holds be

15 4   Me, O my God deliver
From wicked, wayward hand
5.   God my help giver
On whom I stand
And stood since I could understand
20 Nay since by life I first became
What now I am.

6   Since prison'd in my mother
By Thee I prison brake
I trust no other
25   No other make
My stay, no other refuge take
Void of Thy praise no time doth find
My mouth and mind.

7.   Men for a monster took me
30   Yet hope of help from Thee
Never forsook me
8   Make then by me
All men with praise extolld may see
Thy glory Thy magnificence
35   Thy excellence

9.   When feeble yeares do leave me
No stay of other sort
Do not bereave me
Of Thy support
40 And fail not then to be my fort
When weakness in me killing might
Usurps his right

10.   For now against me banded
         My foes have talkt of me
         Now unwithstanded   45
         Who their spyes be
         Of me have made a firm Decree
11.   (Lo!) God to him hath bid a-Dieu,
         Now then persue.

      Persue say they and take him   50
         No Succour can he win
         No refuge make him
12.   O God begin
      To bring with speed Thy forces in
      Help me my God, my God, I say   55
         Go not away

13.   But let them be confounded
         And perish by whose hate
         My Soul is wounded
         And in one rate   60
      Let them all share in shamefull state
      Whose counsells, as their farthest end
         My wrong intend

14.   For I will still persever
         My hopes on Thee to rayse   65
         Augmenting ever
         Thy praise with praise
15.   My mouth shall utter forth alwayes
      Thy Truths, Thy Helps, whose summ surmounts
         My best accounts.   70

16.   Thy force keeps me from fearing
         Nor ever dread I ought
         Thy justice bearing
         In mindfull thought
17.   And glorious Acts which Thou hast taught 75
      Me from my youth, and I have shown
         What I have known

48 (Lo!)] *B notes:* MS. but the verse lacks it.

18.   Now age doth overtake me
And paint my head with Snow
80   Do not forsake me
Untill I show
The ages, which succeding grow
And every after living wight
Thy Pow're and might.

85   19   How is Thy Justice raysed
Above the height of thought
How highly praised
What Thou hast wrought
Sought let be all that can be sought
90   None shall be found, nay none shall be
O God like Thee

20.   What if Thou down didst drive me
Into the Gulf of woes
Thou wilt revive me
95   Again from those
And from the Deep, which deepest goes
Exalting me again wilt make
Me comfort take.

21.   My greatness shall be greater
100   By Thee: by comfort Thyne
My good state better
22.   O lute of mine
To prayse his truth thy tunes incline
My Harp extoll the Holy One
105   In juda known

23.   My voice to my Harp join thee
My Soul Sav'd from decay
My voice conjoin Thee
24.   My tongue each day
110   In all mens viewe his justice lay
Who hath disgrac'd and shamed so
Who work my woe.

[*Variant: MSS B, I, K, N*]

Psalm LXXV
Confitebimur.

1. Wee O God to Thee do sing
    Wee to Thee do prayses bring
        For Thy name is nigh
    When our cause assistance needs
        Us with succour to supply   5
        Therfore saved wondrously
    We recount Thy wondrous deeds

2. As for me, whenso thy shall
    Under my direction fall
        Who to me pertain   10
    Righteous dome shall bannish wrong
3.   This loose land I will again
        Into sounder site restrain
    I will make her Pillars strong

4. I will say to braggards then   15
    Bragg no more: to wicked men
        Set not up your horn
5. Set not up your horn on high
        Be no more perversly born
        Onward with rebellious scorn   20
    Thus to speake repiningly!

6. East whence climing Sun ascends
    West where sliding Sun descends
        South his standing tide
    Can to no man honour bring   25
7.   Only God who all doth guide
        Makes men climb, or stand or slide
    Makes the Caitife and the King

Psalm LXXV [*Variant*]. *Copy-text: B. B notes*: Cross'd in the MS. *I notes in pencil in a later
hand*: Printed in Sidneiana. *K notes:* This is otherwise translated. *After the variant, N notes*:
The same, another way. *B places verse numbers 3–8 by* 15, 18, 22, 26, 29, 32, *respectively.*
9 direction] directions *I*   11 dome] doome *K, N*; do\o/we *I*   16 more:] ~: *K, N*;
~, *I*; ~∧ *B*   17–18 up . . . up] ope *altered to* upp *in different ink in each line in K*
20 Onward] onwardes *K*   21 Thus] *om. I, K, N*   speake] speake still *N*   25 man]
more *K, N*

8.   Then not me, God you withstand
30   Him whose ever right right hand
                Holds a filled cupp
            Not of wine but winey lees
                Of the which they all shall supp;
                Supp, said I? nay suck it up
35   Whom unjust his justice sees

9   So then I will spend my dayes
            In recording still his prayse
                Still my Song shall flow
            From the land of Jacobs God
40 10.   I will crop ill doers low
                I will make well doers grow
            Spreading branches farr abroad.

[*Variant: MS B*]

Psalm LXXX
Qui regis Israel.

1.   Thou which dost Jacob keep
            Attend and heare
        Who guidest Joseph as Thy sheep
        From Throne of Cherubims appeare
5   2.   Manasse now begin
                Thy strength to show
        Make Ephraim make Benjamin
        O make us all Thy safty know.

3   O God of greatest might
10   Turn us again
        Make shine on us Thy faces light
        That wee by Thee may safty gain
    4.   O lord whom hosts attend
                How long shall smoake
15   The flames, which from Thy wrath ascend
        Against their cryes Thy name invoke

---

33 they] thew *I*   34 I?] *I, K, N;* ~, *B*   35 Whom] whome *I;* When *K, N*
Psalm LXXX [*Variant*]. *Copy-text: B. B notes:* Cross'd in the MS. *B places verse number 4 by 14.*

5.   Thou dost Thy people feed
        With bread of teares
And teares they drink, when drink they need
And still their cupp full measure beares   20

6.   Thou makst that for our goods
        Our neighbours braule
Thou mak'st of them that thirst our bloods
The fowle derision, on us fall

7.   O God of greatest might   25
        Turn us again
Make shine on us Thy faces light
That we by Thee may safty gain

8.   A vine Thou broughtst of Old
        From Zoan Plaines   30
And weeding them the place did hold
Didst here implant with pruning pains

9   It stands enrooted fast
        The land it fills

10.   It branches doth like Cedars cast   35
With pleasing cold it cloakes the hills

11.   This way her loving leaves
        Do kisse the Sea
On t'other side her hands she heaves
On old Euphrates hold to lay   40

12.   How happs, That now this Vine
        Dishedgd doth ly
That Thou dost it in prey assign
Abandond to all passersby?

13.   How happs it, from the woods   45
        The wastfull boare
Destroyes it thus, that field-born broods
Of greedy beasts yet spoile it more?

14   O God of hosts the guide
        Again return   50
Behold us thence where Thou dost bide
And to Thy vine Thy count'nance turn

15   Behold the vineyard made
        By Thy right hand

55   Behold the plant, which not to fade
                 Thou once didst will but firm to stand.

16   Consum'd they ly with fire
                 With Axes hewn
               At chiding of thy awfull Ire
60   To unrepaired ruine thrown
17   The man of Thy right hand
                 O lord support
               And who doth in Thy favor stand
               Ordaind by Thee our fence and fort.

65   So we O God from Thee
                 Will never fall
               By Thee restor'd our lives shall be
               Who on Thy name with praysing call
19   O God of greatest might
70   Turn us again
               Make shine on us Thy faces light
               That we by Thee may safty gain.

[*Variant: MS B*]

Psalm LXXXVI
Inclina Domine

1.   Lord bend to me Thyne eare
                   And me heare
            Most poore, and most oppressed
2.   O save my soul distressed
5   Who deeply am Thy debtor
       Save me and make my badd state better
                For Thee my God I serve
         From Thee my hope doth never swerve.

3.   Lord pitty of me take
10   For I make

Psalm LXXXVI [*Variant*]. *Copy-text: B. B notes:* This Psalm also is Crossed. *The indentation in B is inconsistent: 17 is singly indented; 23, 31, 33, 39, triply. B places verse numbers 2, 6, 7, 13, 16 by 5, 20, 22, 46, 59.*

                    To Thee my dayly crying
4.   My heart in sorrow lying
                    With joy O Lord recomfort
            For unto Thee my only comfort
                    My Soul doth strive to rise   15
            With stretched hands and bended eyes.

5   For Thou art good and kind
                        Myld of mind
                    To all their prayërs sending
                    To Thee then well attending   20
6.   Thy servant heare his praying
            Gravely his petitions weighing
7.   I cry, but when I need
            I therfore of Thy help shall speed

8   Compar'd with other gods   25
                        By great odds
                    Thou Lord excell'st: none taketh
                    In hand, what thy hand maketh
9.   All nations by Thee framed
            Praising the Name, that Thou art named   30
                    Shall come and as his right
            Shall fall adoring in Thy sight

10.   Thou great in deed dost stand
                    From whose hand
                    O only God still floweth   35
                    Each work that wonder showeth
11.   Thy path to me discover
            And I O lord with walking hover
                    Still in thy truth: O frame
            My heart to love and feare Thy name.   40

12   My heart, lord, all my heart
                        Shall take part
                    In praysing Thee: Thy glory
                    Shall be my endlesse story
13.   Thou art a gracious giver   45
            Of good to me, Thou dost deliver
                    My Soul from pitt of woe
            Even from the pit that lyes most low

14   Se, God, how proud men arm
50   To my harm
          See how the mighty number
          My chased Soul incumber
          Who Thee from eyes repelling
       Reserve Thee in their sight no dwelling
55   15.   But Thou lord God, my King
          Most mercyfull, wilt mercy bring

            Thy Pardon prone thou art
                  To impart
            To anger slowly going
60   With truth and mildness flowing
16   With pitty then behold me
       With Thy Support, my lord, uphold me
            For I Thy servant am
          And of Thy handmaids body came

65   17.   O set on me some Sign
                  To define
            Me one by Thee embraced
            That they with shame amated
          May fall by whom my Soul is hated
70   Seing my Succour brought
       By Thee, by Thee my comfort wrought.

[*Variant: MS I*]

Psalm: 89: Misericordias

Gods boundles bownties gods promise ever abyding
shall bee my songs eternall theme still gladly recording
of fowloing ages, while ranged in absolute order
gold armed squadrons of stares shall muster in heaven

Psalm: 89 [*Variant*]. *Copy-text: I. I notes in the margin:* idem. [*then in pencil in a later hand*]
Printed in Sidneiana[.] *Line 12 is added between 11 and 13; 86 (after* lighted*) is added between 85 and 87; 87 (beginning with* thow*) is written on the same line with* lighted *and* But *is on a line by itself.*
Incipit: Misericordias *I*
2 theme] them *I*

yea this sooner I think that stares best ordered order   5
shall to disorder fall, confusd in contrary courses
then that league be reverst, that sacred treatye repealed
thus by thy selfe sometime confirmd, thus sworn to thy David
while earth, while waters, while palace of heev'n abideth
stablish I will thy elected seed and loftily seated
on throne will hold them, till endles eternities ending   10
O father highe heavens at thee most worthily wonder
O father earth Dwellers, whose hearts al on god bee reposed
Bend to thy truthe their praise, when so their company meteth
who is above that may compare with mighty Jehova?   15
who can among th' exalted train of gloriows angells
like to Jehova be fownd? all him with an awfull obeisance
terrible acknowledge, and flock affrighted abowt him,
thow comander of hosts, indeed most mighty Jehova
seest not a match in powr in verity knowst not an equall   20
Thow of foaming seas, dost still the tumultuows outcries
thow their high swelling, dost coole with lowly residing
prowd Phæroa hath felt thee: all enemies all thy resisters
felt thy revendging hand, disperst and bloudily wounded
thow thow only the fownder of earth, and former of heaven   25
framer of all this vawted rownd, which hanged on hindges
north and south sustain thie benignity, Thabor and hermon
that where sunn falleth, this where his charret ariseth
testify with praises: thee, thee, all only belongeth
all powre, all puisance, makes earth with wonder amazed   30
thow sitte on justice and suply severyty throned
yet so these holding as truth and mercy beholding;
what shall I say? o blest thrice blest, who hastily hy them
unto thy joyfull feasts, with trumpets harmony rowzed
who lighted by thy wholsome face, kept glad by thy gladnes   35
rising from thy renowned name, advanc'd by thy justice

frankly receave from thee great lord strength Dignity empire
lastly a king, as a sheild, strenght empire Dignity guarding
These things in visions to thy prophets plainly revealed
40   thus were uttred againe, on a man very mighty reputed:
one exalted, I have, Devoted, wholly to serve mee
David I meane, whose head hath streamd by my sacred anointing
force and strength from me, shall mightily ever uphold him
no manifest violence no cloaked villany hurt him
45   his cruel oppressors prickt on by malicious envie
prostrat in his presence will I lay past hope of rissing
never shall hee my kindnes want my fidelity never
raisd to that haight of rule that from seas watery border
unto the streames Eufrates rolls, all lands shall obey him
50   His father his fortress, his gracious god shall he call mee
and him againe I my first born sonn will grace to bee called
placed above all earthly monarchs by my mercy for ever
and constant covenant in state most happy remayning
yea such bliss to his heirs as a legacy shall be bequeathed
55   They shall sitt kings loftily thrond, and loftily throned
their thrones continuance a paragon to the ages of heeven
yf so my laws they leave and bend not their steps to my judgments
yf they breake my beheasts what I bidde perversly relinquish
their misdemeanors, their sinns, with a whipe with a scourging
60   visit I will indeed; yett as unto my Dearly beloved
kind will I ever abide, in truth and mercy for ever
holding firmlye my league not a jot my true promises altring
Once this I sware this I holily sware, nor can be remedied
David I will not faill his progeny shall bee eternall
65   his seate mayntaind while sunns most glorious ardor
guilds the rejoicing Day: while night in unaltred order
Hides the repining day with moons pale silver adorned
which of this covenant, still shines a true witnes in heaven

---

39 to] *written above stricken* th *in* I   40 man~ ... reputed:] ~: ... ~~ I   42 David] i *written over* e *(?) in* I   43 him] *illegible character (resembling* W) *stricken or false start in* I   50 gracious] gricious I   52 placed] e *dotted (?) in* I   54 yea] yee I 55 and *stricken at the beginning of the line in* I   56 thrones] thones I   a paragon] aparagon [*first* a *unclear*] I   57 judgments] judg=ments [ments *written above the line*] I 58 breake] *a letter stricken before* k *(?) in* I   59 a whipe] awhipe I   60 visit] e *altered to* i *before* t *in* I   61 ever abide] everabade I   62 true] tre [e *written over an illegible letter (?)] I*   63 holily] hol\i/ly I   65 sunns] o *altered to* u *in* I (?)   ardor] ador I   68 a true] atrue I

Yet now alas: thie annointed king thow angry rejectest
pulst of his Diadem, his alliance wholy refusest   70
his bulwarks raisest, ruinest his mighty defences
left for a pray to the passengers of a scorn to the neighbours
victory crowns his foes proud joy possesseth his haters
his sword quite blunted, from field with filthie Dishoner
chased hee flies, his throne thrown down his glory defaced   75
spring of his age is winter grown disgraced hee pineth
How long ever alas? wilt thow most mighty be hidden
shall once kindled fire, still flame in furiows ardor
Thinke o think yet again how short our earthly residing
think whether all to bee speedily slayn, were rashly created   80
who is he now living, but death prepareth his harbor
in toombs cold bosome whither hevy nesessity sends him
Lord wher is old kindnes in verity sworn to thy David
our foule disgraces, sweet lord in mercy remember
whose laps are filled with words of many reproches   85
lighted on us but bent at thee and at thine anoyntet
But thow mighty Jehova eternall eternities author
blessed eternally bide and yeeld those blissed a blessing.

[*Variant: MS B*]

Psalm CV
Confitemini Domino.

1.   O pray's th' Eternall, invocate his Name
     Make all Nations under sunn
     Of his works may understand
2.   To him your Songs, your Psalms unto him frame
     Speake of all the Actions done   5
     Wondrously by his right hand.

---

70 refusest] st *written over* th *(?) in* I   71 defences] *first* e *added above* df *in* I
73 crowns] r *altered in* I   74 field] flld *[?]* I   78 once] onc *I*   81 living]
third letter unclear in I   82 hevy nesessity] hevynes ssity *[?]* I   83 David] *an*
extra stroke between i *and* d *in* I *(?)*   84 lord] k *stricken before* lord *in* I   86–7 on
. . . anoyntet *written above* thow . . . author, *which is placed after* lighted *as the continuation of*
86; But *is thus alone on* 87.   86 bent at] bent ata *[?]* I   88 bide] d *written over* b
(?) in I   blissed] blisses *I*

Psalm CV [*Variant*]. *Copy-text: B. B notes:* This Psalm is crosst. *B places verse numbers 8, 30,*
31 by 21, 81, 84.

3. O make his Sacred Name your Reverend boast
    In th' Eternall let them joy
    Who are bent to seek his Place
4. O seek th' Eternall, seek from evry coast
    His Ark, his strength! O employ
    Dayly pains to find his Face

5 Remember well the Wonders He hath wrought
    Deeds beyond all wonder don
    Judgments, which did justly passe
6 For we from Abraham his servant brought
    We the Sons of Isa'aks Son
    Him, that once his chosen was

7 So He our God, though all the Earth He guide
8.   Minding ay the League He swore
    Endless Ages should endure
9 Bound first to Abraham, then faster tyde
    To his Son with yet more care
10   Made again to Jacob sure,

11 In these plain words, To thee this land I give
    Canaän, which I award
    Thy Self, thy ay-succeding heir
12 And this, when yet but few of them did live
    Scarce an handfull in regard
    Yea, that handfull strangers were.

13 They strangers were, and roam'd from land to land
    Destitute of the Seat they sought
    Many wheres aboad to make
14 So farr was it by meaner hurting hand
    Wrong mean while to them was wrought
    Kings he thus checqu'd for their Sake

15 Abstain I charge you ev'en from hurt of these
    Who my Priests anoynted are
    Do my Prophets none Offence
16 A Famin then to call it did him please
    Want of bread bred hungry fare
    Bread for famin best defence.

40 him] he *B*

17. But He before them into Egypt sent
     Joseph, who a slave was sold
     For their coming to prepare   45
18. Whom fettred fast in stocks they strongly pent
     As his foot in Irons hold
     So his heart lay cloggd in care.

19. Till turning time the day about did bring
     That for Wisdom mentioned   50
     Speech Divine him Wise did show
20. Then mighty Pharäo that Countrys King
     Sent and streigh delivered
     Him not only freeing so

21. But into his most wisely carefull hands   55
     Yeilding house, and household care
     All he hath, and all he may
22. He Rulers rules, Commanders he commands
     He them guides, they guided are
     He prescribes, they all obey   60

23. Lo Israël at length to Egypt comes
     Jaacob sojourns in that land
     Cham sometime his dwelling chose
24. O how encreased shortly he becomes
     How the lord his loved Band   65
     Stronger makes than all their foes

25. For Foes they had, God turning love to hate
     In their hosts, whose malice bad
     Sought they guests to circumvent
26. But A'aron he to them in that bad state   70
     Aa'ron whom he chosen had
     With his Servant Moses sent

27. These among them by word of heavnly might
     Did his Wonders, shew'd his Signs
     In the Country Cham possest   75
28. Where Darkness called came, and chasing light
     Working that which God assigns
     Prov'd no rebell to his hest.

62 Jaacob] Jaäcob *B*

29   He made their Rivers blood, their fish he slew
80   30   Earth-bred Froggs he causd to craule
             Where their Kings embowred were
31.   He bad and streight upon his bidding flew
             Flocks of flyes, yea lice did fall
             Thickly swarming every where

85   32   Their watry rain he chang'd to stoney haile
             Lightnings were instead of light
             Over all the Region seen
33   With these as darts he did their vines assaile
             These did on their figg trees light
90   These did blast each growing green

34   His word from heaven grasshoppers did shower
             And for yet a further spoile
             Caterpillers numberless
35   Which did the grasse, the grace of fields devoure
95   Which the hopeless ploughmans toyle
             Wastfull owners did possesse

36   Their Eldest born, the prime of all their land
             Deadly stricken, of their strengh,
             All the stayes were overthrown
100 37   So richly loaden guided by his hand
             Jacobs race escap'd at length
             Weake among their troops was none

38.   And glad was Egypt they were so escap'd
             Feared much by Israël
105   Israël farr more they feard
39   Whom He from heat by day with clouds enwrapt
             Fire by night to lead them well
             In unfailing flame appeard

40   When male-content they flesh of him did crave
110   Quailes on them with Angels bread
             Doun he did from heaven rain
41   Wounding the rock to them he waters gave
             Water which in rivers spredd
             Plotted Islands on the Plain.

108 In unfailing] *B notes: Evermore in* expunged:

42.   Oblivion could not cancell out of thought   115
          That which once by Holy Him
          Had to Abraham been sworn

43   So then with joy his People forth he brought
          All they all in mirth did swimm
          Who his choyces badg had worn   120

44   To them He gave the neighbor nations lands
          Painless harvests of whose paines
          Frankly he did them afford

45.   Only to hold, the statutes he commands
          Only what his law containes   125
          Still to keep. O Prayse the lord

[*Variant: MS B*]

Psalm CVIII.
Paratum Cor meum

1.   My heart prepar'd, præpared is my heart
           To spredd Thy prayse
           With tuned layes

2.   Wake my tongue, my lute awake
           Thou my Harp the Consort make   5
           My self will beare a part.

      My self the first when Morning shall appeare
              My voice and string
              So will Thee sing
       That this Earthly globe and all   10
       Treading on this earthly Ball
           My praysing notes shall heare

4.   For God, my only God Thy gracious love
              Is mounted farr
              Above each starr   15

Psalm CVIII [*Variant*]. *Copy-text: B. B notes:* This Psalm is crossed. I beleive because at the 6th verse [*of the Psalm*] the measure is changed. Sed Quaere. the staffe being of 4 verses in the LX Psalm. And this Psalm being made out of the LVII and the LX. Possibly the Author observd in it the different measures which were putt to those Psalms. *B places verse numbers 3, 11, 12 by 7, 45, 47.*
12 My] By *B*

Thy unchanged Verity
Hev'nly wings do lift as high
As clouds have roome to move

5.   As high as highest heavn's can give Thee place
20   O lord ascend
                       And thence extend
         With most bright most glorious show
         Over all the Earth below
                   The sun beames of Thy Face

25   6   Come forth O God set Thy beloved free
            Be deafe no more to what I pray
      7.   Hark hark I heare so shall it be
            God from his Temple say

         Go then no further, make a merry stand
30   There will I part out Sichems fields
         By perch and pole I'll mete the land
            That Succoth vally yeilds.

      8.   Mine Gilead, Manasseh also mine
            Ephraïm yeilds more men for Warr
35   Judah shall Right by law define
               When strife breeds doubtfull jarr.

      9.   Moab shall wash my feet in Servile place
            At Edom I my shoe will fling
            Thou Palestine (O alterd case!)
40   Shalt of my Triumph sing.

      10. But who will lead us to the Walled town?
            But who will cause us Edom take?
      11   Who but the God that threw us down
            And did our hosts forsake.

45   Long, long wee thus in Servitude have layn
      12.   Come heavnly God, O come at length
            And ridd us out for vain, most vain
               Is help of humane strength.

13.   Then Victory shall us with glory crown
              When not in men, in God we trust   50
              And then our foes by him cast down
              Shall lick the deadly dust

[*Variant: MS I*]

Psalm: 113 Laudate dominum.

Yow that the life of servants doe professe
Jehova's name in worthie praise expresse
Jehova's name to blesse wee must indever
from this age to the next, both now and ever
Jehova's name to praise our thought devises   5
from whence it sets, to where the sunn arises
high is Jehova over all the nations
yea high above all heavnly habitations
with our Jehova who can bee compared
our lord whose dwelling is in height prepared   10
yet doth vouchsafe to make himselfe so low
things done in heav'n things done on earth to know
that lifts the weake, that lay in dust dejected
and ev'n from dongue the poore man hath erected
to make him with the greatest peers to sitt   15
to sway the state, with courage and with witt
by him the barren womb hath beene so blest
to bee of many babes a joyfull nest
    To father sonn and spryte of both proceeding
    there was and is and shalbe praise exceeding.   20

[*Variant: MS B*]

Psalm CXVII
Laudate Dominum

P raise, prayse the lord, All that of lowest sphere
R eside on any side

Psalm: 113 [*Variant*]. *Copy-text: I. I notes in pencil in a later hand:* Printed in Sidneiana.
17 womb] o *written over* h *(?) in* I
Psalm CXVII [*Variant*]. *Copy-text: B. B notes:* This Psalm is crossed.

A ll you I say
I n Countrys scatterd wide
5   S e in your joyes Jehovas prayse appeare
T hat worthily your songs display
H is worth whose every way
E xceding grace
L ayd upon us doth overlay
10   O ur greatest force; whose promise ever true
R estraind within no space
D ecayeth not, He needs it not renew.

[*Variant: MSS B, K, χ*]

Psalm CXIX

G

Grave deep in Thy remembrance lord
Thy promise past
To me whose trust on Thy true word
Thou builded hast
5   For in my Woes
Hence my only comfort growes
That when I grieve
Still Thy word doth me relieve

Most fowly those that proudly swell
10   Did me deride
Yet I from what thy teachings tell
Did never slide
For I did hold
Mindfully Thy wreakes of Old
15   And That O Lord
Comfort did to me afford

Yea trembling horror seisd on me
And I did quake

4 I n] I m [?] *B*

Psalm CXIX G [*Variant*]. *Copy-text:* B. *B notes:* Crost and in the margin written *Quære*
Incipit: Memor esto *N, H* (e *of* esto *altered*), *E*
9 fowly] fowle *K*   10 Did] doe *G*   14 wreakes] workes *N, E*   18–25 *om.* θ

When I did wicked wretches see
    Thy lawes forsake   20
    Who though I stand
Farr exild from native land
    Yet still Thy law
Songs of mirth from me doth draw

Each night præsents unto myne eye   25
    Instead of sleep
Thy awfull name and soundly I
    Thy Doctrin keep
    The spring I know
Whence to me all blessings flow   30
    I firmly stand
In the deeds Thy words command

[*Variant: MSS B, K, χ*]

Psalm CXIX

H

Have Others other choyse
I have irrevocably giv'n my voice
    That my lot in Thee O Lord
My wealth shall be in following Thy Word

    Before Thy præsence I   5
Poure out my heart I pray unfeignedly
    Promise me good hope doth give
let with good help performance me relieve!

    All, all my walks and wayes
My thoughts sharp censure carefully survayes   10

20 lawes] *B*; lawe *K, χ*   23 still] *om. M*   25 præsents] presents *K, χ*   32 the
deeds] thy deeds *θ*; the deed *σ*
Psalm CXIX H [*Variant*]. *Copy-text: B. Stanzas spaced in χ, but not B. B notes: This staffe
or* [i *altered to* o (?)] *part (H) is also crost.*
Incipit: Portio *[final* o *altered]* mea *N*; Portia mea Domine *H, E*
2 irrevocably] irrevocable *θ, H, Q*   3 lot] lott's *N, C*   4 Thy] of thy *Q, E*
5 præsence] presence *K, χ*   6 Poure] power *C*; powre *D, N, σ, G, M*   I] and *G*
unfeignedly] unfainedlie *K, χ*   8 performance] perforance *M*

All my stepps to that I move
Wherto Thy Doctrin testifys Thy love

Nor walk I slack or slow
Nor day from day do I deferring go
15   But with hearty hast do hye
To keep the Words where Thy commandments lye.

Indeed the wicked pack
To stopp my passage wrought my spoile and wrack
But to me that was no cause
20   Why once I should the more forget Thy lawes

Nay then even then when night
Hides in her darkness most remote from light
Rising I my bed forsake
To prayse Thy judgments justly Thou dost make

25   To all that Thee do feare
I a companion fellowship do beare
All I say that feare Thee so
That Thy commandments they observing go

Since all the Earth O Lord
30   Flowes with the goods Thy Goodness dos afford
This one good thing grant to me
That in Thy lawes I may Thy Scholar be

[*Variant: MSS B, K, χ*]

Psalm CXIX

S

Sure lord Thy Self art just
And sure Thy lawes be right

13 or] nor *M*   16 Words] *word G, M*   18 wrought] sought *K, χ*   22 Hides in her] Hides her in *K, χ*; Holdes her, in *E*   light] light [*long* s *altered to* l] *D*; sight *O, E* 24 Thy] the *M*   28 commandments] Covenents *E*   30 goods] good *θ*   dos] doth *K, χ*

Psalm CXIX S [*Variant*]. *Copy-text: B. B notes:* This whole part is crossd and in the margin *Quære* is written.
Incipit: Justus es Domine *N, H, E*

Which justly Thou and rightly dost
　　Command us still to lay
　　Before our carefull sight　　　　5
To rule our words, and guide our way.

　　How neare my heart it goes
　　And pains me to endure
Thy Words forgotten by Thy foes!
　　Whose pureness doth excell　　　10
　　What is of all most pure
By me Thy Servant loved well

　　Who though to them most base
　　And most despisd I grew
Oblivion yet could not deface　　　15
　　Thy Statutes in my breast
　　For ay Thy Truth most true
And justice still most just doth rest

　　Oppression heavy lay
　　And anguish wrung me sore　　　20
Yet were Thy præcepts still my joy
　　Thy præcepts which remaine
　　Most just for ever more
O teach me, and my life sustaine.

[*Variant: MSS B, K, χ*]

Psalm CXIX

W

Without all cause, the mightyest Peeres
Do me persue but all my Feares

---

17 Thy] the *E*　　　20 wrung] wronge *K, C, σ*　　　21 were] weare *H, Q*　　　Thy] my *C*
præcepts] precepts *K, χ*　　　joy] staie *Q*　　　22 præcepts] precepts *K, χ*

Psalm CXIX W [*Variant*]. *Copy-text:* B. *Stanzas spaced in* χ; *not spaced but marked with vir-gules in B. Indentation irregular in B: 1, 2 not indented; 3 singly indented; 9, 10, 12 doubly indented; 11 triply indented. B notes:* This Part Crost *and in the margin* Quære.
Incipit: Principes persecuti sunt *N*; Princeps persecuti sunt *H*; Prinsepes persecuti sunt *E*;
1 mightyest] mighty *G, M*

Herin do end
Least that I should against Thy Word offend

5   Thy word wherin I so delight
As he who after happy fight
Finds precious spoiles,
Sweet recompense of painfull passed toiles

It canot be but I must hate
10   And hate in more than common rate
What fals doth prove
Since on Thy Doctrin true is built my love

The Sun his light doth never bring
But seven times Thy prayse I sing
15   My Theme I make
The punishments Thou dost in justice take

I know to him that loveth Thee
Shall peace, and peace in plenty be
That no unrest
20   To him shall fall, no trouble him molest

That makes I never make an end
Thy saving succour to attend
Performing still
All that I find præscribed by Thy will.

25   That makes my carefull heart doth hold
The Words Thy wittnesst will enfold
Loving them so
That greater love in heart can hardly grow

That makes my self well keeping stand
30   Both them and that Thy Words command
Knowing to Thee
No deedes of mine unknown can ever be

4 Word] lawes *G*; *B notes: law* expunged: 5 so] *B notes: do* expunged   6 fight]
flight *K*, χ   8 painfull passed] *reversed in B, but marked* 1 *and* 2, *respectively*   toiles] *B
notes: foiles* expunged   14 But...I] But I...doe *M*   18 and...in] in...and σ,
G, M   20 trouble] troubles *C, G*   22 attend] defende *Q*   24 I find] I saide σ,
G; is said *M*   præscribed] prescribed *K*, χ   26 Words] workes *O*   wittnesst will]
st *added in B*; wittnes will *K*; wittnes doth σ, *G, M*   enfold] unfolde *E*   28 can]
could *G*   hardly] never *C*   30 Words] word *N, Q, E*   32 deedes] deed *E, G*

[*Variant: MSS G, M*]

Psalme. *120. Ad Dominum./*

In deepe distresse, and trouble when I laye
Unto my God, I calld, and thus did praye:
Preserve my *Soule* (Ô lord) from lipps that lye
And guilefull tongues that harbour trechery.

What proffit (thinkst thou) can redound to thee   5
O truthles tongue, even like to Shaftes that flee:
Of strongest size, and arm'd as sharpe as *Brire*
Or as consuming burning Coales of fire./

Aye me, that thus, am still constrain'd to bide
With wretched *Mesech*; and thus long reside   10
Among the *Tents* of *Kedar*, tird with woes
And compast round with cruell hatefull foes

Too long, (alas too longe) my *Soule* remaines
With theise uncivill rowte, who peace disdaines,
Who, when I labour quietnes to make,   15
To battell straight they doe themselves betake

[*Variant: MSS G, M*]

Psalme. *121./* Levavi Oculos

Unto the hilles I now will bend
   And lift with joye my hopefull sight
To him who me doth comfort send
   My gracious God, the Lord of might

Psalme. 120 *[Variant]. Copy-text: M. In G, the third and fourth lines of each stanza are indented.*
1 laye$_\wedge$] laie; *G*   2 my God,] the lord$_\wedge$ *G*   praye] saie *G*   3 Ô lord] O God *G*
5 redound] redoune *G*   thee$_\wedge$] ~? *G*   7 strongest] mightie *G*   9 me,] mee,! *G*
am still constraind] constrained am *G*   bide$_\wedge$] ~, *G*   12 foes$_\wedge$] ~. *G*   13 long,]
~$_\wedge$ *G*   14 theise] this *G*   15 Who,] For$_\wedge$ *G*   make,] ~$_\wedge$ *G*   16 they doe
themselves betake$_\wedge$] themselves they doe betake./ *G*

Psalme. 121 *[Variant]. Copy-text: M.*
1 hilles$_\wedge$] hills, *G*   2 sight$_\wedge$] ~: *G*   4 God,] ~$_\wedge$ *G*   might$_\wedge$] ~. *G*

5   Even he (for ever blessed be he named)
    Who *Heaven* and *Earth*, and all therein hath framed./

  By him thy foote from slipp shall staie
    Nor will he sleepe, who thee sustaines
Israels greate God by night or daye,
10   To sleepe or slumber aye disdaines
    For he is still thy guard for ever waking
    On thy right hand, thy safety undertaking/

  So undertake, that neither *Sunne*
    By daye with heate shall thee molest
15   Nor *Moone* by night when daye is don
    Offend thee or disturb thy rest
    Yea from all evill, thou still in his protection
    Shalt safely dwell, from harme, or fowle infection/

  This Lord, (who never failes his flocke)
20   shall thee in all thy wayes attend:
  At home, abroade, thy *Fort* thy *Rock*
    From all annoye shall thee defend./.
    Yea from this tyme, to after age for ever
    Thy God wilbe, and thee forsaking never

[*Variant 1: MSS B, I, σ*]

Psalm CXXII
Lætatus sum

O what lively delight, O what a jollity
This newes unto me brought newly delivered
That Gods house ruined should be reedifyd
And that shortly we should evry man enter it

---

5 Even] Ev'n *G*   he (for] he, (who *G*   named)] *G*; ~ₐ *M*   6 *Heaven*] *Heav'n G*
7 foote ₐ] ~, *G*   8 sleepe,] ~ₐ *G*   9 daye,] daie ₐ *G*   12 hand,] ~ₐ *G*
14 molest ₐ] mollest, *G*   15 night ₐ] ~, *G*   16 thee ₐ] ~, *G*   rest ₐ] ~. *G*
17 evill,] ~ₐ *G*   18 fowle] ill *G*   infection/] ~./ *G*   19 Lord,] lord ₐ *G*
flocke)] ~,) *G*   20 attend:] ~ₐ *G*   23 tyme, to after] time ₐ from age to *G*
24 Thy God wilbe] Wilbe thy God *G*

Psalm CXXII [*Variant 1*]. *Copy-text: B.* Lines *13–16, 17–20, 21–4 spaced in I. B notes:* Carmen Asclepiadæum [?] —/-ˇˇ/-/-ˇˇ/-ˇˇ/[.] In the margin *Quære the Psalm itself crost.*
3 reedifyd] reedifield *I*   4 evry] every *σ*

O now Thy galerys lovely Jerusalem   5
Thy gates shall be my rest, now not unordered
Nor wide scatred as erst, but very citty-like
All conjoined in One shall be Jerusalem
   Now there convenient place to the company
Gods hand hath gathered shall be alotted out   10
His passed benefitts jointly to testify
And so prayse him as once praysed him Israël
   Now there shall be the seat, where to be justiced
All shall freely resort weary of injuryes
Seat, whose lofty receit loftily may receive   15
Davids posterity royaly honored
   Pray then, pray we I say Peace to Jerusalem
To you Prosperity friends to Jerusalem
Thy walls thy joïfull fortifications
Peace and plenty betide never abandoning   20
   With good reason I now wish Thee al happyness
Whose blisse is generall unto my Countrymen
With good cause shal I pray dayly thy bettering
Where Gods Mansion is now to be edifyd.

[*Variant 2: MSS G, M*]

Psalme. 122 Lætatus sum.

Right gladd was I in heart and minde
  When thus I heard the people saye
With one assent so well enclinde
  To serve the Lord, and to him praie/
    Unto Godes *Temple* let us goe   5
    And there our service to him showe/

7 erst] east *I*   8 conjoined] conjoyned *I, σ*; commoned *B*   10 gathered] gathred *E*
out] how [*added in a different hand*] *I*   12 Israël] Isarell *I*   13 justiced] justified *σ*
14 All] and *I*   19 thy] e *stricken after* h *in B*   joïfull] joyfull *I, σ*   21 now wish
Thee] wish thee now *I, σ*   al] all *I, σ*   24 is_∧] ~, *Q, E*   edifyd] edified *I, σ*

Psalme. 122 *[Variant 2]. Copy-text:* M.
1 heart_∧] ~, *G*   2 thus] as *G*   saye_∧] saie: *G*   4 the] thee *G*   5 Unto
Godes *Temple* let us goe_∧] Come let us to his *Temple* goe, *G*   6 showe/] ~. *G*

Within thy gates (O Citty faire)
Sweete *Salem* now wee will abide
Since wee to thee have made repaire
10   Our feete from thee shall never slide./
For thou in *Union* peace and love
Art now establisht from above:

For unto thee with mirth and joye
The tribes of *Israel* flocking goe:
15   With earnest zeale there to employe
Theire thankfullnes, and there to showe
In humblest manner they can frame
All praise to Godes most holy name

The *Seate* of *judgment* there doth rest.
20   Even *Davids Throane*, (thy servant deare,)
Ô let your praiers be addrest
That *Salems* peace may still appeare
For who true love doth beare to thee
In prosperous state shall live and be

25   Within thy walles, let peace for aye
And plenteousnes thy howses store
This wish I thee, and still will praye
Thy blisse may stand for evermore.
Yea for theire sakes, whome there I love
30   That thy good state maye never move.

Not for theire sakes alone that feare
(Yea truly feare) and God doth serve.
But for the zeale his howse I beare
Thy safety still he will preserve
35   And for his holy *Temples* sake,
I care of thee will ever take./

[*Variant: MSS G, M*]

Psalme. 123. Ad te levavi oculos./

To thee greate God of Skies
   (Who dwellst in *Heaven* above)
To thee my ernest eyes
   Are fixt without remove.

For as a Servantes care   5
   Attendes his Masters hand
Or as a Maidens faire
   Which by her Mistris stand.

Even so, our eyes wee bend
   And on our God doe place   10
Untill to us he send
   his *mercy*, and his grace.

Have mercy therefore Lord
   And cast thine eyes on us
Thy servantes so abhord   15
   Despiz'd and hated thus

Our *Soule*, with skorne o'reflowes
   (For rich men us deride)
And with despight of those
   That swell in height of pride./   20

[*Variant: MSS G, M*]

Psalme. 124. Nisi quia Dominus/

If thou (O lord) hadst not our right
Upheld by thy greate power and might

Psalme. 123 *[Variant]. Copy-text: M.*
2 *Heaven*] Heav'n *G*   above~] ~,) *G*   5 care~] ~, *G*   8 stand.] ~~ *G*   9 so,]
~~ *G*   10 place~] ~: *G*   12 grace.] ~~ *G*   15 abhord~] abhor'd, *G*   16 thus~]
~. *G*   17 *Soule*,] ~~ *G*   o'reflowes] ore'flowes *G*
Psalme. 124 *[Variant]. Copy-text: M. In G, the third and fourth lines of each stanza are
indented.*
1 right~] ~, *G*   2 Upheld] Maintaind *G*   might~] ~: *G*

If thou with us hadst not uprose
Against our mortall deadly foes

5   Wee swallowed up alive had beene
(So wrathfull was theire rage and spleene)
The waters on us had prevail'd
Our *Soule* had sunck, our life had faild

The waters deepe of proude men high
10   O'rewhelm'd our *Soule* had suddenly
But (prais'd be God) not as a *praye*
Unto theire teeth cast us awaye

Our *Soule* hath now escaped free
Even as poore birdes from Fowlers be
15   The *Snare* is broke, and wee are fledd
And from theire handes delivered

Our hope and help therefore shall rest
In thee our God for ever blest,
Who *Heaven* and *Earth*, and all of nought
20   By thy greate power hast made and wrought./

[*Variant: MSS G, M*]

Psalme. 125:/ Qui Confidunt./

Who trusts in God, and him doth love
As *Sion* mount shall allwaies staie
Whose firme foundation nought can move
But stedfast shall abide for aye.

5   For as the hilles which *Salem* round
Encompasseth: So God his flocke

---

4 foes₍] ~: *G*   5 swallowed] swallow'd *G*   6 (So wrathfull]] ₍So bitter *G*   rage₍
and spleene)] ~, ~: *G*   7 prevail'd] ' *above stricken* e *M*   8 sunck,] ~₍ *G*
faild₍] ~. *G*   10 O'rewhelm'd] Orewhelm'd *G*   *Soule*] Soules *G*   11 (prais'd
be God)] ₍praisd be God, *G*   12 awaye₍] ~./ *G*   14 be₍] ~: *G*   16 deliv-
ered₍] ~. *G*   17 hope and help₍] help and hope, *G*   18 our God] O lord
G   blest,] ~: *G*   19 *Heaven*] Heav'n *G*

Psalme. 125 [*Variant*]. *Copy-text: M.*
1 love₍] ~, *G*   2 staie₍] ~: *G*   3 foundation] foundacions *G*   move₍] ~, *G*

About doth stand, and still is found
    Theire Refuge sure, theire fence and *rocke*.

The scourge ungodly men deserve
    shall not the righteous portion be:
Least they (too much afflicted) swerve
    From *truth*, and unto falshood flee

                                10

Lord unto those that perfect bide,
    Extend thy favour and thy grace:
But as for them who backward slide
    And runne a wicked Godles race

                                15

Leade them with those that evill affect
    And follow theire owne filthy wayes
But *Israel* still in peace protect
    And blesse with many happy daies./

                                20

[*Variant: MSS G, M*]

Psalme. 126. In convertendo.

When thou (O lord) to *Sion* free
    From Captive thralldome didst us send
Wee were as those that visions see
    Or dreames which doe vaine fancies spend
        Our Mouthes with laughter did abound
        Our tongues with joye did then resound

                                5

Then said the *Heathen* (who beheld
    This greate deliverance now wee have:)
The Lord this *Nation* hath upheld
    And don greate thinges, theise folkes to save

                                10

---

11 (too much afflicted)] ∧too much afflicted∧ *G*   swerve∧] ~, *G*   12 flee∧] ~. *G*
13 bide,] ~∧ *G*   14 favour∧] ~, *G*   17 those∧] ~, *G*   18 And] to *G*
wayes∧] waies: *G*

Psalme. 126 *[Variant]. Copy-text: M. The incipit, lacking in M, is supplied from G.*
2 send∧] ~: *G*   3 as] like *G*   4 Or like to *dreames* that vainely end *G*
5 abound∧] ~: *G*   6 resound∧] ~. *G*   7 who beheld] as Compell'd *G*   8 This
greate] by this *G*   have:)] ~∧) *G*   10 thinges,] things∧ *G*   folkes] folke *G*   save∧]
~. *G*

The Lord indeede for us hath wrought
Which makes us joye, as now wee ought

Turne therefore Lord our bondage so,
(As thou for us hast well begun)
15   Like Southerne Rivers, where they flowe
And to refresh drye *Desarts*) runne
Who sowes in teares ofte with annoye
Shall reape and gather home with joye

And he that foorth doth (goeing) mourne
20   Yet beares with him of seede the best:
Shall doubtles home with joye returne
So well his labours shalbe blest
Yea he shall finde a happy yeare
And bring home sheaves with joyefull cheere./

[*Variant: MSS G, M*]

Psalme. 127./ Nisi Dominus./.

Except the lord himself, the howse doth build
The builders labour's lost, and all theire paine
Except the lord from harme the Citty Shield
The carefull watchmen, watcheth but in vaine/

5   So is theire toile, who early doth arise
And late sittes up with ernest restles care
To eate theire bread, when all will not suffize
With anguish mixed is theire daiely fare

But those who feare, and high *Jehova* serve
10   (Which his beloved servantes he doth name,
In quiet rest and sleepe he will preserve
From danger trouble, care distresse and shame

---

12 joye,] ~‚ˌ *G*   ought‚ˌ] ~. *G*   13 Lord‚ˌ] lord, *G*   so,] ~‚ˌ *G*   15 flowe] goe *G*
16 runne‚ˌ] ~. *G*   17 teares‚ˌ] ~, *G*   18 reape‚ˌ] ~, *G*   joye‚ˌ] ~. *G*   19 foorth
doth (goeing)] going foorth, doth *G*   20 ‚ˌYet] (yet *G*   best:] ~) *G*   22 blest‚ˌ]
~, *G*   23 Yea‚ˌ] ~, *G*

Psalme. 127 [*Variant*]. Copy-text: M.
2 paine] paines *G*   3 lord‚ˌ] ~, *G*   4 vaine/] ~. *G*   6 care‚ˌ] ~. *G*   7 when]
yet *G*   9 serve‚ˌ] ~, *G*   10 name,] ~) *G*   11 rest‚ˌ and sleepe‚ˌ] ~, ~, *G*
12 care‚ˌ distresse‚ˌ and shame‚ˌ] ~, distress, ~, *G*

The fruite of blessed wombe, are Children bowld
  An heritage and gifte from God on high:
Like Shaftes a *Giant* in his hand doth hould   15
  Which strongely shott, doth foorth as fiercely flye

He happy is, who hath his quiver full
  And stor'd with such in tyme of deepe debate
They shall not be ashamed, nor looke dull
  But meete theire foes with courage in the gate.   20

[*Variant: MS N*]

Psalm 131./
Domine, non est./

Thou Lord, for thou dost know
  Canst well my witnes bee
    My heart was never apt to clime
      Nor I at anie time
Did arrogantlie goe   5
  Medling in things too great, too high for mee.

Naie thou canst witnes well
  So farre was thought of pride,
    As proud the wained infant is
      Who first the brest doth misse   10
Such pride, I saie, did dwell
  In mee, as doth in wained babe abide.

Unmov'd I quiet laie
  With care but how to rest:
    And now I wish, that as did I,   15
      All Jacob would relie
And make their trustfull staie
  On him, now still, who greatest is, and best./

14 heritage‸] ~, *G*   high:] ~‸ *G*   16 flye‸] flie. *G*   18 debate‸] ~: *G*   20 foes‸]
~, *G*   gate.] Gate./ *G*
Psalm 131 *[Variant]. Copy-text: N. Psalm number in left margin opposite incipit.*

Manuscripts of the *Psalmes*

The seventeen extant manuscripts of the *Psalmes* are listed in the order in which they appear in the reconstructed stemma described in 'Relationship of the Texts of the *Psalmes*'.[1] Readers can find a particular manuscript in the list by noting the alphabetical siglum at the beginning of each description. Our attempts to describe the manuscripts have been complicated at times by the varied practices of different foliators, sometimes at the same library. We report the current foliation or pagination (whether contemporary or modern), but note anomalies and also acknowledge unfoliated leaves with lower-case Roman numerals in square brackets and, adopting the method of the foliator of MS *K* (BL MS Additional 46372), number those at the back continuously with those at the front. Such a procedure permits description of leaves with, we hope, a minimum of confusion. At some points, our reported foliations differ from those in Ringler and Rathmell, who occasionally use different approaches to the problem of describing these complex documents. However, we would emphasize that our work has drawn heavily from the findings of both of these editors, whose pioneering work on the manuscripts has put all students of the *Psalmes* greatly in their debt.

The *beta* (β) Tradition

B Bodleian, MS Rawl. poet. 25 (*Summary Catalogue*, 14519).

i–vii + 157 ff. (158 folios, counting the stub, but not the seven preliminary leaves: i.e. 1–85 + [86] + 86–135[= 136] + [137(stub)–141, not foliated] + 140[= 142] + [143–145, not foliated] + 145[= 146]–157[= 158]). Text of *Psalmes* on 1– 82v, 100[= 101]–131v[= 132^v]. Collation: a^6 (ff. ii–vii), A^{10}, B^{12}, C–D^{10}, E–I^8, i^{10}, ii^8, K–N^8, iii^{10}, iv^4, v^{10}. The copyist, Samuel Woodforde, signed the gatherings through I; another hand has added K–N in pencil (the blank gatherings i–ii and iii–v were ignored). Paper and old, but later, parchment

[1] Some of the details in the following descriptions were generously provided, as noted, by Gavin Alexander, Peter Beal, John Gouws, Daniel Huws, Hilton Kelliher, and Henry Woudhuysen in correspondence with Noel Kinnamon, who alone takes responsibility for any errors or oversights.

or vellum binding, *c.*294 × 205 mm. (ff. i and 157 contemporary with the binding). On the back cover of the binding, reused from another book, is written, upside-down in faded ink, 'Oxon [...?] Acc[ount?] Book 1742'. Beal, SiP 73. The two watermarks in the body of the manuscript only generally resemble Heawood 358 (London, 1695) and 1780 (London, 1680). A third mark resembling Heawood 3149 (1753) is on the front flyleaf and back pastedown, with countermark on the back flyleaf.

Transcribed by Woodforde in 1694/5 from a mutilated, now lost manuscript designated β, MS *B* contains Psalms 1–87 and 102. 73–130 (Psalms 88 and 131 are represented by the numbers only). As Ringler says, Woodforde's own notes indicate that the original volume 'contained numerous interlineations, strike outs, and marginal corrections' which suggest that it 'must have been the Countess of Pembroke's own working copy'.[2] From this working copy descend all the extant manuscripts, after at least three revisions and usually through intermediaries. After the first revision, β^1, another working copy, χ, was produced, apparently from the intermediary δ (ancestor of *I*, *K*, and Psalms 1–26 in *F*); χ was itself frequently revised and led to at least two other lost intermediaries, θ (source of *O* and *D*) and σ (source of *H*, *Q*, *E*, and the descendants of the latter, *L* and *P*) and to four other extant manuscripts *N*, *C*, *G*, *M*. MS *A* was copied after the second revision, β^2, and was itself transcribed in *F* (Psalms 27–150) and *J*. There was a final revision, β^3, before Woodforde made his transcription. The note following Psalm 43, 'hitherto Sir Philip Sidney', associates the text with *J* (and, in a Latin version, with *O*, *N*, *H*, *E*). The verse numbers by certain lines must also have been in β for they correspond with the numbering of the Geneva Bible and were thus probably not added by Woodforde, who would presumably have followed the numbering of the Prayer Book (as in *K* and *I*) or the Authorized Version (which differs at one point, at least, from Geneva). Folios 146–56 contain original verses by Woodforde: an ode to John Wilmot, Earl of Rochester (ff. 146–54, title only on 146; 146 also has the initials 'SW'[3] and the name 'Mary Woodforde') and

---

[2] Sidney, *Poems*, 547.

[3] The *Summary Catalogue* states that the reference is to a 'T' Woodforde, but this unconfirmed assertion is probably based on a misreading of the letter 'S' as 'T'. *First-Line Index of English Poetry 1500–1800 in Manuscripts of the Bodleian Library, Oxford*, ed. Margaret Crum, 2 vols. (Oxford, 1969), L563 and S890, attributes both poems to Samuel Woodforde.

an epitaph on a daughter (who died in 1683), 'quoting', says the *Summary Catalogue*, 'a Latin votive tablet' (f. 155, which is pasted onto f. 156).

Woodforde notes that the following Psalms had crosses by them, apparently because they were to be revised: 44, 46, 53, 58, 60, 62, 63, 64, 68, 69, 71, 75, 80, 85 (not listed in Ringler), 86, 105, 108, 117, four sections of 119 (G, H, S, W), and 122. All of these Psalms, as well as Psalm 50, are preserved in *B* in earlier drafts than the versions contained in the other manuscripts. Woodforde's usual practice was to put the revisions recorded in the original of *B* in the body of the text and note the deleted text in the margins. In the case of Psalm 85, however, he put the revisions themselves in the margins. The lacuna in the original manuscript between Psalms 87 and 102. 73 is explained by Woodforde's note on f. ii: 'The Originall Copy is by me[,] Given me by my Brother Mr. John Woodford who bought it among other broken books to putt up Coffee pouder as I remember.' The two blank gatherings in the Psalms section—ff. 83–91 and 92–9—correspond to the lacuna in the original manuscript. (For Woodforde's other notes on Psalms 44–150, see textual notes.) It is generally assumed that the original has perished.

Grosart used *B* as copy-text for his edition of Psalms 1–43; he emended *B* by referring to *G*, but introduced errors of his own.[4] He claimed to include variants from *A*, but in at least some cases he depended on the unreliable 1823 Chiswick printing of *A* (see e.g. the notes on Psalms 1. 3, 3. 6, 4. 10). He also assumed, along with Woodforde, that the original was the work of a scribe 'who copied under the superintendence of Sir Philip Sidney himself. In certain places . . . Sir Philip writes, "Leave a space here", for a variant stanza, and there are occasionally alterations in his own autograph.'[5] Ringler skilfully reconstructed the texts of Philip's Psalms from *B* for his 1962 edition of *The Poems*. Most of the variant Psalms in Rathmell's 1964 dissertation and Waller's edition of the countess's *The Triumph of Death* were printed from *B*.

A Viscount De L'Isle, MBE. Penshurst Place, Kent.

[i–iii] + 1–135 + [iv–viii] ff. The tight binding prevents close examination of the gatherings, but the following is a probable

---

[4] *The Complete Poems of Sir Philip Sidney*, 3 vols. (London: Chatto & Windus, 1877), III. 72, 74. See Grosart's note on his use of *B* and *G* (II. 204–5).

[5] Ibid., III. 72.

collation, proposed by Gavin Alexander (in personal correspondence), based on the occurrence of watermarks: i–ii^6 (allowing for two missing leaves at the beginning of i), iii–iv^8 (allowing for an anomaly in iii, perhaps caused by cancellation of one half-sheet and insertion of another), v–vii^6, viii^8, ix^{10}, x–xiv^8, xv^{10}, xvi^6, xvii–xviii^8, xix^2 (containing only f. 135; second half-sheet cancelled). Paper *c.*290 × 195 mm.; binding *c.*300 × 209 mm. Beal, SiP 84, dated late 16th century. A descendant of β after the second set of revisions, *A* was itself copied at least twice: it is the source of Psalms 27–150 in *F* and all of the Psalms in *J*, probably including Psalms 1–3 which it now lacks.^{6} Folios 2^v–38^v are numbered according to a clear, but interrupted, pattern in which alternating pairs of *pages* are marked thus: 8 (f. 2^v) [9 was inadvertently skipped?], 12 (f. 4^v), 13 (f. 5), 16 (f. 6^v), 17 (f. 7), 20 (f. 8^v), 21 (f. 9), and so on through 82 (f. 38^v), although 56 and 57 were also skipped (the pattern resumes with 58, 59). This numbering supports Ringler's speculation^7 that at least two of the original folios are lacking, just enough for the missing Psalms 1–3 (which are written on two leaves in MS *J*). Ringler also suggests that there were six additional leaves containing the title and prefatory matter now preserved only in *J*. But, if there were, they were not numbered with Sidney's Psalms (which may once have been bound separately). Catchwords are usually only on the verso of alternate leaves. The pages are ruled in red along the sides, the top and bottom margins, and usually under the Latin incipits and Psalm numbers; a second rule aligns the text on the left. The large initial capitals in gold often extend to the left of the second rule so that all subsequent lines (including rhyming lines) are slightly indented. The volume is now bound in dark red leather (of later date) and contains Psalms 4–150 (ff. 1–135^r), written in an Italian hand by the poet John Davies of Hereford (*c.*1565–1618), who enjoyed the countess's patronage and who is identified as the scribe in the subscription on f. 135^r: 'John Davies of the Citty of Hereford hand-writer hereof'. He added most of the capitals in gold after writing the main text and gilded most of the clubbed ascenders and looped descenders of other letters. There are two watermarks, posts with grapes on blank leaves ([iv] and [v]) at the end and a circumscribed crossbow flanked by what appear to

---

^{6} The relationship of MS *A* to MSS *F* and *J* is discussed in more detail in Noel Kinnamon, 'The Sidney Psalms: The Penshurst and Tixall Manuscripts', *English Manuscript Studies* 2 (1990), 139–61.

^{7} Sidney, *Poems*, 547.

be a 'G' and a '3' or large, reversed Greek 'ε' (?) on leaves between 1 and 135. Folios [i–ii] and [vii–viii] are contemporaneous with the binding. Folio [ii] now bears the De L'Isle catalogue number U1500 Z53. The leaf preceding the text, f. [iii], and ff. [iv–vi] at the back are older, but apparently not part of the original manuscript. The same paper seems to have been used to repair the edges of ff. 1–2. Neither watermark corresponds precisely to marks in Heawood or Briquet (though the second does resemble Briquet 755, dated 1592). Some corrections and additions were clearly made by Davies during or after the transcribing of the text from β. Examples are Pembroke's revisions of some of Sidney's final stanzas (Psalms 22. 73–6, 23. 19–24, and 26. 31–6, written in each case in different ink, without gilding), as well as corrections like 'he^l pe', 12. 1; 'neig^h boure', 15. 6; 'do^th', 17. 29; and so on. Other alterations that were made in a hand resembling that of the *J* scribe (who may or may not have been Davies) include the added final stanzas of Psalms 16 (37–42) and 55 (61–72, written on a separate piece of paper which is pasted onto the original leaf). Also preserved in this manuscript (and its descendants, *F* and *J*) are some post-β revisions, e.g. octaves G, H, S, W of Psalm 119.

Davies began his task, not with Philip Sidney's Psalms, but with the first of the countess's paraphrases, Psalm 44 (f. 39^r). This is indicated first of all by variations in the character of the hand (which is mainly Davies's throughout) and the colour of the ink, but also by the different states of wear and discoloration of the paper on which the two sets of paraphrases are written. Differences in the ink, gilding, and spacing show that the incipits and numbers were added after most of the countess's Psalms were copied.

Ringler suggests that *A* 'was probably originally prepared for presentation to Queen Elizabeth, but was not presented because the many corrections made in the process of copying marred its appearance'.[8] Aubrey asserts in *Brief Lives* that the library at Wilton (where he was a visitor in 1652) held 'a Manuscript very elegantly written, viz. all the *Psalmes of David* translated by Sir Philip Sydney, curiously bound in crimson velvet';[9] in *Memories of Naturall Remarques in the County of Wilts.*, he claims that the volume was sold by the fifth Earl of Pembroke.[10] The passage from the *Memories* is quoted in a

[8] Ibid.
[9] See Aubrey, *Brief Lives*, 139.
[10] *The Natural History of Wiltshire*, ed. John Britton (London: Nichols, 1847), 85–6.

note on [iii^r]: 'Aubrey, in his Natural History of Wilts, MS. in the Library of the Royal Society, p. 240, speaking of the library at Wilton, the seat of the Pembrokes, mentions as being preserved there, "a translation of the whole Book of Psalmes in English verse by Sir Philip Sydney, *writt curiously*, and bound in crimson velvet and gilt: it is now lost." There is every probability of this being the identical manuscript which was missing from Wilton in Aubrey's time, for though the original binding is not preserved, the description *writt curiously* so aptly applies to the present manuscript, which is entirely in the neat handwriting of John Davies, the celebrated writing-master of Hereford, that it almost of itself establishes the identity of the volume, for it is unlikely that two copies of so large a work would be preserved to which the same description could be given.' Anthony à Wood repeats Aubrey's description in *Athenæ Oxoniensis*.[11] The manuscript had surfaced again by 1823, when it was used as the copy-text for Singer's error-ridden, often silently emended edition of the poems published by the Chiswick Press. The dealer Thomas Thorpe listed the manuscript for sale in catalogues dated 1843 (p. 25) and 1844 (item 463), where it is said formerly to have been owned by Mr Lloyd. In 1844 it was sold as lot 241 in the library of Benjamin Heywood Bright. The catalogue of the sale (18 June 1844) notes that the volume was 'from the collections of Boswell and Heber' and that it was bought by Thorpe. Folio [iii^v] contains a note by 'Wylimot De Marisco, Banchor: Monach:' (dated 1845) stating that not all the capitals in the added passages are in gold (e.g. Psalm 144) and that the volume 'was at Penshurst the Antient and Modern Seat of the Sidneys, till a few years ago'. Ringler casts doubt on the latter claim and also refutes the suggestion that the additions were made in a Sidney hand ('for it would shew carelessness in the Copyist to write a MS which required so many Corrections') by observing that the alterations are 'obviously in Davies' hand' (and, he might have added, a hand similar to that of MS *J*). Kelliher reports (in personal correspondence) that *A* was also owned by Thomas Rodd, in whose sale catalogue (Sotheby's, 4–9 Feb. 1850) it is listed as lot 881: '*Written in a fine Italian hand*, by John Davies, of Hereford... the numerous capitals are gilt throughout: *wants first leaf*. fol. ✲✲✲ This interesting volume is from Penshurst Castle.' The buyer was Payne of Payne and Foss, who paid £5. 5s.

---

[11] *Athenæ Oxoniensis*, ed. Philip Bliss, 4 vols. (London, 1813), I, col. 522.

In 1877 Ruskin published an eccentrically annotated selection from Singer's 1823 Chiswick edition as *Rock Honeycomb*.[12] Feuillerat (who assigned the sigla to MSS *A–I*) chose *A* as the copy-text for Philip's Psalms 4–43.[13] He printed Psalms 1–3 from *B*. Rathmell used *A* (supplemented for Psalms 1–3 by *K* in 1963 and *J* in 1964) for both his 1963 printed edition and his 1964 Cambridge dissertation.

F Trinity College, Cambridge, MS O. 1. 51 (James 1075). THE | PSALMS OF DAVID | TRANSLATED | INTO | ENGLISH VERSE | BY | That Noble and Virtuous Gentleman | Sir PHILIP SYDNEY.

[i] + a–b + 1–169 + [ii] ff. Collation: i^r (−1), ii–xliii^4. Paper *c*.190 × 150 mm.; binding *c*.197 × 155 mm. Beal, SiP 86, dated late 16th century. Psalms 1–150 are written in a secretary hand, but some alterations are made in a different hand and ink. Psalms 1–26 descend from β through a lost intermediary, σ, which, revised, was also the ultimate source of *K* and probably the same twenty-six Psalms in *I*. The later Psalms were copied from *A*. There are two watermarks: a pot and grapes (on the endpapers) resembling Heawood 3665 (of 1616) and an armorial device resembling Heawood 546 (1607; also in *K*). James remarks on the binding: 'Of cent. xvii with good gold tooling'.[14] The volume was presented to Trinity College Library by Roger Gale in 1738. Ringler notes that 'Thomas Zouch printed Psalms 93 and 137 from this manuscript in the second edition of his *Memoirs of . . . Sidney* (1809), pp. 398–400'.[15] A Trinity College bookplate is pasted inside the front cover.

J Bent E. Juel-Jensen, DM, FRCP. Headington, Oxford. The Psalmes of David translated | into divers and sundry kindes of | verse, more Rare and Excellent | for the Method and Varietie | than ever yet hath been | done in English. Begun by the Noble and Learned gentleman | Sir Phillip Sidney knight. | and finished by the Right Honorable | the Countess | of Pembroke his | Sister. | [1599.]

i–vi + 1–53 + 53 [in pencil] + 54–137 + [i–iii] ff. Conjectural collation (based on sequence of watermarks): i^2 (modern paper), ii–iii^6,

---

[12] Published as vol. II in the series, *Bibliotheca Pastorum* (London: Ellis & White, 1977).

[13] Sidney, *The Complete Works*, 4 vols. (Cambridge: Cambridge UP, 1923), III. 410.

[14] M. R. James, *The Western Manuscripts in the Library of Trinity College, Cambridge: A Descriptive Catalogue* (Cambridge: Cambridge UP, 1900–4), III. 50, item 1075.

[15] Sidney, *Poems*, 549.

iv^{10}, v^8, vi^{16}, vii^4, viii^6, ix–x^4, xi^{10}, xii^4, xiii^{10}, xiv–xv^4, xvi^{10}, xvii^{16}, xviii–xix^{10}, xx^4 (−3 or 4?). Folios i–vi are foliated in pencil; the paper of ff. i–ii is later. John Gouws observes (in personal correspondence) that ff. [i–ii] following f. 137 (i.e. 138) are a single sheet, ruled differently, with a sewing thread in the gutter, and that a sewing thread is showing between ff. [ii] and [iii]; that f. [iii] is a singleton is supported by the sequence of the watermarks. Paper *c*.337 × 221 mm.; binding *c*.341 × 223 mm. Beal, SiP 81, dated early 17th century. Juel-Jensen describes the binding as 'contemporary vellum...powdered all over with small gilt tools'.[16] The old silk ties are missing, but small stubs remain. The armorial watermark, with a single fleur-de-lis, is similar to Heawood 1768 (*c*.1616) and is the same in all parts of the volume (and is also found in *C*), except for the title page, which has a mark (NCE) that Ringler associates tentatively with 'Thomas or Edmund Valence who manufactured from 1781 to 1816'.[17]

J contains all 150 Psalms (ff. 1–137), transcribed from *A* (presumably including the first three now missing in *A*). But it also preserves on four preliminary leaves some matter not in *A*: a title page (apparently copied from the 1823 Chiswick Press edition, which borrowed it from *C*) on what is probably early nineteenth-century paper and two long independent poems, one of them addressed to Queen Elizabeth ('Even now that Care', ff. iii–iv), the other, 'To the Angell spirit of the most excellent Sir Phillip Sidney' (ff. v–vi^v), written on older paper. An earlier draft of 'To the Angell spirit' was mistakenly attributed to Daniel in the *Whole Workes of Samuel Daniel* (sigs. 2M7^v–8^v) published posthumously in 1623. After Psalm 43 is written, 'Hitherto Sir Phillip Sidney', a note which associates the volume with *β*, for it is also in Woodforde's transcription, *B*, but not *A*. On ff. [i–ii^v], after Psalm 150 on f. 137, there is an alphabetical list of Latin incipits (not always correct and occasionally misnumbered).

The date 1599 (in a different hand) on the title page, as Ringler suggests, was probably taken from the end of the dedicatory poem to the queen. There, however, it was originally 1699 (not 1600), with the 6 altered to 5. Dr Juel-Jensen observes that the manuscript was once part of the Tixall library, which was originally formed in the early seventeenth century by Sir Walter Aston (1583–1639), and suggests

[16] 'Contemporary Collectors XLIII', *BC* 15 (1966), 157.
[17] Sidney, *Poems*, 551.

that it may have come into his possession as a gift from the Pembroke family (Aston was a friend of William Herbert, the son of the Countess of Pembroke) or from either Queen Elizabeth or King James, perhaps for services rendered as ambassador to Spain.[18]

Because *A* lacks the dedicatory poems and Psalms 1– 3, *J* has special value as the only source of the *A* version of these texts. Particularly important is the fact that, as Ringler observes, 'It is the only manuscript to preserve...[the countess's] revised conclusion to the first Psalm'.[19] Ringler also notes that the volume was probably written by a single scribe, 'in an early seventeenth-century Italian hand',[20] even though the formation of individual letters in the two sets of dedicatory verses is not always exactly the same as that used in the text of the Psalms (where, for instance, the descenders of 'y' and 'p' are more horizontal than diagonal).

Inside the front cover are a pencilled note, 'THE TIXALL MANUSCRIPT ONCE SIR WALTER ASTON'S' and the following statement of provenance, also in pencil, in the hand of Bent Juel-Jensen:[21] 'This fine manuscript was once in the Library formed by Sir Walter Aston (1583–1639). Aston was Michael Drayton's patron, when he was knighted in 1603, Drayton was one of his esquires. Aston was companion to Henry, Prince of Wales, in 1613 Gentleman of the Privy Chamber. He was ambassador to Spain twice. William Herbert, Earl of Pembroke, son of Mary Sidney was his friend. The MS remained at Tixall til 1844 when the library was moved to Wycliffe in the North Riding and came into the possession of the Constable family. Sir Talbot Constable moved the library to a house he bought at Ferriby near Hull—Aston House. Sold Sotheby's—The Tixall Library, late the property of Sir T. C. Constable, Bt of Burton Constable and Aston Hall, North Ferriby Yorks. 7th November 1899, lot 598.' A printed slip, 'TIXALL LIBRARY', is pasted in between the two pencilled notes, and a printed label is pasted in at the bottom, 'FROM THE LIBRARY OF LAURENCE W. HOBSON, COMPTON HALL, NEAR WOLVERHAMPTON'. The volume was purchased at Sotheby's, 8 April 1957, by Dr Juel-Jensen, whose signature, in ink, is on f. i. It had been offered for sale in a spring

---

[18] 'Note 314: The Tixall Manuscript of Sir Philip Sidney's and the Countess of Pembroke's Paraphrase of the Psalms', *BC* 18 (1969), 222–3.

[19] Sidney, *Poems*, 551.

[20] Ibid., 550.

[21] 'Note 314: The Tixall Manuscript.'

1900 catalogue by Ellis and Elvey, with the suggestion that the first leaf of the poem to Queen Elizabeth may be lacking (although there seems to be no textual support for such a view, except, perhaps, for the lack of a title). In May 1987 there were, between the final leaf and back cover, two small sheets of paper containing an 'Extract from a Letter from Col. Raleigh Chichester Constable ['Raleigh' added above a caret] to Philip Chichester' (dated 6 Jan. 1930) which confirms some of the information about provenance cited above. In the upper left corner of the inside of the back cover is the pencilled note, 'w/b/c'.

The *delta* (δ) Tradition (see also MS *F*)

I British Library MS Additional 12047.

[i] + 1–3 + [3a] + 4–95 + [ii–iv] ff. Folios 2–3 are inlaid; f. [3a] is an original preliminary leaf, ruled as the subsequent leaves are, signed A (but not foliated; f. 4 is signed A.2.); f. [ii], the last ruled leaf, contains a foliator's note. Collation (based partly on six visible contemporary signatures in ink): A–M^8. Paper *c*.187 × 145 mm.; binding *c*.194 × 153 mm. Beal, SiP 74, dated late 16th century. *I* contains Psalms 1–26 (from δ) in versions similar to those in *F* and *K*, then a miscellaneous selection of 85 later Psalms or 88 poems (there are two different versions of Psalms 75, 89, and 122) appearing as follows: 1–26, 51, 69, 104, 70–1, 75–6, 80, 83, 86, 89 (two versions), 91, 93–4, 96, 98–100, 105, 108, 110, 112, 117, 128, 120–1, 122 (two versions, the second the same as the original draft in *B*), 124–7, 129–34, 138, 147, 148, 149, 58, 85, 123, 73–4, 75 (the original draft, as also in *B*), 68 (the original draft, as also in *B*), 109, 142, 77, 88, 84, 102, 111, 143, 150, 78, 113, and 137. (Pss. 94, 128, and 148 are missing from Ringler's list on 550.) The text is written mainly in a single secretary hand. Like *K*, *I* has been rubricated for use as a devotional text with references to Morning and Evening Prayer,[22] although the mainly random order of the Psalms does not match the order in the Prayer Book. Someone cancelled at least one alteration of the text by writing in 'stet' (f. 38) in

---

[22] The British Library *Catalogue of Additions* attributes the rubrication in both MSS *I* and *K*, as well as annotations on ff. 8^v, 9, 18^v, 44, 51^v, 62, 63, and 95^v in MS *K*, to Sir John Harington of Kelston. Except for ff. 8^v, 9, 18^v, however, the identification seems less than certain. On the difficulty of identifying Harington's hand, see P. J. Croft, 'Sir John Harington's Manuscript of Sir Philip Sidney's *Arcadia*', *Literary Autographs* (Los Angeles: Clark Memorial Library, 1983), 37–75, and R. H. Miller, 'Sir John Harington's Manuscripts in Italic', *Studies in Bibliography* 40 (1987), 101–6.

an Italian hand similar to that of Sir John Harington of Kelston; 'punnished' was thus restored (over 'sundered') to 76. 20 ('venomd' was also apparently restored to Ps. 3. 29—where 'infect' had been added—but only by underlining, so whether Harington is responsible for the restoration there is still more uncertain).

While Psalm 113 and the second version of Psalm 89 are unique to *I*, the other texts are occasionally related to *O* and *D* (especially 104 and 137)[23] and thus suggest a connection with θ. *I* is a highly eccentric copy, not only because of its haphazard arrangement of Psalms, but also because of its occasionally illegible handwriting and its numerous, clearly non-authorial variants (as well as many unusual spellings, such as 'fowloing', 'thruthe', and 'anoyntet', all in the unique version of Psalm 89). It is tempting to speculate that the text derives from a very rough working draft, especially because all of the Psalms after 26 that were added to *K* (except for 113, which is unique in *I*) are missing in *I*, as if the author had been working on them separately. The watermark, grapes with posts or pillars, does not precisely match anything in Briquet or Heawood (but cf. Heawood 3485 ff.)

The numerous annotations on the preliminary leaves provide information about provenance, summarized thus in Ringler: 'Formerly owned by Joseph Haslewood (d. 1833), and Bishop Butler (d. 1839), from whose estate it was acquired by the British Museum in 1841. Haslewood wrongly thought that Sir John Harington was the author of this version; and Bishop Butler suggested that Harington was the transcriber, though the British Museum cataloguer disagreed with this identification of the hand. The manuscript, however, probably descends from a Harington source, for its text of Psalm 69 agrees in error with the text printed from family papers by Henry Harington in *Nugæ Antiquæ*.'[24] The means by which Harington acquired the manuscript are uncertain; neither *I* nor *K* is in the hand of any of the scribes he is known to have employed. The Psalms printed by

---

[23] In the following examples, the *A* reading is given first, followed by the variant in *I* and θ (and sometimes other manuscripts): Ps. 104. 15 'as'/'and'; 53 'thence'/'Then' ('ce' is stricken in *K*); 59 'on'/'in'; 60 'while'/'whiles'; 66 'unconstant'/'inconstant'; 82 'Sea'/'seas'; 102 'his worth in song'/'in song his Worth' (including *B* and *K*); 109 'uncessantly'/'incessantly'; Ps. 137. 21 'and'/'yea'; 23 'with in me'/'in mee doe'; 25 'shalt'/'wilt'; 32 'platt pais'/'flat, plaine' *I*, 'flatt plaine' *O*, *D*; 36 'unto us'/'to others'; 38 'cause'/'make' (including *E*). Particulary significant is 104. 36, where *A* has 'mansions', *I* has 'stations', θ has 'stacion', and *B* notes that 'stations' has been expunged and replaced by 'mansions'.

[24] Sidney, *Poems*, 550.

Henry Harington in 1775 are 51, 104, 137, 69 (II. 57–69); in 1779, he added 112, 117, 128 (misnumbered 120) (I. 277–96). As Kelliher suggests (in personal correspondence), *I* may also be the item listed in the sale catalogues of Charles Meige (Evans, 25, 26, 28 Feb. 1831) as lot 612 (described only as 'The Psalms of David translated into English verse *by Sir Philip Sydney and the Countess of Pembroke*. A Manuscript of the time of Elizabeth, beautifully written, formerly in the possession of Dr. Harrington, of Bath, to whom it descended from Sir J. Harrington, the Poet'; sold possibly to 'McKinny' (according to an indistinct MS annotation in the catalogue) and later listed in a catalogue of Thomas Rodd's (1836) as lot 161 ('a beautiful Manuscript of the time of James the First, *small* 4to, *blue morocco, gilt leaves*... It was formerly in the Harrington collection'). Haslewood's bookplate on the inside of the front cover is the same as that in two other manuscripts owned by him and now also in the British Library, Additional MSS 11307 and 19269. The binding is still the blue morocco referred to in Rodd's catalogue. Bishop Butler printed the texts of the Psalms in *I* that differ from the *A* versions in *Sidneiana*.[25] The British Museum purchased *I* (lot 404), along with *H*, from the son of Bishop Butler, the Revd Thomas Butler, on 5 July 1841.

K British Library MS Additional 46372.

    i–ii + [iia] + 1–111 + iii ff. A slip pasted in the manuscript notes that the following collation should be substituted for that published in the *Catalogue of Additional Manuscripts*): i–iii², iii¹⁰, iv–vi¹², vii¹⁴, viii¹⁸, ix¹², x¹⁰. Hilton Kelliher explains (in personal correspondence) an anomaly in the eighth gathering: 'a gathering that started out with a regular twelve leaves (ff. 80–89, 95, 96) was increased by the addition of three bifolia (ff. 90–stub following 94), comprising sections N to Y of Psalm 119'. The foliator assigned ff. i and iii to the front and back parchment or vellum covers; the torn leaf, f. [iia], before the text (beginning on f. 1) is blank. Paper *c.*323 × 199 mm.; binding *c.*325 × 201 mm. Beal, SiP 76, dated late 16th century.

    The original number of leaves is difficult to determine because there are several stubs of various sizes, some of which are numbered in pencil, while others are ignored. Stubs of leaves originally numbered 4, 13, and 74 remain; they all contained text (another stub after the original f. 74 must not have been numbered because it was

---

[25] Published for the Roxburghe Club (London: William Nicol, 1837), 57–66.

blank). Fragmentary text remaining on the currently foliated stubs 110–11 indicates that two additional, probably originally numbered leaves have indeed been lost. (Folio 110^v contains the last few words of 150. 5–8 and the catchwords 'Lett ringinge', the beginning of 150. 9.) Three other leaves, not originally numbered, were deliberately torn out before currently foliated leaves 74, 95, and 102 because they had been left blank and were thus not needed when Psalms 103, 118, 119, 135, and 136 were added to the manuscript later in different ink and a slightly different hand. Fifteen other Psalms were also added at the same time: 95, 97, 101, 106, 107, 113, 114–16, 139–41, 144–6. Large blank spaces are particularly noticeable after Psalms 95, 101, and 119 (following 119 is a whole blank page, f. 94^v, the last leaf of the three bifolia inserted to accommodate the text of that unexpectedly lengthy paraphrase). All of the Psalms before Psalm 95 (many of them missing in *I*) were apparently copied about the same time, in the same hand, but not in the same ink; the scribe must then have had to wait to copy the twenty additional poems until the countess had composed or revised them. The hand of these twenty Psalms is probably the same as that of the others, but it is more angular (perhaps because of a new or sharpened pen), especially in 'd' and a new 'r' (which occurs along with the regular secretary 'r'). The loss of the last several folios (like ff. 4, 13, 74, and 110–11) was not related to the adding of the twenty Psalms beginning with Psalm 95; lost also were the last part of Psalm 148 (ll. 17 ff.) and all of Psalms 149–50. Also lacking, because of torn or missing leaves, is all or part of the text of Psalms 6. 29–8.16 and 10. 19–24, 61–4 (f. 4), 21. 17–22. 36 (f. 13), 103. 65–96 (the original f. 74, between f. 73 and the current f. 74). The scribe has not been identified, but Kelliher has partly deciphered an erased inscription on f. 43^v: 'John D[. . . ?] his hande'. Henry Woudhuysen suggests (in personal correspondence) that the second name may have been 'Dauies'. Although the hand of the text is not that of John Davies of Hereford, the note may refer to a place in the text of the manuscript that was being transcribed into *K* or to a point in another manuscript to which a scribe or reader was to turn.

The text of *K*, like that of Psalms 1–26 in *F* and *I*, descends ultimately from revisions of δ (itself probably copied from the original of *B*), which represents a preliminary stage in the χ tradition. The existence of this conjectural manuscript is proved by the agreement of all three manuscripts at many points in the early paraphrases.

Most of the paraphrases in *K* are those of the revised *A* version, with the exception of Psalm 75 (the original draft, preserved also in *B*, *I*, *N*) and octaves G, H, S, W of Psalm 119 (the original drafts, also in *χ*). Although *K* is much closer to the *χ* text than Ringler seems to imply, it does occupy an intermediate position between the *β* and *χ* traditions as indicated by several distinctive readings shared with both sets of manuscripts. For example, *K* has *β* readings at 102. 5; 123. 4, 9, 10; 129. 11; 147. 30; 148. 37; 149. 22; and the places cited by Ringler (502, n. 1). Significant *χ* variants appear in *K* at 48. 9–10, 12, 24, 27; 70. 2–5, 13; 146. 10–16 (an extended omission); and many other places. As in *I*, *K* contains rubrics for Morning and Evening Prayer, as well as verse numbers from the Prayer Book Psalter, all of which were added later. The verse numbers are, thus, different from those in *B*, which correspond more frequently with the numbering in the Geneva Bible. A note, 'This is otherwise translated', is written by Psalms 68, 75, 89, and 122. Someone has also added the incipits to Psalms 114–16 and made some correction marks (e.g. 141. 14) and other marks indicating where the biblical verses begin within, rather than at the opening of the line (e.g. 49. 21, 53. 5, 55. 41, etc.). Other notes, perhaps in the hand of Sir John Harington of Kelston, appear opposite the last two stanzas of Psalm 14 (f. 8ᵛ) and at the end of Psalm 22 (f. 14ʳ); Harington may also have written a revision of Psalm 16 (lines 31–2, where Philip Sidney had written, 'For I know the deadly grave | on my soule noe pow'r shall have'): 'ffor I know that thow in hell | wilt not leave my sowle to dwell' (f. 9).[26] At Psalms 30. 7, 49. 26, 86. 28, and 88. 12 someone has also glossed words like 'pit' and 'grave' as 'hell'. Numerous corrections in unidentified hands are not usually cited in the textual notes unless they are part of a crux. As in the case of *I*, the main text is not written in the hand of any of the scribes known to have worked for Harington.

On Harington's association with the manuscript, Ringler notes: 'This is the seventh volume of a collection of Harington family papers acquired by the British Museum in 1947. Sir John Harington in 1610 noted that he possessed "Countess of Pembr: psalms: 2 copies" (British Museum MS. Additional 27632, f. 30) of which this manuscript is doubtless one.'[27] The parchment or vellum binding, recently resewn, is formed of a document from the time of James I referring to 'the

[26] See n. 20 above.
[27] Sidney, *Poems*, 552.

Lands of Thomas Childe Late of Croydon' and to Thomas Catchmay, Robert Corbett, and William Milles. Numbers that appear to be a shelfmark, 1.48 or 4.48, are written on the spine. According to the British Library catalogue, the passages of religious prose and verse on ff. ii^r and 111 (the latter a stub) are in the hand of John Harington, MP (d. 1654), the son of Sir John of Kelston. See also the textual notes to 145. 29–33 (f. 107^v, where lines have been added in the hand of John Harington, MP). A partly indecipherable quatrain is stricken in brownish ink at the bottom of f. 1^r: 'hapes [?] be hard and [. . . ?] have no peare | riches is a nigard and frendshipe is deare | doe yow loke ere yow lep for fere yow doe falle | if yow loke yow maie loes all'.[28] The armorial watermarks resemble (1) Briquet 2291 (1587) and Heawood 481 (1602), similar to the marks in *C*, *H*, *N*, and (2) Heawood 546.

The *chi* (χ) Tradition

The *theta* θ Group

O Huntington Library MS EL 11637.

[i–ii] + 120 ff. Ff. 1–120^r are ruled in red in all four margins; f. 1 is blank but ruled, and f. 120 is a pastedown. Paper and binding *c*.296 × 198 mm. Dutschke's collation[29] (partly confirmed by visible threads): i–iv^6, v–vi^4, vii^6, viii^4, ix–xviii^6, xix^2, xx^{16}. Beal, SiP 78, dated *c*.1605–20. *O* includes all 150 Psalms, ff. 2–118^r, copied from θ, the same exemplar as *D* (not directly from *D*); these two manuscripts are the earliest of those descended from χ, the source of θ. After Psalm 43 the scribe has written, 'hactenus sir Phillip Sydney'. The incipits are frequently lacking in both (as at Psalms 17–26—as well as 2–16 in *O*—and 82–99, 104). There are variant incipits at 62 and 69 (as in *K*, *N*, and σ) and 76 (as in *I*, *N*, *C*). The first five pages of text, ff. 2–4^r, are numbered 1–5 in a similar hand and ink (1 is preceded by 'Page'). Inside the front cover and on a label pasted there, 35 is written above a line and C39 below it. On f. [i^r] is written 'Henry Platt [then in lighter ink] Henricus Platt./ ffoelix quem

---

[28] R. H. Robbins and John L. Cutler, *Supplement to the Index of Middle English Verse* (Lexington: U of Kentucky P, 1965), item 1088.5; and William A. Ringler, *Bibliography and Index of English Verse in Manuscript, 1501–1558* (London and New York: Mansell, 1992), item TM520.

[29] C. W. Dutschke, *Guide to Medieval and Renaissance Manuscripts in the Huntington Library*, 2 vols. (San Marino, Calif.: Huntington Library, 1989), I. 70.

faciunt aliena pericula caut | ./' Platt has not been identified; the Latin
is listed as item 6345 in Walther's *Initia carminum*,[30] with references
to *Gesamtkatalog der Wiegendrucke*, which lists some late fifteenth-
century volumes printed by Félix Baligault with title pages containing
a fuller form of the quotation: '*Foelix quem faciunt aliena pericula cau-
tu*m | *Est fortunatus foelix diues*que *beatus* | *Foelici monumenta die foelix*
| *Pressit et hec vitii dant retine*nt *ve nichil* [one title page reads in the
second line: *Est felix faustus cui sit fortuna fecunda*]'.[31] There is also a
reference to Hervieux's *Les Fabulistes latins*, where the line quoted in
the manuscript is found as the penultimate line in one of the fables of
Walter of England, '*De Niso et Columba*', which Hervieux prints as
item IX in an appendix.[32] Immediately to the right of the quotation
in MS *O* is a shelfmark, 'P:2.', which Dutschke notes is in the hand
of John Egerton (1579–1649), first Earl of Bridgewater; Dutschke
also says that an addition to the shelfmark, '/7.', is in the hand of
the second earl (1622–89). Henry Huntington purchased the manuscript with the Bridgewater Library in 1917. The Huntington shelfmark, 11637, above stricken 6711, is written on the same folio. The
three watermarks are only generally similar to Heawood 3500 (post,
1623), 3499 (post, '1617'), 2094 (grapes, *c*.1590), 2101 (grapes,
Rochester), and 2106 (grapes, 1622). The binding is old, limp parchment. *O* has been described more fully by Cecil C. Seronsy.[33] A
detailed summary description is provided by Dutschke.[34]

The text of MS *O* was probably written in a single early seventeenth-century secretary hand. Seronsy says that 'the text itself
appears to be in more than one hand',[35] but it is uncertain whether
he means by 'hand' script or scribe. In any case, his observation that

---

[30] H. Walther, *Initia carminum ac versum medii aevi…posterioris latinorum*, 2nd edn.,
Carmina Medii Aevi Posterioris Latina I/1 (Göttingen: Vanderhoeck und Ruprecht, 1969).

[31] 2nd edn., Stuttgart: Hiersemann; New York: Kraus, 1968, vols. II (items 2533, 2535–
47) and VI (items 6137, 7039 [not 7037]). Item 2533 is an edition of Arnoldus de Villa
Nova's *Regimen senum et seniorum* ([Paris: Félix Baligault for] Claude Jaumar and Thomas
Julian, *c*.1500); items 2535–47 are various editions up to *c*.1500 of Arnoldus de Villa Nova's
De vinis. Item 6137 is an edition of Johannes Caron's *Carmina tumultuaria* ([Paris: Félix
Baligault, *c*. 1496/7]), with the variant second line in the quotation on the title page. Item
7039 is an edition of Pseudo-Cicero, *Synonyma* ([Paris: Félix Baligault, *c*.1497–1500]).

[32] See *Gualteri Anglici Romuleæ, e Romuli Prosa in Elegiacos Versus Versæ* in *Les Fabulistes*
(Paris: Librairie de Firmin-Didot, 1884), II. 424. An enlarged edition in four volumes,
containing fables by other writers, was published in 1893–9 (rpt. New York: Burt Franklin,
1965).

[33] 'Another Huntington Manuscript of the Sidney Psalms', *HLQ* 29 (1965–6), 109–16.

[34] Dutschke, *Guide*, 69–70.

[35] 'Another Huntington Manuscript', 112.

an Italian hand is occasionally used in the catchwords does not necessarily suggest the presence of a second scribe because key words in the
main text are also sometimes written in an Italian hand (e.g. 'Chariotts' and 'Chivalrie' in Psalm 20. 27). While it is true, furthermore,
that the last three lines of Psalm 23 are added in different ink and a
slightly different hand, there are enough shared features ('r', 'g',
Greek 'ε' (?)), especially in comparison with the later Psalms, to suggest that the scribe is the same. An example is the first stanza of Psalm
116, where there are two related forms of 'g', one with a descender
curving to the left with a slight flourish and one with a straight descender sometimes ending in a similar flourish. The 'g' in Psalm 112.
4 has a form that is halfway between the two distinct forms. Further
evidence is in alterations, such as that made at Psalm 8. 12, where the
double addition of 'light' is made in dark ink similar to that of both
the original text there and the addition to Psalm 23. Such changes
were probably made by the copyist after the transcription was first
completed.

D Wadham College, Oxford, MS A 21.25 (formerly 25).

[i–xxii] + 116 + [xxiii–xxvi] ff. There is also a contemporary numbering of alternate leaves (7–64) in the same ink and hand as the text.
The tight binding clearly reveals sewing only between ff. 89 and 90;
paper stubs are apparent between ff. 24 and 25 and between ff. 28
and 29. Paper *c.*292 × 183 mm.; binding *c.*297 × 188 mm. Beal, SiP
88, dated early 17th century. The revised shelfmark, A 21.25, is written inside the front cover above 'Coxe Mss. 25', the number as listed
in Coxe's *Catalogue*.[36] *D* contains only Psalms 17–150, copied like *O*
from *θ* and written in a rounded Italian hand. Folios [ii–xxii] are
blank. Because of the contemporary numbering of every other leaf
(f. 1 is numbered 7; 3, 8; etc.), it is possible to speculate that at least
12 folios (originally containing Psalms 1–16) are missing (the paper of
the blank leaves is later). A note pasted on f. [i] comments on the
lacuna: '(The old Title) A Translation of the Book of Psalms into
English Verse By the most noble and Virtuous Gentleman Sir Philip
Sidney Knight NB. 16 Psalms are wanting in this MSS.'[37] An addi-

---

[36] H. O. Coxe, *Catalogus Codicum MSS qui in Collegiis aulisque Oxonienibus...*, 2 vols.
(Oxonii: E Typographeo Academico,1852).

[37] The 'old title' probably comes from Steele's essay in *The Guardian* (No. 18, 1 Apr.
1713), where he says, 'I am particularly pleased that he [Sidney] hath translated the whole
Book of *Psalms* into *English* Verse. A Friend of mine informs me, that he hath the Manu-

tional note, in pencil, attributes the poems 'probably' to the Countess of Pembroke and cites the 1779 edition of *Nugæ Antiquæ* and Grosart's edition of Sidney's works. The text is closely related to *O* (the two manuscripts were transcribed from the same exemplar) and *D* is thus one of the earliest of the χ copies through the conjectural intermediary θ. *D* is distinguished by Latinate spellings such as 'neclegt' (Psalms 50. 44, 52. 12, etc.). (For more details, see the description of *O*.)

The binding is brown leather, blind stamped. The crowned garter watermark on the newer, mainly blank paper is similar to Heawood 450 (1760), but with a crown and 'G R' countermark more similar to Heawood 477. One mark on the paper containing the text is a flag with 'G' and '3' or reversed Greek 'ε' (?) resembling Heawood 1369 (cf. 1370 of 1630–40); the other is a crossbow resembling Briquet 763 (1597?), except that Briquet does not show the letters 'P' and 'B'. At the top of the inside front cover is written (above Warner's book-plate): 'Richard Warner 1738 Bought at the Auction of Sir Joseph Jekyll's MSS etc collected by the late Lord Somers'. Ringler notes: 'Lord Somers (d. 1716) bequeathed his books to Sir Joseph Jekyll, and Richard Warner (d. 1775) bequeathed his books to Wadham.'[38] As Henry Woudhuysen notes (in personal correspondence), however, no reference to the manuscript has been found in Sir Joseph Jekyll's sale catalogue. On f. [i] is the note, 'A rare Mss. not published Mr Heber has one', along with references to Park's edition of H. Walpole's *Royal and Noble Authors* and Bliss's edition of Anthony Wood's *Athenæ Oxonienses*.[39]

MSS *N* and *C*

N Bibliothèque de la Sorbonne, MS 1110. The | Psalmes of David: | donne | Into English Verse, | by | The most noble and vertuous | Gentleman Sir Philip | Sydney knight./

[i–iv] ff. + 1–370 380–96 [i.e. 371–87] pp. [v–vi] ff. Collation: i⁴ (−1), ii–xxv⁸, xxvi⁴ (+1, f. 196 pasted onto ff. 197, 200). Paper

script by him, which is said in the Title to have been done *By the most noble and virtuous Gent. Sir PHILIP SIDNEY, Knight*' (see the description of MS *L* below). The phrase 'Translation of the Book of Psalms' may be particularly significant because no other title in the extant manuscripts describes the metrical Psalter in just that way. The closest parallel is in MS *F*, which, however, like the other manuscripts, has 'Psalms of David' for 'Book of Psalms' and was thus probably not the source of the title as quoted in MS *D*.

[38] Sidney, *Poems*, 549.
[39] See the 1806 edition of Walpole (London: John Scott), II. 190–8, and the 1813 edition of Wood (London: Rivington), I, col. 522.

*c.*226 × 175 mm; binding *c.*235 × 178 mm. Beal, SiP 83, dated early 17th century. The title is on f. [iv^r]; Psalms 1–150 are written on pp. 1–396 in an Italian hand. All the leaves, ruled in red, are original. After Psalm 43 is written the note, 'Hactenus, Sir P. Sidney'. After Psalm 150 is written, 'The End'. *N* is part of the χ group and is related to *C* through single-word and whole-line variants. *N* is generally closer to the earlier texts, and it contains alternative paraphrases of Psalms 75 (also in *B*, *I*, *K*) and 131 (unique to *N*). There is even a point where *N*, alone among all the other copies, preserves another reading that Woodforde notes was expunged from β: at 106. 37, *N* has the cancelled phrase, 'With scope t'experiment', rather than the clause, 'That they (forsooth) might trye', which occurs everywhere else, including *C*. *N* also bears some resemblance to the σ group (through textual variants, its title, and the incipits of the various sections of Psalm 119). Both *N* and *C* may have been copied in part from more than one source.

There are two armorial watermarks, one (single fleur-de-lis) resembling Briquet 7210 (1585) and Heawood 1721 (1609; cf. 1721^a of 1614), the other resembling Briquet 2291 (1587) and Heawood 481 (1602). Both marks are similar to those in *H* and *C*. The binding is old calf; the original ties or clasps are missing. On f. 1, the title page, is the inscription, 'Vacate et videte Kenelme Dig[by] M.S. 1110. [a former shelfmark is stricken after 'M.S.']'. Ringler notes that the manuscript was 'first noticed by A. W. Osborn in 1932'.[40]

C Bodleian, MS Rawl. poet. 24 (*Summary Catalogue* 14518). THE | Psalmes of David tra= | =nslated into divers and sundry = | kindes of verse, more rare, and exce= | =llent, for the method and varietie | then ever yet hath bene don in | English: begun by the | noble and learned gentleman | Sir Philip Sidney knight, | and | finished by the Right honnorable | the Countesse of Pembroke, his | Sister, and by her dirrection | and appointment./ | [ornament] | [rule] | Verbum Dei manet in æternum/

i + [ii] + iii–iv + 1–59 + 60–1 + 62–227 [i.e. 61–226] numbered pages (p. [ii] is not numbered). On page 60, '-1' is added after 60 because 61 was omitted during the original pagination; hence, the pagination is one number short after 60, so that there are only 226 pages of text (after the title page): title page on iii; text of Psalms on

---

[40] Sidney, *Poems*, 552.

1–220 (i.e. 219); page 221 (i.e. 220) and 3 folios at the end blank (but for paginator's note on 226–7, i.e. 225–6). The gatherings are unclear because of the tight binding and apparently haphazard pattern of watermarks. The recto pages are ruled in red (four lines on the left and two on the right); the verso pages are ruled similarly, but in a different shade of red, from page 168; up to that page, versos have three rules on the left. Pages 223– 7 (i.e. 222–6) are not ruled. Paper *c*.300 × 192 mm.; binding *c*.305 × 202 mm. Beal, SiP 72, dated early 17th century. Psalms 1–150 are written in a secretary hand, with Italian elements. The text is closely related to *N* and to *G*, *M* and is thus part of the χ group of manuscripts. Study of the variants suggests further that *C* lies between *N* and the other two copies; like *N* it may have been copied in part from more than one source. The final phrase of the title (shortened versions of which appear in *G*, *M*) indicates that the deliberate alterations in *C* may not be authorial, but scribal or editorial. The tight binding (marbled boards and a newer leather spine) is apparently later; pages i–ii are a different kind of paper, presumably contemporary with the binding. Inside the front cover is a Rawlinson bookplate and, twice, the current Bodleian shelf-mark. There is a later signature on the title page: 'W. Barkwithe [*or* Barkwith]' (p. iii). One watermark (armorial, single fleur-de-lis) is on the title page only and is similar to Briquet 7210 (1585) and, suggests Ringler (548), Heawood 1768 (*c*.1616). The Briquet mark resembles one in *N* and *H*; the Heawood mark resembles the one in *J*. One other armorial mark is similar to Briquet 2291 (1587; cf. Heawood 481 [1602]). A third, bunch of grapes, resembles Heawood 2094 (*c*.1590).

The *sigma* (σ) Group

H British Library MS Additional 12048. The Psalmes of David | done into English verse | By the moste noble and | vertuous gentellman Sir | Phillipp Sidney | Knight

[i–iii] + 1–148 + [iv–vii] ff., all inlaid. Contemporary foliation, 1–146, in ink similar to that of the text appears on ff. 3–148 ('Fol:' or 'Foll:' is used before the numbers from 1 to 29); '20' is trimmed away, but 'Foll:' is still visible on f. 22). The collation is difficult to determine because of the inlaying of the leaves, but the following gatherings (ff. 10–15, 16–29, 32–45, 48–53, 54–7, 58–67, 70–7, 78–85, 86–93, 94–101, 102–7, 108–17, 118–23, 125–32, 133–40, 141–8) have been preserved in the new binding: i⁶, ii–iii¹⁴, iv⁶, v⁴, vi¹⁰, vii–x⁸, xi⁶, xii¹⁰, xiii⁶, xiv–xvi⁸. Paper *c*.196 × 149 mm. Beal, SiP 75, dated early 17th century. The title is on f. 2^r; Psalms 1–150, headed 'Davids Psalmes', are written on ff. 3–148 in an Italian hand; some alterations have been made in different ink. After Psalm 43 is the note, 'Hactenus Sir Phillip Sydney'. On f. 148 is written, 'Finis The .7. Penitentiall Psalmes of David vizt: Psal:: 6: 32: 38: 51: 102: 130: 143' and on the verso, 'Μονώ τό [*sic*] Θεώ [*sic*]'. *H* is part of a sub-group, containing *Q, E, L, P*, that derives from χ through σ. Alterations of some χ readings—either undertaken to make them conform with later readings that appear in *Q* and subsequent manuscripts or transferred to those copies—suggest that *H* is the earliest in its sub-group. The handwriting in *H* and *Q* is so similar that it may be the work of the same scribe. These two manuscripts (and sometimes *E*) also share some distinctive spellings ('strenght', 'lenghe', 'seaes', 'tounge', and some consistently doubled letters as in 'thuss', 'hol-lines', 'yeet' for 'yet', and 'ytt' for 'it', but also a peculiar use of the hyphen as in 'de-sent', 'Lea-vie', 'dismay-ed', and 'ruin-s'). MSS *H, Q, E* also sometimes spell 'plague' as 'plauge', a spelling which Mary Hobbs says she has found 'only in documents and verse manu-scripts connected with the Inns of Court'.[41] The incipits (in red) are sometimes written in such small spaces that they seem to have been added after the writing of the text (*Q* lacks all incipits).

The volume was rebound in 1986. There seem to be four distinct watermarks. Four resemble marks previously recorded: (1) Briquet 1369 (1593), similar to the eagle mark in *Q*, (2) Briquet 2291 (1587) and Heawood 481 (1602), similar to the armorial mark in *C* and *N*, (3) Briquet 7210 (1585) and Heawood 1721 (1609; cf. 1721^a of 1614), similar to the single fleur-de-lis mark in *C* and *N*, (4) an armorial device with three fleurs-de-lis, which is visible only on the contiguous ff. 58–67 and which is not similar to other marks in Briquet and Heawood.

In addition to the current shelfmark and the numbers 26 and 1804, there are notes on f. 1^v referring to at least three owners: Dr Taylor, Richard Heber, and Samuel Butler, Bishop of Lichfield and Coven-try. (The names of the booksellers 'Leigh and Sotheby' are written to the left of 'Dr. Taylor's Sale'.) According to Taylor's sale catalogue (6 June 1793), the manuscript, lot 175, was sold to Dr Dalrymple. Philip Bliss notes in his edition of Anthony Wood's *Athenæ Oxoniensis*

---

[41] *Early Seventeenth-Century Verse Miscellany Manuscripts* (Aldershot: Scolar, 1992), 45. See also the textual notes on Pss. 73. 14 (where *O* agrees with σ); 74. 59; 81. 16; 91. 11, 19; 104. 107; 105. 74; 106. 105; 109. 18; 112. 28 (where *J* agrees with *H, Q*); 128. 23; 135. 42; 149. 17.

that it was in Dalrymple's collection at the time;[42] no manuscripts are listed in the Dalrymple sale catalogue of 1809. It was later sold by Evans for £2. 12s. 6d. to the dealer Payne of Payne and Foss as part of Heber's extensive collection (lot 1434, Part XI) on 10 Feb. 1836 (see A. N. L. Munby's annotated copy of the sale catalogue in the Cambridge University Library). Ringler notes that the British Library acquired it from Butler's estate in 1841.[43]

Q Robert H. Schaffner, Johannesburg. THE PSALMes | off David Done into English | verse, By the moste noble and | vertuouse gentellman Sir | Phillipp Sydney knight.

[i–iii] + 114 + [iv–v] ff. (numbered in the same hand and ink as the text, in the top right corner). On [ii] is the mark '$\frac{K}{7}$'; on [iiv] is written 'Warwick'. The title is on [iii] ([i] is blank, as is [v] at the end of the volume). Paper 306 × 195 mm.; binding 313 × 213 mm. (30 mm. thick). Beal, SiP 77, early 17th century. The volume was purchased in 1980 by Robert H. Schaffner, who has graciously provided the descriptive details above (in private correspondence). The manuscript was given the siglum, 'G¹', by Waller and described by him in *Triumph*.[44] The text is part of the σ subgroup. Similarities with *H* suggest that a single scribe may have written both manuscripts (see the description of *H* above). There are no incipits. Waller describes the decoration of *Q*: 'The title-page is decorated with flowers and insects, including a thistle, roses, caterpillars, snails, and bees. Each psalm has its initial capital letter in gold or other colours; various shades of blue and green are especially common. Sixty-eight of these letters are further decorated with such motifs as eagles, gryphons, salamanders, mice, snails, flies, and numerous flowers, almost one quarter of which are thistles.'[45] Waller also suggests that the manuscript 'was the work of someone associated with Esther Inglis (1571–1624)'.[46] So far, no evidence has been found to corroborate that association.

The binding, rebacked and repaired (original clasp positions can still be identified), is contemporary leather, blind stamped; according to Sotheby's sale catalogue for 22 July 1980, it 'is very similar to those on the Queen's College Oxford and Helmingham Hall manuscripts of

---

[42] Vol I, col. 522, n. 5.
[43] Sidney, *Poems*, 550.
[44] Sidney, Mary. *Triumph*, 211–21.
[45] Ibid., 213.
[46] Ibid., 215.

Sidney's *Arcadia*' (330). There is also a 'gilt lozenge-shaped center-piece flanked by initials, "T.M."' (Sotheby's). T.M. has not been certainly identified, although one candidate is Thomas Moffet (1553–1604), the Herbert family physician (Sotheby's). Henry Woud-huysen has proposed (in personal correspondence) Tobie Matthew (1546–1628), Archbishop of York and friend of Sir John Harington, but that would require dating the manuscript binding in the mid-1590s.[47] The coloured initials on the title page, 'WH', may refer to William Herbert (1580–1630), son of Mary Sidney. According to Peter Beal (in personal correspondence), however, similarly written initials also appear in manuscripts owned by Lord William Howard (1563–1640). The Sotheby's catalogue comments on the inscription, 'Warwick': 'probably related to Warwick Castle, seat of Sidney's life-long friend and biographer Sir Fulke Greville, Lord Brooke (1554–1628). The volume might conceivably have come into this library at a later date, although it is not listed among the Elizabethan collections sold to Lord Brooke by J. O. Halliwell-Phillipps (1820–1889) at the time when the earlier Warwick collections were most substantially enlarged. Unrecorded sales from Warwick Castle library have occurred during the present century.' The first nineteenth-century owner to be identified with certainty is Thomas Thorpe, whose 1836 sale catalogue includes the following as lot 1170: ' "Psalmes of David done into English Verse, by the Most Noble and Vertuous Gentleman Sir Phillipp Sydney Knight." Folio. Original binding, with W.H. on the title, and J.M. [*sic*] on the covers.' The manuscript was owned before 1976 by John Goelet and subsequently by Colin Franklin of Abingdon, Oxford, who purchased it at Sotheby's on 22 July 1980, after which it was sold to Mr Schaffner. The primary watermark (as shown in photographs supplied by Mr Schaffner) is an eagle similar to the one in *H*, Briquet 1369 (1593) or, according to Sotheby's, 1370 (1595–1605; cf. Heawood 1248 of 1618). A second watermark in the final blank leaf contains the letters 'C', 'Z', 'O' in the upper left corner and 'R' and 'E' in the lower right corner and has not been identified. Inside the back cover are the numbers '726'.

E The Queen's College, Oxford, MS 341. The Psalmes of David | done into English verse | By the most noble and vertuous | gentle-man Sir Phillip: | Sydney knight.

---

[47] See '*Astrophel and Stella* 75: A "New" Text', *RES* NS 37 (1986), 390.

[i–iii] + [1] + 2–130 + [131] + 131–158 + [iv–xxii] ff. There are
159 folios of text altogether. Two narrow parchment pastedowns containing Latin text, ff. [i] and [xxii], have become detached from the
boards, but remain partly pasted onto the first and last blank leaves.
Folio [ii] bears the Queen's College shelfmark 341 in pencil, as well
as some early scribblings in ink (apparently imitations of the decorative initial H of Psalm 1). Folios [xvi], [xviii], and [xxi] are torn. There
is no clearly visible sewing. Paper *c*.223 × 156 mm.; binding
c.228 × 165 mm. Beal, SiP 85, dated early 17th century. Psalms 1–
150 are written in a rounded secretary hand, with Italian elements.
After Psalm 43 is the note, 'Hactenus Sr Phillip Sydney' (f. 43^v).
Psalm 44 begins on f. 44^r. On f. [iii] is written, 'Queens College
Library Oxon. 1697'. On f. 158 (i.e. 159) is written (as in *H, L, P*):
'Finis The 7: penitentiall psalmes of David. Psals: 6: 32: 38: 51: 102:
130: 143:'. The text descends from the conjectural intermediary σ and
is thus closely related to that of *H* and *Q*. Variants shared with *H* and a
few errors that could have been caused by ambiguously formed letters
in *H*, suggest that *H* was the source of *E*, but the latter may have been
copied from the same exemplar as *H* and *Q*. *E* itself was the source of
L, from which *P* was transcribed. The probably original gold-tooled,
leather-covered boards have been rebacked. The centre motif is very
similar to that of item 18, the *Works* (1616) of James I, in G. D. Hobson's *English Bindings*.[48] Hobson notes that 'in general lay-out, and in
the treatment of the spine, the binding [of his item 18] closely resembles two books which bear the arms of Anne of Denmark'. The tip of
an unidentified watermark is barely visible on some of the inner,
tightly bound margins.

L Huntington Library MS HM 100. The Psalmes of | David done
into | English Verse by | the Most Noble | and Vertuous gentleman
| Sir Phillipp | Sidney Knight
[i–iii] + 1–164 + [iv–vi] ff. Dutschke's collation[49] (partly
confirmed by visible threads): i^2, ii^4, iii^{12} (minus a leaf in the second
half not affecting the text), iv^6, v^8, vi^6, vii^{10}, viii^6, ix^{10}, x^6, xi^{10}, xii^6,
xiii^{10}, xiv^6, xv^{10}, xvi^6, xvii^{10}, xviii^6, xix^{10}, xx^6, xxi^{10}, xxii^6 (−6). Beal,
SiP 79, dated early 17th century. Paper *c*.218 × 158 mm.; binding
c.223 × 170 mm. The paper is ruled in red on all four margins; the

[48] London: Chiswick Press, 1940.
[49] Dutschke, *Guide*, 143–4.

first and last of the unfoliated modern leaves are marbled recto and verso, respectively, as are the pastedowns. Psalms 1–150 are written in an Italian hand. *L* is a copy of *E*, as numerous shared variants and other readings based on ambiguously formed letters in *E* indicate. For example, *L* has 'parte' at 48. 13, where *E* has 'yt:' which, in E's hand, resembles the abbreviation, 'pt:'; at 41. 13, *L* has 'say', an error based on an unusually open secretary 'd' in 'said' in *E*; and other errors based on unusual spellings in *E*. Shared variants in *E* and *L* include the following: 'is my delight' in *E* and *L* for 'he is my light', 27. 1; 'out' for 'hence', 44. 6; 'so feirce doe' for 'doe fiercely', 57. 6; 'melt with sweating' for 'sweat with melting', 68. 19; 'doeth faye but lame' for 'as lamely fares', 77. 23; 'a Larrum' for 'alarum' (or 'alarm'), 78. 198; and 'life' for 'death', 143. 35. On f. 164 is a list of the Penitential Psalms, as in *E, H, P*.[50]

On f. [ii] is an excerpt from Sir Richard Steele's essay in *The Guardian* (No. 18, 1 Apr. 1713) that praises the Sidney Psalms: 'Guardian Vol. 1 P. 81. Our gallant Country man Sir P. Sidney was a a [*sic*] noble example of Courage and devotion: I am particularly pleas'd that he hath translated the Whole Book of PSALMS into English Verse: A Friend of mine informs me that he hath the M̲S̲: by him which is said in the Title to have been done, by *the most noble and virtuous Gentleman. Sir Philip Sydney Knight*: They having never been printed, I shall present the publick with one of them, which my Correspondent assures me he hath faithfully transcribed, and wherin I have taken the liberty to alter only one word:—the 1st word *nigh*, for *High*.' Following the quotation is the note: 'This the very *MSS*. alluded to as above'. On f. [iii] is the note in pencil, 'W. A. White April 10, 1922', a reference to an American owner. The modern binding is dark red morocco, with gold tooling around the edges; the paper edges are gilt, and the endpapers are marbled. There seem to be two distinct watermarks. On the four newer front and back leaves is an armorial mark (crowned garter) similar to Heawood 450 (*c.*1760). The armorial mark (horn) in the paper containing the text, ff. 1–164, resembles Heawood 2654 ('1616').

P National Library of Wales, Peniarth MS 374B. The Psalms of David done | into English Verse by the | Most Noble and Vertuous | Gentleman Sir Phillip Sidney | Knight.

---

[50] See also n. 37 above.

1–191 + [i–ii] ff. Collation: i^8 (−1–3, stubs), ii–xii^8, xiii^8 (−8), xiv–xxiv^8, xxv^6 (−6, stub). That one additional gathering has been lost at the end is suggested by the presence of thread and at least six stubs. Paper *c.*185 × 145 mm; binding *c.*190 × 155 mm. Beal, SiP 82, dated 18th century. *P* contains Psalms 1–150 written on ff. 1–191^r in a single, early eighteenth-century hand (except for a few alterations and annotations in different hands and in different ink and in pencil); ff. [i–ii] are blank and not foliated. The watermark is an armorial device resembling Heawood 454 (1700) or 461 (1713), but with a countermark similar to that in Heawood 353 and a Pieter van der Ley mark in Churchill 135.[51] The text, bound in old parchment or vellum, was copied directly from *L*, as numerous shared variants clearly indicate (e.g. 'Perill' for 'ill' at 23. 12; 'hostes' for 'us', 7. 46; 'I live I' for 'they live and', 38. 55; 'thigh' for 'side', 45. 9; 'parte' for 'it' (*E* has 'yt:' which, in *E*'s hand, resembles the abbreviation, 'pt:'), 48. 13; 'Mirh' for 'mirth', 65. 44; 'Draw' for 'Drave' ('Draue' in E), 76. 6; 'Marsha' for 'Masha', 95. 24; 'by' for 'from' (Variant Ps. 119H. 14). Two inscriptions provide clues to the volume's earlier history: 'Ex dono Roberti Wynn' (inside the front cover) and 'Ex Libris Griffithii Roberts 1791' (top of f. 1). According to a personal letter from Daniel Huws, Keeper of Records and Manuscripts at the National Library of Wales, Griffith Roberts (1735–1808) probably acquired the manuscript from Robert Wynn, the son of William Wynn (1709–60), who owned as many as thirty manuscripts which later became part of the Hengwrt-Peniarth library. (The reference to Wynn's 'gift', says Huws, is in Roberts's hand.) It was probably through Roberts, directly or indirectly, that the copy of the *Psalmes* found its way to Hengwrt. According to the *Handlist of Manuscripts in the National Library of Wales*,[52] he was prominent among those who had special interest in and access to the library there in the late eighteenth century, and his name is written in a number of the manuscripts (xiv–xvii; see xiv for a partial list). In any case, the metrical psalter was at Hengwrt when Aneurin Owen originally compiled his catalogue in 1824.[53] Owen based his work on a 1658 list of 158 items; among the 203 titles he added was *P*, listed then according to

---

[51] W. A. Churchill, *Watermarks in Paper in Holland, England, France, etc., in the XVII and XVIII Centuries and Their Interconnections* (Amsterdam: Hertzberger, 1935).

[52] Aberystwyth: National Library of Wales, 1943.

[53] It was subsequently published as 'Catalogue of Welsh Manuscripts, etc., in North Wales', *Transactions of the Cymmrodorion, or Metropolitan Cambrian Institution* 2 (1843), 410.

what became its Hengwrt number, 192, the same number used by
W. W. E. Wynne in his catalogue, published in *Archaeologia Cambrensis*.[54] Wynne (1801–80) had himself inherited the library in 1859 on
the death of 'his distant kinsman Sir Robert Williames Vaughan'
(*DNB*). It then came to be called the Peniarth collection after the
Wynne estate near Merioneth. After the death of Wynne's son,
Robert, in 1909, the volumes were acquired as the founding collection
of the National Library of Wales through the agency of Sir John Wil-
liams (1840–1926).[55]

MSS *G* and *M*

G Trinity College, Cambridge, MS R. 3. 16 (James 596). THE |
Psalmes of David | metaphrased into sundry | Kindes of verse, |
By the noble and famous gentleman: | Sir Philip Sidney | Knight.

[i–ii] + 301 numbered pages + [iv–vi]. Collation (not counting ff.
[i–ii], the title page, or [iv–vi]): i–xix^6, xx^4, xxi–xxv^6, xxvi^6 (–6).
There is a stub between pp. 238 and 239 in gathering xxi; gathering
xxvi is conjectural because of an apparently missing leaf after f. [iv].
Paper *c*.270 × 190 mm.; binding *c*.280 × 200 mm. Beal, SiP 87,
dated early 17th century. Psalms 1–150 are written in secretary
hand, with Italian elements; the title is in a somewhat different hand
(similar to that of the added attribution to Philip Sidney on 301), but
probably that of the scribe who wrote the text. The title is within a
decorative border. *G* is one of the later χ copies and is most closely
associated with *M*, especially because of their shared rhymed versions
of Psalms 120–7. It may have been copied directly from the heavily
altered χ, with some poems (such as the rhymed Pss. 120–7) perhaps
taken from another source, or it may have been copied from yet
another intermediary that served also as the source of *M*. (For more
information about the relationship of *G* and *M*, see the description
of *M* below.) The grapes watermark in the paper containing the text
is similar to Heawood 2095 (1616) or 2178 (1627). Folio [iv] is apparently part of the original manuscript (it has a similar watermark). The
armorial mark on f. [v] is generally similar to Heawood 1730 (1646).
There are no marks on the endpapers. Folios [i] and [v–vi], as well

---

[54] 'Catalogue of the Hengwrt MSS. at Peniarth', *Archaeologia Cambrensis*, 3rd ser., 15
(1869), 371.
[55] A fuller description of the Peniarth MS is given by Noel J. Kinnamon, 'The Text of
the Peniarth Manuscript of the Sidneian Psalms', *National Library of Wales Journal* 28
(1993–4), 279–84.

as the pastedowns, all seem to be later. According to James,[56] the
volume was given to the college in 1664 by W. Lynnet, whose name
(followed by 'T[rinity] C[ollege]') is on the front binding. Under
the title is written, 'Trin. Coll. Cant. Anno Domino 1664', all within
a double ruled border. At the bottom of the title page is a reference to
the donor: 'Ex dono Magistri Lynnett STB huius Collegij Socij'. On
f. [iv] is written, 'I haue perused this Metaphrase of the Psalmes by
that Worthy, whose happy meditations may yield others content,
and a precedent worthy imitation, Which I desire may be published,
in Print. John Langley. [Something is stricken under the name.]'[57]
This is apparently the manuscript which Samuel Woodforde says
he saw at Trinity before he made his transcription, MS *B*, of a now
lost copy.

M Huntington Library MS HM 117. THE Psalmes of David |
metaphrased into verse by | the noble, learned, and famous | gentle-
man Sir Philip Sidney | Knight
    [i–iv] ff. + 1–161 + 161[i.e. 162]–215[i.e. 216] + 217– 321 pp. +
[v–vi] ff. The number 161 is used twice and 216 is omitted in the contemporary foliation so that the pages between the actual pages 161 and
216 are numbered one lower than they should be. Page 322 is blank
and not numbered. Dutschke's collation[58] (partly confirmed by visible
threads): i–xiii[12], xiv[6] (−5). Paper *c*.167 × 108 mm.; binding
c.190 × 140 mm. Beal, SiP 80, dated early 17th century. The title is
on f. [iv[r]]; Psalms 1–150 are written on pp. 1–321 in a secretary
hand, with Italian features. Several contemporary page numbers are
stricken or altered; f. 161 is numbered in different ink. There are
two watermarks (pots) resembling Heawood 3631 (undated; cf. 3579
[1619] and 3623 [early seventeenth century] and 3601 [seventeenth
century]).
    One of the last copies in the χ tradition, *M* is closely related to *G*
especially because of the rhymed versions of Psalms 120–7 they both
contain. *G* and *M*, especially the latter, are also related to *C* through
numerous common, otherwise unique readings. Perhaps the most
intriguing link, however, is in the title pages of the three manuscripts.

---

[56] James, *Western Manuscripts*, II. 66, item 596.
[57] On Lynnet's preparation of the text for printing in the mid seventeenth century, see
Michael G. Brennan, 'Licensing the Sidney Psalms for the Press in the 1640s', *N&Q*, 31
(1984), 304–5.
[58] Dutschke, *Guide*, 153.

Although *G* and *M* lack the reference to an apparent editor in the final phrase of the title in *C*, their deliberate and systematic variants are often different in style from the texts in the other manuscripts, and they are more often based on the Prayer Book Psalter than the Geneva Bible. (For a fuller discussion of *M*, see 'Relationship of the Texts of the *Psalmes*'.) Like *G*, *M* may have been copied from χ (supplemented at points from another source) or from a lost intermediary derived from χ.

M is probably the item listed in Thomas Rawlinson's sale catalogue (Ballard, 4 Mar. 1733/4) as lot 139 (quarto): 'The Psalmes of David metaphras'd into Verse by Sir Philip Sidney, Knight' (sold to Mr Calamy). Folio [iiiv] is signed, 'W Hayley 1789', in whose sale catalogue (Evans, 13–27 Feb. 1821, 12th day) the manuscript is listed as lot 2389; under the signature is written in pencil 'William Hayley, Poet. b. 1745. d. 1820'. The volume was included in the B. H. Bright sale on 18 June 1844 (Sotheby's, lot 242). According to Ringler the manuscript was also owned by Thomas Corser;[59] Dutschke adds a reference to Corser's sale catalogue, 11 July 1870, part V, lot 556 (Sotheby's) and notes that the buyer was Ellis. Dutschke also notes that W. C. Hazlitt later sold the volume to Henry Huth and that it was bought by Quaritch in Alfred H. Huth's sale of 11 July 1917 (Sotheby's, part VI, lot 6023).[60] Inside the front cover is a Huth bookplate ('Ex Musæo Huthii Animus non res'). The brown morocco binding, with gold tooling, is by Francis Bedford, who was active in the third quarter of the nineteenth century and whose name appears in gold on the inside bottom edge of the front cover.

---

[59] Sidney, *Poems*, 552.
[60] Dutschke, *Guide*, 154.

Relationship of the Texts of the *Psalmes*

Overview

The relationship of the seventeen extant manuscripts of the Sidneian *Psalmes* is exceedingly complex, involving a series of copies made during various stages of revision; those transcriptions were then recopied, with the introduction of many types of variants. There are instances of apparently authorial revision, undertaken at different times, resulting not only in replaced single words, phrases, and lines, but also entire poems, some of which exist in two or more versions. There are also the inevitable scribal errors, some of them immediately corrected or otherwise altered, others showing evidence of correction (sometimes mistaken) by later hands. While such details often obscure textual relationships, it is possible to draw some general conclusions about the development and transmission of the *Psalmes*.[1]

The manuscript that provides the most important evidence is MS *B*, a transcript made in 1694/5 by Samuel Woodforde (1636–1700). Woodforde worked from a mutilated and now lost manuscript— here called *β*—which was given him by his brother, John Woodforde, 'who bought it among other broken books to putt up Coffee pouder' (f. ii). In spite of the late date and imperfect condition of Woodforde's transcript (*β* had already lost numerous leaves), it proves invaluable in helping sort out the often conflicting details contained in the other copies, for the 'broken book' he had received was probably a set of the countess's working papers. As he writes in reference to the much corrected variant of Psalm 49, 'The very manner of this Psalms being crossd and alterd almost in every line and in many words twice makes me beleive this was an originall book that is [,] the book before me was so for none but an author could or would so amend any Copy.' Instead of simply preserving what remained of the countess's working copy (Psalms 88 to 102. 1–72 and Psalm 131 to Psalm 150 had been torn out), Woodforde undertook the labour of copying the whole volume, including (he says) all the variants. The disappearance of

---

[1] The textual relationships of various manuscripts are discussed in Sidney, *Poems*, 500–16; Rathmell (Ph.D. diss), 353–64; G. F. Waller, 'The Text and the Manuscript Variants of the Countess of Pembroke's Psalms', *RES* ns 25 (1975), 1–7; Waller, *Mary Sidney*, 152–8; and Sidney, Mary. *Triumph*, 18–36, 211–21.

the original working copy complicates the process of reconstructing the countess's methodology, for we have only Woodforde's authority for the substantive variants he records. Fortunately, the independent witness of differing manuscript traditions indicates that his transcriptions are reliable on the whole, despite some verbal errors and occasional omissions that can be reconstructed from collation with other manuscripts.[2]

The countess must have had three working copies, all now lost. In addition to what we call β (the lost original of Woodforde's transcript, B), there were two other hypothetical copies which we call δ (an intermediate copy) and χ. At first, the copying of the emerging *Psalmes* must have been done directly and exclusively from β, the ultimate source of δ and its descendant χ. If the procedure of copying from continually and clearly revised working copies had been maintained, the variants would have accumulated in a relatively orderly fashion as each new transcript was made in either the β or the χ tradition. (Tracing at least two levels of transcription from δ in the early K is, in fact, relatively easy and is discussed more fully below.) The numerous revisions preserved in B and the hundreds of variants in the other surviving manuscripts suggest, however, that the working copies were not always easy to read and the scribes were occasionally obliged to choose from among alternative readings. At times they even had access to more than one manuscript which offered still more choices. As Ringler suggests,[3] new versions of particular paraphrases may also have been supplied on slips of paper which were occasionally lost from exemplars, so that a manuscript which is otherwise demonstrably late may suddenly agree in certain details with an earlier one.

Woodforde's marginal notes make B the single most important document for tracing the complex textual history of the poems. It is possible to detect at least two major stages of revision (a few minor changes were also made later, as at 119Q. 14 and 22, where Woodforde notes deletions of readings that are retained everywhere else). As Ringler and Rathmell observe, it was after the first set of revisions (β^1) that another working copy (which we call δ, leading to χ) was

---

[3] Ibid. Supplying text on slips of paper was a common method of revision in the English Renaissance. A revision of Ps. 55. 61–72 is written on a piece of paper pasted to f. 45^v in MS *A*. See also Anne Lancashire's discussion of the revision slips included in the manuscript of *The Second Maiden's Tragedy* (Manchester: Manchester UP; Baltimore: Johns Hopkins UP, 1978), 4–5.

begun. But refinement of β and δ continued and resulted (through δ^{1-2}) in the making of finished scribal copies (K, then χ and the first of its descendants, the lost θ and its extant copies, O and D). It may have been about that time that χ became more or less independent, for none of the χ copies contains the relatively large-scale revisions of Psalm 119 (octaves G, H, S, and W) noted or incorporated in B, A, F, and J. The χ tradition itself also continued to develop, probably through several reworkings and perhaps additional intermediaries.

The countess has been described, in William Ringler's oft-quoted judgement, as 'an inveterate tinkerer who found it difficult to make up her mind'.[4] Certainly she did undertake many large and small revisions that were incorporated into the text at an early stage of its development, but these almost invariably represent stylistic improvements rather than indecision, and a large proportion of the variants recorded in later manuscripts are attributable to scribal error or sophistication, not authorial revision. Indeed, as will be argued below, the very extensive variations in single words and phrases recorded in G and M are almost certainly the result of alterations, often of questionable value, made at some date after 1611 by a hand other than that of the Countess of Pembroke. Such non-authorial intervention is often encountered in the manuscript culture of the English Renaissance, as Harold Love and Arthur Marotti, for instance, have recently demonstrated.[5]

Date

Most scholars have assumed that Pembroke began work on her paraphrases sometime after Philip Sidney's death in 1586. Her dedicatory poem to Queen Elizabeth, 'Even now that Care', however, may suggest that she was somehow involved in the project from the beginning. In presenting her work to the queen she says that the *Psalmes* 'once in two, now in one Subject goe, | the poorer left, the richer reft away' (21–2). Taken literally, this statement would imply that the poems originally had two authors, but since the death of Sir Philip, only one. Further ambiguity is supplied in the next stanza, which seems

---

[4] Sidney, *Poems*, 502.
[5] Love, *Scribal Publication in Seventeenth-Century England* (Oxford: Oxford UP, 1993), 119–23; Marotti, *Manuscript, Print, and the English Renaissance Lyric* (Ithaca and London: Cornell UP, 1995), 150.

to indicate that her work came after his. He 'did warpe', or set the structural vertical threads on the loom, and then she 'weav'd this webb to end' (27).

The latest possible date for the completed *Psalmes* is 1599, as recorded in *J* (where, however, it is altered from 1699 and may be of questionable authenticity); the countess probably completed the *Psalmes* well before that date, allowing time for the making of several copies, perhaps even as early as 1593 or 1594. (MS *J* is a copy of *A*, which is a fair copy of the countess's working papers.) Because Samuel Daniel mentioned the *Psalmes* in dedicating his *Cleopatra* to her, Ringler suggests that the countess's first draft was completed by 1593.[6] A complete manuscript seems to have been circulating at Wilton by 1594 because Henry Parry, in dedicating *Victoria Christiana* to young William Herbert, says 'that sacred poetical work of King David, left unfinished by her brother Philip, has at long last received its final polishing'.[7] Less conclusive evidence of dating is provided by Thomas Moffet's injunction to the countess to 'Let Petrarke sleep, give rest to Sacred Writte' in his dedication of *Silkewormes and their Flies*, since he lived at Wilton and would have known her works in progress.[8]

Most of the manuscripts in the χ tradition are dated by Ringler and Beal in the early seventeenth century.[9] Because of references to the 1611 King James Bible, manuscripts *G* and *M*, with their rhymed versions of Psalms 120–7, seem to postdate the text preserved in *A*, which earlier editors considered to be the final one.

Provenance

The seventeen manuscripts of the *Psalmes* yield little information about the identity of their contemporary owners and scribes. Only MSS *I* and *K* can be traced with certainty to an early owner, Sir John Harington of Kelston (*c*.1561–1612), Pembroke's cousin,

---

[6] Sidney, *Poems*, 501.

[7] Michael G. Brennan, 'The Date of the Countess of Pembroke's Translation of the Psalms', *RES* ns 33 (1982), 434–6.

[8] The date of *Silkewormes* is itself problematic. Katherine Duncan-Jones argues for a date late in the 1590s in 'Pyramus and Thisbe: Shakespeare's Debt to Moffett Cancelled', *RES* ns 32 (1981), 296–301, but Roger Prior has given new evidence for a date prior to 1594 in ' "Runnawayes Eyes": A Genuine Crux', *Shakespeare Quarterly* 40 (1989), 191–5.

[9] Sidney, *Poems*, 548–52; *Index of English Literary Manuscripts* (London: Mansell; New York: Bowker, 1980), I. 475–6.

whose distinctive hand can be discerned at least in MS *K*.[10] It is likely, however, that neither manuscript was prepared for him because the hands of the main text are not those of scribes known to have worked for him. MS *N* at the Sorbonne was owned by Sir Kenelm Digby (1603–65), whose signature is on f. 1, but nothing is known about how he acquired it. MS *Q* has some intriguing initials on the binding—T. M.—and the title page—W. H.—which may point to an association with Thomas Moffet (less likely, Bishop Tobie Matthew) and William Herbert, Pembroke's son, or Lord William Howard (1536–1640), but those identifications remain speculative. Dr Juel-Jensen argues that MS *J* may have entered the Tixall Library through Sir Walter Aston (1583–1639), who may have been given it by William Herbert or King James or Queen Elizabeth (to whom one of the prefatory poems is addressed).[11] Without further corroborating evidence, however, the matter remains open. MS *A*, the source of *J*, has also been thought to have been intended as a presentation copy for the queen,[12] a suggestion supported by its elaborate gilding and by the likelihood that it also originally contained the dedicatory verses to Elizabeth. On the authority of John Aubrey, it is supposed to have been in the library at Wilton at least as early as the middle of the seventeenth century. The binding of MS *E* may also suggest a royal association, for its centre motif is very similar to that of item 18, the *Works* (1616) of James I, in G. D. Hobson's *English Bindings*, which notes that 'in general lay-out, and in the treatment of the spine, the binding [of item 18] closely resembles two books which bear the arms of Anne of Denmark'.[13] Further details of the subsequent history of all the manuscripts are provided in 'Manuscripts of the *Psalmes*'.

Still less is known about the scribes who wrote the manuscripts. Only two can be certainly identified: John Davies of Hereford, who signed his work at the end of the Penshurst manuscript, and Samuel Woodforde, who copied MS *B* from *β*. The hand of *J*, transcribed from *A*, does sometimes resemble Davies's hand, but they have not yet been proven identical. The hands of MSS *H* and *Q* are still closer; these copies even share (sometimes with *E*) what are for the *Psalmes*

---

[10] See above, 'Manuscripts of the *Psalmes*', n. 22.

[11] 'Note 314. The Tixall Manuscript of Sir Philip Sidney's and the Countess of Pembroke's Paraphrase of the Psalms', *The Book Collector* 18 (1969), 222–3.

[12] Sidney, *Poems*, 547.

[13] *English Bindings in the Library of J. R. Abbey* (London: Chiswick P, 1940).

manuscripts some distinctive spellings (see the description of *H* in 'Manuscripts of the *Psalmes*'). If a single scribe did write them both, he remains unidentified.

Some of the manuscripts are particularly interesting for the light they shed on scribal practices and the ways contemporary readers used their copies. For example, one of the manuscripts is clearly a hybrid, and another was intended to be one. The first of these, MS *F*, includes Psalms 1–26 in a version ultimately descended from a lost intermediary, whereas Psalms 27–150 were copied directly from MS *A*. The second is Woodforde's transcript of *β*. Because Woodforde was copying a manuscript with large lacunae, he left pages blank to be filled in later from another manuscript, noting after Psalm 87, 'But here all the leaves are torn off, to the 23 verse of the CII. Psalms, to be supplyd if possible from some other Copy, of which there is a fayre one in Trinity Colledg library in Cambridg, and of which many yeares since I had the sight when I first began my Paraphrase'.[14] He concludes his transcription with the note, 'Sam: Woodforde who for sir Philip Sidnys Sake, and to preserve such a remaine of him undertook this tiresome task of transcribing. 169$\frac{4}{5}$' (f. 131). What happened to his original is unknown.

Two manuscripts owned by Harington, *K* and *I*, show how readers adapted the poems for personal use. Both of these copies have been rubricated for devotional reading at Morning and Evening Prayer.[15] In MS *K* someone has also added verse numbers from the Prayer Book Psalter (even when the textual source of the poem is the Geneva Bible or another translation or commentary). At a few places there are marks which indicate that the verse begins within the line, not at the beginning of it. Occasionally the scribe's work has been corrected by another hand. MS *I* is an anthology containing a large number of selected Psalms, in random order (after Psalm 26), perhaps copied from more than one source. It preserves alternative renderings of several Psalms, including the only transcription of an early draft of Psalm 89, which may also have been in the folios missing from *β*, and a unique version of Psalm 113. Harington's interest in the *Psalmes* is

---

[14] Woodforde's own *Paraphrase upon the Psalms of David*, first published in 1667, mentions a Cambridge manuscript, sig. B4^v–C1.

[15] The Bodleian manuscript of Harington's own metrical paraphrase of the Psalms (MS Douce 361) has also been rubricated for devotional use. See D. H. Craig, *Sir John Harington* (Boston: Twayne, 1985), 105. On Harington's hand in the manuscripts, see 'Manuscripts of the *Psalmes*', n. 21.

also demonstrated by the three Psalms that he sent to Lucy, Countess of Bedford, along with the translation of Petrarch's '*Trionfo della Morte*' and some miscellaneous pieces (Petyt MS 538.43.14).[16]

Two other manuscripts noted by Peter Beal provide further evidence of the wide circulation of Pembroke's Psalms. A manuscript of miscellaneous prose and verse (copied in the later seventeenth century) in the library of All Souls College, Oxford, MS 155, contains Psalms 51, 104, and 137 (ff. 123–7). Psalm 137 is also written on a folded half-sheet, preserved in the Clifton Collection, MS Cl Lm 50, at the University of Nottingham. In all three cases, the text is close to that of MS *I*, which suggests a Harington source or one associated with him.[17] Another manuscript in the British Library, Additional MS 15117, contains versions of the countess's Psalms 51 and 130 set to music (the text is not clearly related to any other extant manuscript).[18]

The many instances of non-authorial intervention in the text of the manuscripts are recorded in the apparatus (which also, of course, records variants that cannot always be classified with assurance as authorial revision or non-authorial intervention). Whether the changes were made independently by scribes (as unnoticed errors, as means of covering errors thus silently acknowledged, or as emendations) or at the direction of readers who, perhaps like Harington, had taken a proprietary or editorial interest in the manuscripts is not always clear. The rhymed versions of Psalms 120–7 in MSS *G* and *M* to be discussed fully below are, if indeed they are not authorial,

[16] According to Beal, Hr 25, this Petyt manuscript is probably only a copy of what Harington sent to the Countess of Bedford; it is neither in his hand nor in the hands of the scribes known to have worked for him.

[17] Beal, I. 466. MSS *O* and *D* (which derive from a lost intermediary, *θ*) contain similar versions of these three Psalms. The following are significant points of agreement among MSS *I*, *O*, and *D* and the Petyt, Nottingham, and All Souls manuscripts: Psalm 137. 21 'yea' ('and' in *A*), 23 'in mee doe' ('with in me' *A*), 25 'wilt' ('shalt' *A*), 32 'flatt plaine' ('flat, plaine' *I*; 'platt pais' *A*), 36 'to others' ('unto us' *A*), 38 'make' ('cause' *A*). *θ* is further distinguished by lacking the following variants common to the other four manuscripts: 17 'be' ('ly' *A*), 37 'miseries' ('bitternes' *A*). Unique variants in all six manuscripts prove that none of them was the source from which the others were copied and that they all derive from at least one more lost intermediary. A full collation of Psalms 51 and 104 leads to the same conclusions. For a description of All Souls College, Oxford, MS 155, see *The Poems of Sir John Davies*, ed. Robert Krueger (Oxford: Oxford UP, 1975), 445–6.

[18] David Greer includes a transcription of the setting of Psalm 51 in *Songs from Manuscript Sources, Volume 1* (London: Stainer and Bell; New York: Galaxy Music Corp., 1979), 12–15. Greer notes (p. 31) that the music is attributed to Anthony Holborne by Brian Jeffrey in *Musica Disciplina*, xxii (1968), 174, but adds that it is not found in editions of Holborne's works.

the most extensive examples. A more concise and admittedly extreme
set of variants in the constantly fascinating MS *I* probably also shows
the effects of a reader creating his own text as he reads. Twice *I*
replaces the word 'daunce' which Pembroke has added to the biblical
text. At Psalm 51. 28, *I* has 'leave' for 'daunce' in the speaker's joyful
assurance of the forgiveness of sin:

> make over me thie mercies streames to flow,
> Soe shall my whitnes scorne the whitest snow.
> > to eare and hart send soundes and thoughts of gladdnes,
> > that brused bones maie daunce awaie their saddnes. (25–8)

At Psalm 75. 12, *I* substitutes 'glaunce' for 'daunce' in a passage
rebuking the ungodly:

> bragg not you braggardes, you your saucy horne
> lift not lewd mates: no more with heav'ns scorne,
> > daunce on in wordes your old repyning measure. (10–12)

That both changes are non-authorial is indicated by their ill-fitting
intrusion into the text and also by their uniqueness (although the
lack of corroboration in other manuscripts is by itself insufficient evidence, given the existence of numerous variant poems in MS *B* especially). The motive for the alteration was probably to some extent
doctrinal. The person responsible for it was likely troubled by the
presence of an apparently secular image in a scriptural context, even
though in Psalm 75 it is not the godly who are depicted as engaging
in such frivolous activity. (At Psalm 96. 36, 'daunce' is allowed to
stand in *I* in a passage describing the joy of the natural world in
God's presence, but the repetition, 'ô daunce', in the same line is
replaced by 'advance'.) Additional examples of variants that probably
did not result from Pembroke's own revision are cited in the next
section.

Manuscript Transmission

Because the early provenance of the manuscripts is obscure, study of
their relationship depends on textual evidence. Comparison of the
Penshurst manuscript (MS *A*) with the other manuscripts reveals a
gradual deterioration of the text, sometimes because of careless
scribes, but also, particularly in *G* and *M*, because of apparent 'tinker-
ing' by someone other than the author. A full collation confirms that
the work of Ringler and Rathmell is correct in the broad outlines they

drew of the relationship of the manuscripts. There are two main groups, β and χ, and a third, δ, that links them to some extent.[19] There are also various subgroups.

We retain the traditional sigla for extant MSS. The sigla of MSS *A* through *I* were assigned by Albert Feuillerat;[20] additional manuscripts have been labelled in sequence as discovered or newly reported by Ringler, Rathmell, Seronsy, Waller, and Beal. To avoid confusion, we have used Greek letters for conjectural manuscripts, replacing the Roman capitals used by Feuillerat and others.

All of the manuscripts descend ultimately from one of the countess's own working copies, here designated β (Ringler and Rathmell's B^0), which was revised on at least three separate occasions. Although the multilayered β is now lost, Woodforde's transcript of it, *B*, provides an early (as well as later) record of the text, for it preserves the original endings and other elements of some of the first forty-three Psalms which were subsequently revised (and which thus appear only in revised form in the later copies). *B* also contains several early drafts of Pembroke's own paraphrases (whole alternative poems), as well as numerous words, phrases, and lines which were, as Woodforde continually notes, 'expunged' and altered directly in the manuscript or replaced by other revisions in later copies (and not recorded in β or at least missing by 1694).

As Ringler and Rathmell conjectured, another working copy must have been prepared, perhaps for use at one of the countess's other residences. This lost manuscript, which we call χ (Ringler and Rathmell's X), probably descends from β after an early point in the revision process (β^1), for all the copies that derive from it lack not only many of Philip Sidney's original lines, but also nearly all of Pembroke's own early drafts as preserved in *B*.

Yet a third important lost copy, δ, was first conjectured by Rathmell (who called it Z) to account for the similarities of the three extant manuscripts which are related to both the β and χ traditions and which represent an intermediate stage in the transmission of the text from the former to the latter of those lost working copies. The diagram is a hypothetical reconstruction of the stemma (explained more fully below). Additional evidence to support the reconstruction

---

[19] Following Ringler in Sidney, *Poems*, 502, we use superscript numbers with lost intermediaries to indicate stages of revision. Whether a particular stage existed as a separate manuscript is not clear.

[20] In vol. III of his edition of Philip Sidney's *Complete Works* (Cambridge, 1923), 408–10.

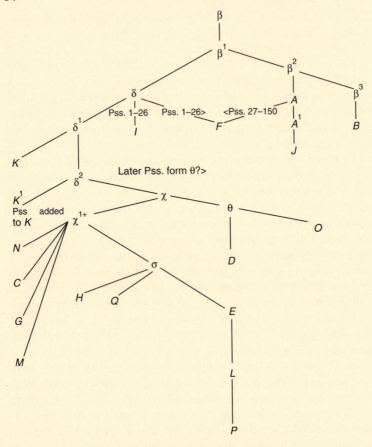

The Stemma of the Sidney *Psalmes*
Philip Sidney's Psalms 1–43/Mary Sidney Herbert's Psalmes 44–150

is provided in the details of the apparatus and in the descriptions of the manuscripts above.

The *beta* (β) and *delta* (δ) Traditions

The β group is the one over which Pembroke seems to have exerted the most direct control. It is represented by the extant MSS *B*, *A*, *F* (Pss. 27–150), and *J*. The second of these, *A*, was copied from β² by John Davies of Hereford (*c*.1565–1618). Proud of his splendid transcription in the Italian style with gilding, Davies signed his

work 'John Davies of the Citty | of Hereford hand-writer hereof'
(f. 135).

Ringler and Rathmell knew of the close relationship of *A* with *J* and
the later Psalms in *F*, but it is now also clear that *J* was copied after
F.[21] Close study of the various stages in the transcribing of *A* clarifies
the sequence. Most of the initial capital letters in *A* are gilded, but
when the gold was being added (after the writing of the main text)
some of the letters were inadvertently omitted. At a few places *A*, *F*,
and *J* are all similarly defective (e.g. 58. 5 and 131. 6 where the vocative 'O' is missing). At other places, *F* lacks a letter, which is in *J*
because it was added to *A* in ink, not gold, apparently by the *J* scribe
(see, for example, the whole of Pss. 132 and 144). The *J* hand seems to
be discernible in lines that were added to *A*: 16. 37–42, 55. 61–72, and
59. 53–90. (Davies may have written both *A* and *J*, in spite of slight
differences in the hands, but he is identified as the scribe only in the
former.) *J* has special value because it preserves two long preliminary
poems and the first three Psalms, all of which are lacking in *A*, from
which at least three folios are missing at the front.

While the greater part of *F* descends ultimately from β, the first
twenty-six Psalms apparently come from δ, which represents a preliminary stage to the χ tradition. The existence of this conjectural
manuscript is suggested by the agreement of *F* with *K* and *I* at a
place like 16. 37–42, the revised final stanza, which all three manuscripts lack. The correspondence of *F* and *I* is so strong (with more
than fifty points of correspondence) as to suggest that δ was revised
and corrected before the transcription of *K*. (Ringler and Rathmell
account for the correspondence by means of the conjectured intermediary *Y*, but the differences can also be explained as the result of
revisions and corrections in δ.) The early state of *I* and *F* (1–26) is
indicated partly by their omission of 'own' at 4. 34. It appears in all
the other manuscripts (including *K*), but it was at first also missing
in β for Woodforde notes that it is 'added above the line by another
hand'.

δ seems to have been a partial draft at this point. Such a condition,
not unexpected in an intermediate copy, would account for the hybrid
nature of *F*, the incomplete state of *I* (really a miscellany containing
only Psalms 1–26 and a selection of other Psalms in random order),

[21] Noel J. Kinnamon, 'The Sidney Psalms: The Penshurst and Tixall Manuscripts',
English Manuscript Studies 2 (1990), 139–61.

and a further peculiar feature of *K*, which was transcribed in two
stages. In any case, *F* was completed from *A*, and the rest of the
eccentric *I* may have come from a further state of δ or it may have
been drawn from a variety of sources. *K*, however, seems to have
been copied from δ after a revision ($δ^1$) and then on a second occasion
after δ was completed ($δ^2$). Such a possibility is suggested by the fact
that twenty miscellaneous Psalms were added to *K* in blank spaces
clearly left for them (most noticeably in the case of Psalm 119). It
may be significant that nearly all of the added Psalms are the ones
lacking in *I*; the only exception is Psalm 113, which *I* preserves in a
unique version.[22]

The *chi* (χ) Tradition

The existence of χ is proved by the agreement of the eleven remaining manuscripts at more than thirty points in Psalms 44–150 against
those in the β and δ groups. There are four main subgroups of χ
manuscripts, and one of those may be further subdivided: *O* and *D*;
N and *C* (which are more loosely connected); *H*, *Q*, *E*, *L*, and *P*,
descended from the hypothetical σ; and *G* and *M*. All of these
manuscripts seem to descend from successive states of the same exemplar, that is, χ and subsequent revisions of it ($χ^{1+}$), occasionally
through lost intermediaries. (It is also possible, however, that *N* and
C descend from a separate intermediary, and *G* and *M* from yet
another.)

---

[22] *I* and *K* may have been copied (perhaps indirectly in the case of *I*) from the same
working draft (δ), which either lacked some Psalms (i.e. those missing in *I* and added in
K) or contained early drafts of those Psalms with notes to scribes indicating that the drafts
were not ready for transcription. They were still missing or not ready when *I* was copied and
when the first set of Psalms was copied in *K*. When they were completed, they were given to
the scribe of *K* (either on separate sheets or in their proper places in δ), who added them in
spaces that had been left for them in *K*. The variant status of Psalm 113 in *I* seems to
confirm that the other Psalms in question were also either not in final form or not yet composed in an early state of δ. The random ordering of the later Psalms in *I* also suggests that
Psalm 113 was transcribed from a working copy or from loose sheets. Further evidence that
I and *K* were transcribed from a working copy is that one or the other or both manuscripts
contain variant incipits to Psalms 62, 69, 76, 80, 85, and 91 (see textual notes) taken from the
interpretationes ('translations') by Heinrich Moller (1530–89) included along with Bèze's
freer *paraphrases* and *carmina* in his *Paraphrasis*, but not translated by Anthony Gilby in
his English version, *The Psalmes of David*. See Noel J. Kinnamon, 'God's "Scholer": The
Countess of Pembroke's *Psalmes* and Beza's *Psalmorum Davidis . . . Libri Quinque*', *N&Q* 44
(1997), 85–8. At some point the variant incipits (some of them also present in certain χ
manuscripts, cited in the textual notes) were 'corrected' to conform to the more familiar
Vulgate wording.

At first glance *D* seems to have been copied from *O*, as Cecil Seronsy suggests.[23] In the countess's Psalms alone, they share not only
more than thirty otherwise unique readings, but also some major
omissions, most notably 119G. 13–25 (a passage which is not lacking
in *K* or the other χ copies). On the other hand, the variants in these
two very similar manuscripts show that neither could have been copied from the other: *O* has additional omissions at 55. 25, 69. 12, 98. 4,
115. 20, 124. 4 and so on; *D* lacks 45. 53 and 59. 85–90, as well as the
whole of Psalms 1–16. The correspondences between them suggest,
rather, that they descend from the intermediary, *θ*.

The beginning of χ as a separate working copy at this point is indicated by a number of details. All eleven manuscripts after *K* share
more than twenty distinctive readings. They also contain lines 37–
44 of Psalm 16, which were missing in *δ*. They all have the erroneous
omission of 'now' in 88. 22 and of the repeated 'most' as well as 'my'
in 102. 5. A few other shared alternative readings are also demon-
strable errors: e.g. 'doth' for 'do', 73. 27; 'dusky' for 'dusty', 77. 89;
'his' for 'this', 78. 165 ('t' was added later in *D*); 'turnless' for 'tearmlesse', 89. 96; 'them ill' for 'their ill', 94. 45. Such errors suggest the
work of a scribe preparing a new transcript of what, by that time, must
have become a heavily marked working copy (some state of *δ*).

From here on, however, the precise nature of the development of
the χ text is often perplexing, for the subgroups and individual manuscripts within them are connected to one another in complicated,
overlapping ways. *N* and *C* are obviously related through single-
word and whole-line variants, and *N* bears some resemblance to the
σ group (for example, through its title and the incipits of the various
sections of Psalm 119),[24] while *C* still more closely resembles *G* and
M. And yet *G* and *M* relate to the *σ* group in ways that *C* does not.

One way to account for the apparent anomalies in these later manuscripts is to try to imagine how χ (like *δ* before it) must have appeared
when copyists sat down to transcribe it. If it looked anything like *β* as
preserved in *B* (and χ, too, must have been cluttered, since it also
seems to have been frequently copied from and altered), the scribes
must sometimes have been confronted with a bewildering set of

---

[23] Cecil C. Seronsy, 'Another Huntington Manuscript of the Sidney Psalms', *HLQ* 29
(1965–6), 109–16.

[24] The incipits seem to have been supplied on separate sheets to the copyists of *N* and *σ*,
but lost before the writing of *C*, *G*, and *M*. They were apparently added later in sometimes
cramped spaces in *H*, and they are lacking altogether in *Q*.

choices to make. Such a condition would account for what is at first most puzzling about these manuscripts: the shifting groups, with the variants showing up in new combinations. The best illustration is the table of passages cited by Ringler for Sidney's Psalms (502).[25] The same shifting pattern—which includes, however, the relative homogeneity of the σ group (and of O and D)—occurs in the later Psalms as well, although there the variants are in single words and phrases, not whole lines (except, of course, for the rhymed versions of Psalms 120–7 and the restoration of lines to Psalm 146 in G and M). Thus, both N and C retain the A readings, 'stout' and 'kneele', in 89. 27 and 95. 15, where the σ group and G, M have 'proud' and 'fall'; N and C share the unique phrases, 'To him most fearful' and 'our praise', in 76. 27 and 89. 15, in contrast to 'unto the fearefull' and 'praises' elsewhere; C has the unique reading, 'I will hould, yea', in 119F. 14, where N agrees with A ('sure I hold, will') and G, M share the phrase, 'Sure will hould, yea'; N, C, G, M all have 'voice' in 149. 15 rather than 'throat' in A and the σ group; and so on. Such regrouping, joined with the constancy and greater similarity of the members of the σ group, does suggest that manuscripts like N, C, G, M, and σ were still being copied directly from χ.

While it is not possible to state with certainty the exact chronological sequence in which the various χ copies were made, there is a discernible direction in the general development of the text so that the revisions might be numbered as χ^{1-3}. That there was a revision of χ after θ, for instance, is implied by a place like 104. 36, where I, K, O, and D have a reading expunged in β, 'stations' ('stacion' in O, D), which was corrected to 'mansions' (as in A) before the transcribing of N, C, and later copies. The nature of many other variants in N and C—substantive, obviously deliberate changes—suggests, however, that the manuscripts contain departures from the χ text which were not always recorded directly in the working copy, but were taken directly from another manuscript or were written on slips of paper subsequently lost, as Ringler suggests,[26] and apparently were never supplied to the copyists of the σ group. Certainly N and C are sometimes very different. N is generally closer to the earlier texts, and it contains alternative paraphrases of Psalms 75 (also in B, I, K) and 131 (unique to N). There is even a point where N, alone

---

[25] MS D should not be singled out in the reference to 42. 53–6; it does not contain a unique revision, but agrees with B, K, and A. See Ringler's textual note to the passage (335).
[26] Sidney, *Poems*, 503.

among all the other copies, preserves another reading that Woodforde
notes was expunged from β: at 106.37, N has the cancelled phrase,
'With scope t'experiment', rather than the clause, 'That they (forsooth) might trye', which occurs everywhere else, including C. That
N and C do share six substantive, otherwise unique variants in this
Psalm, however, implies that it may have been given to the scribes
on separate sheets or that they worked from other manuscripts. The
version given to the N scribe at least must have been copied from a
source close to β, not only because of the cancelled phrase in 37,
but also because of the phrase, 'to our good' in Psalm 106, which is
found elsewhere only in A, F, $\mathcal{J}$, and probably β (Woodforde's omission of 'good' is surely an error; K and χ have 'Unto our'). The association of C with G and M is discussed later.

The *sigma* (σ) Group

That the manuscripts in the σ group are next in the sequence is suggested by the version of Psalm 122 they contain and also by some
changes made directly in H. There are three paraphrases of Psalm
122 altogether: the original draft in quantitative verse preserved in
B and I, a revision of it contained in A, F, $\mathcal{J}$, I (which thus has both
versions), K, O, D, N, and C, and the rhymed alternative poem in G
and M. The version in the σ group, however, is the early β draft. The
reason may be that the revision was written on a separate slip of paper
which was lost from χ after the copying of N and C, but before H.
Furthermore, a few places in H have been altered to create readings
which turn up, not only in Q and E, but also in G and M. Thus,
'floweinge...flockinge' (the A reading at 88.70–1) is changed in a
similar hand in H to 'flockinge...floweinge' (the reading in Q, E,
G, M), 'Isakes' (A 105.19) becomes 'Jacob' (as in Q, E, G, M),
'roote outright' ('hate outright' in A, 'roote owt-right' in K and χ,
101.23) becomes 'roote outquight' ('roote out quite' in Q, E, G, M),
and 'Nature grounde' ('native gown' in A through K, 'Nature ground'
in χ, 148. 37) becomes 'Nature growne' (as in Q, E, G, M). Along
with the evidence of Psalm 122, the clear sequence of these alterations
from H through Q and E to G and M seems to indicate that both
source texts, the revised χ and σ, were altered and that the changes
were then transferred to H (or that changes made in H were transferred to them).

The large quantity and complex nature of the variants in the σ
group of manuscripts has led to more than one attempt to describe

their relationship.[27] It now seems probable that *H* and *Q* were copied directly from the same exemplar, perhaps by a single scribe; not only are the hands nearly identical, but there are many similarly distinctive spellings (especially, consistently doubled letters as in 'thuss', 'hollines', 'yeet' for 'yet', and 'ytt' for 'it', and also a peculiar use of the hyphen as in 'de-sent', 'Lea-vie', 'dismay-ed', and 'ruin-s'). *E* may have been copied from the same source, but it may also have been copied from *H* because certain unusual spellings, ambiguously formed letters, and other peculiarities in the latter may have led to some scribal errors in the former. Certainly such conditions explain the relationship of *E* to the other manuscripts in this subgroup,[28] for it is precisely the errors and occasionally careless handwriting of *E* that show that it was the direct source of *L*, which was even more clearly the source of *P*, an early eighteenth-century transcript recently reported anew by Peter Beal.[29]

Manuscripts *G* and *M*

The remaining manuscripts, *G* and *M*, are among the most interesting of all because, while they contain their share of the usual scribal errors, their texts have been extensively reworked in ways that imply conscious effort. The most noticeable feature of these copies is their rhymed versions of Psalms 120–7 which were composed to replace the quantitative experiments in the other manuscripts. Gary Waller suggests that 'these neo-classical experiments' in quantitative verse were replaced because of Samuel Daniel's 1603 *Defence of Rhyme*.[30] *G* and *M* also contain expansions of the third and sixth lines of Psalm 23 (which are changed from dimeters to trimeters), new stanzas for a few other Psalms, and many smaller, deliberate alterations. They even restore from the β tradition seven lines of Psalm 146 (10–16) which had been missing since the preparation of δ (or at least since the transcription of *K* which is the first extant manuscript to lack the passage; the Psalm is lacking altogether in *I*). Even so, *G* and *M* are far from perfect and are considerably less reliable than the Penshurst manuscript.

[27] See the proposed stemmata in Rathmell (Ph.D. diss.), 357; and Sidney, Mary. *Triumph*, 220, also in Waller's 'The Text and the Manuscript Variants of the Countess of Pembroke's Psalms', *RES* ns 25 (1975), 3; and Waller, *Mary Sidney*, 286.

[28] Noel J. Kinnamon, 'The Text of the Peniarth Manuscript of the Sidneian Psalms', *National Library of Wales Journal* 28 (1993–4), 279–84.

[29] *Index*, SiP 82.

[30] Waller, *Mary Sidney*, 176–7.

More important is the question of the source and character of the extensive variants in *G* and *M*, as well as *C*, for they may not be authorial. *G* and *M*, especially the latter, are related to *C* through numerous common variants. Perhaps the most intriguing link, however, is in the title pages of the three manuscripts. *G* and *M* read thus: 'The Psalmes of David metaphrased into sundry kindes of verse, By the noble and famous gentleman: Sir Philip Sidney Knight' (*G*); 'The Psalmes of David metaphrased into verse by the noble, learned, and famous gentleman Sir Philip Sidney Knight' (*M*). Both titles seem to be based on the first part of the title as preserved in *C*: 'The Psalmes of David translated into divers and sundry kindes of verse, more rare, and excellent, for the method and varietie then ever yet hath bene don in English: begun by the noble and learned gentleman Sir Philip Sidney Knight . . .'. But *C* then adds the following important statement: 'and finished by the Right honnorable the Countesse of Pembroke, his Sister, and by her dirrection and appointment'. The final phrase is a clear acknowledgment that, while Pembroke may, in some sense, have authorized the changes recorded in *C*, she did not necessarily make them herself. In view of the close association of *C* with *G* and *M*, it seems reasonable to speculate that the extensive changes to the text in those two manuscripts may also be non-authorial.

Most of the substantive variations in single words and phrases in *G* and *M* and sometimes *C* are stylistic in nature, but not characteristic of Pembroke's poetic practices or scholarly revisions elsewhere. Often the motive was to eliminate the skilfully varied repetition that is a prominent feature of her paraphrases. At other times, her appropriation of unusual but, in context, evocative biblical thought and language is replaced by more conventional diction and phrasing. The overall effect is the opposite of what one notices in the revisions that seem to be her own. In those cases there is often evidence that the biblical texts or commentaries have been consulted anew and the result is usually greater strength and clarity of expression than in the earlier drafts (see e.g. 44. 45–8, 46. 10, 58. 1–4, 76. 1).

Some of the deliberate changes in *G* and *M*, however, seem to have been made because of a misreading of the exemplar or because of a scribal error in it, but not in the β (or earlier χ) text (e.g. 61. 21, 23; 75. 5; 79. 3; 95. 25; 143. 18). On the two or three occasions where *G* and *M* do seem to return to the biblical text, it is likely that a familiar passage has been recalled from memory. At 51. 33, 'ah! cast me not from thee' (*A*), both manuscripts replace 'from thee' with the quoted phrase, 'not away' (v. 11), the translation of this well-known Penitential Psalm in both the Geneva Bible and the Prayer Book Psalter. When *G* and *M* replace 'side' with 'hand' in 45. 35, they again agree with the biblical text, but also reveal ignorance of the probable source of the original word in Marot's paraphrase in *Psaumes*: '*à ton costé*'.

Evidence of the effort to purge the poems of figures of repetition is not hard to find in *G*, *M*, and, though to a less degree, *C*. Thus, 'god ... god' (*A* 54. 7–8) is replaced by 'God ... lord' (*C*, *M*); 'praise, praise' (*A* 66. 61) by 'O praise' (*G*, *M*); 'come come' (*A* 69. 55) by 'Lord come' (*M*); 'thee, thee' (*A* 73. 74) by 'O God' (*M*) and 'my God' (*C*); 'god, the god' (*A* 85. 12) by 'Thou the God' (*G*, *M*); 'he he' (*A* 108. 40) by 'Even he' (*M*); and so on.

Dissatisfaction with the metaphorical language in the paraphrases is reflected in the change in *G* and *M* at 65. 23–4. Pembroke wrote, 'When stormy uproares tosse the peoples brayn | that civill sea to calme thou bringst agayn' (*A*). But *G* and *M* substitute a new couplet that dispenses with the poet's image of the 'civill sea': 'The raging *Sea*, to calme thou bringst againe | And tumults which disturb the peoples braine'.

The various sections of Psalm 119 provide examples of more directly biblical or biblically based metaphors that are altered in *G* and *M*. The Psalmist often speaks there of walking in the way of right-eousness, and Pembroke accommodates the imagery, as at 119A. 1–2: 'An undefiled course who leadeth, | and in Jehovas doctrine treadeth, | how blessed he?' But *G* and *M*, perhaps because of a lack of aware-ness that 'course' paraphrases 'way', replace it with the conventional substitute, 'life'. Similar examples are at 119A. 7 (*M*) and 119D. 28 (*G*, *M*). The opposite occurs at 119L. 8, where *G* and *M* substitute 'waie' for 'wine', which is part of the author's elaboration of the image of a 'smoked bottle' (v. 83). This preference for the more ordinary word or phrase can be detected in other kinds of alterations such as 'am' (*C*) for 'stand' (*A* 56. 36), 'pursue' (*C*, *M*) for 'ensue' (*A* 70. 15), 'promise' (*G*, *M*) for 'biddings' (*A* 71. 11), 'is' (*G*, *M*) for 'stands' (*A* 95. 11), 'pleasant songes' (*M*) for 'mery shout' (*A* 100. 2), 'verie' (*G*) for 'gaping' (*A* 106. 44), 'woefull' (*C*) for 'waylfull' (*A* 106. 107), 'Accord' (*C*) and 'Joine you' (*G*, *M*) for 'be prest' (*A* 118. 10), 'life' (*G*, *M*) for 'time' (*A* 119F. 16), 'Netts' (*M*) for 'toiles' (*A* 142. 8).

Rhymed Versions of 120–7

The most important implication of these questionable alterations is that the authenticity of the rhymed versions of Psalms 120–7 may be open to doubt. But that is less surprising when one considers the difference in style between those poems and the rest of the *Psalmes* which can, with more certainty, be attributed to Pembroke, for her verse, including the independent preliminary poems in *J*, is more vigorous and rhetorically amplified than the simple, straightforward new paraphrases of *G* and *M*.

The countess's normal pattern of composition, as preserved in Woodforde's transcription, was to begin with a fairly straightforward paraphrase of the biblical text. Her revisions reveal close study of her Genevan sources, as well as greater sophistication in rhyme, metre, metaphor, and phrasing. (See 'Methods of Composition and Translation'.) Psalms 120–7 reverse this pattern. There is little evidence that the Geneva text and Bèze's commentary were consulted during the composition of the new, rhymed Psalms, which are based on the Prayer Book Psalter (perhaps at some points on the 1611 translation, as well, such as 'distresse' 120. 1, 'the thrones of . . . David' 122. 20, 'let us goe' 122. 5, 'And late sittes up' 127. 6). The quantitative versions are far closer to her usual Continental sources. For example, the earlier version of Psalm 121, line 5, 'March, march, lustily on', comes from Marot's '*Marcher*'. She also chose to follow Bèze's interpretation of Psalm 121, with the journey of exile, whereas the revision removes the idea of the journey. The idea of God's 'saving shadow' and explanations of what the sun and moon could do to harm them, both taken from Bèze, are removed in revision. 'Gulphes' is also from Calvin, 'howe deepe a gulf', and 'furious' comes from Marot, '*la fureur*'. All are removed in the variant. Even simple words are revised away from the Genevan sources, as the 'mountains' of Bèze and Geneva become 'hilles'.

Her typical compound words and neologisms are removed as well. For example, 'well-workers' in Psalm 125 is changed to 'those that perfect bide', and 'sunn-burnt regions' in Psalm 126 becomes 'Desarts'. In Psalm 121 'redoubt no falling' becomes the conventional 'from slipp shall staie'. The description of the deceiver 'whose wryed footing not aright directed | wandreth in error' in Psalm 125 becomes the clichéd those 'who backward slide'. 'Business' in Psalm 126 is an original choice for 'harvest', whereas the variant uses the familiar word 'sheaves' from the Prayer Book.

Other strong words removed from the original versions are also of interest. Psalm 125, for example, uses the verbs 'braveth', 'enforted', and 'closeth'; these vigorous words were replaced by 'encompasseth', 'stand', and 'is'. The 'angry gulphes' of Psalm 124 become the innocuous 'waters'. The metaphoric power of the phrase 'Though Tirantes hard yoke with a heavy pressure | wring the just shoulders' in Psalm 125 is completely eliminated, becoming merely 'the scourge ungodly men deserve'.

The removal of repetition, noted in other revisions in *G* and *M*, is coupled here with the addition of redundancy, an interesting juxtaposition. The uninspired revision of Psalm 124, for example, replaces the skilful repetition of 'had drownd us: soe drowne us', with 'the waters on us had prevail'd'. Yet this revision includes the empty doublet 'made and wrought' in line 20.

Alliteration, so typical of the countess's style, is also reduced. For example, in Psalm 121, God's 'saving shadow' which protects from 'present perrill' is completely removed. In Psalm 124, the enemies 'soe fell, soe furious' become merely 'wrathfull'.

In all these ways the revisions in the rhymed versions of Psalm 120–7 reverse the countess's usual process of composition. If *G* and *M* are correctly dated as after 1611, then they are probably not authorial.

Copy-Text

While *G* and *M* are interesting as the record of at least one reader's responses and do seem in one sense to represent the final stage in the developing textual history of the Sidneian *Psalmes*, they do not necessarily represent a reliable final state of the text as the author herself left it. The rhymed versions of Psalms 120–7 are questionable, and the majority of the smaller variants, which do not fit the wider contexts of lines and stanzas, are the result of scribal error or sophistication. Rathmell was right, then, to choose *A* as the basis of his edition. *B* is incomplete and marred by many of Woodforde's own slips, although it is still crucial for reconstructing Philip Sidney's Psalms 1–43. *K* already shows deterioration from the β text and adds more errors, as do *O* and *D*. The miscellany, *I*, can have no serious claim to authority, except in its few variant poems. *N* contains a large number of errors or gratuitous emendations, and the percentage of errors rises steadily from *H* and *Q* through the rest of the *H* subgroup (*L* and *P* can, of course, be wholly disregarded). *C*, *G*, and *M*, while freer of careless errors than some other χ manuscripts, remain doubtful as records of the poet's own work. As for *F* and *J*, not only were they copied from *A*, but they also sometimes misrepresent their original.

On the other hand, the Penshurst text has everything to recommend it. It was probably prepared more directly under the guidance of the author than were any later manuscripts. We know that Davies, the copyist, was regularly employed by her, and study of the text shows that he did his work with care. The very appearance of the poem on the page sometimes authenticates *A*. For example, the even stanzas of Psalm 79 are indented farther to the right because they are written in a slightly different metre.[31] Davies is also fairly scrupulous in indicating contractions when the metre requires them. And while *A* is not flawless, it is demonstrably the most reliable of all the copies, so reliable that some previously proposed emendations may be rejected (although a few others may be necessary). Unlike most of the other copies, it may even be dated with some assurance or at least given a *terminus ad quem* because of the date '1599' in its descendant, *J*, at the end of the dedicatory poem to Queen Elizabeth (which may originally have been included in *A* as well). For all these reasons, we have followed Rathmell in adopting *A* as our copy-text. However, in order to establish and preserve the social history of the manuscripts, we have also included in this edition the texts of variant poems (even when probably non-authorial) and provided in the textual notes a detailed report of other manuscript witnesses. Our intention is thus to offer an edition of the Sidney *Psalmes* that is equally useful to readers seeking the authorial version and to those interested in the contemporary reception of the poems.

[31] At two places *A* has a significant lack of indentation. Like most other manuscripts, *A* has no indentation for the alphabetical Psalm 111, a formal imitation of the Hebrew original in which each line begins with a sequential capital letter (gilt in *A*). The lack of indentation in Psalm 117 emphasizes the acrostic formed by the spaced initial letters 'PRAISTHE-LORD', a feature found otherwise only in *F*, *J*, *D*, and *B* (which has a variant paraphrase). While most manuscripts divide Psalm 150 into an octave and sestet, *A* divides it, according to the rhyme scheme, into two quatrains and a sestet.

Although the evidence is inconclusive, the revisions of Philip Sidney's Psalms involving two lines or more seem generally to fit the pattern of revision in Pembroke's Psalms. Many of the variants in *A* (usually also in *B*), especially the new final stanzas composed to replace the partial stanzas of Psalms 1, 16, 22, 23, 26, 29, and 31, reveal some similarity to the *A* versions of earlier drafts of Pembroke's Psalms preserved in *B*. Alternative passages in *G*, *M*, and sometimes *C*, however, resemble more the rhymed Psalms 120 to 127 and other less extensive variants. (Ringler prints most of the relevant passages in his apparatus.[1])

Most of the β and χ revisions represent condensation rather than expansion of Sidney's text. For example, in *A* the five concluding lines of Philip's paraphrase of Psalm 31 are reduced to two. The opposite procedure was used for the same passage in *G* and *M*: in their distinct versions, the three final lines of the original swell to six. On the other hand, the expanded χ version of the last three lines of Philip Sidney's Psalm 26 reads like an intermediate attempt at replacing the partial stanza, which was later condensed for *A*.

The revisions in *A* also reveal the use of sources other than the Prayer Book Psalter. The opening of the new final stanza of Psalm 1 preserved only in *J*, 'Not soe the wicked', is adapted from the Geneva Bible: 'The wicked *are* not so'. The phrase, 'one age shall to another send', in the final lines of Psalm 22 comes from Bèze's paraphrase: 'from age to age'. The switch to direct address at the end of Psalm 23 may also be indebted to Bèze ('. . . to dwell in thy house all the dayes of my life'), although the Prayer Book Psalter has the second person in the first half of the verse ('But thy loving-kindness . . .'). The rhyme word 'gifts' in the revised final stanza of Psalm 26 prob-

---

[1] In addition to the revised partial stanzas, see Psalms 22. 7–8 (the C lines are also in *N*; *M*, in *G*), 27. 33–4, 31. 58–9 (in *G*, as well as *M*), 32. 10–11, 42. 53–6. Ringler notes, but does not print, variant lines in Psalms 23 and 25; he ignores Psalm 27. 25–30 in *G*. Most of these last instances are discussed below. The following are variant lines in Psalm 25 not printed elsewhere: vv. 15–16, 'the God who still provides | to succour mee from smarte' (*C*); 11, 'Lorde unto me thy wayes now showe' (*G*, *M*; *C* has 'still' for 'do' in *B*); 47–8, 'O who doth feare this God of might | He shall him teach his waies aright' (*C*; the use of 'shall' suggests that this variant is based on the Prayer Book Psalter, which is otherwise identical with Geneva).

ably came from the Prayer Book Psalter (although Bèze's *carmen* has 'dona'), but 'publique place' was suggested by Bèze ('publique congregations'), as was 'on plaine ground' ('*in via plana*' in the *interpretatio*) and 'Jehova' (in all three Latin texts). The expanded version of the passage in χ was influenced by the Geneva note, 'I am preserved . . . by the power of God', or by Bèze, 'that I do stand upright in the way, I doe attribute to thee, O Lorde'.

The variant revisions in MSS *G*, *C*, and *M*, however, are distinguished by the apparent use of a different source (the Authorized Version of 1611) and by a different method of paraphrase. There is one unique correspondence of a *G* variant and Bèze—'confidence' in the expanded final lines of Psalm 31—but that may be the exception that proves the rule ('hope' in *A* parallels the same place in Bèze). 'Want' (3) and 'o'reflowd' (21) among the *G* and *M* variants of Psalm 23 correspond to the biblical text as translated in both Geneva and the Authorized Version. The evidence of the rhymed Psalms 120 to 127 suggests, however, that the source was probably the latter, which is not used in the other *Psalmes* manuscripts. 'Praise' in the final lines of Psalm 42 in *C* and *G* also suggests the use of the Authorized Version.

The types of paraphrase used in the variants in *G* and *M* (sometimes *C*, more rarely *N* and the *H* group) not related to the partial final stanzas are also characteristic of the texts at other places in those manuscripts. The dimeters in the third and sixth lines of Psalm 23 are expanded to trimeters, mainly with pleonasms ('onely' 6; 'owne' 9; 'any' 12; 'Allwaye' 15; 'With griefe' 18; 'ever' in *G*, 'allwayes' in *M*, 24; '*heavenly*' in *G*, 'sacred' in *M*, 27). As in other places in *G* and *M*, some lines were changed to remove repetition:

Psalm 25. 71–2

    B, *A*, *K*, χ: For Thou the Lord, Thou only art

               Of whom the trust lyes [*A*, *K*, χ: lives] in my heart

    M, *G*: Lord, let not me confusion see

               Because my trust is all in thee. [*C*: The God on whome

                  depends my harte.]

Psalm 31. 58–9

    B, *A*, *K*, χ: Then prayse, then prayse I do the lord of Us

               Who was to me more than most gracious

    M, *G*: Then let me ever praise the Lord, who thus [*G*: Then

           praise for aye (my *Soule*) the lord who thus]

          Was unto me more then most gracious

The change in the *C, G, M* version of 25. 77–8 was perhaps made to remove what may have been considered the unconventional phrase, 'in fine', the equivalent of 'enfin' which appears occasionally in the Marot–Bèze Psalms (though not here):

B, A, χ: In fine [*I, F*: tyme] deliver Israël
      O Lord from all his troubles fell.

  C: Lastly, from troubles, (lord) I crave
      Let *Israell* deliverance have./

  G: And let thy *Israell*, (still increase
      From all his troubles,) live in peace/

  M: Lastly O Lord, let *Israel*
      In rest from all his troubles dwell./

The multiple revisions of the end of Psalm 42 in *N* and the *H* group, *C, G,* and *M* all remove the same phrase. Preference for more conventional diction may have led to the variant line 23 in the *M* version of Psalm 25, where the *B* text, 'Let those things Thy remembrance grave', is replaced by 'Let thy remembrance them ingrave'. The countess herself uses the apheretic form 'grave' in the first line of both versions of octave G of Psalm 119.

Two other variants in Sidney's Psalms in the later manuscripts are apparently the result of attempts to cover errors in transcription. Sometime before the copying of the *H* group, *G*, and *M*, a scribe seems inadvertently to have written line 11 of Psalm 32 before line 10, a mistake he dealt with by slightly rephrasing 10 so that it could follow 11. There can be little doubt that a unique, extended variant in the *G* version of Psalm 27. 25–30 did originate as *ad hoc* scribal intervention. The *B* text begins, 'For when great griefes to me be ment | In Tabernacle His hee [*B*: I] will | Hide me ev'n closely in his Tent ...' An eye-skip must have caused the *G* scribe to reverse the last two phrases in 25, which then required a change in 27 for the sake of the new rhyme:

        For when greate griefes are meant to mee,
          In *Tabernacle* his \he/ will [he *added above caret*]
        In *Tent* of his preserve mee free
          on height of *rocky* safest hill.
            In secret place
            kept by his grace:/

The last two lines also had to be altered (with recourse to the biblical text, where both the Prayer Book Psalter and Geneva have 'in the secret place') to avoid repeating the new rhyme introduced in 25. The awkwardness of '*rocky* safest hill' alone attests to the probably impromptu nature of the passage.

On the whole, then, the revisions of Sidney's Psalms seem to fall into two main categories: those composed by Pembroke and preserved in the β tradition and those probably by another hand preserved in the later χ manuscripts. That distinction corresponds to the one between Pembroke's revision of her own Psalms and the probably non-authorial revisions found in *G* and *M*.

Commentary

Space constraints normally prevent the citation of Pembroke's sources, except to elucidate difficult passages. See 'Methods of Composition and Translation' and *Psalmes*: 'Literary Context'.

Psalm 44

A statement of God's mercy to his people in the past, a complaint that God appears to have deserted them despite their faithfulness, and an appeal for mercy in their present distress. [Variant: MS *B*.]

7 *that braunch*, i.e. 'the Pagan foe' (5). See Zim, *Psalms*, 188–9.

8 *this*, i.e. 'thie folke', the new 'braunch'. See Variant Ps. XLIV. 8.

14 *favors treasure*. Cf. Calvin (v. 4): 'the lyght of thy countenaunce' means 'the declaration of his favour'.

17–18 Pembroke adds transition, making clearer the connection between God's defence of Israel in the past and the speaker's trust that God will deliver him.

28 *that*, i.e. that sword, the means by which I might be made safe.

29 *every*. Davies is ordinarily careful to note contractions for the sake of the metre. His failure to do so here (and at a few other places) may have been a simple oversight.

39 *Loe*. 'Soe' in *K* suggests that 'See' in χ may be a scribal attempt to emend an earlier scribal error or an illegible exemplar.

44–8 Cf. Geneva (note v. 12): 'As sclaves which are solde for a low price, nether lokest thou for him that offreth moste, but takest the first chapman'.

60 *blush*. Characteristic addition where the biblical sources speak of shame. See also Pss. 50. 55, 69. 20, 88. 36, 119F. 24, 119K. 24, etc. Cf. Sidney's Pss. 34. 20 and 40. 52: 'blush for shame'. The figure appears frequently in Bèze's *carmina*.

Psalm 45

Traditionally interpreted as an epithalamium for Solomon's marriage to a young Egyptian princess, the Psalm was read by Genevan commentators as a figure for 'Christ and the Church his spouse'.

13–14 'right' here seems to have a partly moral sense, as in 22–4. Cf. Calvin (v. 5): 'whatsoever Salomon attempteth, shall have luckye successe, if hee temper his warlyke stoutnes with justice and meeknesse... Therfore a ryghtfull and even measurablenes maketh the handes of the valeant to be dreadfull'.

25–8 *thou*, i.e. the king. God's anointing is the cause of the king's properly directed love and hate. Cf. Geneva (v. 7): 'Thou lovest righteousnes, and hatest wickednes, because God, *even* thy God hathe anointed thee with the oile of gladnes above thy felowes'.

29 *Sabean*, i.e. Arabian. Cf. Ps. 72. 34n.

33 *courtlie band*, 'honourable women' (Psalter v. 9); 'honourable *wives*' (Geneva). Bèze also avoids the reference to polygamy; Calvin acknowledges it, but claims that Solomon's indulgence was contrary to the law of God. In Pembroke's version, the women are the 'maides of honor' (54), the first usage of this phrase recorded in the *OED*.

35 *side*. Cf. *Psaumes* (v. 9): '*à ton costé*'. 'Hand' in *G, M* agrees with the English sources.

36 *Ophir*. Geneva (v. 9); not in the Psalter. Often mentioned as a source of gold in the Bible; otherwise not certainly identified.

37–64 See 'Methods of Composition and Translation', I.72.

41–4 An anticipation of v. 16 (ll. 60–1), where 'breed', or children, are first alluded to in the Psalm. Cf. Geneva (v. 11): 'So shal the King have pleasure in thy beautie: for he is thy Lord, and reverence thou him'.

Psalm 46

A song of Thanksgiving, attributed in Geneva to the deliverance of Jerusalem from Sennacherib, 'or some other like sudden and marvelous deliverance by the mightie hand of God'. [Variant: MS *B*.]

18 Pembroke adds the idea of the besieged city to the biblical text, perhaps from the Geneva heading or from Calvin's identification of 'gods citie' with the Church (v. 7), thereby connecting with God's presence in the midst of the city (v. 5).

29 Cf. Geneva (v. 9): 'He maketh warres to cease unto the ends of the worlde'.

Psalm 47

A song of praise for God's mercies; Pembroke does not add an explicit Christological interpretation, as do Geneva, Bèze, etc.

3 *song of triumph*. An anticipation of vv. 3 and 5, ll. 6–8, 11–12 (see 11n.).

6 *it*, i.e. both the conditions in 8–9: it is through God's grace that nations are oppressed by our power and humbled under our feet.

9 *Jacobs honor*. Note that Pembroke does not make explicit the identification of Israel with the Church that is present in her Genevan sources.

11 *There past hee by*. Perhaps an implicit reference to the Ark of the Covenant. Bèze interprets the Psalm as David's song when the Ark was brought into Jerusalem, although he is careful to say 'this is that Jehovah, not closed up in this Arke, for he is higher then the very heavens' (v. 2).

14 A difficult line, but verbal emendation may not be necessary. Cf. Geneva (v. 7): 'For God *is* King of all the earth: sing praises *everie one* that hathe understanding'. Thus, 'you judgments sound' is probably a synecdoche for you people who have the capacity to judge, to make sound judgements.

18–19 That is, He gains great princes to befriend the folk of Abraham's God.

20 Cf. Geneva note (v. 9): 'He praises Gods highnes, for that he joyneth the great princes of the worlde, whome he calleth shields to the felowship of his Church'.

Psalm 48

A celebration of Jerusalem, God's holy city, which God protects.

1 Probably a 'translation' of 'Jehova', which is not in the English sources, but only the *paraphrasis* and *interpretatio* in Bèze. See Ps. 68. 7n. and *Psalmes*: 'Literary Context'.

5 Hypermetric in all manuscripts, including *G*, *M* with their unique variants intended to reduce repetition. The first 'Hill' is probably a scribal error, perhaps repeated from 4. See II.18.

of fairest seeing. Cf. Geneva (v. 2): 'faire in situation'.

8 Cf. Geneva (v. 2): '*it is* the joye of the whole earth'. Geneva note: 'Because the worde of salvation came thence to all them that shulde beleve'.

9–10 The revision in *A* seems intended to make God, not His palace, the source of refuge and defence. Cf. Geneva (v. 3): 'In the palaces therof God is knowen for refuge'.

13 *it*, i.e. the city. Cf. Geneva (note v. 5): 'The enemies were afraid at the sight of the Citie'.

19 *Tarshis*. Geneva (note v. 7): 'That is ... Cilicia or ... the sea called Mediterraneum'.

20 *blasts of Eurus.* Pembroke adds the classical reference for the 'East winde'. Cf. Geneva (v. 7).

21 Cf. Geneva (v. 8): 'As we have heard, so have we sene'.

24 *holds.* Psalter (v. 7): 'upholdeth'. Pembroke expands the metaphor of the city in the hands of God.

27 *both*, 'fame' and 'name' (28). Geneva (v. 10): 'O God, according unto thy Name, so is thy praise unto the worldes end'.

32 Cf. Calvin (v. 13): 'marke wel the walles theof, exalt hir Towers, that ye may make report to the generations that commeth after you'.

Psalm 49

Psalm 49 is the most heavily revised of all the paraphrases in *B*. For instance, Woodforde records four distinct alternatives for the opening of line 19. It was revised again before *A* was copied and yet again before *K* and χ. The earlier versions stay close to the biblical text, whereas the *A* version departs significantly from it, even omitting the sheep metaphor in v. 14 that was in lines 15–30 of *B*.

In the opening, the poet calls together an audience comprised of people of all social classes, and sings the Psalm with instrumental accompaniment. The theme of the Psalm is the mutability of wealth and power.

1 *heede.* 'Give eare', the Geneva reading (v. 1), may have been replaced to avoid the repetition in 5.

4 Cf. Geneva (v. 3): 'My mouth shal speake of wisdome, and the meditation of mine heart *is* of knowledge'.

6 *ridled speech.* Cf. Calvin (v. 5): 'and I will open my riddle upon the harp'. Calvin notes that 'the Hebrews' understood riddles to be 'grave sentences, bycause they most comonly are garnished with figures and borowed speeches'.

7–8 The expunged lines are more directly indebted to Geneva (v. 5): 'Wherefore shulde I feare in the evil daies, *when* iniquitie shal compasse me about, *as* at mine heles?'

9 *wealth*, i.e. goods. Cf. Geneva (v. 6): 'trust in their goods'.

11 *out-beare*, usually meaning 'sustain', but perhaps here 'prolong' as in the Geneva note (v. 6).

13–16 The difficult original version may reflect the lack of clarity in the Psalter (vv. 8–9). The revision is a logically and poetically superior free paraphrase based more on Geneva and perhaps Bèze. See 'Methods of Composition and Translation', I.71.

15 *hee*, 'death' (14).

16 *tombe.* The substitution for the biblical word, 'grave', underscores the futility of attempting to escape death by means of wealth; a glorious tomb does not prolong life. Cf. 30.

17 The first half of the line in *A* and the second half in *K*, χ are both free paraphrases of the statement that all must die.

18 *others.* Geneva (v. 10); the Geneva note is the source of the expunged 'strangers' in *B*: 'That is, not to their children, but to strangers'.

21–4 Unlike her usual sources, Pembroke renders the refrain exactly in 39–42, as does the Hebrew original.

21 *nam'd proudlie.* Cf. Geneva (note v. 11): 'labor that their name may be famous in earth'. That is, neither wealth nor fame will last. Cf. Pembroke's translation of Petrarch's famous *ubi sunt* passage in *The Triumph of Death*, 1. 79–100.

25 *peevish,* 'foolish' (*OED*, citing this line). Geneva (v. 13): 'This their waie *uttereth* their foolishnes'. The variant in *K*, χ alludes to the second half of the verse as well: '*yet* their posteritie delite in [Psalter: 'praise'] their talke'.

26 *pitt.* 'Grave' in Geneva (v. 14); 'hell' in Psalter (whence, the later note in *K*).

Carrion foode. Cf. Psalter (v. 14): 'death gnaweth upon them'. Pembroke omits the comparison in this verse, 'Like sheepe thei lie in grave' (Geneva v. 14) and the promising metaphor of death as shepherd (Psalter v. 14).

29 *farr his prince,* 'far above his lord' (Rathmell) once the lord has died.

34 *glories seede.* Geneva (v. 16): 'the glorie of his house'.

35 Revision was needed because of the extra syllable in the original line.

37–43 Revised as part of the general plan to remove all partial or extended stanzas from the metrical Psalter. Cf. note on Variant Ps. XLVI. 41–4.

39 *must.* 'Shall' in *B, K*, χ is the biblical verb (Geneva v. 19): 'He shal enter into [Psalter: 'follow'] the generacion of his fathers'.

39–42 Psalter (v. 20): 'Man being in honour hath no understanding: but is compared unto the beasts that perish'. Geneva: 'Man *is* in honour, and understandeth not'. Cf. lines 21–4, virtually repeated here.

Psalm 50

Bèze explains in his Argument that the Psalm, concerning 'the abuse of the outward worship' appointed by God himself, is particularly 'necessarie for this our time' because Sacraments become idols 'by taking way the difference of the signes and the thinges signified'. Salvation comes by faith, not by works, and the appropriate sacrifice is praise. Cf. Psalm 51. [Variant: MS *B.*]

2 *uttermost confines.* Cf. Geneva (v. 1): 'and called the earth from the rising up of the sunne unto the going downe thereof'.

3 *pursevant,* 'messenger', perhaps also in this context 'warrant-officer' (*OED*). A courtly image added by the countess. Cf. 'garde' and 'usshers', l. 6.

his worde. Pembroke's rendering of the biblical 'hath spoken' (v. 1) connects the giving of the law and the coming of Christ, the word as Logos. John 1: 1. See *Psalmes*: 'Literary Context', II.20.

4 That is, God shines out of beauty's beauty, Sion. Cf. Geneva (v. 2): 'Out of Zion, *which* is the perfection of beautie, hathe God shined'.

5 Cf. Bèze (v. 3): 'Beholde I say that same our God commeth and will be, no longer dumbe...that hee may shewe himself such one now in declaring the meaning of the law...as he declared himselfe of old'. Bèze and Geneva (note v. 3) also mention the thunder and lightning storm that accompanied the giving of the law on Mt. Sinai.

eare and tongue. Pembroke adds God listening, as in Vatablus, to God speaking, as in the biblical text.

7 *apparrance,* used as in a legal context. Heaven and earth (8) are called as 'witnesses' (Geneva note v. 4) at the appearance of the 'nations' (2), at which time they have testified, here rendered 'subsigned with their handes' (13) in written testimony, as in Vatablus.

13 *then when,* i.e. at the time when the 'eternall league' (12) was formed.

17 *me your god.* 'What I teach' in *K,* χ suggests that the decision that had to be made in revising the passage was whether to paraphrase 'I wil speake' in the first part of v. 7 or 'I am thy God, *even* thy God' in the last part.

33 *O no.* Added to emphasize God's rejection of animal sacrifice (v. 14). Cf. line 62; Ps. 51.

34 *vowed debts.* Cf. Geneva (v. 14): 'paie thy vowes'. Bèze, *paraphrasis,* '*laudes mihi debitas*'. 'Heasts' in *K,* χ may be a scribal error or sophistication.

49–50 The repetition reflects the biblical parallelism (v. 20).

57 *marking memorie.* Cf. Geneva (note v. 21): 'I will write all thy wicked dedes in a role and make thee to read and acknowledge them whether thou wilt or no'.

59 *release.* 'Releif' in the later χ tradition is exposed as a scribal error by the image in 60.

61–2 The idea of the sacrifice of praise is not explicit in v. 23 as in v. 14 (ll. 33–4), but it is emphasized at the conclusion of the Psalm by Calvin and Bèze.

61 *And know the rest.* Transition added for clarity; God turns from the wicked to 'the rest', i.e. the godly.

Psalm 51

This most familiar of the seven Penitential Psalms is usually known by its
Latin incipit, '*Miserere mei*'. (The others are 6, 32, 38, 102, 130, and 143.)
The Psalm is traditionally interpreted as David's confession after the prophet
Nathan has confronted him with his adultery with Bathsheba, an interpretation included as the first two verses of the Vulgate, '*Psalmus David, cum venit
ad eum Nathan propheta, quando intravit ad Bethsabee*'. The Bishops' Bible
(1568) retains the emphasis on 'his great offence in committyng adulterie',
as do most other English translations.

In his argument, Bèze acknowledges the special theological significance of
the Psalm: 'And there are joyned in the Psalm also two principall pointes of
true religion: the one, of Originall sinne [v. 5, ll. 15–18], the other of the
abuse of sacrifices [vv. 16–19, ll. 45–56], as though the purgation of sinne
consisted in that outwarde ceremony'. In all the Genevan versions of the
Psalm, the treatment of these central doctrines is nearly identical, emphasizing the need for contrition and for the acceptance of God's grace. See
Psalmes: 'Literary Context'. Like Psalm 130, this penitential Psalm was set
to music in BL Additional MS 15117. Psalm 51 is printed in *Songs from
Manuscript Sources* 1, ed. David Greer, *The English Lute Songs* (London:
Stainer and Bell; New York: Galaxy Music Corporation, 1979), 12–15.

1 *grace*. The emphasis on grace was present in Pembroke's sources, including the heading for the Old Version, which shows David promising 'that he
will not be unmindful, of those great graces', but it is not usually included in
the opening of the Psalm itself, except in Wyatt's opening, 'Rue on me, Lord,
for thy goodness and grace'.

2 *mercies stand*. The phrase in *A* corresponds to the biblical text (v. 1): 'the
multitude of thy mercies' (Psalter). A Geneva note stresses that David's
'manifolde' sins required 'abundant mercies'.

4 *sinnes*. Again, the plural is corroborated by the biblical sources. The
plural emphasizes David's multiple sins, not just his adultery with Bathsheba, but also his murder of her husband Uriah, emphasized in a Geneva
note. Cf. 41.

6 *still wash*. The need for repeated washings, present in Bèze and *Psaumes*, is
emphasized by Calvin and Vatablus. Pembroke's rendering connects the idea
of clean garments with clean 'registers' in 30 and with the 'spottles hart' in 31.

11 *done to thee*. The conjunction of God as offended party, judge, and witness is also present in Calvin and Bèze.

confesse. David confesses to God only, emphasizing the nature of penance
and confession from a Protestant perspective.

12 *Just, judge*. God will give a just 'doome', not the unjust doom of the civil
courts. Cf. Ps. 58 and 82. The necessity for judgement on the ruler is

acknowledged, so that all may recognize God's justice is not influenced by rank.

15–21 Calvin expounds verse 7 as 'a lightsome text for the proof of original sin, wherin Adam hath wrapped all mankynd'.

21 *hid schoole.* Cf. Geneva (v. 6): 'therefore hast thou taught me wisdome in the secret *of mine heart*'. Hunnis: 'Then secretely I shall receive | thy wyse-dome in my hart'. Pembroke's juxtaposition of the child cherished within the womb with the hid school may imply that God imparts knowledge *in utero* even though the child is stained by original sin. See 'Methods of Composition and Translation', I.72.

22–4 The use of hyssop in 'cleansing' leprosy is explained in Leviticus 14, cross-referenced in a Geneva note (v. 6). Cf. Wyatt (43–4) and Lok (Son-net 9).

30 *registers.* 'Sinns' is the object of 'containe'. Cancel the registers that con-tain my sins. Pembroke's phrase amplifies the legal metaphor implicit in Bèze (v. 9) and Parker. Cf. 'Angell Spirit', 56.

32 *love of right.* An expansion of the usual 'right spirit' (Geneva v. 10) to emphasize the will that chooses right.

33–4 *take not againe | thie breathing grace.* Psalter (v. 11): 'take not thy holy Spirit from me'. Pembroke's repeated 'againe' implies that on other occasions God had taken away His grace and then had sent comfort.

35 *free sprite.* Geneva notes (v. 12): 'Which maie assure me that I am drawen out of the sclaverie of sinne'.

37–8 The hand guiding the feet is not really a mixed metaphor, for the speaker will guide those whose 'faultie feete have wandred from thie way', a phrase derived from Calvin (v. 15), 'wanderers' from 'the way'. The speaker is a sinner who has experienced God's forgiveness and is now qualified to teach others.

40 *O god, god of my health.* A direct quotation from Lok (211), one that echoes the content of other Psalters but here connects with the healing of bruised bones and leprosy. Cf. Ps. 88. 1n. See *Psalmes*: 'Literary Context'.

41 *bloodie crime.* Geneva notes (v. 14): 'the murder of Uriiah...2. Sam. 11.17'.

43 *Unlock my lipps.* An original rendering of the usual 'open thou my lips'. God's forgiveness will enable, and entitle, the speaker to sing God's praise. Cf. Ps. 119B. 7–15.

45 *bleeding fuell.* Animal sacrifice. Cf. Bèze (v. 16): 'the bloud of beastes'.

46 *to gaine thy grace.* The Psalmist does not need sacrifice, because grace is not earned, a clear statement of a central Protestant doctrine. Cf. 1.

50–1 *how soe I stand or fall.* Pembroke's version is an original statement of David's concern for Israel, or, in the Protestant reading, for 'the whole Church, because through his sinne it was in danger of Gods judgement' (Geneva note v. 18).

54–6 The final verse, now generally believed to be a late addition to justify temple sacrifice, is problematic since it appears to contradict verses 16–17. The sacrifices can be interpreted metaphorically as 'the calves of mens lippes', Calvin suggests, but concludes that God will accept the 'solemne Ceremonies' so long as they 'are joyned with the pure affection of the harte'. Cf. Ps. 116. 46 and 119O. 10–12. Pembroke does not here speak explicitly, as does Wyatt, of 'Inward Zion' and the 'heart's Jerusalem'. Cf. Stephen J. Greenblatt, *Renaissance Self-Fashioning: From More to Shakespeare* (Chicago: U of Chicago P, 1980), 115–21. But see her stress on 'inward sight' and 'inward part' in Ps. 73. 48, 63.

Psalm 52

An address to the wicked, depicting his destruction, and rejoicing in the security of the godly.

1 *Tyrant.* Geneva Argument: 'David describeth the arrogant tyrranie of his adversarie Doeg: who by false surmises caused Ahimel[e]ch with the rest of the Priests to be slayne'. The Geneva note on v. 1 also calls Saul a tyrant, for he conspired with Doeg. See 1 Sam. 22: 9–23.

27–8 Cf. Geneva (v. 7): 'trusted unto the multitude of his riches, *and* put his strength in his malice'.

Psalm 53

A meditation on the folly of the wicked, who eat up the godly, not realizing their own coming destruction. Nearly an exact duplicate of Psalm 14 in the biblical text, but given different paraphrases by the Sidneys. See 'Methods of Composition and Translation', I.70. [Variant: MS *B*.]

1–4 Pembroke expands the analysis of the mind or heart of the wicked (v. 1); their 'fancie' and their 'studies' of evil are eventually revealed by their deeds. Cf. Ps. 119 on those who study God's law.

5, 10 *not one doth good.* The more exact repetition in the revision matches that of the biblical text (vv. 1, 3).

12 *cursed.* 'Sinnefull' in *G* matches the sense of the biblical text (v. 4).

15–16 Geneva notes (v. 5): 'When they thoght there was none occasion to feare, the sudden vengeance of God lighted upon them'.

18, 19 *thy, thee,* i.e. 'My people' (cf. 13). God speaks in stanza 2; stanzas 1 and 3 are in the voice of the Psalmist.

21–2 Cf. Psalter (v. 7): 'Oh, that the salvation were given unto Israel out of Sion'.

Psalm 54

A prayer for God's help and vengeance against enemies. Bèze's Argument attributes this Psalm to David 'when his secret holds were betrayed to Saul' and warns that 'faithful pastors must looke even for the same conflictes of domesticall enimies, as we have experience in this age'.

4 Pembroke adds the word play in the plea that 'heavie', or mournful, words not be taken lightly.

10 *pay them home.* Colloquial expression for giving deserved punishment.

14–15 Pembroke adds the image of flight to the biblical text (Geneva v. 7): 'For he hathe delivered me out of all trouble'.

Psalm 55

Another prayer for deliverance and vengeance, this time against a betrayer who had been 'my soule, my other self, my inward frend' (39). Pembroke's uncle John Dudley wrote a poetic version when imprisoned for supporting Lady Jane Grey as queen (Arundel MS 289). On parallels with *Psaumes,* see *Psalmes:* 'Literary Context'.

4 *jestures.* Cf. Calvin (v. 3): 'I will wring my hands'.

6 The idea of tearing the body, an ancient form of lamentation, is not in the biblical text (v. 2) or in her usual sources.

19 Pembroke renders the biblical 'Destroye' (Geneva v. 9) to fit the mouth imagery of the passage.

20–30 Pembroke expands the biblical personifications and adds the image of the masque.

39 *my other self.* Cf. *Psaumes,* 'second moy-mesme' and Correspondence: Printed Letter I.

45 *buried breathing in theyr beare.* Calvin connects verse 16 to the punish-ment of 'Corah, Dathan, and Abirom, and the reste of that faction' when the earth swallowed them (Num. 16: 31). Pembroke's alliterative phrase explains that they have been buried alive and that the earth has therefore become their 'beare', or bier.

53 *Athists.* Geneva (v. 19): 'they feare not God'.

54 *still one*, always the same. Bèze (v. 19): 'seeing these men continue in their wickednesse'.

60 *balme from wounded Rind.* An elaboration of 'oil' (v. 21) in reference to a tree which is the source of an aromatic substance, consisting of resins mixed with volatile oils.

71–2 *life-holding threed.* Pembroke adds the classical reference to the Fates, who spin, measure, and cut the thread of life. Cf. Ps. 85. 17n.

Psalm 56

A prayer for deliverance from enemies, a declaration of trust in God, and a promise to perform the vows of praise.

2 *gaping*, i.e. to 'swallow me up' (v. 1).

3 *spies*. Pembroke adds to biblical 'enemies' (v. 3) the concept of spies who had been watching the Psalmist. Cf. Ps. 71. 32.

6 *Still*, i.e. yet. Cf. Bèze (v. 3): 'Notwithstanding'.

11–12 Psalter (v. 5): 'They daily mistake my words'. Cf. Bèze (v. 5): 'whatsoever I entende, I speake or doe, they may pervert it'.

17 *they presse me neere.* Geneva (v. 6): 'kepe themselves close'.

18 *slight*, i.e. sleight or craft. Cf. Bèze (v. 7): 'they hope by their craftes to escape thy handes'.

27 *these*, i.e. 'these matters' (25).

36 *bound.* Cf. Bèze (v. 12): 'O howe greatly do these so many and so great benefites binde me unto thee?'

37 *that*, i.e. thou that.

42 *whether*, i.e. whither.

45 *light of life.* Cf. Geneva (v. 13): 'in the light of the living'. Cf. Ps. 55. 69.

Psalm 57

A prayer for deliverance from enemies and a song of praise.

4 *hive*, 'To shelter as in a hive' (*OED*, first recorded usage). Pembroke leaves implicit the bird imagery from the Psalter (v. 1): 'under the shadow of thy wings shall be my refuge'.

5 Geneva (v. 1): 'til *these* afflictions over-passe'. Geneva notes: 'He compareth the afflictions . . . to a storme, that commeth and goeth'.

10–12 Pembroke omits part of v. 3 that refers to 'the reproof of him that would swallow me up'.

14–15 Cf. Geneva (v. 4): 'the children of men, that are set on fire'. Pembroke adds the hands (possibly by analogy with Bèze (v. 4): 'the pawes of the Lyons') to parallel the teeth and tongues in the biblical text.

24 *sunn-beames of thy face*. Geneva (v. 5): 'thy glorie'. Cf. 54.

25–6 Cf. Geneva (v. 6): 'They have layed a net for my steppes'.

31–6 Cf. Ps. 108. 1–8. On parallels to Wyatt and Parker, see *Psalmes*: 'Literary Context', II.17.

35 *harp*. Emended. 'Hart' in *A* is plausible, but unlikely, because of Pembroke's characteristic fidelity to the biblical text, which here has 'harp', and because of her allusion to Wyatt's 'Awake my lute'. See *Psalmes*: 'Literary Context'.

44–5 *farr/starr*. Added to biblical 'heavens'. Cf. Sidney Ps. 10. 1–2.

47–8 Cf. Geneva (v. 10): 'For thy mercie is great unto the heavens, and thy trueth unto the cloudes'.

49–55 Refrain (19–24) repeated, as in biblical verses 5 and 11.

Psalm 58

The Psalm was seen as David's words against those who had falsely condemned him. Bèze's heading explains that Saul gathered 'a counsell of the states' to prosecute David as a traitor: 'now there is no greater injury than that, which doth oppress under the cloak of Law'. Calvin (v. 2) calls them 'rather a rowt of murtherers, than a Session of Judges'. Pembroke's version is closely linked with Psalm 82, on the unjust judges. [Variant: MS *B*.]

1–5 Pembroke emphasizes the rhetorical structure of question, answer (Sidney, *Psalms*, xxi), perhaps from Bèze's *carmen* (v. 1). Cf. the series of questions asked of unjust judges in her Psalm 82.

3 *sonnes of dust*. Pembroke's original use of the biblical metaphor from Gen. 2: 7 , the creation of mankind from the 'dust of the grounde', is a subtle reminder of the tree of the knowledge of Good and Evil in 2: 9. The unjust judges choose to know only evil. See II.17.

5 *long*, i.e. in duration. Their will, 'long malicious', has now been made known by their actions.

7 *whose*. 'What' in *O, D* is plausible and less ambiguous, but Geneva seems to support 'whose', meaning the world's oppression (v. 2): 'your hands execute crueltie upon the earth'. The Psalter puts the last phrase in the first half of the verse, as Pembroke does in Variant Ps. LVIII. 9.

8 Line added by Pembroke to explain that they give justice only to themselves, not to others. Cf. Old Version (v. 2): 'And where ye should true justice use, | your handes to bribes are bent'.

9–10 Geneva notes (v. 3): 'enemies to the people of God even from their birth'.

15 *skillfuls't*. A fourth 'l' is altered to long 's' and a 't' is added in *A*, perhaps by a later hand; hence, the variant in *F, J*.

16 *shee self-deaff*. Geneva notes (v. 4): 'They passe in malice, and subtilitie the craftie serpent, which colde preserve him selfe by stopping his eare from the inchanter'. Cf. Variant Ps. LVIII. 16–20. The serpent is female in the Psalter, as in many medieval and Renaissance pictures of the serpent in the Garden of Eden.

17–30 A curse against enemies.

25 *brood of springing thornes*. Pembroke's metaphor, connecting the thornes to the untimely birth and to the unripe fruits of line 29, comes from Bèze (v. 9): 'And their posterity even worthy children for such fathers, like thornes growing out of the bush'. The closely worked metaphor replaces awkward repetitions of 'just' in Variant Ps. LVIII. 36–8.

28 *of*, i.e. off. According to the *OED*, this is the regular early form. See also, for example, Ps. 88. 24. For an error or emendation similar to the one in *B*—'oft'—see Ps. 78. 141.

31–2 The epigrammatic close recalls the opening lines and is an idiomatic restatement of Bèze (v. 11): 'surely ther is a God in the earth, that doth also give to every man his owne'.

Psalm 59

Another personal prayer for deliverance and vengeance, notable for the emphasis on God's 'free grace' (43, 89), and for the vivid dog imagery, expanded by Pembroke (25–30, 67–78).

5–6 Pembroke amplifies the biblical 'blooddie' (Geneva v. 2) or 'bloodthirstie' (Psalter) men, to explain that they have been raised in the family profession, murder.

7–10 The specific categorization was suggested by Bèze (v. 3): 'they partly lye in waite for my life, and partly the most mightie of them doe gather their power against me'.

13 That is, but what does it matter if I am free from fault? An added transitional line. Cf. Old Version: 'Yea for no fault that I did make, | I never did them ill'.

24 *malice*, i.e. active ill-will or hatred; thus the phrase is not redundant: such as are wicked through active ill-will. Cf. Bèze (v. 5): 'being given up willingly to all wickednesse'.

26 That is, the dog-like foes return at sunset.

30 *maw*. The appearance of 'mawes' in the parallel passage below (72) suggests that Woodforde's transcription may be correct in having the plural here, as well, even though all the other manuscripts but *O* agree with *A*. What makes the plural in 72 problematical, however, is that it is in the extended passage that was added later in *A* (in the *J* hand) and that *K*, *χ* again have the singular.

32 *they*. Emended. 'Their' is Davies's error; 'prate' is a verb both here and in 35. Emendation is supported by other manuscripts.

41, 42 *wait, wait*. Wait as planning entrapment and as patient expectation. Cf. Bèze (v. 9): 'wherefore though these do lye in waite about my house, so againe I will diligently waite for thy helpe'.

43–4 An interpretative reference to the doctrine of prevenient grace (v. 10). Cf. 89. See *Psalmes*: 'Literary Context', II.20.

54 The alteration from 'amazed' in *B* to 'debas'd' adds a kinetic image to go with 'overthrowne'.

55 Cf. Bèze (v. 12): 'there neede no other witnesse, but their owne wordes to convince them of wickednesse'.

67–72 Virtually repeats lines 24–32, as do vv. 6 and 14.

73–9 Expands dog metaphor, contrasting the barking of the dogs with the singing of the Psalmist.

89 *free grace*. Pembroke's sources again have 'mercy' or 'merciful', as in v. 10 (ll. 43–4).

Psalm 60

A national prayer for an end to God's wrath, demonstrated by defeat on the battlefield, and a request that God will once again lead the armies of Israel to overcome their enemies. [Variant: MS *B*.]

6 *and gaping lay*. The variant phrase, 'as gaping clay', is likely a scribal error, not an authorial revision. Geneva (v. 2) reads: 'Thou hast made the land to tremble, and hast made it to gape'. Geneva also notes: 'As clefte with an earth quake'. See Variant Ps. LX. 5–6.

13–16 Cf. Bèze (v. 4): 'But nowe againe . . . thou givest unto us being converted unto thee thy standart, and thy trueth to goe before us, and commaundest us to followe our captaine, and bring foorth the armie'.

18 *I*. King David, speaking for the people.

25–40 God will triumph over Israel's traditional enemies and establish his kingdom in Judah. Almost literal paraphrase of vv. 7–9.

29 Cf. Bèze (v. 8): 'But the straungers howe fierce so ever they be, shall do all servile work unto me, the Moabites shall holde the basen to wash my feete'.

Psalm 61

The exiled Psalmist prays for God's protection.

5 Cf. Geneva (v. 2): 'From the ends of the earth wil I crye unto thee'. Geneva notes: 'From the place, where I was banished, being driven out of the Citie and Temple by my sonne Absalom'.

8–10 Cf. Geneva (v. 2): 'bring me upon the rocke that is higher then I'. Geneva notes: 'Unto the which without thy helpe I can not atteine'.

22–5 Cf. Bèze (v. 5): 'For thou O God hast graunted my desire, and haste appointed me the kinge of thy holy people'.

32 *gard.* Cf. Bèze (v. 7): 'two keepers . . . thy mercie, and thy trueth'.

Psalm 62

A song of confidence in God, instructing the people to rely on God only, not on fraud, on force, or on riches. [Variant: MS *B*.]

The incipit in *A* is the usual Vulgate version. '*Tamen ad Deum*' is the opening of the *interpretatio* of Mollerus printed with Bèze's *paraphrasis*.

1, 3 *Yet . . . yet.* Geneva notes (v. 2): 'It appeareth by the oft repetition of this worde, that the Prophet abode manifolde tentations, but by resting on God and by patience he overcame them all'.

17–20 The opening quatrain is virtually repeated, as vv. 5 and 6 repeat vv. 1 and 2.

20 Geneva (v. 6): '*therefore* I shal not be moved'. Pembroke's characteristic word play and rhetorical question add emphasis and a sense of the speaking voice. Cf. 4.

28 *Adams sonnes.* Cf. Geneva (v. 9): 'children of men'.

31–2 Psalter (v. 9): 'lighter than vanitie it selfe'. Cf. Bèze: 'yea if thou would waigh in ballance nothing it selfe with mortal men . . . nothing woulde waigh them all downe'.

35 *when.* Cf. Psalter, Geneva (v. 10): '*if* riches increase'. A revealing class statement by Pembroke. See 'Methods of Composition and Translation', I.73.

Psalm 63

The exiled Psalmist longs for God's sanctuary, praises God even in the wilderness, and prophesies the destruction of his enemies. [Variant: MS *B*.]

5–6 The Argument and title in Geneva state the occasion as David's exile 'in the wildernes of Judah' or 'Ziph', when he was 'in great danger by Saul'. The heavy alliteration was deliberately added in revision.

10–11 Cf. Geneva (v. 4): 'Thus wil I magnifie thee *all* my life, *and* lift up mine hands in thy Name'.

12 Cf. Geneva (v. 5): 'My soule shal be satisfied, as with marow and fatnes'.

15 *heer*. An allusion to the speaker's presence in the desert (5). Even here, in the wilderness, the Psalmist will praise God. Thus, 'now' in *C, G* is unnecessary.

19 Cf. Bèze (v. 8): 'For I am farre absent in deede in my bodye from thy house'.

21 *right right*. Probably not a redundancy: just or righteous right hand. Cf. Ps. 45. 13–14.

27 *all that god adore*. The king will conceive high joy in God and in all those who adore God.

Psalm 64

A prayer for personal deliverance against slanderers. [Variant: MS *B*.]

25–6 Cf. Psalter (v. 7): 'But God shall suddenly shoot at them with a swift arrow: that they shall be wounded'.

33–6 That is, there is no one who shall witness this event and not tell of it. Cf. Geneva (v. 9): 'And all men shal se it, and declare the worke of God, and thei shal understand, what he hathe wrought'.

37–40 Cf. Geneva (v. 10): 'But the righteous shal be glad in the Lord, and trust in him: and all that are upright of heart, shal rejoyce'.

37–8 That is, the just shall joy and hope in God, who reigns timeless.

Psalm 65

A Psalm of thanksgiving for God's protection and for a bountiful harvest.

5 *sinns*. The singular in *B, K, χ* is a scribal error; the sources have '[mis]-deeds', 'transgressions', 'sins' (v. 3).

6 The paraphrase suppresses the shift to the second person in the biblical sources.

5–6 Pembroke adds the metaphor of sins turning into the smoke of sacrifices, apparently derived from paying vows in v. 1, connected in Ps. 51 with animal sacrifice.

10 *thy checkrole*. Pembroke intensifies the courtly imagery in the biblical 'dwell in thy courts' (Geneva v. 4) by adding that they will be enrolled on the court payroll.

11–12 A metaphorical paraphrase of the biblical text (Geneva v. 4): '*and* we shal be satisfied with the pleasures of thine House'.

18 *cradle . . . of restlesse wavy playn*, i.e. the sea (v. 5).

23–4 *stormy uproares, that civill sea.* Geneva (v. 7): 'the tumultes of the people'. Psalter, 'the madnesse of the peoples' (v. 7). Pembroke equates God's stilling of the storm with His calming of the people.

24 'That' is a demonstrative pronoun: 'that civill sea' refers to the stormy uproars.

25 Cf. Geneva (v. 8): 'in the uttermost partes *of the earth*'. The paradoxical paraphrase acknowledges the spherical shape of the earth.

28 *both howses of the sonn*, i.e. 'the East and West' (v. 8).

29–30 Cf. Geneva gloss on 'the East and West' (v. 8): 'Ebr. The going forthe of the morning and of the evening'. The variants in *K*, χ avoid the repetition of 'both' (28).

36 Cf. John 12: 24 (Geneva): 'Except the wheate corne fall into the grounde and dye, it bideth alone: but if it dye, it bringeth forthe muche frute'.

37 Cf. Geneva (v. 10): 'Thou waterest abundantly the forrowes'.

42 *thy goings fatt the ground.* Geneva (v. 11): 'thy steps drop fatnes'. Psalter, 'thy cloudes droppe fatnes' (v. 12).

44 *hedg of mirth.* Psalter, 'the little hilles shall rejoyce' (v. 11). Note Pembroke's sense of celebration, amplified throughout this stanza.

45–6 Geneva (v. 13): 'The pastures are clad with shepe: the valeis also shal be covered with corne'.

46 *clotheth.* The inexact rhyme with 'encloseth' (44) seems to be intentional, adding a clothing metaphor for the valleys, as does Parker, 'the vales with wheat ful clad' (v. 13); the variant in χ may be an attempted scribal emendation.

Psalm 66

A Psalm of praise for God's deliverance, first of Israel and then of the speaker; the speaker presents a sacrifice to fulfil an earlier vow.

8 *frown, fawn.* The idea of hypocrisy is in the Geneva note (v. 3): 'the infidels for feare shal dissemble themselves to be subject'.

19 Pembroke supplies the name 'Jordan' for the 'river' (v. 6).

23–4 Cf. Geneva (v. 7): 'the rebellious shal not exalt them selves'.

29 *re-given.* Cf. Bèze (v. 9): 'For he hath restored our life when it was lost'.

34–8 Cf. Geneva (vv. 11–12): 'Thou hast . . . laied a strait *chaine* upon our loins. 12 Thou hast caused men to ride over our heades: we went into fyre and into water.' Pembroke retains the biblical metaphor and interprets the chain as 'sadles' to make the image consistent. Her closest source is Parker, 'Our loynes and backs: bare painful loades: of griefs in hevy wayt'.

36 Cf. Geneva (v. 12): 'men to ride over our heades'.

43–4 A development of the biblical phrase (Geneva v. 13): 'and wil paie thee my vowes'.

54 *from.* Emended. That 'in' is probably Davies's error is suggested by the presence of 'from' in *B*, as well as *K* and χ.

55–6 Cf. Geneva (v. 18): 'If I regarde wickednes in mine heart, the Lord wil not heare me'.

61 *what is left me*, i.e. what remains for me to do but to give praise to Him?

Psalm 67

A Psalm of praise for God's blessings, a prayer that they may continue, and a promise that all nations will praise God.

13 *them*, i.e. themselves.

25 *blisse.* Cf. Calvin (v. 7): 'God shall blisse us'.

28 *the father of the yeere*, i.e. the sun.

30 Pembroke adds the classical refence to Zephyrs.

32 Cf. Geneva (v. 7): 'and all the ends of the earth shal feare him'.

Psalm 68

A Psalm of liturgical praise. Bèze's Argument praises the beauty of this Psalm, wherein David 'added marvellous artificiall colours, rather painting it foorth then writing it'. He applies the Psalm to David bringing in the Ark to Jerusalem. This is generally considered the most difficult of the Psalms to interpret and therefore to translate. [Variant: MSS *B*, *I*.]

6 *daunce.* Geneva (v. 3): 'leape for joye'. An allusion to David's dancing with joy when the ark was brought to Jerusalem (1 Chron. 15: 25–9, mentioned by Bèze).

7 *nam'd of eternall essence.* Geneva (v. 4): 'in his name Jah'. Geneva notes: 'Jah and Jehováh are the names of God, which do signifie his essence and majestie incomprehensible, so that herby is declared, that all idols are but

vanitie, and that the God of Israél is the onely true God'. See Ps. 72. 81–2n. and *Psalmes*: 'Literary Context', II.24.

12 Bèze (v. 5): 'he [God] . . . hath nowe chosen amongest us holy and stable habitations unto him selfe'.

15 *barain sand*. Geneva reads 'drye land' and glosses it (v. 6) 'Which is baren of Gods blessings'. Pembroke explains what it would have been like to farm such land.

19 *did sweat with melting feare*. Cf. Bèze (v. 8): 'the heavens being afraide . . . are dissolved as it were in a sweate, and dropped downe'.

25–6 Cf. Bèze (v. 11): 'And also thou hast given the cause to the great multitudes of our virgines, to rejoyce and sing of thy victories'.

25 *Ther*. Because *F*, *J* have 'They', the alteration in *A* may not be contemporary. However, the phrasing in Bèze (see 25–6n.) suggests that 'ther' is the correct reading: there in the desert where God gave them victories. Cf. Variant Ps. LXVIII. 31.

28 *we*. Note the possible identification of the speaker with the women, referred to in the second person in the sources and in the rest of this passage. Cf. the more open statement in Variant Ps. LXVIII. 33–40, with its sense of release from confinement. See 'Origins, Early Reception, and Influence', I.25.

29–30 Cf. Bèze (v. 13): 'O ye damsels, ye have lived hetherto amongest the soote of the pots, even sitting at home, but nowe ye may come foorth, shining and glittering no otherwise then the doves as white as snowe, doe cast foorth a certaine golden glistering as they flee in the aire'.

32 *wavy*, 'full of waves', 'said of the air, clouds, etc.' (*OED*, citing this line). Along with 'fethered Oare', 'wavy' is part of Pembroke's metaphorical paraphrase of the Psalmist's description of the dove as silver and gold.

33 *that this may not seeme strang*, i.e. that the 'land of Canáan' (Geneva note v. 13) may not seem hostile and inhospitable to the Israelites as the new inhabitants.

35–8 Pembroke explains the pathetic fallacy in her rendition of v. 14, present in her sources in v. 16.

35 *ground*. The reference is to the land itself, not the atmosphere. Cf. Calvin (v. 15): 'And the similitude will fit the place very well, that like as the Snowe maketh the darksome hill white even so the countenance of the Lande shyned whyte ageine, when the darksomnesse of it was wyped away'.

36 *Salmon*. Cf. Calvin, 'thou shalt be made white in Salmon', explaining that Mount Salmon 'is well knowen to be snowy'. Geneva (v. 14) glosses 'Zalmón' as 'Canáan'.

37 *Basan*. See 59n.

41 *This Mountainett*, i.e. Sion, not noted for its height, but for 'the inwarde grace of God, which there remaineth' (Geneva note v. 16).

49–56 Possibly a reference to the traditional reading of v. 18 as Christ's harrowing of hell, although not usually so designated in Protestant commentaries. Geneva, Calvin, and Bèze do, however, cross-reference to Eph. 4. Cf. Spenser, *Amoretti* 68. Anne Prescott, 'Triumphing over Death and Sin', *Spenser Studies* 11 (1994), 230–2.

52 Geneva (following Calvin) notes (v. 18): 'God overcame the enemies of his Church, toke them prisoners, and made them tributaries'. Thus, 'tenants' more precisely fits the context than 'servants' in *K*, χ. But see 'service' (84) in a similar context. Cf. Variant Ps. LXVIII. 94.

59 *Basan*, an area east of Galilee. Cf. Geneva (note v. 22): 'As he delivered his Church once from Og of Bashan [Num. 21: 33; Deut. 3: 1; Ps. 135: 11; Ps. 136: 20], and other tyrants, and from the dangers of the red Sea, so wil he stil do as often as necessitie requireth'.

67 *battaile maides*. The subject of both 'did play' (66) and 'did . . . ring' (67). Cf. Variant Ps. LXVIII. 31–2, 79–80. Pembroke adds the identification to the biblical 'maides playing with trimbrels' (Geneva v. 25). Bèze attributes the succeeding song in the rest of the Psalm to the maidens, as does Pembroke; Calvin attributes it to the Psalmist; Parker to damsels and minstrels; most other sources just present the song without attribution. See 'Origins, Early Reception, and Influence', I.25.

71 *little*, i.e. 'the yongest' (Geneva note on v. 27). Benjamin was the youngest son of Jacob. Benjamin was the tribe of Saul; Judah, the tribe of David.

73 *Nepthaly, Zabulon*. Two tribes from Galilee, Naphtali and Zebulun.

77 *ending*. The object of 'shall take'.

91 *loved*. The word corresponds to nothing in the biblical text (v. 34), but it is more implicit in the context than 'lovely' in the later χ tradition.

93 *shryne*, 'Tabernacle' (Geneva note). Geneva, Psalter (v. 35): 'holie places'. Thus, 'throne' in the manuscripts after *H* is probably not authorial.

96 *his force*. Cf. Geneva (v. 35): 'the God of Israel is he that giveth strength and power unto the people: praised by God'.

Psalm 69

An individual prayer for deliverance from enemies. Pembroke does not make explicit either the attribution to David or the Christological application present in many of her sources. [Variant: MS *B*.]

The incipit in *A* is the usual Vulgate version. '*Serva me*' in χ (though not *G*, *M*) is the opening of the *interpretatio* by Mollerus published in Bèze's *paraphrasis.* Other variant incipits from the Mollerus translation appear with Pss. 62, 85, 91, and perhaps 76 and 80.

23 *Note*, perhaps from the Latin, *nota*, a mark of infamy. It would be tempting to adopt the emendation, 'mote', as in *I*, the 1823 Chiswick edition, and Rathmell. But the scribes of the fourteen other manuscripts let 'note' pass (*B* has the variant paraphrase), so it is probably not a scribal slip. The relevance of the Latin sense is further indicated by the corresponding line in the variant paraphrase: 'Thy cause it is I this disgracefull blame | And noted blot susteine' (23–4). Shakespeare uses note in a similar sense in *Love's Labour's Lost*, IV. iii. 123. See also II.22.

29 Cf. Geneva (v. 9): 'For the zeale of thine house hathe eaten me'.

30 *thy slanders scourges.* Probably to be understood as an objective genitive: the scourges of the slander directed toward God, but also felt by the speaker. Cf. 31–2.

35–40 Pembroke emphasizes both public and private mockery, as in Bèze (v. 12): 'So that in the publike assemblies also they ceased not to prate on me, and feasting merily they made songes of me'. The biblical text, however, speaks of drunkards, not feasters; hence, 'wyny tast' (40).

45 *from such and myred.* 'Such' refers to the drunken, jesting, 'prating' enemies of the preceding stanza. The sense of 45–6 is thus: keep me safe from such people, and, mired as I am, keep me safe from foes surrounding me like a flood. Cf. Variant Ps. LXIX. 42–3. The altered original in *A* seems to be 'from such a mynd', a manifest error that violates the rhyme scheme. The reason for and source of all the subsequent changes made in the passage are uncertain. The alteration of 'such' to 'sunck' in *A* (in a hand similar to that of *J*) is particularly baffling because the *OED* records no contemporary sense of 'sunk' as a noun that would fit here.

52 *told by none*, i.e. innumerable.

65 *not seene before.* That is, I had not previously seen such behaviour in them.

66–8 Verse 21 is mentioned by all the gospels, describing the crucifixion (Matt. 27: 34, 48; Mark 15: 36; Luke 23: 36; and John 19: 29).

69–70 Geneva (v. 22): 'Let their table be a snare before them'. Cf. Bèze: '. . . that they may be snared like beastes which are deceived by the baites of meat set before them'.

79–80 Cf. Geneva (v. 26): 'For thei persecute him, whome thou hast smiten: and they adde unto the sorowe of them, whome thou hast wounded'.

82 *Cyphers*, zeros, which increase a number to which they are added.

85–6 Cf. Calvin (v. 29): 'the booke of lyfe is nothing else, than the eternall purpose of God, wherby he hath predestinate his children to salvacion'.

89–92 Thanksgiving is superior to animal sacrifice. Cf. Pss. 40, 50, and 51.

89 *his.* The biblical text (v. 30) also shifts to the third person here.

98 *thine, yours,* i.e. your inhabitants, creatures. Cf. Variant Ps. LXIX. 100–1.

Psalm 70

A prayer for deliverance of the godly and punishment for the wicked. Calvin notes that this Psalm is related to part of Psalm 40 (vv. 13–17). Geneva has a cross-reference to 40: 14.

1 *Lord.* The variant, 'God', is also in the biblical texts (v. 1) and the Latin incipit. The change avoids repetition in 2.

2 *to help me hast.* Psalter (v. 3): 'make haste to help me'.

3 Cf. the line in *K,* χ with Sidney's Ps. 40. 52: 'blush for shame'.

4 *and of.* The variant in *K,* χ was required by the change in 3.

6, 9 *forced.* 'Turned' in *B* is also in Geneva (vv. 2, 3; the Psalter has 'turned' in v. 2).

Psalm 71

A prayer for God's deliverance in old age. The musician/poet vows to praise God to future generations. Bèze attributes this Psalm to David in old age, after he had been driven out by Absalom. [Variant: MS *B.* Revised extensively in *K,* χ. Note the condensation to 78 lines in *A,* from 112 in the earlier variant.]

16–18 The Psalmist stresses reliance on God from birth through old age. Cf. Bèze (v. 5): 'For I depend wholy on thee alone, uppon thee I say O Lord I have set all my hope, from my first childhoode'. Cf. 28, 55.

24 *hope.* 'Trust' in *K,* χ is the biblical word (v. 7).

25 *thankfull.* 'Praisefull' in *K,* χ corresponds to the biblical sources (Geneva v. 8): 'Let my mouth be filled with thy praise'.

28 *Do.* Emended. There seems to be no syntactical position for 'no' in the passage. The repetition of 'do' is not unexpected and is supported by the other manuscripts.

31 *life.* As rendered by Calvin (vv. 10 and 13) and Bèze (v. 10). 'Soul' in *K,* χ is again the biblical word (v. 13).

32–3 The enemies have discussed their hatred with their spies and, thinking that God has abandoned their victim, order the spies to set upon him.

Pembroke adds the idea of spies to the biblical 'enemies' (v. 10), probably from her own knowledge of the court. Cf. Ps. 56. 3.

32 *my*. Rathmell's emendation to 'their' is supported by *K*, χ, as well as by the corresponding passage in the Variant Ps. LXXI. 46. But 'my spies' could mean those who are spying on me. Geneva (v. 10): 'for mine enemies speake of me, and they that laie waite for my soule, take their counsel together'.

40 *full*, *adv*., fully, completely. 'Fall' in *K*, χ is a scribal error or gratuitous emendation.

44 *my trust*. Cf. Bèze (v. 14): 'for I will never leave of to trust in thee'.

46–7 Cf. Bèze (v. 15): 'I have bene delivered by thee a thousand times, and comforted with innumerable benefites' (the Geneva note also speaks of 'benefites'). The variant in *K*, χ reflects the wording of the biblical text (Geneva v. 15): 'My mouth shal daily rehearse thy righteousnes, *and* thy salvacion: for I knowe not the nomber'.

49 *my god*. Pembroke personalizes the cry. 'Lord God' in *K*, χ is quoted from Geneva (v. 16).

50–1 Emended. The parallelism of the biblical verse and the revision of 51 in *K*, χ (which comes closer to the sense of the Psalm text) support emendation of 50 so that 'assured' goes with the rest of the line and not the new, though related, unit of thought in 51. Geneva (v. 16): 'I wil go forwarde in the strength of the Lord God, *and* wil make mention of thy righteousnes, *even* of thine onely'. But cf. Variant Ps. LXXI. 71–4.

52–4 Pembroke adds the image of the cradle to the biblical 'youth' (v. 17). As the speaker has grown older in experience, he has been able to tell of more wonders God has done for him.

54 Geneva (v. 17): '*therefore* wil I tel of thy wonderous workes'. The variant in *K*, χ was required by the changes made in 51.

58 Bèze (v. 18) explains that his praises could 'be broken off by my miserie, or else by my death'.

64 *into these woes*. The variant in *K*, χ anticipates the last part of the verse—'*and* [wilt] take me up from the depth of the earth'—which is also paraphrased in 66.

69 *ring*. The version in *A* seems to make the playing of the instruments the act of praise. The *K*, χ variant seems intended to return to the biblical text (Geneva v. 22): 'unto thee wil I sing upon the harpe'. Cf. Variant Ps. LXXI. 102–5.

73–4 The transposition in *K*, χ may be a scribal error resulting from an eye-skip. 'No honor sparing' seems to have been suggested by the Geneva note (v. 23): 'he promiseth to delite in nothing, but wherein God maie be glorified'.

Psalm 72

A prayer that God will bless the king and teach him to rule justly.

1 Geneva note on the title ('A Psalme *of Salomón*'): 'Composed by David as toaching the reigne of his sonne Salomón'. Bèze's Argument calls it 'a most pretious jewel' for his son, 'for it contained all things that appertaine to the office of a true king', and notes that they pray for their own profit when they pray for such a king. Pembroke's parenthetic comment fills in the implication, the reason the king's son should be taught the correct way to rule.

3 *thy Realme*. Cf. Bèze (v. 2): 'that he may justlie governe not his people but thine'.

4–7 Pembroke makes explicit the connection between the treatment of the poor and the prosperity of the land.

19 *meades new mown*. Cf. Bèze (v. 6): 'new mowne meddowes'.

23 *many-formed queene*, the moon.

29 *Physons*. 'Pison' or 'Pishon' (Geneva spelling) is the 'first' of the rivers of Eden (Gen. 2: 11). 'Peráh' or 'Peráth' (Geneva spellings) is the 'fourth' (Gen. 2: 14), glossed in Geneva as 'Euphrates', the translation later used in the 1611 Bible. The revision is thus an ingenious and economical attempt to make the paraphrase more precise.

32 *them*, i.e. themselves.

34 *Seba, Saba*. Geneva notes (v. 10) on 'Kings of Sheb and Seb ': 'That is, of Arabia that rich countrie, wherof Sheb was a parte bordering upon Ethiopia'.

35–40 Pembroke sets up a parallel between the kings falling prostrate and those that 'stand', or maintain their positions at court, at their command. There is no mention of the nobility in the biblical text (Geneva v. 11): 'all Kings shal worship him: all nations shal serve him'.

61–4 An original poetic amplification of the phrase, 'like *the trees* of Lebanón' (Geneva v. 16).

81–2 Although only *A* and *J* have a semicolon at the end of 81, it is probably authorial, intended to make the line self-contained and parallel to 82. Thus, 'eternall lord' is not a subjective complement, but another vocative phrase. The lines emphasize God's eternal existence as the ground or source of all being. Cf. Ps. 68. 7n.

83 *all*. Emended. 'And' does not seem to fit into the syntax of the passage and is thus probably Davies's error. 'All' in *B*, *K*, χ matches Bèze's paraphrase (v. 18): 'the author of all things so wonderfull'.

87 *blessing*. The plural is plausible, but it would be more convincing if it were in *K*, as well as *B* and χ.

88 *all this Round*, i.e. 'all the earth' (Geneva v. 19). Cf. 76, 'earthly ball'.

90 To close this second of the five books of the Psalms, Pembroke chooses the Geneva rendering 'So be it, even so be it' (instead of the 'Amen' of the Psalter v. 19), as Sidney had done to close the first book, Ps. 41. 48. Geneva closes the second book of Psalms in the Septuagint with a note 'HERE END THE praiers of David, the sonne of Isháí' (Ps. 72: 19). Cf. the doxologies added at the close of the third and fourth books, 89: 52 and 106: 48.

Psalm 73

This wisdom Psalm addresses the same question as the book of Job: Why do the righteous suffer? As in Psalm 37, the speaker learns not to be disquieted by the temporary prosperity of the wicked.

The incipit in *N, C* may reflect a scribe's omission of part of the beginning of the verse in the Vulgate: '*Quam bonus Israel Deus*' ('How good God is to Israel').

1 *most true.* Pembroke quotes from the opening phrase of *Astrophil* 5 and also paraphrases Bèze's verse 1: 'It must needes be true and inviolable, that God can not be but favorable towards Israel, that is, to them that worship him purely and devoutly'. On extensive parallels with Bèze and Sidney, especially *Astrophil* 5, see 'Methods of Composition and Translation', I.68.

9 *still.* The continuing prosperity of the wicked (cf. 29, 36) is contrasted with the speaker's continual reliance on God (67–70).

16–18 Pembroke uses the chain and robes of office as symbols of the wicked.

21 That is, their desires are fulfilled beyond their expectation.

28–36 The godly, seeing the prosperity of the wicked and their own suffering, question God's providence.

29 *their horne of plenty,* i.e. that of the wicked.

38 *In vain.* The speaker believes that godliness has been in vain, but learns that it is the wicked whose work is vain (59).

50 *stepps.* Added to contrast with 'thoughtes' (46). The speaker could not understand until he went to God's house; human understanding by itself is insufficient.

61–3 The added rhetorical questions lead to self-revelation.

73–85 Pembroke adds an original coda, implying that the ascent will be difficult and require a teacher. See I.69.

Psalm 74

A prayer for God's deliverance from present distress, traditionally interpreted as the destruction of the Temple at Jerusalem. Praise for past blessings leads to a request, as Bèze says, that God will 'continue his accustomed goodnes' in the future for the 'deliveraunce of the people' and for God's own 'glorie and majestie'.

6 *flock*. Emended. While 'folk' could easily be mistranscribed as 'flock' (as it was at times in the other manuscripts), the *A* reading of 'folk' may be Davies's error. The authenticity of 'flock' in *B*, *I*, *K*, χ is supported by the biblical text (Geneva v. 1), 'the sheep of thy pasture', and Bèze's paraphrase, 'thine owne flock'. Cf. Ps. 105. 75.

9 Cf. Psalter (v. 2): 'purchased, and redeemed of old'.

30 Pembroke emphasizes the craftsmanship being destroyed as though it were a forest.

40–1 *house... of god*. Psalter (v. 9): 'houses [Geneva 'Synagogues'] of God'. Thus, 'gods' is an error or sophistication by the χ scribe.

48 Cf. Bèze (v. 9): 'we shoulde have some one prophet who ... might signifie unto us what end would be to these calamities'.

52–4 Emended. The many variants in 52 and its omission in *N* are indications of its difficulty. Geneva reads, 'shal the enemie blaspheme thy Name for ever?' (v. 10). The construction is probably incremental, but Davies seems to have misread his text. The original is probably not 'hatred', but 'hated', which refers to 'name'; 'paintes with shame' refers to another act of the 'foe'. Whoever attempted the emendation in *C*, *G*, *M* failed to consider the syntax of the whole passage. 'That' is the subject of both 'hates' and 'paintes'.

58–60 Cf. Geneva (v. 11): '*drawe* [thy right hand] out of thy bosome, *and* consume them'.

73 *that monsters head*. Geneva (v. 14): 'the head of Liviathán' ('whale' in Bèze). The Geneva notes, like Calvin's commentary, interpret vv. 13–15 (ll. 67–84) as referring to the deliverance of the Israelites from the Egyptians (Leviathan is said to represent Pharaoh).

80 Cf. Bèze (v. 15): 'contrary to the course of nature'. Cf. Exod. 17: 5–6.

103 The image of the hawk is added, probably from Bèze's *carmen*. See *Psalmes*: 'Literary Context', II.23.

120 *their*. The biblical sources have the third person throughout v. 21.

Psalm 75

A national and personal song of praise. [Variant: MSS *B*, *I*, *K*, *N*.]

4–8 Cf. Bèze's Argument: 'This Psalme... doth wholy agree unto those times when David reigned in the citie of Hebron, when he was ready to receive the kingdome of the whole nation by the common consent of all the tribes'. Pembroke seems to accept this interpretation rather than that of the

Geneva note which identifies the speaker ('I') in vv. 2–3 (ll. 4–8) as God Himself.

6 *my.* Cf. Geneva (v. 2): 'I wil judge righteously'.

13 *Where.* Line 15 suggests that the image is spatial, not temporal. Thus, the variant, 'When', is an error.

19–24 Cf. Calvin (v. 9): 'there is in Goddes hande wyne of a sumishe taste, wherewith too make the ungodly drunken untoo death'. Old Version (v. 8) has 'lees and filthy dregs'.

25–6 Pembroke adds the statement about lowly but 'never-dying rymes', a statement that characteristically masks self-assertion as self-deprecation. The idea of spending 'happie tymes' writing is hers as well.

Psalm 76

A national song of praise for God's deliverance in battle. According to the Geneva heading, the Psalm celebrates the 'defence of his people in Jerusalem, in the destruction of the armie of Saneherib'.

The variant incipit in *I*, *N*, *C* (probably also the similar one in *O*, *D*), 'In Judæa', is from Bèze's *paraphrasis* (v. 1), '*In Judæa demum verus ille Deus quis sit intelligitur*'.

1 *Only.* From Bèze (v. 1): 'That true God of Israel is onely knowne in Judea'. Cf. I.69.

2 *Jacob.* The reading in *B*, 'Israel', matches the biblical text.

5 *Their.* Probably a spelling variant of 'there', which is the word in *B* and most of the χ copies, as well as the Psalter (v. 3): 'There brake he the arrows of the bow: the shield, the sword, and the battle'. That Davies transcribed the word correctly, however, is suggested by its appearance in *O* and by 'the' in *D*, which looks like an attempted scribal emendation.

11 Cf. Geneva note (v. 5): 'as thogh their handes were cut of'.

13–18 Woodforde's 'or' suggests that he mistook the last line of the original recorded in his marginal note for an alternative to the preceding line. He was misled by the repetition of 'it self', which was the apparent reason for recasting the lines.

19, 21 The metre requires feminine rhyme in these lines; thus, the contraction of the final syllables may be Davies's error.

20 In this case, the 'good' were preserved and the 'bad were punished'. Cf. Ps. 73.

23–4 In Woodforde's note, '(b)' represents the original second half of 23; '(c)' is the original 24; '(d)' is an intermediate version of 24, composed before the current line was adopted.

28 Cf. Geneva note (v. 12) on cutting off the princes as gathering grapes. Bèze amplifies the vineyard analogy.

30 *doth*. The use of singular verbs in plural senses is not so unusual in Renaissance verse as to require emendation. That is, God terrifies the kings who terrify the earth.

Psalm 77

The speaker's doubt, presented in the past tense, was allayed by remembrance of God's past blessings.

1–2 *crying call/ calling cry*. Polyptoton, used extensively in this Psalm.

11–12 Cf. Bèze (v. 3): 'For the remembrance of God was so farre away from pacifying myne unquiet mynde'.

17–24 Amplifies the biblical text (Geneva v. 4): 'Thou keepest mine eyes waking: I was astonied and colde not speake'. Note effective use of polyptoton in 19–20.

25–32 Expands the meditation of the Psalmist as writer, recalling not only God's former blessings but the Psalmist's own earlier writings. Cf. Geneva (vv. 5–6): 'Then I considered the daies of olde ... I called to remembrance my song'. Geneva explains the song 'Of thankesgiving, which I was accustomed to sing in my prosperitie'.

36 *plaine*. Pembroke adds the emphasis on writing formal complaints, as does Parker (v. 7): 'And thus I playne'.

51 *chang*. Cf. Beze (v. 10): 'the change of things dependeth in thy hand'.

62 Note caveat. The biblical text reads (Geneva v. 13): 'who is so great a God as *our* God'.

67 *do*. Davies has correctly transcribed his text (or, as the other manuscripts suggest, judiciously emended it). The subject of 'do' is 'wonders' (66).

68 *as when*. Pembroke makes explicit the simile implicit in the biblical appeal to history.

73–88 Expands the accounts of a thunderstorm in vv. 16–18, connected in v. 20 to Moses and Aaron leading out the people of Israel 'like sheepe'.

84 *earth*. While the possessive without '(e)s' occurs at other places in the Sidneian *Psalmes*, it usually immediately precedes a noun. On the other hand, the scribes of *A*, *F*, *J* all let the uninflected form stand, and its presence in *B* indicates that it was in at least one working copy.

85–6 Parenthetical. The lightning flash encleares the clouds while the thunder roars and rattles.

89–96 Pembroke adds the path leading through the dry sea bed to 'glad pastures'. Cf. Old Version v. 19.

95 *with Aron Moises.* The original phrase recorded by Woodforde must have been revised for the sake of the metre. The variant in *K*, χ sacrifices the metrical regularity for clarity.

Psalm 78

Bèze's Argument praises the usefulness of this long historical Psalm in recalling God's blessings to those who keep his covenant and his 'wrath' against those who break it. 'And would to God that all men could marke in their minds how necessarie this doctrine is in our times, and howe wonderfull examples God hath set before us to both these purposes by the space of these 40 yeares, even as great as ever before'. Cf. Psalms 105, 106, 135, and 136, which also recall the history of Israel.

1 *A grave discourse.* Cf. *Psaumes* (v. 1): '*Graves propos*'. The biblical title is 'A Psalme *to give instruction*' (Geneva). On the Psalmist instructing the congregation, cf. Pss. 45 and 49. Verse 2 was applied to Jesus's teachings in Matt. 13: 35.

2 *renew.* The Psalm recounts God's past blessings in order to encourage God's people to follow His commandments.

11 *praises of Jehova.* Cf. *paraphrasis* and *interpretatio* (v. 4): '*laudes Jehovæ*'.

15–16 Pembroke renders the 'children' in her sources as 'sonnes'.

21 The image of hope as an anchor is added from Heb. 6: 19. Cf. George Herbert's 'Hope'.

32 *offending bowes.* Bows for offence, armour for defence.

33 Characteristic addition of rhetorical question. Why did they flee, although well equipped? Because they had abandoned God.

40 *Zoan fields.* Zoan was a city in Egypt, called by Calvin (v. 12) 'the famousest place of the Realme'.

42 Begins the familiar account of God's deliverance from Egypt, necessary to be recounted because it had been forgotten by the Israelites. Geneva note (v. 9) explains that children of Ephraim means 'also the rest of the tribes'.

uncouth, i.e. marvellous. Cf. Calvin (v. 13): 'the order of nature was altred, so as the waters were . . . raized up into huge banks as it had ben mountains'.

67 *who*, i.e. 'Jacobs race'.

69–70 Geneva (v. 21): 'Therefore the Lord heard and was angrie, and the fyer was kindled in Jaakób'.

74 *Ambrosian Manna.* Pembroke adds the classical term to the biblical manna or 'heavenly breade' (Bèze v. 24).

77 *princes dearest*. The transposition in *I, K, χ*; is almost certainly an early scribal error. It is the bread that is dear, not the princes, whose worth is taken for granted.

82 *raines, n.*, reins. God's control of the elements is stated metaphorically. Geneva (v. 26): 'He caused the Eastwinde to passe in the heaven, and through his power he broght in the Southwinde'. The biblical image of the rain of 'flesh' and 'feathered fowls' ('quayles' in Bèze) is found in 84–6.

117 *mercy*. Geneva (v. 38): 'Yet he being merciful forgave *their* iniquitie'.

119 *oft*. Geneva (v. 38): 'oft times'.

135–6 Geneva (v. 44): 'And turned their rivers into blood, and their floods, that thei colde not drinke'. In Bèze, 'they' are the Egyptians.

141 *of*. i.e. off. For an error or emendation similar to the one in *B*—'oft'— see Ps. 58. 28.

148 *angry Angells*. The sources (v. 49) have 'evil angels', but Calvin insists (and the Geneva note suggests) that they are evil only in the effects of their executing God's judgement.

151–2 Cf. *carmen* (v. 50): *'effusis Mors undíque fertur habenis'*.

153–4 The reference to the fertile Nile is added. Cf. *Antonius*, 751–806.

158 *Cham*, 'Ham' (v. 51) or Egypt. Pembroke uses Bèze's spelling. Cf. Ps. 105. 48, 56.

161 *while*. The emendation to 'when' in *F* is tempting, but unsupported by any other manuscripts, even though it also matches the corresponding passage in Bèze's *carmen* (v. 52).

168 *their wolves*, i.e. 'their enemies' (Geneva v. 53), the pursuing Egyptians. The image was suggested by the reference to the Israelites as 'a flock' in v. 52.

180–2 Cf. Bèze (v. 57): 'they turned them selves aside contrarie from the marke, as deceitfull bowes use to doe'.

188 The mark following 'converse' in *A* is ambiguous and could be read as either a full point or a comma. We have chosen to read a comma because of the context: 'right well content...' modifies 'god' in line 188.

189–90 Cf. Bèze (v. 61): 'he delivered into the handes of their ememies [*sic*] to be carried into captivity, that Arke his moste sure pledge of his presence and of his power, even that his honour and dignitie'.

193 Cf. Psalter (v. 64): 'The fire consumed their young men'. Bèze interprets 'fire' as 'The flame of his [God's] wrath'.

194 The description of the young women is given in the passive voice in Pembroke's usual sources. She makes the verse active, presenting it from the standpoint of the young women, who must live without hope of marrying because the young men have been killed in battle.

196 *no widow left*. The Geneva note explains (v. 64): 'Either they were slaine before or taken prisoners of their enemies, and so were forbidden' to mourn.

197 *a knight*. Pembroke adds the image of chivalry; cf. 'a strong man' (Geneva v. 65), 'a mighty man' (Bèze), 'a giant' (Psalter v. 66). Cf. 205, with the reference to a castle.

202 *Ephraim*. The biblical text (v. 67)—'Yet he refused the tabernacle of Joseph, and chose not the tribe of Ephraim'—and the agreement of *J* with the variant manuscripts, not *A*, suggests that 'Ephraims' is not authorial, but a mistaken scribal emendation.

207–8 Cf. Bèze (v. 69): 'he builte unto him a sanctuary, as a moste stronge Tower, as stable as the body of the earth'.

209–16 Pembroke expands the pastoral image that concludes this Psalm. Cf. 161–8. See I.71.

Psalm 79

Prayer for national deliverance and vengeance against their enemies. Bèze's Argument notes that this Psalm has the 'same use' as Psalm 74, 'the which none of the Godly can reade without great comfort, neither any of the enemyes of the Church without horrible terrour'.

3 The line in χ and originally *K* is hypermetric and thus clearly an early scribal error.

10 On the crow image, see *Psalmes*: 'Literary Context'.

25 *furies*. Geneva (v. 6): 'Powre out thy wrath'.

32 *desert laid*, made desolate, destroyed (as in 'laid waste').

33 *cumbers*, *n.*, hindrances, burdens. Cf. Bèze (v. 8): 'And we . . . have heaped sinne upon sinne of old'.

34 *passed*, *adj.*, former. Psalter (v. 8): 'O remember not our old sins' (cf. Geneva: 'the former iniquities').

Psalm 80

A national prayer for deliverance, emphasizing God's past blessings. Bèze's Argument says that the 'beginnings, the encreasings and also the calamityes of the Church of Israel are most elegantly described under the similitude of a Vine', a metaphor emphasized in Pembroke's paraphrase. [Variant: MS *B*.]

The incipit in *I*, *K*, '*Qui ducis Israel*', may come from the *interpretatio* (v. 1) in Bèze's *paraphrasis*: '1 *Qui pascis Israel ausculta: qui ducis tanquam oves Joseph* . . .'.

2 *shine*. Her usual sources have 'shew thy brightnes' (Geneva v. 1). Bucer has 'thou which sittest betwene the Cherubims shyne unto us'. Crowley also has 'shine'.

6 *Reduce us*. *Interpretatio* (v. 3): 'reduc nos' ('lead us back'). The Variant quotes the biblical (Psalter and Geneva), 'Turn us againe'.

7–8 Virtually repeated at 15–16 and 38–40 to render the repetition of v. 3 at vv. 7 and 19.

7 Cf. Geneva (v. 3): 'cause thy face to shine'. Cf. 15, 39.

9–10 Cf. Geneva (v. 4): 'how long wilt thou be angrie against the praier of thy people?'

10 *thy wrathes fume*. Cf. *interpretatio* (v. 4): '*Quousque fumabis adversus preces populi tui?*' Golding's translation of Calvin (v. 5) is very similar to the text of the *interpretatio*: 'Howe long wilte thou fume at the prayers of thy people?' ([Ccc.vii.]) *Psaumes*: '*Jusques à quand* ... | *Seront tes fureurs allumees* | *Conte la priere des tiens?*'

13–14 *and to dwellers by*, | *a field of brall*. Bèze (v. 6): 'the people that are our neighbours, doe nowe contend amongest them selves for the partition and dividing of our ground'. 'Brall' is a sixteenth-century spelling variant of 'brawl' (as in some of the χ manuscripts).

13 *to foes of laughter*. Cf. Geneva (v. 6): 'our enemies laugh *at us*'.

17 Bishops' Bible (v. 8): 'Thou dydst translate a vine out of Egypt'. Cf. *interpretatio*: '*Vitem ex Aegypto transtulisti*'.

Zoan playnes, i.e. Egypt (Zoan is properly a city in Egypt). Cf. Ps. 78. 40n.

20 *hir*, i.e. the vine's, Israel's.

21 Cf. Psalter (v. 10): 'The hills were covered with the shadow of it'.

27 *woodbred swine*. Geneva notes of the 'wild bore' (v. 13): 'That is, aswel they that hate our religion as they that hate our persons'.

30 *Review*. See again. 30–1 reflect the biblical parallelism (v. 14).

34 *they*, i.e. God's people. Geneva note (v. 16): 'Onely when thou art angrie, and not with the sworde of the enemie'.

36 *that stablisht man*. The participle is supported by the construction in the biblical sources (Geneva v. 17): '*and* upon the sonne of man, *whome* thou madest strong for thine owne self'.

Psalm 81

A liturgical song of praise for a festival, explained in Bèze's *Argument* as the 'feast of the vintage that was of the Tabernacles'.

1–12 A Geneva note (v. 1) explains that 'for a time these ceremonies were ordeined, but now under the Gospel are abolished'. Pembroke, in contrast, emphasizes the joyful use of music in praising God. See *Psalmes*: 'Literary Context', II.28.

10 *tymes.* The singular verb in *O, D* looks like an attempt to correct an error in χ (and *K*). But cf. the biblical text (Geneva v. 3): '*even* in the time appointed'.

17–18 Pembroke explains the change in speakers. Cf. Bèze (v. 5): 'when he [God] did rise up against the Egyptians for their sake, at the which time also he called upon us with such a terrible voyce, as was never heard before'.

20 *baked clay.* Psalter, 'from making the pottes' (v. 6).

22 *thunder-hid.* Cf. Geneva (v. 7): 'in the secret of the thunder'.

23–4 Psalter (v. 8): 'I proved thee also: at the waters of strife'. Geneva, Bèze have 'the waters of Meribáh', but Geneva glosses the word as 'contention'. See Exod. 17: 7, where Geneva glosses 'Meribáh' as '*Strife*'.

34 The original line recorded by Woodforde was based on the Psalter (v. 12): 'and Israel would not obey me'.

37 *had.* The construction is subjunctive here and throughout the rest of the Psalm, as in the biblical text (Geneva v. 13): 'Oh that my people had hearkened unto me'.

44 *lease of blisse.* Pembroke adds the image of God as the landlord granting bliss.

47 *them from.* 'From ye [i.e. 'the']' in *B* is surely Woodforde's alteration of the text based on the phrasing in the well-known final verse of the Psalm (v. 16): 'honie out of the rocke'.

Psalm 82

God's warning to unjust judges, with a concluding prayer that God himself will judge the earth.

1–5 Pembroke emphasizes the duty of magistrates to the poor, stating that God will judge the unjust judges. Geneva (v. 1): 'God standeth in the assemblie of gods: he judgeth among gods'. Geneva notes: 'The Prophet sheweth that if princes and judges do not their duetie, God, whose autoritie is above them, wil take vengeance on them'.

2 *gods.* Calvin (v. 1): 'But in this place, like as also a litle after, and in other places, the name of "gods" is taken for Judges, in whom God hath imprinted a speciall marke of his glorie'. Cf. 21–2.

gods vicegerents. God is the rightful ruler (29–30). Princes serve by God's will and their authority is dependent on just rule. Cf. the doctrine of conditional obedience in Bèze, Languet, and Mornay, as expressed in *Droit des magistrats* and *Vindiciae contra tyrannos*.

18 Rejecting God's word, they lack the light of God's law. Cf. Ps. 119O. 1–3.

ground, n., that on which a system is founded. Most translations present the movement or shaking of the earth, as Geneva (v. 5): 'They knowe not and understand nothing: they walke in darknes, *albeit* all the fundacions of the earth be moved'. Pembroke, focusing instead on the moral failings of the judges, develops the implications of the Geneva note (v. 5): 'That is, all things are out of ordre, ether by their tyrannie or careles negligence'.

20 Cf. Bèze (v. 5): 'For what can remain safe amongest men, when the difference of right and wrong is taken away'.

23–5 Pembroke's original kinetic imagery emphasizes the ephemeral power of the judges, who themselves are mortal, as they progress from sitting high, to falling (in all the theological connotations of that word), to lying dead 'as others'.

25 Clarified by the cancelled revision recorded by Woodforde in *B*.

Psalm 83

A prayer to save the true faith from the machinations of the Amalekites and the Moabites, who were, like the Philistines, identified with the Catholics in Protestant literature but not explicitly here. Most of the incidents cited come from the book of Judges. Pembroke develops the bird imagery in the Psalm, showing a struggle between the people hidden under God's wings and the falconer who attempts to ensnare them.

9 *traines, n.*, snare in falconry, but also with a secondary meaning of treachery or stratagem.

11 *thy hid ones.* Geneva (v. 3): 'thy secret ones', with a note: 'The elect of God are his secret ones: for he hideth them in the secret of his tabernacle, and preserveth them from all dangers'.

19 ff. Most of the nations mentioned are frequently referred to in the Hebrew scriptures as enemies of the Israelites.

23 *Palestina.* The *interpretatio* (v. 7) has 'Palestina'; Crowley and Parker also have 'palestines', but the biblical sources and the *carmen* have 'Philistines'.

26 *Lotts incestious brood.* Cf. *carmen* (v. 8): '*Et Assur orbe ab ultimo,* | *Incestuousæ qui Lothi propagini* | *Armata brachia commodat*' ('And Assur who, from the farthest point of the earth, brings battle-equipped arms to the incestuous offspring of Lot'). A reference to Moab and Edom, or the Ammonites, supposedly descended from Lot and his daughters (Gen. 19: 36–8).

27–8 *Jabin* and *Sisera*. Cf. Judg. 4 and 5.

29–32 Gideon's victory over Midian (Judg. 6–8), including slaying the princes Oreb and Zeb, and the warriors Zeba and Salmuna.

50 *deface, v.*, discredit or defame. Also a continuation of the imagery in 45–8, the artist damaging the portrait.

Psalm 84

A celebration of God's temple in Sion, interpreted by Geneva and Bèze as David's song in exile.

5–6 Explains 'living God' (Geneva v. 2) as the eternal being who imparts life. Cf. Pss. 68. 7, 72. 81–2.

12 *sonnes*. Characteristically used instead of 'young' (Psalter v. 3, Geneva) or 'yong ones' (Calvin), or 'children', as in Ps. 78. 15–16.

15–16 Pembroke adds both the question and the personal application. Cf. Geneva note (v. 3): 'Soe that the poore birdes have more libertie then I' and Bèze (v. 3): 'Oh alas, is my condition worse then that of the sparrowes and swallowes?'

20 The variant line in *K*, χ; is closer to the biblical text (Geneva v. 5): 'in whose heart *are thy* ways'. The revision is intended to reinforce the idea of the exile longing to return home.

22 *mulberies*. The word in Geneva is 'Bacá', but the gloss to v. 6 explains: 'That is, of mulberie trees which was a baren place' (hence, the need to dig for water).

27 *wherto*. The unique variant in *J*, 'where, to', helps to explain this construction as a separate adverb and preposition.

31 *heare what I begg*. Geneva (v. 8): 'heare my praier'. 'Mark what' in *G*, *M* is not corroborated in any of the known sources.

42 *thou*. Emended. The agreement of *B*, *I*, *K*, and χ and the sense of the passage suggest that Davies erred in writing 'that' for 'thou'. The parallelism of the lines is also characteristic of Pembroke's style and of the biblical text, which here, however, has the third person (v. 11): 'For the Lord God is the sunne and shield *unto us*: the Lord wil give grace and glorie.'

Psalm 85

Corporate prayer that God will deliver them, as He has in the past.

The variant incipit in *I* and *K*, *Benevolus fuisti*, is from the *interpretatio* by Mollerus in Bèze's *paraphrasis*.

5–8 Cf. Geneva (v. 2): 'Thou has forgiven the iniquitie of the people, *and* covered all their sinnes'.

8 Pembroke adds the rather Petrarchan wounds and dart.

9 *still.* 'All' in *B* may have been picked up from 8, but it is in the original line recorded by Woodforde and also in both Geneva and Bèze (v. 3): 'all thine angre [Bèze: 'wrath']'. Thus, 'still' may be a revision.

11 *as heretofore.* Pembroke characteristically connects the revelation of God's past actions with the prayer for present mercy.

17 *threed.* The mythological thread of life, spun by Klotho, measured by Lachesis, and cut by Atropos. Cf. Ps. 55. 71–2n.

21 *What speake I?* The transitional question is not in the biblical text. 'Why' in *B* is supported by Bèze (v. 8): 'But why shoulde I use many woordes unto God?' 'What' is repeated in 22, but whether it is an eye-skip or intentionally parallel with 21 is unclear.

31–8 Pembroke expands the agricultural metaphor, suggested by the biblical phrase (Geneva v. 11) 'Truthe shal bud out of the earth', and adds the characteristic clothing metaphor. She does not here adapt Calvin's statement (v. 13) about God working in Nature.

35 *Jehova.* The word in the *paraphrasis* and *interpretatio* (v. 12); the English sources have 'Lord'. Pembroke's characteristic wording. Cf. Ps. 87. 17.

Psalm 86

Personal prayer for deliverance. Pembroke adds a courtly context to this Psalm, not present in her biblical sources. [Variant: MS *B*.]

3 *Client.* Cf. Bèze (v. 2): 'him that is promoted by thy benefit'. Pembroke interprets in a court context, as 'suites' in 12. See also 39–40, with the idea of family service, present in the biblical phrase (Geneva v. 16): 'sonne of thine handmaid'.

7–8 The 'saddnes'/'gladdnes' rhyme, used also in Pss. 48. 29–30 and 51. 27–8, sums up a major theme in the Psalms.

36 *full with.* 'Full' is probably an adverb here—'fully'—not an adjective as in the variant phrase, 'full of' in *I, K, χ*;. The sense is that God flows plenteously with truth and mercy. Cf. Variant Ps. LXXXVI. 60.

40 *of thy handmaid.* By eliminating the 'son' in the biblical phrase, Pembroke maintains ambiguity in the gender of the speaker, but cf. Ps. 116. 42.

42 *eye taught.* That is, the oppressors will see with their eyes how God delivers the faithful. Cf. v. 17, asking that his enemies will 'see' God's goodness towards him. Also a pun: eye-taught and I-taught.

Psalm 87

A celebration of Sion, God's city, which includes people from all the world.

2 *who*, i.e. God.

4 Cf. Calvin's comment (v. 2): 'wheras God had sanctified al Jewrie: yet is he sayde to have rejected all other cities, and to have taken this one [Jerusalem] to him self to reign in'. The phrase 'Gates of Sion' is 'a double Synecdoche', standing for the rest of the city of Jerusalem, as well as the walls ('the whole circuit') surrounding it.

8 *Egipt and Babell*. Geneva (v. 4): 'Raháb and Babel'. Geneva adds a note, 'That is Egypt and these other countreis'.

12 *as borne from hence*. Cf. Calvin (v. 4): 'Those which heretofore were deadly enemyes, or utter straungers, shall not only become familiar frends, but also be ingraffed into one body, so as they shall be accounted for Citizens of Jerusalem . . . as yf they were Jews born'. Thus, those who are now the enemies of God's people shall, though born in Ethiopia and other places, be joined with the citizens of Jerusalem as if they had also been born there (as a synecdoche for the nation of Israel).

17–20 Continues the idea of God's adoption of Gentile peoples, who will be treated as though they were native born. Bèze (vv. 5–6): 'they shall be the native citizens of Zion . . . For God accounting the people, will write them all in his booke'.

Psalm 88

A personal prayer for deliverance, full of agony and despair. See 'Origins, Early Reception, and Influence', I.50 and 'Table of Verse Forms' for parallels with Herbert.

1 *my health*. Cf. *interpretatio* (v. 1): '*Jehova Deus salutis meæ*'. Geneva: 'O Lord God of my salvation'. Characteristic use of 'health' when the Latin and English sources have 'salvation'. Cf. Pss. 51. 40, 62. 3, 91. 56, 96. 5, 119V. 10, etc. The Hebrew can be so translated.

5–6 Pembroke adds the idea of locking up treasure to the simple biblical statement 'daye and night' (v. 1).

20 *in the grave*. Geneva (v. 3) has 'nere to the grave'; the Psalter has 'nigh unto hell' (the apparent source of the gloss in *K* on *grave* in l.12).

31–6 Cf. Bèze (v. 8): 'Thou hast put all my familiars from me, unto whome I am so loathsome . . . so that I keepe my selfe within my house, as it were in a prison'.

43 *wilt*. The apostrophe in *J* shows that it means 'will it' and that no emendation to 'will' (as in *K*, χ) is needed.

54 *oblivions, n.* Cf. Geneva (v. 12): 'in the land of oblivion'.

55 *Good reason.* Pembroke characteristically supplies a connection between the lack of praise in the grave and the speaker's entreaty.

68–9 Cf. *interpretatio* (v. 16): '*terrores tui constrinxerunt me*' ('thy terrors bind me').

69 *fretting.* While 'fettring' is plausible, it would result merely in doubling the sense rather than enriching it as Pembroke's figures of repetition usually do. Fretting is probably intended here in the sense of vexing.

78 *darknesse.* Geneva gloss on 'hid them selves' (v. 18): '*Ebr. were in darknes*'. Cf. Crowley, 'haste caused myne acquayntaunce into darknes to fall'; Parker, 'My frendes that were: familiar, | in darke fro me they stray' (v. 18).

Psalm 89

The Geneva heading says that 'the Prophet' praises God's 'testament and covenant, that he had made betwene him and his elect by Jesus Christ the sonne of David'. Pembroke follows this Christological interpretation, more obviously in *A* than in the variant. [Variant: MS *I*.]

1 *constant promises.* Cf. *carmen* (v. 1): '*illam* | *Constantem cantabo fidem*' ('I will sing of thy constant faithfulness').

3 *still void.* The substitution, 'endles', in *K, χ*, is intended to convey more exactly the sense of eternity implied in Geneva (v. 1): 'I wil sing the mercies of the Lord for ever'. But 'still' may here be used in the sense of 'quiet'. Cf. Buchanan, '*dum sidera mundo* | *Voluentur tacito*'.

6 *It,* i.e. 'bounty' (cf. '*Immensæ benefactæ meæ bonitatis*' in *carmen* and '*les bontez*' in *Psaumes*). The biblical sources (v. 1) have 'mercy'.

8 If 'theirs' refers to 'heav'ns', then Pembroke seems not to make as clearly as Calvin (v. 2) does the distinction between the 'visible skyes' and the invisible heaven. Cf. Variant Ps. 89. 5–7.

9–13 God's promise is quoted (vv. 3–4).

13 In her rendering of v. 5, 'even the heavens shall prayse thy wonderous worke', Pembroke makes allusion to the chariot of the sun. Cf. Variant Ps. 89. 28 and Ps. 104. 67.

13–14 Cf. *carmen* (v. 2): '*divina semel statuit clementia cursu* | *Pergere perpetuo, quales servare videmus* | *Illa rotata suos constanter sydera motus*'.

16 *the holy troopes.* Geneva notes (v. 5): 'Meaning, the Angels'.

thy Court attending. Cf. Geneva (v. 5): 'the Congregacion of the Saints'. Pembroke characteristically adds a courtly context. Cf. Bèze (v. 8), which renders the biblical 'Lord God of Hosts' as 'the emperour of those heaven armies'.

18 *angell.* Cf. Geneva (v. 6): 'sonnes of the gods' with a note, 'Meaning, the Angels'.

19–20 Geneva notes (v. 7): 'the Angels tremble before Gods majestie and infinite justice'. The subject of 'declareth' is 'awe'.

24 *armor-like apparrell.* Pembroke adds the reference to the armour of faith (Eph. 6: 11–17), but here God's own faithfulness is His armour.

30 That is, everything that the earth encompasses belongs to God. Cf. Psalter (v. 12): 'the earth also is thyne, thou hadst layd the foundation of the round world, and all that therein is'.

34–6 Geneva notes (v. 12): 'Tabór is a mountaine Westwarde from Jerusalem, and Hermón Eastwarde: so the Prophet signifieth that all partes and places of the world shal obey Gods power'.

41–2 *Happy the people.* Cf. Bèze (v. 15): 'O Blessed is the people also being stirred up with the sound of thy trumpets O Lord, doth goe foorth, the light of thy countenance shewing them the waie'; Crowley, 'happie people'.

49 *Jehovas shield.* The ruler. Cf. Ps. 47. 20.

52–96 God is imagined speaking in these lines, which recount what God said to the Prophet Samuel (Geneva note on v. 19). The return to the second person is preceded by 'Selah' at the end of v. 37 in the biblical text.

54–6 Cf. Geneva (v. 20): 'I have founde David my servant; Wyth mine holie oyle have I anointed him'. Calvin (vv. 19–21) discourses at length on the question of the legitimacy of the monarch, emphasizing the difference between David and other kings, because David was appointed by God.

55 *the.* Emended. The repetition of 'the' is Davies's error.

62 *all that him hate.* Geneva (v. 23): 'them that hate him'.

63 *my clemency. Paraphrasis, interpretatio* (v. 24): '*clementia mea*'.

64 *hed.* Bèze (v. 24) has 'head'. The biblical sources have 'horn', glossed in Geneva as 'power, glorie and estate'.

71 *my first-bornes roome,* i.e. the room (in the palace) intended for my firstborn child. The image, unique to Pembroke, is of a king honouring his eldest son with the choicest lodging he can provide. It may have been suggested by '*primogenitum*' (hence, the privilege of primogeniture) in the *paraphrasis* and *interpretatio* (v. 27). In any case, emendation is unnecessary.

73 *circling time.* Cf. 13.

75–6 That is, God's bounty will not cease, nor be bound by a term of years.

79–80 David's kingdom will endure until the spheres of the Ptolemaic universe grow weary. Their circling becomes a measure of time, as in 73–4. Cf. Pss. 139. 24, 148. 13–14.

83 *prophanely*. 'And plainlie' in *K*, χ is not corroborated by any of the sources (v. 31).

87 Geneva notes (v. 33): 'Thogh the faithful answer not in all points to their profession, yet God wil not breake his covenant with them'.

94 *their enduring*, i.e. the enduring of the sun and moon. The heavens shall last no longer than the faithful seed of David. Geneva (v. 36): 'his throne *shalbe* as the sunne before me'. As the heavens turn endlessly, so God's truth will endure (96).

95 *wittnesses*. Cf. Calvin (vv. 36–7).

97 *abjected*, 'rejected' (Geneva v. 38), 'cast away' (Bèze). Cf. *paraphrasis*: '*ut Regem nunc illum tuum iratus repulsum abjeceris*'.

97–128 The prophet bewails the present state of David's descendants, caused by their sin, and prays that God will nevertheless honour his covenant with them.

105–9 Rhetorical questions characteristically added to provide immediacy.

109–10 The seasonal imagery is added to the biblical text (v. 44). Cf. *Psaumes*, '*la fleur de sa jeunesse*'.

115 *short*, i.e. 'short is', as in *G*, *M*.

115–20 Pembroke expands the meditation on mortality. Cf. Geneva (v. 48): 'What man liveth, and shal not se death? shal he deliver his soule from the hand of the grave?'

120 *age*. 'Aid' is a plausible alternative, but 'age' probably means here simply 'number of years' or 'length of life': no matter how long one lives, death is sure to come in the end. Cf. Calvin (v. 47): 'Remember of what age I am'. See also Pss. 94. 21n and 104. 112n. The unusual correspondence of *A* and *M* here attests to the authenticity of the *A* reading.

123–5 Cf. Geneva (v. 50): 'the rebuke of thy servants, which I beare in my bosome of all the mightie people. Geneva notes: 'He meaneth that Gods enemies did not onely sclander him behinde his backe: but also mocked him to his face, and as it were cast their injuries in his bosome'.

126 *thy Christ*. Cf. Geneva (v. 51): 'thine Anointed'. Geneva notes: 'They laugh at us, which paciently waite for the comming of thy Christ'. Calvin and *Psaumes* also mention Christ here.

128 Pembroke's rendering of 'Amen' (Psalter v. 52) or 'So be it, even so be it' (Geneva).

Psalm 90

A meditation on mortality as contrasted with God's eternity and a prayer for God's protection. Attributed to Moses in the biblical sources. Bèze uses it to confute pagan philosophers on the nature of death.

9–12 As people were first created of the dust of the earth, so will they return to the earth as dust ('in equall state') when God has determined the length of their life. Cf. Bèze (v. 3): 'And men . . . as at the first they were created by thee of an handfull of dust, so as soone as . . . thou biddest them retourne thether again, they are forthwith resolved into a small quantity of dust againe'.

14, 16 *Adams heyre, dust.* Emphasizes the Hebrew pun on 'Adam' as dust. Cf. Ps. 58. 3n. Pembroke here alludes both to Adam's creation from dust in Gen. 2: 7 and to Adam's punishment after the Fall in Gen. 3: 19 (Geneva): 'thou art dust, and to dust shalt thou returne'.

19 *thee.* 'Bee' in *K*, *χ*; fails to fit the syntax. While the comparison should more precisely be between man's brief life and God's eternal being, the *A* reading is partly corroborated by the phrasing in Bèze (v. 4): 'how little is this space being compared with thine eternitie'.

20 *one quarter of a night.* Cf. *Psaumes*: '*une nuict seulement un quartier*'. Geneva (v. 4): 'a watch in the night', with a note: 'as the watche that lasteth but thre houres'.

23–4 *fancy, substance.* Pembroke develops the idea of the dream from the biblical 'slepe' (Geneva v. 5) and from Bèze, 'their life seemeth to be like a dreame that soudenly vanisheth away'.

25 *As the hearb.* Pembroke develops the metaphor from v. 6.

34 *his*, i.e. its, life's (measure of days). In *P* 'its' has been added above 'his', a further indication of the lateness of that manuscript, since the change points to a reader who was uncomfortable with 'his' as an early regular neuter form.

36 *a sound that sounded ends.* Psalter (v. 9): 'a tale that was told'.

40 *in poast.* From the French '*en poste*', in the manner of a courtier; hence, at express speed, in haste.

41–2 Bèze (v. 11): 'yet how few do consider the power of thy wrath'. Geneva notes: 'If mans life for the brevitie be miserable, muche more, if thy wrath lie upon it, as they, which feare thee, onely knowe'.

Psalm 91

A wisdom Psalm, meditating God's protection of His people. Bèze's Argument contextualizes the Psalm to the pestilence in 2 Sam. 24 and applies it to contemporary plagues. He includes a moving reference to his 31 years of exile and to his own experience with the plague.

The variant incipit in *I*, 'Habitans in', is from Mollerus' *interpretatio* in the *paraphrasis*. See 'Relationship of the Texts of the *Psalmes*', II.348 n. 22.

4 I, for one, dare affirm.

9–14 Pembroke expands the bird imagery of vv. 3–4, paralleling her treatment in Ps. 57. 4 and throughout Ps. 83.

13 *soft hiv'd*. Cf. Geneva (v. 4): 'sure under his feathers'.

19 *I say*. God speaks in lines 17–56. Cf. 49, 'saith god'.

24 *no*. Perhaps Davies's error for 'nor', as in *K*, *χ*;.

41–4 Quoted in gospel accounts of the temptation of Christ, Matt. 4: 6 and Luke. 4: 10–11.

55 *fill of life*. Cf. Bèze (v. 16): 'I will likewise prolong his life to the full'. Geneva notes on 'long life' (v. 16): 'For he is contented with that life, that God giveth: for by death the shortnes of this life is recompensed with immortalitie'.

Psalm 92

A Psalm of praise. The Geneva heading declares 'This psalme was made to be sung on the Sabbath, to stirre up the people to acknowledge God and to praise him in his workes'.

4 *spring*, 'day-spring'. Psalter (v. 2): 'early in the morning'.

7–9 Pembroke makes no apology, as does the Geneva note on v. 3, for using music to worship God.

13–15 Pembroke characteristically adds questions, as Parker does here (v. 5).

13 Inexpressibility topos appropriate to encomium.

15 That is, no one can understand thy thoughts. Cf. Psalter (v. 5): 'thy thoughts are very deepe'.

20 The biblical text has grass but not flowers. The flowering grass probably comes from Calvin, 'When the ungodly florish as grasse, and all the workers of wickednesse do blossome' (v. 8) or from Parker, 'When evill men flour: as (doth the) grasse: and wicked workers bud' (v. 7). Pembroke develops the plant metaphor here to connect with the rest of the Psalm, particularly lines 35–43, which expand the biblical metaphor in vv. 12–14.

24, 25 *loe*. The repetition in 25 is biblical (Geneva v. 9): 'lo, thine enimies . . . lo, thine enimies'. Thus, 'low' in *K* and some of the *χ* copies is the result of scribal error or emendation (probably because of 'high' in 23). The occurrence of 'loe' in the *H* group helps authenticate it as the correct *χ* reading.

26 *all*. 'Shall' in *C* is likely scribal or editorial even though it is supported by the biblical text (Geneva v. 9): 'shal perish'. But cf. Parker (v. 9): 'thy foes shall perish all'.

28 Cf. Geneva (v. 10): 'anoynted with fresh oile'.

35 *Date-bearing tree.* The biblical sources have 'palm', but Calvin (v. 13) calls it a 'date tree'.

36 *for greene, and growth,* i.e. with regard to greenness and growth (the righteous shall be like the cedar and the palm).

38 *his,* the just man's.

Psalm 93

A Psalm praising God as King. Pembroke's paraphrase emphasizes the eternal, unchanging nature of God's reign.

1 Cf. Geneva (v. 1): 'clothed with majestie . . . and girded with power'.

5 *throne.* Although Geneva (v. 2) says, 'Thy throne is established of olde', the retention of the third person was probably suggested by Bèze: 'Therefore is his kingdome much more stable and unmoveable'.

9–12 The lines conform to Bèze's interpretation (v. 3): Even though rivers roar and roaring waves rise, trouble the sea, and break upon the shore, God on high is more powerful than them all. Pembroke does not read the storms allegorically as a reference to the wicked, however, as does Bèze (vv. 1 and 4). The unusual phrasing of 9 seems to be an attempt to match the Geneva translation: 'The floods have lifted up, ô Lord: the floods have lifted up their voice'.

Psalm 94

This prayer for vengeance was frequently applied to contemporary situations. Pembroke's uncle, Robert Dudley, wrote a poetic version when imprisoned for supporting Lady Jane Grey as queen (Arundel MS 290), for example, and Bèze's Argument applies the Psalm to Europe 'at this day'.

1–8 Here and throughout the Psalm Pembroke renders more of the text in the interrogative than do the biblical sources, making the Psalm a dramatic monologue.

1 *God of revenge.* Cf. Geneva (v. 1): 'O Lord God the advenger', with a note 'Whose office it is to take vengeance on the wicked'.

6 Pembroke, like Bèze, adds the connection between doing and boasting (vv. 4–5).

11 *then.* 'God shall not see' is to be construed as direct discourse; thus 'them' in *O, D, G, M* represents a scribal slip or misinterpretation.

13 *you.* The sources have 'ye' (v. 8) as in some of the χ copies, though probably not χ itself.

17 *Who checks the world.* Cf. Parker (v. 10): 'he that checkes: the heathen'.

19–20 *who raignes above,/he knowes*, i.e. he who reigns above knows.

in thy schoole. Cf. Calvin (v. 12): 'if god trayne us up in his schoole'. On God's school, see particularly Ps. 51 and 119.

21 *his age*. His life. Cf. Pss. 89. 120 and 104. 112n.

24 *such men*, i.e. 'the wicked' (Geneva v. 13).

32 *held my soule in mew*, i.e. confined my soul. Pembroke's usual sources have the soul being silenced rather than confined. Cf. Geneva (v. 17): 'If the Lord had not holpen me, my soule had almoste dwelt in silence'. Pembroke, however, presents silence itself as confinement, as in Ps. 68.

35 *quailed in mind-combats*. Pembroke adds the martial imagery.

38 *throne of missery*. Cf. Geneva (v. 20) 'throne of iniquity', glossed as the seat of 'wicked judges'. Pembroke's term includes the results of that unjust judgement, misery for the godly. Cf. Ps. 82.

39 The unjust judges pretend to administer the law, but intend only to injure the righteous.

Psalm 95

A Psalm praising God as King and calling on the people not to repeat past mistakes.

15 *kneele*. 'Fall' in the later χ copies probably results from a scribal eye-skip (cf. 'fall' in 14). The biblical text (v. 6) has both 'fall' and 'kneel', interpreted allegorically in a Geneva note, 'thei muste give them selves to serve God'.

20 *pasture*. Possessive, as the spelling in *O, D* indicates; the sheep of his pasture.

24 *Masha…Meriba*. Geneva (v. 8) glosses the words as 'tentacion' and 'strife' and refers to Exod. 17: 7, part of the account of the Israelites' dissatisfaction with their wanderings in the desert: 'And he called the name of the place [where Moses struck the rock to obtain water], Massáh and Meribáh, because of the contention of the children of Israél'. Cf. Ps. 78. 49–56.

25 *god doth say*. Pembroke explains the switch from the Psalmist's voice to that of God in the biblical text.

38 Pembroke adds the explanatory parenthesis to v. 11.

Psalm 96

A Psalm praising God as King. Pembroke's version is notable for its emphasis on sacred song and dance.

10–12 That is, because Jehova, who alone is great, doth hold his throne for awe and glory far above all the (false) gods.

13 *For but.* Emended because the phrase, 'But for', in *A, F, J* is probably Davies's error. The question is, What are all the false gods (whom the people of the earth adore) except lifeless idols?

14 *besides.* Emended. The misspelling in *A* is Davies's.

16–18 Pembroke develops the personification implicit in the bibical text, (Geneva v. 6), 'Strength and glorie *are* before him: power and beautie [Bèze: 'Majesty'] *are* in his Sanctuarie'.

20 *give.* Emended. The vocative 'O' is added in *A* in gold, but mistakenly because it makes the line hypermetric. Neither the *F* nor the *J* scribe noticed the error.

24–6 Pembroke expands the courtly imagery of v. 8 (Geneva): 'into his courtes'.

27 *goe with quaking pace.* Geneva (v. 9): 'tremble'.

29 *staylesse, adj.,* without stay or permanence, ever-changing. Cf. Geneva (v. 10): 'the worlde shalbe stable, *and* not move'.

Psalm 97

A Psalm praising God as King, using the image of thunder and lightning to demonstrate his vengeance on idol worshippers.

1 *Jehova.* Bèze's Argument says the Psalmist portrays 'the divinitie of Christ by the repeating of the name Jehovah 6 times, and by attributing al glory and power unto him'.

2 *Earthy.* 'Earthly', properly 'pertaining to the earth' rather than 'consisting of earth', is probably a scribal error in the later manuscripts; the sources have 'the earth'.

7–8 Cf. Bèze (v. 2): 'sitting upon a throne, stayed as it were, with two unmoveable pillers, namely justice . . . and most severe judgement'.

12 That is, his flashings maketh lightnings. Cf. Bèze (v. 4): 'The lightenings breaking foorth from his judgement seat shall fill the world with glittering light . . . and [the wicked] shall tremble throughout the compasse of the earth'. Thus, 'lightning' in *N, C, G* may be a scribal slip or a mistaken emendation based on the misunderstanding of the sentence structure.

23 *you.* The biblical texts (v. 7) have 'they' as in *G, M* (Geneva: 'they that serve graven images'). But the source of Pembroke's paraphrase here is Bèze: 'O ye slaves of the idols'. Cf. 24, 'Idoll-servers'.

27 *all Angells.* The biblical texts have 'all ye gods', which Geneva interprets as 'all that which is estemed in the worlde'. Cf. Bèze (v. 7), 'the very

Angels', and Parker, 'Ye angels all ... bowe downe your knee'. Bèze's Argument stresses the 'worshipping of the very Angells' as a proof of the divinity of Christ, but Pembroke does not make the Christological interpretation explicit here, as she does in Ps. 89 and 132.

31 The source is Bèze (v. 8), who interprets the biblical phrase, 'daughters of Judah', metaphorically as cities.

34–5 God is the ruler over the rulers. Cf. Ps. 82, where God is presented as the judge of judges.

41–2 Cf. Geneva (v. 11): 'Light is sowen for the righteous, and joy for the upright in heart', glossed, 'Though Gods deliverance appeare not suddenly, yet it is sowen and laied up in store for them'.

Psalm 98

A Psalm calling on God's people and all nature to praise God as King.

2 *newnesse.* Pembroke's rendering of the familar biblical text, 'Sing unto the Lord a new song' (Geneva v. 1) may be self-reflexive, for that is what she is doing in these *Psalmes.*

5–7 God has revealed that long-hidden salvation for which His elect wait. Pembroke, like Geneva and like Bèze's Argument, interprets the Psalm as 'the prophecie of the spreading of the kingdome of the Messiah' to the Gentiles. Cf. Eph. 3: 5–7.

7 *taught,* i.e. Jehovah hath taught the nations His justice.

9 *the motives were,* i.e. the motives for God's revealing His salvation. Cf. Bèze (v. 3): 'And if any demaund what hath moved him ... to so great bountifulnesse: let him knowe ... that he is myndfull of the promise that he hath made'.

11 *Margine.* Cf. Geneva (v. 3): 'all the ends of the earth'; Crowley, 'coastes'.

15 *Lute.* Pembroke replaces the biblical 'harp' (v. 6) with the lute as accompaniment for vocal music. See *Psalmes:* 'Literary Context', II.28.

18 *totall globe.* Cf. Psalter (v. 8): 'round world'.

20 *echo.* Pembroke's sources (v. 8) command the mountains to be 'joyfull' (Psalter), to 'rejoyce' (Geneva), to 'skippe' (Calvin), or even to 'daunce' (Parker). She adds the more realistic touch.

21 *you,* i.e. the sea, rivers, and so on. The command to the heavens and the earth to rejoice parallels Isa. 44: 23.

22 *who,* i.e. the Lord.

Psalm 99

A Psalm praising God as King, recounting past blessings to Israel.

4 *rideth*. The biblical texts (v. 1) have God 'sitteth *betwene* the Cherubins'. Crowley says God 'sate upon' them, an image also present in the Old Version, which may have prompted the idea of riding them, echoing Ps. 18: 10.

5–6 Cf. Psalter (v. 2): 'The Lord is great in Sion: and high above all people'.

15–16 Geneva (v. 5): 'and fall downe before his fotestole'. 'Sett' in MS *A* fits the context of the paraphrase; the petitioner would not 'sitt' (as in *I, K, χ;*) before the Lord. The parenthesis comes from Geneva (v. 3): 'praise thy...Name (for it is holie)'.

18 *there*, i.e. at God's footstool. Emendation to 'these' is thus unnecessary, in spite of the testimony of most other manuscripts.

20 *their sutes*. Courtly imagery is added.

21 *But*. 'But' is justified by the context established by the last part of line 20: God did not in the past deny the suits of his people, but deigned to talk with them from a pillar of cloud. Cf. *paraphrasis*: '*Sed et iliis olim patribus nostris ex columna nubis loquutus est*'. 'Out' (as in *I, K, χ;*) matches the Psalter (v. 7).

Psalm 100

A Psalm of praise, explained in Bèze's Argument as a hymn of praise for God's creation and for his adoption of the Church.

1 *you*. 'You' is used as a nominative form elsewhere, e.g., Ps. 98. 20.

2 *mery shout*. The exuberance of this rendering surpasses the Psalter (v. 1), 'come before his presence with a song', or even Geneva, 'Sing ye loude unto the Lord'. The phrase is closer to the Bishops' Bible, 'a joyfull noyse', or Crowley, 'Come merily into his syght, rejoyceynge hertily'. 'Pleasant songes' is characteristic of the more conventional phrasing in *M* and sometimes *G*.

Psalm 101

Psalm 101 is traditionally interpreted as David's meditation on the duties of kingship, justice and mercy (as in the Vulgate incipit, '*Misericordiam et judicium*'). Geneva particularly emphasized the king's duty to encourage true religion by 'rooting out the wicked, and cherishing the godly persons' (Heading, the Old Version.) These duties are to be undertaken, not on his own initiative, but in his role as vice regent to God.

1 *now appointed king*. David writes between his anointing by Samuel (1 Samuel 16) and his accession (2 Sam. 5). Calvin's heading says, 'Although

David were not yet settled in the kingdom, yet... as he was alredy created king by gods apointment, he frameth and addresseth himselfe to the best maner of governement'. Cf. Bèze, 'O Lorde I being appointed King by thee'.

4 *Till that day come.* Pembroke follows Geneva by reading 'Till thou comest to me' as a subordinate clause instead of the more traditional question, 'When wilt thou come unto me?' as in the Great Bible. That is, David is not personally ambitious, but is waiting with patience and certainty for his destined role as king.

5 *deepe study.* Cf. *interpretatio* (v. 2): '*Graviter studebo viae integrae*'. Pembroke portrays this time of exile from court as a period of deliberate preparation for public service. See *Psalmes*: 'Literary Context', II.22.

6 *pure in hart.* Begins a series of allusions to hearts, particularly contrasting David's pure heart with the 'malicious hartes' (11) of the slanderers and the 'puffed hartes' of the 'proud ambitious band' (13–14).

12 *whisp'ring biters.* Whispering is used in its secondary meaning of 'secret slander', and 'biter' in its obsolete sense of 'deceiver' or 'trickster'.

16 *my Counsailors.* Pembroke here is closer to the Hebrew text than to most earlier English Psalters, such as Crowley, wherein David promises 'such wyll I take to dwell with me', obscuring the political impact present in the Vulgate ('*hic mihi ministrabat*'). See Theodore Steinberg, 'The Sidneys and the Psalms', *SP* 92 (1995), 1–17. Marot and Calvin also give a political reading.

18 David vows to study virtue himself and to appoint officers who both speak truth and do justice.

23 *hate outright.* 'Root out quite' is probably not the authorial revision it at first appears to be. As the intermediate version in *H* suggests, it is more likely an attempt to correct the apparent error in *K* and *χ*, 'roote owt-right'. The Psalter does have 'roote out' in the second part of the verse. For the first part, however, both the Psalter and Geneva have 'destroy'.

Psalm 102

A prayer for personal deliverance from sickness and national deliverance from enemies. Geneva interprets vv. 1–12 as a personal plea for deliverance and vv. 13–28 as the cry of the Church, and Bèze's Argument presents the entire Psalm as the lamentation of the Church, but Pembroke renders it all in the first person.

1 *praying.* The sequence, 'my praying' and 'my cry', corresponds to the parallelism in the sources. The Psalter (v. 1) has 'my crying' as the second element. The variant in *χ* may be the result of a scribe's eye-skip or recall of the Psalter phrasing. The alteration in *K* seems to support the authenticity of the *A* reading.

5 *most most.* The metrically defective line in χ may have come from a scribe's misreading and consequent mistaken emendation.

17 *lonely Pellican.* Cf. *paraphrasis* (v. 6): '*Ononcrotalo* [*sic*] *per deserta mugienti . . . similis*' ('Like the pelican bellowing in the desert places'). 'Lovely' in *K*, χ;, which does not fit the pelican image, is clearly a scribal error resulting from the frequent similarity of 'u' and 'n' in nearly all hands of the period. Hunnis much expands the Pelican image, giving the entire legend.

desert Owle. Henry Sidney quoted this phrase from the Vulgate in a letter to Francis Walsingham, explaining his wife's isolation after she was disfigured, or defaced, by smallpox. (1 Mar. 1583, PRO SP 12/159, f. 38ᵛ.) See 'Life', I.3.

19–24 Cf. Bèze (v. 7): 'I pass the nights like a birde under the house eaves, bereaved of her mate, or spoiled of her yong ones taken forth of the nest'.

29–30 Cf. Bèze (v. 8): When the enemies 'wish evill' to anyone, they 'abuse the example of my calamity, if they wish evill or curse any'. Calvin (v. 9): 'the ungodly beare themselves so reprochefully ageynst the chosen people of god, that they borow their misfortunes as in pattern to sweare by'.

32 *wine.* Cf. v. 9, 'mingled my drinke with weping'.

50 *like a Carcasse.* The metaphor comes from Bèze's Argument, saying that the Church is 'most like a dead carkasse then to a living body'.

51 *in.* The preposition need not be emended to 'on' if the sense of 'beare' is here a 'tomb'.

65 *heav'nly hall.* Pembroke adds the courtly image to the biblical phase (v. 19): 'out of the heaven'.

69 *they,* i.e. the prisoners, who, when freed, may become 'fitt meanes' (72) of honouring God's name.

74 *in the mid way.* Cf. Psalter (v. 24): 'in the middest of mine age'. The Psalmist contrasts human mutability with God, who is 'endlesse' and 'aglesse', 78.

85 *one, still one.* Cf. Parker (v. 27): 'thou art still: as we behold, | And art that art; Perpetuall', and Bèze, 'the self-same'. All seem to be attempts to render into the second person 'I am that I am'.

Psalm 103

A Psalm of praise for God's forgiveness of sins and care for his people.

9 *free grace.* Calvin (v. 3) writes of God's grace in 'freely forgiving and wyping away our sinnes'. Pembroke also uses the phrase in Ps. 56. 43, 59. 43, and 119D. 40, etc.

19 *Eagle-like*. Geneva note (v. 5) explains that the eagle sucks blood, 'and so is renewed in strength, even so God miraculously giveth strength to his Church'. Cf. Isa. 40: 31.

40 The metaphor of the balance is added (v. 10).

41–3 Geneva (v. 11): 'For as high as the heaven is above the earth'. Cf. Bèze: 'Nay, looke howe much more greater the heaven is then the earth both in largenesse and in height'. Pembroke adds the Ptolemaic sphere.

45 *his*. God's.

47 *his synnes*. The sins of the one who fears God with 'due devotion'.

53–6 This extended paraphrase may contain allusions (especially in 56) to Calvin's use of the verse (12) to refute the view of 'the Papists ... that the free remission of sinnes is given but once onely, and that afterwarde righteousnesse is gotten ... by desert of works'. Calvin argues that 'wee see here, that the mercy of God ... in not laying our sinnes to our charge, is not shet up by David within a moment of tyme, but is extended even too the ende of our lyfe'.

65 Perhaps because of Bèze's reference to 'earthen vesssels', Pembroke adds the metaphor of God as potter to the biblical text (v. 14): 'he remembreth that we are but dust'. Cf. Isa. 64: 8, Rom. 9: 21, Jer. 18: 1–6.

68 *glasse*. Perhaps a scribal error for 'grasse', as in all the sources. Cf. Geneva (v. 15): 'The daies of man are as grasse'. Or perhaps Pembroke is continuing the potter image with reference to the glassblower.

73–4 Pembroke characteristically adds a transition.

75 *Justice ... mercy*. The transposition in *C* and *N* matches the sequence in the sources (v. 17). 'Bounty', which appears for 'mercy' in other places, may have been suggested by 'grand' bonté' in *Psaumes*.

78 *uncontrol'd*, 'Not subjected to control' (*OED*, citing Ps. 75. 9 to illustrate the attributive use). The more specific sense here is probably 'unlimited' or 'numberless'. Cf. Calvin (v. 17): 'Also he sayth that the same [righteousness] shall be spred forth upon their children, and children's children ... God sheweth mercy to a thousand generations.'

80 *doe*, follow, abide by. Cf. Calvin (v. 18): 'But David sayeth that this mindfulnesse dooth then florish when men occupie themselves in doing'. The angels in 84–8 give an example of obedient deeds.

Psalm 104

A celebration of God's act of creation, in language that Bèze's Argument praises as 'this heavenly poeticall invention'.

1–8 Pembroke expands the courtly imagery, as the 'curtain' of the biblical text becomes a canopy of state.

10 *in Chev'ron*, in the shape of a chevron, 'consisting of a bar bent like two meeting rafters' (*OED*).

14 *from*. The *A* reading is not implausible. Still, the agreement of *B* with the other copies suggests that Davies may have made the same error as the *H* scribe, who caught and corrected it.

13–16 The obedience of the winds and of the angels is emphasized by Bèze and Calvin; the Geneva note refers to Heb. 1: 7.

19 *once*. At creation. Cf. Bèze.

24 *haste*. The polyptoton is so characteristic of Pembroke's style that the variant in *O*, *D* and the alteration in *I*, *K* seem unlikely to be authorial.

28 *where*. The spatial context of the biblical texts supports the *A* reading over 'When' in *B*.

bounding describes God's action in fixing limits to the seas.

36 *mansions*. Cf. Psalter (v. 12): 'the fowls of the air have their habitation'.

39 In expanding the metaphor of v. 12, Pembroke adds the Art/Nature topos.

43 The metaphor of pregnancy is intensified by Pembroke. Cf. Geneva (v. 14), 'that he maie bring forthe bread out of the earth' and Bèze, 'of the bowelles of the earth'.

50 *folded*, i.e. wrinkled because of care. Cf. Geneva (v. 15): 'And wine that maketh glad the heart of man, and oyle to make the face to shine, and bread that strengtheneth mans heart', with a note commenting on God's providing man with necessary things like food, but also things 'to rejoyce and comforte him, as wine and oyle or ointments'. The oil may have a cosmetic effect on wrinkles.

54–61 Following Calvin (v. 15) in interpreting the Psalm as a commentary on the duty of the rich to 'releeve the want of their brethren', Pembroke emphasizes the responsibility of the cedars to demonstrate *noblesse oblige* by helping the 'small birdes'. See I.74.

56 *that*. Emendation (see Woodforde's note and Rathmell) is unnecessary if 'that' is taken here as introducing a clause. The point is that the tall cedars (like princes) are given more moisture precisely because of their greater height (rank). The elaborate paraphrase was suggested by Bèze (v. 16), but the class reference is original. See I.73–4.

62 *traces*. Woodforde's proposed emendation to 'tresses' seems to be based on a misreading; the 'heads' are simply the tops of the hills which the goats have worn with their paths. There may be a pun, however, because of the

image of the heads; 'trace' could mean 'tress', although the *OED* cites no examples of that precise use after 1400.

65–6 Pembroke expands the description of the moon, using phrasing traditional in secular poetry.

67 Pembroke adds the classical image of the chariot of the sun. Cf. Ps. 89. 13.

68 *knowe*. Emended. The exactly parallel constructions of 65–6 and 67–8 suggest, along with the evidence of *B* and even *I*, that Davies erred in making the verb indicative rather than subjunctive at this point.

70 When the sun sets, the 'wood-burgesses', or nocturnal citizens of the forest, delight in going abroad.

72 *crave*. The variant in *K* and most χ copies—'clayme'—seems to be a gratuitous emendation influenced by 'right'.

73 *he*. The Sun. Cf. Geneva (v. 22): 'When the sunne riseth, they retire, and couch in their dennes'.

78 *I*. The personal pronoun is added to the biblical text, v. 24. The Geneva note explains that God's works are beyond mankind's ability to express, but Pembroke personalizes the inexpressibility topos.

81–2 By adding the two imperatives, Pembroke clarifies the structure of the biblical text.

86 Pembroke's description of the sea monsters characteristically conflates the 'play' of Geneva with 'pastime' of the Psalter (v. 26).

92–6 The recycling of old substance into new form parallels Spenser's Garden of Adonis in *The Faerie Queene*, III. vi. 35–8.

91–3 The sudden transition from the abundant life of the creatures to their death seems indebted to the literal translation of Calvin (v. 29): 'Thou shalt hide thy face, they shalbe afrayd: thou shalt take away their breath, they shall dye and turne ageine to their dust'.

101–5 The switch to the first person echoes the biblical text (Geneva v. 33) 'I will sing', but Pembroke intensifies the focus on the speaker and the poet's need for 'good acceptance'. Cf. Geneva (v. 34): 'let my wordes be acceptable unto him'.

111 The added parenthesis characteristically explains the reason all should praise God.

112 *nor*. Emendation to 'noe' would make the construction too elliptical even for the concentrated verse Pembroke often writes; 'bandes' would require a preposition such as 'with'.

The distinction between 'time' and 'age' may be that the former refers to the general concept of time (as opposed to eternity) and the latter to the personal limits of existence. Cf. Pss. 89. 120 and 94. 21.

Psalm 105

Historical Psalm, emphasizing God's goodness. [Variant: MS *B*.]

8 *inquest*. Geneva (v. 4): 'seeke his face'.

11–14 The distinction is between the special covenant God made with the children of Abraham and His general, eternal lordship over the whole world. Cf. Bèze (v. 7): He is 'Lord over all the earth, but he is our God by a peculiar right'.

19 Note that two generations are cited in the Variant, but three here, as in biblical text (the Bible mentions Abraham and Jacob in v. 6 and adds Isaac in v. 9). Jacob is 'god-beholding' because of his vision of God, Gen. 28: 12–16, 35: 1, and 48: 3.

21 Pembroke adds the contractual language.

25–30 Although they had no seat, or permanent dwelling, they were secure because God protected them and punished even kings who would molest them.

29 *anointed band*. The revision of a phrase originally borrowed from Bèze (v. 15), 'Priests anoynted' (*B* variant 38), in light of the Geneva note: 'Those whome I have sanctified to be my people'.

31 *spake*. Geneva (v. 16): 'he called a famine upon the land'. 'Sent' in *C* is probably not authorial.

33–40 Note the concise presentation of Joseph's story: sold as a slave by his jealous brothers, he was imprisoned, but set free because of his interpretation of dreams ('divining'), and providentially empowered to save his family from famine.

42 *doth*. The whole stanza is in the present tense.

48 *Cham*, 'the land of Ham' (v. 23) or Egypt. Pembroke uses Bèze's spelling. Cf. Ps. 78. 158.

51–2 Cf. Bèze (v. 25): 'For God did change their mindes against his people, that [the Egyptians] beganne to hate them, whom they loved so greatly before, and they nowe laboured by subtiltie to circumvent them'.

53 *he*. God. 'Herewith' in *K* and the later χ manuscripts results from misreading or ignorance of the source (v. 25). It is God who 'wills', not Aaron; furthermore, Aaron is God's choice (54), not Moses's.

59 *late watry*, i.e. recently flowing with water (rather than blood as now).

60 Pembroke adds the personal voice, reluctant to tell these horrors.

62 *where their princes sleepe*. Cf. Bèze (v. 30): 'the verie chambers of their king'. Pembroke vividly images the impact of frogs, lice, and vermin in the royal bedchambers.

75 *folk.* Emended. The *A* reading of 'flock' is not implausible, but it is not corroborated in the major sources (v. 37), which have 'people' (Bèze) and 'them' (Geneva and Prayer Book). Thus, in spite of the agreement of *M* (which is often unreliable), Davies may have made an error in transcribing 'folk' (the reading in *K*, χ;), which is also the word used in Bucer. Cf. Ps. 74. 6 and Variant Ps. CV. 100–1.

82 *Beavies,* a company of quails. Thus 'levies' in the later χ copies is indefensible.

87–8 Cf. Bèze (v. 42): 'And this did he, even mindfull of those thinges, which he the holy one in times past had covenanted with his servaunt Abraham'.

91–3 Cf. Bèze (v. 44): 'Unto whom he gave those countries that were possessed of sundrie people, having obteined with great ease, what soever the inhabitants thereof had gotten with great travell and paines'. Thus, 'their' in 92 refers to the neighbouring peoples, while 'their' in 93 refers to the Israelites.

Psalm 106

Historical Psalm, emphasizing God's faithfulness and the rebellion of the people, 'these Mutiners' (23).

1–4 Pembroke amplifies the biblical statement of the inexpressibility topos and expands the interrogative mode.

2 *to our good.* The direct source of the *A* version is Geneva (v. 1): 'Praise ye the Lord because he is good'.

3 *force. Interpretatio* (v. 2): '*vires*'. Calvin: 'mightie power' (cf. 'power' in *N*, *C*).

6–7 Pembroke, who learned archery as a child, adds the metaphor to v. 3.

6 *doe.* 'Doth' in some of the χ copies does clarify the subject, which is 'sight'. But the agreement of *K*, *H*, *G*, *M* with *A* suggests that 'doe', which is not unusual in such a construction, is the authentic reading.

10 *liv'ry.* Pembroke adds the courtly imagery. Cf. 'badg' in Variant Ps. CV. 120 as a mark of God's elected (16).

17–18 A difficult passage syntactically, although the transitional parenthesis clearly points to Bèze (v. 7) as the source: 'For to begin the matter from the first originall, those our Fathers neither had any regarde of so many myracles wrought in Ægypt, neither were they mindefull of the multitude of thy benefites'.

17, 21 Pembroke adds the personal voice.

20–1 The repetition reflects the similar phrasing of the biblical sources (v. 7): 'at the Sea, even at the red Sea'.

22 *for.* Geneva (v. 8): 'for his Names sake'.

26–7 Pembroke expands the biblical image (v. 9): 'he led them in the deepe, as in the wildernes'. But cf. Parker (v. 9): 'And through great deepes he led them dry: as desert men do passe'.

28 *setting.* 'And sett' in *N* seems intended to restore regularity to the metre, which is mainly iambic (but cf. 14, 'boasting').

haters. Emended. Inadvertently omitted by Davies, the word is in *B*, *K*, and χ.

39 Explains the reference to 'gluttons' in 38. Even though they are fully fed, they continue complaining on their journey. Thus, 'But' in *N*, *C* seems unlikely to be an authorial revision. The substitution of 'liv'd' for 'far'd' (travelled) casts further doubt on the variants.

43–9 Dathan and Abiram were among those who challenged the authority of Moses and Aaron. Their rebellion caused them to perish in an earthquake and then 'came out a fire from the Lord' and consumed 250 additional men. See Num. 16: 1–3, 27–35. Cf. Calvin (v. 17): 'swalowed up Dathan, and over covered the Tente of Abiram'.

50–5 While Moses was on Mt. Horeb (or Sinai) receiving the Command-ments, the people convinced Aaron to make a golden calf and then wor-shipped it: Exod. 32: 1–35. Pembroke wryly comments that the highest form of worship to such a god would be to make offerings of hay. Cf. Psalter (vv. 19–20): 'They made a Calfe in Horeb, and worshipped the molten ymage . . . of a Calfe that eateth haye'.

56–60 That is, They forgot God, who had preserved them through mighty miracles in the plains of Egypt; and wonderful works, like the opening and closing of the Oker (or Red) Sea, which let them safely pass and then closed over the Egyptian armies.

57 The description of the Nile as fertile may come from *carmen* (v. 21): '*Nili ad fluenta fertilis*' ('by the streams of the fertile Nile'). Cf. Ps. 78. 153–4.

60 *passage.* Emended. The word is added in *A* above underlined 'ferry', which probably means here a passage or crossing over a river. The authenti-city of 'passage' as a revision (rather than an editorial emendation) is cor-roborated by its appearance in *B*, as well as *J* and all other manuscripts except *F*. 'Ferry', however, is used in a similar way in *A Discourse of Life and Death*, line 540.

61–3 Psalter (v. 23): 'So he said, he would have destroyed them, had not Moses his chosen stood before him in the gap: to turn away his wrathful indignation, lest he should destroy them'.

71 *Pehor*, i.e. Baal-peór 'Which was the idole of the Moabites' (Geneva note v. 28).

72 *dead things*, i.e. 'dead idoles' (Geneva note v. 28).

76–7 Cf. Geneva (v. 30): 'But Phinehás stode up, and executed judgement, and the plague was staied'. Geneva notes: 'When all other neglected Gods glorie, he in his zeale killed the adulterers and prevented Gods wrath'. See Num. 25: 11–13. Bèze (v. 31): 'And Phinees was counted to have done that thing justly, and thereby did obteine the prayse that should remaine to all posterity'.

79 *the brooke of brall*. Psalter: 'the waters of strife'. Geneva (v. 32) has 'the waters of Meribáh' and a marginal reference to Ps. 95: 8, where the transliterated Hebrew word is glossed as 'strife'. See Ps. 95. 24n.

80 *his*, i.e. the brook's. Calvin (v. 32): 'they quareled with God at the waters of strife, wheruppon the place tooke his name'.

81 Geneva (v. 32): 'so that Moses was punished for their sakes'.

93 Pembroke follows Geneva in identifying the pagan gods as devils (v. 37).

105 *worthy plagues*, i.e. plagues they had deserved (v. 43).

109–12 They were repentant, and so changed that not only God, but also their captors, had pity on them. Cf. Geneva (v. 46): 'And [God] gave them favour in the sight of all them, that led them captives'.

119 *approve my word*. Pembroke adds the emphasis on the poet/speaker. Cf. Bèze (v. 48): 'agree unto me'.

Although this is the end of the fourth book of the Psalms, Pembroke does not include a doxology, as at Pss. 72. 90 and 89. 128.

Psalm 107

An exhortation to praise God for His providential care, structured liturgically with verse and refrain.

1 *Paraphrasis, interpretatio* (v. 1): 'Celebrate *Jehovam*'.

3 Pembroke adds the idea of space to the biblical time (Geneva v. 1): 'for his mercie *endureth* for ever'.

9 That is, how many people God has saved and how many times He has acted to save them.

11 *coastes*. Woodforde, in substituting 'wastes', seems to have assumed that the poet meant 'deserts'. But Pembroke is thinking of Geneva (v. 3): 'And gathered them out of the lands, from the East and from the West, from the North and from the South'. On the last phrase, Geneva notes: '*Or*, from the Sea: meaning the red Sea, which is in the South parte of the land'.

12 *dispersed*, i.e. those who have been dispersed.

13 *who*. Emended. 'How' seems to be Davies's error, as *B*, especially, suggests. The complex parallelism is between the 'many ... dispersed' whom

God has brought to rest (12) and the 'many... distressed, | And straying' whom God has saved (13–14). The last part of 13 thus begins a relative clause describing the condition of those who have been delivered. Cf. the similar parallel construction of Bèze's paraphrase of vv. 2–3.

14 Cf. Geneva (v. 4): 'out of the way, *and* found no citie'.

16 Pembroke adds the paradox of drought drowning, or destroying, them.

17–23 The refrain, varied to fit the verse, is repeated three times (33–8, 49–54, and 81–6), as in the original, cf. Geneva vv. 6–8, 13–15, 19–21, 28–31.

19 *error train'd* and 42, *Follies traine.* Cf. Spenser, *The Faerie Queene* I. i. 18. 9, '*Errours* endlesse traine'.

27–8 Cf. Bèze (v. 10): 'chayned in their minde with sorrowe, and in their bodyes most strictly with yron fetters'.

33 *They.* The 'Rebells' (29) who, when God humbles them, cry to Him for aid.

36 *broken boltes.* Pembroke renders the biblical 'bonds' as 'boltes', thereby connecting with the gates in v. 16. God breaks the bolts of the gates of brass and iron (39–40), releasing them. Cf. Crowley, 'and the great barres of Iron he hath in sunder broken'.

44 *this gwerdon,* this reward, i.e. confinement to bed in illness. The immediate source is Bèze (v. 17): 'the reward of their madnesse'.

57–84 Pembroke expands the biblical description of shipwreck.

57 *mounting winged tree,* i.e. boarding ship.

67 *bedasht with raine.* Pembroke adds to the scriptural hyperbole (Geneva v. 26): the storm makes the ship 'mount up to the heaven, and descend to the depe'. Here, the storm is so severe that even the stars get wet.

76 *head-lame feete,* i.e. their heads, through fear, make their feet lame.

77 *Pilot.* Not in biblical text, but cf. Calvin (v. 27): 'although the masters of shippes that have the guiding of the sternes bee never so skilfull: yet are they utterly set beside their knowledge'.

77–80 What good is it to have a skilful pilot when the storm is so great that even 'wisdomes ey' can see nothing?

87 *peoples presse.* Bèze (v. 32): 'the... multitude of the people'. The variant in *B* reflects the apparent distinction in the parallelism of the biblical text: 'the Congregation of the people' and 'the assemblie [Psalter: 'seat'] of the elders' [Bèze: 'their chiefe men']'.

91 *saltes the soile.* Geneva glosses 'barrennes' in v. 34 as 'saltenes'. Cf. Calvin (v. 34): 'and a fruteful land into saltnesse for the wickednesse of them that dwell therein'.

109 *nor strang.* Pembroke adds the transitional comment. It is not strange that God can change plenty to want, or the reverse; the idea in the Psalm here (vv. 33–40) is something like the Wheel of Fortune.

112 *like heards their howses.* Cf. Bèze (v. 41): 'spreadeth their families like a flock'.

114 *aright.* Bèze (v. 42) has 'upright judgement', but the syntax in Pembroke's phrasing is different and better allows for the adverb, 'aright', than the adjective, 'upright', in *B*.

119 *light.* Cf. Geneva note (v. 43): 'whose faith is lightened by Gods Spirite'.

Psalm 108

A national hymn of praise for God's deliverance, composed of vv. 7–11 of Psalm 57 and vv. 5–12 of Psalm 60 (q.v.). Pembroke's first version, recorded in MS *B*, combined her previous paraphrases of these passages; see Variant: MS *B*. The revised version in MS *A* is a new poem.

4 Once again Pembroke has lute in place of 'viol' in the biblical sources (v. 2). Crowley also has lute.

8 Cf. Bèze (v. 5): 'to the whole compasse of the earth'.

16–17 Emended. Davies failed to notice that the sentence is continued by the next stanza. Geneva (vv. 5–6): 'and *let* thy glorie *be* upon all the earth, That thy beloved maie be delivered'.

19 Added to v. 6. Cf. the Old Version (v. 6): 'harken unto mee'.

25 *Manashe.* Not only is this closer to the spelling in Geneva and Bèze ('Manasséh'), but it also more clearly indicates that the name is trisyllabic. The spelling in *G, M* is the same as in the Psalter. The claim for 'Manasse' in *K, χ;* is that it is used in the *paraphrasis* and *interpretatio.*

32 *triumphed,* i.e. when I have triumphed over you. Cf. Bèze (v. 9): 'I will triumph over proud Palestina with joyful acclamations, as she hath triumphed over us before'. Israel will force all these nations to demonstrate their subjection by participating in a triumph. Cf. Ps. 110. 9–16, Variant Ps. LX. 32, Petrarch's *Trionfi,* and *Antonius* (see I.264).

34 *strongest.* Emended. Correction of another spelling error in *A.*

Psalm 109

A Psalm of vengeance, cursing enemies and praying for deliverance.

6 Pembroke adds the military imagery of 'engins' and 'battry'.

7–8 Pembroke intensifies the biblical idea (Geneva v. 3): 'fought against me without a cause'.

12 Cf. Bèze (v. 4): 'there remaineth nothing unto mee, but onely to flee to my prayers'.

13–42 A series of dependent clauses answering the question in 13.

13–54 The curse against the enemy. Perhaps believing the curse may be efficacious, Bèze in his Argument cautions about the use of this Psalm of vengeance: 'it must be used in prayer, and also reade with great judgement'. He applies it to the persecutors of the Church in 'this daye' more explicitly than does Geneva—or Pembroke.

15–16 Cf. Bèze (v. 6): 'and cause him to have envious men againe at his elbowe, which may let his purposes'.

17 Cf. Geneva (v. 7): 'When he shalbe judged, let him be condemned'.

32 *fathers*. The change to 'father' (as in *G*, *M*) is not necessary if 'fathers', like 'forefathers', is possessive: father's hand.

39–40 A difficult passage, because of the unusual placement of 'for' (which may be an error for 'soe'). The sense is that the speaker's enemy disregarded even the most basic human impulses to decent behaviour.

42 *humbled*. The error is in χ; 'humbled' refers to the condition, not the quality, of the heart. Cf. Geneva (v. 16): 'the sorowful hearted' man.

45–8 Cf. Bèze (v. 18): may 'calamitie . . . cleve unto him like a garment, and invade him wholly, as the drinke received into the body entreth into the bowels and the strength of oyle doth pearce unto the very bones'.

47–8 The repeated use of 'as' in parallel clauses echoes Parker (v. 18). 'And' in *B* comes from the biblical sources.

51 Added intensification.

62–3 Bèze (v. 23): 'and I leape here and there like a grashopper'. Geneva note: 'Meaning, that he hathe no staie nor assurance in this worlde'.

64 *fast*, i.e. fasting.

69 *thou, thou*. Emended. The omission of the repeated 'thou' is Davies's error. The construction is clearly imperative, as in all the sources (v. 26), and is corroborated by other manuscripts.

77–8 The clothing metaphor is expanded. Cf. Geneva (v. 29): 'Let mine adversaries be clothed with shame, and let them cover themselves with their confusion, as with a cloke'.

Psalm 110

'David prophecieth of the power and everlasting kingdome given to Christ', according to the Geneva heading and Pembroke's other usual sources. The Psalm is so interpreted in the New Testament, particularly in Heb. 1: 13. Bèze terms it 'an epitome of the Gospell'.

1 According to Pembroke's interpretative sources (v. 1), David here presents God the Father ('my lord') as speaking to Christ ('the lord'). Cf. Jesus'
comment on the verse in Matt. 22: 43–5. See also Acts 2: 34–5.

5 *from me.* The *A* version maintains consistency in the use of the first-per-
son point of view. The other manuscripts are closer (by implication) to the
biblical text (Geneva v. 2): 'The Lord shall send the rod of thy power out
of Sion'.

10 *in solempne robes.* Bèze (v. 3): 'in garmentes of triumph which shall be
holy'. The phrase in *B* may owe something to the *paraphrasis* (or *carmen*): '*tri-
umphalibus . . . vestibus sacris*' (*carmen*: '*Sacris . . . vestibus*').

15–16 Pembroke adds the classical reference to dawn. Cf. *carmen* (v. 3): '*Et
qualis auroræ ex sini* [?] | (*Cæleste donum*) *prodiens* | *Ros prata pingit gemmea*'
('And just as the dew—a heavenly gift—flowing from the bosom of dawn
embellishes the jewelled meadow').

19 *Melchisedech.* A priest-king honoured by Abraham in Gen. 14: 18–20
and mentioned as a type of Christ in his eternal priesthood in Heb. 7, especially v. 21, which quotes Ps. 110: 4.

Psalm 111

A Psalm of praise for God's care of His people.

7 *and working.* Geneva (v. 4) confirms this reading: 'He hathe made his
wonderful workes to be had in remembrance: the Lord is merciful and ful
of compassion'.

13–14 That is, now what (besides his works and attributes) could confirm
each promise, doom, or decree to be sure, just, and unmoved.

18 Characteristic word play on the proverb, 'The fear of the Lorde, is the
beginning of wisdom' (Psalter v. 10). See I.62.

Psalm 112

A wisdom Psalm meditating on God's blessings of the righteous, with a concluding note on the punishment of the wicked. Although this is also an alphabetical Psalm, it is not so noted by Calvin, and Pembroke does not render it as
alphabetical.

5 *branches.* An adaptation of the plant imagery implicit in the biblical 'seed'
(Geneva v. 2): 'his seede shallbe mightie upon the earth'. Pembroke's plant
imagery parallels the description of the just man in Ps. 1: 3 (Geneva) as a
'tre planted by the rivers of water'.

13 *he.* God. Cf. Bèze (v. 4): 'God . . . commandeth the light to arise unto
them that walke uprightly'.

17 *He.* The just man.

19 *businesses.* Cf. Crowley (ll. 18–20): 'The good man...lendeth plentuously | And doeth all hys owne busines, excedynge equally' .

25, 27 *staied, displaied.* Emended. The extra syllables are required by the metre and are corroborated by other manuscripts.

29 *straweth,* i.e. distributes widely. As in the Geneva note (v. 5), Pembroke stresses generosity to the poor.

32 *applause.* An original rendering of the exalted horn of Geneva and Psalter (v. 9).

33–5 *fume,* to demonstrate anger (as in Ps. 80. 10), but here retains a hint of the original sense of 'smoke' (cf. 'consume' in 35 and Geneva v. 10). The wicked and their 'fetches', or tricks, will consume themselves until there is nothing left; they will dissipate like smoke. Cf. Geneva note (v. 10): 'the blessings of God upon his children shal cause the wicked to dye for envie'.

Psalm 113

A hymn of praise for God's providence towards the 'needy soule' (13). Bèze's head note stresses God's love 'toward the miserable and poore', such as Joseph, Moses, David, and Daniel, and to 'barren women', such as Sara, Rebecca, and Anna. [Variant: MS *I.*]

3 *Jehovah.* Cf. Bèze (v. 2): 'The blessed name of Jehovah'.

10 *highly mounted,* i.e. placed high in the mountains. Cf. Bèze (v. 5): 'sitteth most gloriouslie in a most highe place'.

15–16 That God makes kings of 'the needy soule' and the 'wretch' is not precisely the sense of the biblical text (Geneva v. 8): 'That he maie set him with the princes'. The interpretative source may be the *carmen* (vv. 7–8): '*Atque attollit humi prius iacentes,* | *Fimoque tergit obsitos,* | *Rectores populi sui futuros,* | *Regumque sessuros throno*'. Cf. also the Old Version (vv. 7–8): 'The needy out of dust to draw...And so him set in high degree, | With Princes of great dignitie'.

Psalm 114

Praise for God's mercy in delivering Israel from Egypt which, the Geneva heading declares, 'put us in remembrance of Gods great mercie toward his Church'.

3 *elected.* Calvin (v. 1) discourses on the choosing of Israel.

4 *there,* i.e. among the people of Israel, 'Jacobs race' (1).

5–6 Jordan participates in the opening of the Red Sea. Cf. Bèze (v. 3): 'The sea did flye at his [Israel's] sight, comming forth of Egypt, least it should hinder his passage, Jordan driving her waters backwarde made itselfe passeable, that he might come over'.

5–10 Repeated as questions in lines 11–16 as in the biblical original, vv. 3–4 and 5–6.

Psalm 115

Prayer for deliverance from idol-worshipping oppressors, contrasting the power of God to the weakness of idols.

7–12 Pembroke clarifies the sense of her originals by setting up parallel questions. The idolaters ask *where* God is, and the godly ask *what* the idols are. The dramatic monologue sets up the contrast between the invisible but powerful Jehovah, and the visible but impotent idols. Cf. questions in 43–4.

35 *thrice blest.* Pembroke adds the number as an intensifier, as in the opening of 'Even now that Care'.

39 *vaughted roofe*, i.e. vaulted. Pembroke expands the metaphor of the earth as the floor and the heaven as the roof of God's dwelling. God dwells in the upper chambers and gives the 'lowly ground' to men.

Psalm 116

A Psalm of praise for God's deliverance from suffering and from doubt.

11 *prone.* As in the biblical text (v. 5) the emphasis is on the reliability, not the speed, of God's help (as in *M* with its variant, 'quick').

14, 16 *esteemed, redeemed.* Emended. The third syllable is required by the metre and is supported by other manuscripts.

25–32 Cf. Geneva note (v. 11): 'In my great distresse I thoght God wolde not regarde man, and is but lies and vanitie, yet I overcame this tentacion, and felt the contrarie'.

29 *finding false*, i.e. it is false that all men are liars.

33–6 As in ritual sacrifice. Pembroke adds the detail of throwing the cup into the fire, whereas the sources (v. 13) speak only of lifting up or drinking the cup as part of a thanksgiving banquet. Cf. Exod. 29: 40.

41 *taste*, i.e. experience. Cf. Pembroke's metaphorical use of 'taste' in Ps. 119N. 19–20 (v. 103) and Ps. 34. 8 in the biblical sources and as paraphrased by Philip Sidney in Ps. 34. 29–30.

44 *fettring*, i.e. fettering. The variant 'fretting', or chafing, is also plausible.

43 *bands.* Pembroke follows Geneva, Bèze, and Calvin (v. 16) rather than the misprinted (and later corrected) 'bones' of the Psalter. But cf. Ps. 51: 8 which does present God as breaking the Psalmist's bones in Geneva as well as Psalter; Pembroke does not render that phrase either.

46 *sacrifice of praising.* Calvin (v. 17) has a note on the 'calves of his lips' as a sacrifice. Cf. Pss. 51. 43–9, 55–6 and 119O. 10–11.

55 *midle space.* Cf. Geneva (v. 10): 'in the middes of. . . Jerusalem'.

Psalm 117

Unlike her sources, Pembroke renders the repeated phrase, 'Praise ye the Lord', as an acrostic in the initial letters: PRAIS THE LORD. This is much more concise than the earlier, less successful attempt at an acrostic in MS *B.* Bèze's headnote says that this shortest Psalm gives 'the summe of the gospell'. Explained by Paul in Rom. 15: 11, as noted by Geneva and Bèze. [Variant: MS *B.*]

4 *I ehovas.* 'I' preserved here for the acrostic.

7 *H is.* Emended. The repeated 'h' is another obvious slip by Davies.

Psalm 118

A Psalm of praise, with the refrain 'For his mercie *endureth* for ever' in verses 1–4 and 29 rendered as a chorus in the final couplets of stanzas 1–4 and 20, with different groups being called upon to sing the refrain. See also the rendering of 'in the Name of the Lord shal I destroie them' in verses 10–12 as the final couplet in stanzas 8–10. Because v. 22 is applied to Jesus in the New Testament (as in Matt. 21: 42, Acts 4: 11, and 1 Pet. 2: 7) and because v. 26 is quoted in the Palm Sunday account (Matt. 21: 9, Mark 11: 9, Luke 19: 38, and John 12: 13), Psalm 118 is given a Christological interpretation in Christian sources.

20 *unlarging,* i.e. enlarging. Cf. Geneva (v. 5): 'the Lord . . . *set me* at large'.

41 *thou.* On the sudden shift to the second person, Geneva comments (v. 13): 'He noteth Saúl his chief enemie'.

53–4 That is, Who opens to me Justice's gate so that, entering in it, I may relate God's praise? The Geneva note (v. 19) explains, 'He willeth the dores of the Tabernacle to be opened, that he may declare his thankeful minde'.

57 *Here, here.* In the Tabernacle. Cf. Bèze (v. 21): 'Here will I praise thee'.

67–8 *rideth. . . bideth.* Pembroke retains the distinction in Bèze and Geneva (v. 26) between the one who is coming to God's house to govern (the king) and those who dwell in God's house (the priests).

Psalm 119

A meditation on the law of God as a guide to faith and practice. The 176 verses of Psalm 119 are arranged in 22 groups of eight verses, each octave beginning with a successive letter of the Hebrew alphabet (the transliterated names are printed in Geneva and *paraphrasis*). Pembroke adopts this feature in her paraphrase and also uses 22 different stanza forms (plus the unique forms of the variants of four octaves G, H, S, W). She also begins each octave with the appropriate English letter, so that A opens 'An undefiled', B opens 'By what', and so on. Of her sources, only Parker attempts such alliteration, although he alliterates almost every line. Nearly every line of the original includes a reference to God's law; Pembroke uses many synonyms, including hests, edicts, statutes, lectures, biddings, commandings, learning, and ordinances.

Psalm 119A

Pembroke adds questions at lines 3 and 6, making the Psalm a dramatic monologue.

1 *course.* Like the biblical 'way', which Pembroke uses in line 7, 'course' emphasizes the image of the path that recurs through this Psalm. 'Life' in *G, M* is a more conventional alternative.

6 *harty seeking.* Cf. biblical phrase (v. 2): 'seke him with their whole heart'.

7 That is, for the one who relies on God's way, or commandments, to direct his walk, or behaviour.

8 *sinnfull blott infecteth.* Not in any of the sources. Geneva (v. 3): 'worke none iniquitie'. Parallels presentation of sin as disease in Ps. 51. 22–6, 40.

24 *in whole,* i.e. wholly. The variants in *C, M* seem to indicate ignorance of or discomfort with the idiomatic phrase.

Psalm 119B

1–3 Pembroke's 'correcting line' and 'levell' use metaphors from carpentry instead of 'cleanse' (Psalter v. 9) or 'dresse' (Geneva). The image may come from Calvin (Alpha, v. 1): 'levell their lyfe at the marke'. Cf. Ps. 146. 15, 17.

8 *Caskett.* The *A* reading is supported over 'closett' in *O, D, C, M* by the amplification of the image of God's word as a 'pretious treasure' in Bèze (v. 11).

15 *teach all nations.* Pembroke adds the quotation from Christ's instructions to the apostles in Matt. 28: 19: 'Go therefore, and teache all nacions'.

Psalm 119C

3 *and.* The biblical text (v. 17) also has a paratactical construction. Thus 'to', as in the later χ copies, is likely not authorial.

9 *statutes light.* The light of God's statutes. Cf. Bèze's request (v. 18) for God to remove the veil which keeps out 'true light'.

13–14 God will make those who are high become low, and the proud lowly, or humble.

21 *thoughts shall walk.* Pembroke carries through the image of the godly life as a journey on the path depicted in God's word, so that thoughts and speech also 'walk'. Cf. Ps. 119D. 28n.

Psalm 119D

22 *wreathed,* i.e. twisted or crooked. The word appropriately describes the path of error; thus, 'wretched' in χ is probably a scribal slip. 'Writhed' in *B* is probably a spelling variant.

28 *tread.* The reviser of *G, M* again shows discomfort with the dominant image of the Psalm. The image of the tongue treading appears grotesque if taken literally, but paraphrases Parker (v. 3): 'To talke thy wondrous steppes'. Cf. Ps. 119C. 21.

Psalm 119E

4 *blinded eyes.* Cf. Calvin (v. 34): 'blynded with fleshly reason'.

14 *falsed face.* Original addition to 'vanity' (v. 37).

15 *trade,* i.e. way or path. Cf. Old Version (v. 33): 'Instruct me . . . in the right trade, of thy statutes'.

20 *comming,* i.e. anticipated. Woodforde's note, 'forte comming', is mistaken, and his emendation to 'cousning' is unnecessary. Cf. Bèze (v. 39), 'Turne away that reproche, which I do not feare without cause' and Old Version, 'Reproach and shame which I so feare | from me (O lord) expell'.

24 *my will.* 'Me still' in *B* may be another of Woodforde's emendations or errors. The emphasis is on 'strength to continue in thy worde even to the end' (Geneva note v. 40).

Psalm 119F

19 *their.* Lines 19 and 20 reverse the normal order of the clauses. The true antecedent is 'my thoughts' and is therefore more precise than 'my' in *G, M*.

23 The antecedent is 'I'. Cf. Geneva (v. 46): 'I wil speake also of thy testimonies before Kings, and wil not be ashamed', with a note, 'He sheweth the children of God oght not to suffer their Fathers glorie to be obscured by the vaine pompe of princes'.

29 *will either*. Woodforde's suggested emendation of 'with' is ingenious, but the former may not have been written, as Woodforde says, 'accidentally for' ('*forte pro*') the latter, in spite of the testimony of *K* and χ. The compound subject and repeated auxiliary make an acceptable syntactical construction. Cf. Bèze (v. 48): 'I will holde with both mine handes thy commaundementes'.

Psalm 119G

[Variant: MSS *B*, *K*, χ.]

1 *Grave*, i.e. engrave. Cf. Parker (v. 7): God's word 'Graven depe in mynd'.

2 *my trust*, i.e. God.

11 *in exile*. Pembroke follows Bèze's phrase (v. 54) 'being an exile', instead of being on pilgrimage (Geneva; Psalter) or 'among the straungers' (Old Version). The image is clearer in Variant line 22.

16 *this*. Geneva note, following Calvin (v. 56): 'That is, all these benefits'.

Psalm 119H

[Variant: MSS *B*, *K*, χ.]

4 *sute*. The image of the courtier making 'hott and harty sute' to God comes from Calvin (v. 58): 'made sute untoo thy face'.

13–15 That is, he was robbed. His losses did not result from neglect of God's laws. Cf. Geneva (v. 61): 'bands of the wicked have robbed me'. Here, as occasionally elsewhere, Pembroke uses a Latinate structure with the verb at the end of the sentence.

Psalm 119I

13 Cf. Geneva (v. 69): 'The proude have imagined a lie against me'.

16 Cf. *carmen* (v. 70): '*Delitiis illi corpusque animumque saginent*'.

23 *Mines*. Added to the biblical image of gold and silver (v. 72).

Psalm 119K

1–4 Pembroke intensifies the biblical 'fashioned' (v. 73) in this description of creation *in utero*. 'Conceiving' is a pun.

1 *conformed*. 'Confirmed' in *M* misrepresents the metaphor. Cf. Geneva (v. 73): 'thine hands have made me and facioned me'.

20 *in*. 'On' in *B*, *K*, χ is a plausible alternative, but the biblical sources seem to corroborate *A* (Psalter v. 78): 'I will be occupied in thy comandments'.

Psalm 119L

8 *wine*. Added to the biblical metaphor of the smoked bottle in v. 83, connecting it with the wine of the gospel that cannot be contained in old bottles (Matt. 9: 17), probably because of the Latin '*uter*' used in commentaries by Bèze and Vatablus, and in both passages in the Vulgate. Characteristically, *G* and *M* supply a conventional, more literal substitute, 'waie'.

15–18 Cf. Geneva (v. 86): 'All thy commandements *are* true: they persecute me falsely'.

Psalm 119M

1–2 In his 100–word paraphrase of v. 89, Bèze says, 'in the frame of the heaven . . . there is as it were ingraven a sure stability of that thing which thou has once spoken'.

3 *earth*. Emended. The capital 'E' was probably added later by mistake.

5 *they*. Earth and sky.

9 *revived*. The biblical sources have 'quickened' (v. 93); thus, 'relieved' in *K*, χ is probably a scribal error.

14 Cf. Old Version (v. 95): 'the wicked men do seeke my bane'.

16 Cf. Geneva note (v. 96): 'There is no thing so perfite in earth, but it hathe an end: onely Gods worde lasteth for ever'.

Psalm 119N

23 *true wisdom*. In opposition to the 'false waies' of 24. 'Sure' in *B* is probably another error.

Psalm 119O

5 *the*. The *A* reading seems to be authentic, part of an elliptical construction: the statutes . . . (which) thou justly dost ordain. The variant, 'thy', in *B*, *K*, χ is thus probably an error.

10–11 Geneva stresses offering sacrifices of praise instead of animals. A Geneva note and Calvin's commentary on v. 108 both mention the 'calves of my lipps'; Geneva cross-references to Hos. 14, where the phrase becomes a page heading. The note explains, 'Declaring, that this is the true sacrifice, that the faithful can offer, even thankes and praise' (Hos. 14: 2). Cf. Pss. 51. 43–9, 55–6 and 116. 46.

13 *naked*, i.e. exposed to danger. Cf. Bèze (v. 109): 'my life is exposed to all casualties as though I did cary it in my hande'.

Psalm 119P

5 *clossett*. The biblical 'refuge' (v. 114) is variously rendered, such as 'hid and secret place' (Old Version) or 'bower' (Parker). 'Clossett' would be the usual term for an aristocratic woman's private room.

14 Cf. Bèze (v. 116): 'and do not shame me, by making my hope frustrate'.

15 *Piller*. Original, metaphorical addition to the biblical prayer to 'stablish me' (v. 116).

23 *abjected*, i.e. cast out. Cf. Ps. 125. 17. All three parts of the *paraphrasis* have '*abjicis*' (v. 119).

Psalm 119Q

6 *baile thy servant. Interpretatio* (v. 122): '*Sponde pro servo tuo*', with the legal sense of providing bail or security.

9 *Eye doth*. Pembroke's sources have the plural (v. 123), as in *G, M*, but the plural eliminates the pun.

14 *at thy mercies hand*. Geneva (v. 124): 'according to thy mercie'. The omission of 'thy', as in Woodforde's note, makes the reference to mercy too general.

22 *the time requires*. In spite of Woodforde's note that 'the' has been expunged, the definite nature of the statement matches Bèze (v. 126): 'For the time it selfe requireth'.

24 *they*. Cf. Geneva (v. 126): 'For they have destroyed thy law'. 'Doth' in *B, K, χ* is probably an error.

30 *all thy precepts*. Quoted from Geneva (v. 128), although Woodforde notes that 'all' has been deleted.

Psalm 119R

6 *babes*. The biblical sources have 'the simple', which Geneva interprets in a note as 'the simple idiots' (v. 130), rendered by Old Version as 'the very ideots'. Pembroke follows an alternative tradition given in *carmen*, '*infantes*';

interpretatio, '*parvulis*'; Calvin, 'little ones'. Both readings stress the educative function of God's word.

7 Cf. Bèze (v. 132): 'I have greedily swallowed thy precepts'.

10–12 That is, as ordained and taught by thee, I see that thou hast earlier had pity for them whose hearts embrace thy name. Cf. Geneva (v. 132): 'as thou useth to do unto those that love thy Name'.

22 *welling*. The emendation of 'swelling' in *K* and χ eliminates the water metaphor in 21–4, wherein Pembroke amplifies the image of tears as 'rivers of water' (Geneva v. 136) or 'great floudes' (Old Version).

Psalm 119S

Variant: MSS *B*, *K*, χ.]

5 *flame*. Cf. Bèze (v. 139): 'inflamed with love of thee'; Geneva: 'My zeale hath even consumed me'.

9 *debast*. Cf. Old Version (v. 141): 'as one of base degree'.

11–12 Follows Bèze (v. 142) in contrasting God's eternal laws with the laws of men that 'are subject unto change, and . . . come to nought'.

Psalm 119T

1 *harty plaint*. Cf. Geneva (v. 145): 'with *my* whole heart'.

4 *bend*. Cf. Bèze (v. 145): 'am bent to keepe thy statutes'.

9–10 A convoluted rendering of the biblical text (Geneva v. 147): 'I prevented the morning light, and cryed: *for* I waited on thy worde'. But cf. Parker: 'The dawning day: preventingly I creied most earnest than: | Trust fast I did: thy words for why: my hope theby I wan'.

21 *gracelesse crue*. The godless, those without grace.

22 *pursue*. Emended. Correction of a misspelling.

29–30 That is, I know now, although I also knew it long ago. Cf. Geneva (v. 152): 'I have knowen long since by thy testimonies'.

Psalm 119V

5–6 The Psalmist prays that God will serve both as his 'deemer', or judge, and as his redeemer, or his advocate against those who falsely accuse him. Cf. Bèze (v. 154): 'Even thou, unto whom I appeale from the most wicked judgements of other men, plead my cause and be my judge'.

10 *health.* Pembroke frequently uses this rendering of the biblical 'salvation' (v. 155), here supported by Crowley, Old Version, Parker, and the Psalter, where Geneva has 'salvation'. Cf. Ps. 88. 1n.

11 *sole.* The context supports the *A* reading because of the emphasis on the word of God as the only means of salvation.

16 *revive.* Pembroke's usual rendering of the biblical 'quicken' (v. 156). Cf. Ps. 119M. 9n.

20 *declined.* Cf. Bèze (v. 157): 'Yet have not I declined from those things which thou hast testified unto us'.

Psalm 119W

[Variant: MSS *B, K, χ.*]

Parker omits 'W', as a double-V, and forges bravely ahead with 'X', which he solves by writing a large E in the left margin, so that each line begins with X, but the words are 'extremely', 'exactly', *etc.* Pembroke includes W and omits X.

18 Cf. Geneva (v. 168): 'for al my waies *are* before thee'.

Psalm 119Y

11 *thy scholer.* Cf. Geneva note (v. 169): 'As thou hast promised to be the scholemaster unto all them, that depend upon thee'. As in Ps. 51, Pembroke emphasizes the sequence present in her biblical sources: God will teach the Psalmist, and then that Psalmist will be empowered to speak God's praise.

Psalm 120

Bèze's lengthy Argument for Psalm 120 terms Psalms 120–34 'Psalmes of Ascensions', although the common Hebrew title is literally interpreted (by Calvin and Geneva, for example) as 'songs of degrees'. Bèze notes that they 'were peculiarly consecrated to celebrate the retourne of the Israelites out of Babylon' and that they were usually sung by those who 'went up to the temple at solemne feastes'. Calvin rejects Bèze's interpretation and interprets them as songs about David's wanderings, sung in the temple after his return. In either case, the theme of exile made them particularly relevant to the Genevan community, as Bèze notes: 'nowe also there is great use of this Psalme, seeing that the Godly are compelled oftentimes to flee into farre countries by the crueltie of the wicked'. [Variant: MSS *G, M.*]

1–4 Pembroke added to the biblical text the idea of repeated past answers as an indication of future answers .

5–8 The 'forgers' and the 'poisoned abuse' retain Calvin's distinction between the two ways deceitful tongues work (v. 2): 'eyther in compassing them by wyles and captiousnes, or by deffaming them falsly'.

13–16 Bèze combines the two metaphors (v. 4): the wounds made by the deceitful tongues are like those of burning darts made from juniper wood, known to be difficult to extinguish.

19 *Kedar, Mesech.* The Psalmist, exiled from his homeland, wanders in remote regions of northern Arabia and Asia Minor.

20 Emphasizes the nomadic life of the speaker.

22 That is, the furious enemies to friendly peace.

Psalm 121

A Psalm of praise, interpreted in Bèze's Argument as the song of the people as they come within sight of the hills of Judaea. God's protection of them in their long journey from Egypt has application to 'all the Godly'. [Variant: MSS *G*, *M*.]

1–4 Pembroke's dialogue format clarifies the sense of the biblical text, interpreting the biblical 'whence' interrogatively, as does Parker (v. 1), and supplying a reason for looking to the mountains, which are, as Bèze explains, the mountains of Judaea and the site of the Temple. The Old Version (v. 1) gives a concise version of this argument in 'Lift mine eyes to Sion Hill'.

5 *March, march.* From *Psaumes* (v. 3), *'marcher'*, emphasizing the idea of journey, explicit also in Bèze. Cf. 13.

11 *thy saving shadow.* Geneva (v. 5): 'the Lord is thy shadowe', as also rendered in Bèze, as opposed to 'thy defense' in the Psalter .

13 *boldly.* God's people should set forth boldly, knowing that God will protect them as He has done in the past. Bèze's Argument emphasizes the appeal to history to establish God's faithfulness: God's people comfort themselves by remembering another journey, when God brought them out of Egypt 'with a cloude in the day time against the burning of the sunne, and a piller of fire against the discommodities of the night'.

13–16 The explanation of how the sun and moon could potentially injure them comes from Bèze (v. 6): the heat of day and 'the noysome humours which the moone useth to raise in the night time'.

15 *night: the.* Emended. The punctuation is clearly misplaced in *A* and can be corrected from the other early texts, *B* and *K*.

Psalm 122

A Psalm of praise for Jerusalem and the temple, rendered 'Salem' (peace) by Pembroke, thereby emphasizing the theme of the Psalm. [Two other versions are extant. Variant: MSS *B*, *I*, *σ*; and Variant: MSS *G*, *M*.]

6 *gods holy people.* The scribes of *F* and *J* may have misread and mistakenly emended. Cf. Bèze (v. 4): 'But especially that that people which is holy unto God, might assemble together by tribes'.

6–10 Cf. Bèze (v. 5): 'tribunall seates are there placed of God for David and his posterity, to minister justice'.

14 *pray.* Suggested by Bèze (v. 8): 'I powre forth these prayers'. 'Wish' in 13 and 16, and here in 14 in *C*, is from the biblical text (v. 8).

Psalm 123

A prayer for God's deliverance. This highly original treatment stresses the court context. [Variant: MSS *G*, *M*.]

1–2 *oppressed* and *heav'nly good attending* modify 'I'.

5 *erected face.* Implies that the speaker, like a servant or courtier, is on bended knee looking up. On class consciousness, see 'Methods of Composition and Translation', I.73.

Psalm 124

Psalm of praise for God's deliverance. Bèze's Argument establishes contemporary parallels: 'we have seene many such like examples of the goodnesse of God, in this our age howe miserable soever, and our posterity doubtlesse in their time shall beholde the same'. See *Psalmes*: 'Literary Context', II.6. [Variant: MSS *G*, *M*.]

1 *Say Israel.* Cf. Psalter (v. 1): 'Nowe may Israel say'.

7 *gulphes.* Calvin (v. 4), commenting on the water imagery of this passage, declares that God has saved the faithful from 'howe deepe a gulfe'.

13 *grynn*, or snare to catch birds, from Old Version and Calvin (v. 7), the 'grinnes of theire enemyes', explaining that they are threatened both by violence, under the metaphor of the teeth of wild beasts, and by craft, under the metaphor of the snare.

Psalm 125

Praise for God's protection of His people and a prayer for the punishment of the wicked. [Variant: MSS *G*, *M*.]

12–17 The Lord will favour, further, and give peace to those who believe and act rightly, but the 'vaine deceiver' (or hypocrite), who wanders from the way, whose doings are lawless and bent to mischief, he has 'abjected', or rejected.

Psalm 126

A celebration of the return from Babylonian exile and a prayer that God will bring home the rest of the exiles. [Variant: MSS *G, M.*]

2 *lords conduct.* Pembroke adds the metaphor of the 'lords conduct' or passport that was necessary for travel abroad.

4 Pembroke adds the idea of visions produced by fancy, or the imaginative part of the brain, to 'dreame' in the biblical sources (v. 1).

5–6 Cf. Bèze (v. 2): 'Then began the mouthes to be filled with laughter, then began the tongue to testifie gladnesse'.

8 *roially.* The court context of Pembroke's paraphrase may have been suggested by Parker (v. 2): 'For them the Lord: wrought royally'.

9 *Most true.* The reassurance that this is truth and not a dream comes from Bèze (v. 3), 'and surelie so it is', but the wording comes from *Astrophil*, Sonnet 5. Cf. Ps. 73. See 'Methods of Composition and Translation', I.68

15–16 Cf. Bèze (v. 4): 'refresh them, being burnt up with the heate of that most miserable captivitie, even as though thou shouldest send upon the dry countries of the South, rivers of waters'.

Psalm 127

A wisdom Psalm describing home and family as God's blessings [Variant: MSS *G, M.*]

14 On Pembroke's editing of Bèze's phrase, see II.25.

Psalm 128

A wisdom Psalm on children as God's blessing.

4 *by him first troden*, i.e. the paths that God, in the person of Christ, has already walked. Cf. Geneva (v. 1): 'and walketh in his wayes'.

5 *the labours of thy handes.* Cf. Geneva note (v. 2): 'the world esteemth them happie, which live in welth, and ydlenes: but the holy Gost approveth them best, that live of the meane profit of their labours'. Pembroke does not carry through these class implications.

10 *parlor.* Pembroke adapts the biblical metaphor (Geneva v. 3), 'Thy wife *shalbe* as the fruteful vine on the sides of thine house', sensibly placing the wife in the parlour.

17–24 As in Bèze (v. 6), these lines distinguish between private and public blessing, with 'peace and tranquilitie' both for the family and for the state.

18 Pembroke adds the biblical metaphor of life as a race (1 Cor. 9: 24–6 and Heb. 12: 1). Cf. Ps. 145. 64.

Psalm 129

Prayer that God will deliver His people, as He has done in the past.

5 *their force*, i.e. the force of Israel's enemies. The biblical sources also begin with an unspecified 'they' (v. 1), eventually defined in the Psalter as 'the ungodly' (v. 4).

7–12 Expands the biblical metaphor (Geneva v. 3): 'the plowers plowed upon my backe, *and* made long forrowes'. Rather than following the Genevan note (v. 4), explaining that God freed Israel as the oxen from the plough, Pembroke follows Calvin's interpretation, that by cutting the lines that bound the plough to the oxen, God stopped the ploughing, i.e. brought relief to the afflicted. Calvin here supplies a connection between the ploughing of the back and the harvest metaphor in the rest of the Psalm.

8 A characteristic added parenthesis. Cf. 'Even now that Care', 23.

13–14 Pembroke characteristically adds questions here and at lines 19–20 to make the poem a dramatic monologue, addressing enemies of the godly.

17 *wheate*. Pembroke follows Calvin's explanation (v. 6) that the corn on rooftops may be higher, but it is 'unprofitable' and soon withers.

21–2 Cf. Calvin (v. 7): 'wherof the reaper filleth not his hand, nor the gleaner his lappe'.

23 *who you*. The phrase in *A* is correct, because it is the wicked who are being harvested. The transposition in *N*, *C* reveals a scribal misunderstanding of the text.

24 *common kindnesse*. Supplied by Pembroke as a transition to the following stanza, taken from Bèze's explanation (v. 8) that the wicked, like the herb on the housetop, will not be harvested, so 'Neither, for the cause thereof, shall the passengers ... crie unto the reapers, the Lord blesse you from heaven with most plentiful harvest'.

Psalm 130

A penitential Psalm, crying for God's forgiveness and expressing confidence in God's mercy. Like Psalm 51, this penitential Psalm was set to music in BL Additional MS 15117. Roy T. Eriksen argues for the influence of Gascoigne in 'George Gascoigne's and Mary Sidney's Versions of Psalm 130', *Cahiers Elisabethains* 36 (1989), 1–9.

Incipit: *De profundis*. Emended. There is an error in the spacing in *A*.

1 *depth of grief.* Clarifies the metaphorical nature of 'Out of the deepe places' (v. 1), as the Geneva note explains, 'Being in great distresse and sorowe'. On the drowning imagery, see Sallye Sheppeard, 'On the Art of Renaissance Translation: Mary Herbert's Psalm 130', *Texas College English* 18 (1985), 1–3.

5–6 Pembroke adds the lists of adjectives and adverbs, perhaps influenced by Calvin (v. 1), who says that we 'pray but coldly' in prosperity, but 'the Prophet taketh more corage to praye by reason of the trubbles, care, daungers, and heavines under which he was drowned'.

12–13 We print the text recovered from the multi-layered alteration in *A*, which is fully reported in the textual notes.

30 *often, often.* Pembroke usually avoids empty repetition; thus, the sense may be that God has often redeemed the current nation of Israel just as He often redeemed it formerly. Cf. Bèze (v. 7): 'wait uppon the Lord ... whome thou has experienced so oft to be thy deliverer and advenger'. Cf. 36.

Psalm 131

A song of trust, comparing the Psalmist to a weaned child. [Variant: MS *N*.]

5 *wained babe.* Pembroke uses the same spelling for weaned as in Geneva and Bèze. Most sources, including Geneva, Psalter, Old Version, Vatablus, and Calvin, assume that the mother has nursed her infant, but Bèze (v. 2) explains that the weaned child has been returned to its mother, and must learn 'to forget the nourse and to regarde the mother alone'.

6 *O.* Emended. Another inadvertent omission in *A*, revealed by comparison with the other manuscripts.

Psalm 132

Pembroke follows Bèze's interpretation of the Psalm as Solomon's consecration of the Temple to God, rather than making it the generalized speech of 'the faithful', as in the Geneva headnote. The connection to Solomon is scriptural; 2 Chron. 6: 41–2 reports verses 8, 9, 10, and 16 as Solomon's words. Pembroke has Solomon speak in lines 1–42 , with an embedded quotation of David's earlier vow in 7–18. The rest of the Psalm is God's response.

3 *othe and vow.* Cf. 40. David vowed to build God a house (temple), but God made an oath to build David's house (lineage) instead in 2 Sam. 7. His son Solomon was directed to build the temple (1 Chron. 17; II Chron. 2–7).

6 *the.* 'The' is corroborated in 18, a repetition of 6 (as 17 repeats 5).

20 *it.* Geneva notes (v. 5) that 'it' is 'the Arke, which was a signe of Gods presence'. But here the antecedent is 'plott'. Thus the search seems to be, not for the ark, but for the place named as the site for building the temple. Cf. Calvin (v. 5): 'Untill I have found a plotte for the Lorde'.

24 *Jear.* A transliteration of a disyllabic Hebrew word (sometimes also spelled 'Jaar' in English) translated as a place name in Bèze (v. 6), although it was also rendered as 'forest' (Geneva) or 'wood' (Psalter), a double sense captured in Pembroke's phrase, 'woody Jear'. According to 1 Sam. 7: 2, the Ark 'abode in Kiriath-jearim' for twenty years before it was taken to Jerusalem. 'Kiriath-jearim' was often identified with Jear in Psalm 132 (the plural form of Jearim was retained by Bèze in the *carmen 'in planitie Jari-meorum'*) and glossed in Geneva as 'the citie of woods' in Josh. 15: 9. (See also Josh. 9: 17, 18: 14–5 and Judg. 18: 12.) 'Feare' in *E* is an obvious scribal error.

25–6 That is, we have found what we sought here (Mt. Zion in Jerusalem), not in either Ephrata or Jear. Cf. 49–54.

56 *a.* 'A blisse' is the subject of 'shall blesse' (57), making emendation to 'as' unnecessary.

64 *tenants.* Pembroke adds the metaphor of God as landlord who gives tenure to his 'fields of blisse'.

67–8 Choosing the word 'scepter' rather than the usual 'horne', Pembroke alludes to Aaron's rod that bloomed to indicate that he was chosen to be the chief priest (Num. 17: 8). Aaron's rod was thereby a rod of office, and thus a synonym for sceptre. The rod was placed in the Ark of the Covenant, mentioned in line 32.

69 *my Christ.* The establishment of the temple and of the Levitical priesthood serve as figures 'both of the kingdome and of the Priesthoode of Christe' (Bèze's Argument). The Geneva head note for 1 Chron. 17 says that 'Christ is promised under the figure of Salamón'.

73–8 That is, God will cast down the wicked but will crown Christ. Cf. Bèze (v. 18): 'his crowne shall flourishe in the end with most great glory'. Despite her frequent expansion of clothing metaphors, Pembroke here omits the metaphor 'clothe with shame' (Geneva v. 18) that directly contrasts with the priests clothed with righteousness in the biblical sources (v. 16).

Psalm 133

A wisdom Psalm, praising 'brotherlie amitie' (Geneva heading).

5–12 The images of oil and dew are interpreted variously in the sources. The oil represents the Holy Spirit (Bèze's Argument), 'the graces, which come from Christ' (Geneva note v. 2), or 'the peace which issueth from Christ' (Calvin v. 2).

11 *empearled,* i.e. formed into pearl-like drops. A neologism coined by Pembroke to parallel 'embalmes' in 8.

12 Geneva notes (v. 3): 'By Hermón and Zion he meaneth the plentiful countrei about Jerusalém'. Hermon is a mountain in Syria.

13 *there with,* i.e. with brotherly concord.

15 *it,* i.e. concord. Cf. Geneva note (v. 3): 'where there is suche concorde'.

Psalm 134

The priests are exhorted to praise God and to bless the people.

1 *Jehovas servants.* Cf. Calvin (headnote): This 'exhortation to prayse God: which though it belong generally to all the godly: yet is it peculiarly directed to the prests and levites'.

20 *of nought.* Pembroke adds the emphasis on creation *ex nihilo,* not present in her usual sources (v. 3).

Psalm 135

An exhortation to praise God for His works and His providential care of His people.

2 *servants.* Both the Levites 'in his howse' (3) and the people, who come to the 'courtes before his howse' (4). Cf. Geneva note (v. 2) and Calvin, emphasizing the distinction.

9 *Domain,* i.e. demesne, in the original sense of a lord's lands or possessions. Emphasizes courtly context.

12 *inviolate,* i.e. not violated. The heavens, earth, and sea do not violate God's decree.

17 *incorporate.* The mists and vapours take corporeal form as clouds and then as rain.

20–1 That is, God in his pleasure lays waste (causes destruction) by the breathing blasts drawn forth as wind.

26–8 Pembroke emphasizes the courtly context and class distinctions between the 'meaner men' and 'the best'. Cf. Psalter and Geneva (v. 9): 'Pharaóh and ... all his servants'.

30–1 Sehon, King of the Amorites, refused to give the Israelites permission to cross his land. When Sehon attacked them, Moses and the Israelites were victorious, as they were when they were attacked by Og, the King of Bashan. See Num. 21, cross-referenced in Geneva. Cf. Ps. 68. 59n.

40–4 Questions characteristically added to create a dramatic monologue.

44 *Idolls*. Cf. Ps. 115.

56 *Salem*. Pembroke frequently uses this term, meaning peace, for Jerusalem. (Cf. Pss. 76. 3, 102. 71, 122. 4, 12, 125. 5, etc.) The sources here (v. 21) have Zion (Geneva) or Sion (Psalter, Bèze, Calvin).

Psalm 136

An exhortation to praise God for His creation and for His salvation of Israel. The long series of 'who' clauses matches the biblical original. Throughout this Psalm the biblical refrain that concludes each verse, 'for his mercy endureth forever', is rendered in the second and fourth line of each quatrain, retaining the antiphonal quality of the original.

7 *only*. Cf. Geneva (v. 4): 'Which onelie doeth great wonders'.

25 *russhy sea*, i.e. the Red Sea. Bèze explains (v. 13) that the 'Rushie sea ... is called the red sea'. 'Ruddie' (red) in *N* is a logical scribal emendation by someone unfamiliar with Bèze. A less logical emendation is 'rushing' in *G* and *M*.

37–8 *Sehon*, *Ogg*. See Ps. 135. 30n.

49 *each feeding thing*. The biblical sources (v. 25) have 'all flesh' and Bèze, 'all living creatures'. The conventional 'living' in *K*, *O*, *M* is likely a scribal or editorial emendation which removes the alliteration and the succinct statement of which creatures (beasts and also God's people) need God's provision. Cf. Geneva note, Calvin's commentary on v. 25.

Psalm 137

Lament of those exiled in Babylon who have been commanded to sing for their captors; prayer for vengeance.

26 *Edoms race*. The Geneva note (v. 7) explains that the Edomites, children of Esau, 'conspired with the Babylonians against their brethren', referring to Ezek. 25: 13, Jer. 49: 7, and 'Abdias' [Obadiah] 10.

32 *platt pais*, i.e. the French for 'flat place', which is, however, not used in *Psaumes*. The variant, 'flat plaine', would make a tempting emendation, as in Rathmell, but apparently few of the scribes were bothered by the phrase in *A*. Cf. Variant Ps. LXXI. 48.

Psalm 138

A Psalm of praise, which Pembroke adapts to emphasize the personal vow of the speaker to praise God in His court.

1–2 The biblical text has 'before the gods', interpreted in a Geneva note (v. 1) as 'Angels and of them, that have autoritie among men'.

3 *I will... tell.* Pembroke adapts the biblical 'I will praise thee', which occurs in v. 1 only, into a series of promises to praise God (lines 7, 10), and to tell the story so that 'all Kings' will understand God's grace and 'sing' with the speaker (13–15).

4 *pallace.* Pembroke again emphasizes a courtly context in this rendering of the biblical 'Temple' (v. 2), as did Bèze.

13–15 Cf. Geneva (vv. 4–6): 'All the Kings of the earth ... shall sing of the waies of the Lord, because the glorie of the Lorde *is* great'.

14 *contract.* Pembroke adds the legal metaphor to the biblical phrase, 'the wordes of thy mouth' (Geneva v. 4).

16–18 Pembroke expands the eye imagery, present in the biblical text only in the verb 'beholdeth' (v. 6). Cf. Bèze: 'though thou sit in a most high throne, yet doest thou beholde all the base and most low things, and ... those that proudly lift up themselves, although thou may seeme to wincke at both twaine for a time'.

18 *aspiring thing*s, i.e. 'the proude' (v. 6). Cf. Ps. 140. 18.

Psalm 139

A meditation on God's omniscience and omnipresence, emphasizing God's knowledge of the speaker. Includes a prayer for deliverance.

6–7 With typical word play, Pembroke adds the metaphor of the private closet contrasting with the open window to render the biblical phrase (v. 2): 'thou understandest my thoght a farre of'.

12–14 Pembroke amplifies the idea of the biblical text (v. 4), 'For there is not a worde in my tongue, *but* ... thou knowe it wholly', explained in a Geneva note, 'Thou knowest my meaning before I speake'. Pembroke sets forth Sidney's idea of the 'fore-conceit' (*Defence of Poetry, Miscellaneous Prose*, 79; *Old Arcadia*, 242). The Sidneys evidently assume that the thought exists prior to the language that frames it.

15–18 Geneva note (v. 5): 'Thou so guidest me with thine hand, that I can turne no waie but where thou appointest me'. Cf. the labyrinth image in Wroth's 'A Crowne of Sonetts dedicated to Love', *Pamphilia to Amphilanthus*, [P77–90].

24 *starry Spheare.* Ptolemaic spheres. Cf. Ps. 89. 79–80 and 148. 13–14.

29–35 Like Bèze (v. 9), Pembroke interprets the biblical phrase (Geneva v. 9) 'the uttermost partes of the sea' as 'the formost partes of the west'. The

West (probably the New World) would, from their perspective, be the farthest imaginable earthly distance.

36–9 Cf. personification of Night in Wroth's *Pamphilia to Amphilanthus* and in Daniel's *Delia* (1592), no. 49: 'Care-charmer Sleep'. See I.66.

42 *father of all lights.* Jas. l: 17.

55–6 The basic imagery is embroidery stretched on a frame, probably derived from Bèze (v. 15): 'when I was fashioned in the darke cave, as it were with needleworke'. See also Calvin for the images of 'raftring' and embroidery.

59 *shaplesse shape.* Cf. Bèze (v. 16): 'unfashioned lumpe without shape'.

61–3 God, creating the embryo, is described as a craftsman who plans a project in his order book, indicating appropriate times for each task. Cf. Bèze v. 16.

64 *these studies.* Continues the metaphor of the poet as God's scholar (cf. Pss. 51 and 119), but here with particular emphasis on the scientific knowledge that shows God's 'hidden workings' (65). See 'Methods of Composition and Translation', I.73.

71 *but one.* See *Psalmes*: 'Literary Context', II.17.

76 Typical word play. The ungodly lack God's grace, even while they attempt to disgrace God's name (v. 20).

88–9 Pembroke adds the idea of finding a cause for the anger of the wicked against the speaker, as does Bèze (v. 24): 'Finally consider whether I have provoked them with giving any offence'.

Psalm 140

Prayer for deliverance from enemies, with concluding assurance that the wicked will be punished and the godly delivered.

3 *force and fraud.* Cf. Geneva note (v. 3): the wicked use the tongue as a weapon 'when power and force fayle them'.

6 *poisons hurd*, i.e. hoard of poison. Thus, 'poisonous' in K, χ is an unnecessary scribal emendation.

10 *fowle misshape.* Foul mishap. Cf. Ps. 141. 29n.

14–15 My stay (support) is in thee.

18 *aspire.* Cf. Ps. 138. 18.

22 *shall*, i.e. shall be stung.

23 *flames shall fling them low.* As by lightning. Cf. Calvin (v. 11).

24 Pembroke once again adds the idea of drowning where the biblical text (Geneva v. 10) has the wicked cast 'into the depe pittes'.

Psalm 141

Prayer that God will watch the speaker's words, will help him to accept just words of rebuke, and will deliver him from the enemy.

4 *perfume.* Cf. Geneva (v. 2): 'Let my prayer be directed in thy sight *as* incense, and the lifting up of mine hands *as* an evening sacrifice'.

7–9 Cf. Calvin (v. 3): 'David desireth too have his mouthe guarded with watche and warde . . . as if a porter shold watche at the comming in of a gate'.

12 *flattring baites*, i.e. beguiling refreshments. Cf. Bèze (v. 4): 'entised by tasting their delicates'.

13 *the good-man wound.* The rebukes of the righteous.

15 *him*, i.e. 'the good-man'. The part of v. 5 that corresponds to this line is interpreted in the biblical texts as referring to the wicked, who seem not to be included in the paraphrase until 16 ('these').

28 *thy self a fowler be.* Cf. Bèze (v. 10): 'they shall rather fall in the nets of God'.

29 *fowly fall.* For 'fowl' puns, cf. Ps. 140. 10.

Psalm 142

A prayer for deliverance. A freer translation than most of her paraphrases, adapting the past tense of the biblical sources to the present, as does Bèze.

4 *mapp.* The metaphor is added to the biblical text (Geneva v. 2), in which the speaker has 'declared mine affliction in his presence'.

5 *painted.* Cf. Parker (v. 2): 'My troublouse state: I did depaynt, | before himself in light'.

8 *toiles*, i.e. nets, the more conventional variant in *M*.

danger. Emended. The 'r' was lost in trimming the right margin for binding.

10 *lights.* The eye lights, but may also be directed by lights, or lighthouses. Cf. Parker, note on 5 above.

on. Emended. Without 'on', which can be supplied from the other manuscripts, the metre is defective (as is the sense).

23–4 Cf. Geneva (v. 7): '*then* shal the righteous come about me', with a note 'ether to rejoyce at my wonderful deliverance, or to set a crowne upon mine head'.

Psalm 143

A prayer for deliverance.

1–6 Pembroke emphasizes the courtly context implicit in Parker (v. 1): 'heare my sute'.

20 *nor hart, nor hedd.* Cf. Bèze (v. 4): 'for I am in minde utterly amased, and I tremble being striken in mine heart'.

26 *hand-writyng.* An original metaphor for 'the workes of thine hands' (Geneva v. 5). Cf. Sidney's Ps. 19. 15–16.

37 *my hope,* i.e. God. Cf. 'my help', 39.

48 *Meander.* A winding river in Phrygia. This is the first metaphoric use of the name as a 'winding or labyrinthine course' cited in the *OED*.

55–6 Pembroke continues the water imagery introduced by 'Meander' (48) to render the biblical phrase, 'slay mine enemies' (v. 12).

Psalm 144

A Psalm of praise and a request for future blessings. Attributed to David.

8 That is, because of whom my realm obeys me. Geneva (note v. 2): 'He confesseth that nether by his owne autoritie, power nor policie his kingdome was quiet, but by the secret grace of God'.

30–2 Pembroke supplies the explanation, that their mouth forges the intent that is carried out by their sword hand. Cf. 39.

43–9 Virtually repeats 25–31, as v. 11 repeats parts of vv. 7 and 8.

53–6 The daughters are described as caryatids, both bearing and garnishing the palace.

58 Emended. The addition of 'finde' in a different hand shows that Davies erred in ending the line after 'fullnes'. The correction supports moving the comma from after 'fullnes' to after 'finde'.

63 That is, such will be the press, or mass, of sheep that the streets will scarcely hold them.

Psalm 145

A hymn vowing and giving praise. Like Psalms 111 and 112, this is acrostic in the Hebrew original.

1–21 Pembroke expands the Psalmist's vow to sing God's praises.

6 *praise past-praise.* The topos of inexpressibility.

11 *all excell,* i.e. which excel all excellences. The topos of outdoing.

24–5 Cf. Bèze (v. 8): 'a man may almost doubt, whether he be more slow to wrath, or more prone to pardon'.

29–35 As in the biblical text, there are two levels of praise, the sound made by dumb creatures, and the highest praise from those who have 'speciall bonds' to God, i.e. the godly.

33 Cf. Bèze (v. 11): 'For these alone do know and declare by experience what thy dominion is, and what is thy power'.

38–42 Cf. Bèze (v. 13): 'For in deed, thy kingdome is not limitted in any bounds of time, for that it alwayes endureth one, and unchangable from all eternitie'.

39–41 The sense generally is that time ('ages' 39), in spite of its mutability ('unsteedfast chang' 41), cannot bring closure to God's kingdom.

58 Emended. In spite of abundant manuscript evidence to the contrary, the syntax requires some punctuation at this point.

60 *thou.* 'Thou' often resembles 'then' in the Psalms manuscripts. The appearance of 'then' in *K*, *χ*; at this point is thus probably the result of a scribal error. Although figures of repetition are frequent in the paraphrases, they are not usually so empty as the redundance would be in this passage.

64 Life as a race. Cf. Ps. 128. 18n.

Psalm 146

A hymn of praise, beginning with 'Hallelujah', as do Psalms 147–50.

1 Like Bèze, Pembroke begins with the imperative.

5 *this decree*, that is, the speaker's declared intention to praise God continually.

12 *him, his.* Emended. 'His, his' in *A* is probably Davies's error; because there seems to be no noun for the first 'his' to modify, the whole construction collapses. Cf. Bèze (v. 4): 'they are resolved againe into dust, and all their cogitations doe vanish away together with them'. The apparently correct reading in *G*, *M* (if it is not only a scribal emendation) may indicate that the common exemplar of those copies was corrected, not from *A* (or one of its descendants), but from another manuscript in the *β* tradition.

15, 17 *level'd, built.* Pembroke adds the carpentry metaphor. Cf. Ps. 119B. 1–3.

Psalm 147

A hymn of praise for God's providential care.

2 Questions are added here and throughout the Psalm to make a dramatic monologue.

11–12 Cf. Bèze (v. 4): 'there is nothing which thou art not able to do, for thou knowest the number of the verie starres'. Pembroke adds a courtly image with the 'torches' in the 'heav'nly hall'.

28 *mountaine*. 'Maintaine' in χ is probably an error or unnecessary emendation. Cf. Geneva (vv. 8–9): 'and maketh the grasse to growe upon the mountaines: 9 Which giveth to beastes their fode'.

29–30 That is, God feeds the croaking young ravens who are forsaken by the careless old ravens. Cf. Bèze (v. 9): 'being forsaken of their dammes'.

60 That is, except Israel, there is no nation that is not blind to His light. Cf. Bèze (v. 20): 'he hath lefte other men without this most true, and most just doctrine'.

Psalm 148

An exhortation to all people and all of Nature to praise God.

9–10 The polyptoton presents the sun as the origin of light, whereas the reflected light of the moon lights the sea.

13–14 In this paraphrase of v. 4a, 'Praise ye him, heavens of heavens', the poet is following Calvin's Ptolemaic interpretation in which the 'spheare' (13) is that of the fixed stars and 'the rest' (14) are the planets which 'play' (14) in spheres beneath the fixed stars. Cf. Geneva note; Pss. 89. 79–80, 139. 24.

15 Cf. Geneva (v. 4): 'waters, that be above the heavens'. Calvin and the Geneva note identify the waters with rain. Thus, the waters are 'banck'd with', contained by or within the spheres, not beyond them.

26 Pembroke makes sense of the biblical phrase (Geneva v. 7), 'ye dragons and all depths', drawing on the Geneva note that the dragons are whales and other 'monstruous fishes'.

35 Pembroke adds personifying adjectives to the biblical 'mountaines and all hilles' (v. 9).

37–40 Cedars and fruit trees, respectively. Cf. Bèze (v. 9): 'trees laden with fruites, the Cedars mounting up with such mervellous height'.

47–8 Cf. Geneva (v. 12): 'Yong men and maidens, also olde men and children'. Pembroke adds space for adult women to praise God.

Psalm 149

An exhortation to praise God through music and dance.

2–3 That is, make His praise be sounded with cheerful noise among His favourites. The elliptical passive construction corresponds to the phrasing in Geneva (v. 1): 'let his praise *be heard* in the Congregation of Saints'.

6 *refram'd*. The variant in *O, D*, 'reform'd', is plausible. Cf. Bèze (v. 2): 'whose worke thou art as it were newly formed'.

10 Geneva (v. 3) quietly omits the sacred dance; Bèze meditates on the power of music but concludes that such forms of worship are currently inappropriate (Argument). See *Psalmes*: 'Literary Context'.

14 Geneva notes (v. 5): 'He alludeth to that continual rest, and quietnes, which they shulde have, if they wolde suffre God to rule them'.

16 *twice-edged*. The biblical sources (v. 6) have 'two-edged', as in *G, M*.

17 That is, so that they may plague and chastise with the two-edged swords. Cf. Geneva (vv. 6–7): 'and a two-edged sworde in their hands, 7 To execute vengeance upon the heathen'.

21–2 That is, so that no stay may prevent ('lett' 21) the judgement ('doom' 21) set on them by God's sentence. Thus, 'aye' in χ is probably scribal or editorial.

Psalm 150

Final doxology, concluding the Psalter.

2 *holynesse*. See *Psalmes*: 'Literary Context'.

13 *conclud*. Added to the text to provide closure, summing up the entire Psalms with an admonition of praise.

aire, or life. Maintains Calvin's distinction between humankind and other sentient beings (v. 6): 'the talk is here directed unto men, who (although brute beastes have the breth of lyfe as well as they) doo notwithstanding obteyn the name of "breathers, or living wyghtes," above all the others'.

Variant *Psalmes*

See also corresponding notes in *Psalmes*: Commentary [MS *A*].

Variant Psalm XLIV

This early draft is far closer to the Psalter and to Geneva than is the revised version in MS *A*.

1–2 Cf. Psalter (v. 1): 'We have heard with our ears, O God, oure fathers have told us'.

5–6 Cf. Geneva (v. 2): '*How* thou hast driven out the heathen with thine hand, and planted them'. Glosses in Geneva explain that the 'heathen' who are uprooted are 'the Canaanites' and 'them' that are planted are 'our fathers'.

48 *despised*. Emended. The extra syllable is required by the metre and rhyme.

81–2 That is, for Thy sake, we thus endure being killed daily.

87–8 An elliptical construction required by the metre. 'Thou' is understood after 'dost'.

93 *Succours*. The spelling recalls the French origin of the word, i.e. *secours*. Cf. Ps. 71. 39 and Variant Ps. LXII. 25, where the spelling with final 's' also occurs.

Variant Psalm XLVI

3 *ready to be found*. Quoted from Geneva (v. 1).

14 Emended. 'Wash' is required by the syntax of the passage beginning with line 13—'shall . . . wash'—and is supported by the biblical text: '*Yet there is* a River, whose streames shal make glad the Citie of God' (Geneva, v. 4).

21 Geneva (v. 6) reads, '*When* the nations raged'. Pembroke alters the verb 'rage' to a noun, so that the emphasis is not on the anger of the nations but on God's protection of the holy city against their rage. Cf. Ps. 46. 17–20.

32 *his*, i.e. his people.

33 *dread*. Emended. That is, wars are everywhere made by (the active power of) God dreadful, terrible. It is possible, however, that Woodforde mistook 'dread' for 'dead'. See *A* version 29n.

41–4 Partial stanzas are used by Marot and Bèze (as in this Psalm), as well as by Sternhold and Hopkins. Pembroke later removed this one and all others that she and Sidney had written. See 'Major Revisions of Psalms 1–43'.

Variant Psalm L

This early version recorded by Woodforde is far closer to Geneva and to the Psalter than is the revised version in MS *A*.

7 Cf. Geneva (v. 3): 'Our God shal come and shal not kepe silence'.

14 *Saints*. Geneva notes (v. 5): 'God in respect of his elect, calleth the whole bodie holie, Saints and his people'.

43 *This to the Good*, i.e. what has just been said is directed towards the righteous. Cf. *A* version 39. God now turns 'to the Godles sort'.

51 The image of the serpent is added (v. 17), perhaps from analogy with other Psalms that connect slander with the serpent, such as Pss. 58 and 140.

52 Cf. Geneva (v. 19): 'and with thy tongue thou forgest deceite'. Pembroke uses the image of the forge as casting coinage here, but not in the *A* version.

54 *one*, i.e. one woman. That is, they are brothers. Cf. Geneva (v. 20): 'thy mothers sonne'.

Variant Psalm LIII

Closer to the Bible than the *A* version. Line 12, for example, is almost an exact quotation from Psalter v. 4.

9 *any*, i.e. any of 'them' (8), 'the Witless train' (3).

13 Exclamations added to text here and at 22.

14 *as*, i.e. as if.

15 *Wolvish Canibals.* Cf. Geneva (v. 4): 'they eat up my people *as* they eat bread'. 'Canibals' is adapted from Sidney's Ps. 14. 14; the specific image of bestial cannibalism is probably derived from accounts of the New World.

21 *them*, i.e. 'his people' (19). See *A* version 18, 19n.

23 The biblical text cries for 'salvation', with no specific mention of the Messiah. Bèze refers to the 'saviour' who will come 'out of Sion' (v. 6). See *A* version, 21–2n.

24 The period suggests that the last three lines are exclamatory, not interrogatory (cf. 'Ah!' in 22).

Variant Psalm LVIII

4 *Adams.* The phrase from *Psaumes*, '*Enfans d'Adam*', is a more explicit reference to Genesis than the 'sonnes of dust' in the revision. Pembroke reminds the unjust judges that they are still merely human, despite their rank. Cf. Ps. 82.

9 *whom.* 'the World'. See *A* version 7n.

12–13 *since the shape you took | Of men.* Since your birth.

19 The image of the tail used to stop the ears is from a bestiary such as the twelfth-century compilation of Philippe de Thaon.

26–30 On the embryo image, see, I.73.

36–8 Note replacement of this empty repetition with a metaphor in MS *A*.

34 *topside turfway blown.* Upside-down, with the top blown toward the turf. See *OED*, 'topsy-turvy'.

Variant Psalm LX

This early version is much closer to the Psalter than is version *A*.

8 *Stay, stay.* Polyptoton. Keep her in her former stay, or state.

23 Explains how he will divide the land, using the perch and pole, or measuring rods.

31 Pembroke adds explanatory parenthesis, providing transition between their present servitude and their future conquest

32 *triumph.* In the Roman sense of a formal triumph. Cf. Bèze (v. 8): 'thou proude Palestina prepare triumphes for me, and joyfull songs, as thou hast a little before triumphed over us'. Cf. Ps. 108. 32n.

Variant Psalm LXII

7–12 Pembroke expands the metaphor, probably inspired by Bèze (v. 3): 'to drive me downe, whome ye account like a wall readie to fall of its owne accord, or an heape of stones slyding downe'. The crumbling wall is contrasted to the 'rock' of God throughout the Psalm.

25–6 *him that is.* Intended to convey the idea of God's eternal being, Pembroke's occasional translation of the name 'Jehovah' (which, however, is not found at this point in the usual sources). Cf. Ps. 68. 7n.

32 A characteristic addition of the clothing metaphor. The biblical text (Geneva v. 8) has 'powre out your hearts'.

34–5 See *A* version 28n. Cf. Parker (v. 9): 'Adams broode'.

39, 40 *slight, ravin.* Pembroke characteristically turns a direct biblical statement into a poetical metaphor (Geneva v. 10): 'Trust not in oppression nor in roberie: be not vaine'. 'Ravin' corresponds to 'roberie' and 'slight' has here its basic meaning of craft or cunning, which corresponds to Bèze's paraphrase of the verse: 'Dreame not therefore as madde men use to doe, that you can growe more great by force or by deceite'.

42 *on such sand build not.* Pembroke adds the analogy to the wise man and the fool. Cf. Matt. 7: 26 (Geneva): 'But whosoever heareth these my wordes, and doeth them not, shalbe lickened unto a foolish man, which hathe buylded his house upon the sand'.

Variant Psalm LXIII

14 *life joyes,* i.e. life's joys.

23 *light,* i.e. light of day.

26 *Hiv'd.* See Ps. 57. 4n. Pembroke characteristically uses the term for the biblical phrase, 'under the shadowe of thy wings' (Geneva v. 7).

Variant Psalm LXIV

In the revision in MS *A* Pembroke changes the stanza form, metrics, and length, and removes some of the alliteration and internal rhyme. See, for example, Variant Ps. 6–7 and MS *A* 7–8; Variant Ps. 9 and MS *A* 11.

9 *fretted*, i.e. chafed or worn. Cf. Geneva (v. 1): 'whet their tongue like a sworde'.

Variant Psalm LXVIII

3 *Who*, i.e. those who.

12 *but*. Woodforde's suggested emendation to 'both' is plausible. If 'but' here means 'only', however, it may be intended to convey the sense of contrast with the punishment of the wicked in the preceding verse (2). Cf. 'Meane while' 9.

14 *his name Who is*. See *A* version 7n.

22 *wastfull wayes*, i.e. 'wildernes'. Geneva (v. 7).

23 *heavns*. Geneva (v. 8).

27 *Who*. The *I* reading 'and' may be correct because there seems to be no verb for 'Who' in *B*.

soyle. 'Land' in *I* seems to represent an attempt to make the phrase more conventional. Psalter (v. 10) does have 'thine inheritance', but Pembroke seems to be focusing more on the agricultural context.

29 *ther for*. Emended. Woodforde's suggested emendation here is convincing. Even if 'Thy sheep distrest' could be taken as an absolute construction, the causal relationship implied by 'therfore' would still be inappropriate in the passage. 'Ther' is thus probably parallel with 'there' earlier in the line.

31–2 Pembroke attributes the rest of the song to the women, with a departure from direct quotation at 77–80 to describe the company of singers.

34 *Wee house=confined maids*. The speakers are women, with whom Pembroke seems to identify. The distaffs are added to the biblical text, as is the sense of confinement. The soiled feathers become the silvered wing once they are permitted to try 'freer skyes'. The passage may have been too bold for her to let it stand. See, I.25.

38 *With*. Perhaps Woodforde's error for 'which' (as in *I*).

47 *perking*. Applied to persons, 'to perk' means to exalt oneself or thrust oneself forward ambitiously or presumptuously. This seems to be the sense intended here because Basan is personified.

68 *growing Perrukes*. A natural head of hair as distinguished from a false peruke or wig. The sense seems to be that the bloody streams that flow (from their wounded heads 65) shall water their hair hanging in tresses.

69 *self*. Likely an error by Woodforde. The reading in *I* functions as the object of 'bring' (69). 'Folk' is also possible because of 'my people' in the Psalter (v. 22).

75 *And*. Emended. The emendation of 'An' is supported both by the context and by the reading in *I*.

82 *root*. Probably Woodforde's error; 'root' hardly fits the context. 'Brood', as in *I*, is more likely correct: Geneva (v. 26): '*ye that are* of the fountaine of Israel'. Geneva notes: 'Which come of the Patriarke Jaakób'.

Israël. Emended. Emendation is supported by Woodforde's correct placement of the diacritic in other places. such as at Variant Ps. L. 20.

83 *sword*. Parallel with 'sling' (84). But 'force' in *I* is plausible because of Bèze's phrase (v. 27), 'hath mightily overcome the enemies'.

92 *furious wanton*. Emended. Woodforde notes his inadvertent transposition of the words with numerals.

107 *Israels*. Geneva (v. 34).

109 *things didst show*. Geneva (v. 35): 'thou art terrible'. Geneva notes: 'in shewing fearefull judgements against thine enemies'.

Variant Psalm LXIX

9–11 That is, there are not enough hairs on my head for me to give one to each of those who hate me.

24 *noted blot*. See *A* version 69. 23n.

44 *banckless*. Cf. *Psaumes* (v. 14): '*Délivre moi quand on me veut confondre,* | *Et de ces eaux qui n'ont rive ni fons*'.

57 *my ignominious disgrace*. Cf. *interpretatio* (v. 19): '*et ignominiam meam*'.

65–8 Pembroke provides connection between the drunken banquets of the wicked and the metaphoric gall and vinegar (v. 21).

70 Cf. Geneva (v. 23): 'Let their eyes be blinded, that thei se not'. Cf. *interpretatio*: '*Obtenebrentur oculi eorum*'.

81–5 The accounting metaphor is more obvious here than in the revision.

91 *Which*. Emended. The context requires a pronoun (with 'Song' and 'prayses' as antecedents). Cf. Geneva (vv. 30–1): 'I wil praise the Name of God with a song, and magnifie him with thankesgiving... *This* also shal please the Lord better than a yong bullocke.'

111–12 Cf. Geneva (v. 36): 'and thei that love his Name, shal dwell therein'. The sense of the paraphrase seems to be that all those who have a love of God's name deserve well and thus need no other seat than that provided by Him.

Variant Psalm LXXI

This is obviously a draft, since stanza 5 does not fit the rhyme scheme.

27–8 Cf. Geneva (v. 6): 'my praise shal be alwaies of thee'.

32–5 That is, cause all men, therefore, to see Thy glory extolled with praise by me, etc.

45–6 That is, now that those who are their spies are unopposed. It is unclear whether the foes or the spies have made the decree, but cf. 50. See *A* version 32–3.

48 *(Lo!)*. Woodforde's unusual note seems to mean that 'lo' is not in the biblical verse (11), but he marks it in the same way he notes expunged readings: *(Lo!)'. Perhaps he misunderstood the punctuation; the word may have been intended to be parenthetical.

a-Dieu. Pembroke uses the French phrase, which is not in *Psaumes*. Cf. Ps. 137. 32.

93 *the Gulf of woes*. The biblical text speaks separately of 'adversities' and 'the depth of the earth' (Geneva v. 20). Cf. *Psaumes* (v. 20): '*Des creux abysmes de la terre* | *Me tirer il t'a pleu*'.

104 *Harp*. In the revision (line 69), Pembroke adds her characteristic 'lute'.

Variant Psalm LXXV

16 *more:* Emended. The punctuation after 'more', as in *K* and *N*, is needed to clarify the construction in which the second half of 16 is continued by 17. That all the copies but *B* have some punctuation suggests that it was in β and that Woodforde overlooked it.

34 *I?* Emended. The exceptional correspondence of *I, K, N* at this point suggests that Woodforde failed to copy the question mark in β.

Variant Psalm LXXX

40 *Euphrates*. Geneva gloss on 'the River' (v. 11): 'To wit, Euphrates'.

Variant Psalm LXXXVI

17–22 Cf. Psalter (vv. 5–6): 'For thou, Lord, art good and gracious, and of great mercy unto all them that call upon thee.   6 Give ear, Lord, unto my prayer: and ponder the voice of my humble desires.'

20 Because God is good and kind to all who attend to Him, then the Psalmist will pray to Him with confidence.

22 To complete the metre of this line, 'petitions' is probably to be pronounced with four syllables. Cf. Sidney's syllabification of 'motion' and 'potion' in *Defence of Poetry, Miscellaneous Prose*, 120.

25–7 Note disclaimer added in revision, line 15.

31 *his*. Probably Woodforde's mistake for 'is'. There is no clear antecedent to 'his' in *B*.

38 *with*. Perhaps Woodforde's error for 'will'. The verb sequence seems to require the future here.

67–8 This final stanza is short by one line which would be expected after 67 to rhyme with 'embraced'. It is not likely that Woodforde has dropped a line, however, because the passage makes sense as it stands. Still, the revised version in *A* suggests intriguing possibilities because of its rhyme words, 'placed' (42) and 'graced' (44).

Variant Psalm 89 [copy-text MS *I*]

The eccentric nature of the spelling throughout *I* seems to justify more extensive emendation than usual, particularly when the emended spellings can be found at other places in the manuscript.

2 *theme*. Emended. That 'them' is probably a scribal slip is suggested by the fact that MS *I* has 'theame' in line 4 of the *A* version of Ps. 89. Cf. Attridge, *Syllables*, 205.

3 *of*. Perhaps an error for 'to'.

5 *sooner*. Emended. The form with 'a' is not recorded in the *OED* and is probably another scribal slip. Cf. Waller's silent emendation (in Sidney, Mary. *Triumph*).

think. Emended. There is no place for 'thing' in the syntax or sense of the passage. Cf. Attridge, *Syllables*, and *A* version: 'for of thy bounty thus my thoughtes decree' (5).

13 *hearts*. Emended. The context supports the supplying of the missing 't'. The corresponding line in the A version refers to 'mind' (15) rather than 'heart'. Cf. Attridge, Waller, and H. R. Woudhuysen (ed.), *The Penguin Book of Renaissance Verse 1509–1659*, selected and introd. David Norbrook (Harmondsworth: Penguin, 1992; ret. 1993), 679.

reposed. Emended. The past tense is required by the sense and the metre. Cf. Woudhuysen.

14 *truthe*. Emended. A similar extra 'h' has been stricken in the same word in Ps. 71. 46 in *I*. And cf. 'truth' in line 32 below. The spelling with the extra 'h' is not recorded by the *OED*.

17 *be*. Emended. The auxiliary verb is required by the construction, which will not accommodate the pronoun at this point. Cf. Attridge, Waller, Woudhuysen (note to 13).

29 *only*. Emended. *I* has 'oly' for 'only' also at Pss. 108. 39 and 122. 8. 'Oly' is glossed in *Sidneiana* thus: 'ὁλος, totus—all wholly belongeth to thee'. Cf. *A*

version 37–8. Calvin has the same emphasis (v. 14): 'But God who is sufficient of himself, and wanteth none other helps'.

30 *makes*, i.e. that makes.

33 *hy*. Emended. Cf. *A* version: 'Happy the people, who with hasty run-
ning | poast to thy Court' (41–2).

40 *man...reputed:* Emended. The shifting of the colon is required by the
sense of the passage.

42 *sacred*. Geneva (v. 20): 'with mine holie oyle have I anointed him'.

49 *Eufrates*. Calvin (v. 25): 'the people shal possesse the whole countrie
from the sea, even unto Euphrates'. Cf. *carmen*: '*et occidui* [?] *dominantem à
littore ponti,/Assurii latè rapidas Euphratis ad undas*'.

54 *yea*. Emended. The *A* version has a complementary negative construction: 'nay more' (77). Cf. Waller (Sidney, Mary. *Triumph*).

56 *thrones*. Emended. Cf. *A* version: 'a stedfast throne' (79). Cf. Waller.

62 *true*. Emended. Cf. *A* version: 'my word persist unchanged' (89). Cf.
Waller.

65 *ardor*. Geneva: 'his throne *shalbe* as the sunne before me' (v. 26 [i.e. 36]).
Cf. the *A* version, line 93, where there is a more indirect reference to the sun.
If the *I* scribe intended 'adore', the need for emendation is even more apparent because there seems to be no place for that word in either the syntax or
the context.

74 *field*. Emended. *A* version: 'comes [he] to the field to fight?' (106). Cf.
Waller.

78 *once*. Emended. The form without 'e' is not recorded by the *OED*
(which does, however, cite 'ons').

82 *hevy nesessity*. Emended. Waller's reading.

Variant Psalm CV

17 *Isa'aks Son*, i.e. Jacob, the name in the sources (v. 6).

24 There is also a comma at the corresponding point (the end of v. 10) in
Geneva; the next stanza (like the next verse) continues the construction
begun with 19.

27 The extra syllable in this line, which ought to be headless like the corresponding lines, is probably 'thy'.

32 *of the Seat*, of the place of settlement. See *A* version 26. The phrase is an
anapaestic substitute for the expected iamb.

33 *wheres aboad*, places abode. The *OED* cites several instances of the
substantival use of 'where'. The sense is that in roaming from land to land

(31), the Israelites made their (temporary) abode in many places. Cf. *A* version 25–6.

34–5 That is, the Israelites were allowed to live in the lands they roamed because the inhabitants were far from able to do them wrong. Cf. *A* version 27–8.

40 *him.* Emended. Woodforde seems to have erred in transcribing 'he' for 'him' and thus changing the originally impersonal construction. Otherwise, 'it' is hard to account for because there seems to be no antecedent.

50 *for Wisdom mentioned,* i.e. cited for his wisdom (by one of his fellow prisoners who had been released). See Gen. 41: 9–13.

62 *Jaacob.* Emended. The diacritic is probably Woodforde's mistaken addition. The name here is disyllabic. The double 'a', however, suggests a source in Geneva.

68 *whose malice bad.* Probably an elliptical absolute construction: whose malice being bad. In any case, the revision (*A* version 51–2) removes the awkward apparent tautology, which may have been caused by the search for a rhyme word. Cf. faulty rhymes at 20, 23, etc.

79 *their fish.* Cf. Geneva (v. 29): 'and slewe their fish'.

81 *embowred,* lodged in inner apartments, bedrooms. Geneva (v. 30): '*even* in their Kings chambers'.

110 *Angels bread.* Cf. Parker (v. 40): 'sweete aungels foode'. The *A* version (line 84) emphasizes the sweetness without angels.

114 *Plotted,* delineated, charted, mapped out. Thus, the reading in *B* is acceptable as part of an image in which streams of water flow over the land dividing it into parcels or plots.

120 *badg,* a distinctive device, emblem, or mark, used originally to identify a knight or distinguish his followers, which could be figuratively applied in the sixteenth century. Cf. the variant phrase, 'deaths badg', in Ps. 49. 17 as recorded by Woodforde.

121 *the neighbor nations lands,* that is, the lands of neighbouring nations.

Variant Psalm CVIII

1–16 Cf. Ps. 57. 31–54. Since we lack an early version of Ps. 57 in MS B, this is good evidence that these lines remained essentially the same.

12 *My.* Emended. 'By' is Woodforde's error for 'My'. See Ps. 57. 42.

15 Cf. Sidney's Ps. 10. 1–2 where 'star' is added to the Hebrew text, as Katherine Duncan-Jones has noted in *Sir Philip Sidney Courtier Poet* (London: Hamish Hamilton, 1991), 277.

25–52 Cf. Variant Ps. LX. 17–44.

33 *Gilead.* Trisyllabic.

34 *more.* Because the Variant Ps. LX has 'me' (26), it is possible that Woodforde misread it here as 'mo' or 'moe'.

41 *will lead.* The words in the early version of Ps. 60 are 'shall bring' (33). The authenticity of 'will lead' as a revision is indicated by the agreement with the biblical text, v. 10. The variants rejected above (in 7, 8, etc.) are not so corroborated.

42 *who.* The reason for the square brackets around 'who' in *B* is unclear. Certainly there is need for such a word, both metrically and syntactically. If Woodforde is emending the text, he fails to acknowledge his intervention as he usually does.

Variant Psalm 113 [MS *I*]

The Variant found in MS *I* is closer to the Psalter and to Geneva than is the revision, retaining such wording as the 'dongue' of verse 7.

1 *professe.* Used in the Protestant sense of those who are faithful servants of God as 'professors'.

17 Cf. Bèze (v. 9): 'Finally he causeth, that they that were barren before . . . soudenly being made mothers of manie children, were filled with joye'.

19–20 The Gloria, to be said or sung after the Psalm in the Book of Common Prayer, is here added to the Psalm itself as an extension of 'Praise ye the Lord' in Geneva (v. 9). Parker's Psalter includes the 'Gloria Patri for divers Metre' (sig. SSi), although this does not duplicate any of his six renditions. Similarly, Hunnis adds a Gloria at the end of his rendition of Ps. 51, to be included in his other Psalms as well, but the Gloria is not this one.

Variant Psalm CXIX H

22 *in her.* Woodforde is surely correct to place 'in' before 'her'. It is unlikely that Pembroke intended to say, tautologically, that night hides itself in darkness. Rather, it hides people in darkness.

32 *Thy Scholar.* The image of the Psalmist as God's scholar, or a student in God's school, runs throughout Calvin's commentary on Ps. 119, although it is not present in this verse. (See v. 98 'a scholer of Gods law', for example). Cf. Ps. 51. 21n. and Ps. 119Y. 11.

Variant Psalm CXIX W

8 *painfull passed.* Emended. The inadvertent transposition is marked by Woodforde with numerals.

Variant Psalm 120 [MS *G, M*]

1–4 Pembroke's addition about reliance on past answers is removed; the opening lines simply paraphrase the Psalter, with a word added from the 1611 Authorized Version: 'When I was in trouble [1611 'distress'], I called upon the Lord: and he heard me. 2 Deliver my soule, O Lorde, from lying lips: and from a deceitfull tongue'. That same pattern of revision recurs throughout Ps. 120–7 in *G* and *M*.

9 *Aye me*. An exclamation characteristic of Pembroke's style, although usually written 'Ah me!'

15 Cf. Psalter (v. 6): 'I labour for peace'.

Variant Psalm 121 [MS *G, M*]

5 *named)* Emended. The right parenthesis was omitted by the *M* scribe.

7 *slipp*. Geneva (v. 3): 'He wil not suffer thy fote to slippe'.

12 *undertaking*. This stanza is linked to the following both syntactically and rhetorically.

18 *fowle infection*. Added to biblical text.

19 *who never failes his flocke*. The sheep metaphor is added (Psalter v. 8): 'The Lorde shall preserve thy going out and thy comming in: from this time forth for ever'. Cf. *The Mindes Melodie* (l37–8): 'The Lord doth keepe | Israell his sheepe'. Cf. Ps. 122 Variant 2. 14 and Variant Ps. 125. 6.

21 *Fort, Rock*. Added to biblical text (v. 7): 'preserve thee from all evil'.

Psalm CXXII Variant 1

7 *very citty-like*. Cf. Bèze (v. 3): 'Neither shalt thou nowe seeme like a village dispearsed, thy houses being scattered . . . but built up with houses joyned one to another like a city'.

8 *conjoined*. Emended. The sense of the verb, 'common', as 'agree' (*OED*) is not impossible here, but 'conjoined' fits more precisely and is corroborated both by the agreement of *I* and *H* and by Bèze (v. 3), cited above. Woodforde may have misread the multiple adjacent vertical strokes in the likely original, 'conioined'.

9–12 The sense is that now, as before, there will be a convenient place for the company that God has gathered to praise him, just as Israel formerly did.

Psalm 122 Variant 2 [MS *G, M*]

1 *Right gladd was I*. Psalter (v. 1): 'I was glad'.

5 *let us goe*. Cf. 1611 AV (v. 1).

7 *Within*. Cf. 1611 AV (v. 2).

11 *in Union*. Psalter (v. 3): 'at unitie in it selfe'.

14 flocking. The implied sheep metaphor is in Parker (v. 4): 'I meane gods flocke: of Israel'. Cf. Variant Pss. 121. 19 and 125. 6.

19 *Seate of judgment*. Psalter (v. 5).

20 *Davids Throane*. Cf. 1611 AV (v. 5): 'For there are set thrones of judgment, the thrones of the house of David'.

21 *praiers*. Emended. Psalter (v. 6): 'o pray'. 'Praises' in *M* is a likely scribal error.

26 *plenteousnes*. Psalter (v. 7).

Variant Psalm 123 [MS *G*, *M*]

This expanded and simplified rhymed poem diminishes the court context and stays close to the phrasing of the Psalter.

6–8 The hand/stand rhyme is in Crowley, st. 2. Echoes of other Psalters intended for singing may indicate that these simplified, rhymed versions were intended for congregational use.

18 *rich men us deride*. A lower-class perspective is implied, unlike version *A*, where the speaker's position as servant is merely metaphorical. Such identification with the poor may suggest that the revision is not authorial.

Variant Psalm 124 [MS *G*, *M*]

4 *mortall deadly*. Probably redundant, although it could mean that the foes are mortal themselves, though deadly to others.

6 *wrathfull*. Psalter (v. 2; Geneva v. 3): 'wrathfully'. 'Bitter' in *G* may have been intended to reduce the redundancy of a line that already contained 'rage' and 'spleen'. Cf. the *A* version, line 6.

9 *of proude men*. Psalter (v. 4): 'The deep waters of the proud'.

20 *made and wrought*. Although Pembroke frequently uses repetition for rhetorical effect, this is an uncharacteristic redundancy.

Variant Psalm 125 [MS *G*, *M*]

6 *flock*. The sheep metaphor is added, as at Variant Ps. 121. 19 and Ps. 122, Variant 2. 14.

9 *ungodly men*. Replaces 'Tirantes' in version *A* (9) with the 'ungodly' from the Psalter (v. 3), thereby removing the political implications.

13 *perfect*. Cf. Parker (v. 4): 'right up men: of parfyte hart'. Psalter: 'those that bee good and true of heart'

Variant Psalm 126 [MS *G*, *M*]

2 *thralldome*. Cf. Psalter, Geneva 'captivitie' (v. 1). Parker (v. 1) has 'Sions thrall'.

4 *M* avoids *G*'s illogical and non-biblical comparison of the Israelites to dreams. 'As' in 3 (where *G* has 'like') also helps to avoid ambiguity, which may have arisen from a misunderstanding of Parker (v. 1): 'Appeare shall we: then dreamingly'.

7 *Heathen*. Altered from 'Nations' of *A*, line 7, to match the biblical text (v. 2).

17–18 *annoye/joye* rhyme echoes Old Version (vv. 5–6).

19–24 Becomes a simple account of the harvest, replacing the metaphor of *A*, lines 17–24.

24 *sheaves*. Uses the biblical word (v. 6) instead of the metaphoric 'business' of *A*, line 23.

Variant Psalm 127 [MS *G*, *M*]

2–4 *paine/vaine* rhyme of first stanza matches Crowley.

3 *Citty Shield*. Cf. Parker (v. 1): 'Except the Lord: be cityes shielde'. The Psalter has 'the Lord keepe the citie'.

6 *And late sittes up*. The source may be 1611 AV (v. 2): 'to sit up late'. Cf. Psalter (v. 3): 'and so late take rest'; Geneva (v. 2): 'lye downe late'.

15 *Giant*. Cf. Parker, v. 4. Other sources have a 'strong' or 'mighty' man.

20 *But*. 1611 AV may again be the source (v. 5): 'but they shall speak with the enemies in the gate'. Geneva and the Psalter have 'when'.

Variant Psalm 131 [MS *N*]

10 Adds phrase from Old Version (v. 2): 'But as a child that wayned is | even from his mothers brest'.

15–16 Appeal to the speaker's own experience as a model for the godly to follow is an original addition.

GLOSSARY

We have attempted to gloss unusual words or words used in senses that may be unfamiliar to most twentieth-century readers; words which cannot be easily glossed with synonyms or brief phrases are explained in the commentary; some words used in unusual senses only in oblique forms are cited in those forms (e.g. 'noies', 'stoode'). Definitions are based on the *OED*.

abidden, pa.p.   Endured, borne (Ps. 66. 35).

aby, v.   Purchase; pay penalty for, suffer, endure (Ps. 59. 60).

affy, v.   Trust, confide (Pss. 80. 36, 91. 16).

alay, v.   Dilute (Ps. 102. 32); satisfy (Ps. 55. 70).

amaine, adv.   In, or with, full force; at full speed (Ps. 59. 28).

amate, v.   Dismay, daunt, dishearten, cast down (Ps. 129. 15).

ambassage, n.   The sending or dispatch of ambassadors, a mission (*Discourse* 873).

annoy, n.   Annoyance, vexation (*Discourse* 52).

apace, adv.   Swiftly, fast (Ps. 59. 73).

appast, n.   Food (Ps. 148. 32).

aread, v., imp.   Read, interpret ('Dolefull Lay' 65).

arrest, n.   Resting or dwelling upon a subject ('Angell Spirit' 21).

aspect, n.   Appearance, countenance, look or glance (Ps. 68. 4).

aspick, n.   Asp ('by-form . . . used chiefly in poetry', *OED*) (Ps. 58. 13).

attainted, pa.p.   Hit, struck; affected with sickness (Ps. 71. 55).

awhit, adv.   A whit, the least amount (*Discourse* 885).

back, v.   Support at the back (Ps. 144. 22).

baile, v.   Deliver, liberate (Ps. 119Q. 6).

bate, n.   Strife, discord (*Antonius* 1731).

bay, n.   Position when hunted animal, unable to flee, turns to face hunter and defends itself at close quarters (Ps. 59. 78).

bay, v.   To obstruct, dam (water) (Ps. 69. 47).

beare, n.   Bier (Ps. 55. 45).

become, v.   Befit ('Angell Spirit' 49).

bedasht, pa.p.   Dashed against (Ps. 107. 67).

beningly, adv.   Benignly (Ps. 119H. 23).

betaken, pa.p.   Entrusted, committed; commended (Ps. 44. 75).

bewraie, v.   Reveal, expose (Ps. 53. 3).

blank, v.   Frustrate (Ps. 69. 18).

blase, v.   Proclaim (Ps. 145. 34).

blocke, n.   A lifeless body (as inert as a block of wood) (*Antonius* 1960).

blockish, adj.   Excessively dull, stupid (*Discourse* 796).

boorde, n.   Board, table (Ps. 78. 59).

borderer, n.   One who dwells near the border of a (neighbouring) country (Var. Ps. XLIV. 51).

bowe, n.   Bough (Ps. 92. 39).

bowl, n.   Ball (as in the game of bowls) (*Antonius* 994).

breathe, v.   Pause, take rest (Ps. 89. 80).

breathed, v.   Paused, took rest (Ps. 89. 80).

breathing, n.   Short time for breath, pause (*Discourse* 248); *first breathing* life (Ps. 87. 14).

brickle, adj.   Fragile, brittle (Ps. 104. 59).

bring under, v.   Subject, conquer, defeat (Ps. 66. 7).

brook, v.   Possess, hold (Ps. 68. 11).

buckler, n.   Small, round shield (Ps. 84. 42).

business, n.   Activity (Ps. 112. 19).

cancred, pa.p.   Infected with evil, corrupt; malignant, ill-natured (Ps. 53. 9).

candy, v.   Cover or encrust (with a crystalline substance) (Ps. 105. 64).

capreoll, v.   Leap, skip, caper (Ps. 114. 10).

careage, n.   Conduct, behaviour (Ps. 53. 12).

cark, n.   Burden (Ps. 130. 10).

carr, n.   Chariot (Ps. 76. 14).

casia, n.   Cassia, a variety of cinnamon; a fragrant shrub or plant (Ps. 45. 30).

cassere, v.   Disband, banish (*Discourse* 541).

cast, v.   Plan, scheme; purpose, intend (Ps. 45. 18).

chafe, n.   Rage, fury (Ps. 56. 19).

chafe, v.   Become warm, be angry or vexed (Ps. 73. 7).

chaling, v.   Challenge, demand, claim (Correspondence: MS Letter VII).

chap, n.   Open fissure, crack (Var. Ps. LX. 6).

chapps, n.   Jaws (Ps. 78. 98).

cheat, n.   Wheat; booty, prize (Ps. 78. 77).

checkrole, n.   A list of servants to the sovereign or in a large household (Ps. 65. 10).

chink't, pa.p.   Cracked (Ps. 60. 6).

chose, pa.p.   Chosen (Ps. 47. 10).

client, n.   Dependant, follower, he whose cause an advocate pleads (Ps. 86. 3).

clipp, v.   Clasp, embrace; surround or encircle (Ps. 89. 30).

clive, v.   Cleave (Ps. 45. 17).

clog'd, pa.p.   Fettered, encumbered (Ps. 105. 36).

close, v.   Enclose (Ps. 125. 7).

coast, n.   Seaside, but also border, region, district (Ps. 66. 22).

coine, v.   Fabricate (Var. Ps. L. 52).

combersome, combrous, adj.   Obstructing, troublesome (*Discourse* 7, Ps. 73. 48).

compassion, v.   Pity ('Dolefull Lay' 2).

conduction, n.   Guidance, leadership (Var. Ps. LX. 15).

conning, adj.   Cunning (Ps. 140. 12).

coozen, v.   Cozen, deceive (*Antonius* 886).

cope, v.   Encounter, contend, engage in battle (*Antonius* 1180).

corosive, n.   Something that corrodes by chemical action; a grief, annoyance (*Discourse* 88).

couler, n.   Colour (*Discourse* 166).

countermande, v.   Revoke, counteract (Ps. 50. 15).

counterpoize, v.   Counterbalance (*Discourse* 655).

coyning, pr.p.   Lying (Ps. 101. 20).

crazed, pa.p.   Broken, impaired (Var. Ps. L. 61).

cumber, n.   Burden, restraint (Ps. 79. 33).

cumber, v.   Harass, trouble (Ps. 119V. 18).

curiace, n.   Cuirass (*Antonius* 75).

curious, adj.   Elaborate (Ps. 74. 30).

deemer, n.   Judge (Ps. 119 V. 5).

define, v.   Set the limits of, end (Ps. 79. 59); perceive the limits of (Ps. 108. 27); represent the extent of (Ps. 89. 110).

denizend, pa.p.   Naturalized, made a citizen ('Even now' 30).

descryed, pa.p.   Perceived from a distance (*Discourse* 4).

devotion, n.   Disposal (*Discourse* 334).

disgestion, n.   Digestion (*Discourse* 82).

dishowsed, pa.p.   Ousted, dispelled (Ps. 58. 21).

dowries, n.   Endowments ('Dolefull Lay' 62).

drave, v.   Drove (Ps. 76. 6).

dropsie, n.   Insatiable thirst or craving (*Discourse* 177).

eager, adj.   Intense (*Antonius* 263).

eake, adv.   Eke, also (Ps. 111. 6).

edifyd, pa.p.   Built, furnished (Var. Ps. CXXII. 24).

ell, n.   Unit of measurement (*Discourse* 229).

embush, n.   Ambush (*Discourse* 428).

embusht, pa.p.   Ambushed (Ps. 64. 16).

empeach, v.   Hinder, prevent (*Antonius* 489).

empt, v.   Drain, exhaust (*Antonius* 342).

encleare, v.   Light up, illumine (Ps. 77. 86).

engrain, v.   Dye (scarlet or crimson) (Var. Ps. LXVIII. 73).

enlaced, enlast, pa.p.   Entangled (*Antonius* 1109); encircled, surrounded (*Antonius* 1663).

enlarged, pa.p.   Set at large, released from confinement (Var. Ps. LXVIII. 36).

enriven, pa.p.   Split, torn apart ('Dolefull Lay' 4).

envieng, pr.p.   Contending for mastery, vying (*Antonius* 1768).

environned, pa.p.   Surrounded (with hostile intention) (*Antonius* 569).

espial, n.   Act of spying (*Discourse* 545).

extirpate, v.   Root out, destroy completely (Var. Ps. LXVIII. 42).

fare, n.   Journeying, passage, way (Ps. 144. 10, Var. Ps. CV. 41).

farme, n.   A fixed yearly amount, payable as rent, tax, or the like (*Discourse* 929).

fatt, adj.   Fertile, rich (Var. Ps. LXVIII. 45).

fatt, v.   Anoint, enrich, fertilize (Ps. 65. 42).

feeding, n.   Grazing-ground or pasture land (Ps. 100. 7).

ferry, n.   Passage, crossing, especially over a river (Ps. 106. 60, *Discourse* 540).

fetch, n.   Trick (Ps. 112. 35).

filde, pa.p.   Dishonoured, defiled (*Antonius* 74).

fin'd, v.   Paid a penalty, ransom (Ps. 55. 49).

fingred, pa.p.   Plundered, pilfered (*Antonius* 859).

flayed, pa.p.   Stripped of possessions (*Discourse* 198).

flower, n.   Flour (Ps. 81. 45).

foile, n.   Disgrace (*Antonius* 74).

forcing, pr.p.   Convincing, commanding, forceful (*Antonius* 729).

foreslow, v.   Be slow (Ps. 49. 32).

foretaken, pa.p.   Concerned beforehand; preoccupied (*Discourse* 684).

forgo, v.   Neglect, overlook (*Discourse* 576).

fray, v.   Frighten, disperse (*Discourse* 357).

freat, v.   Devour (*fig.*), waste away, diminish (Ps. 102. 42).

frett, v.   Worry, chafe, vex oneself (Ps. 99. 1).

fretting, pr.p.   Rubbing, chafing (Ps. 88. 69, Var. Ps. LXVIII. 18).

fry, v.   To burn with strong passion or emotion (Ps. 119D. 17).

fume, n.   Smoke (*fig.*) (Ps. 80. 10).

fume, v.   Exhibit anger or irritation (Ps. 73. 62).

gage, n.   Pledge, security (*Discourse* 621).

gape, v.   Be eager, as with an open mouth (*Discourse* 848).

gaping, pr.p.   Shouting, pursuing with open mouth (Ps. 56. 2); with open cracks and fissures (Ps. 60. 6).

gatt, v.   Got, received (*Antonius* 1142).

glaive, n.   Sword (Ps. 78. 195).

glosse, n.   Deceptive appearance; superficial lustre or covering (Var. Ps. LXVIII. 35).

ground, n.   Cause, basis (*Discourse* 819).

grutch, v.   Complain, repine (Var. Ps. LXII. 1).

grynn, n.   Snare (Ps. 124. 13).

handstroke, n.   A stroke or blow with the hand (*Discourse* 103).

hearse, n.   Hearse cloth, funeral pall (*Antonius* 1589).

heritage, n.   The people chosen by God as his peculiar possession (Ps. 106. 100).

hid, v.   Hide (Ps. 44. 88).

hinge, n.   The axis of the earth (Ps. 89. 32).

holpe, v.   Helped (*Antonius* 1174).

horne, n.   An emblem of power and might (Ps. 75. 10).

imaginate, adj.   Imaginary (*Discourse* 397).

impackt, pa.p.   Packed up, bound (*Antonius* 1658).

impostume, n.   A swelling or abscess (*Discourse* 36).

imprest, v.   Imprinted ('Angell Spirit' 4).

indiffr'ent, adj.   Impartial, even-handed (Ps. 58. 8).

indued, pa.p.   Endowed (*Discourse* 377).

insolencie, n.   Insolence; pride; offensive contemptuous presumption (*Discourse* 91).

instant, adj.   Urgent, now present (Ps. 59. 18).

intreated, pa.p.   Treated (*Discourse* 304).

jealous, adj.   Vehement in feeling (Ps. 78. 184).

large, adj.   Lavish (Ps. 109. 49); *at large* spaciously (*Discourse* 286).

levell, n.   An instrument for determining what is 'level', 'right', 'true' (Ps. 119B. 3).

levell, v.   Aim (Ps. 101. 7).

licourishe, adj.   Greedy, lickerish (*Antonius* 1190).

lightsom, adj.   Radiant with light (Ps. 44. 15).

limme, *lymm*, n.   Limb (Ps. 66.1).

linning, pr.p.   Ceasing, ending (Ps. 89. 75).

loadstarr, n.   Guiding star (Ps. 78. 48).

loose, v.   Lose; set free, release (Ps. 69. 93).

madde, adj.   Stupefied, dazed (*Antonius* 60).

maigrim, n.   Megrim or migraine headache; whim, fancy (*Discourse* 356).

maine, n.   Mainland (Ps. 97. 2).

mainly, adv.   Loudly, vehemently (Ps. 78. 111).

make, v.   Bring it about (Ps. 45. 26).

mary, n.   Marrow (*Antonius* 1196).

mated, pa.p.   Confounded, amazed (Ps. 48. 14).

meander, n.   Labyrinth, maze (Ps. 143. 48).

mew, n.   Cage, place of confinement (Ps. 94. 32).

middleward, n.   Middle body of an army (Var. Ps. LXVIII. 79).

morion, n.   Helmet (*Antonius* 1785).

mortifide, v.   Killed; humbled; subdued, restrained (Ps. 76. 14).

motion, n.   Bidding, urging (Ps. 55. 53); agitation, change (Ps. 93. 6).

needles, n.   Rural equipment, agricultural or pastoral implements (*Antonius* 1884).

noies, n.   Troubles, annoyances (Ps. 115. 14).

oblivion, n.   Something forgotten (Ps. 88. 54).

obstinate, v.   Make or be obstinate (*Antonius* 2).

of, adv.   Off (Ps. 58. 28).

oppilation, n.   Obstruction (*Discourse* 146).

ought, v.   Owed (Ps. 69. 14).

ougly, adj.   Frightful or horrible (*Discourse* 682).

out-beare, v.   Support, sustain (Ps. 49. 11).

outface, v.   Contradict (Ps. 139. 77).

out-rase, v.   Root out, destroy (Ps. 74. 106).

partag'd, pa.p.   Divided into portions (Ps. 45. 62).

passe, v.   Exceed, surpass (Ps. 72. 68).

passing, pr.p.   Surpassing (Var. Ps. XLIV. 14).

past, pa.p.   Passed (Ps. 44. 69).

peevish, adj.   Senseless, foolish (Ps. 49. 25).

percell, n.   Portion or piece of land (Ps. 60. 23).

perch, n.   Unit of measure (Var. Ps. LX. 23).

perking, pr.p.   Projecting boldly or proudly (Var. Ps. LXVIII. 47).

perruke, n.   Natural head of hair (Var. Ps. LXVIII. 68), as opposed to the more common usage of a skull-cap covered with hair so as to represent the natural hair of the head; a periwig or wig.

pight, v.   Pitched, placed; established (Pss. 82. 3-4; 93. 3, Var. Ps. LXII. 27).

pill, v.   Plunder, pillage, steal (*Antonius* 790).

pin'd, pa.p.   Tormented, troubled (Ps. 55. 63).

pininglie, adv.   Wastingly, languishingly (*Discourse* 824).

plaie, n.   Source of delight (the latest citation, 1503), joy (*Antonius* 1242).

plaine, v.   Complain, lament (*Antonius* 390).

pleurisie, n.   A disease characterized by pain in the chest or side (*Discourse* 32).

pointed, pa.p.   Appointed (Ps. 81. 14).

pole, n.   Unit of measure (Var. Ps. LX. 23).

practize, v.   Associate, have dealings (with) (*Antonius* 891).

pray, n.   Booty, spoile, plunder (Ps. 78. 93); prey, victim (Ps. 69. 48).

prease, presse, n.   Crowd (Ps. 144. 63, *Discourse* 551).

presse, v.   Assail, crowd upon; push or strain forward (Ps. 56. 17).

prest, adj.   Eager, ready (Ps. 118. 6).

prest, pa.p.   Driven (Var. Ps. XLIV. 84).

pricking, pr.p.   Causing sharp pain, tormenting; pressing forth, piercing, pointed (Ps. 58. 27).

pudled, pa.p.   Rendered muddy, dirty (Var. Ps. LXIX. 42).

purling, pr.p.   Rippling, gurgling (Ps. 46. 10).

pursevant, n.   Messenger (Ps. 50. 3).

racke, n.   Intense pain or torment (*Discourse* 667).

raine, n.   Rein (Ps. 78. 82).

raise, n.   Rays (Ps. 74. 88).

raise, v.   Rase, erase (*Antonius* 298).

raked, pa.p.   Drawn together, covered up (Ps. 78. 69).

rampier, n.   Rampart (*Antonius* 110).

rased, raste, pa.p.   Rased, erased (Ps. 74. 34, Var. Ps. LXIX. 85).

ravin, n.   Robbery (Var. Ps. LXII. 40).

reaking, pr.p.   Being emitted, rising, emanating (Ps. 135. 16).

rebate, v.   Make dull, blunt (the edge of a weapon) (Ps. 89. 105).

rebecome, v.   Become again (*Antonius* 101).

re-chearing, pr.p.   Encouraging (Ps. 60. 14).

recur'd, pa.p.   Restored (*Antonius* 84).

redemaund, v.   Ask for again (*Discourse* 850).

redoubt, v.   Fear, stand in awe of, doubt again (Ps. 89. 21).

redownd, v.   Result (Ps. 120. 11).

reduce, v.   Lead or bring back (Ps. 80. 6).

redus'd, pa.p.   Led or brought back (*Antonius* 1410).

reedifyd, pa.p.   Rebuilt, restored (Var. Ps. CXXII. 3).

relation, n.   Account, report (Ps. 44. 1).

rent, v.   Rend or tear (Ps. 46. 19).

repine, v.   Complain; feel or manifest discontent or dissatisfaction (Ps. 111. 19).

repining, pr.p.   Complaining (Ps. 75. 12).

represent, v.   Bring into sight, present (Ps. 84. 27).

repris'd, pa.p.   Withdrawn from trouble or punishment; reprieved (Ps. 106. 76).

rereward, n.   Part of an army stationed behind the main body (Ps. 68. 66).

rest, v.   Stop, check, arrest; remain, remain to be done (Ps. 144. 60).

retch, v.   Reach (*Antonius* 184).

retrait, n.   Retreat (*Discourse* 927).

revolve, v.   To turn over something in the mind; consider, ponder (Var. Ps. LVIII. 7).

rew, v.   Rue, sorrow ('Dolefull Lay' 30).

rift, v.   Split, cleaved (Ps. 78. 49).

right, v.   Avenge, redress (Ps. 68. 11).

rost, v.   Roast, dry up (*Discourse* 940, Ps. 90. 28—the latter instance cited in the *OED*, however, to illustrate 'rost' as a variant of 'rust').

round, v.   Surround, encircle (Ps. 97. 5).

roundly, adv.   In a circular manner; completely (Ps. 125. 6); plainly, openly; sharply (Ps. 119F. 6).

runne, v.   Expose oneself, or be exposed, to a chance, danger, fortune, etc. (*Discourse* 144).

rusty, adj.   Rust-coloured; *fig.*, morally foul or corrupt (Ps. 140. 5); rusted (suggesting age) (Ps. 77. 43); rough, surly (*Antonius* 1297).

saints, n.   God's chosen people (Var. Ps. L. 14).

sawe, n.   Command, saying (Ps. 105. 38).

scilence, n.   Silence (Ps. 94. 32).

seedy, adj.   Containing seeds (Ps. 78. 154).

seeing, n.   The action of seeing (Ps. 48. 5).

seely, adj.   'Silly'; innocent, 'poor' (Ps. 80. 101); foolish, simple (*Discourse* 165).

sepulture, n.   Burial (Ps. 79. 16).

shend, v.   Put to shame, disgrace (Ps. 129. 16).

signe, v.   Assigne, appoint (Ps. 89. 68).

skilles not, v.   Makes no difference (*Discourse* 880).

skumme, n.   Foam, froth (*Antonius* 789).

slipt, v.   Let go (Ps. 78. 82).

sone, soner, adv.   Soon (*Antonius* 1607), sooner (*Antonius* 540).

speaking, pr.p.   Expressive, eloquent (Ps. 45. 8).

speed of, v.   Succeed in getting (Ps. 86. 14).

spill, v.   Perish (intrans.) (Ps. 119C. 10); slay (trans.) (Ps. 109. 41).

spoile, v.   Pillage, plunder (Var. Ps. LXXX. 48).

spring, n.   First sign of day (Ps. 92. 4); young person, youth (Ps. 105. 73); source or flow of water (Ps. 65. 40).

stand, n.   A holding one's ground against an opponent or army (Ps. 144. 22).

stay, n.   Fixed abode, residence (Pss. 60. 21; 80. 29); support (Pss. 62. 25; 69. 43); stop, end (Ps. 149. 21).

stay, v.   Stop (Ps. 55. 15); support (Ps. 59. 40).

stayne, v.   Throw into the shade, eclipse (Ps. 72. 73).

stoode with, v.   Was consistent with (Ps. 106. 87).

stout, adj.   Splendid (Var. Ps. LX. 16); *stoutest*   strongest (Ps. 144. 22).

strait, adv.   Immediately ('Astrea' 26).

strange, adj.   Exceptionally great (in intensity, amount, degree, etc.), strong (*Discourse* 179).

strayne, v.   Restrain (Ps. 118. 34).

stuffe, n.   Fabric, matter (Ps. 45. 52).

succours, n.   Aid, help, assistance (*Old French*, '*succurs*') (Ps. 71. 38, *Antonius* 1512).

sufferance, n.   Patient endurance (*Discourse* 890).

surcease, n.   Stop (Ps. 65. 22).

tables, n.   Writing tablets (Ps. 74. 107).

target, n.   Small, light shield (Ps. 63. 17).

tast, n.   Judgement (Ps. 119 I. 4).

taste, v.   Experience (*Discourse* 95); attest to (Ps. 116. 41).

tearme, n.   Period of time (Ps. 74. 48).

tearmlesse, adj.   Boundless, endless (Ps. 89. 96).

terme, n.   Limit (Ps. 100. 13).

thorne, v.   Prick as with a thorn; vex (*Antonius* 228).

thunderbolt, v.   To strike with a thunderbolt (*Discourse* 336).

thunderstriketh, v.   Strikes with thunder (*Discourse* 413).

tire, n.   Attire, clothing ('Angell Spirit' 9).

toile, n.   Snare, trap (Ps. 142. 8).

tonne, n.   Cask for making wine (*Antonius* 640).

trace, n.   Way, path (Ps. 59. 75); course of action (Pss. 78. 25; 119D. 21).

trade, n.   Practice, habit (Ps. 59. 5).

traile, v.   Mark out a trail (Ps. 59. 75).

traine, v.   Lead, conduct (Ps. 106. 112).

training, pr.p.   Alluring (*Antonius* 728).

traitres, n.   Traitress (*Antonius* 18).

travaile, n.   Journey (*Discourse* 25); labour, trouble (*Discourse* 58).

traveiler, n.   One who travels, wayfarer (*Discourse* 4).

travell, n.   Labour (*Discourse* 145).

unbroaded, pa.p.   Unbraided, loose (*Antonius* 306).

unsounded, pa.p.   Unfathomed (Ps. 135. 14).

unstate, v.   Deprive of state, rank, estate (Ps. 89. 107).

untearmed, pa.p.   Unbounded, unlimited (Ps. 105. 16).

unwares, adv.   Without warning; suddenly, unexpectedly (*Discourse* 606).

usury, n.   Interest ('Dolefull Lay' 22).

vittaile, n.   Victual, food (Ps. 132. 57).

vizarde, n.   A mask or visor (*Discourse* 680).

waide, pa.p.   Weighed (Ps. 103. 40).

wained, pa.p.   Weaned (Ps. 131. 5).

waiter, n.   Servant (Ps. 123. 3).

waitresse, n.   Waiting-maid, handmaid (Ps. 123. 4).

ward, n.   Place for guarding (*Antonius* 110).

warp, v.   Contrive, devise (*Antonius* 304).

wast, n.   Wasting of the body (Ps. 91. 20).

wearing, pr.p.   Fatiguing, wearying (Ps. 142. 18).

weele, v., contr.   We will (*Antonius* 670).

where, conj.   Whereas (*Discourse* 298).

whers, *wheres*, n.   Places (Ps. 107. 89, Var. Ps. CIV. 33).

wilt, v., contr.   Will it (not cited in the *OED*) (Ps. 88. 43).

wolle, n.   Wool (*Antonius* 1761).

woold, v.   Would (Correspondence: MS Letter II).

wordle, n.   World (*Antonius* 491).

wordlie, adv.   Worldly (*Antonius* 1134).

wrack, n.   Downfall, misfortune (*Antonius* 301).

wreake, n.   Vengeance; instance of taking vengeance (Ps. 71. 77).

wreake, v.   Avenge, revenge (Var. Ps. LIII. 19).

wreakfull, adj.   Vengeful (Ps. 44. 63).

wryed, pa.p.   Diverted (Ps. 125. 15).

TABLE OF VERSE FORMS

In this table we have sought to define the Countess of Pembroke's verse forms as closely as possible, citing the varying interpretations of other critics where relevant. However, the experimental nature of much of her verse sometimes renders it difficult to offer a single and comprehensive way of describing her forms through standard methods of metrical description. See I.57–60.

'Astrea'
Ten stanzas of 6 lines, each speaker in each stanza given two lines of iambic tetrameter followed by one line of trimeter with a feminine ending, rhymed *aabccb* in a form of caudate or tail rhyme. Cf. *Antonius*, Chorus Act III.

'Even now that Care'
Twelve stanzas of 8 lines, iambic pentameter, rhymed *ababbcbc*. Cf. Psalm 45.

'To the Angell Spirit'
Thirteen stanzas of 7 lines, iambic pentameter, rhymed *abbabba*.

'To the Angell Spirit: Variant'
Ten stanzas of 7 lines, and one concluding stanza of 5 lines, iambic pentameter, rhymed *abbabba*.

'The Dolefull Lay' (Disputed)
Sixteen stanzas of 6 lines, iambic pentameter, rhymed *ababcc* (except for stanza 3, rhyming *ababaa*).

Antonius
Antonius employs a variety of literary forms. Like Garnier, Pembroke prefaces the play with a prose Argument. For the body of the play Pembroke renders Garnier's rhymed hexameters in blank verse, with periodic rhymes for emphasis, particularly at the close of paragraphs and for stichomythia and *sententiae*. For the choruses Pembroke retains the same number of lines used by Garnier and approximates the effect of his forms; only the chorus in Act III is identical.

Chorus, Act I
    Garnier: Eleven stanzas of 8 lines, iambic tetrameter, rhymed *ababcdcd*.
    Pembroke: Eleven stanzas of 8 lines, iambic trimeter, with varying use of 4 rhymes: *abcdadcb*, *abcbadcd*, *abcbcdad*, *abacdcbd*, etc.

First Chorus, Act II
    Garnier: Eleven stanzas of 6 lines, iambic tetrameter for lines 1, 2, 4, 5 and iambic trimeter for lines 3, 6, rhymed *aabccb*.
    Pembroke: Eleven stanzas of 6 lines, iambic trimeter, rhymed *ababcc*.

Second Chorus, Act II
   Garnier: Eleven stanzas of 11 lines, alternating iambic tetrameter and iambic trimeter with feminine rhyme, rhymed *ababcddcece*.
   Pembroke: Eleven stanzas of 11 lines, headless iambic tetrameter with a trochaic effect, rhymed *ababcddcede* or *ababcddcece*.

Chorus, Act III
   Garnier: Sixteen stanzas of 6 lines, iambic tetrameter, rhymed *aabccb*.
   Pembroke: Sixteen stanzas of 6 lines, each two lines of iambic tetrameter fol-lowed by one line of trimeter with a feminine ending, rhymed *aabccb*. Cf. 'Astrea'.

Chorus, Act IV
   Garnier: Ten stanzas of 8 lines, iambic tetrameter, rhymed *aabbcdcd*.
   Pembroke: Eighty lines, iambic trimeter, rhymed couplets.

The Triumph of Death
Petrarch: *Terza rima*, i.e. rhymed *aba, bcb, cdc*, etc.
Pembroke: *Terza rima*. Cf. Psalm 119H.

Psalmes

Psalm 44
Twelve stanzas of 8 lines, trochaic tetrameter (lines 2, 4, 5, and 7 catalectic—i.e. dropping of the unstressed syllable at the end of a line), rhymed *ababbcbc*. Cf. Variant: MS *B*.

Psalm 45
Eight stanzas of 8 lines, iambic pentameter, rhymed *ababbcbc*. Cf. 'Even now'.

Psalm 46
Five stanzas of 8 lines, 44443343, rhymed *ababbcbc*. Cf. Variant: MS *B*.

Psalm 47
Four stanzas of 5 lines, iambic tetrameter, rhymed *ababa*.

Psalm 48
Four stanzas of 10 lines, 4443444344, lines 2, 3, 6, and 7 catalectic, rhymed *abbcaddcee*.

Psalm 49
Seven stanzas of 6 lines, iambic pentameter, each stanza with the same rhymes, *abcdef*.

Psalm 50
Eight stanzas of 8 lines, iambic pentameter, rhymed *ababacac*. Cf. Variant: MS *B*.

Psalm 51
Pembroke's choice of *rhyme royal* (seven-line stanzas of iambic pentameter rhymed *ababbcc*; feminine rhyme in lines 6 and 7) emphasizes the importance of this Psalm. See Commentary.

Psalm 52
Eleven stanzas of 4 lines, 3232 with feminine rhyme in lines 2 and 4, rhymed *abab*.

Psalm 53
Three stanzas of 8 lines, iambic tetrameter, rhymed *ababbcac*. Cf. Variant: MS *B*.

Psalm 54
One stanza of 16 lines, iambic pentameter with the rhyme *ab* repeated throughout.

Psalm 55
Six stanzas of 12 lines, iambic pentameter. The same three rhymes are used in each stanza, with the first three stanzas rhyming *abccbaacbbca*; *baccabb-caacb*; *cbaabccabbac*. The last three stanzas reverse the entire rhyme scheme, beginning *cabbaccbaabc*, forming 'a perfect palindrome' (Waller, *Mary Sidney*, 198). There are many verbal parallels with *Psaumes*; see particularly 6, 14, 17, 39, 41.

Psalm 56
Nine stanzas of 5 lines, iambic pentameter, lines 3 and 4 headless iambic tetrameter with trochaic effect, rhymed *aabba*.

Psalm 57
Nine stanzas of 6 lines, 522443, lines 4 and 5 headless iambic tetrameter with trochaic effect, rhymed *abbcca*.

Psalm 58
Four stanzas of 8 lines, iambic pentameter, rhymed *ababcbcb*. Cf. Variant: MS *B*.

Psalm 59
Fifteen stanzas of 6 lines, 424244, rhymed *ababcc*.

Psalm 60
Six stanzas of 8 lines, iambic trimeter, rhymed *ababbcbc*. Cf. Variant: MS *B*.

Psalm 61
Five stanzas of 7 lines, 2244334, rhymed *ababcca*.

Psalm 62
Five stanzas of 8 lines, iambic tetrameter, rhymed *ababacac*. Cf. Variant: MS *B*.

Psalm 63
Four stanzas of *rhyme royal*, seven lines of iambic pentameter rhymed *ababbcc*. Cf. Variant: MS *B*.

Psalm 64
Five stanzas of 8 lines, 44443333, rhymed *ababbcbc*. Cf. Variant: MS *B*.

Psalm 65
Eight stanzas of 6 lines, 444455, feminine rhyme in lines 1–4, rhymed *ababcc*. According to Waller, *Mary Sidney*, 199 this poem could also be read as iambs and anapaests.

Psalm 66
Eight stanzas of 8 iambic tetrameter lines, feminine rhyme in lines 3, 4, 5, and 7, rhymed *aabbcdcd*.

Psalm 67
Four stanzas of 8 lines, 44232223, rhymed *aabcbddc*, lines 1 and 2 headless.

Psalm 68
Twelve stanzas of 8 lines, iambic pentameter, feminine rhyme in lines 5 and 7, rhymed *ababcbcb*. Cf. Variant: MSS *B, I*.

Psalm 69
Thirteen stanzas of 8 lines, headless iambic tetrameter, feminine rhyme in lines 5 and 6, rhymed *ababccaa*. Cf. Variant: MS *B*.

Psalm 70
Three stanzas of 8 lines, iambic trimeter, rhymed *ababcddc*.

Psalm 71
Thirteen stanzas of 6 lines, trochaic tetrameter—lines 3 and 6 catalectic, rhymed *aabccb*. Cf. Variant: MS *B*.

Psalm 72
Nine stanzas of 10 lines, 5555223223, rhymed *ababccdeed*.

Psalm 73
Seven stanzas of 12 lines, iambic pentameter, rhymed *abbaccaddaee*.

Psalm 74
Twenty-one stanzas of 6 lines, 334334, rhymed *aabccb*.

Psalm 75
Five stanzas of 6 lines, iambic pentameter with feminine rhyme in lines 3 and 6, rhymed *aabccb*. Cf. Variant: MSS *B, I, K, N*.

Psalm 76
Five stanzas of 6 lines, iambic hexameter, rhymed *ababcc*.

Psalm 77
Twelve stanzas of 8 lines, iambic trimeter usually rhymed *abcdacbd*, although final quatrain varies.

Psalm 78
Twenty-seven stanzas of *ottava rima*: 8 lines, iambic pentameter, rhymed *abababcc*.

Psalm 79
The reason for the double indentation is that the paraphrase is written in stanzas of alternating metrical patterns: the odd stanzas are iambic tetrameter with feminine rhyme in lines 1–5 and 8 and iambic dimeter in lines 6 and 7; the even stanzas are iambic tetrameter in lines 1–5 and 8 and iambic dimeter with feminine rhyme in lines 6 and 7. Eight stanzas of 8 lines, rhymed *aabbcddc*.

Psalm 80
Five stanzas of 8 lines, iambic pentameter, feminine rhyme in lines 6 and 8, rhymed *ababbcbc*. Cf. Variant: MS *B*.

Psalm 81
Six stanzas of 8 lines, iambic tetrameter, lines 5–8 headless with trochaic effect, feminine rhyme in lines 7 and 8, rhymed *ababccdd*.

Psalm 82
Six stanzas of 5 lines, 44524, rhymed *aabbb*.

Psalm 83
Nine stanzas of six lines, 443344, rhymed *abccab*.

Psalm 84
Six stanzas of 8 lines, 35543344 with feminine rhyme except in lines 7 and 8, rhymed *ababccdd*.

Psalm 85
Four stanzas of 10 lines, headless iambic tetrameter with a trochaic effect, rhymed *ababcddcee*.

Psalm 86
Six stanzas of 8 lines, iambic tetrameter with feminine rhyme in lines 2, 4, 7, and 8, rhymed *ababccdd*. Cf. Variant: MS *B*.

Psalm 87
Four stanzas of 6 lines, 545444, with feminine rhyme in lines 2 and 4, rhymed *ababcc*.

Psalm 88
Thirteen stanzas of 6 lines, 422334, rhymed *abbcca*. A much freer paraphrase than most of Pembroke's Psalms, the form anticipates Herbert's psalm-like lyrics, such as 'Longing', 'Home', Dullnesse', 'Giddiness', 'The Method', 'Complaining', and 'The Glance'. See also I.50–1.

Psalm 89
Sixteen stanzas of 8 lines, iambic pentameter with feminine rhyme in lines 1, 3, 6, and 8, rhymed *ababbcbc*. Cf. Variant: MS *I*.

Psalm 90
Seven stanzas of 8 lines, tetrameter, alternating trochaic and iambic lines, with the second quatrain reversing the movement of the first; lines 1 and 3 are fully trochaic, 6 and 8 are headless iambic, rhymed *ababcdcd*. 'The metre is difficult because initial feet in iambic lines often have syllables of nearly the same value (e.g. ll. 2, 5, 7) and lines 1 and 3 tend to make the reader expect a continuing trochaic movement.' Pembroke may well have been working with a hymn form or even trying some sort of quantitative experiment here (Susanne Woods, in personal correspondence).

Psalm 91
Seven stanzas of 8 lines, 33433343, rhymed *ababcbcb*.

Psalm 92
Five stanzas of 9 lines, 234234234, rhymed *abbaccadd*.

Psalm 93
Two stanzas of 8 lines, headless iambic tetrameter with a trochaic effect, rhymed *ababbaba*.

Psalm 94
Six stanzas of 8 lines, iambic pentameter, rhymed *ababbccb*.

Psalm 95
Five stanzas of 8 lines, 42254445, rhymed *abbaccdd*.

Psalm 96
Seven stanzas of 6 lines, headless iambic tetrameter with a trochaic effect, feminine rhyme in lines 2 and 5, rhymed *abacbc*.

Psalm 97
Five stanzas of 9 lines, iambic trimeter with feminine rhyme in lines 3 and 4, rhymed *aabbccddc*.

Psalm 98
Three stanzas of 8 lines, iambic pentameter, rhymed *ababbcac*.

Psalm 99
Eight stanzas of 4 lines, headless iambic tetrameter with feminine rhyme in lines 3 and 4, rhymed *aabb*.

Psalm 100
Spenserian sonnet, 14 lines of iambic pentameter, rhymed *ababbcbccdcdee*.

Psalm 101
Eight stanzas of 3 lines, iambic pentameter, with an unusual interlocking rhyme scheme, which is almost a delayed *terza rima*: aba cdc, beb, dfd, ege, faf, ghg, aha.

Psalm 102
Fifteen stanzas of 6 lines, 343354, rhymed *aabcbc*.

Psalm 103
Twelve stanzas of eight lines, 23523235, rhymed *aabccddb.*

Psalm 104
Fourteen stanzas of 8 lines, iambic pentameter, rhymed *ababbaba.*

Psalm 105
Twelve stanzas of 8 lines, iambic pentameter with feminine rhyme in lines 7 and 8, *ottava rima.* Cf. Variant: MS *B.*

Psalm 106
Seventeen stanzas of 7 lines, iambic pentameter, rhymed *ababcbc.*

Psalm 107
Fifteen stanzas of 8 lines, iambic tetrameter, rhymed *ababbcbc.*

Psalm 108
Five stanzas of 8 lines, iambic tetrameter, rhymed *ababbccb.* Cf. Variant: MS *B.*

Psalm 109
Fourteen stanzas of 6 lines, 543355, rhymed *abcacb.*

Psalm 110
Four stanzas of 8 lines, 44443343, rhymed *abbacdcd.*

Psalm 111
One stanza of 20 lines, iambic pentameter couplets. As Calvin's headnote records, the Hebrew original has the form of an 'Apcee' (ABC), or alphabetical acrostic, 'in such wise that every verse conteyneth two letters' except the last two, which have three letters each. Unlike her usual sources, Pembroke retains the alphabetical form, allotting two letters per verse until verse 7.

Psalm 112
Nine stanzas of 4 lines, 4343 with feminine rhyme, rhymed *abab.*

Psalm 113
Three stanzas of 6 lines, iambic trimeter with feminine rhyme in lines 3 and 4, rhymed *aabbcc.* Cf. Variant: MS *I.*

Psalm 114
One stanza of 20 lines, alternating iambic hexameter and tetrameter, rhymed couplets.

Psalm 115
Eight stanzas of 6 lines, 353544, rhymed *ababcc.*

Psalm 116
Seven stanzas of 8 lines, iambic trimeter with feminine rhyme in lines 6 and 8, rhymed *ababcdcd.*

Psalm 117
Acrostic poem. One stanza of 12 lines, iambic dimeter, rhymed *ababcdcdefef.* Cf. Variant: MS *B.*

Psalm 118
Twenty stanzas of 4 lines, iambic tetrameter with feminine rhyme in lines 3 and 4, rhymed *aabb*.

Psalm 119A
Four stanzas of 6 lines, 442244 with feminine rhyme in lines 1, 2, 5, and 6, rhymed *aabbcc*.

Psalm 119B
Four stanzas of 6 lines, 354354, rhymed *abacbc*.

Psalm 119C
Four stanzas of 6 lines, 234234, rhymed *abacbc*.

Psalm 119D
Four stanzas of 10 lines, 3341333414, lines 1 and 6 headless iambic trimeter with trochaic effect, rhymed *abbacdeedc*. Woods, *Natural Emphasis*, 296, terms this 'an incredible *tour de force*; strophic construction (rather than meter/rhythm tensions) [going] beyond simple iambic metricality'.

Psalm 119E
Four stanzas of 6 lines, iambic tetrameter, rhymed *abcabc*.

Psalm 119F
Eight stanzas of 4 lines, headless iambic tetrameter with a trochaic effect, each stanza with a single rhyme.

Psalm 119G
Two stanzas of 8 lines, 43434343, rhymed *ababcaca*. Cf. Variant: MSS *B*, *K*, *χ*.

Psalm 119H
One stanza of 25 lines, headless iambic tetrameter with a trochaic effect, *terza rima*, *ababcbcdc*, etc. Cf. Variant: MSS *B, K, χ*.

Psalm 119I
Four stanzas of 6 lines, headless iambic tetrameter with a trochaic effect, rhymed *aabcbc*.

Psalm 119K
Three stanzas of 8 lines, iambic tetrameter, headless with a trochaic effect in lines 2, and 5 through 8, rhymed *abaabcbc*.

Psalm 119L
Four stanzas of 6 lines, 555235, rhymed *abaccb*.

Psalm 119M
Two stanzas of 8 lines, iambic tetrameter with feminine rhyme in lines 2, 4, 5, and 7, which repeat the b and c rhyme words in both stanzas, rhymed *ababcaca*.

Psalm 119N
Four stanzas of 6 lines, 335335, rhymed *abcbca*.

Psalm 119O
Four stanzas of 6 lines, 535353, rhymed *abacbc*.

Psalm 119P
Two stanzas of 14 lines, in complex repeated patterns of seven, six lines of tetrameter followed by one of pentameter: lines 1, 2, 8, and 9 headless iambic tetrameter; lines 3, 4, 10, and 11 trochaic tetrameter; lines 5, 6, 12, and 13 iambic tetrameter; lines 7 and 14 (which repeat rhymes between stanzas) iambic pentameter. Rhymed *aabbccdeeffggd*.

Psalm 119Q
Four stanzas of 8 lines, 44442444, lines 1, 3, and 5 headless iambic metres with trochaic effect, rhymed *ababccdd*. In *A*, *K*, χ line 6 has seven syllables, but the parallel lines 14, 22, 30 each have eight. *B* notes that one syllable in each of these octosyllabic lines has been expunged. It is not impossible that 6 is simply defective through a scribal slip and that the alteration of the other lines to match is not authorial.

Psalm 119R
Four stanzas of 6 lines, 554225, rhymed *abccab*. As Woods, *Natural Emphasis*, 297, notes, the second line in the stanza has 9 syllables 'with accent-wrenching'.

Psalm 119S
Two stanzas of 8 lines, iambic trimeter, rhymed *ababbcbc*. Cf. Variant: MSS *B*, *K*, χ.

Psalm 119T
Four stanzas of 8 lines, 42244444, rhymed *abbaccdd*, lines 5 and 6 headless.

Psalm 119V
Eight stanzas of 4 lines, 3344 with feminine rhyme, rhymed *aabb*.

Psalm 119W
Three stanzas of 6 lines, headless iambic tetrameter with a trochaic effect, rhymed *ababaa*, lines 2 and 4 feminine. Cf. Variant: MS *B*, *K*, χ.

Psalm 119Y
Eight stanzas of 4 lines, 3443, rhymed *abba*.

Psalm 120
The *A* versions of Psalms 120–7 are written in quantitative metre, following Sidney's experiments. The later variants in *G*, *M* are written in rhymed iambic metre, with simplified diction, usually taken directly from the Psalter (and a few quotations from the 1611 Authorized Version), with little reliance on scholarly commentary. They read as if they had been revised for congregational singing and may not be authorial. See 'Transmission and Authority of Texts'.

Six stanzas of 4 lines, unrhymed quantitative verse. Attridge, *Syllables*, 203–4, notes that it combines the 'regularity achieved by the method of *OA*

32 with the irregularity typical of classical stress-patterns'. Although it maintains 'coincidence of stress and quantity', its alcaic stanzas include 'three different types of line, so that no sense of accentual regularity is set up'. Cf. Variant: MSS *G, M*.

Psalm 121
Five stanzas of 4 lines, unrhymed quantitative verse, in 'phalaecian hendecasyllables very similar to those of Sidney's *OA* 33' (Attridge, *Syllables*, 203). Cf. Variant: MSS *G, M*.

Psalm 122
One stanza of 17 lines, unrhymed hexameters, which demonstrate 'a substantial degree of coincidence [of stress and quantity], and careful attention to vowel-tenseness' (Attridge, *Syllables*, 203). Two other versions are extant. Cf. Variant: MS *B, I, χ* and Variant: MSS *G, M*.

Psalm 123
One stanza of 10 lines, unrhymed quantitative verse. Unlike Sidney, Pembroke retains the classical short, stressed, disyllables in elegiacs (Attridge, *Syllables*, 204). Cf. Variant: MSS *G, M*.

Psalm 124
One stanza of 16 lines, iambic, unrhymed quantitative verse. Attridge, *Syllables*, 204, notes that the iambics here compare favourably with Spenser's '*Iambicum Trimetrum*' in their attention to 'native English stress-rhythms'. Cf. Variant: MSS *G, M*.

Psalm 125
Five stanzas of 4 lines, sapphics, unrhymed quantitative verse. Cf. Variant: MSS *G, M*.

Psalm 126
Six stanzas of 4 lines, unrhymed quantitative verse. Attridge, *Syllables*, 204, notes that the Psalm lacks a consistent metrical pattern; 'Woodford's scansion is incorrect'. Cf. Variant: MSS *G, M*.

Psalm 127
Six stanzas of 4 lines, unrhymed quantitative verse. 'Incorrectly scanned by Samuel Woodford', the poem is in anacreontics like *Old Arcadia* 32, 'one of the rare occasions on which Sidney made stress and quantity coincide', as does Pembroke here (Attridge, *Syllables*, 203). Cf. Variant: MSS *G, M*.

Psalm 128
Three stanzas of 8 lines, 43433333, rhymed *ababcbcb*.

Psalm 129
Five stanzas of 6 lines, headless iambic tetrameter with a trochaic effect, rhymed *ababcc*.

Psalm 130
Six stanzas of 6 lines, 222244 with feminine rhyme in lines 5 and 6, rhymed *ababcc*. (On the metrics and the distribution of 'each verse equally among eight stresses', see Sallye Sheppeard, 'On the Art of Renaissance Translation: Mary Herbert's Psalm 130', *Texas College English* 18 (1985), 1–3).

Psalm 131
One stanza of 10 lines, iambic tetrameter, rhymed *ababbabacc*. Cf. Variant: MS *N*.

Psalm 132
Thirteen stanzas of 6 lines, caudate rhyme, or tail-rhyme (see 'Astrea') iambic 444423, rhymed *ababcc*.

Psalm 133
Four stanzas of 4 lines, 4224, rhymed *abba*.

Psalm 134
One stanza of 20 lines, 44333322111134224444, rhymed *aabbccddefefcghhgiic*.

Psalm 135
Eight stanzas of *rhyme royal* (seven-line stanzas of iambic pentameter rhymed *ababbcc*), except that line 6 is dimeter.

Psalm 136
Thirteen stanzas of 4 lines, tetrameter with alternating lines of iambs and trochees, rhymed *abab*. Throughout this Psalm the biblical refrain that concludes each verse, 'for his mercy endureth forever', is rendered in the second and fourth line of each quatrain, retaining the antiphonal quality of the original.

Psalm 137
Five stanzas of 8 lines, iambic tetrameter variant of *ottava rima*.

Psalm 138
Eight stanzas of 3 lines, iambic pentameter, rhymed *aab*, *bcc*, *dde*, *eef*, etc. An unusual feature is that all lines have feminine rhyme, except those that link rhymes between stanzas: lines 3 and 4, 9 and 10, 15 and 16, 21 and 22.

Psalm 139
Thirteen stanzas of 7 lines, 4422444, rhymed *abccbab*.

Psalm 140
Five stanzas of 6 lines, iambic pentameter. The colons are retained in the middle of the lines because they mark the elaborate internal rhyme scheme: *ab/bc/cd/de/ef/af*. The opening line of each stanza is a cry to the Lord; the final line of each stanza has an internal rhyme with Lord.

Psalm 141
Five stanzas of 6 lines, iambic hexameter with feminine rhyme in lines 3 and 6, rhymed *aabccb*.

Psalm 142
Two stanzas of 12 lines, 555533355535 with feminine rhyme, rhymed *ababcdcdefef*. A freer translation than most of her paraphrases, adapting the past tense of the biblical sources to the present, as does Bze.

Psalm 143
Six stanzas of 10 lines, 5233333333 with feminine rhyme in lines 3, 5, 7, and 8, rhymed *aabcbcddee*.

Psalm 144
Nine stanzas of 8 lines, iambic trimeter, rhymed *ababcdcd*.

Psalm 145
Nine stanzas of *rhyme royal* (seven-line stanzas rhymed *ababbcc*), except that the meter is iambic tetrameter.

Psalm 146
Three stanzas of 9 lines, 555533535, rhymed *ababbccdd*.

Psalm 147
Six stanzas of 10 lines, iambic pentameter, rhymed *ababbcacdd*.

Psalm 148
Seven stanzas of 8 lines, 44444343, rhymed *ababbcbc*.

Psalm 149
Three stanzas of 8 lines, trochaic tetrameter (lines 1, 3, 5, and 6 catalectic), rhymed *ababccdd*.

Psalm 150
Sonnet, 14 lines of iambic pentameter, rhymed *abbaabbacdcdee*.

Variant Psalms

Variant Psalm XLIV
Twelve stanzas of 8 lines, 33434343 with feminine rhyme in lines 1, 3, 6, and 8, rhymed *abacbdcd*. Metrics and rhyme altered in MS *A*.

Variant Psalm XLVI
Five and one-half stanzas of 8 lines, 43344334, rhymed *abbaccdd*. Metrics and rhyme altered in MS *A*; partial stanza is removed.

Variant Psalm L
Six stanzas of 12 lines, iambic pentameter with feminine rhyme in lines 6 and 12, rhymed *aabbbcddeeec*. Stanza form and length altered in MS *A*.

Variant Psalm LIII
Two stanzas of 12 lines, 444443444443, rhymed *aabbbcddeeec*. Metrics and stanza form altered in MS *A*. Closer to the Bible than the *A* version. Line 12, for example, is almost an exact quotation from Psalter v. 4.

Variant Psalm LVIII
Nine stanzas of 5 lines, 35544, rhymed *aabbb*. Stanza form, metrics, and length altered in MS *A*.

Variant Psalm LX
Eleven stanzas of 4 lines, 5443, rhymed *abab*. Stanza form, metrics, and length altered in MS *A*.

Variant Psalm LXII
Two stanzas of 24 lines, iambic pentameter, rhymed *abbabbbaabaa* (repeated). Stanza form, metrics, and length altered in MS *A*.

Variant Psalm LXIII
Ten stanzas of 4 lines, 5425 (line 2 headless iambic tetrameter with a trochaic effect), rhymed *abba*. Stanza form, metrics, and length altered in MS *A*.

Variant Psalm LXIV
Five stanzas of 7 lines, iambic tetrameter rhymed *abbaacc*. Stanza form, metrics, and length altered in MS *A*.

Variant Psalm LXVIII [MSS *B*, *I*]
Fourteen stanzas of 8 lines, 66676667, rhymed *abbacdcd*. Stanza form, metrics, and length altered in MS *A*.

Variant Psalm LXIX
Fourteen stanzas of 8 lines, 55353553, rhymed *aabcdcbd*. Stanza form, metrics, and length altered in MS *A*.

Variant Psalm LXXI
Sixteen stanzas of *rhyme royal* (seven-line stanzas rhymed *ababbcc*), except that the metre is iambic 3322442 with feminine rhyme in lines 1 and 3. This is obviously a draft, since stanza 5 is *aaaaabb*. Stanza form, metrics, and length altered in MS *A*.

Variant Psalm LXXV [MSS *B*, *I*, *K*, *N*]
Six stanzas of 7 lines headless iambic tetrameter (trimeter in line 3) with a trochaic effect, rhymed *aabcbbc*. Stanza form, metrics, and length altered in MS *A*.

Variant Psalm LXXX
Nine stanzas of 8 lines, 32443244, rhymed *ababcdcd*. Stanza form, metrics, and length altered in MS *A*.

Variant Psalm LXXXVI
Nine stanzas of 8 lines, 32333434 (line 2 headless iambic dimeter with a trochaic effect; feminine rhyme in lines 3, 4, 5, and 6), rhymed *aabbccdd*. A line is missing in the final stanza. Stanza form, metrics, and length altered in MS *A*.

Variant Psalm 89 [MS *I*]
88 lines of unrhymed quantitative hexameter. Attridge, *Syllables*, 205, concludes that, 'when allowances are made for errors in transcription, [this

Psalm] can probably be considered as the most successful Elizabethan attempt to naturalise the hexameter—though it is still, of course, far inferior to the best verse of the native tradition'. Stanza form, metrics, and length altered in MS *A*.

Variant Psalm CV
Twenty-one stanzas of 6 lines, 544544, lines 2, 3, 5, and 6 usually headless iambic tetrameter with a trochaic effect, rhymed *abcabc* with some defective rhymes as lines 104/7. Stanza form, metrics, and length altered in MS *A*.

Variant Psalm CVIII
Eleven stanzas. Psalm 108 is composed of vv. 7–11 of Ps. 57 and vv. 5–12 of Ps. 60. For this first version, recorded in *B*, Pembroke combined the paraphrases she had already made of the relevant portions of those Psalms, each in a different stanza form. She also made some minor changes as at Ps. 108. 25, 29, 41. MS *A* records a different poem.

Variant Psalm 113 [MS *I*]
One stanza of 20 lines, iambic pentameter with frequent feminine rhyme, rhymed couplets. Stanza form, metrics, and length altered in MS *A*.

Variant Psalm CXVII
One stanza of 12 lines, 532354324535, rhymed *abcbaccdcede*. This acrostic Psalm is much improved in version *A*.

Variant Psalm CXIX G [MSS *B*, *K*, *χ*]
Four stanzas of 8 lines, 42422424 (lines 6 and 8 headless iambic tetrameter with a trochaic effect), rhymed *ababccdd*. Stanza form, metrics, and length altered in MS *A*.

Variant Psalm CXIX H [MSS *B*, *K*, *χ*]
Eight stanzas of 4 lines, 3545 (line 3 headless iambic tetrameter with a trochaic effect), rhymed *aabb*. Stanza form, metrics, and length altered in MS *A*.

Variant Psalm CXIX S [MSS *B*, *K*, *χ*]
Four stanzas of 6 lines, 334334, rhymed *abacbc*. Stanza form, metrics, and length altered in MS *A*.

Variant Psalm CXIX W [MSS *B*, *K*, *χ*]
Eight stanzas of 4 lines, 4425, rhymed *aabb*. Stanza form, metrics, and length altered in MS *A*.

Variant Psalm 120 [MSS *G*, *M*]
Four stanzas of 4 lines, iambic pentameter, rhymed *aabb*. Altered from quantitative verse in MS *A*.

Variant Psalm 121 [MSS *G*, *M*]
Four stanzas of 6 lines, 444455 with feminine rhyme in lines 5 and 6, rhymed *ababcc*. Altered from quantitative verse in MS *A*.

Psalm CXXII Variant 1 [MSS *B, I, σ*]
Unrhymed asclepiadic quantitative verse. Attridge notes that the variant is
'in verse like that of *OA* 34'. Note the correspondences with the version in
A, demonstrating a process of revision. The rhymed alternative in *G, M* is
virtually a different poem.

Psalm 122 Variant 2 [MSS *G, M]*
Six stanzas of 6 lines, iambic tetrameter, rhymed *ababcc*. Altered from quantitative verse in MS *A*.

Variant Psalm 123 [MSS *G, M]*
Five stanzas of 4 lines, iambic trimeter, rhymed *abab*. Altered from quantitative verse in MS *A*.

Variant Psalm 124 [MSS *G, M]*
Five stanzas of 4 lines, iambic tetrameter, rhymed couplets. Altered from
quantitative verse in MS *A*. This simplified poem stays close to the Psalter.

Variant Psalm 125 [MSS *G, M]*
Five stanzas of four lines, iambic tetrameter, rhymed *abab*. Altered from
quantitative verse in MS *A*.

Variant Psalm 126 [MSS *G, M]*
Four stanzas of six lines, iambic tetrameter, rhymed *ababcc*. Altered from
quantitative verse in MS *A*.

Variant Psalm 127 [MSS *G, M]*
Five stanzas of 4 lines, iambic pentameter, rhymed *abab*. Altered from quantitative verse in MS *A*.

Variant Psalm 131 [MS *N*]
Three stanzas of 6 lines, 334335, rhymed *abccab*. Stanza form, metrics, and
length altered in MS *A*.

INDEX OF FIRST LINES AND
TITLES OF POEMS

GENERAL INDEX TO INTRODUCTIONS AND TEXTUAL ESSAYS

This selective index includes significant references to individuals and literary works, with more extensive sections on Mary Sidney Herbert and Philip Sidney. It is designed to be used in conjunction with the commentaries to the individual works, which contain cross-references to other parts of the edition.